PSYCHOLOGY AND AGING

Diana S. Woodruff-Pak
Temple University

PRENTICE HALL, Englewood Cliffs, New Jersey 07632

Library of Congress Cataloging-in-Publication Data

WOODRUFF-PAK, DIANA S., 1946–
    Psychology and aging/Diana S. Woodruff-Pak.
    p.   cm.

    Includes index.
    ISBN 0-13-733064-2
    1. Aged—Psychology. 2. Aging. I. Title.
BF724.8.W66 1988   87-36134 CIP
155.67—dc19

Editorial/production supervision and
Interior design: Robert C. Walters
Cover design: Ben Santora
Manufacturing buyer: Raymond Keating

Cover illustration: The photographs on the cover represent almost 100 years in the life of Florence Knapp, the oldest living American. Miss Knapp was 114 years old on October 10, 1987. The large photograph was taken on the boardwalk in Atlantic City, in the 1890s when Miss Knapp was in her late teens or early twenties. The insert shows Miss Knapp's happiness at the celebration of her 110th birthday. Her remarkable ancestry along with some details of her fascinating long life are presented in Chapter 6.

© 1988 by Prentice-Hall, Inc.
A Division of Simon & Schuster
Englewood Cliffs, New Jersey 07632

Printed in the United States of America

10 9 8 7 6 5 4 3 2 1

ISBN 0-13-733064-2   01

Prentice-Hall International (UK) Limited, *London*
Prentice-Hall of Australia Pty. Limited, *Sydney*
Prentice-Hall Canada Inc., *Toronto*
Prentice-Hall Hispanoamericana, S.A., *Mexico*
Prentice-Hall of India, Private Limited, *New Delhi*
Prentice-Hall of Japan, Inc., *Tokyo*
Prentice-Hall of Southeast Asia Pte. Ltd., *Singapore*
Editora Prentice-Hall do Brasil, Ltda, *Rio de Janeiro*

To Grandmother Helsel.
You have inspired me to study psychology and aging.

Contents

Preface

This is an exciting time to be writing a book about *Psychology and Aging.* I have been working in this field now for twenty years and can clearly recognize the progress we have made in that relatively short period of time. Although the psychology of aging is still a young field, it is a rapidly expanding discipline which is attracting to its ranks psychologists from other areas of expertise as well as new young scientists. Undergraduates and graduate students in increasing numbers are also recognizing the relevance of gerontology to many subdisciplines within psychology as well as disciplines outside of psychology.

The focus of this book is on the psychology of aging. However, gerontology is by nature multidisciplinary, and this book includes biological and social science perspectives beyond those typically encompassed by psychology. Thus, *Psychology and Aging* presents a thorough grounding in the psychology of aging plus an overview of gerontology as a whole.

A special focus of this book is the rapidly growing field of neuroscience with its dramatic implications for the field of aging. A number of neuroscientists have been attracted to the field of aging, and their work is of great significance to the behavioral capacities of older adults. For example, neuroscientists are in the process of unlocking the secrets of the neurobiology of memory. Our understanding of the brain is accelerating to the point that memory drugs and brain implants are within the domain of mainstream science rather than merely in the realm of science fiction. Some older adults suffering from Parkinson's disease have already benefitted from brain implants, and patients with Alzheimer's disease may be the next to have their capacities improved with this technique. And who among us would refuse the opportunity to improve our memory with a pill? Aging does not have to be very far along before many of us want to eliminate our memory lapses.

The psychology of aging is a fascinating field with great social and personal relevance, and this book is written to generate genuine excitement for this field. The first two chapters provide an overview of psychology and aging by discussing the advantages of studying aging from personal, social, and scientific motivations. A brief history of the scientific study of aging and the special research techniques required to study aging are also presented. The next two chapters present a social scientific perspective of aging. An overview of the demographic characteristics of the aged in the United States and in the world is presented in Chapter 3, and in Chapter 4 social and environmental influences on the aged with special emphasis on aging in the context of the family are discussed.

Physiological aging is the topic of Chapter 5 with a focus on aging in the central nervous system. Theories of biological aging are also presented in this chapter. Longevity and health are personalized in Chapter 6 with a life-expectancy test. The remarkable life of the longest-lived American, Florence Knapp, who was 114 years old on October 10, 1987 is presented. Miss Knapp graces the cover of this book in her youthful beauty in her late teens and as a beautiful example of a dynamic centenarian celebrating her 110th birthday.

Sexuality and aging is the topic of Chapter 7. Reported in this chapter is something that contemporary older adults have made very clear: Sexuality is a significant aspect of life until the day we die.

Arousal and sleep and the speed of behavior are the topics for the next two chapters. These topics have received a great deal of research attention in the psychology of aging because changes in arousal level, sleep and speed dramatically affect behavior in later life. Changes in these basic aspects may contribute greatly to what differentiates behavior in old age from behavior at early periods of the life span.

The next series of chapters addresses a number of behavioral processes as they age. Among them are sensation and perception, learning and memory, cognition, intelligence, and personality. Data contained in these chapters comprise the central core of psychology and aging. Chapter 15 considers work and retirement and focuses on how social norms involving work and retirement shape individuals' lives.

The only chapter in *Psychology and Aging* which focuses on abnormal aging is Chapter 16 on psychopathology and intervention. A very small percentage of older adults are mentally ill. Most of them have been mentally ill since at least young adulthood and have simply aged. When psychopathology appears for the first time in later life, it usually takes the form of depression. Thus, Chapter 16 discusses depression in later life along with interventions for this psychopathology. The other major topic in this chapter is Alzheimer's disease or senile dementia of the Alzheimer's type (SDAT). SDAT is the most frequent cause of senility in old age, and it is a dreaded disease for which there is currently no cure.

Later adulthood is a time to review life and reminisce about previous experience. Chapter 17 addresses this aspect of aging and discusses autobiography and life review. Several autobiographies are presented to provide the flavor of what it is like to look back over a full life and extract meaning and satisfaction (or despair) from it. Living, dying, and death are the topics of Chapter 18. While death can be experienced at any point in the life span, it is most likely to be faced in late life. For this reason the topic of death and dying is usually associated with the study of aging. In this chapter the many aspects of death and dying from cryonics to euthanasia are considered.

The last chapter in *Psychology and Aging* deals with aging in the future. All of us face aging in our own personal future. The aging of our grandparents, parents, and our own aging happen more rapidly than we would have anticipated. Indeed, the aged is the one minority group to which we will all belong. The final chapter explores some considerations about our own personal aging along with what the experience of aging may be like in the twenty-first century.

For the student of psychology and aging I have tried to make the material interesting by presenting examples and including case studies of some of the many fascinating older adults I have come across. To highlight the important points in each chapter, a comprehensive chapter-end summary is included. I would also encourage students to read further about topics of special interest to them, and in that regard an extensive list of up-to-date references in psychology and aging has been included. For colleagues teaching the course I have written a series of multiple-choice and short essay questions for each chapter which are included in the Instructor's Manual.

There are many people who have helped me at some point while I have been writing *Psychology and Aging*. In particular, I want to express my appreciation to the following scholars who reviewed the manuscript in depth and made many valuable suggestions to improve the content of the book. They are: Steven W. Cornelius (Cornell), Nancy W. Denney (University of Wisconsin), Irene M. Hulicka (State University College at Buffalo), Joan McDowd (University of Southern California), Victoria J. Molfese (Southern Illinois University), Marion Perlmutter (University of Michigan), and Russell Ohta (University of Southern California). In addition, one person has given me encouragement and direct assistance on a daily basis from the inception of this project to its completion. In this regard I express my gratitude to my husband, Hyung Woong Pak.

Diana S. Woodruff-Pak

CHAPTER 1

The Study
of Psychology and Aging

Why study aging? This has been a question asked for decades by laypeople, students, and scientists alike, and the answer to the question gets more and more lengthy as the years pass. One of the most dramatic ways in which we can answer that questions is to point out that within 40 years the population in the world will include over 1 billion people 60 years of age or older (Shuman, 1987a)! Perhaps first and foremost, we need to study aging because of the rapidly expanding world population of older adults.

    A century ago, we may have studied aging because of simple human curiosity and the challenge presented by observations of the passage of time on living organisms. Aging is a phenomenon which exists as a part of nature and, therefore, it is important to understand its causes. Recently, as people have become more interested in understanding their own personal development and their relationships with others, the study of aging has come to involve the goal of understanding the changes individuals experience and the nature of different perspectives attained at different ages.

    Perhaps the most compelling reason for studying aging in the late 1980s is the fact that there are so many in our population who are in their sixties or older. With the alleviation of the high mortality rates of infancy and youth in the twentieth century in developed nations, a much greater proportion of the population is surviving to old age. For Third-World countries, aging of the population will be a phenomenon of the twenty-first century.

Problems and issues of having a major segment of the population over the age of 65 simply did not trouble nations, whether developed or undeveloped, much before the mid-twentieth century. Confronted with the prospect of continued growth in the numbers of individuals attaining their eightieth and ninetieth birthdays, social planners have been forced to direct resources into the study and care of an elderly population. This means that gerontology is an expanding discipline, and it will continue to offer career and service opportunities to growing numbers of individuals who become interested in answering the questions and addressing the problems of aging.

WHY STUDY AGING?

It appears that the reasons to study aging fall into at least three categories: (1) scientific, (2) personal, and (3) social. A central goal of this volume is to enhance the understanding of adulthood and aging. Therefore, it is important to examine these three major reasons for studying aging in greater detail.

Scientific Reasons

One of the mysteries of life is the effect of the passage of time on living organisms. In many respects, aging is one of the most complicated of all nature's puzzles. While processes of development proceed in a fairly regulated and predictable fashion from a relatively undifferentiated to a highly complex state, processes of aging begin in the already developed organism and proceed in a much less regular manner. In answering the question, "Why study aging?" in his presidential address to the American Psychological Association Division on Maturity and Old Age in 1957, James Birren raised the question of whether or not the complexities of aging could even be delimited by scientific understanding. He stated:

> From the viewpoint of science the question might be asked: "Is aging an orderly process susceptible to reduction to a series of rational principles?" To some extent a question of this nature is premature, but progress can come from premature and embarrassing questions. Aging is one of the problem areas in science that stands in need of much clarification, because there is a tendency on the part of some scientists to shy away from research on aging because it has not been neatly conceptualized (Birren, 1958, p. 292).

In the three decades which have elapsed since Birren's statement, great progress has been made in the scientific understanding of aging. Nevertheless, aging has yet to be reduced to a series of rational principles. In that sense, aging is a challenge to scientists because it poses questions difficult if not impossible to answer. To the scientist, aging might be what Mt. Everest is to the mountain climber. Only the hardiest and most willing to take risks will accept the call. Success is by no means guaranteed, but on the other hand, the attainment once achieved is supreme.

Success in the scientific understanding of aging has a variety of rewards. To untangle one of the knottiest problems life presents is a reward in and of itself. Additionally, an understanding of aging can lead to very direct benefits to humankind. For example, basic research on the biological effects of the hormone DES being conducted at Temple University by Dr. Arthur Schwartz has led to the discovery that this hormone retards cancer in aging mice as well as lowering the fat content in the bodies of the animals. If, after many additional scientific steps, it is discovered that the hormone exerts a similar effect in human aging, many lives may be extended and numerous individuals may be spared the agony of cancer. Basic research on aging has a tremendous potential to impact our lives, and this is why in some respects it is impossible not to consider the social reasons for the study of aging when discussing the scientific rationale. The social pressures to study aging have led to greater resources being directed to scientists interested in problems of aging so that the scientific study of aging is no longer purely a pursuit for the purpose of knowledge itself.

In addition to impacting society, the scientific study of aging also impacts understanding of basic processes themselves. The understanding of how aging affects memory lends insight into processes of memory. The pieces of knowledge generated by the description and explanation of aging changes add to the knowledge about general phenomena. In this regard, the study of basic processes and the study of the aging of those processes augment one another. Each draws from the other to lead to a more complete understanding. In the psychology of aging, scientists do not simply begin in a vacuum when they study aging. They build upon the knowledge which has already developed in a behavioral domain by adding to that knowledge the effect on that behavior of the aging process.

The organization of this book is based on the premise that research on aging and study of basic psychological processes enhance one another. Thus, the chapters are organized around basic behavioral processes studied in psychology: arousal, sensation and perception, learning and memory, intelligence, personality, and psychopathology. In a sense, aging is a natural manipulation of these behavioral phenomena and in that manner serves as a test of the understanding of the basic processes. For example, in Chapter 11 on the psychobiology of learning, memory, and aging, a model of the neurobiological circuit for a simple form of learning is presented. Age differences exist in this simple form of learning. Thus by determining if aging processes affect the neurobiological circuit, a test of the basic model is made.

It must be acknowledged that this method of moving from nondevelopmental to developmental perspectives of behavioral phenomena is not without problems. For example, we will find in Chapter 13 on intelligence and aging that the premise of applying intelligence tests created for a specific purpose to the more general use of assessment across the life span may have yielded an unrealistic perspective of intelligence in old age. Nevertheless, the interchange between the study of basic processes and the study of their development and aging often augments understanding in both domains.

Personal Reasons

The decade of the 1970s was a period of egocentrism on the part of many Americans, and indeed this decade has frequently been labeled the "me" decade. It is not surprising that in their quest to understand their lives, people took a developmental perspective to look forward and backward at themselves. It was a period when books such as *Roots* and *Passages* were best sellers because they emphasized self-understanding through an intergenerational and developmental perspective. Particularly in the case of *Passages,* the neglected middle-aged years and the people experiencing them were finally given attention. In discovering what Havighurst (1972) has called the "developmental tasks" of adulthood and the common phases which individuals experience in the various adult decades, many adults were relieved to find how much they shared with others of their age group. They also took comfort in the insights they gained about what they could expect to experience in subsequent years.

It turns out that adjustment in old age involves the development of habits and interests much earlier in life which will be adaptive later. Planning for retirement is actually most effectively carried out if it is initiated in early adulthood. In addition to the financial provisions which must be made, the establishment of activities which can be pursued when more leisure time is available aids in the transition from work to retirement. While many firms are recognizing the importance of preretirement counseling in helping their employees to achieve satisfaction in retirement, most initiate the counseling at a point when the employee is about to retire. A personal reason for understanding more about aging and the aging process is to facilitate adjustment in the later years.

Individuals often study aging to gain personal insights to aid them in dealing with their parents and grandparents. One of the developmental tasks of middle age is to become the parent to one's parents. At some ponit in time, the middle-aged individual has to become more responsible for the welfare of his or her parents. For some, this is the point at which they become interested in the study of aging.

Another personal reason for studying aging is to develop a career in gerontology. In many fields involving service delivery, a knowledge about aging including a certificate in gerontology can advance a career. Physicians and nurses and other health delivery services personnel are more likely to deal with aged patients than with any other age group, and geriatrics is becoming an increasingly important specialty in health care. Adult education is one of the few domains in which the field of education is growing, and teachers are requiring training in the different methods needed to educate effectively adults and the elderly. Counselors and therapists are being met with increasing demands from an aging population, particularly as the more highly educated middle-aged cohorts attain older adulthood. As a significant segment of consumers, the aged are of consequence to business as well. Knowledge of aging is sought for developing and marketing new products targeted for the aged. Thus, gerontology is a relevant discipline to almost any professional specialization, and it is also a field which provides a significant number of careers in and of itself.

In the last 20 years, there has been a rapidly expanding development of curricula directed to the study of aging (Douglass, 1987). Programs of education in aging began in the early 1950s. In 1976 the Association for Gerontology in Higher Education surveyed academic institutions in the United States and found that 1,275 colleges and universities offered courses in aging or provided special educational opportunities for older persons. In the period between 1966 and 1984, the Administration on Aging (AoA) career training program supported educational programs on aging in over 200 universities and colleges. The staff at AoA estimate that 25,000 students received concentrated training in aging from these programs which resulted in a certificate or degree in gerontology. Nevertheless, the number of trained personnel in the field of aging continues to fall far short of need.

Social Reasons

The aged have become such a major segment of the population that it is simply no longer possible to ignore them. At the turn of the century, the aged comprised only 4 percent of the population of the United States, and the life expectancy was 47 years. Given the urgency of other health and social issues of the time, aging was the least of the concerns of social planners. This is still true in developing nations where life expectancy is similar to what it was in the United States a century ago. The urgent problems of poverty, high birth rate, public health, and social order are more pressing than the problems of old age. However, in the United States where half of the population born today can expect to live 75 years and where we have great numbers of adults in their thirties who will increase the percentage of the population in 2020 which is over 65 to as much as 16 percent, aging is an issue which cannot be ignored.

There is a great demand in modern society for knowledge about aging. It is essential for the welfare of a large segment of our population—a segment to which we will all one day belong—that we develop a better understanding of the processes involved. To a great degree medical research made it possible for so many of us to survive to old age, and now we require a great deal more of medical as well as psychological and social research to maximize the lives of all those reaching old age.

DEFINITIONS IN THE STUDY OF AGING

When and where do aging begin and what does it encompass? This is one of the first and most often asked questions about aging, and the answer begins to illustrate the complexity of the issue. One of the first points necessary to establish is that aging occurs on many levels. It can be conceptualized on at least three primary dimensions: biological, psychological, and social. Biological aging is inevitably viewed in terms of decline. It is conceptualized in terms of the nearness to death or an individual's position relative to his or her potential life span. Psychological aging refers to the adaptive capacity of an individual as observed in terms of behavior. It may also refer to subjective reactions and to self-awareness. Social aging deals with the social habits and roles of the individual in relation to the expectations of various groups and of society.

With regard to when and where aging begins, it begins at different points of the life span depending upon whether one is dealing with biological, psychological, or social age. If one is thinking in terms of catabolic processes and decline, then aging does not begin until some apex has been attained whether it be at the point of seven to nine months in the fetus in terms of the total number of nerve cells which will ever exist in the organism, or at the age of 30 or beyond when physiological systems such as the cardiovascular, pulmonary, or nervous systems begin to show a loss in efficiency of approximately 1 percent per year. It could be argued that social aging begins at birth or perhaps at one year of age when certain social expectations and norms begin to be established on the basis of age. Psychological aging might be viewed to begin at a variety of different times depending on the behavior being assessed.

One of the important differences between psychological age functions and biological age functions is that psychological age functions include the possibility of increment while biological age functions by definition involve decline. Psychological aging includes concepts of maturity and wisdom in addition to concepts of senility. Typically, psychologists take a life-span approach and consider aging to begin after adulthood has been attained.

It may seem unusual in a textbook about aging to avoid presenting a specific and quotable definition of aging. However, a major point to be made is that aging is not one single process but a number of processes which are not well understood. Furthermore, a definition of aging at one level may be inaccurate when applied at another level. To state, for example, that the aging process begins at conception would suit some, but it would not be accurate for many phenomena which simply do not exist at conception or for many years after conception. Thus, we will consider components of aging, such as biological, psychological, and social aging, and refrain from specifically defining aging as a whole.

While we will refrain from presenting a specific definition of aging, it is important for the student to know what we mean when we use the term *aged*. In discussing humans, the most commonly accepted age at which the term aged applies is the retirement age of 65 years. This age was set by the founder and first chancellor of the German Empire, Otto von Bismarck, in the late nineteenth century. Von Bismarck chose the age of 65 arbitrarily as the retirement age because so few people in that period survived that long. Indeed, the age of 65 in contemporary American society means something very different from what it meant 100 years ago, and it must be made explicit that the acceptance of this number of years as the demarcation of an aged individual is arbitrary. In this regard, we will consider it merely an operational definition of aged.

It is important to stipulate from the very beginning of this book that the aged are not a homogeneous group. Quite to the contrary, individual differences increase with age, and many geropsychologists have chosen to differentiate between the young old and the old old (Neugarten, 1974). Indeed, each decade beyond the age of 65 probably could be delineated as a new phase. The typical 65-year-old is quite different from the typical 75-year-old who also stands apart from the typical 85-year-old.

Another point which is important to understand when studying aging is that *aging* is simply a general marker term for something else. One of the goals of gerontologists is really to eliminate the term *aging* altogether and replace it with the process or processes responsible for the change under examination. Aging denotes the passage of time and whatever processes occurring over time which result in change in the organism.

The term used to denote the scientific study of aging is *gerontology*. This term is more general than geriatrics because it is meant to encompass the entire scope of aging processes, both normal and pathological. Geriatrics, on the other hand, is the study and treatment of pathological processes of aging. The medical model of aging, like the biological perspective, deals totally in terms of decline. Aging is viewed as synonymous with pathology.

HISTORY OF GERONTOLOGY

Although the history of interest and speculation about aging is ancient, the scientific study of aging is a relatively recent development. Some of the earliest writings which have been discovered have involved myths and ideas about aging, indicating that this has been a topic of significance from the time humans recorded their thoughts. In a treatise about conceptions of aging in ancient history, Gruman (1966) pointed out that aging was a phenomenon dealt with in myths. Before humans began thinking systematically about nature and attempting to explain natural phenomena, they considered these topics to lie within the domain of religion. Gruman identified three myths that were popular in earlier times and used to help people deal with the mysteries of aging and long life.

The first myth was the *antideluvian* theme that sometime in the past people had lived longer and that they had somehow lost that power in the present. The Biblical Adam and Eve story is one example of this theme. In northern Japan it was believed that people had lived longer by shedding their skins like snakes.

The *hyperborean* theme had more of a geographical flavor and was initiated by the Greeks. The idea was that somewhere in the world there existed people who lived a long time. These remarkable people were thought to be favored by the gods and blessed with abundance, tranquility, and good health. According to an ancient source quoted by Gruman, "they hold glad revelry; and neither sickness nor baneful eld mingleth among that chosen people; but, aloof from toil and conflict, they dwell afar" (Gruman, 1966, p. 22).

The third theme characteristic of early attempts to explain aging and longevity is the *rejuvenation* theme. Often the rejuvenating source was water as in Ponce de Leon's long-sought fountain of youth. However, sexual activity also was given a great deal of attention as a rejuvenator. A Biblical example comes from the first book of Kings in which David in his old age was given a young virgin to sleep with in hopes of helping him to regain vigor.

> Now King David was old, advanced in age; and they covered him with clothes, but he could not keep warm.
>   2 So his servants said to him, "Let them seek a young virgin for my lord the king, and let her attend the king and become his nurse; and let her lie in your bosom, that my lord the king may keep warm."
>   3 So they searched for a beautiful girl throughout all the territory of Israel, and found Abishag the Shunammite, and brought her to the king. (I Kings: 1–3)

While all of these themes were developed in the prescientific era before empirically derived answers to questions were sought, these myths are not without their counterparts in contemporary society. Evangelical Christians who hold to an absolutely literal interpretation of the Bible believe that Adam lived 930 years, Seth for 912 years, Noah for 950 years, and Methuselah, the best-known longevous individual, for 969 years. In the sense, they exemplify contemporary believers in the antediluvian myth. In the Soviet Union it is claimed that many citizens of the region in the Georgian republic known as Abkasia live to be 160 years or beyond. This exemplifies the hyperborian myth in contemporary life, which was popularized several years ago in commercials for Dannon yogurt.

The most common myth which has been carried into modern times is the rejuvenation theme. Numerous spas and clinics throughout the world offer treatments to prolong life. The rich and the hopeful can travel to Rumania to be treated with the procane and vitamin injections of Dr. Ana Aslan, trek to Switzerland for injections from the cells of a lamb fetus as prescribed by Dr. Paul Niehans, or visit the Peter Stephan Private Clinic in London where they will receive "body servicing," which includes injections of genetic material and enzymes from fetal cells. While many clients of these various treatments feel that the travel and expense were worth the results, there is little evidence that any known substance or treatment actually serves to extend life.

The beginning of an empirical attempt to manipulate individual life expectancy was actually an extension of the dream of rejuvenation. The beginning of experimental gerontology is cited by some (Comfort, 1964) as occurring on June 1, 1889 at the public lecture when the 73-year-old French physiologist, Charles Brown-Sequard revealed that he had been experimenting on himself by injecting extracts from the testicles of monkeys. He was searching for what we now know as hormones, and he hoped to use them to retard the aging process. His research was ridiculed and he was accused of being senile. Brown-Sequard claimed to feel like a man of 30 as a result of the treatment. Nevertheless, he died five years later at the age of 78.

The French professor's concept was not forgotten, however, and Eugen Steinach attempted to stimulate proliferation of the testicular hormone cells by operating on the testicles. More radical was the Russian surgeon, Dr. S. A. Voronoff, who transplanted the testicles of chimpanzees onto men. With our present knowledge of the immune system, it seems remarkable that the men survived the surgery. Apparently the transplants fell off, and the recipients were left in about the same state as when they came into the operation. While these pioneering attempts seem laughable to us in the 1980s, they represent serious efforts to discover a "cure" for aging. Indeed, in tampering with hormones and the endocrine system which is involved with the production and control of hormones, these early scientists were exploring the system currently believed by many gerontologists to hold the key to aging.

In leaping through history from the original thoughts of humans about aging and longevity to contemporary manifestations of the compelling power of the myths and to the first acknowledged attempt by a scientist experimentally to extend life, we have overlooked the significant historical developments which led to the scientific study of aging. Prescientific thinking and the delegation of natural phenomena to the domain of religion prevailed until relatively recently in the history of ideas. It was not until the seventeenth century that individuals began to break with tradition, sometimes at the risk of their lives for religious heresy, and attempt to invoke the scientific method to explain nature.

Francis Bacon was one of the early advocates of the scientific method who also considered aging to be within the domain of science. The scientific method advocated the systematic observation of phenomena in order to discover the underlying laws governing behavior. Bacon's implication for gerontology was that by undertaking a systematic study of the processes of aging, one might discover the causes of aging. He thought that poor hygienic practices had the most significant effect on the aging process. Thus, he was one of the first to hypothesize a cause for aging which could potentially come under human control and which was clearly set apart from the will of God.

One of the most famous of American scientists in the eighteenth century was Benjamin Franklin, and Franklin's active mind considered and tested hypotheses about aging and rejuvenation. Like Bacon, Franklin hoped that science would be able to discover the laws governing the aging process and that it might, ultimately, discover a way to rejuvenate people. In this regard he stated:

> I wish it were possible, from this instance, to invent a method of embalming drowned persons, in such a manner that they may be recalled to life at any period, however distant, for having a very ardent desire to see and observe the state of America a hundred years hence, I should prefer to any ordinary death, the being immersed in a cask of Madeira wine, with a few friends, till that time, to be then recalled to life by the solar warmth of my dear country. But...in all probability we live in an age too early and too near the infancy of science, to hope to see an art brought in our time to its perfection,...(Franklin quoted in Gruman, 1966, p. 84).

Franklin's wry wit should not obscure the fact that he was serious about the potential of various methods of rejuvenation. He explored the possibility that lightning might be used to resurrect deceased animals and eventually humans. It was thought at the time that since electricity had a stimulating effect, it could have a direct influence on the life span. Of course this method of rejuvenation, as so many others, failed.

Bacon and Franklin can certainly be considered among those who nurtured scientific thinking and its application to aging, but a Belgian named Quetelet is considered to be the first gerontologist (Birren, 1961). Quetelet was born in Ghent in 1796 and received the first doctorate awarded in Science from the University of Ghent in 1819 in mathematics. He created some of the major statistical tools used to analyze data, and he also developed concepts which reshaped notions of the nature of humans and human behavior. He studied probabilities and developed the concept of the average man around which extremes were distributed. This was a revolutionary idea. Up to that point a more Aristotelian concept had prevailed of humans having something or not having it—of being or not being. Quetelet's idea was that there could be a continuum of levels of an ability or trait and that this continuum was distributed around an average. The result of Quetelet's pioneering work was a curve (often called the bell-shaped curve) that we now accept as representing a basic distribution of most human traits.

Measurements distribute themselves in this fashion with regard to such characteristics as height, weight, and intelligence. In 1835 Quetelet published a book entitled *On the Nature of Man and the Development of His Faculties* in which he listed the averages and the extremes he had measured for various traits such as hand strength and body weight. He also published records of variations in the death and birth rates, and he presented some data which have been included as part of the psychology of aging. Specifically, he looked at the age of French and English playwrights and began to analyze their productivity in terms of how old they were. Such notions have been followed up in the more recent work of Lehman (1953), who found that the focus of artistic production changed with the age of the producer. Young poets typically write lyric poems, while many older poets write sagas and epics.

In another manner Quetelet broke with earlier thought and tradition by examining longevity. Before the 1800s, longevity belonged to the domain of theology and was not considered a fitting topic for natural science. However, in Quetelet's mind, little was beyond comprehending if one attended to scientific observation and statistical relationships. Although Quetelet is not a well-known figure in contemporary times, his impact was great, and the many translations of his book attest to the wide dissemination of his ideas in his own time. Thus, his ideas have filtered down to modern scientists, even if his name has not.

From the time Quetelet's book was published in 1935 until the period of the next major contribution to gerontology, 50 years elapsed. Sir Francis Galton succeeded Quetelet as the next prominent contributor to gerontology, and like Quetelet, he was a member of the upper class. Indeed, it was only the members of the upper class who could afford to be educated and to enjoy the luxury of contemplation and scientific experimentation. Galton was a cousin of Charles Darwin. In his own right he was a well-known statistician, responsible for developing the first index of correlation. Galton's fundamental contribution to gerontology is the study he carried out at the International Health Exhibition in London in 1884. For this exhibition he devised and built measuring devices for 17 different abilities and charged individuals a modest sum to test their faculties. Over 9,337 males and females aged 5 to 80 were measured on characteristics such as strength of grip, vital capacity, visual accuracy, hearing acuity, and reaction time. With these data Galton demonstrated that many human characteristics showed differences with age. For example, hearing for high tones was one of the variables which showed a lower capacity with age. Thus, with this massive data collection Galton initiated one of the first major studies of life span development and ushered in an new era in the scientific study of aging.

Study of various aspects of the aging process began to be initiated around the turn of the century and a number of books on aging appeared. In 1908 Minot published *The Problems of Age, Growth and Death,* and Metchnikoff came out with *The Prolongatiaon of Life. Senescence and Rejuvenescence* by Child appeared in 1915, and *The Biology of Death* by Pearl was published in 1922. These books represented the initial attempts of biologists to describe, explain, and to speculate about how to modify processes of aging (Birren & Woodruff, 1983).

Brown-Sequard has been considered the initiator of experimental gerontology, but he did not write extensively about his experiements and his ideas on aging were not taken seriously. The authors of the first books on the biology of aging were in some ways as unsophisticated as Brown-Sequard in their approaches, and what many of the texts had in common was a simplistic approach involving the attempt to explain aging as a single process with a single cause. This had been the weakness of Bacon's explanation—that a single cause such as poor hygienic practice could account for all aspects of aging.

Now, two centuries later, gerontologists had yet to make many advances. Metchnikoff, for example, was impressed by the observation that yogurt eaters of central Europe apparently enjoyed good health and longer lives. He attributed their longevity to the possibility that yogurt cleansed the gastrointestinal tract of bacteria which he thought caused an increasing toxicity of the organism with age. What Metchnikoff did not know was that gastrointestinal bacteria actually perform important functions in the digestive process. On the basis of his observations or correlations between the life expectancies of grandparents, parents, and children, Pearl came to believe that heredity was the sole key for determning longevity. This reasoning represents a violation of one of the major features of the aging process: multiple determination.

Aging is the result of the interaction of biological, psychological, and social forces. This point can be illustrated by the following example. Imagine that you had parents and grandparents who lived to their eighties. This would give you a significant advantage in terms of having a potentially longer life expectancy. (You would add a total of ten years on to your life expectancy according to the life expectancy test presented in Chapter 6). On the other hand, imagine that your personal life style led you to be 30 percent overweight and smoke two packs of cigarettes a day. (You would have to subtract approximately 19 years off your life expectancy according to the life expectancy test). The point is that there does not appear to be one single determinant of long life. Certainly no single gene inherited from our ancestors predetermines our life expectancy. Indeed, the life expectancy test in Chapter 6 includes 32 questions indicating that there are at least 32 empirically demonstrated factors involved in longevity, and undoubtedly the list will lengthen as we learn more about processes of longevity and aging.

In addition to the books on aging that began to appear after the turn of the century, there began to be some data collection which laid the foundation for perspectives of psychological aging. This persisted in some cases for several decades. Intelligence testing which began in France as an effort to predict academic success in children was adapted in the United States to predict success in the armed services and used as a screening device to eliminate those men who might be incapable of following orders and learning new tasks. These data were analyzed by age, and in 1921 Yerkes published a report indicating that after the age of 20, intelligence declined.

This result which was replicated in subsequent studies of the civilian population of that period affected the perspective of many of those who began to study the psychology of aging in the 1920s through the 1950s. It was not until the mid-1960s (Schaie, 1965) that a clear and forceful statement of the weakness of cross-sectional studies which led to the Yerkes (1921) result was published. These developments are addressed in greater detail in Chapter 2 on research methodology in aging and in Chapter 13 on the study of intelligence in adulthood and old age.

The volume which marks the first book-length contribution to the psychology of aging since Quetelet's publication in 1835 was *Senescence, the Last Half of Life.* This book was published in 1922, and its author, G. Stanley Hall, is considered to be the father of developmental psychology. Hall was a psychologist specializing in childhood and adolescence. He published the first book on the latter topic, and actually coined the term *adolescence.* His concern with his own retirement led him to write *Senescence,* and the tone of the book is sometimes bitter, reflecting the reluctance with which Hall approached his own aging. Nevertheless, the book made important contributions. Up to this point, psychologists had regarded old age as but the inverse or regression of development. Hall challenged this notion by stating:

> As a psychologist I am convinced that the psychic states of old people have great significance. Senescence, like adolescence, has its own feelings, thoughts and wills, as well as its own physiology, and their regimen is important as well as that of the body. Individual differences here are probably greater than in youth (Hall, 1922, p. 100)

One of Hall's innovations was a study of old people's religious beliefs and fears of death by means of a questionnaire. Hall found that people did not necessarily show an increase in religious interest as they grew older. He also discovered that the elderly in his sample had not become more fearful of death. Geropsychologists today keep rediscovering the fact that the aged are afraid of the circumstances of dying, but are not more fearful of death itself. Death, as an abstraction, is more a fear of a young person. This point will be elaborated in Chapter 18 on living, dying, and death.

A contemporary of Hall's was a physician named Osler who was an internist at Johns Hopkins University. At that period, medicine had the tradition of looking for a single cause of a disease or disorder. It was thought that the identification of the organism entering the body would lead to the prescription of a specific therapy which in turn would bring the cure. Osler was impressed by a preponderance of arteriosclerosis, or hardening of the arteries, in the aged. His contribution to gerontology was the discovery that aging was closely related to the state of the blood vessels in the body, and he maintained that if the brain did change with age, it was a result of the hardening of the arteries. This position has been maintained by many geriatricians and gerontologists who view aging in the nervous system as secondary and caused by the insufficient oxygen supply to the nervous tissue which is caused by aging in the cardiovascular system.

While Americans studying gerontology in the 1920s stressed the significance of hardening of the arteries and decline in the cardiovascular system in aging processes, Pavlov and his students in Russia emphasized the importance of the central nervous system in aging. From his famous experiments of conditioning in dogs, Pavlov learned that old animals conditioned differently from young ones and that their responses showed a different course of extinction. Pavlov believed that the inhibition process was the first to succumb to old age, and this notion has continued to receive support in subsequent decades. Age changes in inhibitory processes in the nervous system and the implications of these changes are discussed in Chapter 8 on arousal, sleep, and aging.

The question of whether a perfect nervous system ages only because of external influences such as inadequate blood flow which was the focus of early American researchers, or because a "time clock" slows the functions of the nervous system itself as the early Russian scientists emphasized is still viable today. This issue has yet to be resolved, although some answers will be provided in subsequent chapters. What is most clear is that there are multiple determinants of aging. Aging occurs independently at many levels, and at the same time interaction occurs among the various aging phenomena to make the total outcome in the organism more than simply the sum of the individual parts.

In one of his statements, Pavlov presented a fundamental issue of gerontology that has persisted to the present. This issue involves the differentiation between a normal process of senescence and that due to disease. Pavlov observed in his aging dogs both normal physiological and pathological old age (Nikitin, 1958). In geriatrics it is often maintained that only disease or pathology can lead to the demise of an otherwise perfect organism and that it is meaningless to say that someone dies of "old age." This point is currently being challenged even by geriatricians themselves (Fries & Crapo, 1981). In gerontology it has traditionally been maintained that the disease model of aging is inadequate and that there is a normal pattern of aging apart from disease. Normal patterns of aging could be the result of genetic or environmental determinants. To distinguish the inevitable from the avoidable through manipulation of the enviornment is the concern of many researchers today.

During the 1930s the groundwork was laid for many of the developments in gerontology which have flourished in the post-World War II period. Medicine became increasingly interested in the degenerative diseases because dramatic progress was being made in controlling the early-life killers, the infectious diseases. However, studying chronic disease involves examining the physiological changes of the aging host to that disease in addition to studying the disease process itself. In 1933 the Josiah Macy, Jr. Foundation of New York sponsored the publication of *Arteriosclerosis: A Survey of the Problem* edited by Edmund Cowdry. In this volume consideration was given to the relationship between aging and the blood vessels, of which arteriosclerosis is in part a manifestation.

As a result of the activities of the Josiah Macy Jr. Foundation, an interdisciplinary volume was sponsored and devoted to the problems of aging. The activities of this foundation also led to a conference sponsored by the National Research Council and the Union of American Biological Societies in 1937. The National Research Council additionally sponsored a conference of its committee on the biological processes of aging in 1938. The rapid acceptance of another volume edited by Cowdry, entitled *Problems of Ageing,* was evidence that the ideas presented in it were timely. The first edition of 1939 was reprinted in 1940, and a second edition was published in 1942.

Several influential organizations held conferences on aging in 1940 and 1941. Among these were the American Orthopsychiatric Association, the Medical Clinics of North America, the American Chemical Society, and the National Institutes of Health. The Josiah Macy Foundation, an early sponsor of research on aging, provided a grant to aid the Public Health Service in conducting a conference in Mental Health and Later Maturity, and the National Institutes of Health sponsored a conference on this subject in 1941.

Many of the topics of that conference are still contemporary concerns, such as the psychiatric significance of aging as a public health problem, intellectual changes with age, psychotherapy in the practice of geriatrics, and industrial aspects of aging personnel. This conference would have had a considerably greater impact on the concepts, research, and practice of a variety of sciences and professions had not the United States become involved in World War II before these proceedings could be published. The contemporary flavor of the conference can be seen in the opening address presented by the Surgeon General Thomas Parran, who anticipated many of the current concerns of gerontologists:

> The aged are people whereas aging is a process. However, in order to solve the urgent clinical and sociologic problems introduced by the greatly increasing numbers of older people in the country, we need to know more of the processes and the con-

sequences of aging. Not the least important of many questions are those concerned with the mental changes introduced by senescence. Without health, the increasing millions past the meridian represent a potential disastrous economic and social menace to the commonwealth. Thus the maintenance of mental and physical health into true senility is an objective worthy of our most conscientious and extensive efforts....

Senescence is not a disease, nor is it all decline. Some functional capacities increase with the years as others diminish. This is particularly notable with certain mental activities. It is thus of the greatest importance that far more precise information as to the changes in mental capacities which occur with aging become available if we are to employ wisely and utilize the vast reservoir of elderly persons only too anxious to be of use. There is no greater tragedy for the aged than the unnecessary sense of uselessness which society now imposes upon them prematurely (USPHS, 1972, p. 2).

Several of the basic concepts of gerontology were developed in the 1940s. One was that problems of aging are complex and are best studied in an interdisciplinary context. A second concept was that aging represented an interractive process of biological predisposition and the environment. As noted earlier, impetus for the study of aging came from the fact that the focus of medicine was shifting from infectious diseases to chronic diseases, which by their nature are involved in the physiology of aging.

Another impetus was the fact that the proportion of persons over age 65 had dramatically expanded between 1900 and 1940. During the 1930s the number of individuals over the age of 65 increased 35 percent, as contrasted with an increase in the general population of only 7.2 percent. The significance of this point will be elaborated in Chapter 3 on the aging population. There was an increasing realization both of the social consequences of the aggregation of large numbers of older persons and, because of their particular health requirements, of the need for fundamental information on the processes of aging.

By 1940, thinking about problems of aging had become more systematic. Gerontology was receiving recognition as an independent and important field. However, World War II interrupted research pursuits in gerontology as many directed their energies to the war effort. At the same time, the war created the need and the opportunity for the study of aging. Just as World War I had led to the collection of large masses of data on men in the adult-age range, World War II stimulated data collection in this population. For example, in England, where there was a shortage of workers, studies of aging were undertaken with the aim to learn how to best train and utilize older workers in positions which had been previously reserved for the young. In the United States, it was the data James Birren (who was to become one of the preeminent international scholars in the field of gerontology) collected in the military during World War II on servicemen of various ages which convinced him that age was an important variable affecting his results more dramatically than any of his experimental independent variables. Thus, while the war interrupted the development of gerontology as a field, it also served in some ways as an impetus for the study of aging.

TABLE 1.1   Senior Authors of Eight or More Publications in Psychological Gerontology That Appeared Prior to 1968, Ordered By Their First Publication.

1919	S. L. Pressey	1951	R. Albrecht
			J. Botwinick
1926	E. W. Burgess		J. H. Britton
	E. L. Thorndike		M. Cesa-Bianchi
			H. Kay
1927	K. Tachibana		R. W. Kleemeier
			D. O. Moberg
1928	H. E. Jones		H. Thomae
1929	H. S. Conrad	1952	J. Tuckman
1930	E. K. Strong	1953	A. I. Goldfarb
			V. A. Kral
1931	D. Kotsovsky		M. E. Linden
	W. R. Miles		K. W. Schaie
1933	C. Bühler	1954	E. W. Busse
1934	I. Lorge	1955	P. Baumgartner
1935	J. E. Anderson	1956	D. B. Bromley
	W. Dennis		J. Inglis
	J. G. Gilbert		W. Schulte
	H. C. Lehman		G. F. Streib
	D. Wechsler		K. Wolff
1938	G. Lawton	1957	F. Clément
			L. F. Jarvik
1940	O. J. Kaplan		K. F. H. Murrell
	R. G. Kuhlen		
		1958	E. Belbin
1943	R. A. McFarland		S. Griew
			U. Lehr
1945	N. W. Shock		B. L. Neugarten
	A. L. Vischer		K. F. Riegel
1947	C. Fox	1959	W. K. Caird
	R. J. Havighurst		S. M. Chown
			C. Eisdorfer
1948	J. E. Birren		G. A. Talland
	P. Ju-Shu		
	S. Pacaud	1961	I. M. Hulicka
	K. Stern		
		1963	R. N. Butler
1949	W. Donahue		
	H. Feifel	1964	F.I.M. Craik
	J. Szafran		R. Kastenbaum
	A. T. Welford		P.M.A. Rabbitt
1950	N. Bayley	1965	C. L. Goodrick

Source: Riegel, K. F. (1977). History of psychological gerontology. In J. E. Birren & K. W. Schaie (Eds.), *Handbook of the psychology of aging.* New York: Van Nostrand Reinhold, p. 88.

Beginning in 1946, a rapid series of developments occurred which merits a characterization of the postwar years as a period of expansion. Laboratories devoted to the study of aging were started, research societies were founded, and many national and international conferences were held. A detailed description of the growth of the field in this period would be prohibitive, but some examples are appropriate.

In 1940 the Surgeon General, Thomas Parran, appointed a National Advisory Committee to assist in the formation of a unit on gerontology within the National Institutes of Health. This culminated in the creation of the National Institute on Aging, which was signed into law in 1974. In 1946 staffing was started at the Gerontological Unit of the National Institutes of Health and the Nuffield Unit for Research into Problems of Aging at the University of Cambridge. These units attracted many scientists who are now prominent in the field of aging.

A listing of researchers prominent in geropsychology during this period and up to 1968 is presented in Table 1.1. Many of these individuals were present at an international congress of gerontology which was founded in 1946. The first International Congress of Gerontology was held in Liege. The Gerontological Society of America was founded in 1945, and it encouraged discussion among professionals of all disciplines pursuing research in the field of aging.

To illustrate the increase in research output in the postwar years, an examination of the number of publications on aging is appropriate. In 1835 there were but a mere handful of publications, such as the material by Bacon and Franklin. From about 1835 to the early 1900s, there was not much increase. At the turn of the century, there were five or six books published, and this rate continued until 1949, with some interruption due to World War II. The literature generated between 1950 and 1960 equaled the production of the literature published in the entire preceding 115 years. Thus, research and interest in aging have shown an exponential curve of growth which is continuing in the present. Figure 1.1 demonstrates this point by presenting the number of publications per year in geropsychology over the decades between 1920 and 1970. This curve looks even more dramatic as it is presented in Figure 1.2 which illustrates the cumulative number of publications in geropsychology over the hundred-year period between 1870 and 1970.

A sampling of the major studies in geropsychology listed by time of initiation is presented in Table 1.2. This list was compiled by Brumer and published in Riegel (1977). It is limited to the investigations which began prior to 1965 and included persons over the age of 55 years. The studies included represent large cross-sectional or longitudinal investigations, and much of the material presented in this textbook is derived from these data. However, in the period since 1965 there has continued to be an exponential growth in the number of publications in gerontology such that a great deal of data has been added since the studies identified in Table 1.2 were completed. It must be noted that some of the studies on the table are ongoing. In this sense the table represents more than a mere collection of important studies which were completed by 1965.

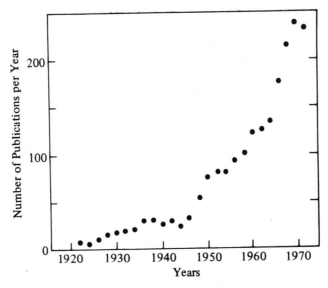

FIGURE 1.1 Publication rate over the 50-year period between 1920 and 1970 in psychological gerontology. Number of publications per year are plotted as averages of two-year intervals. Source: Riegel, K. F. (1977). History of psychological gerontology. In J. E. Birren & K. W. Schaie (Eds.), *Handbook of the psychology of aging.* New York: Van Nostrand Reinhold, p. 93. Reprinted by permission.

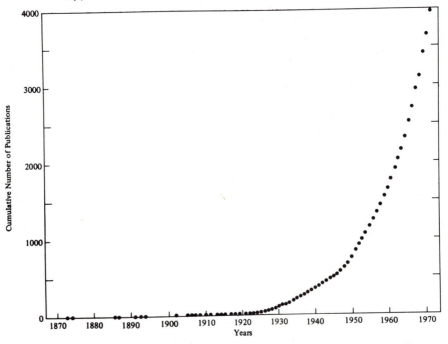

FIGURE 1.2 Cumulative number of publications in psychological gerontology over the 100-year period between 1870 and 1970 Source: Reigel, K. F. (1977). History of psychological gerontology. In J. E. Birren & K. W. Schaie (Eds.), *Handbook of the psychology of aging.* New York: Van Nostrand Reinhold, p. 93. Reprinted by permission.

18

TABLE 1.2   Major Human Studies in the Psychology of Aging.[a]

Beginning Year	Principal Investigator References Title or Place of Study	Subjects (number, type, age range) Procedures	Focus of research
1884	Galton Rutger and Stoessiger (1927), Elderton, Moul and Page (1928) Anthropometric Laboratory, London	9,337 visitors, International Health Exhibition; 5 to 80	anthropometric, sensory perceptual, motor measures
1920	Foster and Taylor (1920) Boston Study	106 hospital patients, 50 to 84; 315 men, 20 to 30; 316 children, 10 to 19	Yerkes-Bridge Point Scale
1922	Terman (1925) Terman and Oden (1959) Genetic Studies of Genius	1,500 school children with IQ's above 140; several follow-up studies into adulthood	Stanford-Binet, Concept Mastery Test, inverview
1925	Jones Jones and Conrad (1933) New England Study	1,191 Ss from rural communities, 10 to 60	Army Alpha, memory tasks
1927	Willoughby (1927) First Stanford Study	141 children, 13; 280 siblings and 190 parents, 5 to 60	Army Alpha
1928	Bayley and Macfarlane Mass and Kuypers (1974) From Thirty to Seventy	142 parents of children from Berkeley Growth Study and Guidance Study; 40 years follow-up	life style, personality, environmental context, health
1928	Miles (1931) Miles and Miles (1932) Stanford Later Maturity Study	863 Ss from two California cities, 6 to 95; 2 year follow-up on subsample	Otis Self Administration Test of Intelligence, perceptual and motor skills
1929	Nicholson (1929) Voluntary Motor Activity	2,000 Ss, 17 to 86	speed and control of motor ability
1930	Babcock (1930), Gilbert (1935) Measurement of Mental Deterioration	185 Ss, 20 to 29, 175 Ss, 60 to 69	Babcock Test of Mental Efficiency
1930	Sorenson (1938) Adult Abilities	5,500 students of evening classes, 15 to 60 +	aptitude test, reading test, vocabulary
1931	Strong (1943) Vocational Interest	1,300 Ss, 15 to 60 +; several retest studies	Strong Vocational Interest Blank
1933	Bühler (1933) Lebenslaufanalyse	256 Ss mainly from Austria and Germany; adults	biographies, life histories, interviews, personal and performance records
1934	Cattell (1934)	1,039 clerks and typists, 15 to 70	Cattell Intelligence Test
1934	Kirihara (1934) Japanese Factory Worker	25,000 workers and children, 6 to 75	intelligence test
1936	Terman and Miles (1936) Sex and Personality	3,000 Ss, 20 to 90	Attitude Interest Analysis Test
1937	Willoughby (1937)	500 women, 20 to 60 +	Personality Adjustment Sexual Attitude Rigidity Tests

TABLE 1.2   (continued)

Beginning Year	Principal Investigator References Title or Place of Study	Subjects (number, type, age range) Procedures	Focus of research
1939	Wechsler (1939) Doppell and Wallace (1955) Standardization WAIS	1,750 Ss from New York area, representative of white U.S. population, 7 to 64; 475 Ss from Kansas City, 68 to 75 +	Wechsler-Bellevue Adult Intelligence Scale
1941	Gilbert (1941) Memory Loss	174 Ss, 20 to 29 matched on vocabulary with 174 Ss, 60 to 69	eleven memory tasks
1941	Heston and Cannell (1941) Adult Performances	643 Ss, 15 to 76	Stanford-Binet, Knox Cubes, Porteus Mazes, Ferguson Form Board
1944	Thorndike and Gallup (1944) Verbal Intelligence	2,906 Ss, national sample, 20 to 60 +	Columbia Arithmetic, Vocabulary, Directions
1947	Gray (1947) Psychological Types	1,000 Ss, 10 to 60	introversion-extroversion questionnaire
1947	Kallman and Sander (1948), Jarvik and Blum (1971) Twin Studies	150 same sex twins from New York area 60 to 89; several follow-up studies	four subtests from WAIS, Stanford-Binet Vocabulary, tapping test
1948	Raven (1948), Foulds (1949) Comparative Assessment of Intelligence	4,000 skilled and unskilled men, administrators, students, 15 to 60	Progressive Matrices, Mill Hill Vocabulary
1950	Owens (1953, 1966) Iowa Study	127 college freshmen of 1919; retested after 31 and 46 years	Army Alpha
1951	Birren and Botwinick (1951a,b) Performance Speed	413 Ss, 16 to 90	addition test, writing speed
1953	Berkowitz and Green (1965) Longitudinal Study of WAIS	205 Ss below 50, 1,026 Ss above 50; retested after 10 years	Wechsler-Bellevue Adult Intelligence Scale
1953	Havighurst and Albrecht (1953) Older People	500 Ss, 20 to 60 +	social roles, interests, activities
1953	Lutze and Binas (1953) Work Intensity	850 Ss, 12 to 60	addition tests
1953	Lehman (1953) Age and Achievement	several thousand exceptional individuals	biographies, performance and production records
1954	Barker and Barker (1961) Psychological Ecology	162 Ss, 65 + from three small cities	recording of action patterns
1956	Blau (1956) Age Identification	450 Ss, over 60	social status, age identification, social roles
1956	Hardesty Wechsler (1956), Riegel and Riegel (1959, 1972) Standardization HAWIE	1,831 Ss, representative of German population, 10 to 60; 360 Ss, representative of Northern German population, 55 to 75 + ; retested after 5 years	Hamburg-Wechsler Intelligence Test für Erwachsene

TABLE 1.2   (continued)

Beginning Year	Principal Investigator References Title or Place of Study	Subjects (number, type, age range) Procedures	Focus of research
1956	Havighurst (1957) Study of Adult Life in Kansas City	124 Ss, 50 to 70, 167 Ss, 70 to 90; seven rounds of retesting	life satisfaction, level of activity, role changes
1956	Heglin (1956) Problem Solving	300 Ss, 15 to 70 +	rigidity tests
1956	Kent (1956) Counseling Study	500 Ss, over 60	attitude toward life and retirement
1956	Kutner, Fanshel, Togo, and Langner (1956)	500 Ss, over 60	attitude toward life and retirement
1956	Riegal and Riegel (1972)[b] Hamburg Study	120 Ss, 16 to 19, 380 Ss, 55 to 75 + representative of population in Northern Germany; retested after 5 years; rechecked after 10 years	Intelligence (HAWIE), verbal abilities (SASKA), word associations, attitudes and interests, social and living conditions
1956	Schaie (1958) Seattle Life-Span Study	500 Ss, 21 to 70; retested after 7 years and 14 years	SRA Primary Abilities Test, behavioral rigidity, social and living conditions
1957	Busse (1970), Maddox (1963), Palmore (1970) Duke University Study of Aging and Human Development	271 community residents, 60 +; ten rounds of retesting	physical, psychiatric, psychological (WAIS) and sociological measures
1957	Phillips (1957) Role Changes	500 Ss, over 60	age identification, social roles, adjustment
1958	Neugarten and Gutman (1958), Neugarten (1964) Age-Sex Roles and Personality	131 Ss, 40 to 70	Thematic Apperception Test
1958	Reichard, Livson and Peterson (1962) Aging and Personality	87 men, 55 to 72	projective tests, interviews
1959	Lowenthal (1964) Social Isolation and Mental Illness	534 patients admitted to psychiatric clinic, 60 +; 600 community residents, 60 +	interviews, social activities, adaptation, interaction and intimacy
1960	Birren, Butler, Greenhouse, Sokoloff, and Yarrow (1963) Granick and Paterson (1971) Healthy Aging Man	47 men, 65 to 91 11 years follow-up	medical records, EEG, psychometric, personality, psychosocial tests
1960	Gurin, Veroff and Feld (1960) Psychological Stress	2,447 Ss, 21 to 65 +	interview of symptoms of distress
1960	Nyssen and Crahay (1960) Language Functions	400 Ss, 21 to 88	word definition tests
1961	Kogen and Wallach (1961) Values and Attitudes	357 college students, 154 Ss, 47 to 85	test of self-confidence and caution, evaluation of life stages

TABLE 1.2   (continued)

Beginning Year	Principal Investigator References Title or Place of Study	Subjects (number, type, age range) Procedures	Focus of research
1961	Lehr (1961) Changes in Themes of Life	350 Ss, 20 to 60	ratings, attitudes toward life, marriage, family, menopause
1961	Wallach and Green (1961) Subjective Time	118 freshmen and sophomores; 160 Ss, 65 to 75	Knapp Time Metaphor Test, intelligence (WAIS)
1963	Bell, Rose and Damon (1966) Normative Aging Study	2,000 men, 24 to 84	various biological, psychological and sociological tests
1963	Lehr and Puschner (1963) Lehr (1964) Attitudes Toward Age	500 Ss, 20 to 80	interviews, questionnaires, awareness of aging
1963	Neugarten, Wood, Kraines, and Loomis (1963) Attitude Toward Menopause	267 women, 21 to 65	interview, Attitude-Toward-Menopause Check List
1964	Canestrari and Coppinger (1964) Word Association	700 Ss, 20 to 69	Kent Rosanoff Word Association Test
1964	Neugarten and Weinstein (1964) Changing Grandparents	140 grandparents, 50 to 69	comfort, significance and style of grandparental roles
1965	Thomae *et al.* (1973)[b] Bonn Studies	222 Ss, 59 to 78, 293 Ss, 62 to 88; retested after 1, 2, 4 and 7 years	intelligence (HAWIE), attitude and interests, social and living conditions, life histories

[a]Initiated prior to 1965 and including persons above 55 years of age.
[b]The studies by Riegel and Riegal (1972) and Thomae *et al.* (1973) have been pooled, see Riegel and Angleitner (1975).
Source: Riegel, K. F. (1977). History of psychological gerontology. In J. E. Birren & K. W. Schaie (Eds.), *Handbook of the psychology of aging.* New York: Van Nostrand Reinhold, pp. 89–92.

To get an even more contemporary impression of the growth of interest and research in gerontology, an examination of the number of doctoral dissertations published in aging has been undertaken. Dissertations reflect the number of students entering a field at a given time rather than the total number of workers in a field. The number of dissertations completed between 1934 and 1982 on any topic in gerontology is presented in Figure 1.3 along with dissertations on psychology and aging. Again it can be seen that the growth rate is exponential. Furthermore, in addition to the new students who are being attracted to the study of aging, many senior scholars are beginning to attend to age as a major organizing variable and are publishing articles on aging in their special areas of expertise.

Another example of the growing size and significance of the study of aging in psychology is the decision of the American Psychological Association, the major organization of psychologists in the United States, to create a journal devoted to

Doctoral Dissertations in Aging
All Aging and Psychology

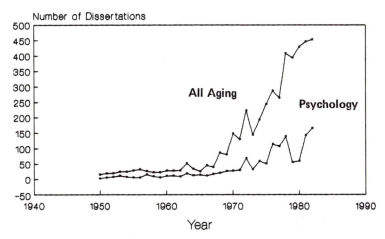

FIGURE 1.3   Number of doctoral dissertations per year on any topic relating to aging during the period between 1934 and 1982. These doctoral dissertations were located by professional librarians working at the University of Southern California Andrus Gerontology Center library and cited in 15 articles published in the *Journal of Gerontology* between 1971 and 1985 (Moore, 1985; Moore & Birren, 1972, 1973; Moore, Tuchin & Birren, 1971; Mueller, 1977, 1981, 1982; Mueller & Kronauer, 1978, 1979, 1980; Mueller & Moore, 1983, 1984; Mueller, Moore & Birren, 1974, 1975, 1976).

research on psychological aging. The new journal, *Psychology and Aging,* published its first volume in 1986.

What is the reason for this awesome growth in gerontological interest and knowledge? In a sense, this question is a rephrasing of the question with which we began this chapter: Why study aging? There we listed the scientific, personal, and social reasons which have led so many to become attracted to research, teaching, and practice in the field of aging. Of course, the major source of growth has occurred as a function of social change. Gerontology is really a product of the twentieth century. Historically, old age was certainly not unknown; it was simply uncommon. The average life expectancy at birth 1000 B.C. is reported to have been about 18 years; in Julius Ceaser's day, approximately 50 B.C., the figure increased to 25 years and stayed about the same until the seventeenth century when the average life expectancy increased to 32 years. Life expectancy in the United States in 1900 was 47 years, but by 1988 it has increased to over 75 years. Thus, there are a great many more of us who are aged, and we are making demands on society to attend to our needs and desires.

While aging of the population has been primarily a phenomenon of developed nations, it is increasingly becoming a relevant issue in all parts of the world. Thus, from July 26 to August 6, 1982, the United Nations General Assembly convened a World Assembly on Aging in Vienna. Delegates from 124 member states were present. The World Assembly on Aging focused on the question of aging within the context of global social and economic trends and addressed these issues in their full complexity. The World Assembly on Aging made clear that the increasing numbers of aged in the world will necessitate fundamental adjustments in social and economic infrastructure (Shuman, 1987b). The meeting was the first of its kind convened on a worldwide level. The meeting of the World Assembly on Aging is yet another clear sign attesting to the scope and import of gerontology as a field. There is no question whatsoever that the need for understanding about aging in general and psychology and aging in particular will continue to expand throughout the twenty-first century.

SUMMARY

We began this chapter with the question, "Why study aging?" The answer to that question lies in three different areas: scientific, personal, and social. The first domain of response is scientific. Two of the major goals of science are to describe and to explain. Aging is a general phenomenon which exists universally in living organisms, and, thus, it is an important topic to explore. A second reason for studying aging is personal in that we all age. To enhance our self-understanding, to plan for the future, and to improve our relationships with others at different points in the life span, it is useful to know about processes of aging. The third reason for studying aging is social. There is a large segment of our population which is elderly and which faces problems unique to that period of life. Provisions must be made for this group. In this regard, the best possible understanding of aging is desirable if not essential to the optimization of society. Indeed, the population of the world is aging, and the issues of aging must be addressed on a worldwide level if major social and economic crises are to be avoided.

Three primary dimensions of aging are biological, psychological, and social. Biological aging is defined in terms of nearness to death and involves decline in the organism's capacity to survive. Psychological aging is the adaptive capacity of an individual's behavior as well as subjective reactions and self-awareness. Social aging involves social habits and roles in relation to expectations of various groups and society.

The scientific study of aging processes is called gerontology. The term *geriatrics* refers to the branch of medicine dealing with aging processes and relates to pathological changes in old age.

The history of human concern with aging dates back to the earliest recorded writings. There was myth and speculation about the causes of aging in prescientific times. From the beginning of experimental gerontology in the late nineteenth century, attempts to extend life expectancy occurred. Charles Brown-Sequard who presented his ideas about aging in 1889 is credited as the first modern experimental gerontologist, although over a century earlier Benjamin Franklin had conducted experiments on rejuvenation. Adolphe Quetelet contributed to the descriptive body of knowledge about aging with his book published in 1835, *On the Nature of Man and the Development of His Faculties.* Sir Francis Galton succeeded Quetelet as the next prominent contributor to scientific knowledge about aging and behavior by collecting data on over 9,000 participants at the International Health Exhibition in London in 1884.

After the turn of the century, a number of books about the biology of aging appeared. In 1922, G. Stanley Hall, a very prominent American psychologist, gave visibility to the psychology of aging by publishing *Senescence, the Last Half of Life.* The 1920s were also a time when the perspective that intelligence declines with age was being formed.

In the early twentieth century the famous physiologist, Ivan Pavlov, focused on an issue that has continued to trouble gerontologists. This is the problem of differentiating between normal aging processes and aging effects resulting from disease. The field of medicine addressed this issue in the 1930s and 1940s, and several conferences were held to examine normal versus pathological aging. It was recognized during this period that gerontology must be studied from a multidisciplinary perspective.

World War II interrupted the scientific study of aging, but with the shortage of workers resulting from the war, it also served as a impetus to understand how to use effectively the skills of older workers. Since 1946, the field of aging has grown at an exponential rate. Research and training in gerontology have expanded dramatically in the last four decades as indexed by research publications and doctoral dissertations completed during this period. Given the continued aging of the population of the world, the need for knowledge about processes of aging and the demand for individuals trained in gerontology will continue to increase throughout the next century.

REFERENCES

BIRREN, J. E. (1958). Why study aging? *American Psychologist, 13,* 292–296.

BIRREN, J. E. (1961). A brief history of the psychology of aging. *Gerontologist, 1,* 67–77.

BIRREN, J. E., & WOODRUFF, D. S. (1983). Aging: Past and future. In D. S. Woodruff & J. E. Birren (Eds.), *Aging: Scientific perspectives and social issues,* 2nd Ed. Monterey, CA: Brooks/Cole.

CHILD, C. M. (1915). *Senescence and rejuvenescence.* Chicago: University of Chicago Press.

COMFORT, A. (1964). *The process of ageing.* New York: New American Library.

COWDRY, E. V. (Ed.) (1933). *Arteriosclerosis: A survey of the problem.* New York: Macmillan.

COWDRY, E. V. (Ed.) (1939). *Problems of ageing.* Baltimore: Williams and Wilkins.

DOUGLASS, E. B. (1987). Gerontological education and training. In G. Maddox (Ed.), *The encyclopedia of aging.* New York: Springer.

FRIES, J. F., & CRAPO, L. M. (1981). *Vitality and aging.* San Francisco: W. H. Freeman.

GRUMAN, G. J. (1966).   A history of ideas about the prolongation of life: The evolution of the prolongevity hypothesis to 1800. Philadelphia: American Philosophical Society.

HALL, G. S. (1922).   *Senescence, the second half of life.* New York: Appleton.

HAVIGHURST, R. J. (1972).   *Developmental tasks and education.* New York: McKay.

LEHMAN, H. D. (1953).   *Age and achievement.* Princeton, NJ: Princeton University Press.

METCHNIKOFF, E. (1980).   *The prolongation of life.* New York: Putnam.

MINOT, C. (1908).   *The problems of age, growth and death.* New York: Putnam.

MOORE, J. L. (1985).   A bibliography of doctoral dissertations on aging from American institutions of higher learning, 1981-1983. *Journal of Gerontology, 40,* 509-519.

MOORE, J. L., & BIRREN, J. E. (1972).   A bibliography of doctoral dissertations on aging from American institutions of higher learning, 1969-1971. *Journal of Gerontology, 27,* 399-402.

MOORE, J. L., & BIRREN, J. E. (1973).   A bibliography of doctoral dissertations on aging from American institutions of higher learning, 1970-1972. *Journal of Gerontology, 28,* 380-386.

MOORE, J. L., TUCHIN, M. S., & BIRREN, J. E. (1971).   A bibliography of doctoral dissertations on aging from American institutions of higher learning, 1934-1969. *Journal of Gerontology, 26,* 391-422.

MUELLER, J. E. (1977).   A bibliography of doctoral dissertations on aging from American institutions of higher learning, 1974-1976. *Journal of Gerontology, 32,* 480-490.

MUELLER, J. E. (1981).   A bibliography of doctoral dissertations on aging from American institutions of higher learning, 1978-1980. *Journal of Gerontology, 36,* 496-512.

MUELLER, J. E. (1982).   A bibliography of doctoral dissertations on aging from American institutions of higher learning, 1979-1981. *Journal of Gerontology, 37,* 496-512.

MUELLER, J. E., & KRONAUER, M. L. (1978).   A bibliography of doctoral dissertations on aging from American institutions of higher learning, 1975-1977. *Journal of Gerontology, 33,* 605-615.

MUELLER, J. E., & KRONAUER, M. L. (1979).   A bibliography of doctoral dissertations on aging from American institutions of higher learning, 1976-1978. *Journal of Gerontology, 34,* 591-603.

MUELLER, J. E., & KRONAUER, M. L. (1980).   A bibliography of doctoral dissertations on aging from American institutions of higher learning, 1977-1979. *Journal of Gerontology, 35,* 603-617.

MUELLER, J. E., & MOORE, J. L. (1984).   A bibliography of doctoral dissertations on aging from American institutions of higher learning, 1981-1983. *Journal of Gerontology, 39,* 631-640.

MUELLER, J. E., & MOORE, J. L. (1983).   A bibliography of doctoral dissertations on aging from American institutions of higher learning, 1980-1982. *Journal of Gerontology, 38,* 497-511.

MUELLER, J. E., MOORE, J. L., & BIRREN, J. E. (1974).   A bibliography of doctoral dissertations on aging from American institutions of higher learning, 1971-1973. *Journal of Gerontology, 29,* 459-467.

MEULLER, J. E., MOORE, J. L., & BIRREN, J. E. (1975).   A bibliography of doctoral dissertations on aging from American institutions of higher learning, 1972-1974. *Journal of Gerontology, 30,* 484-489.

MUELLER, J. E., MOORE, J. L., & BIRREN, J. E. (1976).   A bibliography of doctoral dissertations on aging from American institutions of higher learning, 1973-1975. *Journal of Gerontology, 31,* 471-483.

NEUGARTEN, B. L. (1974). Age groups in American society and the rise of the young-old. *Annals of the American Academy of Political and Social Science,* September, 187–198.

NIKITIN, V. N. (1958). *Russian studies on age-associated physiology, biochemistry and morphology: Historical sketch and bibliography.* Kharkov: A. M. Gorkiy Press.

PEARL, R. (1922). *The biology of death.* Philadelphia: J. P. Lippincott.

RIEGEL, K. F. (1977). History of psychological gerontology. In J. E. Birren and K. W. Schaie (Eds.). *Handbook of the psychology of aging.* New York: Van Nostrand Reinhold.

SCHAIE, K. W. (1965). A general model for the study of developmental problems. *Psychological Bulletin, 64,* 92–107.

SCHUMAN, T. M. (1987a). Third World aging. In G. Maddox (Ed.), *The encyclopedia of aging.* New York: Springer.

SHUMAN, T. M. (1987b). World Assembly on Aging. In G. Maddox (Ed.), *The encyclopedia of aging.* New York: Springer.

U.S. PUBLIC HEALTH SERVICE. (1972). Proceedings of the conference on mental health in later maturity, May 23–24, 1941. Washington. DC: Supplement 168 to U. S. Public Health Reports, Government Printing Office.

YERKES, R. M. (1921). Psychological examining in the United States Army. (National Academy of Science). Washington, DC: Government Printing Office.

CHAPTER 2

Research Methodology in Psychology and Aging

The aim of undertaking empirical research on the psychology of aging is to obtain objective information about behavioral processes in aging. One of the major difficulties in attempting to make psychology an objective science is that it is in the domain of every human's experience, and it is difficult to remove the subjective influences. Everyone considers themselves somewhat of an expert on human behavior, and often the results of psychological research are considered obvious, trivial, or wrong.

In reality, humans are very subjective and biased observers. We select information usually to fit in with our own world views. This is clear when we think about the frequent discrepancies in eyewitness accounts. We experience the world subjectively, and our brains' capacity to select the stimuli we remember is well documented. Thus, when we attempt to make a science out of human behavior and experience, we run into a great number of difficulties.

THE SCIENTIFIC METHOD

Science is the pursuit of objective knowledge gained through observation. Scientific thinking is different from less formal modes of thought. It involves a very deliberate kind of systematic search for knowledge. Compared to the casual, passive observations of everyday life, scientific observation is directed and carried out with care and forethought. The deliberateness and control of the process of observation is what distinguishes scientific observation. Test tubes and chemicals do not make observation scientific. It is not merely the use of special instruments, as important as they are, that makes science. Science is a method.

Requirements of the Scientific Method

There are four major requirements of the scientific method. These requirements identify scientific methodology and set it apart from less rigorous types of problem solving.

The first requirement of the scientific method is that the phenomena be *publicly observable and repeatable.* This poses difficulty for psychologists who are interested in "interior" events such as moods, dreams, and ideas. Making human responses repeatable is also difficult due to the complex nature of our capacity. Subtle differences in environment even so seemingly innocuous as the time of day or the lighting in the room may lead subjects to respond completely differently from the way they initially responded. Indeed, participation in one study may change individuals, so that they are different the next time they are tested. This problem is particularly acute in the study of aging where we are interested in continuity and change in behavior over time. By repeatedly measuring the same people, we may be changing them in a fashion which is different from how they would age in the absence of participation in aging research.

Scientific methodology requires *consistent explanation* of phenomena. It is clearly unscientific to hold to the premise that "absence makes the heart grow fonder," while also asserting "out of sight, out of mind." However, both of these axioms are popular and frequently used to explain the same event—separation. This illustrates how much more rigorous the criteria for scientific explanation are as compared to criteria applied to real-life problem solving.

The scientific method demands *systematic means of observation.* Precise and controlled conditions must be arranged so that data are collected accurately. This frequently poses problems of validity in that the people placed in circumstances where careful measurement is possible may behave totally differently from the manner in which they would behave in nonlaboratory conditions. This is especially true of the elderly. They appear to be more affected by their initial visits to the laboratory in that they are more anxious and variable in their behavior than are the young (Echenhofer & Woodruff, 1980).

The fourth requirement of scientific methodology is that there is *precision in terms.* This poses difficulty for psychologists because we often deal with everyday experiences for which there are common and imprecise terms. Devising an appropriate operational definition (a definition based explicitly on the operations used to derive the behavior (for example, intelligence is what is measured by an intelligence test; reaction time is the number of milliseconds elapsing between the onset of the stimulus and the initiation of the subject's response) is frequently difficult. In psychology there is often a gap between the operational definition and the concept we are trying to capture in our measure. This is especially obvious in the case of our example of an operational definition of intelligence. Most lay-people and psychologists feel that there is much more to human intelligence than what can be measured on a paper-and-pencil test, and they are probably correct!

Prescientific versus Scientific Thought

In Chapter 1 it was pointed out that before the seventeenth century, human thought was prescientific. People did not recognize that they had the capacity to understand natural phenomena, and they assigned nature to the domain of theology and superstition. The twentieth century is touted as the age of reason and science, at least in developed nations where a vast majority of the population receives formal education. While most adults appear to have the capacity to think scientifically—to use hypothetico-deductive logic to solve a problem—we do not always use this method in solving problems. We have islands of prescientific and superstitious thinking which seep into our behaivor. For example, it was said that the five-time Wimbleton tennis champion, Bjorn Borg, never shaved during a tennis match because he believed that he played poorly when he was cleanshaven. It is doubtful that he ever systematically tested the effect of shaving on his playing. Indeed, it would be almost impossible to do so. This is because he believed shaving affected his performance. Even if he shaved for ten tournaments and then remained unshaven for ten tournaments, we would not be able to ascertain if shaving truly affected his tennis playing. Success in any sport is dramatically affected by attitude and self-confidence. Because he believed that his beard made a difference, Bjorn might have been more likely to lose when he shaved. The critical variable is not the beard, it is the confidence it inspires. In this sense, shaving did affect performance, but the effect is indirect.

We all have some quirk reflecting the prescientific nature of our thought, even though we are capable of using the scientific method. The difficulty with approaching psychology scientifically is that our personal biases may often get in the way of our conclusions. When evaluating human behavior, we either do not strictly adhere to the scientific approach or we apply scientific methodology inappropriately.

Steps in Science

The goal of science is understanding. In pursuit of that goal, there are usually several steps: description, explanation, and prediction and modification. The psychology of aging is primarily a descriptive science; that is, we are for the most part at the first step of the scientific endeavor. This is because geropsychology is a relatively new science and because we are usually not able to experiment and manipulate psychological aging phenomena because of pratical and ethical reasons. In this regard, few would volunteer for an experiment aimed at aging them.

However, many might desire to be made younger. Nevertheless, manipulations in either direction might be stressful, life threatening, or impossible to achieve.

In accordance with the steps in scientific study, there are two major methods of psychological research: *descriptive* and *experimental.* Descriptive research involves the description of relationships between two or more variables. In the case of descriptive aging research, age is often one of the two variables and some behavioral measurement is the other. This type of research is also correlational because one variable is correlated with another.

Experimental research involves the manipulation of an independent variable and the measurement of the effect of the manipulation on the dependent variable. Three characteristics of experimental research are: (1) the random assignment of subjects to conditions, (2) the use of controls including a control group, and (3) the existence of some manipulation or several levels of the independent variable. The aim is to hold everything constant but the independent variable in order to observe its effect on behavior as measured by the dependent variable. Descriptive and experimental research takes specific forms when applied to the study of aging.

CLASSICAL
DESCRIPTIVE DESIGNS

The aim of research on the psychology of aging is to evaluate changes in behavior as a function of age. Achieving this aim is problematic for a number of reasons, among them: a vast period of time to be covered (40 or more years), tremendous individual variability, confounds with disease processes, relative uniqueness of each generation or cohort (a group of people born at approximately the same point in time). There have traditionally been two primary approaches used to study psychological aging involving *cross-sectional* and *longitudinal* research design.

Cross-sectional Design

This is a descriptive research design used to measure behavior as a function of age. Since researchers obviously cannot manipulate or assign subjects to different age groups, this is a correlational study, and no inferences about causality should be made. The proper inference is that the subjects are different in the various age groups (if there are in fact statistically significant differences in behavior in the results) rather than that they are changing with age. One of the most common errors made in the psychology of aging is to interpret cross-sectional results as signifying age changes rather than differences between age groups. We will see in Chapter 13 on intelligence and aging what a pervasive mistake this can be and what damage it caused to the image of middle-aged and aging individuals.

The cross-sectional design involves testing at least two age groups at one point in time and comparing the average scores of the two groups. An example of a cross-sectional design covering the adult years is presented in the vertical outlined area of Figure 2.1. While a study can be a cross-sectional design by simply including

Cross-sectional and Longitudinal
Developmental Research Designs

Birthdate				Age		
1890	65	70	b	75	80	85
1895	60	65		70	75	80
1900	55	60		65	70	75
1905	50	55		60	65	70
1910	a	45	50	55	60	65
1915	40	45		50	55	60
1920	35	40		45	50	55
1925	30	35		40	45	50
Time of Measurement	1955	1960		1965	1970	1975

FIGURE 2.1   Examples of longitudinal (a) and cross-sectional (b) designs. Longitudinal designs follow the same people over time, while cross-sectional designs compare different age groups at one point in time.

two age groups, it is far more satisfactory to include at least three points in the adult life span (young, middle, and old adulthood) than to rely simply on two points of measurement. Even better are the seven points represented in the cross-sectional design in Figure 2.1. The goal of studies conducted using this design is to determine if differences occur between the groups as a function of age. The problem is that the groups may differ for many reasons in addition to age.

The characteristics of cross-sectional studies are:

1. Measurement of groups which differ by age. This is a between-subjects comparison.
2. Measurement is made at one single point in time.
3. Usually comparisons are made between group averages on the dependent measure.

The cross-sectional research design is the most frequently used design in the psychology of aging. In spite of its weaknesses and confounds, it is the quickest and most efficient means of gathering data in the adult-age range. Most of the information imparted in this book is derived from the cross-sectional research design.

Longitudinal Design

Like cross-sectional design, the aim of studies employing longitudinal design in the study of psychological aging is to collect descriptive behavioral data as a function of age. The feature which is unique to longitudinal data is that it provides insight about age *changes*. In the longitudinal design, one sample is selected and measured at least twice on behavioral dependent variables. Subjects are tested at several ages at several times of measurement. A longitudinal design is presented in Figure 2.1 in the horizontally outlined section. Usually more than one dependent variable is used because of the major investment in time and other resources required to keep track of a longitudinal sample. Because of the extensive logistical and financial commitment required to conduct longitudinal research, few longitudinal studies are undertaken.

In the past six decades there have been ten large-scale longitudinal studies in the United States. One of these, initiated in 1921 by Louis Terman, identified over 1,500 Californian children of elementary school age who scored 140 or higher on the Stanford Binet Intelligence Test. In addition to testing them a number of times during their elementary and high school years, Terman retested them when they were 27, 39, 50, 55, and 60 years old. After Terman's death, other investigators carried on the study into the old age of the sample. A number of studies and books presenting the data and conclusions of this research called *Genetic Studies of Genius* have been published, first by Terman and his associates (e.g., Terman & Oden, 1947, 1959) and also by others (e.g., Bayley & Oden, 1955; Sears, 1977).

Another series of major longitudinal studies was initiated in the 1920s and 1930s at the University of California at Berkeley. In one of these studies called the Oakland Growth Study, every fifth baby born in the city of Oakland was included in the sample. In addition to the baby who was subsequently followed through adolescence and adulthood, parents and grandparents were interviewed. Now, the offspring of the original babies are included in the sample. Results from this work has provided a major foundation for contemporary knowledge about growth, development, and aging (Bayley, 1955, 1968, 1970; Eichorn, 1973; Eichorn, Clausen, Haan, Honzik & Mussen, 1981).

An example of a longitudinal study of aging is the Duke Longitudinal Study. It was initiated in the 1950s and sampled community residents over the age of 50 in the area of Raleigh-Durham, North Carolina. Biological, psychological, and social aspects of the lives of these individuals were measured over a period of 20 years. We will report results based on these longtitudinal data in a number of the chapters of this book.

Longitudinal data are unique in that they provide us with our only measure of intraindividual change over time. The factors which characterize a longitudinal study are:

1. There is repeated measurement of the same subjects who are followed over a period of time.
2. Frequently the subjects are all born around the same time (within five years of one another).
3. There are usually numerous dependent variables.
4. Data often come from many sources in addition to the subjects themselves.

A modified form of the longitudinal design is the follow-up study. This is a study in which individuals who were tested at a previous point in time are followed up and retested at a later date. While the original intent of the study was not to provide longitudinal data, at a later point in time, the original investigator or another researcher seizes the opportunity to gather longitudinal data.

The present author was involved in a follow-up study in personality. An investigator, Morris Kimber, was careful to save all his data years after he had collected it for his doctoral dissertation. When he passed away, his wife found the data and offered to donate it to the University of Southern California. It had been a study of the personality test performance of 485 students at USC in 1946. Since the university has a strong alumni association, records were available to locate a portion of the original sample. Twenty-five years after the original study when the participants were in their mid-forties, current addresses for 143 of them were obtained, and 105 agreed to take part and were tested in the follow-up study (Woodruff & Birren, 1972; Woodruff, 1983). The substantive results of this study will be described in Chapter 14 on personality.

While there are obvious sampling limitations in a follow-up study in which only one quarter of the original sample is located and retested, there are at least some statistical means which can be used to compare the subjects included with those not participating to determine how representative the follow-up sample is. Because longitudinal data are so valuable and useful in providing insights about aging, extensive effort is expended to control for the biases inherent in longitudinal and follow-up sampling rather than eliminating this mode of data collection from the repertoire of geropsychologists.

Strengths and Weaknesses of Cross-sectional and Longitudinal Designs

Both cross-sectional and longitudinal designs are preexperimental and cannot be used to provide the inference that aging is causing any phenomenon to occur. However, they do provide insights about the descriptive nature of aging processes by giving us information about what may occur as we age.

Cross-sectional designs are appropriate for the purpose of immediate prediction and control. For example, in the case of the need to set immediate social policies based on the population of young, middle-aged, and old adults of the present, cross-sectional studies are extremely useful. However, when cross-sectional data are used to predict the aging of subsequent cohorts, they may introduce biases. Cross-sectional studies are useful in providing normative characteristics of the population to indicate trends of central tendency and variability. They are also a very useful first step in the description of psychological aging phenomena because they may identify behaviors which vary between different age groups.

Unfortunately, despite their strengths, cross-sectional data also have serious limitations. For example, cross-sectional data are limited because they involve a between-subjects design and include interindividual variability. People in two age groups may differ for a variety of reasons apart from age. They may have different educational levels, different socioeconomic status, different world views, and even different genetic constituency. Additionally, there may be so many inter-individual differences wthin one age group that the existing age differences may not emerge when the two groups are compared.

The vast diversity between humans introduces a nuisance variable to cross-sectional designs: interindividual variability. When interindividual variability is systematic according to the period in time in which an age group was born, it is called the *cohort* effect and will be described in a subsequent section of this chapter. Suffice it to say that problems with the cohort variable make it possible only in rare instances for cross-sectional data to be interpreted to reflect true age changes. For this reason we never call the results observed in cross-sectional studies *age changes*. We use the term *age differences* to remind ourselves that the results may not be a function of aging.

One of the reasons longitudinal data are so useful is that the nuisance variable of interindividual variability is less of a problem. The same individual is tested repeatedly, so individual identity is maintained and the same person is compared to himself or herself at subsequent times of measurement. In this way, change can be observed. Another feature of longitudinal data is that they provide a picture of the temporal patterning of developmental and aging events. The rate of change and the actual shape of the individual growth curve can be observed. This is demonstrated in Figure 2.2 (taken from the domain of child development but mean-ingful to the study of aging) which presents data on the growth spurt of physical height in childhood and adolescence. When these data are measured cross-sectionally, they average to a linear function because the spurt occurs in different individuals at different ages. It is only with longitudinal data that the actual shape of the curve is apparent. Children do not grow in a linear fashion as suggested by data collected cross-sectionally. The natural phenomenon is obscured with this method. If the rate of change of one dependent measure is obscured, it becomes obvious that when one wants to determine relationships among change in different dependent measures, one must have longitudinal data. To observe the patterning of relationships between variables over time, longitudinal data are essential.

Although they provide unique and valuable insights, longitudinal data are extremely problematic. There are several categories of difficulties with longitudinal designs, one of which has to do with repeated measures. By recruiting an individual into a longitudinal study and measuring him or her over and over, you change the person. At each time of measurement, the subject is more test sophisticated than the last. Thus, confounded with the natural aging changes of the person are the changes occurring as a function of the testing. While control groups who are tested once or at less frequent intervals can be employed to eliminate this problem, this control is seldom used.

Another category of problems with longitudinal studies is that created by the long time frames required to study adulthood. With time, a field changes and advances are made in measurement techniques. However, to assure comparability, the investigator is usually limited to the tools available at the time the study was

Growth in Childhood
Cross-sectional vs. Longitudinal

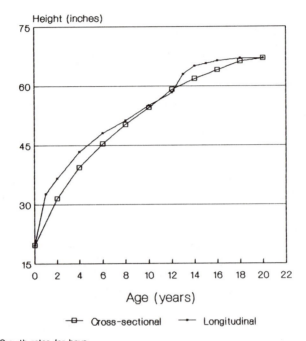

Growth rates for boys

FIGURE 2.2 Comparison of longitudinal data on growth rate including the "growth spurt" with cross-sectional data of the same phenomenon which misrepresents the true age function and yields a linear trend.

initiated. Although new measures can be added, they extend the time required for testing and lead to possible biases resulting from fatigue or boredom.

Another problem introduced by the passage of time is the attrition of the sample. People move away, lose interest, or become ill and die. All of these factors lead to a smaller and less representative sample. It is difficult to get a representative sample to volunteer to participate in a longitudinal study in the first place, and then attrition causes even more sample bias. This makes it more difficult to make valid generalizations to the general population. Time plays havoc with the investigator and staff, as well. Personnel turnover, and the aging and death of investigators all take their toll on longitudinal studies.

A major limitation of longitudinal research is resources. It is expensive to support the staff in keeping accurate records and maintaining contact with subjects. It requires office space and facilities to store records, and laboratory space and equipment is needed to measure subjects. If a large sample is maintained, numerous personnel must be employed to test all of the subjects within a given time period so that they can be tested in subsequent years. The cohort variable affects longitudinal data in that the generalizations based on one longitudinal study of a cohort group may not be valid for another.

Now we can begin to see that the cross-sectional design, despite all of its flaws, has appeal because it avoids many of the problems and biases inherent in longitudinal design. The data are collected at one point in time. There is no problem with time in that measurements can be made with state-of-the-art techniques, and the sample will not suffer from attrition. Repeated measures are not a problem, and the subjects can be totally naive. The logistics and resources necessary to carry out a cross-sectional study are far less than those needed for longitudinal research. Thus, it is not surprising that most of the research in the psychology of aging is cross-sectional. However, given the weaknesses of both cross-sectional and longitudinal designs, can we be satisfied with the inferences derived from either type of study?

One way that we can examine the reliability and validity of cross-sectional and longitudinal data is to determine if the results are repeatable. For example, if we take a number of cross-sectional studies collected over a period of many years and find that the studies consistently yield the same results, we can begin to surmise that the behavior in question may reliably differ and even change with age. For many dependent measures this amount of data is not available, but there are a few behaviors which have shown consistent age differences over a large number of cross-sectional studies.

One such behavior is the personality dimension of extraversion-introversion. Extraversion involves behavior which is gregarious, outgoing, sociable, enthusiastic, assertive, talkative, and adept at personal manipulations. The converse, introversion, involves shyness and a degree of social ineptness. By 1970 there had been one longitudinal and 12 cross-sectional studies which published data on the extraversion-introversion dimension. Nine of the cross-sectional studies presented sufficient data in the published article so that comparisons across articles could be achieved. Six of the nine studies indicated that introversion was greater in old age at a statistically significant level. The scores of older adults in the other three studies were in the direction of greater introversion, but the results did not attain statistical significance.

Over the period between 1955 and 1968, nine studies collected data from cohorts with birth years ranging from 1879 to 1943. When testing a variety of cohorts at different points in the life span, there was replication of the result that there are age differences in extraversion-introversion in the direction of higher introversion scores in old age. This kind of replication reinforces the hypothesis that there *may* be an age change in the direction of increased introversion, but it is not sufficient to lead to the conclusion that interiority increases with age. Longitudinal data are required as well, and the one longitudinal study in which such data were available only included subjects to their 45th birthday. At this point in their lives, the subjects were not more introverted than they had been 20 years previously (Kelly, 1955).

An example of a behavioral domain in which there was abundant cross-sectional evidence consistently pointing in one direction which was later modified by the perspective from longitudinal studies is intelligence. The clash between longitudinal and cross-sectional studies of intelligence and the methodological inadequacies which were identified as functioning in both types of developmental designs are elaborated in Chapter 13. The discrepancies observed between cross-sectional and longitudinal data led to many of the advances achieved in the last several decades in research methodology in developmental psychology and the psychology of aging. One of these advances was sequential designs.

Sequential Designs

In an article published in *Psychological Bulletin,* K. Warner Schaie (1965) responded to the seeming discrepancies in cross-sectional and longitudinal data and proposed sequential designs as an alternative. He argued that in developmental research there are three attributes which operate: *age, cohort,* and *time of measurement.* Age is the variable developmental psychologists and geropsychologists seek to measure. It is the maturational, ontogenetic phenomena which occur with the passage of time. Cohort includes those historical *and* genetic effects associated with being born at a certain point in history. The effect could be genetic in that at a certain point in time, a given gene pool exists.

Consider, for example, the gene pool available in the United States in 1944. It consisted of all men and women capable of conceiving children who were in the country. Unfortunately, this was a very select group comprised of those men who remained in this country because they were not physically qualified for the armed services, those who were too old or too young to volunteer or be drafted, and those who were involved in the war effort and based at home. A vast segment of the gene pool was out of the country, and the size and nature of the cohort born in the United States between 1940 and 1945 reflects this fact. Simply comparing the size of the cohort born between 1950 and 1955 to the cohort born a decade earlier (presented graphically in the next chapter in Figure 3.1) attests to the impact of World War II on the American gene pool and birth rate.

An example of how current events affect the composition of the gene pool can be seen in the Japanese cohort born between 1946 and 1955. Before and to some extent after that period, the cohorts have exclusively Mongolian genes in their background, but the cohort in question has some input from Caucasian and Negroid genes. This is because American soldiers were available in great numbers to contribute to the gene pool of that period in Japan. The outcome of historical events was a Japanese cohort totally unique in the history of that country.

In addition to the genetic component of the cohort variable, there is an environmental and experiential component. Being born at a certain time and growing up during a specific period in history stamps a cohort with certain general common experiences. Those of us born after 1935 have no experience of the tragedy of the Great Depression which indelibly altered the personalities of millions of Americans who suffered through it. Those born after 1945 never experienced the patriotic surges which motivated so many to die for their country in World War II. Instead, they faced the anguish created by the war in Viet Nam and expressed emotions which earlier-born cohorts considered traitorous.

The impact of being born at a certain period appears to have lasting consequences for values such as political party affiliation. Neal Cutler (1969, 1983) has used cohort analysis to demonstrate that party affiliation is usually made when the cohort first comes of voting age, and voting patterns by political party tend to persist in a given cohort. We currently have the perception that people become politically more conservative as they age, but Cutler's analysis demonstrates that the people over age 65 who predominantly vote Republican were actually Republican in their youth. Will we believe that people become more politically liberal as they age when the cohort born between 1945 and 1950 who were the radicals of the late 1960s become the radical elderly of the 2020s? It will be interesting to see what we have learned about the validity of our stereotypes by then. There is a *zeitgeist* or general intellectual, moral, and cultural state of an era which is carried by all of those who have experienced that time. Thus, when we compare people who have been born during different periods, we can never be sure if the differences we observed resulted from differences in their genes and experience (the cohort effect) or from differences in their age.

The third variable identified by Schaie (1965) is time of measurement. This is conceived as an effect involving the environmental context at a particular point in time. All of us who were above the age of four or five in 1963 when John F. Kennedy was assassinated remember what we were doing when we learned of the assassination, and in its aftermath there was a general state of shock and depression in the country. A more recent example of this phenomenon is the explosion during the launching of the Challenger in 1986. The disaster had particular impact on school children who were watching the launching of the first teacher, Christine McCulaffe, into space.

If either cross-sectional or longitudinal measurements were made of psychological variables shortly after the assassination of John F. Kennedy or after the space shuttle disaster, the results might be unusually inflated or depressed as a function of the time of measurement. These events affected the way people felt and behaved. Seasonal fluctuations may have a time-of-measurement effect as well. If during a one-year longitudinal study, adolescents are assessed once at Christmas, a second time right before finals weeks, and a third time in the heat of the summer, the results may not reflect their maturation.

The time-of-measurement effect is thought of as a short-term effect which affects all cohorts at a given point in time, although it may not affect them all equally. A cross-sectional study comparing college students, middle-aged parents, and aged grandparents conducted on April 10th, shortly before income tax is due, may find mood differences in the various cohorts related to the interaction between time of measurement and life stage. The college students may be almost oblivious to the tax deadline, the middle aged may feel harassed, and the aged may fall somewhere in between.

In addition to defining the three variables confounded in cross-sectional and longitudinal data, Schaie (1965) presented designs which he felt could provide estimates of each effect. By selecting populations on the basis of age, time of birth, and time of measurement, it is possible to estimate the magnitude of the various effects. The problem is that once any two of these parameters is stipulated, the third is fixed. For example, if you fix time of birth and time of measurement, age is fixed as well. This means that one of the three variables is always confounded in sequential studies. The assumption always must be made that one of the three components has no effect, and this assumption is problematic.

The three types of sequential designs proposed by Schaie in 1965 are presented in Figure 2.3. Their strengths, weaknesses, and general purpose are outlined in the following sections.

Cohort-sequential design.   This design measures the effects of age and cohort and confounds the effect of time of measurement. Its purpose is to generalize longitudinal findings over several cohorts. It isolates cohort differences and presents them over longitudinal sequences, thus permitting inferences about age changes over the age range covered. These age changes are then generalizable to more than

FIGURE 2.3   Examples of the sequential strategies proposed by Schaie (1965). The time-sequential design (a) explores the effects of age and time of measurement and confounds cohort. The cohort-sequential design (b) examines the effects of age and cohort and confounds time of measurement. The cross-sequential design (c) illuminates the effects of cohort and time of measurement and confounds age.

Sequential Research Designs
Proposed by Schaie (1965)

Birthdate			Age		
1890	65	70	75	80	85
1895	60	65	70	75	80
1900	55	60	65	70	75
1905	50	55	60	65	70
1910	45	50	55	60	65
1915	40	45	50	55	60
1920	35	40	45	50	55
1925	30	35	40	45	50
Time of Measurement	1955	1960	1965	1970	1975

the one cohort, which is the typical sample of longitudinal studies. Using the example of a cohort-sequential design outlined in Figure 2.3, the cohort born in 1910 and the cohort born in 1915 are each followed over a period of five years when they are 50 to 55 years old. There are three times of measurement, and that is the confound. This study will provide information about aging between the period of 50 and 55 years old, and it will identify any cohort differences existing in these groups which differ in birth rate by five years. Including only four cells in the design has been done for the purpose of providing a clear example. In practice, researchers would typically include more cohorts and a wider range of ages in a sequential study. According to Schaie, it is possible to confound the time-of-measurement variable with impunity only in rare instances, such as in the study of physical attributes or in studying infrahuman organisms. In other instances, he recommended alternative sequential designs.

Time-sequential design.   This design provides information about age and time of measurement and confounds cohort. It resembles a cross-sectional study carried out at two points in time. Inferences can be made about age differences at the points of the age range which are covered and information is also available about time-of-measurement differences at the ages covered. It is the net change over one time unit, in the case of the time-sequential design outlined in Figure 2.3, over two times of measurement. Differences between people aged 50 and 55 are replicated twice in our example. The confound is that different cohorts are compared. Four independent samples are drawn.

Whereas in the cohort-sequential design we followed two cohorts longitudinally, in the time-sequential design we are not making repeated measures on any group. Differences between 50- and 55-year-olds are compared at a lag of five years so that we examine the effect of time of measurement as well as the effect of age. Assuming that genetic or environmental effects which operate to create the variable designated as cohort are absent, the estimates of age and time-of-measurement effects are accurate. Schaie (1965) favored this design and felt that many psychological traits such as ability, personality, learning, and interests might not be affected by cohort. In light of the empirical demonstrations that the cohort variable is significant in the measurement of these attributes (e.g., Schaie & Strother, 1968; Woodruff & Birren, 1972), this notion has been revised.

Cross-sequential design.   Cohort and time of measurement are assessed in this design while age serves as a confound. From that point of view, this design holds the least interest for developmentalists. However, it does provide insights about effects impacting on development. In our example in Figure 2.3, two cohorts are examined at two times of measurement. We thus have a means to assess cohort and time of measurement, but we must collapse our data over two age groups in each case, making the comparisons confounded by age. Schaie (1965) argued that the assumption that age could be safely confounded might be tenable for many psychological characteristics which remain stable over a large part of the life span.

However, this assumption is seldom viable during the childhood or adolescent years.

In addition to presenting the three models, Schaie pointed out that in any instance where more than four cells were included in the data collection strategy, at least two of the three sequential analyses could be carried out. In this manner, an estimate could be made of the degree to which the assumptions about the confounded variable was accurate.

While Schaie's suggestions served many useful purposes, they were also criticized on several dimensions. Baltes (1968) argued that it was not useful to hold to a three-dimensional model when one of the dimensions was always confounded. He suggested instead that age and cohort be considered the primary variables and that sequential strategies be carried out in the fashion included in the outlined portions of Figure 2.4. Baltes also pointed out that the designs were descriptive

Sequential Research Designs
Proposed by Baltes (1968)

Birthdate			Age		
1890	65	70	75	80	85
1895	60	65	70	75	80
1900	55	60	65	70	75
1905	50	55	60	65	70
1910	45	50	55	60	65
1915	40	45	50	55	60
1920	35	40	45	50	55
1925	30	35	40	45	50
Time of Measurement	1955	1960	1965	1970	1975

FIGURE 2.4   Examples of the sequential strategies proposed by Baltes (1968). These are essentially combinations of longitudinal (a) and cross-sectional (b) sequences which explore the effects of age and cohort.

rather than explanatory and that the variables of age, cohort, and time of measurement simply described but did not explain the phenomena under study. Schaie and Baltes were able to resolve their differences for the most part (Baltes & Schaie, 1976; Schaie & Baltes, 1975) by agreeing that it was conceptually useful to identify all three variables but more practical to use the designs illustrated in Figure 2.4. That the designs are descriptive rather than explanatory has also been accepted.

The data collected in sequential strategies have supported Schaie's original contention that simple longitudinal and cross-sectional designs hopelessly confound important effects. Results from sequential studies will be presented primarily in Chapter 13 on intelligence and aging.

EXPLANATORY ANALYTIC
DEVELOPMENTAL RESEARCH

The goals of science are to describe, explain, and modify. In psychology and aging, the goal of explanation involves the demonstration of causes of developmental and aging phenomena. This goal must be met primarily through experimental and quasi-experimental strategies. Among the explanatory analytic techniques outlined by Baltes, Reese and Nesselroade (1977) in their text on developmental methodology are experimentation and simulation of development and aging, cross-cultural comparisons, heredity-environment comparisons, learning research, path analysis and structural models as methods leading to explanation. We will examine experimental and simulation techniques in this chapter and refer the interested reader to Baltes, Reese and Nesselroade's excellent book for additional information on other techniques.

Experimental aging research takes at least two primary forms. It can simply include an experimental manipulation within the traditional descriptive design (cross-sectional, longitudinal, or sequential), or it can involve the attempt to manipulate a parameter thought to cause aging. The second type of study is sometimes called age simulation, and it is less common than the use of experimental manipulation within a descriptive design.

Much of the attempt to explain aging phenomena is carried out in cross-sectional designs in which a certain parameter is manipulated. Often this research goes a step beyond the initial description of aging phenomena in an effort to explain underlying causes. On the basis of previously descriptive research, hypotheses are created and tested with experiments. Such a study was carried out by Birren and Botwinick (1955). The descriptive literature on aging had included an enormous number of studies documenting that response speed slowed with age. One of the possible causes for the slowing of response speed was the slowing of neural conduction velocity. It was reasoned that the slowing might be caused by peripheral factors such as conductivity in the nervous system, and Birren and Botwinick devised an ingenious experiment to test this notion. They reasoned that the length of the axon (part of the nerve cell which connects its own cell body to the next nerve cell) traveling from the jaw to the spinal cord was shorter than the axon traveling from the finger to the spinal cord which in turn was shorter than the axon traveling from the foot to the spinal cord. If nerve conduction velocity was an important factor in the slowing of resopnse speed and aging, then the foot reaction time of the aged which had to travel a much longer path than the jaw reaction time should be disproportionately slowed in the elderly. Excessive slowing of neural conduction velocity was predicted to interact with age, and indeed, many of the cross-sectional studies involving experiments predict an age interaction. Hypothetical data which would confirm an age interaction are presented in Figure 2.5.

An interaction occurs when the differences between the old and young in several conditions are not parallel. It serves to demonstrate under what conditions

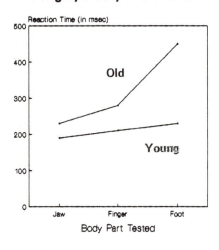

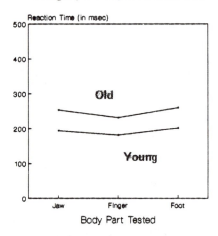

FIGURE 2.5 The panel on the left illustrates hypothetical data from the jaw, finger, and foot reaction-time study which shows an interacation between age and length of the axon. These hypothetical data suggest that conduction velocity affects reaction time in old age because the longer axon is involved in disproportionately longer reaction time. The actual data (in the panel on the right) show no interaction effect. While the old are slower in all three conditions, they are not disproportionately slow on foot reaction time. The data suggest that neural conduction velocity does not play a significant role in the slowing of reaction time with age.

age differences are exacerbated. In this manner, insight may be gained as to what is causing the age differences to occur. The actual outcome of Birren and Botwinick's experiment is also shown in Figure 2.5. The data points for the young and old are almost exactly parallel. The old are slower in every condition, but they are not disproportionately slower as the distance traveled by the neural impulse gets longer. These data have been used to support the position that periphral factors such as neural conduction velocity cannot account for the magnitude of slowing in old age.

Age simulation studies involve time-compressed or short-term modification of age functions by application of behavioral variables, biological variables, or processes assumed to be age associated. In these experiments, age becomes part of the dependent variable. The steps involved in age simulation as identified by Baltes et al. (1977) are:

1. Define an age function to use as a criterion.
2. Develop at least one hypothesis about a key variable or process involved in causing the age function.
3. Design a study to test the hypothesis-finding conditions which vary, or by actually manipulating, the key independent variable.
4. Test the accuracy of the hypothesis.
5. Examine the external validity of the result.

An age-simulation experiment (Woodruff, 1975) involving manipulation of the EEG alpha frequency in young and old subjects will serve to identify how each of the steps are actually carried out. For step 1, the age function serving as the dependent variable was simple reaction time. Numerous studies had indicated that reaction time slowed with age. Step 2 involved adoption of the hypothesis that the slowing of the EEG alpha rhythm might account for the slowing of reaction time. The rationale and empirical support for this hypothesis are presented in Chapter 10 on speed of behavior and aging. The study designed in accordance with step 3 involved the experimental manipulation of the EEG alpha frequency in young and old subjects with the technique of biofeedback. Young and old subjects were trained to modify their alpha activity to produce alpha waves 2 cps slower than their modal activity (as occurs in aging) and 2 cps faster than their modal activity (typifying youth). In this manner both young and old subjects were trained to modify their EEG in the direction of the EEG of younger and older individuals. The test of the accuracy of the hypothesis (step 4) was carried out by examining reaction time during the various EEG states. The results are presented in Figure 2.6.

When they produced slow EEG alpha activity, both young and old subjects had slower reaction times than when they produced fast EEG alpha activity. This suggested that the hypothesis that the slowing of the EEG alpha frequency was

FIGURE 2.6   Reaction time in the young and old and three brain wave frequency conditions.

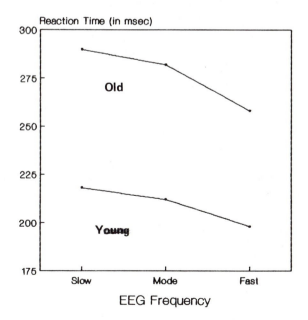

EEG Frequency and RT
Young and Older Adult Subjects

involved in the slowing of reaction time with age was accurate. However, in carrying out step 5 to test the external validity of the results, it was observed that the magnitude of the slowing of the EEG alpha frequency, which is about 1 cps in the average old person, cannot account for the magnitude of slowing of reaction time. Even when old subjects were producing brain-wave activity faster than the brain waves of young subjects, their reaction time was slower than the reaction time of the young. Thus, while the slowing of the EEG alpha frequency may be involved in the slowing of reaction time with age, it cannot account for the magnitude of reaction-time slowing.

It is obvious that there are many studies of the aging process which cannot and should not be carried out. The risk of permanently injuring subjects is simply too great in many cases to attempt to age experimentally or make young the participants. Nevertheless, we are at a point in the history of the psychology of aging where we have amassed a great deal of descriptive data, and we can begin to test some of the hypotheses which have been derived from previous research to lead us to an understanding of the nature of aging processes.

ETHICS IN RESEARCH ON AGING

In discussing experimental aging research, it is difficult to avoid the issue of ethics. On the one hand, we have the prospect of identifying some of the causes of aging processes, and in cases where those processes are deleterious, we have the potential of intervening and altering the course of the age function. With this goal in mind, it is reasonable to consider testing various relationships and attempting to identify phenomena responsible for causing behavioral aging. However, it is essential that we consider the rights of every individual whom we study to be assured that the person's rights are protected. Subjects must feel free to withdraw from a study at any time if it is causing them discomfort, and investigators must make certain that this is communicated to subjects. The problem is that even when these strictures are communicated, certain demand characteristics of the study may cause the subject to suspend judgment about whether the experience is harmful and remain even in a situation which is painful.

In addition to the problems which face investigators in typical psychological research, there are special problems with elderly subjects. In studies of senile dementia and other mind-debilitating diseases, the subject is no longer capable of making decisions about whether to participate. Others must make this decision for him or her, but the patient's rights must be protected. In the case of life-threatening illnesses, researchers have even more control over their patients. If there is a high risk but potentially beneficial cure, the patient must be able to decide whether to risk the cure or die without it. Even the manner in which the researcher presents the options to the patient may influence the decision. Therefore, the researcher must be scrupulous in the effort to present the alternatives.

In their discussion of ethical issues in the study of adulthood and aging, Hultsch and Deutsch (1981) point out that all of the following practices are ethically questionable:

1. Involving individuals in research without their knowledge of consent.
2. Failing to inform participants about the true nature of the research.
3. Misinformng participants about the true nature of the research.
4. Coercing individuals to participate in research.
5. Failing to honor promises or commitments to participants.
6. Exposing participants to physical or mental stress.
7. Invading participants' privacy.
8. Failing to maintain confidentiality of information received.
9. Withholding benefits from participants in control groups.

Hultsch and Deutsch assert that these problems usually do not arise because investigators are evil or uncaring. Scientific observation frequently demands circumstances which do not always include humanistic ideals. To study stress experimentally, stress must be produced in the participants. Since it is unethical to produce any great degree of stress in humans, there have not been many acceptable experimental studies of stress. Stress may be studied as it occurs naturally, but the opportunity to manipulate and control it usually eludes us.

One of the ways in which medical researchers decide whether to carry out a project which involves risks to the subjects is to undertake a cost-benefits analysis. Do the potential risks of the experiment outweigh the benefits to the participants and society at large, or will there be benefits to compensate the participants for their risks? One means devised to balance the costs to participants is to pay them for their work in the study. In high-risk experiments involving the testing of drugs, for example, the pay becomes higher. While many have questioned whether subjects are truly free to make a rational decision when they need money and large sums are offered for their services, this is the means by which we carry out human trials on drugs. Volunteers are paid for loaning their bodies to medical research.

Given the large numbers of research programs carried out in the United States, there are bound to be abuses of ethical principles by some researchers. In the last two decades greater emphasis has been placed on providing rules and guidelines for research with humans and animals, and federal funding of research is contingent upon the approval of the project by human-subject panels in the institutions requesting the funds as well as by panels in the federal government. Additionally, professional societies such as the American Psychological Association have devised their own set of guidelines for ethical research (APA, 1973). These guidelines have led researchers to heighten their consciousness about potential abuses and have led to changes in the design and execution of research which has had to become more sophisticated in teasing out behavior while avoiding stress, embarrassment, or pain.

SUMMARY

Research methodology in psychology and aging is directed toward understanding what happens to behavior as individuals age. A large number of problems make it difficult to derive a clear picture of behavior and aging. Since human behavior is a topic on which anyone may think he or she is an "expert," everyday prescientific thinking becomes confused with scientific approaches to psychology and aging.

The scientific method requires that phenomena be *publicly observable and repeatable,* and this is problematic for psychologists who are interested in internal mental events. However, an aging individual's behavior must be inferred from observable performance. *Consistent explanation* and *systematic observation* are two additional requirements of the scientific method. Often when we bring older adults into the laboratory and systematically observe them, we make them anxious. A fourth requirement of the scientific method is *precision in terms.* In our attempts to develop precision in our terms, we often oversimplify what we are tyring to measure. We end up dealing with something precise but trivial.

Description, explanation, and modification are three steps in science taken to understand phenomena. Psychology and aging is a descriptive science for two major reasons. It is a young science and it is usually not feasible to experiment with human aging. The major classical descriptive designs are the cross-sectional and longitudinal designs. The cross-sectional design involves a comparison of at least two age groups of subjects. Cross-sectional comparisions of younger and older adults are the most common of all research designs in the study of psychology and aging. Longitudinal studies involve following a group of individuals over time as they age. There have been ten major longitudinal studies including adulthood in the United States. Follow-up studies provide longitudinal data, but they involve finding and retesting individuals who have been assessed previously.

There are weaknesses as well as strengths in cross-sectional and longitudinal designs. Cross-sectional studies are useful for immediate prediction and control, but they confound age with cohort. People born at different points in time may differ for a variety of reasons apart from age. Thus, results from cross-sectional studies tell us about age differences. Age changes in people can be isolated only by following them over time. However, measuring an individual many times may change the person to make him or her less representative of the general population. Also, as people drop out of longitudinal studies, the sample becomes less and less representative. Turnover of investigators and expense are additional problems of longitudinal studies. Furthermore, longitudinal data on one cohort may not generalize to another cohort.

Sequential designs were created to minimize the problems of cross-sectional and longitudinal designs. They combine the two types of design in an effort to control for the three main sources of variance in developmental designs: age, cohort, and time of measurement. Sequential designs include the *cohort-sequential* design which measures the effects of age and cohort and confounds the effect of time measurement. The *time-sequential* design cohort and provides information about age and time of measurement. Cohort and time of measurement are assessed in the *cross-sequential* design, and age is confounded.

Explanatory analytic developmental research includes experiments and age-simulation studies. The aim is to test hypotheses about the causes of aging phenomena that have arisen from descriptive research. Age-simulation studies are time-compressed or short-term modifications of age functions. Naturally, it would be unethical to irreversibly age younger adults, and the number of age-simulation studies which can be attempted is limited.

Ethics in research on psychology and aging involve protecting the subject from physical and psychological harm. Subjects must always be aware of the voluntary nature of their participation. In cases in which the subject cannot make a decision to participate due to senility or in which terminal illness motivates a patient to take high risks to find a cure, scrupulous attention to the needs and rights of the patient must be heeded by the researchers. Attention to the rights of human subjects in the last several decades has led to widely recognized and accepted guidelines which are actively enforced in academic and medical research settings throughout the country.

REFERENCES

AMERICAN PSYCHOLOGICAL ASSOCIATION, AD HOC COMMITTEE ON ETHICAL STANDARDS IN PSYCHOLOGICAL RESEARCH. (1973). *Ethical principals in the conduct of research with human participants.* Washington, DC: American Psychological Association.

BALTES, P. B. (1968). Longitudinal and cross-sectional sequences in the study of age and generation effects. *Human Development, 11,* 145–171.

BALTES, P. B., REESE, H. W., AND NESSELROADE, J. R. (1977). *Lifespan developmental psychology: Introduction to research methods.* Monterey, CA: Brooks/Cole.

BALTES, P. B. AND SCHAIE, K. W. (1976). On the plasticity of intelligence in adulthood. Where Horn and Donaldson fail. *American Psychologist, 31,* 720–725.

BAYLEY, N. (1955). On the growth of intelligence. *American Psychologist, 10,* 805–818.

BAYLEY, N. (1968). Behavioral correlates of mental growth: Birth to thirty-six years. *American Psychologist, 23,* 1–17.

BAYLEY, N. (1970). Development of mental abilities. In P. H. Mussen (Ed.), *Carmichael's manual of child psychology.* New York: Wiley.

BAYLEY, N. AND ODEN, M. H. (1955). The maintenance of intellectual ability in gifted adults. *Journal of Gerontology, 10,* 91–107.

BIRREN, J. E. AND BOTWINICK, J. (1955). Age differences in finger, jaw, and foot reaction time to auditory stimuli. *Journal of Gerontology, 10,* 429–432.

CUTLER, N. E. (1969). Generation, maturation, and party affiliation: A cohort analysis. *Public Opinion Quarterly, 33,* 583–588.

CUTLER, N. E. (1983). Age and political behavior. In D. S. Woodruff & J. E. Birren (Eds.) *Aging: Scientific perspectives and social issues* (2nd ed.). Monterey, CA: Brooks/Cole.

ECHENHOFER, F. G. AND WOODRUFF, D. S. (1980).   The effect of repetitive stimulation upon EEG and arousal in young and old adults. *Gerontologist, 21,* 103.

EICHORN, D. H. (1973).   The Institute of Human Development Studies: Berkeley and Oakland. In L. F. Jarvik, C. Eisdorfer, & J. E. Blum (Eds.), *Intellectual funtioning in adults: Psychological and biological influences.* New York: Springer.

EICHORN, D. H., CLAUSEN, J. A., HAAN, N., HONZIK, M. P., AND MUSSEN, P. H. (1981).   *Present and past in middle life.* New York: Academic Press.

HULTSCH, D. F. AND DEUTSCH, F. (1981).   *Adult development and aging: A life-span perspective.* New York: McGraw-Hill.

KELLY, E. L. (1955).   Consistency of the adult personality. *American Psychologist, 10,* 659–681.

SCHAIE, K. W. (1965).   A general model for the study of developmental problems. *Psychological Bulletin, 64,* 92–107.

SCHAIE, K. W. AND BALTES, P. B. (1975).   On sequential strategies in developmental research: Description or explanation? *Human Development, 18,* 384–390.

SCHAIE, K. W. AND STROTHER, C. R. (1968).   A cross-sequential study of age changes in cognitive behavior. *Psychological Bulletin, 70,* 671–680.

SEARS, R. R. (1977).   Sources of life satisfactions of the Terman Gifted Men. *American Psychologist, 32,* 119–128.

TERMAN, L. M. AND ODEN, M. H. (1947).   *The gifted child grows up: Twenty-five years follow-up of a superior group.* Stanford, CA: Stanford University Press.

TERMAN, L. M. AND ODEN, M. H. (1959).   *The gifted group at midlife: Thirty-five years follow-up of the superior child, genetic studies of genius.* Stanford, CA: Stanford University Press.

WOODRUFF, D. S. (1975).   Relationships between EEG alpha frequency, reaction time, and age: A biofeedback study. *Psychophysiology, 12,* 673–681.

WOODRUFF, D. S. (1983).   The role of memory in personality continuity: A 25-year follow-up. *Experimental Aging Research, 9,* 31–34.

WOODRUFF, D. S. AND BIRREN, J. E. (1972).   Age changes and cohort differences in personality. *Developmental Psychology, 6,* 252–259.

CHAPTER 3

Characterizing the Aging: The Aging Population and the Aged As Individuals

More than at any time in the history of the United States, there is an awareness of the significance of aging and the impact of the aged in our society. Individuals over the age of 65 comprised 12 percent of the population of the United States in 1985 (U.S. Department of Health and Human Services, 1987). The aged have become a large and visible segment of the population. In addition to their increasing numbers, they have become organized in groups such as the "Gray Panthers" or the Association for the Advancement of Retired Persons (AARP). As the oldest and largest organization of Americans over the age of 50 years, the AARP has more than 22 million members. It was pointed out in Chapter 1 that the social reasons leading to the increased attention to aging stem primarily from the growth of the aged population. The focus of this chapter is to describe that growth and its causes and to examine the aging population. This broad perspective will help us to focus on the aging individual.

Characteristics of populations are studied by demographers. Demography is a branch of sociology concentrating on the science of population dynamics which operates at a macro level dealing with society as a whole. Psychology focuses on the individual rather than on the population at large. Nevertheless, the demographic perspective is useful to psychologists in delimiting the range in the population in which individuals can fall. It is also relevant in helping us to make predictions about individuals and what their lives might be like in the future.

Demographers project rather than predict in that they base their forecasts on data which already exist. To project how many older people will be in the population in the next century, they base their estimates on the number of people already born. In this manner they have a solid empirical base upon which to project estimates. Figure 3.1 presents an example of a demographic projection. Based on

FIGURE 3.1   Age structure of the population of the United States in 1976 and projected for 2030. Median ages of the population projected between 1970 and 2030. Source: *Newsweek*. (Feb. 28, 1977). "Graying of America." New York: Newsweek, Inc., p. 52. Reprinted by permission.

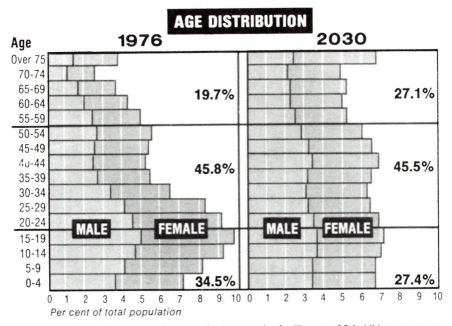

Charts based on U.S. Census projection assuming fertility rate of 2.1 children per woman

A CHANGING PROFILE

If the birth rate stays low, the nation's demographic profile will change shape and the median age (half the population older, half younger) will rise.

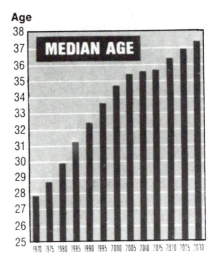

the census data gathered in 1970, projections are made about the age composition of the United States' poulation in 2030.

In addition to the age composition of the population, Figure 3.1 includes projections of the median age of the population. This is the mid-point age in the population. Half of the population is older than the median age, and the other half of the population is younger than the median age. Clearly, the median age in the United States is increasing. In 1820 the median age in the United States was less than 17 years. It was 23 years in 1900 and 30 years in 1980 (Zopf, 1986). As indicated in Figure 3.1, the median age in the United Sates is approaching 40 years by 2030.

Americans have always liked to think of themselves as youthful, and for most of their history they have been. The first American census was taken in 1790, and it indicated that half the people in the country were 16 years old or younger. As recently as 1970, the median age was under 28. But as the nation moves into its third century, its people are also getting older. Over the period between 1980 and 2030, demographers project that the number of people over 65 will more than double to 65 million. About 21.2 percent of the population, or more than one out of every five Americans, may be over the age of 65 by 2030!

In examining the demography of aging to determine the characteristics of the aged population, we have organized the chapter around five major questions. This is done to distill the vast number of facts available in gerontological demography into a focus of five important points.

WHO ARE THE AGING?

The simplest answer to the qustion of "Who are the aging?" is that there are many more of this group in the 1980s than there have been in the history of humankind. The actual number of individuals in the United States over the age of 65 at various times in the twentieth century is presented in Figure 3.2 along with projections for the older population into the twenty-first century. It is obvious from this figure that there has been an incredible growth in the numbers of older adults in our country. In 1985 there were 28.5 million Americans over the age of 65. This is almost ten times as many older adults as there were in 1900. And the older population itself is getting older. In 1985 the 65–74 age group (17.0 million) was nearly eight times larger than in 1900, but the 75–84 age group (8.8 million) was 11 times larger and the 85 + age group (2.7 million) was 22 times larger (U.S. Department of Health and Human Services, 1987). The projections in Figure 3.2 for older adults in the future are based upon the life expectancy of Americans already born. The most rapid increase in the older adult population in the United States is expected between the years 2010 and 2030 when the "baby boom" generation reaches the age of 65.

Another way to conceptualize the vast numbers of older adults in the United States is to compare our older adult population of approximately 28,500,000 people with the populations of other countries in the world. Our population of older adults

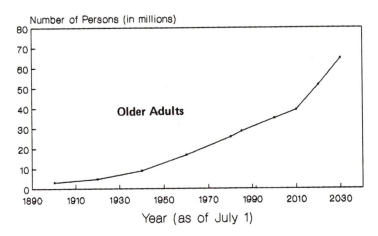

NUMBER OF PERSONS 65+
1900 to 2030

Number of Persons (in millions)

Older Adults

Year (as of July 1)

Based on data from US Bureau of Census

FIGURE 3.2   Number of people in the United States aged 65 and older from 1900 and projected to 2030. Source: U.S. Department of Health and Human Services (1987). *A profile of older Americans.* Washington, DC: Program Resources Department, American Association of Retired Persons (AARP) and the Administration on Aging (AoA).

exceeds the entire population of our neighbor to the north, Canada. It also exceeds the population of countries such as Australia and the Republic of Korea. Indeed, of the 19 foreign countries listed in Table 3.2, the population aged 65 and older in the United States exceeds the total population of 14 of them. Furthermore, our population of aged is growing at a far faster rate than the general population as a whole.

The most dramatic increases in human life expectancy have been achieved in the twentieth century. Today we have the existence of a large population of elderly because many more people are surviving the hazards of birth, infancy, childhood, and youth and are attaining adulthood and old age. It is difficult to imagine that just 90 years ago only half of the people born survived to the age of 47. Think what that would mean to your life. It meant that most couples did not both survive to see the marriages of all of their children. It meant that there were many fewer grandparents. It meant that couples typically lost a partner long before retirement. It meant that the average person could not count on attaining his or her 50th year, a point in life which we now consider to be when a person hits the prime of a career or begins to consider a new career.

Do you realize that as a student between the ages of 18 and 22, you are going to live to be at least 72.5 years if you are a man and 79.3 years if you are a woman?

That means you will still be alive in 2040 with a good chance to live until 2050 or beyond. While you may have not thought much about it, you have probably taken it for granted that your parents and even your grandparents will survive to see your children born, and you undoubtedly expect to see your own grandchildren and great grandchildren. Yet yours is among the first of generations in human which can live with such expectations. Let us examine life expectancy throughout history to begin to recognize what an impact the addition of more than 25 years to our life expectancy has had on our perspective on life.

Life Expectancy Throughout History

A point which must receive a great deal of emphasis is that to have a large proportion of old people in a society is a relatively recent phenomenon. While even in ancient times, people were aware of unique cases of individuals surviving to reach 80 or 90 years of age, most people's efforts through history have been concentrated solely on surviving long enough to raise or at least bear healthy children, and many were not even successful in living that long.

Life expectancy and life span.   In tracing the history of human longevity, it is important to distinguish between the concepts of *life expectancy* and *life span*. Life span is the upper limit set on human life. It is the genetic potential of the human species, and factors that appear to set this upper limit are yet to be discovered.

In their book on medical aspects in vitality and aging, Fries and Crapo (1981) distinguish two concepts subsumed under the term *life span*. They distinguish the maximum life potential (MLP) from life span for the general population with the idea that only a very few of us have the genetic capacity and environmental circumstances to achieve the MLP. The age at death of the longest-lived member of the species, the MLP, is recorded to have been 120 years. No individuals with verifiable birth records have survived beyond that age. (The longest-lived human with a documented birth date was Shigechiyo Izumi, a Japanese man who died on February 21, 1986 at the age of 120 years, 7 months, and 21 days). Life span, according to Fries and Crapo, is the age at which the average individual would die if there were no disease or accidents. They assert that this age is about 85 years for humans and that it has been constant for centuries. It must be acknowledged that Fries and Crapo's position is controversial, and not totally accepted within gerontology and geriatrics. They present a compelling argument for the notion of natural death, a concept which does not exist within the medical model of aging which views aging phenomena totally in terms of disease. We will have more to say about this notion in Chapter 6 on longevity and health.

As distinguished from maximum life potential and life span, life expectancy is the expected age at death of the average individual, granting current mortality rates from disease and accident. Another way to say this is to call it the age by which half of a given birth cohort will survive and half will be dead. For infants born in 1985, life expectancy was 74.7 years. This is almost 28 years longer than life expectancy for infants born in 1900. Statistics on life expectancy are computed annually by life insurance companies as well as by governmental agencies, but it is only recently that public records have been kept in such a way that precise life expectancy for the population could be estimated.

Research on life expectancy throughout history.   One of the earliest studies of birth and death rates in populations was undertaken by Graunt and published in 1662. More recently, scholars have examined records for earlier periods and made rough estimates of life expectancy. These calculations along with estimates based on more poorly documented pieces of evidence gathered from earlier periods have led to the current picture indicating human longevity has changed dramatically since prehistoric times. This is illustrated in Figure 3.3. The changes have not been in life span but in life expectancy. In modern times more people have survived to reach old age. In this way the average length of life for a given period has been extended over the centuries to the present. The average life expectancy in the United States is now almost 75 years.

Louis Dublin and his associates (Dublin, Lotka & Spiegelman, 1949) thoroughly reviewed the research on life expectancy throughout history. Studying the characteristics of human bones from the limited number of fossils of prehistoric humans which have been found, they estimated that very few prehistoric humans survived even to 40 years of age. Most met violent deaths at an early age as indicated by fractures in a large proportion of the fossilized skulls.

FIGURE 3.3   Average length of life from ancient to modern times.

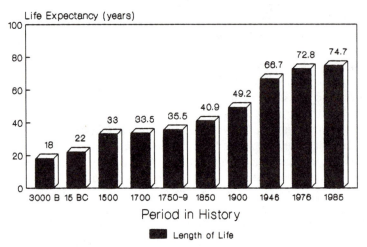

Average Length of Life
Ancient to Modern Times

Pre-1700, Europe; 1700-Present, U.S.

Estimates of average age at death in Greece between 3500 B.C. and A.D. 1300 suggest a gradual improvement in life expectancy from around 18 years in the early periods to 30 years in the period around 400 B.C. Ancient Rome was an even less healthy place to live, with some estimates of life expectancy as low as 20 years. These mortality rates for the highest centers of civilization 2,000 years ago are worse than the mortality rate for any country in present times, but not by much. For example, the United Nations (1982) reports that life expectancy for males in Ethiopia is about 38 years. Life expectancy for females in that country is 41 years.

Studies of life expectancy in the Middle Ages indicate that little improvement had been made since the time of Greek civilization. Estimates for this period range from 30 to 35 years for the average length of life. John Graunt, a haberdasher who lived in England in the mid-seventeenth century, spent much of his spare time analyzing records of christenings and burials in the city of London. While his data are incomplete, they suggest that life expectancy during that period in England may have been as low as 18 years. More sophisticated analyses undertaken later in the seventeenth and eighteenth centuries indicated that life expectancy in Western Europe was between 30 and 37 years, and that in selected cities in the United Staes in this period, life expectancy estimates ranged from 25 to 36 years. In the nineteenth century, health conditions improved enough so that about ten years was added to average life expectancy. In the mid-nineteenth century, life expectancy estimates ranged around 40 years, and by the early twentieth century, life expectancy in the United States was estimated variously between 47 and 49 years.

It is in the twentieth century that we have made the most rapid gains in human life expectancy in the history of humankind. Since the turn of the century, we have added almost 28 years to the average life expectancy in the United States so that a baby born today has a 50 percent chance of surviving to the age of 75. This tremendous leap in the life expectancy has resulted from medical advances, improvements in the standard of living, and improvements in our health care system.

Causes for improvement in life expectancy.   Reductions in mortality in the United States since 1900 have paralleled economic progress. The continued development of agricultural and industrial efficiency has led to affluence which to some degree has been used to promote public and personal health. Public funds have been used to build health facilities, to train health care professionals, and to support medical research. Increased affluence has also made it possible for individuals to purchase better health care and to avoid malnutrition.

Advances in the medical and allied sciences have led to a number of new health goods and services of improved quality. Public health efforts such as the development and application of vaccines, the pasteurization of milk, the chlorination and other protection of water supplies, the improvement of waste disposal, the protection against importation of nonendemic diseases, the improvement of housing (including central heating), the supervision, augmentation, and enrichment of food supplies, and the introduction of air conditioning—all have played a role in making our contemporary life less stressful and more conducive to longevity. Health insurance and welfare have made it possible for a greater proportion of the population to take advantage of health care advances. Additionally, the media has publicized medical advances, and the public has become more health conscious. Indeed, just knowing about factors affecting longevity can extend life expectancy when the individual is willing to take preventive measures to improve health status (Woodruff, 1977).

If the single greatest cause for the strides in life expectancy in the last 90 years had to be named, it would have to be the discovery of certain "wonder" drugs. The development of sulfonamides and antibiotics to combat infectious diseases has virtually eliminated diseases which in previous centuries practically wiped out whole populations. The change in mortality resulting from infectious disease is clearly evident in Figure 3.4 which shows the death rate in New York City over a 150-year period. The tremendous spurts in death rate resulting from epidemics of cholera, yellow fever, and influenza have virtually been eliminated since the advent of sulfa and antibiotic drugs developed in the 1930s and 1940s. The last major surge in the mortality rate occurred in New York (and also across the nation) in 1918 with the devastating influenza epidemic of that year.

Medical and public health advances have had their greatest effect on the early phases of the life span. Infant and childhood mortality rates have been drastically reduced so that more children are surviving to adulthood and old age. While we have not yet conquered the diseases of old age such as coronary artery disease, heart disease, and cancer, we have succeeded in conquering acute diseases that affect mortality most in infancy and childhood. Childbirth has also been changed from a risky to a relatively safe event for women, again improving life expectancy.

Estimates from the U.S. Public Health Service indicate that if the primary cause of death in the United States—heart disease—could be cured, another six years could be added to our current life expectancy. If all diseases of the heart and arteries, along with strokes, were eliminated, 11 years could be added, making life expectancy at birth 86 years. Cures for cancer have been projected to add five years to human life expectancy. While all of these figures are inflated, since it is highly improbable that total cures for heart disease or cancer will be discovered, scientists and physicians have already greatly improved the chances of survival for people with heart disease or cancer, and this progress suggests that more advances will be made. Several years ago the mortality from heart disease began to decline, and it is becoming more likely that the average individual can live to the life span of 85 which appears to be his or her biological endowment. Natural death resulting from processes of aging rather than from chronic disease is a concept gaining increasing credence in the medical profession (Fries, 1980). Thus, in answer to the question, "Who are the aging?" it is clear that they are numerous and they are increasing.

One important point about life expectancy that may not be obvious until one examines the life expectancy tables presented in Chapter 6 is that life expectancy at birth is different from life expectancy at the age of 65. When an individual survives the hazards which have killed some of his or her peers in early life, he or she adds to life expectancy. The life expectancy at age 65 for a man is about

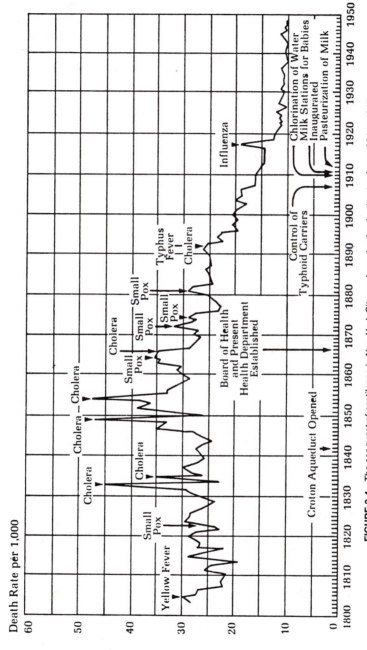

FIGURE 3.4 The conquest of pestilence in New York City as shown by the death rates from 1804 to 1947. (Courtesy of Department of Health, City of New York).

59

14.6 years. If he attains the age of 65, a man has a 50 percent chance of surviving to the age of 80. For a 65-year-old woman, life expectancy is 18.6 years. Thus, she has a good chance of living to the age of 84 years. Mortality rate is high in infancy, but it drops to its lowest point at age 11 and then gradually accelerates until it reaches high rates in the seventh decade and beyond. Mortality rates are plotted by age for the years 1910 and 1970 in Figure 3.5 to demonstrate this force of mortality.

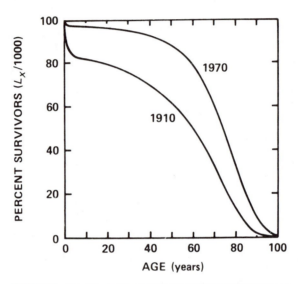

FIGURE 3.5   The age-specific mortality rate (number of deaths per year per 1,000 individuals entering each age) is shown at each age for the United States in the years 1910 and 1970. For both years, the mortality rate is minimal at about age 11 and shows a steady exponential increase following the age of 30. Source: Fries, J. F. & Crapo, L. M. (1981). *Vitality and aging.* San Francisco: W. H. Freeman, p. 30. Reprinted by permission.

It can be seen from the data presented in Figure 3.5 that the advances which have been made in life expectancy have come mostly in the early years of life. Another way to state this fact is to point out that while almost 28 years have been added to life expectancy at birth since 1900, only about five years have been added to life expectancy at age 65.

Much of the material in this book is devoted to answering the question, "Who are the aging?" The simple demographic answer which is being presented is that the aged are many—and many more than they were in previous decades. Later in this chapter we take another perspective to the question by examining characteristics of the contemporary cohorts of the aged.

ARE ALL NATIONS AGING?

Earlier in this chapter data were presented indicating that the median age of the population as well as the proportion of the aged in the population is rising dramatically in the United States. While this is a phenomenon occurring in all developed countries, it is not yet universal. Mortality rates are so high in underdeveloped nations that life expectancy is much lower. Additionally, the birth rates in these countries are high, so that the proportion of the aged in the population and the median ages are much lower than in developed nations. Countries which have developed at a pace approximating that of the United States have shown similar advances in life expectancy. Some underdeveloped countries still have a life expectancy close to that which existed in the United States at the turn of the century. However, many Third World countries anticipate dramatic increases in the percent of older adults in the population in the twenty-first century (Shuman, 1987). Life expectancy at birth and percent of the population over the age of 65 is listed for selected countries in Table 3.1.

The United Nations has categorized countries on the basis of the age of the population. If the population has more than 7 percent aged 65 and older, it is categorized as aged. An older adult population comprising 4 percent to 7 percent of the population is called mature, and a young population has less than 4 percent of its members aged 65 and older. These categories are used in Table 3.1. Countries identified as young are located in Africa, South Asia, and Latin America. Low per capita income, high birth rate, and high mortality rate characterize countries in this category (Palmore, 1987). Life expectancy in such countries is around 52 years at birth. Mature countries are located in the same continents as the young countries, but life expectancy is greater primarily due to lower birth and mortality rates. Income is also substantially higher in mature countries. The aged-population countries are found mostly in North America and Europe. The most notable exception to this is Japan which has the highest life expectancy in the world.

Examination of Table 3.1 reveals that the United States is not the oldest country in the world in terms of having the largest percentage of aged in the population. Zopf (1986) identified 19 countries with a population of one million or more which had a greater percentage of the population over 65 than did the United States. These countries are identified in Table 3.2. Sweden is the oldest country in terms of the percentage of old people in the population.

People born in the United States also do not have the longest life expectancy. Based on data available from the United Nations in 1982 and presented in Table 3.1, the longest life expectancy for both men and women was enjoyed by the Japanese. Japanese men have been credited with the longest life expectancy for at least a decade, and they presently enjoy a life expectancy four years longer than that of American men. Estimates a decade old indicate that women in the Netherlands had the longest life expectancy, followed by women in Sweden. Women in Japan a decade ago had a life expectancy one year shorter than Dutch women (United

TABLE 3.1   Demographic Characteristics of Young, Mature, and Aged Populations

Country	% 65+	Birth Rate	Death Rate	Natural Increase	Life Expectancy M	F	Per Capita GDP ($)
Young populations							
Bangladesh	2.7	47	19	28	46	47	118
Burma	3.5	39	14	24	51	54	133
Columbia	2.6	32	8	24	60	65	890
Egypt	3.6	37	10	27	52	54	485
Ethiopia	3.5	50	25	25	38	41	97
Indonesia	3.3	34	16	17	48	48	340
India	3.4	33	13	20	46	45	159
Iran	3.5	42	12	31	58	58	1,607
Mexico	3.2	38	8	30	63	68	1,413
Zaire	2.5	46	19	28	44	48	148
Average	3.2	39	14	25	51	53	539
Mature populations							
Afghanistan	4.7	48	22	26	40	41	200
Brazil	4.3	33	9	24	58	61	1,635
Chile	4.2	31	6	25	64	68	1,260
Korea, Republic of	4.0	25	8	17	63	69	1,285
Pakistan	4.1	36	12	24	54	49	257
Panama	4.2	31	6	25	64	68	1,260
South Africa	4.1	38	12	26	57	59	1,594
Sri Lanka	4.3	28	6	22	65	67	183
Turkey	4.6	40	15	25	54	54	1,159
Average	4.3	32	11	24	58	60	981
Aged populations							
Argentina	8.2	24	9	15	65	71	1,448
Canada	9.5	15	7	8	70	77	8,735
Czechoslovakia	12.1	15	12	4	67	74	n.a.
England & Wales	15.3	13	12	1	70	77	5,545
France	12.4	15	10	5	70	78	8,851
German Dem. Republic	15.4	14	14	0	69	75	n.a.
Germany, Fed. Republic	15.3	10	12	−2	70	77	10,419
Italy	13.4	11	10	1	70	76	3,472
Japan	9.3	13	7	6	74	79	8,476
Poland	9.9	19	9	10	67	75	n.a.
Spain	10.6	14	8	7	70	75	3,999
USA	11.3	16	9	7	70	78	9,687
USSR	8.0	18	9	9	65	74	n.a.
Average	12.4	15	10	5	69	76	6,737

Source: U.N. 1982.
Countries listed are the larger countries in each category. All figures are for the most recent year available. Birth and death rates are crude rates per 1,000 population. Life expectancy is at birth for males (M) and females (F). GDP = Gross Domestic Product. Average = mean. n.a. = not available. From Palmore, E. B. (1987). International perspectives. In G. L. Maddox (Ed.). *Encyclopedia of Aging,* New York: Springer, p. 362.

TABLE 3.2 Elderly Population of Countries Having 1 Million or More Inhabitants and Higher Percentages of Elderly Than the United States

Country	Year	Total Population (000)	Population 65 + Number (000)	Percent
Sweden	1980	8,310	1,354	16.3
East Germany	1980	16,737	2,661	15.9
Austria	1980	7,505	1,162	15.5
West Germany	1980	61,566	9,550	15.5
England & Wales	1980	49,244	7,424	15.1
Norway	1980	4,086	603	14.8
Denmark	1980	5,123	739	14.4
Belgium	1979	9,855	1,410	14.3
France	1980	53,583	7,535	14.1
Scotland	1980	5,153	724	14.1
Switzerland	1980	6,314	872	13.8
Italy	1980	57,070	7,676	13.5
Hungary	1980	10,711	1,438	13.4
Greece	1979	9,449	1,233	13.0
Czechoslovakia	1978	15,137	1,892	12.5
Finland	1980	4,780	572	12.0
Bulgaria	1980	8,861	1,051	11.9
Netherlands	1980	14,091	1,616	11.5
Northern Ireland	1978	1,539	175	11.4
United States	1980	226,505	25,544	11.3

Sources: United Nations, *Demographic Yearbook, 1979,* table 7; *1980,* table 7; *1981,* table 7. From Zoph, P. E. Jr. (1986). *America's older population.* Houston: Cap and Gown Press, Inc. p. 11. Reprinted by permission.

Nations, 1979). The most recently available estimates (Palmore, 1987) indicate that life expectancy for Japanese women exceeds life expectancy for American women by one year.

WILL THE POPULATION OF AGED IN THE UNITED STATES CONTINUE TO INCREASE?

We already know the answer to this question based on the data presented in Figures 3.1 and 3.2. The answer to the question of whether the aged population in the United States will increase is an emphatic *yes*. Let us examine this phenomenon more closely.

Demographers project that the percentage of the elderly in the population is increasing and will continue to rise until at least 2050. This is because they know the number of individuals who have been born up to the present, and they can estimate the mortality rate and birth rate. Given these numbers, it becomes apparent that the postwar baby boom which has impacted society so greatly in its early years will continue to do so as it ages. This large cohort has affected various institutions and activities in the United States. More elementary schools were built in the 1950s, and this cohort swelled the population in high schools and colleges in the 1960s and 1970s. They increased the ranks of the employed (and unemployed) in the 1970s and 1980s. By 2020 they will become the gerontology boom.

One of the means demographers use to examine the age composition of the population is the population pyramid. This is a figure presenting the size of each cohort by age. In Figure 3.6 the population pyramids for four periods in the United States is presented. Comparison of these pyramids shows rather dramatically how

FIGURE 3.6 Age-sex population pyramids for the United States: 1870, 1940, 1960, 1980. Source: Zopf, P. E., Jr. (1986). *America's older population.* Houston: Cap and Gown Press, p. 10. Reprinted by permission.

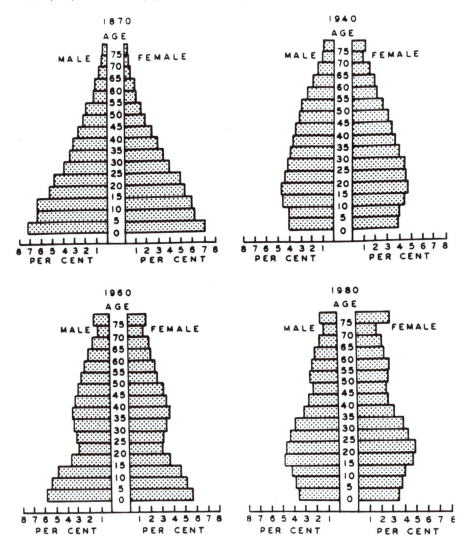

the age structure of our population has changed. The population pyramid of 1870 when people over 65 comprised about 3 percent of the American population was triangular in shape indicating a high birth rate and a high mortality rate. Population pyramids for countries such as Ethiopia which now has a life expectancy lower than American life expectancy in 1870 would be triangular with slopes perhaps even steeper than this curve.

By 1940 life expectancy had increased in the United States and birth rate was also slowing. The pyramid was becoming more rectangular. The pyramid for 1960 refelcts the bulge in the youngest age groups of the post-war baby boom, but at its apex, there is a much wider area indicating the increased number of survivors to the ages of 65 and especially to 75 and beyond.

By 1980 the bulge of the baby boom is seen to move up expanding the 15–30 year age group. Also notable in the 1980 population pyramid is the continued flattening at the top reflecting a larger group of old cohorts, and most apparent is the bulge on the older female side. The sex difference in life expectancy is highly visible in the 1980 pyramid. Several forces are combining in the United States and in most developed countries to make the population pyramid become rectangular— the shape proejcted for 2030 in Figure 3.1.

WHAT ARE THE FORCES AFFECTING THE AGE STRUCTURE OF THE POPULATION?

There are three major forces which affect age structure in any population: *fertility, mortality,* and *immigration* (Cutler & Harootyan, 1975).

Fertility

The childbearing behavior of a person or group is called fertility. The fertility rate affects the number of individuals entering into a given cohort. It is the most important determinant of the size and proportion of older persons in a population (Deming & Cutler, 1983). Fertility varies with the number of women in the childbearing ages and the number and spacing of children they choose to have. If the fertility rate is high, there will be a higher ratio of younger to older people, and the population pyramid will be more triangular in shape. This is the case in countries such as India where the fertility rate is very high. In the case of the United States, the fertility rate lowered after the postwar baby boom in the 1950s. Fertility in the United States has leveled off at replacement-level fertility of 2.1 children per woman.

The projections presented in Table 3.3 provide an example of the profound effect of fertility on the age composition of the poulation. It becomes apparent from the data presented under the heading of "Projections" in Table 3.3 that the same number of older persons (column 1) can constitute different proportions of

TABLE 3.3 Parameters for the Elderly Population Under Alternative Fertility and Mortality Assumptions: 1976, 2000, and 2020

(Numbers in thousands)

Population parameter	1976	2000[2]					2020[2]				
		Census[1] Bureau	Mortality Assumption				Census[1] Bureau	Mortality Assumption			
			Set 1	Set 2	Set 3	Set 4		Set 1	Set 2	Set 3	Set 4
1) Population, 65 years and over	22,934	31,822	30,923	33,278	33,855	65,799	45,102	42,327	49,483	51,301	129,691
2) Percent increase over 1976	(X)	38.8	34.8	45.1	47.6	186.9	96.7	84.6	115.8	123.7	465.5
3) Population, 75 years and over	8,741	14,386	13,791	15,224	15,916	42,583	16,975	15,316	19,458	21,495	90,607
4) Percent increase over 1976	(X)	64.6	57.8	74.2	82.1	387.2	94.2	75.2	112.6	145.9	936.6
PERCENT 65 AND OVER											
5) Series I (High)		11.3	11.0	11.6	11.9	20.1	12.7	12.1	13.6	14.1	28.3
6) Series II (Medium)	10.7	12.2	11.9	12.6	12.9	21.6	15.5	14.8	16.5	17.2	33.0
7) Series III (Low)		12.9	12.7	13.3	13.6	22.8	17.8	17.0	18.9	19.6	36.6
8) Percent, 75 years and over 65 years and over	38.1	45.2	44.6	45.7	47.0	64.7	37.6	36.2	39.3	41.9	69.9
9) Excess of females over males, 65 years and over	4,207	6,388	6,151	6,915	6,181	5,221	8,166	7,544	9,217	7,462	3,865
10) Sex ratio, 65 years and over	69.0	66.6	66.8	65.6	69.1	85.3	69.3	69.7	68.6	74.6	94.2
11) Ratio (per 100) 65 to 79 years 45 to 49 years	156.4	125.5	123.3	128.9	129.5	172.0	215.9	207.6	229.1	229.4	303.1

TABLE 3.3 (continued)

RATIO (PER 100) 65 YEARS AND OVER
                 18 TO 64 YEARS

12) Series I (High)	18.1	19.5	19.0	20.3	20.7	38.7	22.7	21.5	24.5	25.6	60.8
13) Series II (Medium)		19.9	19.4	20.7	21.1	39.5	26.0	24.6	28.0	29.2	69.1
14) Series III (Low)		20.2	19.7	21.0	21.5	40.1	28.6	27.1	30.8	32.2	75.7

x Not applicable.

[1]*Current Population Reports*, Series P-25, No. 704, July 1977.

[2]Set 1 Death rates of 1976 remain unchanged.
Set 2 Death rates decline twice as rapidly between 1976 and 2050 as in latest Census Bureau projections.
Set 3 Death rates of 1976 are reduced by one-half in 2050.
Set 4 Death rates of 2050 are zero.

Source: Jacob S. Siegel, "Prospective Trends in the Size and Structure of the Elderly Population, Impact of Mortality Trends, and Some Implications," *Current Population Reports*, Series P-23, no. 78, (January 1979), Table 12, p. 19.

the total population (columns 2 and 3) depending upon the fertility rate. Under conditions of high-average fertility (3.1 births per woman), the population over 65 would be 13.1 percent of the total in 2020. However, if the average fertility for the next 40 years is around replacement-level fertility of 2.1 births per woman, the number of the aged will become 15.5 percent of the total population. The second figure is closer to what demographers are projecting. Indeed, the percent of the aged in the population in 2020 may exceed the 15.5 percent projection because fertility rate in recent years has dropped even below 2.1 births per woman. Reinforcing the point that fertility is the major determinant of the percentage of the aged in the population is the fact that the differences resulting from these two fertility assumptions are greater than the differences due to alternative mortality or migration assumptions (Deming & Cutler, 1983).

Given that fertility has the greatest impact on the age structure of a population, the graying of America could be slowed considerably (or even reversed) if there were to be another baby boom. For years many demographers have expected this baby boom to materialize. The expectation was based on the premise that once the children born during the postwar baby boom grew old enough to have babies of their own, the birth rate would again soar. This would create an "echo" of the earlier boom. However, the premise appears to be false.

Although the number of women of childbearing age has climbed dramatically over the last decade, the number of births has not followed suit. The total fertility rate has fallen from a postwar high of 3.8 children per woman in 1957 to a record low of 1.8 children per woman in 1976. In the media this phenomenon has been called a colossal baby bust (*Newsweek,* 1977). Currently, most of the factors that have contributed to the baby bust appear stronger than ever. Contraception and abortion have spread, more women are working than ever before, and working women have fewer children. Smaller families have become a part of the American life style. Nevertheless, there are so many potential mothers available in the population that it would take only a small increase in the fertility rate to add a great number of new babies. Perhaps many women have only postponed the decision to have a family.

Mortality

Fertility affects the impact of a given cohort on the age structure of a population, while mortality affects the continued contribution of that cohort to the population. The higher the mortality rate, the steeper the angle of the triangle. This can be seen in the population pyramid for 1870 shown in Figure 3.6. One of the major achievements over the period between 1870 and the present is the decline in infant mortality rate.

A factor which would decrease a cohort in the beginning of its existence is infant mortality rate. Infant mortality rate in 1935 was 55.7 per 1,000 live births. By 1970 this rate had dropped to 19.8 per 1,000 live births, and it was reduced even further in 1977 to 14.1 per 1,000 live births (U.S. Public Health Service, 1979).

The infant mortality rate of 10.8 infant deaths per 1,000 live births recorded in 1984 was the lowest rate ever recorded for the United States (U.S. Public Health Service, 1986). This rate is still not the best in the world, primarily because of the large discrepancy between the infant mortality rate of black and white infants. In 1984 black infant mortality rate was 18.4, while it was 9.4 for white infants. The absolute difference in infant mortality rate between black and white infants has been decreasing since 1960. However, because the infant mortality rates for both the white and black populations have been decreasing by the same average annual percent (3.6 percent per year) between 1960 and 1984, the black infant mortality rate in 1984 was 1.96 times the white rate. This is about the same ratio as in 1960 (1.93) (U.S. Public Health Service, 1986).

High mortality rates at younger ages were common in earlier periods of the twentieth century. In 1900 only 39 percent of the people born would survive to the age of 64, and 33 percent would survive to the age of 80. In 1970, 72 percent of all those born in the United States will survive to the age of 64 and 49 percent will make it to the age of 80. We have conquered most of the life-threatening diseases of infancy, childhood and youth, allowing most to attain adulthood and old age.

The gains against the killers of early life have not been matched by gains against the chronic diseases of old age. We survive our youth to die of the diseases of later life. This can be seen by comparing mortality rates at infancy and heart disease mortality in developed and undeveloped countries. For example, in 1970 the ratio of infant mortality to heart disease mortality was 11/333.9 deaths in Sweden; in the United States the figure was 19.8/326.1. However, this statistic for Mexico was 68.5/18.9. Many more Mexican infants do not survive, and those who do survive in Mexico apparently do not succumb as frequently to heart disease.

The death rates for the ten leading causes of death in the United States in 1900, 1970, and 1984 are compared in Table 3.4. Influenza, pneumonia, and tuberculosis are no longer among the leading five causes of death, while chronic diseases such as heart disease and cancer have taken their place. Of course, this latter group of diseases is concentrated among the older population. More people are living to older ages, so health problems associated with the degenerative diseases have become a major concern. By 1969 diseases of the heart, cancer, and stroke together accounted for three out of every four deaths of persons aged 65 and older (Deming & Cutler, 1983).

Projections involving the interaction between fertility and mortality are included in Table 3.3. Low fertility in combination with low mortality results in the highest proportion of older persons in the United States in the future. This combination could lead to 21.2 percent of the population being over the age of 65 in 2030. This can also be seen in the worldwide figures presented in Table 3.1. Countries with low fertility and mortality rates such as those in Western Europe have a high proportion of aged in their population. On the other hand, the high fertilty and mortality rates in countries in Africa, South Asia, and Latin America lead to very low percentages of elderly in the population.

TABLE 3.4   Death Rates for the Ten Leading Causes of Death in 1900 with Comparable Rates for 1970 and 1984 in the United States

Cause of Death	Rate (deaths per 100,000 population)			Rank		
	1900	1970	1984	1900	1970	1984
Influenza and pneumonia	202.2	30.9	24.9	1	5	6
Tuberculosis	194.4	2.6	0.5	2	—	—
Gastroenteritis (diseases of the stomach and intestine)	142.7	0.9	0.1	3	—	—
Diseases of the heart	137.4	362.0	323.5	4	1	1
Cerebral hemmorhage and other vascular lesions	106.9	101.9	65.3	5	3	3
Chronic nephritis (kidney diseases)	81.0	3.7	8.5	6	—	—
All accidents	72.3	56.4	39.3	7	4	4
Cancer and other malignant neoplasms	64.0	162.8	191.8	8	2	2
Diseases of early infancy	62.6	21.4	8.0	9	—	—
Diptheria	40.3	0.0	0.0	10	—	—

Source: Public Health Service, National Center for Health Statistics, *Vital statistics of the United States, 1970, Volume II—Mortality, Part A,* Washington, D.C.: U.S. Government Printing Office, 1974, Table 1–5; *Monthly Vital Statistics Report,* 27 June 1974, *22,* adapted from Tables 7 and 8; *Monthly Vital Statistics Report,* September 26, 1986, *35,* adapted from Table B.

Immigration

The third demographic factor affecting the population compositon of a country is immigration. Past levels of immigration tend to increase the number of older persons in subsequent years because it increases the size of the cohort. In this manner, immigration works something like fertility. At the same time, since most immigrants are young, the force of immigration works in the present to lower the median age of the population and to decrease the percentage of the aged.

Immigration had a major impact on the population composition of the United States 60 to 100 years ago which is still being felt today, but the impact of current immigration is less because there are proportionately fewer immigrants today. From 1881 to 1930, there were almost 27.6 million immigrants to the United Staes. Most of these individuals were 15 to 39 years old. While immigration continues, the average annual number of immigrants has declined from 879,000 in 1901–1910 to 332,000 in 1961–1970, and the net effect on the total population and its composition is decreasing over time because the population is greater (Irwin & Warren, 1972).

As a result of the high immigration rates earlier in this century, contemporary cohorts of elderly are comprised of many foreign-born individuals. Great waves of young immigrants came to the United States in the early twentieth century. The age distribution of the foreign-born population reflects the trends in immigration. As a result of the sharp curtailment of immigration after World War I, the foreign-born population tends to be concentrated in the older ages. In 1970, about one third of all foreign-born persons were 65 years or older, and about 15 percent of the population aged 65 and older was foreign-born. Europeans dominated the migration patterns early in the century, and one of every three persons of foreign extraction (foreign-born plus native persons of foreign or mixed parentage) from Denmark, Germany, Ireland, Norway, and Sweden were aged 65 or older. Less than 10 percent of the people in the United States from Cuba, China, Japan, or Mexico were aged 65 or older. These countries have contributed immigrants either in smaller numbers or they have contributed them more recently, or both.

The present annual statutory ceiling on immigration is about 400,000 immigrants per year (with some legal exceptions in times of war or special international crises). Thus, population projections into the twenty-first century are minimally affected by immigration. The projections presented in this chapter take into account the assumption that 400,000 immigrants will enter the country annually.

What are Some Characteristics of the Contemporary Aged Cohorts?

One of the aims of this book is to describe the aged as they are today. Another aim is to describe, predict and explain aging phenomena for all cohorts. While a description of the contemporary aged cohorts cannot be used exclusively as a basis on which to describe future cohorts, such a description does provide us with the contemporary picture, and it may give us some clues about aging in the future as well.

Residential Distribution

An initial part of the description involves information about where the older population resides. In 1980, the largest number of individuals over the age of 65 resided in metropolitan areas. This constituted 18.2 million individuals which was 71 percent of the aged population (U.S. Department of Health and Human Services, 1987). Of these elderly living in metropolitan areas, 32 percent lived in central cities, and 39 percent lived in suburbs.

Another interesting distributional characteristic of the older population involves the states in which they are concentrated. Which state do you think is the "oldest" in terms of having the highest percentage of aged? Figure 3.7 illustrating the indivudal states by percentage of adults aged 65 + provides some clues about where the highest concentrations of elderly are. The "oldest" state is Florida. In 1985 17.6 percent of Florida's population was over the age of 65 (U.S. Department of Health and Human Services, 1987). In contrast, Alaska is by far the "youngest" state. In 1985 only 3.2 percent of the population of Alaska was aged 65 or older. The largest states, California and New York, also have the largest

PERSONS 65+ AS PERCENTAGE OF TOTAL POPULATION: 1985

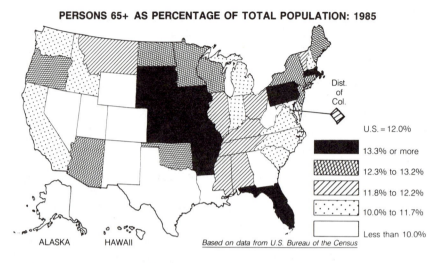

FIGURE 3.7   Persons ages 65 and older represented as a percentage of the total population of each state in the United States. Source: U.S. Department of Health and Human Services (1987). *A profile of older Americans.* Washington, DC: Program Resources Department, American Association of Retired Persons (AARP) and the Administration on aging (AoA).

populations of the aged—2,766,000 and 2,254,000, respectively. However, this constitutes a smaller percentage of the total population (10.5 percent in California, 12.7 percent in New York) than the 2,001,000 elderly of Florida.

In the case of the age composition of a given state, a low percentage of older persons is due to high fertility, in-migration of persons under the age of 65, and the out-migration of persons aged 65 and over. States in the South and West typically have a low proportion of older persons primarily because so many younger people are migrating there. A high percentage of older persons results from low fertility, heavy out-migration of young persons, substantial in-migration of older persons, or heavy immigration of foreign-born persons prior to World War I who remain. Parts of the Midwest and Northeast exemplify this pattern which is apparent in Figure 3.7.

Marital Staus and Living Arrangements

The marital status and living arrangements of the older population are impacted primarily by the dramatic sex difference in mortality. This sex difference will be discussed in Chapter 6 on longevity and health, but it is important to point out that current life expectancy at birth favors females by seven years over males. The sex ratio is computed by taking the number of males, dividing it by the number of females, and multiplying it by 100 as follows:

$$\text{Sex ratio} = \frac{\text{Number of males}}{\text{Number of females}} \times 100$$

A figure over 100 indicates more males than females, while a figure under 100 indicates more females than males. A sex ratio of 50 indicates that there are two females for every male. At birth the sex ratio of 105 indicating that there are more males than females born.

Figure 3.8 indicates the substantially higher death rate for males at every point in the life span. Especially dramatic in this figure is the mortality rate for young black males between the ages of 15 and 30 years. The gap in life expectancy between the sexes has expanded in the twentieth century. Zopf (1986) pointed out that in 1900 the age-adjusted death rate for males was 9 percent higher than that for females, but by 1980 the death rate for males was 80 percent higher.

While mortality rates have fallen dramatically in the United States, the benefit has been greater for women than for men. For example, in the early decades of the twentieth century many women died in childbirth. However, the risk of childbirth has been greatly eliminated, and consequently women are more likely to attain their biological potential and outlive men. Naturally this large difference in life expectancy affects the marital status and living arrangements of elderly women and men.

The average older woman is a widow, living alone. The average elderly man still lives with his spouse. This causes the experience of aging to be dramatically different for women than for men. Figure 3.9 illustrates the living arrangements of older men and women. While 75 percent of older men are married and living with their spouse, only 38 percent of older women fall into this category. In 1978, 52 percent of older women were widows (Deming & Cutler, 1983). In addition

FIGURE 3.8   Sex ratios in the United States in 1980 by age and race. Source: Zopf, P. E., Jr. (1986). *America's older population.* Houston: Cap and Gown Press, p. 10. Reprinted by permission.

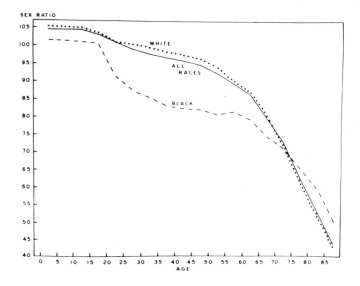

Living Arrangements of People 65+
1985

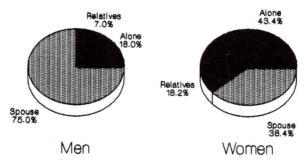

Based on data from US Bureau of Census

FIGURE 3.9   Living arrangements of men and women aged 65 and older in the United States in 1985. Source: U.S. Department of Health and Human Services (1987). *A profile of older Americans.* Washington, DC: Program Resources Department, American Association of Retired Persons (AARP) and the Administration on Aging (AoA).

to the sex differences in longevity, women usually marry men older than themselves, and men have higher remarriage rates than women. These three factors account for the dramatic sex differences in marital status in the elderly.

In 1985, 43 percent of older women lived alone (U.S. Department of Health and Human Services, 1987). Cutler and Harootyan (1975) pointed out that there had been some discussion of a trend toward increased "pairing" of older unmarried individuals as a way to pool economic resources and provide compansionship. However, census data did not bear out this phenomenon. No significant change occurred between 1960 and 1978 in the proportion of older persons reported as living with unrelated individuals. To the degree that the census data accurately represent changes in living arrangements, the proportion of people living with unrelated individuals has remained around 2 percent for both sexes since 1960.

Education

The educational level attained by the cohorts aged 65 and above is considerably lower than the level attained by subsequent cohorts. Table 3.5 compares the average education of the cohort 25 years old and slightly older to cohorts between the ages of 55 and 75 and over in 1982. Almost 72 percent of the population aged 25 and over completed high school compared with only 34 percent of the population aged 75 and older. The educational level of the older population has been steadily increasing. Between 1970 and 1985, the median level of educa-

TABLE 3.5 Percentages of People with Specified Years of Schooling, by Sex and Age, 1982

Sex and Age	Percent Completing			Median Years Completed
	8 Years or Less	High School, 4 or More Years	College, 4 or More Years	
Male				
25+	15.7	71.7	21.9	12.6
55–59	18.6	64.4	19.7	12.3
60–64	24.0	59.9	13.7	12.3
65–69	30.9	51.7	13.2	12.1
70–74	40.1	43.0	12.0	10.9
75+	53.1	33.9	10.3	9.4
Female				
25+	15.6	70.3	14.0	12.5
55–59	16.3	67.1	9.5	12.4
60–64	22.6	61.5	8.3	12.3
65–69	27.8	54.2	8.0	12.1
70–74	36.7	46.0	7.9	10.9
75+	47.7	36.1	6.7	9.4

Source: U.S. Bureau of the Census, "America in Transition: An Aging Society," *Current Population Reports,* P-23, no. 128 (1983), table 10. From Zoph, P. E., Jr. (1986). *America's older population.* Houston: Cap and Gown Press. p. 113. Reprinted by permission.

tion for older adults increased from 8.7 years to 11.7 years (11.4 years for males, 11.8 years for females) (U.S. Department of Health and Human Services, 1987).

Projections of the educational attainment of future cohorts of the elderly indicate that these groups will be better educated. For example, by 1990, 65 percent of the cohort aged 65 to 69 will have graduated from high school. This means that the elderly consumers of the twenty-first century will be well educated and perhaps more demanding in terms of the services they expect as part of their rights as contributing members of society.

Economic Characteristics

A major determinant of economic position is employment status, and statistics indicate that labor force participation of older males has steadily decreased from 46 percent in 1950 to 22 percent in 1975, while rates for females have been quite low and have declined to 8 percent in 1975. Figure 3.10 shows labor force participation by age in 1981. The vast majority of older adults are out of the labor force by the age of 65 even though the retirement age has been increased to 70 or eliminated altogether. The decrease in labor force participation by older adults reflects the increase in voluntary retirement programs, the availability of early retirement benefits in Social Security and some private pensions, and the decline in self-employment.

In line with the low and decreasing labor force participation among the elderly

PARTICIPATION
RATE

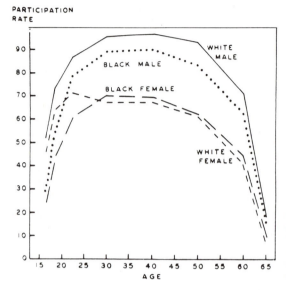

FIGURE 3.10 Labor force participation rate in 1981 by age, race, and sex. Source: Zopf, P. E., Jr. (1986). *America's older population*. Houston: Cap and Gown Press, p. 10. Reprinted by permission.

is a drop in income. This is shown in Table 3.6 in the median income by age and sex. The median income received by individuals aged 65 and older is significantly less than the income of all age groups except the 15–19 age group. One of the major limitations to life satisfaction and a high quality of life in the elderly is income. In 1980, persons aged 65–69 received a median income of $6,150, which was 77 percent of that for all ages. People aged 70 and over received $4,872, which was only 61 percent of the median income for all other age groups.

There is a higher proportion of elderly individuals living below the poverty

TABLE 3.6   Median and Relative Income of Persons, by Age and Sex, 1980

Age	Median Income (dollars) Both Sexes	Male	Female	Percent of median Both Sexes	Male	Female
15+	7,944	12,530	4,920	100.0	100.0	100.0
15–19	1,736	1,801	1,673	21.9	14.4	34.0
20–24	6,612	7,923	5,286	83.2	63.2	107.4
25–34	11,173	15,580	6,973	140.6	124.3	141.7
35–44	12,254	20,037	6,465	154.3	159.9	131.4
45–54	11,927	19,974	6,403	150.1	159.4	130.1
55–64	9,420	15,914	4,926	118.6	127.0	100.1
65–69	6,150	8,953	4,379	77.4	71.5	89.0
70+	4,872	6,545	4,168	61.3	52.2	84.7

Source: U.S. Bureau of the Census, "Money Income of Households, Families, and Persons in the United States: 1980," *Current Population Reports*, P-60, no. 132 (1982), table 50. From Zopf, P. E., Jr. (1986). *America's older population*. Houston: Cap and Gown Press, p. 189. Reprinted by permission.

line. Table 3.7 presents the percentage of individuals falling below the poverty line in 1980 by race and sex. Older women are at far greater risk for poverty than older men, and older blacks are particularly vulnerable to poverty. Hence, close to half of older black women have incomes below the poverty line. Cutbacks in federal aid in the 1980s have exacerbated the condition of the elderly poor, placing many more elderly among those with incomes beow the official poverty level. Of all family status groups, female unrelated individuals are most likely to be living in poverty. These women constitute one half of all the older persons in poverty, although they are only one quarter of the total older population.

Statistics for 1985 indicate that about 3.5 million elderly persons were below the poverty level, and another 2.3 million were classified as "near-poor" (income between the poverty level and 125 percent of this level). In total, 5.8 million elderly or over one fifth (21 percent) of the older population were poor or near-poor in 1985 (U.S. Department of Health and Human Services, 1987).

Addressing themselves to this issue, Deming and Cutler (1983) stated:

The economic situation of older people remains a major problem, despite contemporary increases in benefits from Social Security, private pension plans, Medicare,

TABLE 3.7   Percentages of Persons Below the Poverty Level, by Age, Sex, Race, and Spanish Origin, 1980

Age Sex	All Races	White	Black	Spanish Origin[a]
Male	11.2	8.7	28.7	23.5
Under 15	19.0	14.5	43.6	33.6
15–17	14.1	10.3	35.8	29.1
18–21	10.9	8.5	24.4	21.9
22–24	9.8	8.4	17.6	16.4
25–34	7.5	6.2	17.2	14.9
35–44	7.6	6.2	18.4	16.0
45–54	6.5	5.4	15.2	15.2
55–59	6.4	4.8	22.3	12.7
60–64	7.8	6.2	24.6	19.1
65 +	10.9	9.0	31.5	26.8
Female	14.7	11.6	35.7	27.7
Under 15	19.3	14.8	42.6	33.9
15–17	15.8	11.1	41.5	31.0
18–21	16.0	12.3	36.5	29.2
22–24	15.1	12.0	33.6	20.9
25–34	12.8	10.0	31.1	23.9
35–44	10.6	8.3	26.8	23.1
45–54	8.9	6.7	26.3	22.4
55–59	10.6	8.2	31.8	19.5
60–64	12.6	10.3	35.8	19.6
65 +	19.0	16.8	42.6	34.4

Source: U.S. Bureau of the Census, "Characteristics of the Population Below the Poverty Level: 1980," *Current Population Reports*, P-60, no. 133 (1982), table 11. From Zopf, P. E., Jr. *America's older population.* Houston: Cap and Gown Press, p. 203. Reprinted by permission.
[a]May be of any race.

and other income maintenance and in-kind transfer programs. Food, housing, and health care costs are rising far more quickly than are the economic resources of older people, especially those not in the labor force, those located in central cities, unrelated individuals, women, and black and other races. Indeed, the combination of relatively fixed incomes and substantial annual inflation add to the economic plight of these older persons (Deming & Cutler, 1983, p. 47).

A different perspective on this issue was presented by Rabushka and Jacobs (1980). They pointed out that the common image of misfortune and need underpins the broad-based support that many programs for the elderly enjoy. However, they assert that the negative image is inaccurate and perpetuated by widespread news-media coverage of a select few among the elderly who may suffer from poverty, forced retirement, job discrimination, crime, malnutrition, poor housing, social isolation and serious health impairments. Rabushka and Jacobs believe that this is a stereotyped view of aging suggesting that many of our senior citizens cannot lead independent lives, that they are in desperate need of money, nutritious meals, decent housing, comprehensive health care and other vital social services.

These authors maintain that the preconceptions are largely inaccurate and are contradicted by the facts of aging. Based on their interviews with more than 1,500 elderly homeowners in the United States and in other studies, they sketch a much brighter picture. For example, they point out that the number of officially counted "poor" elderly has fallen since 1959 from 33 percent of the aged population to as low as 6 percent when noncash benefits are added to greatly increased retirement benefits. Fully 70 percent of the aged live in their own houses and nearly nine of every ten elderly homeowners make no mortage payments. Every state has some form of property-tax relief for this group, and all older Americans are eligible for other state and federal tax benefits.

There are other benefits from the public and private sectors as well. Many pharmacies offer prescriptions at a reduced rate to senior citizens, and a number of other businesses offer cost breaks. Public transportation in most cities is available at reduced rates at least during noncommuting hours, and entertainment and cultural events usually cost less for those who can prove they are 65 or above. Social Security recipients are among the very few who receive tax-free yearly increases in cash income indexed to inflation. The Supplementary Security Income program guarantees a minimum income to all older Americans. Food stamps, housing benefits, and Medicare and Medicaid provide in-kind income to millions of older persons.

While these benefits are relatively new, they have been instituted by society to meet the demands of the large cohorts of people over age 65 who are a new phenomenon in the history of humankind. To meet the needs of these groups, annual spending on programs for the aging already exceeds $150 billion, and it has been estimated that by the year 2040 when as much as 20 percent of the population may be 65 and older, 40 percent of the federal budget will be devoted to them. Rabushka and Jacobs feel that with these kinds of prospects in sight, if we do not focus our programs on those truly in need, the bill will be far too expensive to pay.

Interindividual Variability and Aging

One final characteristic of the contemporary cohorts of aged which deserves special emphasis is individual difference. In this book we are attempting to identify psychological aging phenomena. One quality psychologists note repeatedly when they study older adults is their great variability. As we age, we become more unique. We become more like ourselves and more different from anyone else. On any psychological trait that we can measure, individual variability is greater in older adulthood. Undoubtedly as a result of more and more experience, we become more differentiated.

The life of Fay O'Malley Hopkins Tuttle is described to give a flavor of why individual differences become greater with age. Mrs. Tuttle had an extremely varied and diverse life. Indeed, one could say that she led many lives. There is no way that anyone else could be like she was. She was completely unique in her old age due to her extremely individualized life styles. Every time we attempt to characterize older individuals as a group, we should remember uniquely differentiated individuals such as the one we now describe.

Faye O'Malley Hopkins Tuttle.   At the time of the interview, Mrs. Tuttle was sought out by many because of her lively wit and longevity. She was 98 years of age, and she had lived a truly remarkable life.

She was born of Irish immigrant parents in New York City in 1887, but her parents had moved to the Midwest to farm during her early childhood. Life was difficult for the O'Malleys. They were physically weak from years of semistarvation in Ireland, and they were not suited to the strenuous life of farming. It did not take long for this life style to ruin permanently their health. Faye's mother died in childbirth when Faye was 10 years old, and her father never recovered from this loss. By the time she was 12 years of age, Faye was an orphan.

Some kind people in town helped Faye, allowing her to support herself by working in their restaurant until she was 16. Her blossoming beauty attracted a customer at the restaurant who talked her into accompanyng him to Nevada where he planned to strike it rich in the silver mines.

Soon after they arrived in Virginia City, he was shot in a brawl and died. Faye then managed to support herself for the following 12 years as a prostitute in the western mining camps. That vocation introduced her to Frank Hopkins, an old miner who found and claimed a rich vein of silver. He wanted to settle down with Faye, and she agreed to marry him. The Hopkins had two children, one of whom died in infancy. After Frank died at the age of 68, Faye lived with her daughter until the young woman married and moved with her husband to Denver.

After seeing her daughter married, Faye moved to California and invested her inheritance from Frank in a saloon and hotel in San Francisco which she managed. When she had amassed a considerable fortune, she decided to help young orphaned girls who had suffered a plight similar to hers, and she opened a foster home for homeless children.

The widow Hopkins lost everyting she had when the foster home burned to the ground. Consequently, she moved in with her daughter in Denver who by that time was also widowed and suffering from tuberculosis. Mrs. Hopkins contracted tuberculosis herself and moved into a sanitarium for tuberculosis patients. There she recovered from the disease. She met another recovered tuberculosis patient, Joseph Tuttle, at the sanitarium and at the age of 64 she married him. Her third husband owned a ranch in Arizona, and she operated his ranch with him until he died. She continued to ranch in Arizona into her early nineties. Finally, the ranch became too much for her, so she sold it and moved into a retirement community in Flagstaff. At the age of 98 in the retirement community her memory was clear and her sense of humor was wry as she remembered the many different lives she had lived.

Fay O'Malley Hopkins Tuttle's life was unique. Every individual's life is unique. We all may not lead as wild and difficult a life as Faye O. H. Tuttle, but by the time we have attained old age, we have become very individualized and quite different from anyone else. Thus, even as we try to describe psychology and aging, we must continually remind ourselves that aging is a unique experience for every individual. We can identify trends and commonalities in the experience of aging, but a very important generalization is that we become more individually different and unique as we age.

SUMMARY

The age group over 65 years old has become a large and visible segment of the population in the United States and in many countries in the world. In 1985 there were 28.5 million people over the age of 65, representing 12 percent of the population of the United States. Demographers project that 21.2 percent of the population could be 65 or older by 2030. The median age of the American population has increased from less than 17 years in 1820 to over 30 years in 1985.

The answer to the question, "Who are the aging?" is that there are far more aging persons now than at any other time in the history of humankind. Life expectancy at birth in the United States is 75 years, an increase of almost 28 years since the turn of the century. A much greater percentage of Americans are surviving infancy, childhood, adolescence, and young adulthood to reach mature adulthood and old age.

The maximum life potential (MLP) of the human species is the same as it has been for centuries—120 years. Life span for the majority of humans is probably around 85 years. What has changed is life expectancy, the number of years to which half of a birth cohort survive. Life expectancy in ancient times was probably no more than 20 years. Even in the nineteenth century, it was not much more than

40 years. Advances in health care and sanitation, adequate nutrition and heating are some of the factors contributing to our current life expectancy of 75 years.

The aging of populations is occurring throughout the world, but progress is more rapid in developed countries than in Third World nations. Countries can be categorized on the basis of the age composition of their population as aged (over 7 percent 65 + years), mature (4 to 7 percent 65 + years), or young (less than 4 percent 65 +). Young countries have high birth and mortality rates and low per capita income. Mature countries have substantially lower birth and mortality rates and higher income. Aged countries have the lowest birth and mortality rates and the highest per capita income. Aged-population countries are found primarily in North America and Europe while young countries are located mostly in Africa, South Asia, and Latin America.

There is no question that the aged population in the United States and other aged nations is going to increase. Indeed, the aged population in all countries of the world is increasing. Because of the large baby-boom cohort born after 1945 in the United States, there will be a gerontology boom in this country in 2020 and beyond.

Three factors which account for the age structure of a population are fertility, mortality, and immigration. Low fertility rates increase the proportion of older adults in the population because fewer babies are born. Low mortality rates increase the proportion of older adults because more individuals survive into old and very old age. Both fertility and mortality rates in the United States are at an all-time low. Low immigration maintains the status of the population while high immigration increases the proportion of younger individuals. Immigrants tend to be young and in the early phase of their childbearing years. Thus, they increase the number of young in the population. The immigration rate in the United States is so low that it has little impact, at present, on the age structure of the population.

With regard to a characterization of contemporary older cohorts, a majority lives in metropolitan areas, and the highest percentage of older adults lives in states in the Midwest and Northeast. However, the state with the highest percentage of older adults (17.6 percent) is Florida. Three fourths of all men over 65 years old are married and living with their spouse, while only 38 percent of older women enjoy this status. The majority of older women live alone or with relatives. Between 1970 and 1985, the median level of education of the older population increased from 8.7 years to 11.7 years. Educational attainment is increasing with each older cohort, but the average adult over 75 years had completed only nine years of education in 1982. While most older adults have adequate income, about 3.5 million elderly persons were below the poverty level in 1985. The poverty rate for persons aged 65 or older was 12.6 percent in 1985, and another 2.3 million or an additional 8 percent were classified as "near-poor." In total, over one fifth of the older population were poor or near-poor in 1985.

While it is possible to characterize the aging population and to identify characteristics of contemporary older cohorts, these statistics do not adequately portray the vast variety present in older adults. As people age they become more individualized. They become more unique with advancing years. Thus, in the elderly, individual differences are greater than at any other point in the life span.

REFERENCES

CUTLER, N. E. & HAROOTYAN, R. A. (1975).   Demography of the aged. In D. S. Woodruff & J. E. Birren (Eds.) *Aging: Scientific perspectives and social issues.* New York: D. Van Nostrand.

DEMING, M. B. & CUTLER, N. E. (1983).   Demography of the aged. In D. S. Woodruff & J. E. Birren (Eds.) *Aging: Scientific perspectives and social issues* (2nd Ed.). Monterey, CA: Brooks/Cole.

DUBLIN, L. I., LOTKA, A. J. & SPIEGELMAN, M. (1949)   *Length of life: A study of the life table.* New York: Ronald Press.

FRIES, J. F. (1980).   Aging, natural death, and the comparison of morbidity. *New England Journal of Medicine, 303,* 130–135.

FRIES, J. F. & CRAPO, L. M. (1981).   *Vitality and Aging.* San Francisco: W. H. Freeman.

IRWIN, R. & WARREN, R. (1972).   Demographic aspects of American immigration. In C. F. Westoff & R. Parke, Jr. (Eds.), *Demographic and social aspects of population growth.* Washington, DC: U.S. Government Printing Office.

Newsweek, (February 28, 1977).   "The graying of America," 52–65.

PALMORE, E. B. (1987).   International perspectives. In G. L. Maddox (Ed.), *The encyclopedia of aging.* New York: Springer.

RABUSHKA, A. & JACOBS, B. (February 15, 1980).   "Are old folks really poor? Herewith a look at some common views." *New York Times.*

SHUMAN, T. (1987).   Third World aging. In G. L. Maddox (ed.)., *The encyclopedia of aging.* New York: Springer.

SIEGEL, J. S. (1979).   Prospective trends in the size and structure of the elderly population, impact of mortality trends, and some implications. *Current Population Reports,* Series P-23, No. 78.

UNITED NATIONS. (1979).   *Demographic Yearbook: 1978.* New York: United Nations.

UNITED NATIONS. (1982).   *Demographic Yearbook: 1982.* New York: United Nations.

U.S. DEPARTMENT OF HEALTH AND HUMAN SERVICES. (1987).   *A Profile of Older Americans: 1986.* Washington, DC: Program Resources Department, American Association of Retired Persons (AARP) and the Administration on Aging (AoA).

UNITED STATES PUBLIC HEALTH SERVICE, National Center for Health Statistics. (1977)   *Monthly vital statistics report* 27 (11), Supplement, Advance report, final natality statistics. Washington, DC: U.S. Government Printing Office.

UNITED STATES PUBLIC HEALTH SERVICE, National Center for Health Statistics. (1986).   *Monthly vital statistics report,* 35 (6), Supplement 2, Advance report of final mortality statistics, 1984. Washington, DC: U.S. Government Printing Office.

WOODRUFF, D. S. (1977).   *Can you live to be 100?* New York: Chatham Square Press.

ZOPF, P. E., Jr. (1986).   *America's older population.* Houston: Cap and Gown Press.

CHAPTER 4

Social, Cultural, and Environmental Factors in Aging

The story of the *Prince and the Pauper* is a familiar tale to almost everyone. A young prince trades places with a poor boy and each child experiences the other's life. Differences in social class and wealth result in dramatic differences in the daily experience of the two boys. Now imagine what would happen if the switch was for life and that we could observe the boys as old men. We would be able to explore and compare the cumulative effects of poverty and low social status to the effects of wealth, power, and aristocratic social status. In this manner we would have a dramatic view of social and environmental influences on aging. These are the kind of influences to be considered in this chapter.

Investigation of aging processes from a social perspective begins by contrating two levels of social influence in society: (1) *microsocial,* which is the immediate interpersonal environment of individuals as they interact with family, friends, neighbors, and associates in their daily lives, and (2) *macrosocial,* which involves broader social structures such as the political, economic, religious, and cultural forces affecting large groups of individuals (Bengtson & Haber, 1983). In this chapter we will examine microsocial and macrosocial influences on aging as well as explore the physical environment of the elderly in terms of housing and living arrangements. Finally, we discuss social psychological theories of aging including Robert Havighurst's Developmental Task theory, Erik Erikson's Psychosocial Crises theory, Disengagement theory, and Activity theory.

THE MICROSOCIAL ENVIRONMENT
OF OLDER ADULTS

The main focus of our discussion of the microsocial environment is the family. Family ties are particularly important for the aged (Aizenberg & Treas, 1985; Treas, 1983). To compensate for the shortcomings in society's provisions for the well-being of older adults, family bonds of affection and obligation are relied upon. It has been estimated that nearly 80 percent of the care for frail elderly is provided at home by family members (Hagestad, 1987). When help from a spouse is not available, children are by far the most common providers of care. After spouse and children, siblings and grandchildren are the family members most likely to help (Kivett, 1985; Scott, 1983). Siblings are especially relied upon if the older adult is childless (Cicirelli, 1985). Thus, health and financial needs of the elderly are frequently met by resources from their family. Affection and companionship are provided by relatives at a time when the older person's social network may be circumscribed by poor health and low income. While friendships may be transient, familial relationships are enduring. The family is most important in sustaining the individual throughout the life span.

Hagestad (1986) has pointed out that with the aging of the population has come a change in the formation of kin networks. In the 1980s multigenerational families are more common. The term *top heavy* has been used by Hagestad to indicate that contemporary families have more older members. A growing number of relationships exist which bridge generational ties. For example, grandparents are also great-grandparents and thus are members of families with four generations or more. Five-generation families are seemingly more common as well, although estimates of the incidence of five-generation families are not available (Hagestad, 1987). There is a web of roles and relationships in a family with many living generations.

The roles of many aged in our society include spouse, parent, sibling, grandparent, and great-grandparent and some are even great-great-grandparents. Shanas (1980) noted the prevalence of such roles for older adults by providing the following statistics for individuals over the age of 65: More than half are married (spouse role), nearly 80 percent have living children (parent role), almost 80 percent have at least one sibling (sibling role), approximately 75 percent are grandparents (grandparent role), and at least 40 percent of the grandparents also become great-grandparents (great-grandparent role). The majority of older adults also have other kin such as cousins, nieces, and nephews. While most research on social roles and aging has focused on the parent-child relationship, there is also a growing body of research on grandparenthood. However, other relationships in later adulthood such as sibling relationships have been neglected by social gerontologists (Hagestad, 1987).

Most older people live in families. This is shown on Table 4.1. The family in which most older adults live is not an extended one, it consists of only an aged husband and wife. Because women live about 7 years longer than men and because

TABLE 4.1   Living Arrangements of Those Aged 65 and Older By Race, Spanish Origin, Age, and Sex, 1978

	65–74 Years		75 Years and Older	
	Men	Women	Men	Women
White				
In families	86.5	61.6	77.8	49.3
Primary individual[a]	12.6	37.2	21.7	49.8
Other[b]	0.9	1.2	0.5	0.9
Black				
In families	71.0	63.5	65.6	56.3
Primary individual[a]	19.8	34.5	24.6	43.2
Other[b]	9.2	2.1	9.8	0.5
Spanish origin				
In families	85.1	72.5	—[c]	69.8
Primary individual[a]	15.5	25.0	—[c]	26.7
Other[b]	—	2.5	—[c]	3.5

Source: U.S. Bureau of the Census. *Current population reports.* Special Studies Series P-23, no. 85, Social and economic characteristics of the older population, Table 2, 1979.

[a]A household head living alone or with nonrelatives only.

[b]Includes lodgers, resident employees, and those living in group quarters such as convents or rooming houses.

[c]Base less than 75,000 persons, so no results reported due to their low reliability.

women often marry men older than themselves, more women are widowed and living alone, especially at advanced ages.

Treas (1983) defends the contemporary extended family from the criticism that it currently fails to provide for the needs of the elderly as it did in previous generations. While a greater percentage of older adults lived with multigenerational families at the turn of the century (58 percent of those married and aged 65 and older, 65 percent of the unmarried according to Dahlin, 1980), there is little evidence that contemporary older adults would be better off living in extended households. The vast majority of older adults prefer *not* to live with their children, and Michael, Fuchs, and Scott (1980) attribute this trend toward solitary living to rising income in the elderly permitting them to purchase desired privacy in housing. A 1975 national survey of older adults' living arrangements found that only 12 percent of those married and 17 percent of those unmarried shared households with offspring (Shanas, 1975). Treas (1983) concluded that the aged today live apart from offspring because it is their preference to do so. This arrangement seems to have no ill effects on their well-being.

Although older adults prefer separate residences from their children, they do not feel isolated or alienated from their kin. The term *intimacy at a distance* was coined by Rosenmayr. Because of the inevitable ambivalence in family relationships which arise, physical and social distance are necessary. Thus, Rosenmayr

(1984) argued that intimacy is more easily sustained when family members have some distance between them.

Intergenerational Relations

Kin are typically accessible to older adults. According to Shanas (1980), 75 percent of older parents had a child who lives less than 30 minutes away, and more than half of the respondents had visited with a child within two days of the interview. Daughters seem to maintain closer contact than sons, and unmarried offspring are closer than married ones. Indeed, Hagestad (1987) declared that women are the linchpin of family contact. It is women who are the kinkeepers. They orchestrate family activities and get-togethers, keep track of family relationships, and facilitate intergenerational contact. The most centrally involved in kinkeeping are women in the middle generations, and the mother-daughter link is pivotal in this regard.

Contemporary intergenerational relationships involve an increase in the amount of support from the grandparents to the grandchildren (Bengtson, Cutler, Mangen, & Marshall, 1985). A comparable trend was reported by Shanas (1980) who found a decrease in help from children to parents but increased help from parent to child. The picture of older adults dependent on their children is inaccurate. Indeed, elderly with high expectations for children's filial involvement have lower morale (Seelbach & Sauer, 1977). Older adults endorse self-reliance, and they do not want to be a burden to their children. Instead of being passive recipients of assistance from the family, older adults commonly contribute aid to relatives, including children and grandchildren.

Grandparenting

We usually think of grandparents as old. However, grandparenting has become a phenomenon of middle age as well as old age. Troll (1982) pointed out that earlier marriage, earlier childbirth, and longer life expectancy over several cohorts have produced a generation of grandparents as young as their forties. In contemporary times when people become grandparents, they still feel youthful and are likely to be working. Many grandparents may not become involved in grandparenting until they are great-grandparents. At that point in their lives, they are more likely to be retired and in the position to assume the role of the old-fashioned "granny."

Of the people over the age of 65 in the United States, 75 percent have living grandchildren. Three fourths of these grandparents see their grandchildren at least every week or two, and nearly half see their grandchildren almost every day (Harris & Associates, 1975). In spite of visiting and interacting with grandchildren, the role of grandparent is peripheral to many older people. It is not a central source of their identity or life satisfaction. In an oft-cited study of grandparenting, Neugarten and Weinstein (1964) found that only 19 percent of grandmothers and

27 percent of grandfathers felt emotional self-fulfillment in their role as a grandparent.

An important contribution of the Neugarten and Weinstein (1964) study on grandparenting was to identify the variety of styles older adults assumed in this role. From the 70 pairs of grandparents studied, five different styles of grandparenting were observed. They were:

1. *Formal grandparent.* Involves clear demarcations between parents' and grandparents' roles. Grandparents only provide special treats and occasional minor services.
2. *Fun seeker.* Grandparenting is a leisure activity. It is enjoyable and a self-indulgence.
3. *Surrogate parent.* This is typically a role for the grandmother. She becomes caretaker of the grandchild when the mother works or is incapacitated.
4. *Reservoir of family wisdom.* The role usually reserved for grandfathers. He dispenses some special skill or knowledge.
5. *Distant figure.* The grandparent is a benevolent but infrequent visitor. This person appears at family gatherings during holidays or for ritual occasions.

Robertson (1977) proposed an alternative typology of grandparenting based on her observations of role conceptions among 125 grandmothers. A distinction was made by Robertson between the social dimension and the personal dimension of grandmothering. Attitudes and expectations of the grandmother role resulting from macrosocial influences are the social dimension. The personal dimension involves attitudes and expectations deriving from individual needs.

Four types of grandmothers are categorized. The *apportioned* type is the grandmother who has high personal and social expectations and attitudes toward her role. She has the greatest involvement with her grandchildren and tends to be concerned with indulging and enjoying them. At the other extreme is the *remote* grandmother who is detached from her grandchildren. She has low personal and social expectations and attitudes toward the grandmother role. In the middle are the *symbolic* and the *individualized* grandmother types. The symbolic grandmother emphasizes normative or moral aspects of the grandparenting role. She has high social expectations and attitudes toward her role but low personal expectations and attitudes. The individualized grandmother, on the other hand, has high personal expectations and attitudes but low social expectations and attitudes. This type of grandmother emphasizes the personal aspects of the role.

As many as 37 percent of Robertson's (1977) respondents said that they preferred the grandparent role to the parent role. These women perceived grandmotherhood to be an easier role. It is a role that afforded them pleasure and gratification without requiring them to assume responsibility for the care of their young kin. Thus, many grandparents are absolutely delighted to see their grandchildren and interact with them, and they are equally delighted when the grandchildren's parents take them home.

The Later Family Life Cycle

The family undergoes predictable changes in composition, organization, and function as its members age. We call this pattern the family life cycle. The changes typify the average family experience in our society. Deviations from this pattern (such as divorce) or variations in the timing of experience (such as bearing children very early or very late in the cycle) are important determinants of the social context of aging for the individual.

Clearly, the greatest change in the family life cycle in the twentieth century is the prolonged period that a couple may expect to spend together after the children have left home. The typical phases which occur late in the family life cycle are the launching of the children into economic independence, a childless preretirement period, a retirement stage, and ultimately widowhood. While these stages are associated with age to some degree, there is considerable diversity in the timing and duration of each phase of the family life cycle (Neugarten & Moore, 1968; Oppenheimer, 1981). How the individual scheduled earlier life events will affect the timing of the events in the later portion of the family life cycle.

If a couple completed their family at a young age, then the child-launching phase of their family life cycle will occur when they are in their forties. Contrasted to this are the parents who had children late in their lives and thus will be launching children as they retire. If the latter couple had to drain their financial resources to support their children in college, they may not have been able to prepare financially for retirement.

Child launching brings with it the opportunity for increased marital intimacy, travel, and new leisure activities, and many couples experience an increase in marital satisfaction at this time. On the other hand, for some women the launching of the children brings about what has been called the empty nest syndrome. This includes a crisis of purposelessness with the loss of the role of motherhood. In the late 1960s and into the 1970s, the empty nest syndrome was the focus of research. National attention to this phenomenon in the mid- to late 1970s was focused by First Lady Betty Ford when she experienced depression after launching her children and spending a great deal of time alone due to the demanding role of her husband.

A national survey of middle-aged women indicated that the empty nest was not a major crisis for most women (Glenn, 1975). Indeed, in Glenn's survey, women with empty nests actually had higher morale than their counterparts with children still at home. The following statement captures the positive aspects of launching children. While it is probably not typical, it provides a striking contrast to the prospects implied by the empty nest syndrome.

> From the day the kids are born, if it's not one thing, it's another. After all these years of being responsible for them, you finally get to the point where you want to scream, "Fall out of the nest already, you guys, will you?" It's as if I want to take myself back after all these years—to give me back to me, if you know what I mean. Of course, that's providing there's any "me" left (Rubin, 1980, p. 313).

"The middle generation squeeze" is how Brody (1981) characterized the role of middle-aged men and especially middle-aged women. While launching the children, parents are often becoming responsible for their own parents and/or grandparents. Brody suggested that there could be two postparental phases in family life. There is an empty nest when the children leave, and there is a second empty nest when the middle-aged couple's parents die. As the population ages, caring for parents is becoming more and more a preretirement phase duty. Troll (1982) pointed out that one of every ten people aged 65 or older has a child over the age of 65. The growing numbers of very old persons and families with two generations who need care have led to concerns about overtaxing family caregivers (Hagestad, 1987).

Caught in the middle-generation squeeze, couples relate differently in their marriage than they had in the early years of the relationship. The kind of interaction that a married couple has in later life changes. Companionship seems to replace romance and passion. While sexual activity continues, it is not as frequent as in previous decades of marital life. Conversations of older couples are less likely to involve their children and more likely to center on topics such as health, shared activities such as church, and home upkeep.

Retirement brings the couple together for a greater portion of time, and the new life style often requires adjustment. An accountant's wife was overheard to say to her newly retired husband, "I married you for better or for worse, but not for *lunch*." Changing patterns of everyday living which have developed over 40 or more years of marriage is difficult. Eating and sleeping habits need to be readjusted when the couple no longer need to set the alarm for 6:00 A.M. so the husband can get off to work. For the wife who has had the home as her sole domain during the day, it is disrupting to have her husband around to interfere with her schedule.

A study of wives of retired teachers revealed complaints about too much togetherness, too little personal freedom, and too many demands on time (Keating & Cole, 1980). However, these disadvantages were sometimes offset by satisfactions in feeling needed. Treas (1983) reported several studies suggesting that wives become increasingly disillusioned with their spouses' retirement. She also points out that relatively little is known about how women adjust to their own retirement. Since women's lives have traditionally centered on the home, their labor force withdrawal has been viewed as unproblematic and even welcome.

The end of the family life cycle involves the dissolution of the marriage through the death of a spouse. The husband is more likely to be the one to die first, so the new role of widowhood is left to the wife. After the age of 65, less than half of women are living with a spouse. Widowhood touches most aging families and demands dramatic adaptations in the lives of the survivors. For this reason, the last stage of the family life cycle warrants special consideration.

Widowhood

Becoming a widow or a widower involves the loss, reorganization, and acquisition of social roles. Due to the much greater life expectancy of women and to the social custom of women marrying older men, many more women become widowed. Ceasing to be a wife means that the woman can no longer be a nurse, confidante, sex partner, or housekeeper for her husband. Instead, she may have to assume some of the roles he had taken in their partnership: financial manager, handyman, wage earner. Her social relations with others may also change. She may lose contact with her in-laws, and she may become a "fifth wheel" in couple-oriented interactions. Indeed, some of her old female friends may regard her as a potential rival. Friends may also avoid her because they do not know what to say to her. In a society focused on enjoyment, people are likely to withdraw from those who are grieving. Furthermore, if a widow's income changes as a result of her husband's death, social contacts may decrease for financial reasons.

Even in the late 1980s with the aged constituting 12 percent of the population of the United States, there is still a stigma to widowhood, especially for women (Lopata, 1987). In America there is no social role of widow, as there is in some other societies (e.g., India), and the identity can lead to a rather sex-segregated life for women in this status.

Mortality rate increases after the death of a spouse, and older widows have higher rates of mental illness and suicide (Bock, 1972; Gove, 1972, 1973). The most severe aspects of the grief reaction, such as the increase in mortality rate of the bereaved, subside about a year after the death of the spouse. Nevertheless, some widows state that they never recover from the husband's death. Finally, new activity, friends, and gratifications eventually supplant old ones. In Lopata's (1973) study of Chicago-area widows, she found that half of the widows adjusted so well to their new life styles that they actually saw some compensations in widowhood (e.g., independence, a reduction in workload).

Issues in the Environment and Aging

The role of the environment in affectring the qualify of life of the elderly has received increasing attention. For example, research on the impact of housing environments on older people has been undertaken by housing planners, sociologists, and psychologists. In part the impetus has come from commitment at the federal, state, and local levels to improve housing for older individuals. The awareness of the problem and resolve to solve it is at least 20 years old. Additionally, there is an expanding awareness of the importance of the immediate environment on an individual's social and psychological well-being. Lawton (1977) has argued that as people grow older and physical activity and social interaction grow less, the aged become progressively more affected by aspects of their environment. The aged may be more limited by their environment and may spend more time in one localized environment than younger, more mobile age groups. Thus, housing arrangements may be more significant in later life than at any other point in the life span.

Several aspects of older adults' housing environments have been the focus of research. The impact of different densities of age-peers on older residents' social lives and emotional well-being is one important area of research. Other work has examined the potential benefits of physically improved housing on residents' satisfaction with their housing as well as on social and emotional well-being. Two quite different motivations have propelled gerontologists to study the effects of age-peers and physical improvements in housing. One goal has been to test the hypothesis that easy access to age-peers has important social benefits. The other motivation has been the commitment of the federal government to fund the development of new age-segregated housing for the elderly.

Research on the effect of moving into age-segregated publicly supported new housing suggests that such housing has distinctive benefits for older adults including increased housing satisfaction, morale, and social activity (Carp, 1966; Lawton & Cohen, 1974; Teaff, Lawton, Nahemow, & Carlson, 1978). It has also been shown that older people living in age-peer dense commercial and retirement housing appear happier and more socially involved than nonresidents of such housing arrangements (Bultena & Wood, 1969; Rosow, 1967; Sherman, 1975).

While living in environments where they are surrounded by age-peers improves life satisfaction in many aged people, it is important to avoid the conclusion that all older adults would prefer to live in housing or communities in which the majority of individuals are old. We have emphasized from the beginning of the book that individual differences become greater in old age. Individual preferences for housing also become more varied. Some older adults prefer to remain in the neighborhood in which they have lived for many decades, even if that neighborhood has deteriorated. They seek continuity in their lives and value the familiar residence which holds many memories for them. Others prefer to move to retirement communities where they have many age-peers and activities. Still others choose to move to smaller dwellings which are age-integrated. They choose to live surrounded by younger individuals because they dislike an environment overly oriented to older adults. Thus, social planners have to come to recognize that providing one or two types of housing and environments for the elderly is not enough. The aged must be provided with a number of options to fulfill their very individualized needs.

The Neighborhood and the Elderly

As the individual ages, his or her dependence on the local environment increases. In particular, older individuals between the ages of 65 and 85 have a special relationship with the neighborhood (Regnier, 1983). The aged as well as children are more dependent and rely more on the collection of local resources that comprise a neighborhood. It is important that the needs of older people be considered in the design and structure of the optimum neighborhood. Towns such as Reston, Virginia and Irvine, California have located housing projects for older people near their town centers (Wylie, 1976). However, it is far more common for there to be a total lack of planning and urban design guiding improvements for the elderly in existing neighborhoods and even in newly designed neighborhoods.

Research comparing housing with neighborhood concerns has shown that neighborhood issues are even more of a critical consideration than housing satisfaction (Struyk, 1981). While the elderly often live in adequate housing, they frequently live in neighborhoods which they perceive to have critical problems. Complaints about neighborhoods by the elderly include lack of stores, churches, and restaurants as well as fear regarding the potential for crime.

Crime is an extremely important concern of older people. Safe and convenient neighborhoods are often mentioned by older adults as important prerequisites to high life satisfaction. A Harris poll commissioned by the National Council on the Aging documented fear of crime as the highest rated concern of older people (Harris & Associates, 1975). Street assault such as purse snatching is a common crime perpetrated against older people. Fear of such a crime can keep older persons almost prisoners inside their own homes. They are afraid to venture out into the neighborhood even to shop for food.

To improve a neighborhood for its elderly residents is not an easy undertaking. From the perspective of the urban design planner, the improvement process could involve the addition of physical structures including restaurants and stores, the creation of additional transit lines to alleviate transportation problems, and an increase in the number of police patrols to increase the residents' safety. In addition to these changes, the alleviation of environmental hazards such as cracked, uneven sidewalks and poor street lighting is essential. Locating a senior center in an area with a high concentration of elderly facilitates social interaction within their own neighborhood.

Crime Against the Elderly

There is a perception that the aged are the major target of violent crime in the United States. However, annual data from the National Crime Survey between 1973 and 1982 indicate otherwise. Persons aged 65 and older have the lowest personal victimization rates of any age group for the crimes of robbery, aggravated assault, simple assault, rape, and personal larceny without contact (Cutler, 1987). Furthermore, there was no evidence of any trend toward increasing victimization of the elderly over that period. The only category in which older adults have a higher rate of crime is personal larceny with contact, which means purse snatching and pocket picking (e.g., Bureau of Justice Statistics, 1981, 1984; Liang & Sengstock, 1983).

Although older adults are less likely to be victimized by crime, they report a greater fear of crime than younger adults (Harris & Associates, 1975, 1981). Fear is more prevalent among older women and older persons living in the central cities of larger urban areas. Although fear has been alleged to lead the elderly to become prisoners in their own homes, at least one large study of public housing tenants found no support for the idea that older tenants remain housebound out of fear of crime (Lawton & Yaffe, 1980).

Elder Abuse and Neglect

While battered children and wives have been receiving media attention and increasing social supports for close to three decades, it was only in 1978 that the issue of elder abuse and neglect began to receive attention (Quinn & Tomita, 1986). Initial research on elder abuse and neglect provided a profile of the typical victim. This would be a woman aged 75 or older who suffered from significant mental and/or physical impairments which affected her ability to care for herself. When physical abuse is involved, the victim typically lives with the abuser (Pillemer & Finkelhor, 1985). While the abuser is usually a family member, many other individuals having contact with the elderly are guilty of abuse. Among those most commonly cited for elder abuse have been lawyers, nurses, corner grocers, physicians, and bankers (Quinn, 1987).

The initial studies of elder abuse and neglect resulted in hearings before the Select Committee on Aging of the U.S. House of Representatives in 1981. The committee found that the problem was widespread. Abuse and neglect were not limited to isolated cases of frail elders and their pathological offspring. The estimate by the committee of the annual incidence of elder abuse was 4 percent of older adults. If we take 4 percent of the 1985 estimate of the older adult population, 28.5 million, that would mean that 1,140,000 older adults were abused in 1985. The Select Committee on Aging held further hearings in 1985 and found that the abuse of older adults is far less likely to be reported than the abuse of children. Of all adult abuse cases reported annually, 82 percent involved an elderly victim (U.S. House of Representatives, 1985).

Quinn (1987) identified five types of abuse and neglect subjected upon older adults. These include: (1) Physical abuse and neglect resulting in trauma such as bruises, cuts, rope burns (from being tied up), broken bones, blood clots beneath the scalp, dehydration and malnutrition, pressure sores, hypothermia, and death; (2) Financial abuse which is more common with elders than other forms of domestic abuse because older adults are more likely to have assets such as a home, bank accounts, or other valuables; (3) Violation of basic rights which is common and includes not being permitted to vote or to practice one's religion, or to open one's own mail; (4) Psychological abuse which usually occurs in conjunction with other types of abuse and includes threats to abandon the elderly or to put them into nursing homes; (5) Self-abuse and neglect. The last category is not agreed upon by experts, but many states include this category in their reporting.

As of 1986, 37 states had laws mandating that elder abuse and neglect be reported to governmental agencies. Clinical treatment for elder abuse and neglect is in the process of being formulated and tested (Quinn, 1987).

MACROSOCIAL FORCES AND AGING

We now move from issues in the personal environment of the individual such as family, friends, and neighborhood to broader forces in the society and culture which affect aging individuals. How age stages are defined in a culture is one aspect of the macrosocial forces affecting the aging of the individual. Age-status systems vary across cultures, as do the norms set up in a society for behavior and activities at various ages. We explored some aspects of the macrosocial perspective of aging in Chapter 3 when we discussed the aging population. Now we examine additional social concepts about aging.

Social Age and Its Influence
on the Timing of Life Events

The timing of life events are regulated in part by our chronological age. However, there are at least four major social factors which also influence the timing of events in our lives: socioeconomic status, ethnicity, birth cohort, and gender (Bengtson, Kassachau, & Ragan, 1977).

Socioeconomic status can influence the age at which major events occur in life (Neugarten, Moore, & Lowe, 1965). The lower the socioeconomic status, the earlier major events in the life course are reached. In lower socioeconomic status groups, on average individuals quit school earlier, begin work earlier, marry earlier, have children earlier, and retire at a younger age. If you ask members of lower socioeconomic status groups what age is old, they will often say old is 50 to 55 years old. This is at least a decade younger than the age which respondents from higher socioeconomic status groups identify as old.

There appear to be contrasting needs and adaptation to aging among blacks, Chicanos, Orientals, and Anglos in contemporary American society (Bengtson, 1979; Moriwaki & Kobata, 1983; Myerhoff, 1979). For example, when asked about their perceptions of old age, Mexican-American respondents were the most negative, Anglo respondents were the most positive, and black respondents were intermediate in their attitudes. Mexican-Americans were most aware of a stigma attached to the status of old age, while blacks were more likely to express pride in having attained old age (Bengtson, Grigsby, Corry & Hruby, 1977). Old age has high status in Oriental culture, and older Asians in families and communities in which the traditional Oriental values are maintained enjoy special prestige. On the other hand, as younger Asians become assimilated and adopt Western values, there can be serious intergenerational conflict when the elders are not treated according to the traditional Oriental system.

The cohort effect on social age refers to how individuals born during different periods of historical time think about their own age and the ages of those younger and older than themselves. The cohort born in the mid- to late 1940s in their late adolescence became the "hippies" of the late 1960s, and they cautioned, "Don't trust anyone over the age of 30." Contemporary adolescents do not appear to hold such contempt for adults over the age of 30. Indeed, the hippies of the late 1960s are now in their late thirties, and undoubtedly their view of those over the age of 30 has changed. Younger cohorts' attitudes about aging may be changing as well because of the greater visibility of older adults in our culture. *Golden Girls,* the hit television comedy about four older women who live together, has a high rating among adolescents and young adults. It is unlikely that such a program would have been successful with previous cohorts of young people.

Biologically, girls mature more rapidly than boys, so it is no wonder that social age differs for girls and boys and women and men. Because of the earlier maturation rate in females, it is more socially acceptable for women to date and marry men several years older than themselves. In terms of appearance, aging is considered to affect women more adversely than men. Thus, a woman over 50 may be considered "over the hill," while a man over 60 is still "in his prime." While these stereotypes may be changing in the late 1980s when some glamorous actresses look beautiful after 60, for the majority of the population, they still exist.

Thus, the way we perceive social age is affected by a number of influences. Depending on socioeconomic status, ethnicity, cohort, and gender, individuals of the same chronological age may be perceived to be much younger or older. We perceive our own age and the age of others according to the way we have been socialized.

Age-status systems.   The sequence of roles available to an individual through the life course is called an age-status system. A woman's status over the life span might consist of the following roles: daughter, sister, friend, student, wife, intern, resident, doctor, mother, neighbor, colleague, grandmother. An age-status system is developed by a culture to give order and predictability to life for the individual members.

Upon entering many of the statuses in the life sequence just described, a major new stage may begin and/or end. For example, when a woman becomes a wife in our society, her role as a daughter changes dramatically. She is ending one major stage of her life and entering a new and important stage. Bengtson and Haber (1983) stated that the most significant characteristic of an age-status system is that major stages emerge, contract or elongate, and eventually terminate. The 28-year extension to the average life expectancy in the United States since the turn of the century has expanded the period of postparenthood. Early in the twentieth century it was typical that one of the parents would be dead before the last child was launched. Now a couple can anticipate at least 20 years together after the last child has left home.

Childhood did not always exist as a major period in the life cycle. Children in earlier centuries were considered to be miniature adults. It was only after the growth of industrialization reduced the need for child labor that children remained longer in a sheltered status. At that point the idea of an early stage of life became acceptable. We have pointed out in Chapter 1 that G. Stanley Hall created the term *adolescence*. That stage appeared in the early part of the twentieth century as middle- and upper-class young people were encouraged to remain in school for at least 12 years to receive adequate education to succeed in an increasingly complex society.

Late life is emerging as another period which is becoming increasingly differentiated. With a greater percentage of the population attaining old age and with longevity slowly increasing (Fries & Crapo, 1981), many policy makers, researchers, and practitioners are starting to establish categories within the aged. Neugarten (1974) distinguished the old (aged 65–74) from the very old (over the age of 75 or 80) because of the different needs of the two groups of older adults.

Age norms.   An age norm is a designation of behavior which is appropriate at a certain age. In a given society, there is general consensus about what individuals should be doing at certain points in the life span. Age norms differ between societies, and they can also vary by cohort and the period in which they are measured. Consider, for example, the wide variety of age-related characteristics in adulthood on which consensus was reached in the mid-1960s. Neugarten, Moore, and Lowe (1965) asked 93 middle-class, middle-aged individuals their opinions about the appropriate age range for the items listed in Table 4.2. They found very high agreement on the age ranges listed in the table. Have the age norms changed during the 25 years which have elapsed since the data in Table 4.2 were collected? Look at Table 4.2 and decide whether you agree with the age norms described by middle-aged adults in the mid-1960s. With life expectancy continuing to increase, some of the age norms in the late 1980s may be older than they were in the 1960s. Indeed, Neugarten (1979) has stated that chronological age is becoming a poor predictor of the way people live.

In the 1980s an adult's age is less likely to tell you anything about that person's economic or marital status, life style, or health. Neugarten believes that we are becoming an age-irrelevant society. It no longer surprises us to hear of a 22-year-old mayor or a 29-year-old university president, or a 35-year-old grandmother, or a retiree of 50. There are 70-year-old college students taking courses beside the

TABLE 4.2   **Consensus in a Middle-Class, Middle-Aged Sample Regarding Various Age-Related Characteristics**

	Age Range Designated As Appropriate or Expected	Percentage Who Concur	
		Men (N = 50)	Women (N = 43)
Best age for a man to marry	20–25	80	90
Best age for a woman to marry	19–24	85	90
When most people should become grandparents	45–50	84	79
Best age for most people to finish school and go to work	20–22	86	82
When most men should be settled on a career	24–26	74	64
When most men hold their top jobs	45–50	71	58
When most people should be ready to retire	60–65	83	86
A young man	18–22	84	83
A middle-aged man	40–50	86	75
A old man	65–75	75	57
A young woman	18–24	89	88
A middle-aged woman	40–50	87	77
An old woman	60–75	83	87
When a man has the most responsibilities	35–50	79	75
When a man accomplishes most	40–50	82	71
The prime of life for a man	35–50	86	80
When a woman has the most responsibilities	25–40	93	91
When a woman accomplishes most	30–45	94	92
A good-looking woman	20–35	92	82

Source: Neugarten, Moore, & Lowe (1965). Age norms, age constraints and adult socialization. *American Journal of Sociology*, p. 712. Used by permission of University of Chicago Press.

traditional 18-year-olds and the returning to college of 30-, 40-, and 50-year-olds. Some 55-year-old men become fathers for the first time, or start a second family at that age. It is also more and more likely that first-time mothers are over the age of 35. Neugarten (quoted in Hall, 1980) remembered when the late Justice William Douglas, in his seventies, married a woman in her late twenties. The press was shocked and hostile. Neugarten feels that the hostility would not exist in the 1980s. The age discrepancy might be noted, but the outrage which typically occurs when people act contrary to a well-established norm would be gone.

Although we are becoming more of an age-irrelevant society, we still behave for the most part on the basis of age norms as they are identified in Table 4.2. Havighurst (1972) has pointed out in his theory of developmental tasks that adjustment is best when major life events occur during the normative period. For example, if young adults are not married by their 30th birthday, there is increasing pressure on them by parents, relatives, and even friends to marry. That pressure may not be as great as it was for single people in the 1950s, but it still exists. For women, there is the additional biological clock of childbearing running out during the decade of the thirties. A woman becomes concerned that she will never have children if she is not married by her early thirties. Men often experience a crisis in their forties when they contemplate whether they have achieved all of the career goals they set for themselves earlier in life. Sometime before their 50th birthday they face the "moment of truth" about their achievements, and this account of themselves might lead to contentment, depression, or a decision to make a major change, such as a career change, to more deeply fulfill their lives.

SOCIAL PSYCHOLOGICAL THEORIES

Those who have taken a social psychological perspective in devising theories about development and aging have taken into account environmental forces operating on the individual as well as the biological and psychological forces within the person. Such a perspective led Erik Erikson to develop a personality theory postulating eight psychosocial crises which characterize eight different periods across the life span. These crises are generated by the conflicts between the maturing individual and the demands of society. Erikson based his theory on psychoanalytic premises, but he placed much more emphasis on the phases of the life span after childhood than did Freud. Erikson also differed from Freud in his emphasis on the social forces affecting personality. Freud saw the ego as being shaped almost entirely by the parents. Erikson placed more emphasis on the role of peers, teachers, and others outside the family.

Even more emphasis was placed on the environment by Robert Havighurst who devised a theory about adjustment over the life span around what he called the Developmental Tasks of life. The psychosocial crises and developmental tasks of Erikson and Havighurst are presented on Table 4.3. In the following section

TABLE 4.3   The Psychosocial Crises of Eight Life Stages (*Erik Erikson*)

Psychosocial crises refer to individuals's psychosocial efforts to adjust to the demands of the social environment at each stage of development.

Life Stage	Psychosocial Crises
Infancy (birth to 2 years)	Trust versus mistrust
Toddlerhood (2–4)	Autonomy versus shame and doubt
Early school age (5–7)	Initiative versus guilt
Middle school age (8–12)	Industry versus inferiority
Adolescence (13–22)	Identity versus role diffusion
Young adulthood (23–30)	Intimacy versus isolation
Middle adulthood (31–50)	Generativity versus stagnation
Later adulthood (51–)	Integrity versus despair

Developmental Tasks (*Robert Havighurst*)

Tasks individuals must accomplish at given point in the life span. May have biological, psychological, and social components.

Infancy and early childhood (0–4)
  Walk
  Take solid foods
  Language
  Elimination
  Sex differences and modesty
  Concept formation
  Reading readiness
  Morality

Middle childhood (5–11)
  Physical skills for games
  Positive self-concept
  Peer relations
  Masculine-feminine social roles
  Reading, writing, calculating

Adolescence (12–18)
  Relations with age mates
  Sex and social role identity
  Adjust to physical changes
  Emotional independence from parents
  Preparation for marriage
  Preparation for career
  Establish values

Early adulthood (19–29)
  Select mate
  Adjust to living with spouse
  Childbearing
  Childrearing
  Establishment in occupation
  Develop congenial social group

Middle age (30–60)
  Assist teenaged children to become
    responsible adults
  Achieve social and civic responsibility
  Occupational success
  Develop new leisure patterns
  Accept and adjust to physiological
    changes
  Adjust to aging of parents

Later maturity (60–)
  Adjust to decreasing strength and
    health
  Adjust to retirement
  Death of spouse
  Affiliate with one's age group
  Accept death

we will examine Havighurst's theory and his developmental tasks for adulthood and old age and present Erikson's psychosocial crises for these periods as well. The chapter will conclude with social psychological theories created to explain life satisfaction in old age. These are Disengagement theory and Activity theory.

Developmental Tasks

Havighurst (1954, 1972) postulated that throughout life individuals must learn and adapt to new roles, new situations and new relationships. To understand human

development, it is important to be aware that learning and adaptation are con-
tinual processes, even (and perhaps especially) in old age. Havighurst defined a
developmental task as a task

> arising at or about a certain period in the life of an individual, the successful achieve-
> ment of which leads to his happiness and success with later tasks while failure leads
> to unhappiness in the individual, disapproval by society, and difficulty with later
> tasks. (Havighurst, 1972, p. 2).

These tasks usually have biological, psychological, and social components.

Erikson termed middle age the period of generactivity versus stagnation. This
is the time the individual is the most responsible in his or her life. The person is
at the peak of power and influence in society. At this point one may either be productive and "generative" or may falter, fail to develop, and "stagnate." According to Havighurst, middle age is a period in life when biolojgical aging is first being
felt. Men are experiencing health problems such as heart disease and women are
facing menopause. Developmental tasks arise from changes within the person,
environmental pressures, and demands or obligations laid on the individual by
his or her own values and aspirations. The great majority of Americans are in
families at this point in their lives, and the developmental tasks are derived from
the perspective of an individual being a spouse and parent in middle age. Tasks
involve family interaction. Indeed, Havighurst portrays the middle-aged person
being pulled from both sides by the children and by the aging parents.

Among the developmental tasks of this period are assisting the teenage
children to become responsible adults. At this point in their lives, adolescent children
alternate between rebellion and dependence. The middle-aged adult has to be a
strong model and be in control of his or her own feelings to cope with the needs
and demands of the adolescent child. Conflict between parents and children is
almost inevitable at this point as a function of the child's needs to leave home eventually and become independent, and as a function of rapid social change which
produces cohort differences in values.

At the same time the middle-aged parent is dueling with adolescent children,
he or she must adjust to the aging of parents. At some point in life, individuals
become a parent to their own parent. They become the supportive partner in the
relationship, and the parent becomes more dependent on them. This can involve
financial help, physical care, or simply emotional support. It is a developmental
task for both the middle-aged children and the aging parents to adjust to this new
relationship.

Achieving social and civic responsibility is another developmental task of
middle age. This is the point of life when the highest status is attained, and it is
on this aspect of middle age that Erikson focuses when he labels it the period of
generativity versus stagnation. In middle age, people begin to ask themselves if
they have accomplished the goals they set out to achieve in their youth. This point
in life becomes the "moment of truth." It is also the period when people begin

to count their age as the number of years they have remaining rather than the number of years since birth.

Havighurst also calls the need to develop new leisure patterns a developmental task of middle age. This is because the children are leaving home, and the couple must readjust to the new freedom and time they have available in the absence of their children. Leisure patterns developed at this point will be even more important upon retirement when a great deal of free time is available.

Accepting and adjusting to physiological change is another developmental task of middle age, and it is at this point in life that early aging changes are first felt. Decline in energy level, difficulty in remaining slim, and necessity for reading glasses are all signs that the body is changing. An even more dramatic sign is the experience of a heart attack, either personally or in a close friend. It is at this juncture that many middle-aged individuals reevaluate their lives and decide to live as if each day may be their last.

The developmental tasks of later maturity involve major life adjustments, and unfortunately, almost all the developmental tasks of this period involve loss. Decreased income, poor health, and the loss of a spouse are all major changes for the worse in the life of an older person, making this period one of the most stressful. In Erikson's scheme, this is the period of ego integrity versus despair. It is the point when the individual reviews his or her life and integrates it into a meaningful whole or looks back with regret at what could have been.

Adapting to decreasing physical strength and health is a developmental task which is faced by almost all older people. Arthritis, heart disease, arteriosclerosis, and cancer are among the major diseases plaguing the elderly, and many suffer from more than one of these diseases. Additionally, normal aging processes render physiological capacity and sensory function less adequate, so more effort is required for everyday tasks.

Adjustment to retirement is another challenge in old age which may lead to great enjoyment after the adjustment is made. There is no reason to view all of the developmental tasks of old age as negative, when over 70 percent of the elderly in a recent survey viewed their quality of life as good to excellent (Flanagan, 1982). Nevertheless, change is stressful, and adjustment to retirement is a major life change. Affiliating with one's age group is difficult for many people 65 and over. We face this when we search for a name to identify this group. Should we call them senior citizens, old people, or the elderly? None of these names sounds very attractive because of the low status of the aged in the United States. Accepting this loss of status and affiliating with this age group is understandably difficult. The other two developmental tasks, the death of a spouse and the acceptance of one's own death, pose major challenges to the individual. These will be discussed in Chapter 18 on living, dying, and death.

Disengagement and Activity Theories

Working at the University of Chicago in the 1950s and 1960s was a group which made major contributions to the study of personality in adulthood and old age. This group undertook a large-scale longitudinal study of personality in Kansas City, and the empirical results of that work led to the creation of Disengagement theory. Results of projective tests suggested increasing interiority of the aging adults. They appeared to become more introspective and socially introverted with age. Research on the activities of the elderly suggested that there was decreasing role activity and also less ego investment in social roles. There appeared to be a shrinkage in social life space.

These results led Cumming and Henry (1961) to propose Disengagement theory. It stipulates that as individuals age, they are released from social roles and they also withdraw psychological energy from social ties. This was seen as a mutually beneficial disengagement on the part of society and the individual. It was postulated that life satisfaction would be highest if individuals would disengage themselves from society while society carried out this disengagement process as well.

This theory stimulated a great deal of additional research and controversy and led to the creation of its converse, Activity theory. The main premise of Activity theory is that life satisfaction is highest when individuals remain engaged in social roles. This theory was supported by empirical evidence derived from more complex measures of social interaction.

These competing theories led to the study of personality types in old age, and the resolution of the controversy has been that there is diversity in old age resulting in life satisfaction being achieved in many different patterns of social interaction (Neugarten, 1977). For example, all four combinations of activity and life satisfaction have been found. There are people who are actively socially engaged and have high life satisfaction, but there are also dissatisfied people in this pattern. There are people who have withdrawn from social role participation who have high life satisfaction, and there are those who are depressed in this same situation. This has led to the hypothesis that personality type or personality organization is pivotal in determining which individuals will age successfully and achieve high life satisfaction (Neugarten, 1977).

SUMMARY

Social influences on aging are studied from a microsocial perspective examining the immediate interpersonal environment of family, friends, neighbors and associates as well as from a macrosocial perspective involving broad social structures such as political, economic, religious, and cultural forces. The family is one of the most significant social supports for older adults. It is through the family that older adults have most of their social roles. Roles for elders include spouse, sibling, parent, and grandparent. Because people are living longer, there are many more four- and even five-generation families. In this manner, the roles of great-grandparent and great-great-grandparent are being filled more frequently.

While most families prefer a maximum of two generations living together in one household, this does not mean that intergenerational relations are cold.

Intimacy at a distance is what American families prefer. Contact among family members is frequent, with three quarters of older adults living within 30 minutes of at least one child. When older family members need help and a spouse is not available, children respond to the need. In the absence of availability of help from children, siblings and grandchildren step in to help.

Family contact is provided most frequently by women. Kinkeeping is an activity women attend to most faithfully, and it is usually women in the middle generations who are most centrally involved with keeping in touch with the extended family.

Grandparenting is achieved most often in middle age when adults are still busily engaged in work. Seventy-five percent of older adults have living grandchildren, and three quarters of these grandparents see their grandchildren every week or two. There are a number of ways to approach the grandparent role, from being a surrogate parent to being a distant figure. Pesonal and social expectations and attitudes influence how people approach grandparenting. While a minority of grandparents reported that they found emotional self-fulfillment in the grandparent role, over a third of grandmothers said that they enjoyed that role more than they had enjoyed the role of parent.

The family undergoes predictable changes in composition, organization, and function as its members age. A major difference in the family life cycle in the late twentieth century is the fact that the couple lives together at least 20 years after they have launched their last child. In earlier periods when life expectancy was shorter, one spouse typically died before the last child was out of the nest.

The empty nest syndrome of serious depression experienced especially by the mother after her children have left home does not appear to affect many American women. Morale is actually higher among women whose children have been launched than among women of the same age who still have children at home. However, among a small minority of woman, the empty nest syndrome is debilitating in middle age.

In middle age, individuals experience the middle-generation squeeze. They are responsible for launching their children and soon thereafter they may become responsible for the welfare of their aging parents. Adults may even experience a second empty nest at the death of their parents. Some middle-aged grandchildren may have aged parents and grandparents to care for when the aged parents can no longer manage to care for their own parents.

In late middle age and on into retirement, a couple's relationship goes through several changes. Companionship seems to replace romance and passion, and retirement can bring with it too much togetherness for some individuals. On the other hand, the final phase of the family life cycle, the dissolution of the marriage through the death of the spouse brings about a loss and a loneliness that some widows and widowers say they will never overcome.

Far more women than men outlive their spouses, and the status of widow in the United States carries with it a stigma. People are likely to withdraw from someone who is grieving. Widows feel like a "fifth wheel" and often decrease their social contacts. Mortality rate increases after the death of a spouse, as does the rate of mental illness. Eventually many recover from the loss of a spouse, and some even see compensations in widowhood. Nevertheless, the loss of a spouse is one of the most difficult crises to be faced over the entire period of the family life cycle.

The aged become progressively more affected by aspects of their environment. They may be more restricted to their immediate environment, so it becomes more important to them. Some older adults prefer to live among others of their own age group, while other elderly like to remain in their old neighborhood among neighbors of various ages. Since individual variability is greatest in old age, it is important that older adults have a variety of options for their housing. Neighborhoods in which there are stores, churches, and restaurants in close proximity as well as little potential for crime are preferred.

While the aged are portrayed as being major targets of crime, they are actually the least likely to be victimized by any violent crime except purse snatching or pocket picking. As individuals age, they seem to have increased fears of crime. However, they do not appear to respond to this fear by becoming housebound.

Elder abuse and neglect have recently received recognition as a serious social problem. It is estimated that 4 percent of the elderly are abused or neglected. Unfortunately, abuse and neglect of old people are generally committed by those who are trusted by the elderly. The types of abuse and neglect include physical abuse, financial abuse, violation of basic rights, psychological abuse, and self-abuse. Clinical treatment for elder abuse and neglect is in the process of being formulated and tested.

Social age influences the timing of events in people's lives. Factors affecting social age are socioeconomic status, ethnicity, birth cohort, and gender. An age-status system is the sequence of roles available to an individual through the life course. Age norms are designations of behavior which is appropriate at a certain age. Behavior in American society in the late 1980s is becoming more age irrelevant. Age norms are declining in importance.

Erik Erikson's Psychosocial Crises identify eight phases in the life span and the central personal issue of each period. Robert Havighurst's Developmental Task theory identifies challenges individuals must face and overcome to adjust throughout life. Disengagement and Activity theories deal with life satisfaction in later adulthood. Both have been shown to be inadequate to deal with the vast individual differences in the way older adults achieve life satisfaction.

REFERENCES

AIZENBERG, R. & TREAS, J. (1985).   The family in late life: Psychosocial and demographic considerations. In J. E. Birren & K. W. Schaie (Eds.), *Handbook of the psychology of aging* (2nd Ed.), New York: Van Nostrand Reinhold.

BENGTSON, V. L. (1979).   Ethnicity and aging: Problems and issues in current social science inquiry. In D. E. Gelfand & A. J. Kutzik (Eds.), *Ethnicity and aging.* New York: Springer.

BENGTSON, V. L., CUTLER, N. E., MANGEN, D. J., & MARSHALL, V. W. (1985). Generations, cohorts and relations between age groups. In R. H. Binstock & E. Shanas (Eds.) *Handbook of aging and the social sciences* (2nd Ed.)., New York: Van Nostrand Reinhold.

BENGTSON, V. L., GRIGSBY, E., CORRY, E. M., & HRUBY, M. (1977) Relating academic research to community concerns: A case study in collaborative effort. *Journal of Social Issues, 33,* 75-92.

BENGTSON, V. L. & HABER, D. (1983).   Sociological perspectives on aging. In D. S. Woodruff & J. E. Birren (Eds.) *Aging: Scientific perspectives and social issues* (2nd Ed.), Monterey, CA: Brooks/Cole.

BENGTSON, V. L., KASSCHAU, P. L., & RAGAN, P. K. (1977).   The impact of social structure on the aging individual. In J. E. Birren & K. W. Schaie (Eds.), *Handbook of the psychology of aging.* New York: Van Nostrand Reinhold.

BOCK, E. W. (1972).   Aging and suicide: The significance of marital, kinship, and alternative relations. *Family Coordinator, 21,* 71-79.

BRODY, E. M. (1981).   "Women in the middle" and family help to older people. *The Gerontologist, 21,* 471-480.

BULTENA, G. L. & WOOD, V. (1969).   The American retirement community: Bane or blessing? *Journal of Gerontology, 24,* 209-217.

BUREAU OF JUSTICE STATISTICS. (1981).   *Crime and the elderly.* Washington, DC: U.S. Department of Justice.

BUREAU OF JUSTICE STATISTICS. (1984).   *Criminal victimization in the United States, 1982.* Washington, DC: U.S. Department of Justice.

CARP, F. (1966).   *A future for the aged: The residents of Victoria Plaza.* Austin: University of Texas Press.

CICIRELLI, V. G. (1985).   Sibling relationships throughout the life cycle. In L. L'Abate (Ed.), *The handbook of family psychology and therapy,* vol. I. Homewood, IL: Dorsey Press.

CUMMING, E. & HENRY, W. (1961).   *Growing old: The process of disengagement.* New York: Basic Books.

CUTLER, S. J. (1987).   Crime (against and by the elderly). In G. L. Maddox (Ed.) *The encyclopedia of aging.* New York: Springer.

DAHLIN, M. (1980).   Perspectives on the family life of the elderly in 1900. *The Gerontologist, 20,* 99-107.

ERIKSON, E. H. (1959).   Identity and the life cycle. *Psychological Issues, 1,* 18-164.

FLANAGAN, J. C. (1982).   *New insights to improve the quality of life at age 70.* Report prepared for National Institute on Aging. Palo Alto, CA: American Institutes for Research.

FRIES, J. F. & CRAPO, L. M. (1981).   *Vitality and aging.* San Francisco: W. H. Freeman.

GLENN, N. D. (1975).   Psychological well-being in the postparental stage: Some evidence from national surveys. *Journal of Marriage and the Family, 37,* 105-110.

GOVE, W. R. (1972).   The relationship between sex roles, marital roles, and mental illness. *Social Forces, 51,* 34-44.

GOVE, W. R. (1973).   Sex, marital status, and mortality. *American Journal of Sociology, 79,* 45-67.

HAGESTAD, G. O. (1986).   The aging society as a context for family life. *Daedalus, 115,* 119-139.

HAGESTAD, G. O. (1987).   Family. In G. L. Maddox (Ed.), *The encyclopedia of aging.* New York: Springer.

HALL, E. (April, 1980).   Acting one's age: New rules for old. Bernice Neugarten interviewed. *Psychology Today,* 66-80.

HARRIS, L. & ASSOCIATES (1975).   *The myth and reality of aging in America.* Washington, DC: The National Council on the Aging.

HARRIS, L. & ASSOCIATES (1981).   *Aging in the eighties: America in transition.* Washington, DC: The National Council on the Aging.

HAVIGHURST, R. J. (1954).   *Developmental tasks and education.* New York: McKay.

HAVIGHURST, R. J. (1972).   *Developmental tasks and education* (2nd Ed.) New York: McKay.

KEATING, N. C. & COLE, P. (1980).   What do I do with him 24 hours a day: Changes in the housewife's role after retirement. *The Gerontologist, 20,* 84-89.

KIVETT, V. R. (1985).   Consanguinity and kin level: Their relative importance to the helping network of older adults. *Journal of Gerontology, 40,* 228-234.

LAWTON, M. P. (1977).   The impact of the environment on aging and behavior. In J. E. Birren & K. W. Schaie (Eds.) *Handbook of the psychology of aging.* New York: Van Nostrand Reinhold.

LAWTON, M. P. & COHEN, J. (1974). The generality of housing impact on the well-being of older people. *Journal of Gerontology, 29,* 194-204.

LAWTON, M. P. & YAFFE, S. (1980).   Victimization and fear of crime in elderly public housing tenants. *Journal of Gerontology, 35,* 768-779.

LIANG, J. & SENGSTOCK, M. C. (1983).   Personal crimes against the elderly. In J. Kosberg (Ed.), *Abuse and maltreatment of the elderly: Causes and interventions.* Littleton, MA: John Wright-PSG, Inc.

LOPATA, H. Z. (1973).   *Widowhood in an American city.* Cambridge, MA: Schenkman.

LOPATA, H. Z. (1987).   Widowhood. In G. L. Maddox (Ed.) *The encyclopedia of aging.* New York: Springer.

MICHAEL, R. T., FUCHS, V. R., & SCOTT, S. R. (1980).   Changes in the propensity to live alone: 1950–1976. *Demography, 17,* 39-56.

MORIWAKI, S. Y. & KOBATA, F. S. (1983).   Ethnic minority aging. In D. S. Woodruff and J. E. Birren (Eds.), *Aging: Scientific perspectives and social issues* (2nd Ed.), Monterey, CA: Brooks/Cole.

MYERHOFF, B. G. (1979).   A symbol perfected in death: Continuity and ritual in the life and death of an elderly Jew. In B. G. Myerhoff & A. Simic (Eds.) *Life's career: Aging.* Beverly Hills, CA: Sage.

NEUGARTEN, B. L. (1974).   Age groups in American society and the rise of the young-old. *Annals of the American Academy of Political and Social Science,* September, 187-198.

NEUGARTEN, B. L. (1977).   Personality and aging. In J. E. Birren & K. W. Schaie (Eds.) *Handbook of the psychology of aging.* New York: Van Nostrand Reinhold.

NEUGARTEN, B. L. (1979).   Time, age, and the life cycle. *American Journal of Psychiatry, 136,* 887-894.

NEUGARTEN, B. L. & MOORE, J. W. (1968).   The changing age-status system. In B. L. Neugarten (Ed.), *Middle age and aging.* Chicago: University of Chicago Press.

NEUGARTEN, B. L., MOORE, J. W., & LOWE, J. C. (1965).   Age norms, age constraints, and adult socialization. *American Journal of Sociology, 70,* 710-717.

NEUGARTEN, B. L. & WEINSTEIN, K. (1964).   The changing American grandparent. *Journal of Marriage and the Family, 26,* 199-204.

OPPENHEIMER, V. K. (1981).   The changing nature of life-cycle squeezes: Implications for the socioeconomic position of the elderly. In R. W. Fogel, E. Hatfield, S. B. Kiesler, & E. Shanas (Eds.), *Aging: Stability and change in the family.* New York: Academic Press.

PILLEMER, K. & FINKELHOR, D. (1985).   Domestic violence against the elderly: A discussion paper. Prepared for the Surgeon General's Workshop on Violence and Public Health. Leesburg, VA, October.

QUINN, M. J. (1987).   Elder abuse and neglect. In G. L. Maddox (Ed.), *The encyclopedia of aging.* New York: Springer.

QUINN, M. J. & TOMITA, S. K. (1986).   *Elder abuse and neglect: Causes, diagnosis, and intervention strategies.* New York: Springer.

REGNIER, V. (1983).   Housing and environment. In D. S. Woodruff & J. E. Birren (Eds.), *Aging: Scientific perspectives and social issues* (2nd Ed.), Monterey, CA: Brooks/Cole.

ROBERTSON, J. F. (1977).   Grandmotherhood: A study of role conceptions. *Journal of Marriage and the Family, 39,* 165-174.

ROSENMAYR, L. (1984).   Socio-cultural change in the relation of the family to its older members. In *Proceedings from Tenth International Conference of Social Gerontology.* Paris: International Center for Social Gerontology.

ROSOW, I. (1967).   *Social integration of the aged.* New York: Free Press.

RUBIN, L. B. (1980).   The empty nest: Beginning or ending? In L. A. Bond & J. C. Rosen (Eds.), *Competence and coping in adulthood.* Hanover, NH: University Press of New England.

SCOTT, J. P. (1983).   Siblings and other kin. In T. H. Brubaker (Ed.), *Family relationships in later life.* Beverly Hills, CA: Sage.

SEELBACH, W. C. & SAUER, W. J. (1977).   Filial responsibility expectations and morale among aged parents. *The Gerontologist, 17,* 492-499.

SHANAS, E. (1975).   *National survey of the aged.* Final report, grant no. HEW OHD 90-A-369.

SHANAS, E. (1980).   Older people and their families: The new pioneers. *Journal of Marriage and the Family, 42,* 9-15.

SHERMAN, S. (1975).   Mutual assistance and support in retirement housing. *Journal of Gerontology, 30,* 479-483.

STRUYK, R. (1981).   The changing housing and neighborhood environment of the elderly: A look at the year 2000. In S. B. Kiesler, J. N. Morgan, & V. K. Oppenheimer, (Eds.), *Aging: Social change.* New York: Academic Press.

TEAFF, J., LAWTON, M. P., NAHEMOW, L., & CARLSON, D. (1978).   Impact of age integration on the well-being of elderly tenants in public housing. *Journal of Gerontology, 33,* 126-133.

TREAS, J. (1983).   Aging and the family. In D. S. Woodruff & J. E. Birren (Eds.), *Aging: Scientific perspectives and social issues* (2nd Ed.), Monterey, CA: Brooks/Cole.

TROLL, L. E. (1982).   *Continuations: Adult development and aging.* Monterey, CA: Brooks/Cole.

U.S. HOUSE OF REPRESENTATIVES (1985).   *Elder abuse.* Select Committee on Aging, 99th Congress Committee Pub. No. 99-516. Washington, DC: U.S. Government Printing Office.

WYLIE, M. (1976).   New communities. In M. P. Lawton, R. J. Newcomer, & T. O. Byerts (Eds.), *Community planninig for an aging society.* Stroudsburg, PA: Dowden, Hutchinson, and Ross.

CHAPTER 5

Physiological Aging

Identifying and explaining relationships between physiology, behavior, and aging is the goal of this chapter. Psychophysiologists are the scientists concerned with examining how physiological systems, such as the cardiovascular, pulmonary, and nervous systems, affect the way we act, and conversely, how our feelings and actions affect these systems. The application of psychophysiological techniques is especially pertinent in the field of aging as it is clear that physiological functions change with age. Indeed, geropsychologists have tended to be so preoccupied with physiological age changes and how they affect behavior that they have often ignored behavioral influences on physiology.

Behavior has all too frequently been interpreted in terms of the biological decremental model of aging which stipulates that aging is represented by decline in all physiological systems (Woodruff, 1980, 1982). This leaves psychologists in the unfortunate position of merely describing behavioral decrements. If geropsychologists more carefully viewed the interactive nature of physiology-behavior relationships, we would be in a better position to attempt to modify age changes in behavior and even age changes in physiology.

We begin this chapter at a molecular and cellular level to describe some of the basic biological theories of aging. These theories have been postulated to explain physiological aging. Then we examine physiological aging at the organ system level. Emphasis is placed on age changes in the nervous system, since this system most directly affects behavioral aging. In this regard we examine some of the new tools useful in the assessment of behavior, aging, and the nervous system. Next psycho-physiological models of aging are presented, and at the end of the chapter we discuss how behavior and physiology interact in aging along with the implications of this research for old people.

One of the certainties which has emerged from a century of research in gerontology is that aging is a tremendously complex problem for which there is no simple explanation. Thus, when we begin to examine theories of biological aging, it becomes clear that gerontologists do not have any one unifying theory of aging. Aging is such a complex set of processes that no single theory is able to account for all of the phenomena which occur. There are a number of models and theories of aging. Some of them compete to explain the same processes, while others coexist and explain aging at different levels or in complimentary fashions.

We have distinguished at least three levels or categories of aging: biological, psychological, and social. In this chapter theories dealing with biological and psychophysiological aging will be discussed.

BIOLOGICAL THEORIES
OF AGING

Rockstein and Sussman (1979) have identified ten different theories in the biology of aging, and their categories are adopted and used for the purposes of this chapter. These authors point out that a number of the currently proposed theories have common underlying themes. One theme is that aging of organs and ultimately of the entire body is a programmed process. Theories such as the programmed theory, the gene theory, and to some degree the running-out-of-program theory and wear-and-tear theory fall into this category. An alternative model is that aging is nothing more than the accumulation over time of insults from the environment. The somatic-mutation theory, the cross-linkage theory, the free-radical theory, the clinker theory, and the error theory are all variants on this theme. Rockstein and Sussman maintain that it is closer to the truth that the aging processes represent a cumulative, age-related summation of the inherited program for aging, combined with the effect of accumulating environmental insults suffered by an individual from infancy through old age. In other words, it is not simply a program *or* the accumulation of insults that bring about aging; it is probably an interaction of both.

In the biology of aging, there are three criteria which must be met by a theory on aging (Rockstein & Sussman, 1979). These criteria are:

1. The aging phenomenon under consideration must be evident universally in all members of a given species.
2. The process must be progressive with time.
3. The process must be deleterious in nature, leading ultimately to the failure of the organ or system.

These three criteria differentiate biological theories of aging from theories in psychology and social psychology and aging. The latter two categories include theories involving nondeleterious processes and processes which are not universal in all members of the species. Also, psychological and social psychological theories do not really have any specific criteria by which they can be identified as do the biological theories. The following are brief descriptions of the ten major biological theories of aging.

Theories Involving Genetic Programming

The gene theory. This could also be called the "time bomb" theory of aging because it postulates in a variety of forms a kind of genetic mechanism which ticks away in the organism and programs its death. In its simplest form, this theory proposes the existence of one or more deleterious genes within each organism. These genes become active late in life and result in the death of the organism. One form of this theory is the concept that there arc two kinds of genes for aging. The favorabale kind are the juvenescent genes responsible for youthful vigor and mature adult functioning. The unfavorable senescent genes are responsible for decline in function and deterioration in structure. Early in life the juvenescent genes predominate, and the senescent genes take over in middle age and predominate after that.

Another variation of the gene theory is that the same genes carry the juvenescent and senescent functions. Developmental functions are supposedly activated early in life, and aging functions are activated after reproduction. The term used for genes having such a dual role is *pleitrophy.* An example of pleitrophic function in humans is the development of reproductive functions in the woman and their programmed senescence in menopause. Advocates of all variations of the gene theory tend to agree that no single gene programs senescence. Undoubtedly, many genes are involved. Recent evidence for a gene on the twenty-first chromosome involved in senile dementia of the Alzheimer's type (SDAT) provides support for the gene theory of aging.

The programmed theory. This theory is based on the observation that all species show a predictable species-specific pattern of changes in the body which occur with age, and all species have a predictable life span. Such regularities could only result from genetic programming, according to proponents of this theory (Wilson, 1974). Wilson proposed that the aging process which ultimately leads to the failure of the individual to survive, has evolved to maximize the survival of each species. After fulfilling the role of propagating a new generation, the adults of any species undergo a program of aging established by evolution. The death of most of the adults at a given average age permits the survival of the new generation for the purpose of propagation and perpetuation of the species. Unfortunately, this theory is very undeveloped because it simply explains why programming occurs without explaining how it occurs. It totally omits specification of the mechanisms involved in the programming. Thus, at best, the theory is incomplete.

The running-out-of-program theory.   This is a theory involving the concept of scarcity of resources or limitation of products. It postulates that at fertilization each cell of the offspring is endowed with only a prescribed amount of genetic material. As cells age, the basic genetic material of the nucleus, DNA, is ultimately used up, thus leading to cell failure. Support for this theory comes from numerous reports of gradual, age-related diminution of activity or amount of enzymes (catalysts of cellular activity) in organs such as the liver, brain and muscle.

The "Hayflick phenomenon," so named for its discoverer, Leonard Hayflick (1965, 1976, 1977), is another example of this theory. When cells are maintained alive outside the body in tissue culture, they go through a predictable sequence, presented diagrammatically in Figure 5.1. In the proper solution they will double until they cover the bottom of a petri dish, and when half of the cells are removed and put into another dish, they will duplicate until that dish is covered. What Hayflick discovered was that the number of cell doublings has an upper limit which is correlated with the life span of the species whose cells are being cultured. For example, allowed to thrive and multiply in appropriate conditions, cells from human lung tissue multiply rapidly. They double at first at a rate of once every 24 hours.

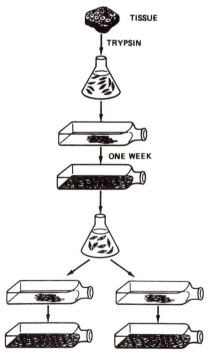

FIGURE 5.1   Serial cultures of human fibroblast cells in the laboratory. These cultures will duplicate just over 50 times before losing the capacity to reproduce Source: Fries, J. F. & Crapo, L. M. (1981). *Vitality and aging.* San Francisco: W. H. Freeman, p. 48. Reprinted by permission.

As the process progresses, the time between successive doublings increases and after about 50 doublings, the cells fail to double again and the cell strain dies. Since there is a relationship between the life span of a species and the number of doubling of that species' cells, it makes it appear as if aging is a programmed phenomenon.

The wear-and-tear theory.   The idea here is that aging is a programmed process, but the theory also stresses that cells are continuously wearing out, just as machines wear out from excessive use. The process is aggravated by the harmful effects of internal and external stress factors, including the accumulation of injurious by-products of metabolism. The accumulation of this combined damage to the cell contents with age, along with the increasing failure of the cells to repair or replace damaged vital cellular components, causes cell death in increasing numbers with advancing age. The theory appears particularly suitable for aging in muscle and nerve cells which do not undergo cell division after birth and are thus subject to wear and tear.

Theories Involving Random Accumulation of Insults

The somatic-mutation theory.   The biologist most closely associated with this theory is H. J. Curtis (Curtis & Miller, 1971). He found that by exposing mice and guinea pigs to X-rays or by the direct application to the liver of certain chemicals like carbon tetrachloride, a considerable number of liver cells were destroyed. Replacement of these cells by cell division resulted in a large number of new liver cells which were abnormal. A high incidence of abnormal chromosomes occurred. In mice which received no treatment, it was observed that older mice had more spontaneous chromosome abnormalities. Also, mice of a short-lived strain had liver cells with more chromosome abnormalities at all ages than strains of mice which had longer life spans. This evidence led Curtis and his colleagues to propose that aging of all cells in the senescent animal is the result of the time-dependent accumulation of mistakes in the chromosomes (somatic mutations). The cause for these mutations was not clearly specified.

The cross-linkage theory.   This theory was proposed and elaborated by Bjorksten (1974) and concerns the aging of proteins like collagen which are held ultimately responsible for the failure of tissues and organs. Collagen is a substance which serves as supportive tissue in the lungs, heart, muscle, and the lining of the walls of blood vessels. Changes in its structure with age are partially responsible for the condition of arteriosclerosis and loss of elasticity of blood vessels. Proponents of the cross-linkage theory suggest that the known accumulation of numerous cross-linking compounds produce the random, irreparable binding together of essential molecules in the cells. This results in the disturbance of normal cell functioning.

The free-radical theory.   This theory is considered to be a special case of the cross-linkage theory. According to Gordon (1974), instead of postulating a number of noxious compounds which can produce cross-linkage, free radicals are identified as the cause of aging. These are chemical components of the cell which arise as a by-product of normal cell processes produced by the action of oxygen. They exist only for brief periods of a second or less since they are highly reactive chemically and interact with other substances, especially unsaturated fats. The membrane of the cell is made up in part of fatty or lipid substances, and it can become damaged if subjected to an excessive number of free radicals. Free radicals can also cause mutations in chromosomes and damage the genetic machinery of cells as well as the membrane. Furthermore, free radicals are self-propagating. They react with a molecule and release several new free radicals which then cause additional chains of reactions. Antioxidants which prevent this process such as vitamins C and E can reduce or inhibit the production of new free radicals, and recently scientists have become interested in determining if these substances have life-prolonging effects. At the present time, the evidence is not conclusive.

The clinker theory.   This theory is in the family of somatic-mutation, cross-linkage and free-radical theories as it involves the excessive buildup in the body of noxious compounds. It suggests that aging involves the time-related accumulation of deleterious substances within various cells of the body. These include by-products of cellular metabolism (such as lipofuscin, histones, aldehydes, quinones, and free radicals) which are known to accumulate in increasing quantities in the cytoplasm of most cells. These substances are chemically inert and do not have the ability to react with other substances. They are like the clinkers, the unburned debris in the coal, which accumulate in the coal furnace and eventually clog it so that it cannot function. With regard to aging, it has been suggested that the accumulation of inert substances interferes with the normal functioning of tissues by displacement of otherwise functional cytoplasmic components of the cells involved.

Error theory.   This is a popular but relatively unsubstantiated theory. It proposes that as cells continue to function, random errors may occur in the process of the synthesis of new proteins. Protein synthesis involves a complex series of steps, beginning with DNA in the nucleus and the transcription of the genetic code, and leading to the ultimate translation of the code in the final steps to the production of protein. The process involves enzymes which are responsible for all cellular activities. Random errors could occur in the synthesis of the enzymes which would then affect the synthesis of other proteins. This would accelerate the accumulation of errors. With time, the result would be a decrease in protein synthesis to a catastrophic failure level. Weaknesses in this theory include the fact that a number of recent studies have failed to show any qualitative changes in enzymes, although the enzymes did show a decrease in activity with age. Thus, errors do not appear to be the complete basis for universal cellular senescence.

The autoimmune theory. This theory postulates that the body fails to recognize itself, turns against itself, and attacks and tears down its own tissue. It was formulated by Walford (1969) and has been supported and extended by Adler (1974). According to this theory, the organism's immune system which is designed to repel or overcome bacterial and viral infection or invasion by foreign proteins fails in its function. From birth, the body's immune system has "memorized" the structural configuration of its own thousands and thousands of proteins, which it continues to recognize at least through middle age. Accordingly, in the normal young person or healthy adult, the immune system will repel or attack only foreign proteins through the production of antibodies or attack by certain white blood cells. The autoimmune theory proposes that, with advancing age, defects arise in the immune system so that the self cannot be distinguished from the nonself. This results in the production of antibodies against the self. The autoimmune theory, like the programmed theory, attempts to explain what happens, but it fails to explain how it happens. Thus, at the present time the theory is not yet substantiated.

It can be seen from this overview of the theories of biological aging that there are a number of theories which attempt to explain aging at different levels. Clearly, there is no one general theory of aging. No single phenomenon can account for the many levels on which aging occurs, and it becomes apparent in this chapter that as gerontologists we consider many different things when we study aging processes. Biologists focus exclusively on deleterious processes, while psychologists examine age functions of a variety of shapes including increment and stability. For the time being, it is useful to examine the various perspectives to acknowledge the range of aging phenomena. At some point in the future of gerontology, we will be able to relate some of these phenomena across several levels of organization. However, at the present time, our theories are as nonconvergent as they are diverse.

Many of the theories of aging are not complete in their explanation of how aging occurs. Descriptive research on the actual changes which occur in physiological aging is more complete. We will turn now to a description of age changes in physiological systems.

AGING IN THE NERVOUS SYSTEM

Measures of the aging brain and nervous system can be made in a variety of ways. The measures we have of the functioning brain in humans are noninvasive, that is, we make the assessments from outside the brain. It is only with animal subjects (and occasionally with human patient populations having therapeutic surgery) that we use invasive techniques to measure the living, responding brain. Three noninvasive measures used on normal aging humans which we discuss here are electrophysiological techniques and the CAT and PET scans. We also assess the aging brain by conducting studies after the individual has died. Analysis of the brain tissue at a cellular and molecular level provides insights about the neurobiological changes which occur with age. Indeed, it is only with such post-mortem analyses that we can confirm a diagnosis such as senile dementia of the Alzheimer's type (SDAT). We will describe some of the brain changes at this level in Chapter 9 on sensation and perception. Here we will discuss measures of the living, functioning brain.

Electrophysiological Measures of the Aging Brain

The brain is composed of billions of nerve cells called neurons. The electrical activity of hundreds of thousands of neurons can be recorded by attaching electrodes to an individual's scalp and amplifying the tiny electrical signals approximately a million times. The characteristic oscillating pattern of electrical activity recorded in this manner is called the electroencephalogram (EEG), and it has been used as a clinical tool to identify abnormal brain activity and as an experimental tool to examine brain and behavior relationships. Since it is not feasible to invade the brain with recording techniques, the EEG is one of the few means available to measure human brain activity.

There are at least four identified rhythms in the EEG. The alpha rhythm is in the 8 to 13 cycle per second (cps) range and is the dominant modal brain wave frequency. Behaviorally, it is associated with a relaxed but alert state and is most prominent in the back parts of the head, especially when the eyes are closed. Beta activity is a faster rhythm, above 13 cps, and is associated with an alert, thinking state of consciousness. Theta activity is in the 4 to 7 cps range and is associated with daydreaming and drowsiness. Activity in the 1 to 3 cps range is called delta and occurs druing sleep. Thus, faster brain waves are associated with alertness and arousal, while slower rhythmic patterns are related to drowsiness and sleep. Clinical uses of the EEG include the identification of tumors and areas of pathology in the brain which are manifested as areas of localized slowing of EEG activity. Thus, slowing is associated with drowsiness, sleep, and brain pathology.

The dominant brain wave rhythm of young adults is slightly faster than 10 cycles per second. One of the best-documented findings in the psychophysiological literature is that this dominant brain wave rhythm slows with age (see Marsh & Thompson, 1977; Woodruff, 1985 for reviews). By the time an individual reaches the age of 60 to 65, his or her dominant brain wave rhythm is probably around 9 cps. Although some 80-year-olds have brain wave patterns similar to those of 20-year-olds, the normal pattern in even the healthiest of aging individuals is for EEG slowing to occur with age. Figure 5.2, taken from the research of Obrist and associates, illustrates slowing in the same individual over a ten-year period.

Obrist, Henry and Justiss (1961) demonstrated that the slowing of the EEG alpha rhythm is a reliable phenomenon occurring in longitudinal as well as cross-sectional studies. In the ten-year period of Obrist's longitudinal study, two thirds of the subjects manifested slowing of the dominant rhythm. Since this slowing has been related to pathology, the subjects may have had some kind of disease,

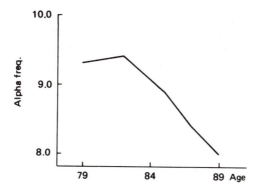

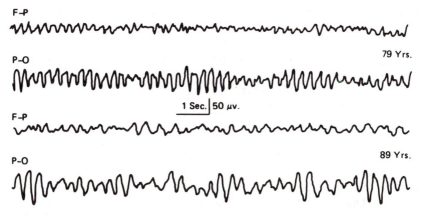

FIGURE 5.2 Alpha frequency plotted as a function of age for a mentally "normal" old man over a ten-year period. The top tracing was recorded at age 79, the bottom tracing at age 89. The latter EEG was associated with mild signs of intellectual impairment. F-P = Fronto-Parietal; P-O = Parieto-Occipital. Source: Obrist, W. D., Henry, C. E. & Justiss, W. A. (1961). Longitudinal study of EEG in old age. *Excerpta Medical Internatinonal Congress,* Serial no. 37, pp. 180–181. Reprinted by permission.

such as cerebral arteriosclerosis, which would cause a slower metabolic rate in the brain and lead to slower brain wave rhythms. It has been demonstrated that senile patients, patients with arteriosclerosis or severe brain atrophy, have very slow brain wave rhythms.

One of the studies which convincingly demonstrated that alpha slowing occurs in even the healthiest of aged individuals was reported by Birren, Butler, Greenhouse, Sokoloff, and Yarrow (1963). An extensive study was undertaken to examine biological and behavioral changes in 47 old men chosen because they were in optimal health. Obrist examined the EEGs of these men and found that even in the healthiest there was a slowing of the EEG alpha rhythm to 9 cps. Thus, alpha slowing, is a phenomenon associated with normal aging and is not necessarily the result of disease.

The slowing of the dominant EEG rhythm is part of the legacy of descriptive studies of aging, and this finding is cited, along with numerous others, to support the biological-decremental model of aging. While there are at least 20 studies documenting deleterious age changes in the EEG, there have been few attempts to determine if these age changes in EEG are reversible. One such attempt (Woodruff, 1975) is described in Chapter 10.

Event-Related Potentials

Brain electrical responses to specific stimuli are usually not apparent in recordings of ongoing EEG, but by taking a number of epochs in which the same stimulus event has occurred and summing or averaging across these epochs, the activity related to the stimulus becomes apparent. The assumption is that random activity not associated with the stimulus cancels to a flat voltage pattern, while activity time-locked to the stimulus cumulates and emerges from the random background "noise" of the ongoing EEG. A number of different bioelectric signals exhibit stable temporal relationships to a definable external event, and these can be elicited in most of the sensory modalities. Most research involves auditory, visual, or somatosensory stimulation. The general term for these signals is *event-related potentials* (ERP), and a number of categories of ERPs exist.

Brain stem auditory evoked responses.   While we still do not have concrete information about the specific location of the neural generators of most ERPs, a type of potential has been identified in the 1970s which can be linked to specific generators and thus provides direct information about the intact nature of the brain pathways. This poential is the very early potential generated in peripheral sensory pathways. The visual and somatosensory pathways have been studied with this method, but the greatest amount of research and excitement has been generated in the auditory modality by potentials which have been named *brain stem auditory evoked responses* (BAERs). These very small (measured in tenths of millivolts) potentials provide information about hearing acuity, about the functional capacity of the auditory pathway through the brain stem, and about the speed of conduction of neural impulses through this pathway.

Figure 5.3 presents the BAER and the brain stem structures which are its generators. This remarkable figure represents a very recent development in the study of human electrophysiological responses—the ability to link individual waves to their generators in the central nervous system. This measure is one of the rare instances in which functional activity from known brain sites can be recorded.

Anatomical mapping of the BAER wave forms in animal and human autopsy data indicates that wave I originates in the auditory nerve, wave II is from the cochlear nucleus, waves III and IV are in the pons, wave V is in the inferior colliculus, and waves VI and VII are in the thalamus and thalamic radiations, respectively. Wave V is particularly well correlated with the intensity of the auditory signal in normal and pathological ears, and therefore it is diagnostically useful. At higher intensities the latency of wave V is shorter, and when the signal is not detected by the nervous system, the wave does not appear. The BAER response to various

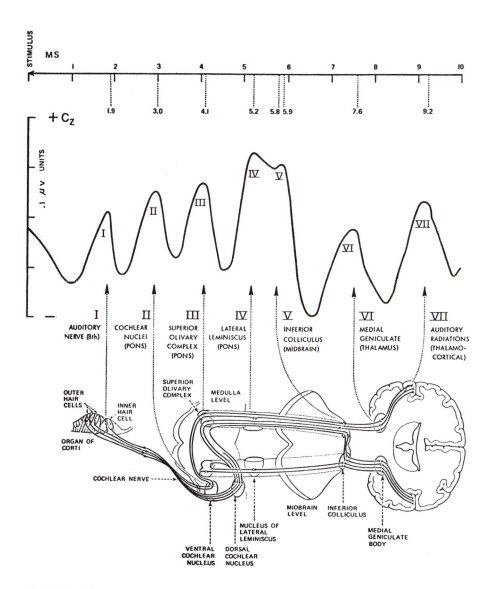

FIGURE 5.3 Diagram of normal latencies for vertex-positive brain stem auditory potentials (waves I through VII) evoked by clicks of 60 dBHL (60 dB above normal hearing threshold) at a rate of 10 per second. Lesions at different levels of auditory pathway tend to produce response abnormalities beginning with indicated components, although this does not specify the precise generators of the response; the relative contributions of synaptic and axonal activity to the response are as yet unknown. Intermediate latency (5.8 msec) between those of waves IV and V is mean peak latency of fused wave IV/V when present. Cz + , Cz − = vertex positivity, represented by an upward pen deflection , and vertex negativity, represented by a downward pen deflection. Source: Stockard, J. J., Stockard, J. E. & Sharbrough, F. W. (1977). *Mayo Clinic Proceedings, 52,* 761–769. Reprinted by permission of Grass Instrument Company, Quincy, MA.

intensities of signals including a 10 dB signal which is not registered in the nervous system is presented in Figure 5.4.

The BAER has been shown to change with development (Hecox & Galambos, 1974). The most rapid development of the auditory system occurs in the first 16 months of life and is reflected in the rapid decrease in wave V latency. Adult values are reached around the age of 16 months and are maintained at least until middle age. Studies of the BAER suggest that wave V latency changes are moderate in old age (Allison, Wood, & Goff, 1985; Harkins & Lenhardt, 1980; Rowe, 1978).

Rowe (1978) demonstrated about .3 msec slowing in all BAER waves when he compared 25 young (mean age 25.1 years) and 25 old (mean age 61.7 years)

FIGURE 5.4 Typical normal brain stem auditory evoked responses (BAER) are shown at six intensities from an adult subject demonstrating hearing within normal limits. Note that the shift of wave V latency in msec is a function of stimulus intensity. Each tracing represents the sum of 4,096 responses to a .1 msec click, presented monaurally at the rate of 30 per second. Time base of each tracing is 10 msec. Source: Sandlin, R. E. & Mokotoff, B. (1976). Brain stem auditory evoked response measurement. *Maico Audiological Library Series, 14,* Report 8. Reprinted by permission.

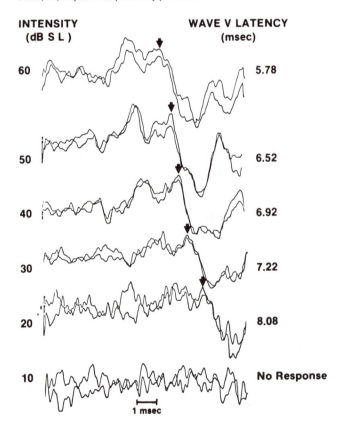

subjects with normal hearing. The emerging picture from the BAER in old age is that at peripheral levels, the older nervous system performs about the same as the younger nervous system. It is when brain potentials are recorded from structures at higher levels of the brain that the slowing is significant.

The gerontological applications of the BAER are primarily clinical, and many such applications have been described by Michalewski, Thompson, & Saul (1980). The BAER is clearly of importance in the evaluation of hearing ability, which declines in a significant proportion of the elderly population. The BAER is particularly useful as a diagnostic tool for hearing in patients who are unable to respond. In addition to its clinical usefulness in hearing assessment, the BAER is a neurological assessment tool in that it provides a measure of the intact nature of the auditory pathway. Brain stem lesions can be detected with this painless measure, and the BAER is an improvement over the EEG in the assessment of brain death.

Sensory-evoked potentials. The most comprehensive study of sensory-evoked responses has been carried out in the Salt Lake City laboratory of Dustman and Beck who, with Schenkenberg, measured auditory, visual, and somatosensory potentials in males and females over the life span. This research began to appear in 1966 (Dustman & Beck, 1966) and was followed by a series of reports (Dustman & Beck, 1969; Schenkenberg, 1970; Schenkenberg, Dustman & Beck, 1971). Figure 5.5 presents a sample of these extensive data. The major change which the Salt Lake City group identified was a greater latency in the wave forms of older subjects, particularly in the later waves appearing after 100 msec. Amplitude in the later waves also decreased in old age. A change limited to the visual-evoked response was an increase in amplitude in an early component.

General hypotheses were advanced to explain these age changes. The slowing in the aged nervous system was associated with latency increases, and decreases in the amplitude and latency of the later components were associated with age changes in the secondary system, the ascending reticular arousal system (ARAS), perhaps involving age changes at the synapse. To explain the increase in visual-evoked response amplitude in early components, it was suggested that a decrease in inhibition was occurring. Both the arousal and the inhibition hypotheses are discussed in greater detail in Chapter 8 along with the ERP evidence which supports them.

Long latency potentials related to complex psychological variables. The P3 wave of the ERP is prominent only when the stimulus which has elicited the ERP has meaning or significance to the subject. A number of studies have indicated that the amplitude of the P3 component, regardless of the stimulus modality, is inversely related to the degree that the subject expects the stimulus to occur (e.g., Duncan-Johnson & Donchin, 1977). The factor which appears to determine the latency of the P3 component is decision time; more specifically, the time required for the subject to perceive and categorize the stimulus according to a set of rules (e.g.,

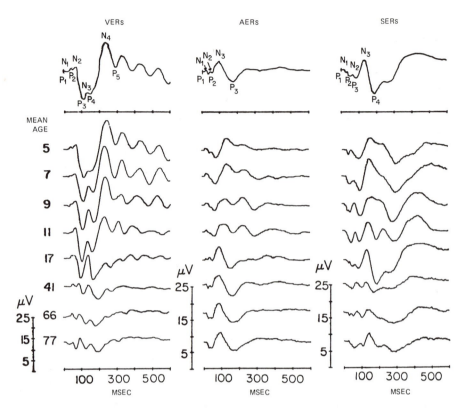

FIGURE 5.5 Composite VERs, AERs, and SERs of subjects in eight age groups. Each plot is a composite of 20 subjects: 10 males and 10 females in each age group. VERs are from left occipital scalp; AERs and SERs are from left central scalp. P = positive peak; N = negative peak. Source: Dustman, R. E., Beck, E. C. & Schenkenberg, T. (1977). Life-span changes in man. In J. E. Desmedt (Ed.), *Cerebral evoked potentials in man: The Brussels International Symposium*. New York: Oxford University Press. Reprinted by permission.

Kutas, McCarthy, & Donchin, 1977). When task difficulty is increased, young subjects have prolonged processing times and longer P3 latencies.

Comparisons of the P3 in young and old subjects have led gerontologists such as Marsh and Thompson (1977) to suggest that the ERPs of the two age groups are more similar during active processing than during passive stimulation. The amplitude and shape of the P3 component have been similar in many of the age comparative experiments. However, the result which has been consistent since the first report of P3 research in aging (Marsh & Thompson, 1972) is the fact that the latency of P3 is delayed in older subjects. Thus, the P3 research offers direct confirmation of the aging phenomenon to which behavioral studies have been pointing for decades. Processing time is slower in the aged central nervous sytem.

Using a task in which the subject is asked to count the number of occurrences of an infrequent tone, Goodin, Squires, Henderson, and Starr (1978) tested 40 healthy subjects between the ages of 15 and 76 years. Data from six subjects

FIGURE 5.6 Rare-tone evoked-potential wave forms for six normal subjects in order of increasing age (top to bottom). The dashed line reprsents 300-msec post-stimulus onset. Source: Squires, K. C., Goodin, D. S. & Starr, A. (1979). Event related potentials in development, aging, and senile dementia. In D. Lehman & E. Callaway (Eds.), *Human evoked potentials.* New York: Plenum Press. Reprinted by permission.

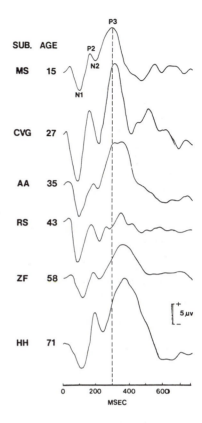

in this experiment ranging in age from 15 to 71 years are presented in Figure 5.6. The primary result of this study was that the latency of the P3 component systematically increased with age. Regression analysis indicated that the P3 component latency increased at a rate of 1.63 msec/year. This result is almost a 100 msec increase in the P3 component in the decades between the twentieth and the eightieth year. Some of the other components increased in latency with age, but the magnitude of these latency increases was not more than half of the magnitude of the P3 latency increase. Goodin et al. (1978) demonstrated that these age changes were not a function of auditory sensitivity by noting that behavioral performance (detection of higher frequency tones) was equal in young and old, all subjects reported that they could hear the tones clearly, and the N1 component which is dramatically affected by tone intensity was only different by 6 msec between the young and old subjects. Thus, ERPs provide differential information about the effects of aging and auditory acuity.

Computerized Axial Tomography (CAT)

Another brain measure which has primarily clinical applications is the CAT scan. Until quite recently, the assessment of patients with behavioral disorders has

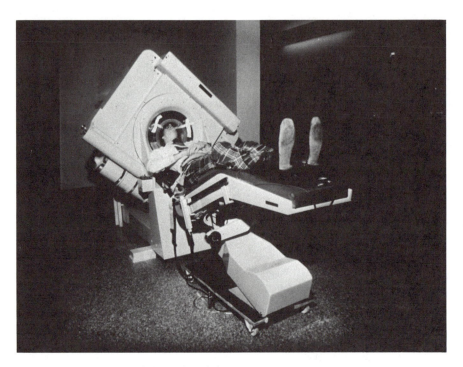

involved indirect measures of nervous system function or dangerous invasive techniques that involved risks and potential complications to patients (for example, angiography, pneumoencephalography). Computerized axial tomography is a safe and painless procedure which provides a picture of the living brain. It is a method of visualizing cerebral structures including the ventricular system and cortical sulci. The value of this technique in neurological assessment of patients of all ages is so great and has been recognized so rapidly that many hospitals throughout the country have installed the relatively expensive apparatus required for this procedure, even though it has become commercially available only since the mid-1970s. Thus, the CAT scan can be used in most large cities in the United States to assess geriatric patients showing symptoms of cerebral impairment, and it can be undertaken upon referral by the attending physician.

The CAT scan involves a rotating X-ray source which takes over 28,000 readings in approximately five minutes. This usually consists of a scan that has viewed two contiguous slices of brain tissue in a transaxial plane at the selected level of the brain. The entire procedure takes less than half an hour. Readings are processed by a computer which calculates 6,400 absorption values for each brain slice. The computer calculates the density of tissue scanned by the X-ray beam, and different densities of tissue are translated into lighter or darker areas on a cathode ray tube display. A photograph is then taken of the display so that a permanent record can be assessed by a neuroradiologist or neurologist. The data are also stored on magnetic tape.

The resultant photograph is essentially a picture of a transaxial slice of the brain. Bone and calcified areas that are dense look white in the computerized tomograms, grey matter of the brain looks grey, and the least dense areas, the ventricles, look almost black.

Huckman, Fox, and Topel (1975) have devised and validated specific quantitative criteria for evaluation of cerebral atrophy and senile dementia. They have indicated that both enlarged ventricles and enlarged sulci are necessary for a reliable diagnosis of senile dementia, and they have provided numerical standards for the width of the ventricles at two points and for the width of the four largest sulci that can be considered atrophied (Huckman et al., 1975). It has also been demonstrated by these investigators that these criteria applied to tomograms yield results as reliable as assessments based on pneumoencephalographic examination and pathologic examination at autopsy.

CAT scans have been used to diagnose senile dementia and to identify geriatric patients with treatable brain pathology (Huckman et al., 1975). This technique has also been used in conjunction with behavioral assessment to determine the relationship between behavioral capacity and brain structure. Kaszniak (1977) assessed the memory of 50 patients for whom a CAT scan was available, and he demonstrated that CAT scans predict behavioral changes. However, his correlations were moderate, and more recent evidence indicates that the severity of dementia cannot be predicted by CAT scan data (Fox, Kaszniak, & Huckman, 1979; Kaszniak, Garron, Fox, Bergen, & Huckman, 1979). In 78 hospital patients aged 50 years or older with suspected changes in mentation in the absence of focal or other organic brain disease, EEG slowing was the strongest and most general pathologic influence on cognition (Kaszniak et al., 1979).

Physiological functioning of the brain as measured by the EEG rather than neuroanatomical structure as measured by the CAT scan was the best correlate of cognitive function. Thus, while the CAT scan is a powerful tool in evaluating patients with dementia and can be used to rule out potentially treatable disorders, it is not terribly useful in demonstrating the severity of dementia or the ultimate prognosis. More recent studies have indicated that ventricular enlargement is more often correlated with cognitive deficits than is cortical sulcal enlargement. Furthermore, changes observable in the older brain are generally not observable among groups of subjects under 60 years of age. The average degree of atrophy measured increases continuously after the age of 60 (Jernigan, 1987).

Shown in Figure 5.7 is the CAT scan at two levels of the brain of a patient who came to the Baer Consultation and Diagnostic Center at the Philadelphia Geriatric Center. The patient, a man of 72, visited the center because he occasionally felt dizzy, and he had experienced one episode in which he had forgotten what he was saying in the middle of a sentence. Since he was a very competent individual who still held a responsible position, he was concerned about this experience and wanted to know if he was neurologically impaired. The CAT scan along with the neurological, psychological, and psychiatric assessments of this man reassured him. All were normal, and the CAT scan in Figure 5.7 shows a normal old brain. The

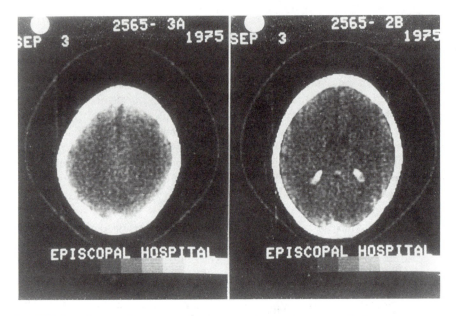

FIGURE 5.7   CAT scan of 72-year-old male showing the absence of any brain pathology.

ventricles (black area in the center) are small and hardly discernable, and no sulci (black lines along the edges) are apparent.

The CAT scan in Figure 5.8 shows a tumor in the right parietal area (lower right side). The tumor shows up as a darker area, being less dense than neural tissue. This patient, a 71-year-old male, was assessed by a psychiatrist and a neurologist as moderately impaired, but his performance on the psychological tests was normal. His neurological impairment is potentially treatable through surgery.

Potential treatment is not available for the patient whose CAT scan is shown in Figure 5.9. She is an 83-year-old woman with a diagnosis of senile dementia. Neurological, psychiatric, and psychological assessment showed this woman to be moderately to severely impaired, and the CAT scan confirmed the diagnosis of senile dementia. The ventricles and a number of sulci are enlarged, indicating rather widespread cerebral atrophy characteristic of most senile dementia patients.

Ford and Pfefferbaum (1980) reported preliminary results of their attempt to correlate ERP changes with structural changes in the brain as assessed by the CAT scan. Among the findings was a higher correlation (r = 0.77) between a CAT scan index of a decrease in brain tissue and longer latency P3 waves. This result linking decreases in brain tissue with longer latency P3 waves is in accordance with other data indicating that P3 latency increases dramatically in dementia patients.

Ford and Pfefferbaum also found a high correlation (r = 0.81) between more negative slow waves recorded over the frontal area and less brain tissue. This result supports the suggestion that behavioral, neuroanatomical, and ERP data are con-

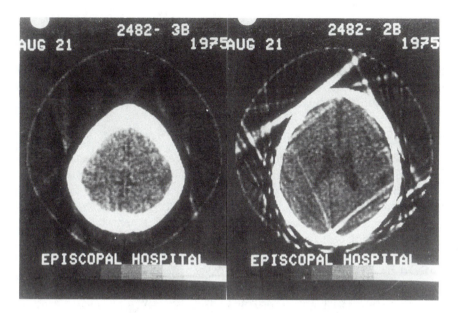

FIGURE 5.8   CAT scan of 71-year-old male showing tumor in the right parietal area. Tumor is shown in about the middle of the far right side of the brain in both photographs.

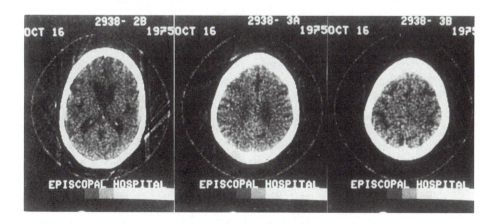

FIGURE 5.9   CAT scan of a 83-year-old woman with a diagnosis of Senile Dementia of the Alzheimer's Type (SDAT). Ventricles (black areas in center) sulci (black areas on edges of brain) are enlarged indicating degeneration of brain tissue.

verging to suggest a deficit with age in the frontal lobes. The evidence for this frontal lobe deficit is discussed in greater detail in Chapter 8.

The main application of CAT scan data may be clinical, and this tool has great significance in the diagnosis of senile dementia. However, CAT scans are beginning to be used in conjunction with ERP and behavioral measures to provide more precise information about brain and behavior relationships in aging.

Positron Emission Tomography (PET)

The PET scan is a method of imaging the brain which measures specific biochemical processes in the living person. The PET techinque requires the integration of three components. It involves the use of compounds labeled with positron-emitting radioisotopes which serve as tracers for physiological processes. It also integrates the use of a positron tomograph (PET scanner) for detecting the tissue distribution of the tracer. Finally, tracer kinetic models for quantifying the physiological processes are used. The aspects of brain function most frequently assessed by PET are blood flow and oxygen metabolism. Rates of glucose metabolism are measured to assess these functions.

PET studies have been carried out to relate cognitive performance in normal aging and SDAT to brain function (Ferris, 1987). PET studies of normal elderly subjects have failed to show reductions in regional brain metabolism (de Leon, Ferris, George et al., 1983; de Leon, George, Ferris et al., 1984; Duara, Grady, Haxby et al., 1984; Hawkins, Mazziotta, Phelps et al., 1983). Although age-associated atrophic changes are visualized by CAT scan technology, metabolic change is not apparent. Ferris (1987) interpreted this result to indicate that the normal aged brain is able to compensate for structural losses and maintain normal metabolic function.

The initial PET studies of patients with SDAT show substantial reductions in regional rates of glucose utilization (Ferris, de Leon, Wolf et al., 1980) and oxygen metabolism (Frackowiak, Pozzilli, Legg et al., 1981). In these studies SDAT patients' PET data were compared to the PET data of normal elderly control subjects. These studies also demonstrated high correlations between the degree of cognitive impairment and decline in brain metabolism. Subsequent PET studies have shown 15 to 40 percent reductions in brain metabolism in SDAT patients for main brain regions (Benson, Kuhl, Hawkins et al., 1983; Chase, Foster, & Mansi, 1983; de Leon, Ferris, George et al., 1983; Friedland, Budinger, Ganz et al., 1983). A relatively greater deficit was indicated in these studies in posterior brain regions (parietal and temporal cortex) than in more anterior regions (frontal cortex).

Studies including CAT and PET assessments in the same SDAT patients indicate that the different patterns observed in PET data on SDAT patients are not simply the result of structural losses. Miller, de Leon, Ferris et al., (1987) reported differences in temporal cortex activation patterns between normal elderly and SDAT patients when these individuals were engaged in a memory task. PET data may be most useful in the assessment of normal aging and SDAT when the subjects are actively processing information. Most of the PET data on older adults to date have been collected while the subjects were passively sitting in the PET scan apparatus. Future studies need to be undertaken in which older adult subjects are assessed during their performance of mental tasks.

AGING IN OTHER PHYSIOLOGICAL SYSTEMS

Extensive research has been carried out on the physiology of aging which simply cannot be represented in this book. Rather, we briefly summarize age-related changes which occur in the various physiological systems and refer the interested reader to volumes such as the *Handbook of the Biology of Aging* (Finch & Hayflick, 1985) and the *Biology of Aging* (Rockstein & Sussman, 1979) for greater details on these topics. All physiological systems except the reproductive and endocrine systems are covered in this chapter. Reproductive and endocrine physiology and aging are discussed in Chapter 7 on sexuality and aging.

Cardiovascular System

Cardiovascular disease is the number one cause of death in the United States. While cardiovascular disease is pathological and not part of normal aging, many normal age changes in the cardiovascular system are simply exacerbated by cardiovascular disease.

Progressive changes associated with aging include the diminished capability of the heart rate to compensate in response to stress. We see this in the psychophysiology laboratory whenever we study cognitive aging in relation to autonomic nervous system measures. For example, if we ask groups of young and old subjects to learn a list of words and then test them on the list, long after the test is over, the heart rate of the older subjects will be elevated. Young subjects will probably show less heart rate elevation to the learning task in the first place. But even if they do, their heart rate will return to its normal level long before the older subjects' heart rates will recover. The older cardiovascular system seems to marshall all of its resources and give a major lasting response to stress. While the younger cardiovascular system is reactive, the reaction to moderate stress is more contained, and heart rate in the young quickly returns to baseline levels after the stress.

The efficiency of the heart as a pump declines. The amount of blood pumped with each beat of the heart (called stroke volume) and other measures of cardiac output decline. Some of this decline is the result of the increasingly sedentary life style individuals lead as they age. DeVries (1970) reported changes in the cardiovascular system in older men with as little as six weeks of exercise three times a week. Cardiac output did not improve over this short a period, but blood pressure decreased significantly. The point is that we simply do not know how much of the decline in the heart's efficiency as a pump is the result of normal aging processes and is irreversible. Longitudinal studies of individuals who remain active over their adult lives into old age have not been undertaken. One would predict that cardiac output might decline moderately in these individuals, but not to the degree that it has been observed to decline in the nonexercising population.

Arteries and blood vessels become less elastic, and the walls harden. This is not just a result of arteriosclerosis. Normal aging processes also affect the vessels, making the interior narrower. This undoubtedly is related to the fact that blood pressure increases with age. While atherosclerosis and hypertension are partially the result of diet and life style, some aspects of normal aging processes are also involved in these diseases. As mentioned previously, physical activity directly affects the cardiovascular system by lowering blood pressure.

Respiratory System

The respiratory system includes the lungs and its associated air passageways. Changes in the structures of the rib cage and of the small air passageways and air sacs of the lungs result in a reduction in the efficiency of the respiratory system. The amount of air breathed in and the amount of air moved by the lungs decreases with age. The total functional respiratory surface also declines, so there is reduced effectiveness in ventilation with each breath taken. This means that less oxygen is transported into the blood stream, and eventually that less oxygen reaches the brain.

Based on the knowledge that less oxygen may reach the aging brain, some experimenters attempted to improve cognitive functioning in older adults by placing them in hyperbaric chambers. It was reasoned that the higher atmospheric pressure in the chamber coupled with filling the chamber with pure oxygen might get more oxygen to the brain and improve cognitive function. Unfortunately, there was no apparent change in the cognitive performance of older adults in these circumstances.

DeVries (1983) noted that one of the major beneficial effects of physical exercise is to improve respiratory functioning in older adults. In his studies of aging men, vital capacity (the volume of air that can be expelled by the strongest possible expiration after the deepest possible inspiration) improved by 20 percent after only six weeks in an exercise program.

Complicating normal age-related changes in the respiratory system is the exposure to air pollution throughout life. Those living in urban industrial areas are particularly affected by the exposure. The cumulative damage resulting from infectious respiratory diseases can exacerbate the normal age-related degenerative changes. Of course, the major damaging habit to the respiratory system is smoking. Heavy smoking is particularly linked with the increasing incidence of emphysema and lung cancer in the aged. Lowered immunity to infection and chronic bronchitis of unknown etiology are common in older adults, and these pathologies make the elderly especially susceptible to viral and bacterial infection, particularly pneumonia.

Gastrointestinal System

The system receiving and digesting nutrients is the gastrointestinal system. The gastrointestinal tract begins with the mouth and ends with the anal opening.

Included in this system are the mouth, esophagus, stomach, small intestine, large intestine, liver, and gall bladder. Atrophy of the mucous lining, the secretory glands, and the smooth muscle of the walls of the system occurs during aging throughout the gastrointestinal tract. Reduced motility results in an increasing incidence of constipation with age. With advancing age there is an increase in the incidence of stomach and colonic cancer along with an increase in a variety of other disorders ranging from intestinal distress to diverticulosis to spastic colitis. Gastrointestinal disorders in the older adult may also be exacerbated by emotional and psychological distress. Proper diet and drug therapy along with stress reduction are helpful in reducing the incidence of gastrointestinal disorders in old age.

Urinary System

Changes in the urinary system do not constitute a major problem in the elderly. The incidence of kidney disease including lower and upper urinary tract and bladder infections increases with age, especially among men. The common bladder function changes with age include an increase in frequency of urination and in the residual volume of urine in the bladder following each urination. Incontinence and bedwetting occur with increasing incidence in old age, especially in individuals with brain impairment. In those elderly who remain alert and suffer from incontinence, biofeedback has been of demonstrated utility in regaining control over bladder function.

Skin, Bone, and Muscle

Probably the best-known physiological age change is the drying, wrinkling, and sagging of the skin. Another well-known age change is the fact that the hair becomes sparser and turns gray. Changes in the skin are the result of lifelong exposure to environmental insults and of a decreased rate of cell division in the outer skin layers. There is a diminished ability to replace damaged or dead cells, and wounds also heal more slowly. Hair changes color because the pigment content of the hair is reduced, usually beginning in the late thirties or early forties.

Aging affects bones in that bone mass diminishes. Bones become more brittle and increasingly subject to fracture. Bone loss affects women more than men, and white women are affected more than black women. In extreme, clinically evident cases, bone degeneration is called osteoporosis. Older women suffering from osteoporosis have been known to break ribs turning over in bed. There have been cases of hip fracture resulting from simply stepping off a curb into the street. Breaking a hip is a real hazard for older women because it confines them to bed for long periods of time and often leads to a downward spiral of health culminating in death.

"Declining speed and vigor of muscle contraction is a universal manifestation of the aging process in all animals including humans," (Rockstein & Sussman, 1979, p. 136). Muscle mass is another structure which can be at least partially retained with physical exercise (deVries, 1983). Aging muscle declines in function because total muscle mass is lost. The number of muscle fibers and the size of the fibers declines.

We have briefly taken an overview of physiological aging in a number of systems. Now we examine some of the psychophysiological models to evaluate how physiological aging affects behavior.

PSYCHOPHYSIOLOGICAL MODELS OF AGING

Because there are no full-blown theories in the psychophysiology of aging, we have instead a number of models or hypotheses about the causes of psychophysiological aging phenomena. Some of the models are briefly examined here. Other models involving psychological and psychophysiological aging are more fully elaborated in subsequent chapters. Such models as the overarousal-underarousal model, the stimulus persistence model, and the loss-of-inhibitory-processes model are discussed in Chapter 8, and the cautiousness model is discussed in Chapter 9.

The Discontinuity Hypothesis

From extensive research with aging individuals, Birren (1963) developed the discontinuity hypothesis which states that it is only when a physiological function becomes abnormal that the physiological variable affects behavioral variables. When a physiological variable enters an abnormal range, then and only then may it affect behavior. In other words, physiological variables which do not affect behavior when they are in a normal range in young subjects may affect behavior in old subjects when the physiological function reaches an abnormal level.

A few examples may help to illustrate the discontinuity hypothesis. In the study of 47 healthy old men in which extensive physical and psychological examinations were administered to a highly screened group of elite elderly men (Birren, Butler, Greenhouse, Sokoloff, & Yarrow, 1963), the investigators used a sophisticated battery of clinical tests. This testing procedure was more intensive than a normal physical examination, and while the investigators had selected a group of what they thought were extremely healthy men, they found that even among these healthiest of aged individuals, about half the group had some subclinical forms of disease, that is, disease that would not be detected by a physician in a routine examination.

In the healthiest group, there were only five statistically significant correlations between all of the physiological variables and all of the behavioral variables. In the less healthy, subclinical pathology group, 26 of the physiology-behavior relationships were statistically significant. This suggests that only when we start getting into poor health or start shading in the range of poorer health does physiology affect behavior.

Another study supporting the discontinuity hypothesis was undertaken at Duke University. Wilkie and Eisdorfer (1971) found in a longitudinal study relating blood pressure to behavioral variables, such as memory and intelligence, that only when blood pressure was elevated did it relate to or affect the behavioral variables. Blood pressure in the normal range did not appear to be related to behavior. So again, only when there was pathology was there a behavior-physiology relationship.

The implication this hypothesis has for daily life is that it emphasizes the adaptability of old people. Although some physiological functions decline, the life styles of the elderly may not have to change dramatically. To exemplify this, Birren tells a story about an experience he had while carrying out research on visual perception. To be in contact with elderly subjects, Birren set up the experiment in a local nursing home. Part of the experiment involved giving the subjects a visual acuity test. One of the volunteers for the project was a man of around 85 years old who was active in the home and was an officer in the residents' organization. The man also had the leading role in the current nursing home play. He was well known by most of the residents, and he was one of the most popular men in the home.

When Birren tested this man for visual acuity, he found that the old man was functionally blind. Birren went to the nursing home administrator and asked if the administrator knew that this particular man was blind. The administrator did not believe Birren. He had been fooled by the man's adaptability as had most of the staff and other nursing home residents. Observing the man's behavior very carefully, Birren found that he was always accompanied by his wife, and she very subtly guided him and gave him cues so that, although he was blind, he functioned as if he were sighted. This remarkable example emphasizes the adaptability of old people.

Sensory-Deprivation Model

The old, relative to the young, have been considered to be in a state of sensory deprivation. It has been determined, according to the biological-decremental perspective, that sensory acuity declines due to deficits in the peripheral sensory systems. In the visual system at a peripheral level the lens thickens, the pupil aperture narrows, and the muscles in the eye function less well so that accommodation is not as efficient. Generally, it takes more light energy to have the same effect on the older eye as on the younger eye. Some studies have indicated that there is no way to compensate for the difference between the old and the young eye. There are physical changes in the eye that make it less responsive to light.

The hearing apparatus also changes. Ability to hear high tones declines with age. So again there is less auditory information available to the older ear. In terms of the skin, receptors for touch and pain are lost. The skin loses its elasticity, and touch is a sense that generally declines in old age. About two thirds of the taste buds in the mouth die by the time an individual is 70 years of age. The sense of smell also declines. A large percentage of the sensory receptors in the nose die with age. Overall, less sensory information is transmitted to the older brain.

Studies on sensory deprivation have indicated that when an individual is deprived of sensory information, he or she experiences some difficulty. The brain appears to need a certain level of stimulation, or a certain amount of sensory input, to function optimally. Relative to the young, the old may be in a state of sensory deprivation, and for this reason they may function less efficiently. A study was undertaken by Kemp (1970) who tried to get at this issue by putting both young and old subjects in a sensory deprivation chamber to see if the old were selectively more affected than the young by this procedure. There were no age differences, so the hypothesis that the old are in a state of sensory deprivation is at this point not well substantiated.

The sensory-deprivation model again suggests that old people need stimulation. Stroke patients who receive additional stimulation appear to recover faster. At the hospital where Kemp carried out his research, a very interesting thing happened as a result of sensory-deprivation studies. While sensory-deprivation research was underway, researchers talked to some of the therapists and explained theoretical issues in the area of sensory deprivation. One of the therapists got the idea that if sensory deprivation does affect people in a negative way, then patients in comas who are unstimulated are perhaps being mistreated. At this hospital they decided to institute a program in which they started talking to patients in comas even though the patients could not respond. As a result of this treatment, there seemed to be a shortening in recovery time.

BEHAVIOR-PHYSIOLOGY
INTERACTIONS

The gerontological literature abounds with references to behavior-physiology relationships. One example of the interactive nature of physiology and behavior is in the domain of intelligence. The notion that intelligence inevitably deteriorates with age is flawed. Intelligence cannot be viewed simply from the point of view of the biological-decremental model. In Chapter 13 on intelligence and aging, it is demonstrated that the aged may score lower on intelligence tests as a result of educational obsolescence or as a result of other noncognitive factors, discussed in Chapter 12 on aging in human learning, memory, and cognition. A number of gerontologists have suggested the application of educational intervention strategies to reduce this obsolescence (e.g., Baltes & Willis, 1982). Others have suggested a restructuring of the intelligence test so that it would not discriminate against the aged person.

It has been suggested as a reaction to the once overwhelmingly biological orientation of geropsychology that much of what is attributed to biological decline may actually result from social and environmental influences. We discovered in Chapter 4 on social, cultural, and environmental factors in aging that the external enviornment takes on added significance in old age. Indeed, social and environmental influences may affect behavior in old age more than does biology. The clear implication is that environmental interventions can successfully alleviate some behavioral deficits in old age.

While social and environmental influences and interventions are certainly critical in reversing decline in old age, it has not yet been conclusively demonstrated that even the biological decline is inevitable or irreversible. Biological decline has been identified in descriptive studies of aging in animals and humans, but few attempts have been made to manipulate biological variables to determine if biological decline can be reversed. We are only begininng to undertake experimental studies to determine if biological changes are really inevitable in old age. When we do try to affect physiological functioning in the aged, we are surprising ourselves at how often we can observe beneficial results (e.g., Dustman et al., 1984; deVries, 1983).

MODIFYING PHYSIOLOGICAL DECLINE

DeVries (1983) has reported physiological functioning in the aged, as a result of moderate exercise. It is not age alone which causes individuals to decline physiologically. Other factors, some of which it may be possible to alter, are associated with declining physiological capacity in the aged. DeVries demonstrated that one of the factors associated with physiological decline is disuse, the lack of exercise in contemporary sedentary life styles. With a modified exercise program, even very old individuals can regain some of the physiological efficiency they had lost with advancing years. Indeed, Dustman and Ruhling (1986) showed that even brain function was more efficient in a group of older runners compared to a control group of sedentary older adults.

If we are searching for new approaches and new information in the psychology of aging and gerontology, we must reexamine some of the changes that we have long thought to be irreversible. This is being done in a number of biology and psychobiology laboratories where investigations of aging are being carried out. For example, in Caleb Finch's laboratory at the Andrus Gerontology Center of the University of Southern California, investigations have been undertaken to examine how hormonal changes in aging rats might be reversed. Estrogenreplacement therapy has been one of the outcomes of this type of research, and progress in the area may lead to the maintenance of optimal hormonal levels in postmenopausal women. Such research has clear implications for sexual behavior in older women who sometimes abstain from sexual intercourse because of pain in the genital region which has atrophied in the absence of normal hormonal levels. Other hormone research is being carried out in the laboratory of Arthur Schwartz at Temple University where a substance has been identified which appears to retard the growth of cancer in laboratory animals.

On the basis of the data on brain trauma, it was accepted as fact that the older brain could not regain any function once it was damaged. Investigators did not include adult or older animals in their brain plasticity studies because they thought it was useless even to test plasticity in older brains. This reluctance to experiment with older organisms in studies of brain plasticity attests to the degree to which scientists and physicians believed there could be no recovery of function in older brains. It was thus extremely unorthodox for Dru and colleagues (Dru,

Walker, & Walker, 1975) to include a group of old rats in their study of recovery of function in the visual cortical areas. This work represents a pioneering study demonstrating plasticity in older as well as young brains.

Dru and colleagues (1975) trained rats to discriminate horizontal bars from vertical bars and required them to perform a discrimination-avoidance task, choosing the appropriate stimulus in order to avoid shock. After the animals had learned the task to criterion, they received ablation lesions on one side of their visual cortices (Krieg's area) and later to the other side. After the surgery they lived in one of four environments: (1) total darkness for the postoperative period; (2) cages with diffuse light for four hours each day and total darkness the rest of the day; (3) a patterned visual environment containing horizontal bars, stripes, and triangles through which the animals were passively transported for four hours each day, with the rest of the day spent in darkness; and (4) access to the same patterned environment described for four hours per day, but with no restrictions on the animals' ability to move around. These various environmental treatments were first used by Held and coworkers (Held & Hein, 1963) who demonstrated that, in young animals, normal visual development was dependent upon unrestricted movement through a visual field. Some kind of experience with visual-motor integration appeared to be crucial to normal perceptual development.

The results of Dru's work with mature animals were consistent with the previous literature on young animals. All animals who had been placed in darkness, diffuse light cages, or passively transported through the patterned environment failed to relearn the task. Only those animals allowed free movement in the patterned environment recovered the avoidance task. Apparently, as in the normally developing brain, voluntary coordination between the visual system and the motor system are necessary for the neural reorganization required to recover the behavioral function.

The crucial aspect of the experiment was the effect of the lesions on the aged animals. The older group performed almost identically to the mature group, in that the older animals with free movement in the patterned environment recovered the task. They relearned the task significantly more slowly than did the younger animals, yet they did recover the function. These results strongly suggest that the aged brain has not declined to the point where it cannot undergo functional reorganization following injury. Further, the age decrement noted in the speed of recovery may be a function of a greater amount of time in the deprived environment of standard laboratory housing before the experiment, rather than a function of aging itself. These results imply that a generalized decremental view of brain status with age is inaccurate. Recovery of function appears possible at any age. More recently, Diamond and colleagues (1985) have demonstrated that providing older rats with an enriched environment stimulates changes in the brain similar to those changes seen in the brains of young enriched rats.

A most important point to be made in this chapter is that physiological age functions may not be fixed and inevitable, and there may be behavioral intervention strategies and biological intervention strategies capable of reversing some of the deleterious performance observed in old people.

SUMMARY

The overall purpose of this chapter is to present the relationships between physiological and behavioral aging. There is criticism of the biological-decremental model which depicts behavioral change in aging always in terms of biological decline. It is pointed out that social and environmental influences may affect behavior even more than physiology, and attempts to manipulate decremental biological age functions have just begun.

The basis of physiological change in aging occurs at genetic and cellular levels. To highlight our current understanding of the causes of aging, ten theories of biological aging are presented. These theories can be categorized into genetic programming theories (gene theory, programmed theory, running-out-of-program theory, and wear-and-tear theory) and random accumulation of insults theories (somatic-mutation theory, cross-linkage theory, free-radical theory, clinker theory, error theory, and autoimmune theory). Genetic programming theories postulate that aging of cells, organs, and ultimately of the entire body is a programmed process. The alternative theme is that aging is nothing more than the accumulation with time of insults from the environment. No one theory encompasses all of biological aging, as aging is undoubtedly a multiply determined set of processes.

Aging in the nervous system can be assessed with several different types of methods. Electrophysiological measures of the aging brain indicate that the EEG alpha rhythm slows with age, and the latencies of event-related potentials related to sensory and cognitive phenomena are longer in older adults. CAT scan measures of the older brain suggest structural changes with some loss of grey matter. Structural losses are exacerbated in SDAT. PET data on normal aging individuals indicate no age-related change in brain metabolism. However, brain metabolism is altered, especially in posterior regions of the cerebral cortex, in SDAT patients. In the future, studies using PET techniques will provide more insights about normal aging and SDAT if subjects are performing mental tasks while they are being assessed with the PET scan.

The cardiovascular system is dramatically affected by aging, and heart disease is the number one cause of death in the United States. Many normal age changes in the cardiovascular system are exacerbated by cardiovascular disease. Among the changes are diminished capacity in the heart to compensate for stress. Heart rate does not return to baseline levels in older adults after stress as quickly as it does in younger adults. The heart pumps less blood, and arteries and blood vessels become less elastic. Physical activity throughout adulthood or even initiated in later life can moderate some of the deleterious changes in the cardiovascular system with age.

The respiratory system is less efficient in older adults. Less air is breathed in and out, and less oxygen is transported into the blood stream in older adults. One of the major beneficial effects of physical exercise is to improve respiratory functioning in old age. Air pollution and smoking are additional hazards which accelerate decline in the older respiratory system.

Reduced motility occurs in the older gastrointestinal system, resulting in an increasing incidence of constipation. Proper diet and stress reduction are helpful in reducing the incidence of gastrointestinal disorders in old age.

Changes in the urinary system do not constitute a major problem for the elderly. However, incontinence and bedwetting occur with increasing incidence in old age. These problems are often successfully treated with biofeedback.

Age changes in the skin are one of the most familiar signs of old age. Hair becomes sparser and turns gray. Aging effects on bone are less visible, but they are more serious to health. Bone mass diminishes in old age, and in extreme cases bone degeneration is called osteoporosis. This condition affects older women more often than it does older men. Muscle mass also declines with age, although physical exercise can maintain to some degree the loss of muscle mass accompanying aging.

Psychophysiological models presented in this chapter include the discontinuity hypothesis and sensory deprivation. The discontinuity hypothesis states that it is only when a physiological function becomes abnormal that the physiological variable affects behavior. One example of this relationship has been documented for high blood pressure. People with normal or slightly elevated blood pressure levels maintain cognitive and memory capacity, but people with high blood pressure show declines in cognition and memory function. The sensory-deprivation model in aging suggests that older adults receive less sensory input and thus may behave like individuals in a relative state of sensory deprivation. This model has not received much empirical testing.

Physiological age functions are not fixed and irreversible. There is plasticity in the brain and behavior of older adults. Physical exercise is one means for modifying physiological functions. Improvements in the cardiovascular and respiratory systems in older adults have been documented as a result of physical exercise. Mood and cognitive functioning have also been demonstrated to be affected positively in older adulthood with moderate exercise. Enriched environments affect the actual brain structure of older as well as younger rats. A generalized decremental view of brain status with age is inaccurate. Recovery of function appears possible at any age.

REFERENCES

ADLER, W. H. (1974).   An "autoimmune" theory of aging. In M. Rockstein, M. L. Sussman, & J. Chesky (Eds.), *Theoretical aspects of aging.* New York: Academic Press.

ALLISON, T., WOOD, C. C., & GOFF, W. R. (1985).   Brainstem auditory, pattern-reversal visual and short-latency somatosensory evoked potentials: Latencies in relation to age, sex, brain and body size. *Electroencephalography and Clinical Neurophysiology, 55,* 619-636.

BALTES, P. B. & WILLIS, S. L. (1982).   Plasticity and enhancement of intellectual functioning in old age: Penn State's adult development and enrichment project (ADEPT). In F. I. M. Craik and S. Trehub (Eds.), *Aging and cognitive processes.* New York: Plenum Press.

BENSON, D. F., KUHL, D. E., HAWKINS, R. A., PHELPS, M. E., CUMMINGS, J. L., & TSAI, S. Y. (1983).   The flurodeoxyglucose 18F scan in Alzheimer's disease and multi-infarct dementia. *Archives of Neurology, 40,* 711-714.

BIRREN, J. E. (1963).   Psychophysiological relations. In J. E. Birren, R. N. Butler, S. W. Greenhouse, L. Sokoloff, & M. R. Yarrow (Eds.), *Human aging: A biological and behavioral study.* Washington, DC: U.S. Government Printing Office.

BIRREN, J. E., BUTLER, R. N., GREENHOUSE, S. W., SOKOLOFF, L. & YARROW, M. R. (Eds.) (1963).   *Human aging: A biological and behavioral study.* Washington, DC: U.S. Government Printing Office.

BJORKSTEN, J. (1974).   Crosslinkage and the aging process. In M. Rockstein, M. L. Sussman, & J. Chesky (Eds.), *Theoretical aspects of aging.* New York: Academic Press.

CHASE, T. N., FOSTER, N. L., & MANSI, L. (1983).   Alzheimer's disease and the parietal lobe. *Lancet, ii* (8343), 225.

CURTIS, H. J. & MILLER, K. (1971).   Chromosome aberrations in liver cells of guinea pigs. *Journal of Gerontology, 26,* 292-294.

DE LEON, M. J., FERRIS, S. H., GEORGE, A. E., CHRISTMAN, D. R., FOWLER, J. S., GENTES, C., RIESBERG, B., GEE, B., EMMERICH, M., YONEKURA, Y., BRODIE, J., KRICHEFF, I. I., & WOLF, A. P. (1983).   Positron emission tomography studies of aging and Alzheimer's disease. *American Journal of Neuroradiology, 4,* 568-571.

DE LEON, M. J., GEORGE, A. E., FERRIS, S. H., CHRISTMAN, D. R., FOWLER, J. S., GENTES, C., BRODIE, J., REISBERG, B., & WOLF, A. P. (1984).   Position emission tomography and computer assisted tomography assessments of the aging human brain. *Journal of Computer Assisted Tomography, 8,* 88-94.

DEVRIES, H. A. (1970)   Physiological effects of an exercise training regimen upon men aged 52-88. *Journal of Gerontology, 25,* 325-336.

DEVRIES, H. A. (1983).   Physiology of exercise and aging. In D. S. Woodruff & J. E. Birren (Eds). *Aging: Scientific perspectives and social issues* (2nd Ed.), Monterey, CA: Brooks/Cole.

DIAMOND, M. C., JOHNSON, R. E., PROTTI, A. M., OTT, C., & KAJISA, L. (1985). Plasticity in the 904-day-old male rat cerebral cortex. *Experimental Neurology, 87,* 309-317.

DRU, D., WALKER, J. P., & WALKER, J. B. (1975).   Self-produced locomotion restores visual capacity after straite lesions. *Science, 187,* 265-266.

DUARA, R., GRADY, C., HAXBY, J., INGVAR, D., SOKOLOFF, L., MARGOLIN, R. A., MANNING, R. G., CUTLER, N. R., & RAPOPORT, S. I. (1984).   Human brain glucose utilization and cognitive function in relation to age. *Annals of Neurology, 16,* 702-713.

DUNCAN-JOHNSON, C. & DONCHIN, E. (1977).   On quantifying surprise: The variation of event-related potentials with subjective probability. *Psychophysiology, 14,* 456-467.

DUSTMAN, R. E., & BECK, E. C. (1966).   Visually evoked potentials: Amplitude change with age. *Science, 151,* 1013-1015.

DUSTMAN, R. E. & BECK, E. C. (1969).   The effects of maturation and aging on the waveform of visually evoked potentials. *Electroencephalography and Clinical Neurophysiology, 26,* 2-11.

DUSTMAN, R. E., BECK, E. C., & SCHENKENBERG, T. (1977).   Life-span changes in man. In J. E. Desmedt (Ed.), *Cerebral evoked potentials in man: The Brussels International Symposium.* London: Oxford University Press.

DUSTMAN, R. E. & RUHLING, R. O. (1986).   Brain function of old and young athletes and nonathletes. Presented at the 39th Annual Scientific Meeting of the Gerontological Society of America, Chicago, November.

DUSTMAN, R. E., RUHLING, R. O., RUSSELL, E. M., SHEARER, D. E., BONEKAT, W., SHIGEOKA, J. W., WOOD, J. S., BRADFORD, D. C. (1984).   Aerobic exercise training and improved neuropsychological function of older individuals. *Neurobiology of Aging, 5,* 35-42.

FERRIS, S. H. (1987).   Positron emission tomography. In G. L. Maddox (Ed.), *The encyclopedia of aging.* New York: Springer.

FERRIS, S. H., DE LEON, M. J., WOLF, A. P., FARKAS, T., CHRISTMAN, D. R., REISBERG, B., FOWLER, J. S., RAMPAL, S. (1980).   Positron emission tomography in the study of aging and senile dementia. *Neurobiology of Aging, 1,* 127-131.

FINCH, C. E. & HAYFLICK, L. (Eds.) (1985).   *Handbook of the biology of aging* (2nd Ed.), New York: Van Nostrand Reinhold.

FORD, J. M. & PFEFFERBAUM, A. (1980).   The utility of brain potentials in determining age-related changes in central nervous system and cognitive functions. In L. W. Poon (Ed.), *Aging in the 1980s: Psychological issues.* Washington, DC: American Psychological Association.

FOX, J. H., KASZNIAK, A. W., & HUCKMAN, M. (1979).   Computerized tomographic scanning not very helpful in dementia—nor in craniopharyngioma. (Letter) *New England Journal of Medicine, 300,* 437.

FRACKOWIAK, R. S. H., POZZILLI, C., LEGG, N. J., DUBOULAY, G. H., MARSHALL, J., LENZI, G. L., & JONES, T. (1981).   Regional cerebral oxygen supply and utilization in dementia—a clinical and physiological study with oxygen-15 and positron tomography. *Brain, 104,* 753-778.

FRIEDLAND, R. P., BUDINGER, T. F., GANZ, E., YANO, Y., MATHIS, C. A., KOSS, B., OBER, B. A. HUESMAN, R. H., & DERENZO, S. E. (1983).   Regional cerebral metabolic alterations in dementia of the Alzheimer type: Positron emission tomography with [18F] fluorodeoxyglucose. *Journal of Computer Assisted Tomography, 7,* 590-598.

GOODIN, D., SQUIRES, K., HENDERSON, B., & STARR, A. (1978).   Age-related variations in evoked-potentials to auditory stimuli in normal human subjects. *Electroencephalography and Clinical Neurophysiology, 44,* 447-458.

GORDON, P. (1974).   Free radicals and the aging process. In M. Rockstein, M. L. Sussman & J. Chesky (Eds.), *Theoretical aspects of aging.* New York: Academic Press.

HARKINS, S. W. & LENHARDT, M. (1980).   Brainstem auditory evoked potentials in the elderly. In L. W. Poon (Ed.), *Aging in the 1980s: Psychological issues.* Washington, DC: American Psychological Association.

HAWKINS, R. A., MAZZIOTTA, J. C., PHELPS, M. E., HUANG, S. C., KUHL, D. E., CARSON, R. E., METTER, E. J., & RIEGE, W. H. (1983).   Cerebral glucose metabolism as a function of age in man: Influence of the rate constants in the flurodeoxyglucose method. *Journal of Cerebral Blood Flow and Metabolism, 3,* 250-253.

HAYFLICK, L. (1965).   The limited in vitro lifetime of human diploid cell strains. *Experimental Cell Research, 37,* 614-636.

HAYFLICK, L. (1976). The cell biology of human aging. *New England Journal of Medicine, 295,* 1302-1308.

HAYFLICK, L. (1977). The cellular basis for biological aging. In C. E. Finch & L. Hayflick (Eds.), *Handbook of the biology of aging.* New York: Van Nostrand Reinhold.

HAYFLICK, L. (1980). The cell biology of human aging. *Scientific American, 242,* 58-65.

HECOX, K. & GALAMBOS, T. (1974). Brain stem auditory evoked responses in human infants and adults. *Archives of Otolaryngology, 99,* 30-33.

HELD, R. & HEIN, A. (1963). Movement produced stimulation in the development of visually guided behavior. *Journal of Comparative and Physiological Psychology, 56,* 872-876.

HUCKMAN, M. S., FOX, J., & TOPEL, J. (1975). The validity of criteria for the evaluation of cerebral atrophy by computed tomography. *Radiology, 116,* 85-92.

JERNIGAN, T. W. (1987). Computed tomography: Cognitive changes. In G. L. Maddox (Ed.), *The encyclopedia of aging.* New York: Springer.

KASZNIAK, A. W. (1977). Effects of age and cerebral atrophy upon span of immediate recall and paired associate learning in older adults. *Dissertation Abstracts International, 37* (7-B), 3613-3614.

KASZNIAK, A. W., GARRON, D. C., FOX, J. H., BERGEN, D., & HUCKMAN, M. (1979). Cerebral atrophy, EEG slowing, age, education, and cognitive functioning in suspected dementia. *Neurology, 29,* 1273-1279.

KEMP, B. J. (1970). Simple auditory reaction time of young adult and elderly subjects in relation to perceptual deprivation and signal-on versus signal-off conditions. Unpublished doctoral dissertation. University of Southern California.

KUTAS, M., MCCARTHY, G., & DONCHIN, E. (1977). Augmenting mental chronometry: The P300 as a measure of stimulus evaluation. *Science, 197,* 792-795.

MARSH, G. & THOMPSON, L. W. (1972). Age differences in evoked potentials during an auditory discrimination task. *The Gerontologist, 12,* 44.

MARSH, G. & THOMPSON, L. W. (1977). Psychophysiology of aging. In J. E. Birren & K. W. Schaie (Eds.) *Handbook of the psychology of aging.* New York: Van Nostrand Reinhold.

MICHALEWSKI, H. J., THOMPSON, L. W., & SAUL, R. E. (1980). Use of the EEG and evoked potentials in the investigation of age-related clinical disorders. In J. E. Birren & R. B. Sloan (Eds.), *Handbook of mental health and aging.* Englewood Cliffs, NJ: Prentice Hall.

MILLER, J., DE LEON, M. J., FERRIS, S. H., RUSSELL, J., GEORGE, A. E., REISBERG, B., FOWLER, J., & WOLF, A. P. (1987). Abnormal temporal lobe response in Alzheimer's disease during cognitive processing as measured by c-2-deoxy-D-glucose ("C-2DG") and PET. *Journal of Cerebral Blood Flow and Metabolism* (in press).

OBRIST, W. D., HENRY, C. E., & JUSTISS, W. A. (1961). Longitudinal study of EEG in old age. *Excerpta Medical International Congress,* Serial no. 37, 180-181.

ROCKSTEIN, M. & SUSSMAN, M. L. (1979). *Biology of aging.* Belmont, CA: Wadsworth.

ROWE, M. J. (1978). Normal variability of the brain-stem auditory evoked response in young and old adult subjects. *Electroencephalography and Clinical Neurophysiology, 44,* 459-470.

SANDLIN, R. E. & MOKOTOFF, B. (1976). Brainstem auditory evoked response measurement. *Maico Audiological Library Series, 14,* (8).

SCHENKENBERG, T. (1970). Visual, auditory, and somatosensory evoked responses of normal subjects from childhood to senescence. Unpublished doctoral dissertation. University of Utah.

SCHENKENBERG, T., DUSTMAN, R. E., & BECK, E. C. (1971).   Changes in evoked responses related to age, hemisphere, and sex. *Electroencephalography and Clinical Neurophysiology, 30,* 163-164.

SQUIRES, K. C., GOODIN, D. S., & STARR, A. (1979).   Event related potentials in development, aging, and dementia. In D. Lehman & E. Callaway (Eds.), *Human evoked potentials.* New York: Plenum Press.

STOCKARD, J. J., STOCKARD, J. E., & SHARBROUGH, F. W. (1977).   *Mayo Clinic Proceedings, 52,* 761-769.

WALFORD, R. L. (1969).   *The immunological theory of aging.* Baltimore: Williams and Wilkins.

WILKIE, F. & EISDORFER, C. (1971).   Intelligence and blood pressure in the aged. *Science, 172,* 959-962.

WILSON, D. L. (1974).   The programmed theory of aging. In M. Rockstein, M. L. Sussman & J. Chesky (Eds.), *Theoretical aspects of aging.* New York: Academic Press.

WOODRUFF, D. S. (1975).   Relationships between age, EEG alpha rhythm, and reaction time: A biofeedback study. *Psychophysiology, 12,* 673-681.

WOODRUFF, D. S. (1980).   Intervention in the psychophysiology of aging: Pitfalls, progress, and potential. In R. Turner & H. W. Reese (Eds.), *Life-span developmental psychology: Intervention.* New York: Academic Press.

WOODRUFF, D. S. (1982).   Advances in the psychophysiology of aging. In F. I. M. Craik & S. Trehub (Eds.) *Aging and cognitive processes.* New York: Plenum Press.

WOODRUFF, D. S. (1985).   Arousal, sleep, and aging. In J. E. Birren & K. W. Schaie (Eds.), *Handbook of the psychology of aging* (2nd Ed.), New York: Van Nostrand Reinhold.

CHAPTER 6

Longevity and Health

Photo of Charles Howard Knapp on the porch of the Knapp farm when he was 93 years old. (Courtesy of Cindy Aiman Stemich and Ruth Knapp Oberholtzer.)

There are several important reasons for studying longevity in the psychology of aging, even though longevity has typically remained in the domain of biology and medicine. The first reason is that the study of longevity emphasizes the significance of multidisciplinary study in gerontology. This topic really involves many disciplines and a need to work with social and biological perspectives as well as with the psychological perspective.

A second rationale for the study of longevity by students of geropsychology is that the longevity data are used as the basis of the biological-decremental model, a model which has pervaded the psychology of aging. The factors involved in physiological aging are important to the study of longevity, and the factors leading to long life are significant knowledge for psychologists to have.

A third reason for the import of longevity to psychologists is that psychological variables are important correlates of longevity in and of themselves. This is a different perspective from the more typical point of view of the psychology of aging—the examination of behavior as a function of time. In studying psychological correlates of longevity, we are treating psychological variables as potential independent variables which we could manipulate to observe the outcome on longevity. Naturally, the aim would be to maximize life expectancy by changing those psychological variables associated with a shortened length of life.

The means we use to study longevity is personal. We begin by taking the Life Expectancy Test (Woodruff, 1977) which is comprised of 32 questions identifying empirically established correlates of longevity. While this test is an exercise designed to teach people about the factors relevant to life expectancy and has not been tested for its validity, it is based on the most accurate information on longevity currently available.

It is noted in Chapter 1 that from the beginning of recorded history, humans speculated on the causes of long life, devised myths, and invented folk remedies to extend life expectancy. More recently, we have used scientific methods to determine and experiment with the causes of long life. While there is still much research to be done before we can accurately determine all of the factors affecting longevity, a large body of data has been collected which gives us some clues. This information can be used to evaluate the life expectancy of an individual.

The actuarial tables or life tables compiled from Federal government data by insurance companies are still one of the best predictors of life expectancy available. For this reason we will use the life tables as a starting point and begin the estimation of personal life expectancy on this statistical basis. Subsequently, in the Life Expectancy Test which follows, we personalize the prediction by taking into account various factors in a person's background and life style which make it possible to individualize the prediction.

Statisticians in insurance companies recognize the fallacy and risk in attempting to predict individual deaths on the basis of a few population parameters, and it is clear that even with the additional personal information gathered in the Life Expectancy Test, totally accurate prediction is impossible. The Life Expectancy Test must not be viewed as a scientific instrument. Rather, it should be viewed as an intellectual exercise. Nevertheless, it is an exercise which should be taken seriously. The test points out those aspects of life style which may serve to lengthen or shorten life expectancy.

It is important to recognize the accuracy limitation of the Life Expectancy Test, and it is also important to understand how most of the data on which the test is based were collected. These data represent the most advanced information available to scientists on longevity, but scientists still have a long way to go before they fully comprehend all the various causes of long life, especially in humans.

Most of the data currently available on human life expectancy are correlational. The research designs have been descriptive rather than experimental, and correlations or relationships have been found to exist between certain factors and long life. For example, people who live longer tend to have x, y, and z characteristics, while people who live a shorter time tend to have m, p, and q characteristics. Such information does not necessarily mean that factors x, y, and z lead to or cause long life, or that factors m, p, and q cause earlier death, although they may. Correlational studies simply show that certain variables are related. Only experimental studies can reveal causes.

It is essential to understand that correlational studies do not provide conclusive evidence about causation. The Life Expectancy Test will be misunderstood if this idea is not clear. When a correlational study is undertaken, the investigator measures at least two variables and then statistically calculates the relationship between those variables. It is entirely possible for two variables to be highly correlated and at the same time be totally unrelated. For example, it might be found that the amount of ice cream eaten on a given day was highly correlated with the number of drownings on that day. Does that mean that eating ice cream causes drowning? No. It simply means that the two phenomena occurred under the same circumstances. In this example, weather is the third variable. On hot days more people eat ice cream and more people also go swimming and drown.

While it is easy to see the absurdity of implying causation on the basis of correlational evidence in the previous example, many people forget or ignore this difficulty with correlational data when variables with some likelihood of being causally related are in fact found to correlate. For example, when high correlations were found between the incidence of lung cancer and the number of cigarettes smoked per day, many were willing to say that smoking causes cancer. Scientists were aware that such an inference was suggested by the data but not proved. Many argued that a third variable (for example, personality) caused people to smoke and also caused lung cancer. The proof came with experiments showing that animals given large doses of nicotine developed cancer, while control animals not given such material did not. The experimental evidence demonstrated the causal relationship.

The obvious reason why it is difficult to establish clear causal relationships in human longevity is that we cannot experiment with human lives. We simply cannot randomly assign some people to one potentially dangerous treatment while assigning another group to a nontreatment condition. Indeed, even when we carry out studies to maximize longevity and provide the experimental group with a known beneficial treatment, ethical questions are raised when we withhold the beneficial treatment from the control group. The most scandalous example of such an experiment was carried out over many decades by government researchers who treated experimental subjects who had syphilis with antibiotics and withheld treatment and even information about antibiotics from a control group who also had contracted the disease. The only alternative to experimental research in human populations is correlational research. You examine those people who by chance happen to be exposed to the dangerous condition, and usually you do not know if the people in the endangered group were different to begin with in terms of longevity. Studying such situations provides us with some information, but it does not necessarily tell us the cause.

The correlation between education and longevity is a good example of the misleading quality of correlational data. Descriptive studies show that people with more education live longer than people with only a few years' schooling. Is giving a person only a few years' schooling a dangerous treatment? Probably not. The education itself, or the lack of it, does not cause an earlier death. The people who were unable to spend a number of years in school are, on the average, poorer, they receive less adequate health care, their nutrition may be inadequate, and they may even have dropped out of school because of poor health. In other words, those who get less education are different in a number of ways from those who get a great deal of education. Education itself does not cause long life, but length of education is related to variables which are causally involved in longevity.

There are a number of variables which are correlated with long life which are difficult to explain at the present time. For example, abstaining from alcoholic beverages is associated with a shorter life expectancy than is moderate drinking. Many find this hard to believe. However, those people who refuse to drink alcoholic beverages live an average of several years less than moderate drinkers. This is true even though we know that *heavy* drinking shortens the life expectancy and that excessive consumption of alcohol has adverse physiological effects. It is conceivable that these correlational relationships occur not because refusing to drink affects longevity, but because there is some other quality apart from abstaining from alcohol which characterizes teetotalers and which shortens their life expectancy.

In addition to the lack of information in many cases as to why certain variables are correlated with longevity, it is impossible to know at the present time how the various factors interact. The model used for the Life Expectancy Test is additive. In other words, the effect of each of the 32 factors discussed in the test is added. There is reason to believe, however, that at least some of the factors may combine or interact to extend or shorten life expectancy in a multiplicative way.

Recent research on the effects of taking birth control pills and smoking on life expectancy in women provides an example. Smoking and the use of birth control pills both individually increase a woman's (particularly an older woman's) chances of having cardiovascular problems. When combined, by women who both smoke and take birth control pills, the risk of death due to heart disease is greatly increased. The risk is much greater than simply adding together the risks of smoking and taking the pill.

When two risk factors interact and magnify the effect of each other, it is called a synergistic relationship. There is evidence that the combined effects of smoking and obesity also have a synergistic relationship, further increasing one's risk of premature death. Such synergistic effects are not taken into account in the Life Expectancy Test because we simply do not have much information about how risk factors (*or* beneficial factors, for that matter) interact and combine to determine life expectancy. The student should keep in mind that if he or she identifies a number of risk factors in his or her background and life style, these factors most probably interact to reduce the number of remaining years to an even greater extent than estimated on the Life Expectancy Test.

THE LIFE EXPECTANCY TEST

Remember that this test is an exercise designed to teach the student about the factors contributing to longevity. There is no test in existence which can tell you with absolute certainty how long you will live. The test presented here is based on the best scientific evidence available today. While scientists still do not know all of the variables causing long life, they are aware of some of the phenomena that seem to be correlated with longevity. The Life Expectancy Test is based on those data.

Begin by finding your life expectancy from the life table presented as Table 6.1 On the basis of your sex, age, and race, you start with this average life expectancy.

TABLE 6.1   Life Expectancy Table[a]

Age	White Male	White Female	Black Male	Black Female
10	72.7	79.6	67.2	75.2
11	72.7	79.6	67.2	75.2
12	72.7	79.6	67.2	75.2
13	72.8	79.6	67.3	75.2
14	72.8	79.6	67.3	75.2
15	72.8	79.6	67.3	75.3
16	72.9	79.7	67.4	75.3
17	72.9	79.7	67.4	75.3
18	73.0	79.7	67.5	75.3
19	73.1	79.7	67.5	75.4
20	73.1	79.8	67.6	75.4
21	73.2	79.8	67.7	75.4
22	73.3	79.8	67.8	75.5
23	73.4	79.9	67.9	75.5
24	73.4	79.9	68.0	75.6
25	73.5	79.9	68.1	75.6
26	73.6	80.0	68.2	75.7
27	73.7	80.0	68.3	75.7
28	73.7	80.0	68.4	75.8
29	73.8	80.0	68.6	75.8
30	73.9	80.1	68.7	75.9
31	73.9	80.1	68.8	76.0
32	74.0	80.1	69.0	76.0
33	74.1	80.2	69.1	76.1
34	74.1	80.2	69.3	76.2
35	74.2	80.2	69.4	76.2
36	74.3	80.3	69.6	76.3
37	74.3	80.3	69.7	76.4
38	74.4	80.3	69.9	76.5
39	74.5	80.4	70.0	76.6
40	74.6	80.4	70.2	76.7
41	74.6	80.5	70.4	76.8
42	74.7	80.5	70.6	76.9
43	74.8	80.6	70.8	77.0
44	74.9	80.7	71.0	77.1
45	75.0	80.7	71.2	77.2
46	75.1	80.8	71.4	77.4
47	75.2	80.9	71.7	77.5
48	75.4	81.0	71.9	77.7
49	75.5	81.1	72.2	77.9

[a]Life expectancies presented here are based on life tables computed by the National Center for Health Statistics for 1983 (National Center for Health Statistics, 1986).

TABLE 6.1   (continued)

Age	White Male	White Female	Black Male	Black Female
50	75.7	81.2	72.5	78.1
51	75.8	81.3	72.8	78.3
52	76.0	81.4	73.1	78.5
53	76.2	81.5	73.4	78.7
54	76.4	81.7	73.7	78.9
55	76.6	81.8	74.1	79.1
56	76.8	81.9	74.4	79.4
57	77.1	82.1	74.8	79.7
58	77.3	82.3	75.2	79.9
59	77.6	82.4	75.6	80.2
60	77.9	82.6	76.0	80.5
61	78.2	82.8	76.5	80.9
62	78.5	83.0	76.9	81.2
63	78.8	83.3	77.4	81.6
64	79.2	83.5	77.9	81.9
65	79.5	83.7	78.4	82.3
66	79.9	84.0	78.9	82.6
67	80.3	84.2	79.4	83.0
68	80.7	84.5	79.9	83.3
69	81.1	84.8	80.4	83.7
70	81.5	85.1	80.9	84.1
71	82.0	85.4	81.5	84.6
72	82.5	85.7	82.1	85.0
73	82.9	86.1	82.7	85.5
74	83.4	86.4	83.3	86.0
75	84.0	86.8	84.0	86.5
76	84.5	87.2	84.6	87.0
77	85.1	87.6	81.2	87.4
78	85.7	88.0	81.8	87.9
79	86.2	88.4	82.4	88.5
80	86.9	88.8	87.1	89.0
81	87.5	89.3	87.8	89.6
82	88.2	89.8	88.5	90.2
83	88.8	90.3	89.3	90.9
84	89.5	90.9	90.1	91.6
85	90.2	91.5	91.0	92.4

[a]Life expectancies presented here are based on life tables computed by the National Center for Health Statistics for 1983 (National Center for Health Statistics, 1986).

By keeping a running score based on your personal attributes, you will end up with a personalized life expectancy and an awareness of what you might do to live even longer. Begin by finding your life expectancy on Table 6.1 Take your present age, and find your starting life expectancy according to what sex and race you are.

Now that you have your starting life expectancy, add and subtract years according to how you answer the questions on the Life Expectancy Test.

LIFE EXPECTANCY TEST

Heredity and Family

1. **Longevity of grandparents**
   Have any of your grandparents lived to age 80 or beyond? If so, *add one year for each grandparent living beyond that age. Add one-half year for each grandparent surviving beyond the age of 70.*

   _____

2. **Longevity of parents**
   If your mother lived beyond the age of 80, *add four years. Add two years* if your father lived beyond 80. You benefit more if your mother lived a long time than if your father did.

   _____

3. **Cardiovascular disease of close relatives**
   If any parent, grandparent, sister, or brother died of a heart attack, stroke, or arteriosclerosis before the age of 50, *subtract four years for each incidence.* If any of those close relatives died of the above before the age of 60, *subtract two years for each incidence.*

   _____

4. **Other hereditable diseases of close relatives**
   Have any parents, grandparents, sisters, or brothers died before the age of 60 of diabetes mellitus or peptic ulcer? *Subtract three years for each incidence.* If any of these close relatives died before 60 of stomach cancer, *subtract two years.* Women whose close female relatives have died before 60 of breast cancer should also *subtract two years.* Finally, if any close relatives have died before the age of 60 of any cause except accidents or homicide, *subtract one year for each incidence.*

   _____

5. **Childbearing**
   Women who have never had children are more likely to be in poor health, and they also are at a greater risk for breast cancer. Therefore, if you can't or don't plan to have children, or if you are over 40 and have never had children, *subtract one-half year.* Women who have a large number of children tax their bodies. If you've had over seven children, or plan to, *subtract one year.*

   _____

6. **Mother's age at your birth**
   Was your mother over the age of 35 or under the age of 18 when you were born? If so, *subtract one year.*

   _____

7.   Birth order

Are you the first born in your family? If so, *add one year.*

_____

8.   Intelligence

How intelligent are you? Is your intelligence below average, average, above average, or superior? If you feel that your intelligence is superior, that is, if you feel that you are smarter than almost anyone you know, *add two years.*

_____

9.   Weight

Are you currently overweight? Find your ideal weight in Table 6.2. If you weigh more than the figure in Table 6.2, calculate the percentage by which you are overweight, and *subtract the appropriate number of years shown in Table 6.3.* If you have been overweight at any point in your life, or if your weight has periodically fluctuated by more than ten pounds since high school, *subtract two years.*

_____

10.   Dietary habits

Do you prefer vegetables, fruits, and simple foods to foods high in fat and sugar, and do you *always* stop eating before you feel really full? If the honest answer to both questions is yes, *add one year.*

_____

TABLE 6.2   1983 Metropolitan Height & Weight Tables

TO MAKE AN APPROXIMATION OF YOUR FRAME SIZE...

Extend your arm and bend the forearm upward at a 90 degree angle. Keep fingers straight and turn the inside of your wrist toward your body. If you have a caliper, use it to measure the space between the two prominent bones on *either* side of your elbow. Without a caliper, place thumb and index finger of your other hand on these two bones. Measure the space between your fingers against a ruler or tape measure. Compare it with these tables that list elbow measurements for *medium-framed* men and women. Measurements lower than those listed indicate you have a small frame. Higher measurements indicate a large frame.

Height in 1' heels	Elbow Breadth
Men	
5'2"—5'3"	2½"—2⅞"
5'4"—5'7"	2⅝"—2⅞"
5'8"—5'11"	2¾"—3"
6'0"—6'3"	2¾"—3⅛"
6'4"	2⅞"—3¼"
Women	
4'10"—4'11"	2¼"—2½"
5'0"—5'3"	2¼"—2½"
5'4"—5'7"	2⅜"—2⅝"
5'8"—5'11"	2⅜"—2⅝"
6'0"	2½"—2¾"

1983 METROPOLITAN HEIGHT AND WEIGHT TABLES

Weights at ages 25–59 based on lowest mortality. Weight in pounds according to frame (in indoor clothing weighitng 5 lbs. for men and 3 lbs. for women, shoes with 1″ heels)

Men

Height Feet	Inches	Small Frame	Medium Frame	Large Frame
5	2	128–134	131–141	138–150
5	3	130–136	133–143	140–153
5	4	132–138	135–145	142–156
5	5	134–140	137–148	144–160
5	6	136–142	139–151	146–164
5	7	138–145	142–154	149–168
5	8	140–148	145–157	152–172
5	9	142–151	148–160	155–176
5	10	144–154	151–163	158–180
5	11	146–157	154–166	161–184
6	0	149–160	157–170	164–188
6	1	152–164	160–174	168–192
6	2	155–168	164–178	172–197
6	3	158–172	167–182	176–202
6	4	162–176	171–187	181–207

Women

Height Feet	Inches	Small Frame	Medium Frame	Large Frame
4	10	102–111	109–121	118–131
4	11	103–113	111–123	120–134
5	0	104–115	113–126	122–137
5	1	106–118	115–129	125–140
5	2	108–121	118–132	128–143
5	3	111–124	121–135	131–147
5	4	114–127	124–138	134–151
5	5	117–130	127–141	137–155
5	6	120–133	130–144	140–159
5	7	123–136	133–147	143–163
5	8	126–139	136–150	146–167
5	9	129–142	139–153	149–170
5	10	132–145	142–156	152–173
5	11	135–148	145–159	155–176
6	0	138–151	148–162	158–179

Source: Metropolitan Life Insurance Company (Health and Safety Education Division).

11. Smoking

How much do you smoke? If you smoke two or more packs of cigarettes a day, *subtract twelve years.* If you smoke between one and two packs a day, *subtract seven years.* If you smoke less than a pack a day, *subtract two years.* If you have quite smoking, congratulations, you subtract no years at all!

TABLE 6.3   Risk to Life of Being Overweight (in years)

Age	Markedly Overweight (more than 30%)		Moderately Overweight (10–30%)	
	Men	Women	Men	Women
20	− 15.8	− 7.2	− 13.8	− 4.8
25	− 10.6	− 6.1	− 9.6	− 4.9
30	− 7.9	− 5.5	− 5.5	− 3.6
35	− 6.1	− 4.9	− 4.2	− 4.0
40	− 5.1	− 4.6	− 3.3	− 3.5
45	− 4.3	− 5.1	− 2.4	− 3.8
50	− 4.6	− 4.1	− 2.4	− 2.8
55	− 5.4	− 3.2	− 2.0	− 2.2

Source: Metropolitan Life Insurance Company. (1976) Longevity patterns in the United States. *Statistical Bulletin, 57,* p. 2.

12.   Drinking

If you are a moderate drinker, that is, if you never drink to the point of intoxication and have one or two drinks of whiskey, or half a liter of wine, or up to four glasses of beer per day, *add three years.* If you are a light drinker, that is, you have an occasional drink, but do not drink almost every day, *add one and one-half years.* If you are an abstainer who never uses alcohol in any form, do not add or subtract any years. Finally, if you are a heavy drinker or an alcoholic, *subtract eight years.* (Heavy drinkers are those who drink more than three ounces of whiskey or drink other intoxicating beverages excessively almost every day. They drink to the point of intoxication.)

13.   Exercise

How much do you exercise? If you exercise at least three times a week at one of the following: jogging, bike riding, swimming, taking long, brisk walks, dancing, or skating, *add three years.* Just exercising on weekends does not count.

14.   Sleep

If you generally fall asleep right away and get six to eight hours of sleep per night, you're average and should neither add nor subtract years. However, if you sleep excessively (ten or more hours per night), or if you sleep very little (five or less hours per night), you probably have problems. *Subtract two years.*

15.   Sexual activity

If you enjoy regular sexual activity, having intimate sexual relations once or twice a week, *add two years.*

16. **Regular physical examinations**

Do you have an annual physical examination by your physician which includes a breast examination and Pap smear for women, and a proctoscopic examination every other year for men? If so, *add two years.*

17. **Health status**

Are you in poor health? Do you have a chronic health condition (for example, heart disease, high blood pressure, cancer, diabetes, ulcer) or are you frequently ill? If so, *subtract five years.*

Education and Occupation

18. **Years of education**

How much education have you had? *Add or subtract the number of years shown in Table 6.4.*

TABLE 6.4   Education and Life Expectancy[a]

Level of Education	Years of Life
Four or more years of college	+3.0
One to three years of college	+2.0
Four years of high school	+1.0
One to three years of high school	±0.0
Elementary school (eight years)	−0.5
Less than eighth grade	−2.0

[a]Estimates based on data presented in E. M. Kitagawa and P. M. Hauser, Differential mortality in the United States: A study in socioeconomic epidemiology. Cambridge, MA: Harvard University Press, 1973 (pp. 12, 18), and in Metropolitan Life Insurance Company, Socioeconomic mortality differentials, *Statistical Bulletin,* 1985, *56,* 3–5.

19. **Occupational level**

If you are working, what is the socioeconomic level of your occupation? If you do not work, what is your spouse's occupation? If you are retired, what is your former occupation? If you are a student, what is your parents' occupational level? *Add or subtract the number of years shown in Table 6.5.*

20. **Family income**

If your family income is above average for your education and occupation, *add one year.* If it's below average for your education and occupation, *subtract one year.*

21. **Activity on the job**

If your job involves a lot of physical activity, *add two years.* On the other hand, if you sit all day on the job, *subtract two years.*

TABLE 6.5   Occupation and Life Expectancy[a]

Occupational Level	Years of Life
Class I —Professional	+ 1.5
Class II —Technical, administrative, and managerial. Also agricultural workers, as they live longer for their actual socioeconomic level	+ 1.0
Class III—Proprietors, clerical, sales, and skilled workers	± 0.0
Class IV—Semi-skilled workers	− 0.5
Class V —Laborers	− 4.0

[a]Estimates based on data presented in E. M. Kitagawa and P. M. Hauser, Differential mortality in the United States: A study in socioeconomic epidemiology. Cambridge, MA: Harvard Unviersity Press, 1973 (pp. 12, 18), and in Metropolitan Life Insurance Company, Socioeconomic mortality differentials, *Statistical Bulletin,* 1975, *56,* 3–5.

22.   Age and work

If you are over the age of 60 and still on the job, *add two years.* If you are over the age of 65 and have not retired, *add three years.*

Life Style

23.   Rural versus urban dwelling

If you live in an urban area and have lived in or near the city for most of your life, *subtract one year.* If you have spent most of your life in a rural area, *add one year.*

24.   Married versus divorced

If you are married and living with your spouse, *add one year.*

A. *Formerly Married Men.* If you are a separated or divorced man living alone, *subtract nine years,* and if you are a widowed man living alone, *subtract seven years.* If as a separated, divorced, or widowed man you live with other people, such as family members, *subtract only half the years given above.* Living with others is beneficial for formerly married men.

B. *Formerly Married Women.* Women who are separated or divorced should *subtract four years,* and widowed women should *subtract three and a half years.* The loss of a spouse through divorce or death is not as life-shortening to a woman, and she lives about as long whether she lives alone or with family, unless she is the head of the household. Divorced or widowed women who live with family as the head of their household should *subtract only two years for the fomerly married status.*

25. **Living status as single**

   If you are a woman who has never married, *subtract one year for each unmarried decade past the age of 25*. If you live with a family or friends as a male single person, you should also *subtract one year for each unmarried decade past the age of 25*. However, if you are a man who has never married and are living alone, *subtract two years for each unmarried decade past the age of 25*.

26. **Life changes**

   Are you always changing things in your life; changing jobs, changing residences, changing friends and/or spouses, changing your appearance? If so, *subtract two years*. Too much change is stressful.

27. **Friendship**

   Do you generally like people and have at least two close friends in whom you can confide almost all the details of your life? If so, *add one year*.

28. **Aggressive personality**

   Do you always feel that you are under time pressure? Are you aggressive and sometimes hostile, paying little attention to the feelings of others? *Subtract two to five years depending on how well you fit this description*. The more pressured, aggressive, and hostile you are, the greater your risk for heart disease.

29. **Flexible personality**

   Are you a calm, reasonable, relaxed person? Are you easygoing and adaptable, taking life pretty much as it comes? *Depending upon the degree to which you fit this description, add one to three years*. If you are rigid, dogmatic, and set in your ways, *subtract two years*.

30. **Risk-taking personality**

   Do you take a lot of risks, including driving without seat belts, exceeding the speed limit, and taking any dare that is made? Do you live in a high crime rate neighborhood? If you are vulnerable to accidents and homicide in this way, *subtract two years*. If you use seat belts regularly, drive infrequently, and generally avoid risks and dangerous parts of town, *add one year*.

31. **Depressive personality**

   Have you been depressed, tense, worried, or guilty for more than a period of a year or two? If so, *subtract one to three years depending on how seriously you are affected by these feelings*.

32. **Happy personality**

Are you basically happy and content, and have you had a lot of fun in life? If so, *add two years.* People with feelings like this are the ones who live to be 100.

_____

TOTAL _____

OVERVIEW OF FACTORS
INVOLVED IN LONGEVITY
AND HEALTH

One of the first things which is notable about the Life Expectancy Test is the information in the life tables. These tables are based on the latest census data and predict life expectancy on the basis of age, sex, and race (National Center for Health Statistics, 1986b). Note that the life expectancy at age 10, which is the age at which the chart begins, is greater than the figure given as life expectancy at birth (71.0 for males and 78.1 for females). The reason that life expectancy increases at older ages is because once you survive certain critical periods, your chances for living longer are greater. For example, infancy is a time when the mortality rate is relatively high. When a baby is alive at the age of 1, he or she has a greater likelihood of surviving longer than a newborn baby. Between the ages of 10 and 25, life expectancy changes very little because fewer people die between these ages. The force of mortality gradually accelerates after that, and a greater and greater percentage of the people remaining alive die with each succeeding year. This automatically (statistically) increases the life expectancy of their surviving peers.

Life tables are based on recorded deaths at each age, and the life expectancy given for each age is the number of years you have a 50-50 chance of living. The statistics are computed in such a way that the figure given for life expectancy at your age is the number of years to which 50 percent of the people alive at that age survive. For example, half of the white American cohort who today are 30 years of age will still be alive 47 years from now when they are 77 years old. Half of all Americans who have already reached the age of 80 years will survive to the age of 88.1 years. Some individuals who are now in their late eighties will survive to 100 years, but there are currently so few Americans in the age categories of 86 and older that the government does not even include life expectancy beyond the age of 85 on the charts.

Notice also in the Life Expectancy Table (Table 6.1) the significant difference in life expectancy between the races. Blacks in the United States have a shockingly low life expectancy when compared to the rest of the population. At birth, a black male has a life expectancy over six years shorter than a white male. The black-white female difference in life expectancy at birth is just over five years. The gap in life expectancy between blacks and whites gradually narrows until the age of 75 when life expectancy for black and white males is equal. For black and white females, equal life expectancy occurs at the age of 78, and after that age, life expectancy for black women is greater. It is likely that life expectancy becomes greater for the remaining blacks who survive to the late 70s because the percentage of blacks surviving to this age is so small that those left are a very select group. Undoubtedly, the lack of social advantages for blacks as a minority group is primarily responsible for this large racial difference in life expectancy.

Oriental Americans live longer than their Caucasian counterparts. This is interesting in light of the fact that old age is particularly respected and revered in Oriental culture. Whether the attitudes of these individuals contribute to their longer life expectancy, or whether diet and genes are the primary causes has yet to be determined. Studies on the causes of greater longevity in American Orientals may help extend life expectancy in all races. However, relatively little research attention has been given to aging in this minority group.

The biggest and most consistent difference in life expectancy is the sex difference. Women of all ages and all races live longer than men of the same age and race. A female child born today has a seven-year advantage over her male counterpart. The gap in life expectancy between the sexes does narrow in later life, particularly after menopause when women become more at risk for heart disease. However, the sex difference is apparent throughout the life table to the oldest entry. The causes of sex difference in longevity—both biological and enviornmental—merit special consideration.

Sex Differences in Life Expectancy

One of the most startling features about life expectancy in the United States and in all developed nations is the large sex difference in life expectancy. A male child born today can expect to live seven years less than his female peer. Furthermore, the gap between the sexes in longevity appears to be widening. In 1900 white females had only a 2.9 year advantage (Zopf, 1986). However, as life expectancy increased over the next 60 years so did the gap between the sexes. By 1959 there was a 6.6 year difference in life expectancy between white females and males, and the most recent American statistics indicate that the difference has increased moderately to 7.0 years (National Center for Health Statistics, 1986b). The gap between the sexes peaked at 8.4 years and has now begun to narrow (Fries, 1987). The most recent federal government predictions are that the gap will remain relatively stable. There is no evidence that the gap will narrow significantly, at least in the next 40 years.

Sex differences in longevity: Genetic or environmental?   Why does this large sex difference in longevity exist? Do we simply stress males more in industrialized societies in which the gap is the greatest? Are there biological explanations based on genetic and hormonal differences? No definitive answers exist yet, but the emerging picture tends to favor biological explanations. Females appear to be the biologically superior sex in regard to longevity.

Evidence to explain sex differences in longevity comes from a wide variety of sources. The starting point favoring a biological explanation is that in most subhuman species females live longer. Since it is difficult to see how the environment favors female animals living in the wild, biologists interpret these data as indicating a genetic and hormonal basis for greater longevity in females.

The most widely accepted biological explanation for sex differences in human longevity involves hormones. Hormonal differences between males and females have a wide range of consequences. The presence of a Y chromosome codes for maleness and causes gonads to form early in fetal development. The gonads produce and secrete androgens or male hormones, and the hormones affect the development of the brain. Indeed, the part of the brain most affected by male hormones is the hypothalamus, that very part of the brain which regulates all further development and which is currently considered by biologists to be the brain center which may pace aging (Finch & Hayflict, 1977, 1985). In the absence of a Y chromosome, the fetus develops into a female. Hormonal differences between the sexes affect phenomena such as behavior, metabolism rate, and body structure, and these secondary sexual characteristics are likely to be involved in sex differences in longevity.

From conception onward throughout the life span, males are more vulnerable. The fact that a much larger number of stillbirths are male than female suggests that biology rather than environment is implicated. It has been estimated that there are 120 males conceived for every 100 females. Many more deaths in the fetal stage are males than females. Thus, at birth the sex ratio is 106 males per 100 females. Boys continue to die in disproportionate numbers to girls throughout childhood and adolescence, with the sex ratio in adolescence being 104 males to every 100 females. By the third and fourth decades, male attrition has been great enough to reverse the sex ratio, and during this period of the life span there are 97 men for every 100 women. The attrition of males accelerates in the fifth and sixth decades leading to a sex ratio of 68 males to 100 females at age 65. By the age of 80, women outnumber men by almost two to one. These data and some of their social consequences are pointed out in Chapter 3 and in Figure 3.9, and the aim in this chapter is to attempt to explain some of the causes for the differences.

One of the emerging problems in an aging society is the great number of single women in late life. Widowhood is problematic not only because of the loneliness and absence of social roles, but also it is the most likely cause of poverty in old age. Men are not the only ones penalized by sex differences in longevity. Women who must spend the last ten or more years of their lives alone (because they married men two to five years older and also outlived them by seven years) certainly cannot be viewed as beneficiaries of sex differences in longevity.

That greater male vulnerability is at least partially a result of differences in sex hormones is supported by several pieces of evidence. While the sex difference in longevity at birth is seven years, if you observe the later years in Table 6.1, you will notice that the gap narrows, particularly after midlife.

While both men and women have heart attacks, the number one cause of death in the United States, women have them later than men. Testosterone and estrogen affect blood-clotting mechanisms which are an important factor in heart disease. Blood which clots more easily makes the individual more prone to a heart attack. The clotting factor in blood, called platelets, is affected by the male hormone, testosterone, so that blood is more likely to clot. The blood of female animals injected with testosterone clots more easily, and clotting is less in the presence of the female hormone, estrogen. Thus, after menopause, when estrogen levels are low and the relative amount of testosterone in women's blood is greater, they are much more likely to have heart attacks. Men are much more prone to heart attacks in the third and fourth decades of their lives when testosterone output is high.

The most dramatic evidence for a hormonal effect on longevity comes from the research on castration in males. Evidence presented by Drori and Folman (1976) suggests that testosterone may be negatively related to longevity inasmuch as castrated male rats had longer than average life expectancies. The investigators interpreted these results as occurring because of the cancer and tumor-inducing properties of testosterone in rats.

Drori and Folman are not the only investigators to have shown that castration in male animals extends life. Hamilton and Mestler (1969), anatomists at the State University of New York College of Medicine, reported that castration prolongs life in some but not all strains or species of animals. To determine the effect in humans, they compared life expectancy of twentieth-century eunuchs to life expectancy of matched male and female groups.

Castration has been practiced since antiquity. In the West it was carried out to produce *castrati* singers, and in the East it was practiced to provide trusted servants for the members of the imperial palace and their harems. However, in the twentieth century only certain cancer patients, psychotics, or mentally retarded individuals have been castrated. Hamilton and Mestler compared life expectancy of 735 intact, mentally retarded men, 883 intact, mentally retarded women, and 297 mentally retarded eunuchs. Not only did the eunuchs outlive the noncastrated men by an average of 13.5 years, they also outlived the women by an average of 6.7 years. This is one of the rare instances in which men outlive women, and Hamilton and Mestler attributed the effect to testosterone. The younger the men were when they were castrated (thus, the less they were exposed to testosterone, especially if castration occurred before puberty), the longer they lived. Even men castrated between the ages of 30 and 39 lived longer than intact men. Since intact women produce some testosterone, the anatomists speculated that the women, like the intact men, may have died earlier as a result of having higher levels of this male hormone than did the eunuchs who had their testosterone-producing glands removed.

It is an understatement to assert that castration is a radical means to achieve longer life in males. Indeed, most men would prefer to die. Fortunately, to live a long time, neither rats nor men need to be castrated. Droir and Folman (1976) demonstrated that male rats that were exercised or that were given the opportunity to mate at least once a week, lived longer than unexercised rats, rats prevented access to females, and castrated rats.

A fact suggesting a positive effect for estrogen is that women who have had children tend to live longer. (That is, they live longer once they survive childbirth.) Since estrogen production increases dramatically during pregnancy, it has been suggested that increased estrogen is responsible for the greater longevity of childbearing women. They are less susceptible to breast cancer, and it appears that they may also be less susceptible to heart disease.

The effect of widespread use of birth control pills (which include estrogen) on longevity in women is too recent a phenomenon to appear in actuarial tables. The Pill seems to carry some risk, but less than the risk of pregnancy. There is suggestive evidence that birth control pills taken in conjunction with smoking greatly increases mortality resulting from heart disease and stroke, and estrogen replacement therapy in later life (after menopause) has been associated in some studies with a higher incidence of cancer. Thus, estrogen has negative as well as beneficial effects. Nevertheless, hormonal differences between men and women probably account for some of the sex differences in longevity.

While the biological arguments for sex differences in longevity are compelling, environmentalists may still want to claim that men are stressed more and that this is what causes their earlier demise, particularly as a result of stress-related illnesses such as heart disease. It is true that men die in greater numbers as a result of violence and accidents, including work-related accidents. More men also smoke than do women, and they inhale more deeply. Some years ago it was estimated that if all men would quit smoking, the sex difference in life expectancy could be cut in half (Rutherford, 1972). Clearly, this is an environmental hazard which could be reduced. Furthermore, as more women become employed, and especially as they enter into hazardous occupations which were formerly reserved for men, and as more women smoke, we might speculate that sex differences in longevity would be reduced. However, the Census Bureau as well as life insurance actuaries do not predict that this will be the case (Auerbach, 1977; Spiegelman, 1966). It is forecast that there will be no narrowing of the gap between the sexes for at least the next 40 years. This trend in the face of social changes which are leading to greater stress for women appears to negate the environmentalist argument even more.

Several studies which provide the most convincing evidence for the powerful effect of biological factors on sex differences in longevity were underatken by Madigan (1957; Madigan & Vance, 1957) under circumstances considered to hold the environment constant for men and women. Social factors in Catholic orders appear to be more or less equated for the sexes. In male and female Catholic teaching orders there are equal health conditions, fairly homogeneous stresses and hazards, and removal from the normal sex roles experienced by individuals who are not cloistered. The nuns consistently showed a longer life expectancy at age 45. This line of research, coupled with the evidence that females of most species in the wild live longer, provides rather impressive evidence that sex differences in longevity result primarily from biological sex differences. Which biological sex differences lead to sex differences in longevity have yet to be clearly determined. The sex hormones, estrogen and testosterone, probably play a role, particularly in heart disease. It is not clear why males are more vulnerable from the moment of conception, but again, it is difficult to explain this vulnerability at the fetal, neonatal, and early childhood stages other than to assert that it has biological determinants.

One hypothesis states that since females have two X chromosomes while males have an X and a smaller Y chromosome, perhaps recessive genes carrying negative longevity factors are expressed in males and not in females. That is, the negative recessive gene on the X chromosome in males would have no analogue on the Y chromosome to counter its damaging effect. Females, on the other hand, would have to have the recessive gene on both chromosomes before the negative effect was expressed.

One argument against this hypothesis is that the negative recessive genes would tend to be eliminated by selection. However, proponents of the hypothesis counter that if the negative effect was expressed only late in life after reproduction, selection could not operate. Another argument against the X chromosome hypothesis is that in species in which the female is the heterogametic (odd-chromosome or Y-chromosome) sex—for example, in the case of birds and butterflies—the males should live longer. This is not the case. Females in most species, even in heterogametic species, live longer. Thus, the most widely accepted biological explanations for sex differences in longevity involve some component of the endocrine system, the hypothalamus, and the hormones.

The growing body of evidence favoring a biological interpretation of sex differences in longevity does not rule out the environment as a potent determinant of life expectancy. Indeed, the extension of life expectancy in the United States and in industrialized countries has resulted from improving the environment. We are beginning to approach our biological potential for life expectancy by removing or controlling hazards in the environment such as infectious diseases, poor sanitation, and malnutrition. As environmental hazards have been removed, the sex differences in longevity have reversed and favored females.

When mortality rates are high and when the social status and health treatment of females are low, females have a higher mortality than males. This is particularly true when birth control is not practiced and females are exposed to numerous pregnancies in environments where little or no medical assistance is available. As of 1968, there were six countries remaining in the world in which males lived longer than females. These countries were Cambodia, Ceylon, India, Jordan, Pakistan, and Upper Volta. By 1974, only in India did males live longer, and by 1982 life expectancy was still greater for men in India. Underdeveloped countries have a short life expectancy for men and women; as of 1982, India had a male life expectancy of 46 years and a female life expectancy of 45 years (United Nations, 1982). As females become more socially equal in these countries, and as environmental conditions become more favorable to longevity in general, sex differences in longevity throughout the world without exception will favor females.

In their book on predicting longevity, Rose and Bell (1971) suggested that the changing sex differential in mortality rates in the United States has been due to the decline in tuberculosis and maternal mortality at younger female ages, and the decline in disease related to high blood pressure at older female ages. All of these advances are associated with social and medical advances. Unfortunately, as the environment has gotten better for women, some aspects of increasing industrialization have made the environment more dangerous for men. Male deaths due to car accidents, lung cancer, and coronary artery disease have increased since 1900, even though male life expectancy at age 45 has gained three to five years. Advances in medicine and in improving the environment have tended to favor female longevity more than male longevity.

The increasing sex differential in longevity has resulted from social change, even though the current explanations for sex differences in longevity are primarily biological. This is because the underlying female advantage for longevity was overwhelmed under adverse environmental conditions targeted primarily at the female (particularly through childbirth). As these conditions were improved, the female biological potential could be expressed. This hypothesis would predict that female longevity will continue to rise over male longevity under conditions of continued or increased preferential social treatment. This is exactly what appears to be occurring in the United States. The latest government figures show that women live seven years longer than men, and demographers have predicted that the gap will be maintained in the future.

Heredity and Family Influences on Longevity

You may have noted on the life expectancy test that the first eight questions involved heredity and family influences on longevity. Many of these items are related to something over which the individual has little control. It has been suggested that if you want to live a long time, one of the things you must do is pick long-lived parents and grandparents. This fact could not be more clear than in the case of Florence Knapp, the oldest living American and the second oldest person in the world.

Florence Knapp: The oldest American.   Miss Florence Knapp, aged 114 years, certainly did an excellent job of "picking" long-lived genes. Examine her ancestry in Figure 6.1 and you will see a pedigree for long life. Remember from Chapter 1 that life expectancy in the late-eighteenth century was estimated to be about 40 years, yet three of Miss Knapp's four grandparents lived beyond the age of 80. Her aunt, Mary Knapp, born in 1826 lived almost 108 years. Miss Knapp's parents were also exceptionally long-lived by nineteenth-century standards. These favorable genes were passed on to Charles and Elizabeth Johnson Knapp's ten children, all

Florence Knapp's Genealogy

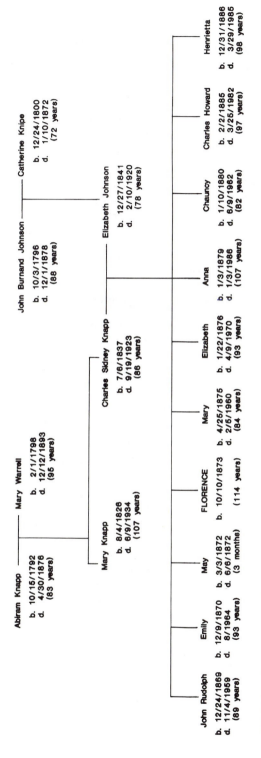

FIGURE 6.1 Genealogy chart of Florence Knapp, at the age of 114 years, the oldest living person in the United States. Chart indicates date of birth (b.) and death (d.) and age at death in parentheses. (Courtesy of Ruth Knapp Oberholtzer, niece of Florence Knapp).

FIGURE 6.2 Florence Knapp celebrating her 100th birthday on October 10, 1976. (Courtesy of *The Reporter,* Lausdale, PA).

born at home on their farm in Montgomery Square, Pennsylvania. Aunt Mary Knapp witnessed each birth and notarized the birth date to make it official. Thus, October 10, 1873, is the birth date of Florence Knapp, recorded in *Guinness Superlative Limited,* the publishers of the *Guinness Book of Records* as the oldest living person in the United States.

Miss Knapp is extremely bright. She graduated from college in 1894 (from what is now West Chester State University in Pennsylvania), and she taught the primary grades for a total of 42 years. For 35 of those years she taught at the exclusive Baldwin School in Bryn Mawr, PA.

As was true for women in those days, choosing a career in teaching meant that the woman did not marry. Miss Knapp has been a lifelong advocate for women's rights. In 1919 she marched down Broad Street in Philadelphia in a demonstration for women's suffrage wearing a white dress and white shoes and stockings and carrying a banner which said, "Votes for Women." At the age of 62, Miss Knapp retired. She lived and worked on the family farm until she was 110 years old. Indeed, at 110 she was still weeding the garden. Only when she began to have difficulty with getting around did she reluctantly move into a nursing home where she lives now. Since the age of 100, she has survived a broken hip and three bouts with pneumonia, again attesting to her remarkable vitality.

Miss Knapp took the Life Expectancy Test and answered favorably to almost all of the questions. Of course her heredity is strongly in favor of a long life based on the life expectancy of her parents and grandparents, and on her outstanding intelligence (as indicated by her being a college graduate in the nineteenth century, a most unusual achievement for those times, especially for a woman). She has been eating health food all of her life, and had fresh fruits and vegetables available from the farm. Miss Knapp never smoked or drank. She was physically active until the age of 110 years, and she has been under the care of a physician all of her life.

About the only aspect of Miss Knapp's life that is not correlated with higher life expectancy is the fact that she remained single throughout her life. She jokingly attributes her longevity to remaining single. However, she did live with her extended family which apparently provided her with high life satisfaction. Her memory is very keen as she can tell many stories of happenings on the farm with the family and friends when she was young. She can still recite many of the old poems she would teach to her little students, and she is remembered by her former students who visit and write to her.

How genes affect life expectancy.   Longevity is transmitted through the genes and through the opportunities and environment which your family provides for you. Grandparents have less of an influence than parents on longevity, and this may result from both genetic and environmental causes. Theoretically, each grandparent contributes only a fourth to the grandchild's genetic makeup. The contribution is made through the parents. Half of an individual's genes come from each parent. Also, parents are more directly responsible for raising the individual, and they usually have a more direct influence on their children's life style, health habits, diet, and outlook on life. The fact that the mother may have the greatest influence in shaping these aspects of her child's life has been used to explain why maternal life expectancy shows a greater relationship to life expectancy in children than does the life expectancy of the father. There may be biological reasons for this greater maternal-offspring longevity correlation as well.

Just as years are added if parents and grandparents were particularly long-lived, so years are subtracted if they died prematurely. The most years are lost if close relatives died prematurely of heart disease or diseases of the arteries. This is because diseases of the heart and arteries are the major cause of death in the United States and because these diseases are to a degree hereditary. Although diabetes mellitus and peptic ulcers cause fewer deaths in the United States each year (ranking seventh and seventeenth, respectively, National Center for Health Statistics, 1986a), they are highly heritable and need to be protected against in the offspring of those suffering from these diseases. Some cancers, such as stomach and breast cancer, also seem to run in families, although the risk of inheriting them is less than the risk of inheriting heart disease, diabetes, or peptic ulcer. Although cancer is the second leading cause of death in the United States, it appears to be less heritable than heart disease.

Optimal care and attention does not appear to be given by young mothers (under the age of 18), whose offspring also have a much greater infant mortality rate and are presumably weaker even if they survive. Mothers over the age of 35 also have a greater incidence of genetic defects and deaths in their infants. Thus, for individuals whose mother was under 18 or over 35 when they were born, life expectancy is somewhat shorter, even though they survived infancy. There is much less evidence that the father's age at birth of children has an effect on the children's life expectancy.

Birth order is also correlated with longevity. The earlier in the family line an individual is born, the greater the life expectancy. It is not clear whether this factor is simply another way of representing the maternal age factor (with later-born children coming when the mother is older and less fit), or whether it is a completely independent factor. It could be a social factor in that the first born may get more of the attention and resources of the parents. It could also be bioloigical, in that mothers become depleted physiologically after a certain number of births.

While giving birth has some risk to life, modern medicine has made the experience relatively safe, and women who have had children appear to live slightly longer than women who are childless. There are several factors involved in this relationship between having children and living longer. First, many women are childless not by choice but because they suffer from poor health. Naturally, women in poorer health are less likely to live a long time. Secondly, women who do not have children, whether it is by choice or for health reasons, have a higher incidence of breast cancer. The surge of hormones released during pregnancy and nursing seem to protect the breasts from cancer.

Contrasted to the moderate benefit to a woman's life expectancy in childbirth, numerous pregnancies place great stress on a woman's body, particularly when the pregnancies are spaced close together. Thus, women who have many children experience more physiological stress on their bodies (and probably more emotional stress as well), and therefore they have a shorter life expectancy. Low socioeconomic status puts people at an even greater risk, and since more mothers of large families are in the low socioeconomic bracket, they are at an even greater disadvantage with regard to life expectancy than mothers of large families in the middle or upper classes.

Intelligence, like so many other traits, runs in families, and very intelligent people live longer than their less bright contemporaries. The advantage may come from being better able to get oneself into an advantaged social position and being more adaptable and smarter at avoiding risks in life. On the other hand, the advantage may come more directly through the genes. A genetic predisposition for higher intelligence may also carry with it a genetic predisposition for greater longevity (Woodruff, 1977).

Heredity and family are aspects of an individual's life which he or she cannot choose. However, being aware of background characteristics and protecting oneself from any negative consequences which may come from it is a way to maximize life expectancy. For example, those people with a family predisposition for heart disease, diabetes, peptic ulcer, or cancer have a higher probability of having these diseases, but they will not contract them with certainty. Awareness of the fact that certain diseases run in a family can alert the individual to take preventive measures.

Health

It is not surprising to adults in the late 1980s that excessive weight shortens life expectancy. Indeed, obesity is one of the best predictors of premature death. Extra weight strains all of the physiological systems described in Chapter 5. The heart and arteries are particularly stressed by excessive weight. In overweight individuals the heart has more body surface through which it must pump blood, and the arteries are likely to be clogged with more fat. Heart attack, stroke, high blood pressure, and arteriosclerosis are more common in overweight individuals, as is diabetes mellitus. Excess weight also prevents individuals from being more active. Inactivity is another predictor of shorter life expectancy. In a number of different ways, excessive weight negatively affects life expectancy.

Smoking is the habit most responsible for shortening life expectancy. There is no single thing an individual can do which will add more years to life expectancy than to stop smoking. In the face of all the evidence, no one can reasonably take the position that smoking does not harm health. When individuals quit, they feel better, their health improves, and their life expectancy is extended.

Excessive alcoholic consumption is yet another life-shortening habit. Alcoholics die usually from cirrhosis of the liver, and excessive alcohol causes brain damage as well as damage to the liver. Alcoholics often also suffer from poor nutrition which accelerates aging processes and death.

While moderate drinking is associated with longer life, it has not been established that the relationship between moderate drinking and longer life is causal. In the final analysis it may turn out that moderate drinkers are a select group of individuals who have other characteristics such as above-average income and occupational levels which combine to lengthen their life. Likewise, people who abstain from alcohol may be those with rigid, maladaptive personalities. Such individuals have a shorter than average life expectancy. Furthermore, the group of abstainers may include former alcoholics who have already damaged their liver, and it may include those with a genetic predisposition to alcoholism. Such genes may also shorten life. All of the statements to explain the relationships between moderate drinking or abstaining and longevity are hypothetical. The only certain thing at this point is that the relationship exists.

Regular physical activity is clearly an activity one can engage in to extend life. The activity must be undertaken frequently rather than just on weekends. A minimum of three exercise periods a week lasting a minimum of a half hour are recommended by exercise physiologists (deVries, 1983).

There are a number of reasons that exercise seems to be related to long life. For one thing, activity affects a number of the organ systems in the body as discussed in Chapter 5. The effect is particularly beneficial to the cardiovascular system. Cardiac output improves as a result of regular exercise, and circulation is improved. Even if a person suffers a heart attack, he or she has a better chance of surviving the heart attack if they exercise.

While activity does not change the level of cholesterol in the blood, it does change the amount of cholesterol laid down in the arteries. Thus, the arteries are less clogged in individuals who exercise. Exercise makes the body more adaptive to all kinds of stressors, including accidents and falls. Reflexes slow less in people who exercise. Strength is also affected, and this may prevent injuries from accidents and falls which injure and kill many older adults. Exercise also facilitates relaxation. A brisk 15-minute walk relaxes an individual as much as does a tranquilizer (deVries & Adams, 1972).

Another way of being inactive is to sleep too much. In very large studies of a number of factors related to longevity, it has been found that people who sleep ten or more hours a day die younger. The studies showed that optimal life expectancy occurred in people who stated that they got seven hours of sleep per night. People who slept very little (less than five hours was particularly bad, while less than six hours showed only a slightly increased risk) also died younger (Hammond, 1964). The reasons for these relationships have not been fully determined. In addition to the inactivity caused by too much sleep, those who sleep a lot may be in poor health or depressed and thus more likely to die younger. The stress of too little sleep may compound the problems of people who are tense and anxious and thus be related to a shorter life expectancy.

The activity and stimulation you get from sexual intimacy appear to extend your life. While there have been no studies demonstrating that humans who engaged in sexual activity lived longer, few studies of older people have provided suggestive evidence that those who continued to engage in sex lived longer. In animals, experiments have shown that sexual activity is effective in lengthening life. Indeed, if we were to interpolate the number of years added to human life from the number of months added to rats' lives due to sexual activity, we would gain 12 years from regular sexual activity! In Chapter 7 we will discuss the research on sex and longevity, pointing out the benefits to quality as well as length of life.

Preventive medicine is stressed in question 16 on the Life Expectancy Test regarding annual physical examinations. Many diseases, particularly cancer, are most successfully treated when they are detected early. By visiting a physician once a year to check on health, an individual prevents any disease from progressing gradually to the point where it can no longer be treated. Practicing preventive medicine extends life expectancy.

Education, Occupation, and Longevity

The reasons that people with more education live longer are complex. Simply going to school for a greater number of years is not what causes people to live longer. However, education does determine to a great degree what occupation an individual will have. And, of course, occupation affects income.

Socioeconomic status is determined by education, occupation, and income. People of higher socioeconomic status live longer because they have more advantages. They can purchase better health care, better housing and food, and they work at jobs which involve less risk. Their lives may be stressed in far fewer ways than the lives of people of low socioeconomic status. Additionally, people who get more education may be brighter to begin with and have a genetic potential for greater longevity.

Success is associated with longer life, and brighter people are more successful. Thus, regardless of education and occupation, if a person is successful at what he or she does, that person will live longer. Unsuccessful people often die prematurely.

Physical and mental activity appear to extend life. Those who are inactive on the job or who are forced into inactivity as a result of retirement seem to live a shorter time than those who stay active. However, it is not true that retirement causes death in individuals. Many people retire because of poor health. Their poor health precedes rather than results from retirement. On the other hand, forced retirement in healthy individuals who enjoy their jobs is a source of extreme stress, and it may cause some individuals to lose interest in life and die at a younger age.

Life Style, Health, and Longevity

Stressors such as pollution and crime are far greater in the city than in the country, and these and other factors contribute to the two-year life expectancy difference between rural and urban dwellers. The pace of life is slower in the country, and it is much easier to be physically active there. More jobs in the country involve physical activities. Nutrition may also be better as people living in the country have easier access to fresh fruits and vegetables.

Just as environmental stresses shorten life, there are also social and psychological stresses which influence health and longevity. Change is stressful, and although change and adaptation to change are critical to life, too much change impairs health. Holmes and Rahe have demonstrated that a great deal of change in the preceding year is associated with a greater amount of serious illness, accidents, and health change of any kind (Holmes & Holmes, 1974; Holmes & Rahe, 1967; Rahe et al., 1964).

One stress clearly documented to impair health and shorten life is living alone. Whether an individual is single or formerly married, if he or she lives alone, life expectancy is shorter. Being married appears to protect an individual against stress. Close friends also serve as a buttress against stress, and people who like others and who are able to develop intimate personal friendships are happier in old age and seem to live longer.

The most extensive research relating personal behavior patterns to life expectancy has been done in San Francisco by cardiologists Meyer Friedman and Ray Rosenman (1974). These physicians developed the concept of the Type A behavior pattern which involves a high-pressured, aggressive, hostile personality and a much greater risk for coronary heart disease. Type B individuals, who enjoy life and are much more concerned about the quality of their lives than they are about the material marks of success, live longer and are to be emulated according to Friedman and Rosenman.

Other dangerous personality traits are tendencies toward risk taking and depression. Such traits lead people to die in accidents, or through suicide and homicide (the fourth, eighth, and twelfth leading causes of death, respectively). Those who are adaptable and easygoing are longer-lived, while rigid, dogmatic people die at an earlier than average age.

The personality quality that has been identified as characteristic of centenarians is happiness. Very long-lived people are more likely to say that their lives have been worth living and that they would do it all over again in just about the same way. They have self-respect and self-esteem, they feel needed, and they are still happy to be alive. The special thing about centenarians seems to be the quality, not the quantity, of their lives.

SUMMARY

Longevity is not often addressed as a topic in psychology and aging, although it has many important implications for psychologists. Many of the changes individuals must make in their lives to maximize their life expectancy involve psychological motivation and attitudes.

Life expectancy is personalized in this chapter by presenting the Life Expectancy Test in which the reader estimates his or her own individualized life expectancy. Thirty-two factors are identified in the categories of heredity and family, health, education and occupation, and life style which affect longevity, and the way these factors affect life expectancy is explained. Most of the data we have on factors related to human life expectancy are correlational. This means that we are not certain if there are direct causal relationships between the 32 factors identified. The evidence we do have suggests that three major factors in human life expectancy about which we can do something are smoking, weight, and exercise. Smoking and being overweight shortens our life and impairs our health, while exercising improves health and longevity.

The life tables document that the longer an individual lives, the longer total life span that individual will have. An infant born in 1985 has a 75-year life expectancy, but a 65-year old in 1985 will live on average to the age of 82 years. Sex and race differences in life expectancy are also notable on the life tables. Women outlive men by seven years, and whites outlive blacks by close to six years. Biological sex differences probably account for much of the seven-year difference in life expectancy between men and women. In particular, the female hormones appear to protect women from cardiovascular disease, the number one cause of death in the United States. Advances in health care such as treatment for breast and ovarian cancer have tended to help women more than men. The racial difference in life expectancy is undoubtedly the result of the lower socioeconomic status of the average black person.

Hereditary and family influences on longevity include a relationship between long-lived parents and grandparents and long life and the shortening of life if heritable diseases run in the family. The oldest living American, Florence Knapp who is 114 years old, is presented as an excellent example of a member of a long-lived family.

Intelligence is also partly inherited, and high intelligence is associated with long life. Other family factors affecting longevity include mother's age at the birth of the child and birth order. Offspring live longer if they were born during a woman's prime childbearing years, and first borns live longer than later-born children.

The worst things an individual can do in the health category are to be overweight and to smoke. Together these two factors can subtract several decades from life expectancy. Eating healthy foods and drinking moderately, on the other hand, add years to life expectancy. Regular exercise is exceedingly beneficial to health and longevity. Sexual activity is another positive correlate with living longer. Sleeping six to eight hours per night and having regular medical examinations are additional prudent health habits which correlate with long life.

People of higher socioeconomic status live longer. Thus, the more education an individual has, the higher the status of his or her occupational level, and the greater the income, the more likely he or she is to realize the genetic potential for longevity.

Life style affects longevity in a number of ways. Living a rural environment gives a slight edge in life expectancy. Being married is especially beneficial to the life expectancy of men, but it also adds years to women's lives. Living with others as a single person is helpful for men. Having friends, avoiding stress, having a relaxed and flexible personality, avoiding depression, and being basically positive and happy are psychological characteristics of individuals who live longer.

REFERENCES

AUERBACH, S. (1977).   Women increase age gap. *Philadelphia Inquirer,* Janaury 11.

DEVRIES, H. A. (1983).   Physiology of exercise and aging. In D. S. Woodruff & J. E. Birren (Eds.), *Aging: Scientific perspectives and social issues* (2nd Ed.), Monterey, CA: Brooks/Cole.

DEVRIES, H. A. & ADAMS, G. M. (1972).   Electromyographic comparison of single doses of exercise and meprobamate as to effects on muscular relaxation. *American Journal of Physical Medicine, 51,* 130–141.

DRORI, D. & FOLMAN, Y. (1976).   Environmental effects on longevity in the male rat: Exercise, mating, castration, and restricted feeding. *Experimental Gerontology, 11,* 25–32.

FINCH, C. E. & HAYFLICK L. (Eds.) (1977).   *Handbook of the biology of aging.* New York: Van Nostrand Reinhold.

FINCH, C. E. & HAYFLICK, L. (Eds.) (1985).   *Handbook of the biology of aging* (2nd Ed.), New York: Van Nostrand Reinhold.

FRIEDMAN, M. & ROSENMAN, R. H. (1974).   *Type A behavior and your heart.* New York: Knopf.

FRIES, J. F. (1987).   Life expectancy. In G. L. Maddox (Ed). *The encyclopedia of aging.* New York: Springer.

HAMILTON, J. B. & MESTLER, G. E. (1969).   Mortality and survival: Comparison of eunuchs with intact men and women in a mentally retarded population. *Journal of Gerontology, 24,* 395–411.

HAMMOND, E. C. (1964).   Some preliminary findings on physical complaints from a prospective study of 1,064,004 men and women. *American Journal of Public Health, 54,* 11–23.

HOLMES, T. H. & HOLMES, T. S. (1974).   How change can make us ill. *Stress: A Report form Blue Cross and Blue Shield of Greater New York, 25,* 66–75.

HOLMES, T. H. & RAHE, R. H. (1967).   The social readjustment rating scale. *Journal of Psychosomatic Research, 11,* 213–218.

KITAGAWA, E. M. & HAUSER, P. M. (1973).   *Differential mortality in the United States: A study in socioeconomic epidemiology.* Cambridge, MA: Harvard University Press.

MADIGAN, F. C. (1957).   Are sex mortality differentials biologically caused? *Milbank Memorial Fund Quarterly, 35,* 202–223.

MADIGAN, F. C. & VANCE, R. B. (1957).   Differential sex mortality: A reserarch design. *Social Forces, 35,* 193–199.

METROPOLITAN LIFE INSURANCE COMPANY. (1975).   Socioeconomic mortality differentials. *Statistical Bulletin, 56,* 3–5.

METROPOLITAN LIFE INSURANCE COMPANY. (1983).   Height and weight tables. New York: Metropolitan Life Insurance Company.

NATIONAL CENTER FOR HEALTH STATISTICS. (1986a).   Advance report of final mortality statistics, 1984. *Monthly Vital Statistics Report,* Vol. 35, No. 6 Supp. (2). DHHS Pub. No. (PHS) 86–1120, September 26.

NATIONAL CENTER FOR HEALTH STATISTICS. (1986b).   *Vital statistics of the United States, 1983,* Vol. II, Sec. 6, Life Tables. DHHS Pub. No. (PHS) 86–1104.

RAHE, R. H., MEYER, M., SMITH, M., KJAER, G., & HOLMES, T. H. (1964).   Social stresses and illness onset. *Journal of Psychosomatic Research, 8,* 35–44.

ROSE, C. L. & BELL, B. (1971).   *Predicting longevity.* Lexington, MA: D. C. Health.

RUTHERFORD, R. D. (1972).   Tobacco smoking and the sex mortality differential. *Demography, 9,* 203–216.

SPIEGELMAN, M. (1966).   *Significant mortality and morbidity trends in the U.S. since 1900.* Bryn Mawr, PA: American College of Life Underwriters.

UNITED NATIONS. (1982).   *Demographic yearbook: 1982.* New York: United Nations.

WOODRUFF, D. S. (1977).   *Can you live to be 100?* New York: Chatham Square Press.

ZOPF, P. E., Jr. (1986).   *America's older population.* Houston: Cap and Gown Press.

CHAPTER 7

Sexuality and Aging

As individuals develop and age, they become more complex and diverse. One of the greatest differentiating factors in human behavior is the capacity for sexual activity. In human adults sexual activity ranges from celibacy to intimacy with many sexual partners. As people develop and age, their capacity and interest for sexual activity show a remarkable range. In sexual behavior there are important changes with age. Our discussion will include aspects of sex differences in aging, but human sexuality will be the focus of this chapter. We will discuss sex differences in behavior in aging primarily as they affect sexual behavior. We will begin by discussing age changes in the reproductive and endocrine systems which affect sexual behavior.

AGING IN THE REPRODUCTIVE AND ENDOCRINE SYSTEMS

Age changes occur in the auxiliary reproductive organs in men and women which are especially apparent after the age of 60. In women the vagina contracts in size and the epithelium lining of the vaginal wall becomes pale, thin, and dry as a result of lower levels of circulating estrogen. A consequence for sexual activity is that there is less lubrication of the vagina, and older women are more likely to experience discomfort during intercourse. This problem can be ameliorated with the external application of lubricants. The external female genitalia, the vulva, change in appearance as estrogen level is reduced. The labial folds flatten, and pubic hair and subcutaneous fat are lost. Vulvitis, infection and inflammation of the vulva, is a common complaint of elderly women.

In men over the age of 60 years, the prostate, seminal vesicles, and bulbo-urethral glands all show regressive changes. The weight of the prostate increases by 100 percent by the seventh to eighth decades. Secretory activity is seriously reduced by these changes after the age of 60. Usually the changes in the prostate are benign, but they can also be malignant. Surgery is often required whether the changes in the prostate are benign or malignant because the bladder is affected. The result is difficulty in urination.

Changes in the penis occur beginning in the third and fourth decade of a man's life. The arteries and veins begin to harden at this time, and the erectile tissue also begins to harden. By the time a man is 55 to 60 years of age, the harden-ing has become more generalized. It has been suggested that sexual impotence in-volving failure of erection in older men may be related to this progressive hardening in both penile blood vessels and erectile tissue (Rockstein & Sussman, 1979).

The hormones secreted by the endocrine system which are involved in human sexuality are primarily estrogen in women and testosterone in men. The levels of these hormones circulating in the blood are reduced in aging.

Menopause occurs in women as early as the forties, although in many women it occurs in the fifties. The menopause begins when women show irregular menses and reduced fertility. While estrogen concentration of the blood decreases, blood levels of luteinizing hormone and follicle-stimulating hormone reciprocally increase. The premenstrual state of the uterus lining becomes less and less fully developed. Eventually menstruation ceases to occur. After menopause has begun, it usually takes two to three years for the process to be completed. During this period the woman experiences irregular menses, follicular exhaustion, failure of ova produc-tion, and eventually, the permanent cessation of menstrual activity. Some women have what are called "hot flashes" during this time. They feel overheated, sweaty, and flushed. However, most women report little discomfort during the menopause, and many feel relieved that they no longer need to concern themselves with avoiding pregnancy.

In men 20 to 39 years old, about 90 percent of the sperm-producing tubules in the testes are functional. By the time men are 50 to 70 years old, the percentage of functional sperm-producing tubules has decreased to 50 percent. Only 10 percent are functional after the age of 80. Thus, fertility declines in men over the age range of 40 to 80 years, but men are still capable of having children even very late in life. The percentage of viable spermatozoa is high in older men. Indeed, there are men in the seventies and eighties fathering children, and in one case a 94-year-old man fathered a child (Rockstein & Sussman, 1979).

The circulating level of testosterone does not change much until men are in the sixth decade. While women experience a rather dramatic decline in estrogen levels in mid-life, there is no such counterpart for men in mid-life. Testosterone level changes for men in the age range of 20 to 90 are shown in Table 7.1. While the level of testosterone in the eighth to ninth decade is only 40 percent of the circulating level of a mature to middle-aged man, the decline has been gradual.

TABLE 7.1 Plasma Testosterone Levels by Age in Men

Age (years)	Ng./100 Ml. Plasma
20–50	633 + 25
50–60	582 + 62
60–70	462 + 70
70–80	373 + 46
80–90	245 + 26

Source: Adapted with permission from Talbert, G. B. (1977). Aging of the reproductive system. In C. E. Finch and L. Hayflick, eds., *Handbook of the biology of aging.* New York: Van Nostrand Reinhold. p. 345.

Significant age changes occur in the reproductive and endocrine systems which affect sexual activity in later life. However, these changes are not so dramatic as to prevent sexual activity. Some of the changes such as the loss of fertility in women after the menopause result in greater sexual freedom. Sexual activity has always been associated with good health and long life. We will now examine the relationship between sexual activity and longevity.

SEXUAL ACTIVITY
AND LONGEVITY

We presented evidence in Chapter 6 that the sex hormones, testosterone and estrogen, are associated with sex differences in longevity. It was also mentioned in that chapter that sexual activity affects longevity. In this chapter we will discuss sexual activity and longevity. The evidence documenting the relationship between sexual activity and longevity is not as clear as we would like it to be. However, the Abkhasians of the Soviet Union who include in their numbers a disproportionate number of long-lived people, expect to enjoy sex into their eighties and nineties, and they apparently do. Indeed, the story has been reported (Benet, 1974) of an elderly gentleman in Abkhasia who became enraged when his daughter told his prospective bride that he was 108 years old rather than 95 as he claimed. The father was angry because it is believed in Abkhasia that a man is capable of sexual activity until he is 100 years old. After that he is considered to be getting old. The bridegroom obviously planned to consummate his marriage.

Since continuing to be active is one of the primary correlates of longevity and since maintaining an interest and a role in life is characteristic of centenarians, it is likely that research in the future will identify continued sexual activity as a factor in long life. However, at the present time, no conclusive evidence for this exists in studies of humans.

The evidence linking sexual activity to longevity is correlational in humans, or it is based on subhuman species. For example, individuals who are married live longer than those who never marry or who are divorced or widowed. Those who are living with a partner probably have more opportunity for sexual activity than those who are single, divorced or widowed. Since married people live longer than unmarried individuals, some of the additional time married people live may result from their continued sexual activity. On the other hand, there are a number of factors in addition to sexual activity which contributes to the correlation between marital status and long life (Woodruff, 1977).

Indian and Chinese sages advocated sex and believed that sexual activity was the means to eternal youth. As noted in Chapter 1 in the discussion of the history of gerontology, some of the remedies for old age and potions for long life involved attempts to return sexual vigor. Western writers, in contrast, have historically taken the position that sexual excess has harmful consequences. At the present time, experts agree that "excess" in sexual activity is not a useful concept due to the tremendous range of individual variation in sexual capacity and interest (McCary, 1973).

In 1964, long before writing about the joys of sex, Alex Comfort suggested that the Indians and Chinese rather than the Western monks were correct. Regularly mated rats stay in far better health than rats which are prevented from mating. Furthermore, Comfort (1964) wryly remarked that what was true of rats was also true of clergymen.

Studies comparing the mortality rates of Anglican and other Protestant clergy who marry to the mortality rates of Roman Catholic clergy who take vows of celibacy indicated that the married clergy died at rates much lower than the population average (Anglican and Protestant clergy's mortality rates were 69 percent and 74 percent, respectively, of the national average). The celibate clergy had shorter than average life expectancies (Roman Catholic clergy had mortality rates 105 percent of the national average). While these data along with data comparing life expectancies of married and unmarried individuals are undoubtedly confounded with factors apart from sexual activity, such data make it appear that the virtues of sexual abstinence, at least as they relate to longevity, have been misrepresented by the moralists.

Authors of the Victorian age were influenced by prevailing social mores to conclude that more than a little sexual activity shortened life expectancy. Authors of the 1960s and 1970s, living in an era of sexual freedom, favored evidence suggesting that sexual activity leads to greater longevity. In the late 1980s we must again return to a more conservative stance about indiscriminate sexual activity due to acquired immune deficiency syndrome (AIDS). While sexual activity with a lifelong partner is associated with longer life, sexual activity with many partners increases the risk for AIDS, thus shortening life expectancy.

The most conclusive evidence on the relationship between sexual activity and longevity comes from animal studies. As early as 1939, research indicated that sexual intercourse increased resistance of male and female rats, mice, and rabbits to toxic substances (Comfort, 1964). At that time, it was believed that testosterone and estrogen had antitoxic effects and that the vitality of mated animals resulted from increased levels of sex hormones. Research discussed earlier on the effects of castration in animals and humans has indicated that the male hormone, testosterone, may be negatively related to longevity. However, high levels of testosterone in male rats cause them to be physically and sexually active. This physical activity resulted in the rats living longer.

In 1969 Drori and Folman had shown that the mean life span of male rats allowed to mate at least weekly was significantly longer than that of their litter mates who were not allowed access to female rats. In the group allowed to mate there was a much higher level of circulating testosterone. Why did these rats live longer if high levels of testosterone shorten life expectancy? Drori and Folman (1969) hypothesized that testosterone is associated with increased activity, and it is the increased activity or exercise that affects longevity.

In a subsequent study, Drori and Folman (1976) demonstrated that mating probably increases longevity by increasing voluntary exercise. They compared mated rats with rats unmated but exercised two minutes daily. Also included in this study were groups of rats which were castrated, groups which were underfed, and groups which received no treatment (including no access to female rats). The exercised rats lived as long as the mated rats. Mating appeared to induce even more exercise than engaged in by the exercised group, and both the mated and the exercised groups had a reduced incidence of pneumonia. The pulmonary systems of these two groups of rats were affected positively. Thus, while circulating testosterone may have deleterious effects on longevity, these effects may be balanced by the activity-inducing properties of the hormone. These data imply that the source of the activity, be it sexual or physical exercise, is not important. The activity itself is the significant factor.

It is simply not valid to interpolate the results of animal studies to humans, but there are extensive data from studies on humans indicating that activity is essential to long life. Hence, we might surmise that the Drori and Folman (1969, 1976) studies provide a means for many of us to extend our lives, either through sexual activity or physical activity.

The prescription of activity, including sexual activity, applies to adults at all points of the life span. Activity in the sixties, seventies, eighties, and beyond is at least as important as it was in earlier periods of life. Unfortunately, many recoil at the thought of sexual activity late in life. It is unfortunate that this dimension of life is abandoned by some people as they age because they (or their physicians) feel that it is unnatural.

SEXUAL ACTIVITY OVER
THE LIFE SPAN

In Abkhasia where there are a disproportionate number of long-lived people in the population, sex is considered a good and pleasurable thing and is guiltless. Sexual matters are extremely private, and young people are encouraged to postpone sexual gratification not as a matter of frustration but as a hopeful expectation of future enjoyment. This is because a continuation of sex into old age is considered as natural as maintaining a healthy appetite or sound sleep (Benet, 1974).

Sexual attitudes have a tremendous impact on the appeal of sex. Whether sex is viewed as pleasurable and matter-of-fact or as sinful and dangerous is determined in part by attitudes formed in childhood. The openness and honesty expressed by contemporary adolescents toward sexual matters suggest that the sexual revolution has been occurring in the United States for several generations. Indeed, it was by the cohorts over the age of 65 today that the sexual revolution in the United States was initiated. This assertion may seem surprising in light of birth control techniques such as the Pill and IUDs which only became widely available in the 1960s. However, while we tend to associate increased sexual activity with younger generations, some of the greatest changes in attitudes along with the acceptance of premarital sexual activity were prompted in the 1920s during the youth of contemporary older cohorts.

The youth of the 1980s have grown up in an atmosphere of less sexual repression than did their parents, who in turn were raised by a generation rebelling against the repression of the Victorian or post-Victorian era. Given the values of contemporary youth emphasizing the importance of affection and maturity in sexual relationships, future generations in the United States may be less likely to experience the guilt and anxiety over sexual matters which still sometimes expresses itself in the behavior and attitudes of middle-aged and aged cohorts. Coupled with a mature outlook in contemporary youth is a growing awareness of the risk of promiscuity due to AIDS.

Sexual activity appears to peak early in life, usually during the first few years of marriage when an interested and available partner is present. The pioneering research of Dr. Alfred Kinsey was among the first to document age differences in frequency of intercourse (Kinsey, Pomeroy & Martin, 1948; Kinsey, Pomeroy, Martin & Gebhard, 1953). These cross-sectional data are presented in Figure 7.1, and they suggest that differences in male patterns of sexual activity pace age differences for both men and women. Both single and married men have fewer orgasms in each successive decade. The age difference for single women is minimal.

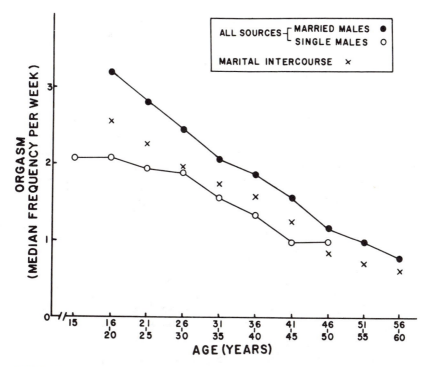

FIGURE 7.1   Age and the median frequency of orgasms per week for men. Orgasms from all (six) sources include marital intercourse. Source: Kinsey, A. C., Pomeroy, W. B. & Martin, C. E. (1948). *Sexual behavior in the human male*. Philadelphia: W. B. Saunders. Reprinted by permission.

Additional cross-sectional and longitudinal studies have supported the cross-sectional picture of decline first presented by Kinsey (e.g., Masters & Johnson, 1966, 1970; Pfeiffer & Davis, 1972; Pfeiffer, Verwoerdt & Davis, 1972; Pfeiffer, Verwoerdt & Wang, 1968, 1969; Verwoerdt, Pfeiffer & Wang, 1969a, 1969b). However, a recent extension of the longitudinal investigations using the Duke sample suggested that sexual activity may remain stable in middle adulthood and old age and then cease abruptly (George & Weiler, 1981).

Weiler (1981) attempts to make a strong case that just as the asexual older person and the sexually dysfunctional older person were myths of the past, the notion of gradual decline in sexual functioning is a myth of present research on sexuality and aging. The picture presented by Weiler is based on one six-year follow up of the Duke sample previously reported on in shorter periods of data analysis by Pfeiffer, Verwoerdt, Wang and their colleagues. Whether the accurate age function is one of gradual decline or whether it is one of stability with abrupt decline is simply not clear at the present time. While George and Weiler's (1981) analysis represents the longest longitudinal study of age and sexuality, six years of longitudinal data in one sample is hardly sufficient to define a norm for the population.

The prevailing picture of sexual function in old age is one of gradual decline which is paced by the decline in performance by the man. At the present time it is thought that a married woman's decline in frequency of orgasm results from age changes in her husband's sexual patterns, as her own sexual capacity continues to increase until mid-life. Indeed, there is evidence that frequency of orgasm for sexually active women increases in each decade of life through the eighties (Starr & Weiner, 1981). An important point made by many counselors and therapists as well as older people themselves is that sexual activity need not be assessed solely on the basis of number of orgasms. There are many components to sexual activity, and there are few limitations to most of these components as individuals age.

In a questionnaire survey of 800 older Americans living in communities throughout the country, Starr and Weiner (1981) identified a number of alternatives to intercourse cited as important by the respondents. Many women facing the problem of sexually inactive partners were willing to accept alternatives to genital intercourse including oral sex. Survey results also suggested that a significant number of older women would consider other means of sexual satisfaction, including masturbation, "sharing" of men, lesbianism and taking younger lovers.

Touching, stroking and kissing were described by those surveyed as important and stimulating aspects of sexuality. However, orgasm was ranked by three fourths of those surveyed as important to a good sexual experience, and many said that simultaneous orgasm was preferred. Masturbation was an acceptable means of sexual satisfaction to 85 percent, though far fewer said that they masturbated. As an enjoyable form of sexual activity, 15 percent spontaneously mentioned oral sex with many ranking it as their favorable sexual experience.

A major limiting factor for older adults in experiencing sexual activity is the availability of a partner. This is especially true for women. Widowers tend to remarry within two years of the death of their spouse, and older men have the availability of the large population of widowed, divorced, and single older women (Starr, 1987). After the age of 65, there are four single women for every single man. Indeed, some widowed older men are overwhelmed by the atteniton they get from their many single female friends.

In contrast to popular myth, when asked to describe the "ideal lover," most of the men and women who specified an age portrayed someone within ten years of their own age. Only 6 percent (and more men than women) said that their ideal was a considerably younger lover.

Another surprising result was that the attitudes of surveyed elderly were quite liberal in terms of their acceptance of nudity. They had little self-consciousness about their aging bodies and little anxiety about the decline of sexuality as they aged. Nearly two thirds of the group and three fourths of those who still reported being sexually active asserted that their lovemaking had actually improved with the years. Among the aspects about sex that those over 60 found more satisfying were: improved techniques making them better lovers, greater appreciation of sex, greater feelings of freedom with no fear of pregnancy, no concern for children's interruption, possibility for having sex at various times during the day, and reduced financial and work pressures (Brecher, 1984; Starr & Weiner, 1981).

Sexual Problems in Middle Age

While many individuals enjoy an active sex life throughout middle and old age, it is in mid-life that individuals often experience their first problems with sexuality (McCary, 1973). Women during this period of their life span are still close to the peak point of their sexual potential, and many women report an increase in sexual interest either because they incorrectly assume that they may soon lose sexual satisfaction with the onset of menopause or because they are relieved not to have to worry about unwanted pregnancy. At the peak of their careers in middle age, men may be less interested in sexual activity and may experience impotence for the first time.

Impotence. The inability for men to have an erection during intercourse increases in incidence during middle age. Masters and Johnson (1970) reported that after the age of 50, the incidence of sexual inadequacy increases dramatically in men. This is not normally due to physiological age changes such as hardening of the penile blood vessels and erectile tissue which is moderate in middle age. Nor is it usually the result of the gradual reduction in testosterone level with age. Impotence in middle-aged men appears to be largely caused by social and psychological factors.

Masters and Johnson (1970) listed six major factors implicated in male impotence:

1. Monotony of a repetitious sexual relationship
2. Preoccupation with career or economic pursuits
3. Mental or physical fatigue
4. Overindulgence in food or drink
5. Physical and mental incapacities of the individual or his spouse
6. Fear of poor performance resulting from any one or combination of the other categories

While there are physical changes occurring in both the male and female which make their sexual responses slower and of less magnitude, these slight and gradual declines can in no way account for the inability to maintain an erection or achieve orgasm.

Menopause. Menopause occurs in the middle-aged female as a dramatic sign that her reproductive years have ended. It is probably the symbolic significance of the menopause that has the most impact on a woman rather than the slight physical discomfort she may experience. Research suggests, however, that even the stressful psychological aspects of menopause are overrated.

Between the ages of 45 and 50 in most women, the menstrual cycle ends and estrogen and progesterone are no longer produced by the ovaries. Since satisfying sexual activity is not affected by estrogen and progesterone levels, sexual pleasure need not decline after menopause; and as mentioned previously, some women experience an increase in sexual interest and activity at this point as they no longer are anxious about pregnancy. The physical symptoms of menopause include hot flashes, breast pains, dizzy spells, headaches, and heart palpitations. The incidence of these symptoms varies among individual women. Depression or anxiety reported by some women do not appear to be inevitable consequences of menopause, as many women are free from such symptoms according to research carried out by Neugarten (1967).

Physical changes such as loss of elasticity of the skin, hot flashes, appearance of facial hair, and changes in the breasts and genitals can be retarded by treatment with estrogen. While many specialists advocate the use of estrogen therapy to retard physical aging in appearance and function, others warn of the danger of increased incidence of cancer. Estrogen replacement also appears to prevent the loss of bone mass which occurs in older women. The risk of osteoporosis without estrogen replacement may be greater than the risk of cancer with estrogen replacement therapy. Women and their physicians should be aware of the benefits of estrogen replacement, but they must also be alerted to the potential danger of this treatment. Additional research is underway to evaluate more clearly the relative costs and benefits of estrogen replacement therapy.

Neugarten and her associates studied the attitudes of women of various ages toward menopause. Results indicated that half of the middle-class women in the sample had extremely negative attitudes toward this change while the other half had more favorable attitudes (Neugarten, Wood, Kraines, & Loomis, 1963). Women beyond the age of 45 (who had presumably experienced menopause) saw more favorable aspects of this period than did younger women. The older women and women of all ages who were better educated also saw the change as less stressful, suggesting that the more that is known about menopause, the fewer problems it creates. Women reported that one of the worst things about menopuase was not knowing what to expect. Also rated as negative aspects were the pain and discomfort and the indication that one was getting older. Most felt that menopause had no effect on sexual relations or on physical and mental health.

While most men do not expereince an analog to menopause in women, men probably experience a climacterium or decrease in reproductive ability late in life when fertile sperm are no longer produced. The rapid decrease in hormone level experienced by women during menopause is responsible for some of the physical symptoms of that period, and Reubsaat and Hull (1975) have reported analogous symptoms in about 10 to 15 percent of men in their mid to late fifties or early sixties. It appears that in this small proportion of men there is a rapid rather than a gradual drop in hormone level, and men who experience this rapid hormone drop experience physical and sometimes psychological discomfort. Hot flashes, dizziness, and depression have been reported by men with this syndrome. Thus, while there is no male menopause involving both the loss of reproductive capacity and the rapid decline of hormones, some men do experience a rapid drop in hormone level (unrelated to the later occurring climacterium), leading them to experience symptoms similar to the symptoms of menopausal women.

Sexual Activity in Old Age

There are a great number of misconceptions about sex in old age held by most laymen, and unfortunately, by many physicians as well. Recent emphasis on sex education may be affecting public awareness of sexual potential in old age.

In the 1950s a study was carried out at Brandeis University to determine students' attitudes about sex and aging (Golde & Kogan, 1959). Students were asked to complete the sentence, "Sex for old people is...." The responses included pessimistic answers such as "unimportant," "past," and "negligible." More recent surveys involving students in gerontology classes taught by the author at the University of Southern California and at Temple University led to a more positive picture. Students polled in the 1970s were unanimous in the acknowledgment that sex continues to play an important role in the lives of old people. Students completed the sentence, "Sex for old people is...." with descriptions such as: "fine;" "important and gratifying;" "good;" "fun;" "a matter of personal ability, attitude and opportunity;" "as important as it is for people of all ages for psychological well being. It depends upon individual needs and appetite;" "whatever they want to make it;" "great if they are both capable of doing it;" "out of sight;" "not necessarily different than for younger people;" "still a part of life and since they are still alive, it's cool."

Such data are encouraging not only because they reflect positive attitudes about aging but because they indicate that future generations of elderly people may have more active and enjoyable sex lives. It appears that the best correlate of sexual activity in old age is the pattern of sexual activity in earlier years. Thus, healthy attitudes about sex in old age decrease the probability of a self-fulfilling prophecy.

Butler (1975) pointed out that those individuals who have a positive attitude about sex and who derive sexual satisfaction in early life will have the best chance to enjoy a rich sex life when they are old. With aging there is a gradual slowing of response, especially in men. Butler and Lewis (1976) viewed this as a process currently described as part of "normal" aging, but perhaps itself eventually amenable to treatment and reversal. A pattern of regular sexual activity, or at least self-stimulation, helps to preserve sexual functioning in both men and women (Butler & Lewis, 1976).

Butler (1975) pointed out that when sexual problems do occur among older people, they should be viewed as the result of physical disease, disability or emotional upset requiring careful diagnosis and treatment to restore functioning. There are several common factors which affect sexuality in old people. These include:

Heart disease. When older people have heart disease and especially if a heart attack has occurred, many older people give up on sex altogether for fear of provoking another attack. According to Butler and Lewis (1976) the incidence of death during sexual intercourse is thought to be very low. They assert that sex usually can and in many cases should be resumed on the average 16 weeks after a heart attack, depending on physical conditioning. An active sex life may in fact decrease the risk of further attack. One test to determine readiness for sex according to Butler and Lewis (1976) is whether or not a person can walk vigorously for three blocks, or climb one or two flights of stairs without pain, abnormal pulse rate or blood pressure, or electrocardiogram changes.

Anemia. One of the most common and easily treated sexual problems is caused by anemia. Found in some form in one out of four persons over 60, anemia leads to fatigue and often a reduction in sexual activity. An improved diet with adequate vitamins and minerals will frequently restore both energy and sexual activity.

Other physical problems. There are a number of other physically debilitating illnesses and surgical procedures likely to occur in middle or old age which impede sexual function. Diabetes and prostatectomy affect male sexuality, and mastectomy, hysterectomy, oophorectomy, and urinary infections may affect sexual function in women; colostomy and ileostomy affect body image and sexuality in both men and women. These problems and their treatment are discussed by Solnick and Corby (1983)

Drugs. Tranquilizers, antidepressants and certain antihypertensive drugs are all problematic for sexual behavior. A doctor can sometimes prescribe a less sexually-inhibiting drug if he or she realizes it is important to the patient.

Alcohol. In excess, this drug reduces potency in men and delays orgasm in women. Butler and Lewis (1976) feel that it is probably the most widespread drug-related cause of sexual problems. In general, an older person should not have more than 1½ ounces of hard liquor, two 6-ounce glasses of wine, or three 8-ounce glasses of beer in any 24-hour period when sex is anticipated.

Emotional problems. The greatest of these is the fear of impotence. When a man is unduly alarmed by temporary impotency, or in the case of older men, by sensing a gradual slowing of sexual response, he may cause, or perpetrate the importance through fear alone. Older women tend to be worried more about the propriety of sex itself in their later lives. They may be the victims of negative stereotypes of old age which include sexual prohibitions. There can also be emotional problems between older sexual partners. They may be bored with one another, or there may be a change in emotional balance due to illness, the unrelenting intimacy of retirement, or simply the same problems that face couples of any age.

Masters and Johnson noted that psychological factors play at least as great a role as hormones in determining the sex drive of older individuals, yet misinformation about sex in the later years often exaggerates fears and misconceptions which sexually incapacitate the aging. There is an amazing amount of misinformation. For example, if intercourse is painful for an older women as a result of slight atrophy in her vulva and vagina, many physicians are apt to ask her what she expects at her age. Hormone therapy might alleviate these problems, but the physician does not consider the issue important enough to consider therapy.

Fortunately, training programs, conferences, and publications for physicians, sex counselors and psychotherapists are beginning to include the problems of older people, as well as those of the chronically ill and physically disabled of all ages who still maintain an interest in sex. Even some nursing homes are relaxing their puritanical standards by introducing "privacy rooms" where older people can be alone together. There is a growing recognition and provision for the fact that romance and sex are still a vital concern for some nursing home residents.

One of the most important features of an active sex life in old age is having an interesting and interested partner. A portion of the Duke Longitudinal Study involved assessment of sexual activity and attitudes in participants. In this longitudinal study of 254 men and women aged 60 to 94, Pfeiffer, Verwoerdt, and Wang (1970) reported that 50 percent of the subjects in their sixties were still engaged in sexual activity and 10 to 20 percent of those in their eighties maintained sexual relations.

The drop in activity in the seventies was due in part to physical illness, but the availability of partners becomes an issue at this age as well. Women are particularly at a disadvantage because they usually outlive their husbands and have little chance of finding a partner. Thus, in addition to the social and economic constraints faced by widows, they also lose the opportunity for sexual interaction. Nevertheless, for those fortunate individuals to whom an active sexual partner is still available, there is no time limit drawn by the advancing years to their sexuality. Furthermore, the activity may extend their lives.

HOMOSEXUALITY AND AGING

Since sexuality is not often associated with old age, it is even less typical to think about homosexuality and aging. However, if the proportion of older gay men and lesbians parallels estimates for younger age groups, at least 10 percent of the elderly are homosexual (Kimmel, 1978). This means that there are close to 3 million gay men and women over the age of 65.

Aging is thought to be difficult for the homosexual, especially the homosexual male who achieves status and partners on the basis of his appearance and vigor (Harry & DeVall, 1978; Solnick & Corby, 1983). Homosexual males are stereotyped as being even more youth oriented than heterosexual males. Because of this supposed orientation to youth, they are stereotypically thought to have more negative views of aging and be more likely to label themselves as old earlier than heterosexual males. Thus, one perspective available on homosexuality and aging is that aging is especially stressful (Weinberg, 1970) and that aging homosexuals are lonely, isolated and despairing (Allen, 1961).

This negative view is called stereotypical because it may not fit all aging homosexual males. The initial studies on homosexuality and aging were carried out on the homosexuals who frequented gay bars where interactions emphasized casual sexual contact and where contacts were made on the basis of youth and physical attractiveness. The AIDS epidemic has threatened this life style and made it less likely that those homosexual men embracing this life style will ever reach old age. Gay men are the highest risk group for AIDS, and tens of thousands of them are dying in young adulthood. The cohorts of gay men that have been born after World War II have been dramatically reduced by AIDS. The percentage of these cohorts to reach the age of 50 years or older will be significantly less than their heterosexual counterparts.

Studies of aging homosexual males in ongoing relationships have also been reported. Friend (1980) interviewed 43 gay men aged 32 to 76, Kimmel (1979–80) interviewed 14 gay men over the age of 55, and Kelly (1977) interviewed 30 gay men over 65. Several themes emerged from these studies. One of the most important points is that like older heterosexuals, older gays are diverse in life style and in psychological well-being. The stereotypes generated in the studies of respondents in gay bars were not representative. The majority of respondents studied by Friend, Kimmel, and Kelly were not lonely, depressed or sexually frustrated. Apparently the experience of growing older as a homosexual has become less stressful since the gay rights movement began in 1969. However, there are some problems as well as some compensations specifically associated with the gay life style.

There are even fewer data available on homosexual women. Those data which were first available suggested that the sexual aging pattern is similar to the pattern of never-married women who tend to discontinue sexual activity early in their lives (Christenson & Johnson, 1973). A more recent study by Raphael and Robinson (1980) who interviewed 20 lesbian women over age 50 changes that perspective. The lesbians were more likely than gay men to be in sexually monogamous rela-tionships. Some lesbians reported feeling their menopause, some reported a decline in sexuality with aging, and several said that they were enthusiastic about sex whenever they had a good love relationship. They felt that any time they desired a sexual relationship they could have one. Furthermore, lesbian women were more likely than heterosexual women to find partners or mates in late-life, if desired (Kimmel, Raphael, Catalano, & Robinson, 1984). Support for this fact was found in a study by DeCecco, Kehoe, and Goldberg (1984) of 100 lesbians over the age of 60. These women were comfortable with their lesbianism and were in excellent mental and physical health. This is quite a contrast to older heterosexual women who are often frustrated due to the lack of available partners.

It has been suggested that one reason that homosexuals in the more recent studies are coping so well with aging may be that revealing their homosexual preference and withstanding the stress of the "coming out" toughened them and taught them new strength (Kimmel, 1979). Kimmel also suggested that those homosexuals who have come out and are willing to admit and discuss their sexual preferences may be better adjusted than homosexuals who would not volunteer for studies and who are unable or unwilling to admit or discuss their homosexuality.

In a comparison of aging for homosexuals and heterosexuals, Teitelman (1987) commented:

> Many of the service needs and aging experiences of homosexuals, then, are virtually indistinguishable from those of the total elderly population. the homosexual individual, however, may bring certain unique strengths and problems to old age that the nongay person does not possess. It is these aspects of gay and lesbian aging that must be accounted for if gerontological research is to be accurate, and service delivery appropriate. (Teitelman, 1987, p. 330).

Closing this chapter with a discussion of homosexuality and aging again points out the diversity in human sexuality. No one life style or sexual preference guarantees life satisfaction, but many different adaptations lead to adjustment and fulfillment. Indeed, in many cases aging brings greater sexual fulfillment to heterosexuals and homosexuals alike. The contemporary cohorts of the aged have been sexual revolutionaries at all points of their lives. They broke the ground for the sexual revolution of the 1920s and forced the cohorts older than they to accept their new values, and they are now forcing younger cohorts to give up the notion that sex is the exclusive domain of the young.

SUMMARY

This chapter has emphasized the diversity of sexual behavior in adults and the continued differentiation of sexual behavior in aging. Aging affects the reproductive and endocrine systems, but it does not necessarily diminish the enjoyment and need for sexual activity. In the forties or fifties in women, menopause occurs which marks the cessation of reproductive capacity. While some mild discomfort may occur during the two- to three-year period that the menopause is occurring, most women report little physical or psychological distress. Quite the contrary, most women are relieved that they no longer need to worry about getting pregnant. In men, age changes in the reproductive and endocrine systems are more gradual, and men can conceive children even into their eighth decade. Physical age changes include the hardening of penile vessels and erectile tissue beginning in the thirties which eventually make it more difficult to have an erection. Testosterone levels gradually decline to 40 percent of their young adult levels by the decade of the eighties.

Throughout history, sexual activity has been associated with longevity. Correlational studies in humans and experimental studies in animals indicate that sexual activity may indeed extend life expectancy. Married people live longer than their single and divorced counterparts, and married clergy live longer than celebate priests and nuns. Animals allowed access to sexual activity live longer than their sexually deprived littermates. In animals, physical activity may be the factor that mediates the relationship between sexual activity and longer life expectancy.

Sexual activity attains its highest frequency early in life, usually during the first few years of marriage. The gradual decline of sexual intercourse in later life appears to be paced by a decline in sexual capacity in the male partner. Sexually active women may actually increase their capacity for orgasm in each decade after the forties. However, older adults often achieve sexual satisfaction even without orgasm. Older women's greatest problem is the lack of available partners. There are four single women over the age of 65 for every single male.

Mid-life is when individuals often experience their first problem with sexuality. Impotency in men can result from monotony, preoccupation with a career, mental or physical fatigue, overindulgence in food or drink, physical and mental incapacities, or fear of performance. Menopause in women is not accompanied by any decline in sexual appetite, and indeed, the end of reproductive capacity may offer the women more sexual freedom.

Sexual activity in old age is best predicted by patterns of sexual behavior in earlier life. Sexually active individuals tend to remain sexually active, while those who have been less sexually active will continue that pattern into old age. Many older adults report that sex is even better after 60. They have had the opportunity to learn more techniques, they have more time to enjoy sex during the day as well as at night, they have more privacy and fewer worries than they did in middle age.

Perhaps 10 percent of adults over the age of 65 are homosexual. Aging may be more difficult for homosexuals who have lived the life style of selecting partners on the basis of appearance and vigor. However, that gay life style has been dramatically affected by the appearance of AIDS. Homosexual men who have developed and maintained ongoing relationships have a wide variety of life styles and, like heterosexuals, generally adjust to aging well.

There are some advantages for aging lesbian women, as it is relatively easy for lesbians to develop relationships in late-life. While the older single heterosexual women has a slim chance of finding a sexual partner since single women outnumber men four to one, the older lesbian has a better opportunity to find sexual outlets.

Sexual behavior is yet another domain in which the diversity of older adults is apparent. Interindividual variability shows a vast range in the sexual behavior of older adults. What is most clear is that for most of us, our sexuality is alive and well until the day we die.

REFERENCES

ALLEN, C. (1961).   The aging homosexual. In I. Rubin, (Ed.), *The third sex*. New York: New Book.
BENET, S. (1974).   *Abkhasians: The long-living people of the Caucasus*. New York: Holt, Rinehart and Winston.

BRECHER, E. (1984). *Love, sex, and aging.* Boston, MA: Little, Brown.

BUTLER, R. N. (1975). Sex after sixty. In L. Brown & E. Ellis, (Eds.), *The later years.* Acton, MA: Publishing Sciences.

BUTLER, R. N. & LEWIS, M. (1976). *Love and sex after sixty.* New York: Harper & Row.

CHRISTENSON, C. V. & JOHNSON, A. B. (1973). Sexual patterns in a group of older never-married women. *Journal of Geriatric Psychiatry, 6,* 80–98.

COMFORT, A. (1964). *The process of ageing.* New York: New American Library.

DeCECCO, J. P., KEHOE, M., & GOLDBERG, S. (1984). Lesbians-over-60: A national survey. San Francisco: Center for Research and Education in Sexuality.

DRORI, D. & FOLMAN, Y. (1969). The effect of mating on the longevity of male rats. *Experimental Gerontology, 4,* 263–266.

DRORI, D. & FOLMAN, Y. (1976). Environmental effects on longevity in male rat: Exercise, mating, castration, and restricted feeding. *Experimental Gerontology, 11,* 25–32.

FINCH, C. E. & HAYFLICK, L. (Eds.) (1977). *Handbook of the biology of aging.* New York: Van Nostrand Reinhold.

FRIEND, R. (1980). Gay aging: Adjustment and the older gay male. *Alternative Lifestyles, 3,* 231–248.

GEORGE, L. K. & WEILER, S. J. (1981). Sexuality in middle and late life: The effects of age, cohort, and gender. *Archives of General Psychiatry, 38,* 919–923.

GOLDE, P. & KOGAN, N. (1959). A sentence completion procedure for assessing attitudes toward old people. *Journal of Gerontology, 14,* 355–363.

HARRY, J. & DeVALL, W. (1978). Age and sexual culture among homosexually oriented males. *Archives of Sexual Behavior, 7,* 199–209.

KELLY, J. (1977). The aging male homosexual: Myth and reality. *Gerontologist, 17,* 328–332.

KIMMEL, D. C. (1978). Adult development and aging: A gay perspective. *Journal of Social Issues, 34,* 113–130.

KIMMEL, D. C. (1979–80). Life history interviews of aging gay men. *International Journal of Aging and Human Development, 10,* 239–248.

KIMMEL, D. C., RAPHAEL, S., CATALANO, D., & ROBINSON, M. (1984). Older lesbians and gay men. In *Sourcebook on lesbian/gay health care.* San Francisco: National Gay Health Education Foundation, Inc.

KINSEY, A. C., POMEROY, W. B. & MARTIN, C. E. (1948). *Sexual behavior in the human male.* Philadelphia: W. B. Saunders.

KINSEY, A. C., POMEROY, W. B., MARTIN, C. E., & GEBHARD, P. H. (1953). *Sexual behavior in the human female.* Philadelphia: W. B. Saunders.

McCARY, J. L. (1973). *Human sexuality.* New York: D. Van Nostrand.

MASTERS, W. H. & JOHNSON, V. E. (1966). *Human sexual response.* Boston: Little, Brown.

MASTERS, W. H. & JOHNSON, V. E. (1970). *Human sexual inadequacy.* Boston: Little, Brown.

NEUGARTEN, B. L. (1967). A new look at menopause. *Psychology Today, 1,* 42–45.

NEUGARTEN, B. L., WOOD, V., KRAINES, R. J. & LOOMIS, B. (1963). Women's attitudes toward the menopause. *Vita Human, 6,* 140–151.

PFEIFFER, E. & DAVIS, G. C. (1972). Determinants of sexual behavior in middle and old age. *Journal of the American Geriatrics Society, 20,* 151–158.

PFEIFFER, E., VERWOERDT, A. & DAVIS, G. C. (1972). Sexual behavior in middle life. *American Journal of Psychiatry, 128,* 1262–1267.

PFEIFFER, E., VERWOERDT, A. & WANG, H. S. (1968) Sexual behavior in aged men and women. I. Observations on 254 community volunteers. *Archives of General Psychiatry, 19,* 753–758.

PFEIFFER, E., VERWOERDT, A. & WANG, H. S. (1969).   The natural history of sexual behavior in a biologically advantaged group of aged individuals. *Journal of Gerontology, 24,* 193–198.

PFEIFFER, E., VERWOERDT, A. & WANG, H. S. (1970).   Sexual behavior in aged men and women. In E. Palmore (Ed.), *Normal aging.* Durham, NC: Duke University Press.

RAPHAEL, S. & ROBINSON, M. (1980).   The older lesbian: Love relationships and friendship patterns. *Alternative Lifestyles, 3,* 207–229.

ROCKSTEIN, M. & SUSSMAN, M. (1979).   *Biology of aging.* Belmont, CA: Wadsworth.

RUEBSAAT, H. J. & HULL, R. (1975).   *The male climacteric.* New York: Hawthorn Books.

SOLNICK, R. & CORBY, N. (1983).   Human sexuality and aging. In D. S. Woodruff & J. E. Birren (Eds.) *Aging: Scientific perspectives and social issues.* (2nd Ed.) Monterey, CA: Brooks/Cole.

STARR, B. D. (1987).   Sexuality. In G. L. Maddox (Ed.), *The encyclopedia of aging.* New York: Springer.

STARR, B. D. & WEINER, M. B. (1981).   *The Starr-Weiner report on sex and sexuality in the mature years.* New York: McGraw-Hill.

TALBERT, G. B. (1977).   Aging of the reproductive system. In C. E. Finch and L. Hayflick (Eds.), *Handbook of the biology of aging.* New York: Van Nostrand Reinhold.

TEITELMAN, J. L. (1987).   Homosexuality. In G. L. Maddox (Ed.), *The encyclopedia of aging.* New York: Springer.

VERWOERDT, A., PFEIFFER, E. & WANG, H. S. (1969a).   Sexual behavior in senescence. Changes in sexual activity and interest of aging men and women. *Journal of Geriatric Psychiatry, 2,* 163–180.

VERWOERDT, A., PFEIFFER, E. & WANG, H. S. (1969b).   Sexual behavior in senescence. II. Patterns of sexual activity and interest. *Geriatrics, 24,* 137–154.

WEILER, S. J. (1981).   Aging and sexuality and the myth of decline. In R. W. Fogel, E. Hatfield, S. B. Kiesler, & E. Shanas (Eds.), *Aging: Stability and change in the family.* New York: Academic Press.

WEINBERG, M. (1970).   The male homosexual: Age-related variation in social and psychological characteristics. *Social Problems, 17,* 527–537.

WOODRUFF, D. S. (1977).   *Can you live to be 100?* New York: Chatham Square Press.

CHAPTER 8

Arousal, Sleep, and Aging

Arousal and sleep represent opposite ends of the behavioral continuum, but it is not unusual to discuss them together. This is because they may be regulated by common mechanisms. Additionally, it is likely that the observed age changes in arousal in the waking state may be related to age changes in sleep patterns and/or that arousal level changes during the waking state alter requirements for sleep.

A typical measure of states of arousal and stages of sleep is electrophysiological activity, and this is the measure of primary discussion in this chapter. The electroencephalogram (EEG) and Event-Related Potentials (ERPs) which were described in Chapter 5 on physiological aging have been useful in elucidating age differences in arousal and sleep in the central nervous system (CNS). Particularly in the arousal literature, the autonomic nervous system (ANS) has also received a great deal of attention. No overview of the literature on aging and arousal would be complete without a discussion of biochemical measures of ANS arousal such as free fatty acid level and bioelectric measures such as galvanic skin response (GSR) and heart rate.

In attempting to understand brain mechanisms in arousal, sleep, and aging, there are a number of related concepts and models. One area of significance is excitability and inhibition in the nervous system. Since the time of Pavlov, researchers have recognized that changes in the aging brain may involve changes in excitation and inhibition, and contemporary research supports Pavlov's initial assertion that inhibitory processes decline in aging. What is less clear is the relationship between decreasing inhibitory processes and arousal. It is possible that a decline in inhibition signifies more excitability and hence overarousal for the elderly. However, many possibly independent changes occur in the nervous system with age which might lead to overarousal in one system and underarousal in another. Furthermore, compensatory mechanisms occur which may result in organization at a new functioning level.

Another related model developed from the behavioral literature on aging and perception involves stimulus persistence. This could be conceived as an excitability model which stipulates that the older nervous system responds in a prolonged fashion to stimuli. A given visual or auditory stimulus persists longer in the older nervous system, implicating greater excitability, and perhaps less inhibition. This phenomenon might be viewed as another form of overarousal in the older nervous system, particularly if arousal is conceptualized to occur in short-term phases as well as existing as a long-term state.

The data on changes in the aging brain are significant to this chapter as they suggest a common origin for observed changes in arousal and sleep. A predominant and oft-cited change is the loss of cortical neurons and dendritic branching in the frontal lobes which probably underlies the observed electrophysiological changes over the frontal cortex (Michalewski et al., 1980; Pfefferbaum et al., 1979; Tecce et al., 1980). Frontal cortex inhibits the ascending reticular arousal system (ARAS) and thus influences arousal.

The frontal cortex has also been implicated in the regulation of sleep (Prinz, 1976b). Thus, age changes in the frontal lobes may account in part for alterations in arousal and sleep. At the same time, other changes in the aging brain including cell loss in various areas in addition to frontal cortex, declines in blood flow, and alterations in neurotransmitters and synaptic mechanisms are undoubtedly involved in age changes in sleep and arousal states. Thus, the observed age differences in sleep and arousal may involve common mechanisms, and they probably also involve independent causes.

The focus of this chapter is on psychophysiological measures of arousal and sleep and biological changes which may cause problems with these capacities. However, it should not be overlooked that social and behavioral phenomena are also causally involved in age differences in sleep and arousal. Retirement is a socially imposed milestone that has profound implications for sleep and wakefulness. The demands of work affect sleep patterns, energy level, attention, motivation, and arousal. The abrupt change in the work cycle caused by retirement leads to alterations in sleep including altered demands for sleep which in turn can affect psychophysiological measures of these activities.

A behavioral phenomenon observed in aging which may profoundly affect sleep and wakefulness is depression. Social and psychological events involving loss preclude the elderly toward depression which in turn can alter sleep patterns and levels of arousal. These social and behavioral phenomena reinforce the point that most data on sleep, arousal, and aging are cross sectional and reflect differences between groups. The age differences are not necessarily a function of biological aging. They may reflect different environmental demands or circumstances of the aging population as well as age changes in the brain.

SLEEP AND AGING

A major impetus to the research on sleep and aging is its clinical significance. Questionnaire surveys have indicated that more than a third of the individuals over 60 years of age complain of problems with sleeping. Some data even suggest that the quality and quantity of sleep are related to life expectancy (Institute of Medicine, 1979; Woodruff, 1977). Earlier studies of sleep and aging focused on EEG measures of sleep and documented the lowered incidence of high amplitude delta wave activity characteristic of deep sleep and the lowered incidence of the sleep stage associated with dreaming.

EEG Measures of Sleep and Aging

The five stages of sleep in a young and old subject are depicted in Figure 8.1. With EEG assessment, normal sleep can be divided into two main categories: nonrapid eye movement (or NREM) sleep which includes stages I to IV and rapid eye movement (or REM) sleep. NREM sleep involves the absence of eye movements and moderately reduced muscle tonus. In stage I the EEG pattern is of low amplitude, irregular, fast frequency activity. Stage II includes synchronous waves of 12 to 16 cps (spindles) which occur against a background of low amplitude, fast frequency activity. High amplitude (75 uv or more) slow waves (0.5–2.5 cps) also called delta waves characterize stage III sleep and comprise 20 to 50 percent of the EEG record during this stage. When these slow waves comprise 50 percent or more of the EEG record, stage IV sleep is achieved. This is qualitatively the deepest sleep.

FIGURE 8.1 The typical appearance of the EEG during waking and the stages of sleep in a young and an aged subject. Although alpha and spindle activities can be seen to be slower in the senescent EEG recordings (C4 referenced to mastoid), the most striking age difference occurs during Stage III and IV sleep. Due to their decreased size (and apparent slowing), the delta waves in this senescent tracing do not meet conventionally defined criteria for Stage IV sleep (waves of 0.5 to 3 Hz; $\geq$ 75 uv for 50 + % of the epoch) (Prinz, 1976a).

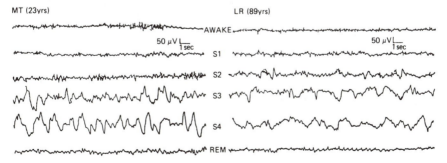

REM sleep is characterized by low amplitude, fast frequency EEG activity, similar to the EEG during wakefulness. For this reason, REM sleep is sometimes called paradoxical sleep. The phenomenon which gives this stage its name is the presence of bursts of rapid eye movements. Just at the onset of a REM sleep period, muscle tonus undergoes a marked decrease which is sustained throughout most of the REM period. REM sleep has been associated with dreaming.

According to Miles and Dement (1980), the most prominent EEG sign of adult aging is the steady decrease in delta wave amplitude during slow wave sleep (SWS). The delta waves that characterize stages III and IV are greatly attenuated in amplitude in older adults. For example, Prinz (1976a) reported in a study of 12 healthy subjects between the ages of 75 and 92 whose EEG was recorded while they slept in their homes, the largest slow wave amplitudes rarely exceeded 150 uv, while 200 uv or greater waves are commonly seen in young adults. There is an overall decrease in the amount of delta wave activity in the all-night EEG record. Deep sleep during the night is not achieved as often by older adults.

In addition to the dramatic delta wave amplitude decrease, there is an overall decrease in the absolute amount of delta wave activity in the all-night EEG records of old people. However, some investigators maintain that the age differences in the incidence of delta wave activity occur almost totally from the decline in amplitude of delta waves and not from differences in their prevalence (Webb & Dreblow, 1982).

Another age change in sleep EEG is the change in spindle activity, 12–16 cps wave seen in stage II. Senescent sleep spindles are often poorly formed and of lower amplitude, resulting in an infrequent occurrence of typical spindling activity (Feinberg, Koresko, & Heller, 1967). Spindle frequencies are often slower in older adults as well (Feinberg et al., 1967; Kales et al., 1967). Feinberg (1974) pointed out that these changes are analogous to the changes in alpha activity which also decreases in frequency, amplitude, and overall amount in senescence.

In addition to the altered EEG characteristics during sleep, there are also age changes in the amounts and patterning of the various sleep stages. Age changes in sleep patterns are shown in Figure 8.2. Most likely as a result of the reduced amplitude of sleep-related EEG slow waves characterizing stage IV sleep, this stage is greatly reduced or absent in senescence (Feinberg et al., 1967; Foret & Webb, 1980; Kahn & Fisher, 1969; Kales et al., 1967; Prinz, 1976b). Hayashi and Endo (1982) demonstrated that this aging phenomenon occurs in Japanese elderly as well. On the basis of three consecutive nights of recording 15 healthy men and women age 73 to 92 years, Hayashi and Endo concluded, "Compared with the young adults, the aged subjects showed extraordinary reductions in Stages III and IV sleep," (Hayashi & Endo, 1982, p. 277).

Sleep deprivation appears to shorten the time it takes to get into deep sleep (stages III and IV or slow wave sleep, SWS). Webb (1981) reported that after two nights of sleep deprivation, groups of subjects in their twenties or forties showed sharply reduced latencies to SWS and increased stage IV sleep. The younger subjects also entered SWS more quickly. Carskadon, Harvey, and Dement (1981) reported

REM SLEEP/NREM SLEEP RELATIONSHIP THROUGHOUT HUMAN LIFE

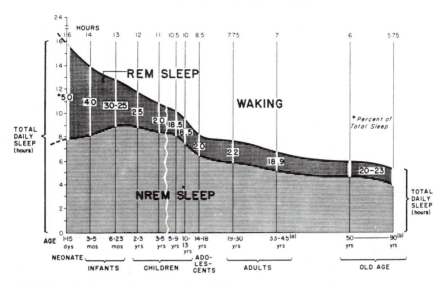

FIGURE 8.2   A diagrammatic representation of REM and NREM sleep (and total sleep) obtained at different ages across the life span. Adapted from Roffwarg et al., 1966, with permission. Stave IV sleep values shown are based on the data of Williams et al. (1974) (Prinz, 1976a).

similar results in a five-night study of sleep deprivation and recovery in adolescents. The greatest change in the sleep pattern appeared to be in stage IV in which there was an almost 100 percent increase after one night of sleep loss.

This same five-night paradigm was used to examine sleep patterns in ten subjects aged 61 to 77 years (Carskadon, 1982). After one night of sleep deprivation, older subjects spent significantly less time in stage I sleep and more time in stages III and IV than they had on a night preceding the sleep loss. Subjects also had fewer wakenings after sleep onset in the two nights following sleep deprivation. These results suggest that a change in sleep scheduling for the aged may be in order.

Older people tend to spend more time in bed (10 to 12 hours) and more time awake in bed. Carskadon (1982) suggested that if older people would spend only six hours a night in bed, the quality of their sleep, including the time spent in deep sleep, might improve. When the need for sleep is increased by sleep loss, stage IV sleep is achieved in old subjects for a period approaching the time adolescents spend in stage IV (Carskadon, 1982).

Time spent in REM sleep also appears to diminish in studies of senescent sleep patterns (Prinz, 1976a). Intensity of the REM sleep state also appears to decline as inferred from the diminished REM activity that normally accompanies this state. These differences in REM activity are related to mental function test scores. Among aged men selected for good health, Feinberg et al. (1967) found a correlation between time spent in REM sleep and WAIS performance and Wechsler Memory Test scores. These results were replicated by Kahn and Fisher (1969) and by Prinz (1977).

Incidence of Awakening

New insights about sleep in old age place emphasis on the large number of awakenings the elderly experience during the night. Such awakenings have disruptive effects. Frequent awakenings correlate with daytime sleepiness to a greater degree than do the other sleep measures, and they are related to elevated levels of norepinephrine and especially to respiratory dysfunction.

Miles and Dement (1980) reported an almost linear increase in waking after sleep onset with age which is paralleed by a very marked increase in the occurrence of brief (10 sec or less) arousals which are not perceived or remembered and may not cause actual wakefulness. The most prominent subjective symptom in older adults is the complaint of increased number and duration of sleep disruptions. This complaint often parallels the objective finding of increased wakings after sleep onset.

One possible cause for the increase in awakenings per night may involve level of arousal. A number of studies have indicated that plasma levels of norepinephrine are increased in the elderly both in the daytime and especially during the night (e.g., Coulombe, Dussault, & Walker, 1977; Prinz & Halter, 1981). Plasma norepinephrine is elevated in humans when the sympathetic nervous system is activated. Hence, heightened plasma norepinephrine levels may represent increased sympathetic activation in the aged. Such sympathetic activation has been associated with an aroused EEG pattern and behavioral alertness; two measures used in sleep research to indicate the waking state.

When heightened activation resulting from increases in plasma norepinephrine occurs at night, it could interfere with sleep and promote nighttime wakefulness. Indeed, Prinz and Halter (1981) found significant correlations between sleep patterns and mean plasma norepinephrine in samples of healthy men in their twenties and sixties. Awakenings caused by a tone stimulus was followed by pronounced surges in plasma norepinephrine in the old but not in the young. Prinz and Halter suggested that determining the role of increased sympathetic activity in sleep abnormalities might provide an impetus for the development of new pharmacological interventions which could counteract nighttime sympathetic hyperactivity and improve the quality of sleep in the aged.

Sleep Apnea

Sleep apnea is the name given to the cessation of air flow in breathing for ten seconds or longer during sleep. An elevated incidence of sleep apnea has been documented in at least one third of the elderly population. The fastest growing body of literature on the topic of sleep and aging focuses on breathing patterns during sleep and implicates respiratory disturbances as a major cause of impaired sleep and frequent awakenings in the elderly (Ancoli-Israel et al., 1981; Bliwise, Carey, & Dement, 1983; Bliwise, Coleman, & Carey, 1982; Carskadon & Dement, 1981; Coleman et al., 1981; Guilleminault & Dement, 1978). These respiratory disturbances are a health risk in themselves. However, more alarming is the evidence that sleeping pills and alcohol increase the incidence and length of these episodes (Guilleminault, 1982).

The occurrence of apnea or several other kinds of abnormal respiratory events at a rate of more than five per hour is considered pathological (Guilleminault & Dement, 1982). Some elderly have hundreds of these events during the night. The incidence of respiratory problems in the sleep of the elderly has been variously reported at 63 percent (Ancoli-Israel et al., 1981), 31.8 percent in women and 44.4 percent in men (Carskadon & Dement, 1981), 44 percent (Coleman et al., 1981), and 33 percent (Bliwise et al., 1983). Longitudinal data collected by Bliwise, Carskadon, Carey and Dement (1984) suggest that increases in respiratory disturbances during sleep may occur primarily during the fourth and fifth decades and remain high in subsequent years.

Coleman et al. (1981) argued that sleep apnea associated with insomnia and hypersomnia might account for the relationship between life expectancy and time asleep. The mortality rate for those over 70 who state that they sleep less than four hours or more than ten hours per night is nearly twice the rate for those of the same age who report sleeping seven to eight hours. Sleep apnea is associated with life-threatening hemodynamic changes during sleep, and thus it may be directly related to life expectancy.

Sleep Patterns in Senile Dementia
of the Alzheimer's Type

Bliwise (1985) argued that sleep measures are useful predictors of senile dementia of the Alzheimer's Type (SDAT), and they are also helpful in assessing the progression of the disease. Relative to aged controls, SDAT patients show decreased sleep efficiency in terms of time in bed actually spent asleep. The sleep of SDAT patients is also more fragmented in that they awaken more than normal elderly adults. Most startling about the sleep of SDAT patients is the virtual absence of stages III and IV sleep. These patients apparently have no deep sleep. They also take longer to get into REM sleep.

A syndrome which is responsible for the institutionalization of many SDAT patients is what has been called *Sundown syndrome*. It refers to the periods of behavioral agitation, confusion, and disorientation occurring during the normal sleep period. SDAT patients often awaken and begin to wander around in the middle of the night. If they go outside, they can get confused and lost. If they remain inside, they can fall, burn themselves on the stove, start a fire and be a danger to everyone living with them. Since a caretaker cannot remain vigilant day and night, he or she must reluctantly institutionalize the SDAT patient. The reason that Sundown syndrome occurs in SDAT patients is unknown, and it is also not understood why some SDAT patients have the syndrome while others do not.

At the time Bliwise (1985) discussed research on SDAT and sleep, about 200 SDAT patients had been studied throughout the world with sleep EEG measures. Bliwise recommended that given the major sleep changes which occur with the disease and given the sheer enormity of the disease, additional research on sleep and SDAT must be undertaken.

Prescription for Sleep in the Elderly

Taken as a whole, the age differences observed in sleep characteristics serve as evidence that the pattern of sleep is altered in the normal aged and even more dramatically altered in patients with SDAT. The age differences are similar in men and women, but impairment may be greater in men (Miles & Dement, 1980). Increased wakefulness and decreased slow wave sleep are subjectively experienced as less sound sleep. However, it is the fragmentation of sleep most frequently caused by disturbed nighttime breathing which has been shown to be most closely related to sleepiness and reduced daytime well-being in the aged (Carskadon, Brown, & Dement, 1983).

It is evident that there is a higher incidence of complaints of poor sleep and a greater usage of drugs to promote sleep among elderly individuals. It has been reported that in the United States, those 60 and older consume 33 percent of all prescriptions for sleeping pills such as secobarbital and diazepam (Institute of Medicine, 1979). Advances in knowledge of respiratory disturbances associated with sleep in the aged indicate that these drugs may increase the incidence of apnea and associated cardiac arrythmia.

Another behavior common in the elderly is to compensate for inadequate nighttime sleep by napping during the day. Like sleeping pills, napping may be counterindicated for the sleepless aged. Sleep deprivation studies have demonstrated that sleep loss actually improves the quality of sleep by increasing the time spent in deep sleep the next night. Thus, by avoiding sleeping pills and staying in bed at night for shorter rather than longer intervals, older adults might improve the quality of their sleep.

AROUSAL

Behavioral relationships with level of arousal had been considered in the 1920s and 1930s (Welford, 1965), but it was in the late 1940s and early 1950s that arousal theory received its major impetus with the discovery of the ARAS in a series of ingenious experiments (e.g., Lindsley et al., 1950; Moruzzi & Magoun, 1949). Moruzzi and Magoun observed the relationship between direct electrical stimulation from electrodes implanted in the reticular formation and behavioral arousal. This relationship is shown schematically in Figure 8.3 with the electrical stimulation to the reticular formation occurring naturally from the sound of a bell input from neural collaterals from the auditory pathway. Furthermore, Lindsley et al.

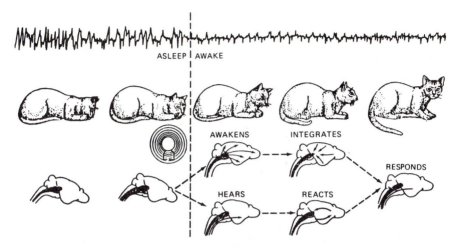

FIGURE 8.3 Schematic drawing of the EEG, brain, and behavior of a cat as it passes through the arousal stages from deep sleep to waking alertness. In the first frame the cat is in deep sleep. The second frame shows the bell ringing which rouses the cat. Collaterals from the primary auditory pathway provide input to the reticular formation (shown in light grey). The cat awakens and integrates in the third and fourth frames and responds in the fifth frame. Coincidentally, in the third frame the ARAS acts (black arrows) to awaken the cortex so that it can "hear" signals arriving in the auditory area. The EEG changes from pattern of sleep to one of wakefulness at the end of frame two. The ARAS then integrates the brain's activity so that the brain can react as a whole. The cat finally responds in frame five with a motor impulse (light grey descending arrow by reticular formation in frame 5). The cat then jumps to its feet and runs away. The entire process takes place in a matter of a few seconds. Source: "The Reticular Formation" by J. D. French. Copyright © 1957 by *Scientific American,* Inc. All rights reserved.

(1950) found that lesions to the midline reticular formation resulted in a permanent sleeping state in the animal, but that the animal could be aroused by stimulation higher in the brain than the lesion.

These discoveries led to the generation of a great body of research, and Lindsley (1952, 1960) reviewed much of this literature and organized it into a general theory of arousal. The main dependent measure in this research was the EEG, and in Lindsley's theory, various EEG frequency bandwidths were associated with stages of arousal ranging from deep sleep to alert problem solving. Arousal states and their EEG correlates are summarized in Table 8.1. In its simplest form the theory associates very slow EEG frequencies called delta waves (1–3 cps) with deep sleep. A bandwidth ranging from 4–7 cps is called theta and is associated with light sleep and the transition between sleep and wakefulness. The 8–13 cps range is called alpha frequency and signifies alert wakefulness. The faster frequencies of 14–30 or more cps are called beta waves and occur during thinking and problem solving.

Arousal theory received considerable attention in psychology in the 1950s, and it began to be considered in relation to aging in the late 1950s and early 1960s. It is interesting to note that in the *Handbook of Aging and the Individual* (Birren, 1959a) the only brief allusion to arousal is Birren's suggestions that the aged person

TABLE 8.1 Psychological States and Their EEG, Conscious, and Behavioral Correlates[a]

Behavioral continuum	Electroencephalogram	State of awareness	Behavioral efficiency
Strong, excited emotion (fear) (rage) (anxiety)	Desynchronized: low to moderate amplitude; fast, mixed frequencies	Restricted awareness; divided attention; diffuse, hazy; "confusion"	Poor (lack of control, freezing-up, disorganized)
Alert attentiveness	Partially synchronized: mainly fast, low amplitude waves	Selective attention, but may vary or shift, "concentration" anticipation, "set"	Good (efficient, selective, quick, reactions). Organized for serial responses
Relaxed wakefulness	Synchronized: optimal alpha rhythm	Attention wanders—not forced. Favors free association	Good (routine reactions and creative thought)
Drowsiness	Reduced alpha and occasional low amplitude slow waves	Borderline, partial awareness. Imagery and reverie. "Dreamlike states"	Poor (uncoordinated, sporadic, lacking sequential timing)
Light Sleep	Spindle bursts and slow waves (larger). Loss of alpha	Markedly reduced consciousness (loss of consciousness). Dream state	Absent
Deep sleep	Large and very slow waves (synchrony but on slow time base). Random, irregular pattern	Complete loss of awareness (no memory for stimulation or for dreams)	Absent
Coma	Isoelectric to irregular large slow waves	Complete loss of consciousness, little or no response to stimulation: amnesia	Absent
Death	Isoelectric; gradual and permanent disappearance of all electrical activity	Complete loss of awareness as death ensues	Absent

[a]From Lindsley, D. B. (1952). Physiological phenomena and the electroencephalogram. *Electroencephalography and Clinical Neurophysiology, 4,* 445.

shows a reduction in excitability of the central nervous system which is manifested in longer latencies of responses and in a relative incapacity to withhold responses. In that handbook the term *arousal* does not appear in the index. By 1977 when the second handbook, the *Handbook of the Psychology of Aging* (Birren & Schaie, 1977), appeared, there were 38 entries under the heading of arousal. Clearly, the decades of the 1960s and 1970s are when the model of aging and arousal received the most research attention.

Underarousal

Birren (1960) first articulated the underarousal hypothesis when he stated:

> There is the possibility that the well-established psycho motor slowing of advanc- ing age is a consequence of reduced physiological activation. This agrees with what limited literature exists on age differences in activity and drive levels. Assuming a less energized or activated organism with age, in any unit of time there will be less interaction between the individual and his environment. This reduces the opportunity for all psychological processes to take place, e.g., perception, acquisi- tion, manipulation of symbols, and storage. (Birren, 1960, pp. 326–327).

At the point in time when Birren made this statement, the major evidence for the underarousal hypothesis was provided by studies of the ongoing EEG of the aged. As discussed in Chapter 5, the alpha rhythm of the EEG slows with age, and the amount of energy in the alpha activity and the abundance of it declines. Data on aging and event-related potentials also suggest a lower arousal level in older adults.

The data on sensory-evoked potentials are consistent in suggesting that the old are in a state of underarousal. However, it has been argued by Marsh and Thompson (1977) that the ERP data involving active processing of information (as opposed to the passive stimulation conditions required in sensory-evoked poten- tial paradigms) does not consistently support the underarousal hypothesis. Smith, Thompson, and Michaelewski (1980) asserted that when stimulated passively or required to perform simple tasks, the elderly show ERP differences consistent with reduced cortical excitability. However, when subjects were actively engaged in cognitive tasks, electrocortical measures indicated that the elderly are not necessarily underaroused and could exhibit levels of cortical excitability similar to those of younger persons.

Galvanic skin response and heart rate.   The first empirical demonstration of the relationship between underarousal and aging was reported by Botwinick and Kornetsky (1959, 1960) and involved the galvanic skin response (GSR). This research initiated a series of studies carried out in a number of laboratories over the next two decades which related ANS activity to underarousal and poorer behavioral performance in the elderly. Much of this literature is excellently reviewed by Marsh and Thompson (1977).

Botwinick and Kornetsky used a classical conditioning paradigm in which shock was the unconditioned stimulus (UCS), a tone was the conditioned stimulus (CS), and GSR was the response. The GSRs of the elderly men (mean age, early seventies) conditioned less readily and extinguished more quickly than the GSRs of the younger subjects, and older subjects also showed less GSR responsivity in the habituation period. The investigators concluded that autonomic reactivity was significantly decreased in the elderly.

The underarousal hypothesis has also been supported by studies of autonomic reactivity in the aged during vigilance tasks. In several studies in which young and old subjects were instructed to report the occurrence of a double advance on the ticks of a clock over a long period of time, the latency of GSR to critical stimuli was longer in the aged (Surwillo & Quilter, 1965a) and the frequency of GSR responses was less (Surwillo & Quilter, 1965b).

Heart rate reactivity has also supported the underarousal hypothesis. Thompson and Nowlin (1973) found heart rate deceleration to be much less in a warned reaction time task for the old subjects than for the young. This result was also reported by Harkins et al. (1976). Thus, taken as a whole, the bioelectric measures of ANS activity indicate that the old are in a state of underarousal. However, many of the studies involving bioelectric measures of ANS arousal have been boring to subjects and have involved relatively passive responses to the experimental conditions. Few of these studies supporting the underarousal hypothesis have involved active information processing on the part of the subjects. In conditions of active information processing, older individuals have been shown in many cases to be equally aroused in comparison to young subjects, or more highly aroused than the young.

Overarousal

One of the first gerontologists to articulate the overarousal hypothesis was Welford (1965) who stated:

> Reduced activation would tend to lower both signal and noise, the former probably more than the latter, rendering the organism less sensitive and less responsive than it would otherwise be. At first sight the changes with age in neural structures make it seem obvious that older people would be likely to suffer from under-activation. Yet both clinical and everyday observation of middle-aged and older people often point rather to *over*-activation resulting in unduly heightened activity, tension and anxiety. (Welford, 1965, p. 14).

The data which have been used most frequently to support the overarousal hypothesis involve the measurement of lipid mobilization, a biochemical measure related to sympathetic nervous system function. It had been demonstrated that the level of free fatty acid (FFA) in the plasma component of blood was intimately related to the level of ANS arousal (Bogdonoff, Estes, Friedberg & Klein, 1961; Bogdonoff, Estes, Harlan, Trout & Kirschner, 1960; Bogdonoff, Weissler & Merritt, 1960). To obtain this measure, an indwelling needle is placed in the subject's forearm and sequential samples of blood are collected during the experimental session. Thus, regardless of the behavioral measure being assessed, there is a certain amount of stress involved in this technique associated with the drawing of blood.

In the studies which have used this measure, results indicated that during serial learning and stressful monitoring tasks emphasizing information overload, aged subjects had initially higher FFA levels, showed increases comparable to the young while performing the tasks, and continued at a significantly higher level for a minimum of one hour following the behavioral tests (Powell, Eisdorfer & Bogdonoff, 1964; Troyer, Eisdorfer, Wilkie & Bogdonoff, 1966). On the basis of these data, Eisdorfer (1968) concluded:

> It has been implicitly assumed, however, that the aged are at a resting state of low internal arousal and sustain a low drive state. Our contention is that the aged may not be at a low state of arousal. Once aroused autonomically, perhaps because of a faulty ability to suppress end organ response or because of an altered feedback system, aged subjects appear to function as if in states of high levels of heightened arousal. In any event, increasing anxiety or further exogenous stimulation has a detrimental effect on performance, as opposed to the incremental effect that we would anticipate from an organism stimulated at lower levels of arousal. It would be predicted, then, that where arousal or anxiety is diminished by experimental manipulation, older persons should improve their performance. (Eisdorfer, 1968, p. 215).

An experimental test of the underarousal hypothesis was undertaken by Eisdorfer, Nowlin, and Wilkie (1970). They administered an adrenergic blocking agent (propranolol) to one group of older subjects and a placebo to another and found fewer errors and lower FFA levels when the experimental subjects performed the serial learning task. They concluded that autonomic end organ arousal accounted for the learning deficits in the placebo-treated group and asserted that the results supported the overarousal hypothesis. Unfortunately, a young control group was not tested, so the effect of the drug on subjects who would not be expected to be "overaroused" was not assessed.

An attempt was made by Froehling (1974) to replicate these results using a within-subject design. The results of this study did not support the hypothesis that excessive end organ activity was associated with learning decrement in the elderly. If overarousal exists in the elderly, it may be a transitory phenomenon occurring only in the older subject's first visit to the laboratory. In a repeated measures design, the overarousal effect was not apparent.

Qualifications of the arousal concept. A comparison of the various studies, which incorporate an arousal dimension as an explanatory construct, is virtually impossible at the present time. For example, studies arguing that older people are underaroused rely heavily on traditional bioelectric measures (EEG frequency, GSR, heart rate) as indicators of physiological arousal, whereas the overarousal position stems primarily from biochemical measures related to ANS function (FFA, urinary catecholamines). Behavioral measures employed in these studies have also been decidedly different. It is obvious that great commonality of methodology and measuring techniques is required before any resolution of the arousal, performance, and aging controversy can be realized.

INHIBITION

A hypothesis which has been advanced to explain behavioral aging phenomena since Pavlov considered classical conditioning in aged dogs is the decrease in inhibitory processes in the nervous system. Birren (1959b) proposed on the basis of admittedly scanty evidence that older persons showed a reduction in inhibitory control over behavior. This was also the explanation used in studies of the classical conditioning of the eyeblink response in humans which is performed much less efficiently in old age (Braun & Geiselhart, 1959; Gakkel & Zinina, 1953; Kimble & Pennypacker, 1963). Jerome's (1959) description of Gakkel and Zinina's (1953) study of eyeblink conditioning differentiation and word association was

> Failure to obtain even the gross differentiation between the sounds of the buzzer and the bell was accepted as indicative of a serious impairment of the process of inhibition, and a high frequency of garrulous responses in the word-association test was regarded as supporting this conclusion. (Jerome, 1959, p. 670).

A review of the evidence for failure of inhibitory processes in the elderly appears in an article on ERP research in adult aging by Smith, Thompson, and Michalewski (1980). They pointed out that the enhancement of ERP wave forms which results from nonspecific cerebral lesions has been attributed to reduced inhibitory control of afferent stimulation. On this basis, high amplitude ERP components observed in some neurological conditions have been interpreted as arising from deficits in central inhibition (Callner et al., 1978; Lee & Blair, 1973). It has been reported that one or more ERP components in the middle-latency range are significantly larger in older than in young individuals. Straumanis et al. (1965) interpreted this difference as due to a reduction in inhibitory activity, and subsequent research has also been interpreted in this manner (Dustman & Beck, 1969; Schenkenberg, 1970).

Event-related potential data provide convincing evidence for a decline in inhibitory function, at least in the visual system of the aging (Dustman & Snyder, 1981; Dustman, Synder & Schlehuber, 1981). In one study (Dustman & Snyder, 1981) the augmenting-reducing phenomenon was investigated in 220 male subjects aged 4 to 90. A predisposition towards augmenting or reducing is related to level of inhibitory functioning (Buchsbaum, 1976; Knorring & Johansson, 1980; Knorring & Perris, 1981). Individuals who reduce their ERP responses to intense stimuli have relatively strong inhibitory functions while those who are augmenters are less able to dampen their responses. Furthermore, Down's syndrome individuals who are described as having cortical inhibitory deficits have abnormally large visual

ERPs, especially in recordings from frontal and central scalp. Individuals with Down's syndrome also have ERPs which augment substantially more in reaction to increased flash intensity in comparison to normal control subjects (Galbraith, Gliddon & Busk, 1970; Gliddon, Busk & Galbraith, 1975). Dustman and Synder (1981) reported that the amplitude of ERPs to flashes was greater in central scalp recording sites at wave form latencies of 90–110 msec, 110–150 msec, and 150–200 msec in very young (4 to 15 years) and older (50 to 90 years) individuals. These data are shown in Figure 8.4.

The very young and old subjects were also greater augmenters. Brighter flashes were accompanied by larger increases in ERP amplitude in these two age groups as compared to subjects of intermediate ages. The researchers reported that the ERPs of Down's syndrome individuals, believed to have inhibitory deficits, are strikingly similar to the ERPs of the young and old subjects in their study. They pointed out that the predominant action of monoamines is thought to be inhibitory, and monoamine levels are low during childhood and old age. Additionally, anterior cortical areas which exert inhibitory control over the ascending reticular formation are immature during development and suffer cell loss in old age. This developmental course parallels the findings of Dustman and Snyder (1981). They suggested that the chemical and structural deficiencies in aging are reflected by a relative inability to suppress brain potentials elicited by repetitive and relatively meaningless stimuli. If their ERP measures do reflect inhibitory

FIGURE 8.4 Amplitude slope values for three VER components from central scalp (C3 and C4 combined). Each age group included 20 male subjects. Source: Dustman, R. E. & Snyder, E. W. (1981). Life-span changes in visually evoked potentials at central scalp. *Neurobiology of Aging, 2,* 303–308. Reprinted by permission.

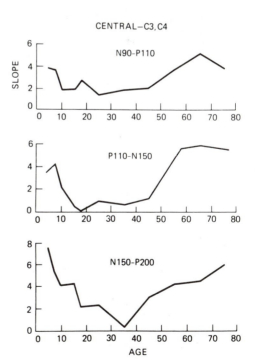

efficiency, loss of cortical inhibition is obvious in the recordings of individuals in the fifties and may be occurring a decade earlier.

Dustman, Snyder and Schlehuber (1981) examined visually-evoked responses (VERs) elicited by patterned and unpatterned flashes in the same 220 healthy males tested in Dustman and Snyder (1981). Dustman et al. (1981) reasoned that inhibition in the visual system is essential for optimal detection of edges and contours. Thus, reduced inhibitory function should result in a less differentiated VER to patterns. In other words, VERs to patterns and to diffuse flashes should be relatively similar, and correlations between the patterned and unpatterned conditions should be higher in those individuals having less inhibitory function. Correlating the digital values comprising the two wave forms, Dustman et al. (1981) found that correlations followed a U-shaped curve over the life span. These interesting data are presented in Figure 8.5

Patterned and unpatterned flash VERs were most alike for the youngest and oldest subjects. The age effect was localized to scalp areas overlying visual cortex where cortical tissue is organized to maximize the detection of lines and edges (Hubel & Wiesel, 1962, 1977.) The effects were much stronger for the earlier VER epochs which encompass wave forms known to be associated with checkerboard stimulation (Harter & White, 1970; Jeffries, 1977). These results are compatible with a concept of reduced inhibitory functioning within the visual systems of the very young and the old. Dustman et al. (1981) suggested that the reduced inhibition

FIGURE 8.5 Life-span changes in similarity of VER waveforms elicited by patterned and diffuse flashes for four time bands. Intensity was two logs above threshold. Each data point represents the mean correlation (r) and equivalent Fisher z-coefficient (z) obtained by correlating digital values within each time segment. Recordings were from occipital scalp. Source: Dustman, R. E., Snyder, E. W. & Schlehuber, D. J. (1981). Life-span alterations in visually evoked potentials and inhibitory function. *Neurobiology of Aging, 2*, 187–192. Reprinted by permission.

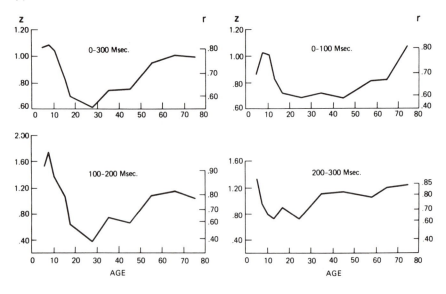

may have been related to reduced catecholaminergic activity, although biochemical measures were not made in this study.

It has been stated several times in this chapter that it is believed that the frontal cortex exerts an inhibitory control over the reticular formation. Recent behavioral and electrophysiological data corroborate the neuroanatomical evidence that the frontal cortex may be an area of particular vulnerability in aging. Albert and Kaplan (1980) reviewed the neuropsychological evidence which suggested that many behavioral deficiencies which are apparent in the elderly resemble behavioral deficits in patients with frontal lobe lesions. Scheibel and Scheibel (1976) identified losses of dendritic masses in prefrontal and temporal areas of aging brains in histological studies. Electrophysiological measures have also implicated selective aging in anterior cortex (Michalewski et al., 1980; Pfefferbaum et al., 1979; Tecce et al., 1980). These data, coupled with behavioral and histological evidence, begin to point rather compellingly to a selective aging of the frontal lobes which impairs the capacity of the elderly to modulate attention. This frontal lobe impairment might result in decreased inhibitory control of the ARAS.

Smith et al. (1980) cautioned that the evidence from ERP studies for a deficit in inhibition with age are provocative, but they are based on ad hoc reasoning and perhaps should not be taken seriously without more direct evidence. What is required at the present time are studies in which independent measures of inhibition are taken in the elderly along with ERP and behavioral recording.

STIMULUS PERSISTENCE

This is essentially an overexcitability hypothesis which could be viewed partly as a lack of inhibitory processes. Basically, the idea is that once the aged nervous system has been stimulated, the stimulation persists longer. It reverberates in the system for a greater period of time, and the system is refractory for a longer time period.

One of the strongest proponents of this hypothesis is Botwinick who has made an extensive review of the behavioral evidence favoring stimulus persistence in the elderly (Botwinick, 1978). Perceptual data which support this hypothesis are studies of aging and stimulus fusion, masking, after-images, and illusions.

Smith et al. (1980) have reviewed the ERP data relevant to the stimulus persistence hypothesis. They cite studies such as Celesia and Daly (1977) in which the cortical frequency of photic driving (CFPD) was examined in subjects in their early twenties and subjects over 60 years of age. CFPD is defined as the highest frequency at which a photic driving response could be obtained as measured by ERPs. In the young subjects CFPD was 72 flashes per second while in the old subjects CFPD was 60 flashes per second.

Further ERP support for the stimulus persistence hypothesis is presented by Smith et al. (1980) from their own data that there is a persistence of electrical positivity during the slow wave phase of the ERP response. Such positivity is generally associated with a decrease in neural reactivity, while slow wave negativity is thought to be associated with heightened reactivity. Thus, persistence in this case may implicate a lowered state of arousal in the elderly.

A SEARCH FOR APPROPRIATE MODELS

Taken as a whole, the evidence which has been reviewed in this chapter indicates that a myriad of changes occur in aging which may lead to contradictory predictions about behavioral outcomes. On the one hand, the aged may be in a tonic state of underarousal, but they show phasic overarousal as well, particularly in novel situations. While they are tonically underaroused, implicating a decline in the efficiency of the ARAS, they are also likely to have poorer inhibitory processes as suggested by degeneration in the frontal lobes. Less effective inhibition should result in greater excitability and a higher state of arousal.

The aged may show greater excitability in response to sensory stimulation because neurotransmitters may be degraded more slowly (resulting in stimulus persistence). However, it is not the case that the elderly are tonically overaroused. Quite the converse, they are in a tonic state closer to the beginning stages of sleep. To explain some of these anomalies, Thompson and Marsh (1973) created the ANS-CNS desynchronization hypothesis. It stipulates that there is poorer integration of these two components of the nervous system in old age.

Another model that appears promising is the one suggested by the data of Bondareff (1980) on age changes in the brain of the rat. He observed what he termed "compensatory" losses of excitatory and inhibitory synapses. If only one type of synapse was lost, the animal might be incapacitated but with the loss of both types of processes, a new balance was attained at a different level of functioning with fewer total synapses involved. If such a model were to be applied to the whole nervous system, it would appear that the aging reticular formation suffers biochemical and synaptic degradation perhaps resulting in slower EEG frequencies, lower amplitude late ERP components, and lowered responsivity as measured by bioelectric indices of the ANS. The anterior cortex which exerts an inhibitory influence on the reticular formation loses cells and particularly the dendrites which provide cortico-cortico connections. Thus, integration in frontal cortex is less efficient and inhibitory control declines. These two age changes could result in a sort of compensation in which a new level of organization is achieved. It may be less efficient, but it may be relatively in balance as compared to a nervous system in which only one process partially fails.

SUMMARY

While arousal and sleep occur at opposite ends of the behavioral continuum, they may be regulated by common mechanisms. Age changes in the brain as well as changing behavioral patterns resulting from retirement probably affect arousal level and sleep efficiency in later life.

At least one third of adults over the age of 60 complain about their ability to get a good night's sleep. One of the most dramatic age changes in sleep is the decrease in the amount of stage IV sleep, the deepest and most refreshing of the sleep stages. Sleep deprivation shortens the time it takes to get into deep sleep, and sleep deprived individuals spend more time in stage IV sleep. Thus, rather than spending more time in bed to make up for the loss of deep sleep, older adults are advised to spend only six hours a night in bed.

Other problems of older adults' sleep include an increased incidence of awakenings, less REM sleep (the period of sleep associated with dreaming), and increased sleep apnea (brief periods when the sleeping individual stops breathing). Sleeping pills and alcohol increase the incidence of apnea and thus represent a risk for older adults.

In senile dementia of the Alzheimer's Type (SDAT), sleep is seriously disrupted. Changes in sleep patterns may be used to assess the progression of SDAT. Often patients with SDAT have no apparent stage III or IV sleep; they are thus without deep sleep. SDAT patients often have Sundown syndrome. They awaken and wander around in the middle of the night.

A large body of evidence suggests that older adults are in a chronic state of underarousal. Brain electrical activity in terms of the slower modal brain wave frequency and lower amplitude ERPs suggest underarousal. Some studies using GSR and heart rate also support the underarousal hypothesis.

Overarousal appears to be a tonic state in older adults. They sometimes overreact to stressful situations, and they take longer to return to normal baseline levels of activation. Once they are familiar with a situation, overarousal is less likely to occur.

Failure of inhibitory processes appears to be another concomitant of normal aging. Age changes in the frontal lobes of the brain may be responsible for loss of inhibition with age. Stimulus persistence may be one aspect of loss of inhibitory processes. Once a stimulus is registered in the older nervous system, it appears to reverberate for a longer period of time.

The nervous system may compensate for changes in it by achieving new levels of excitatory and inhibitory balance. Age changes may combine to result in a new level of organization. This level may be less efficient than the level achieved in the young, but it may be relatively balanced in terms of excitatory and inhibitory control.

REFERENCES

ALBERT, M. S. & KAPLAN, E. F. (1980).   Organic implications of neuropsychological deficits in the elderly. In L. W. Poon, J. Fozard, L. Cermak, D. Arenberg, & L. W. Thompson (Eds.), *New directions in memory and aging: Proceedings of the George A. Talland memorial conference.* Hillsdale, NJ: Lawrence Erlbaum.

ANCOLI-ISRAEL, S., KRIPKE, D. F., MASON, W., & MESSIN, S. (1981).   Sleep apnea and nocturnal myoclonus in a senior population. *Sleep, 4,* 349–358.

BIRREN, J. E. (Ed.) (1959a).   *Handbook of aging and the individual.* Chicago: University of Chicago Press.

BIRREN, J. E. (1959b).   Psychophysiological aspects of aging. *Duke University Council on Gerontology,* 157–173.

BIRREN, J. E. (1960).   Behavioral theories of aging. In N. W. Shock (Ed.), *Aging— Some social and biological aspects.* Washington, DC: American Association for the Advancement of Science.

BIRREN, J. E. & SCHAIE, K. W. (Eds.) (1977).   *Handbook of the psychology of aging.* New York: Van Nostrand Reinhold.

BLIWISE, D. L. (1985).   Sleep patterns in Alzheimer's patients. Paper presented at the annual meeting of the American Psychological Association, Los Angeles, August.

BLIWISE, D. L., CAREY, E., & DEMENT, W. C. (1983).   Nightly variation in sleep-related respiratory disturbance in older adults. *Experimental Aging Research, 9,* 77–81.

BLIWISE, D. L., CARSKADON, M., CAREY, E., & DEMENT, W. C. (1984).   Longitudinal development of sleep-related respiratory disturbance in adult humans. *Journal of Gerontology, 39,* 290–293.

BLIWISE, D. L., COLEMAN, R. M., & CAREY, E. (1982).   Age-related prevalence and natural history of sleep apnea and nocturnal myoclonus. *Gerontologist, 22,* 187.

BOGDONOFF, M. D., ESTES, E. H., JR., FRIEDBERG, S. J., & KLEIN, R. F. (1961).   Fat mobilization in man. *Annals of Internal Medicine, 55,* 328–338.

BOGDONOFF, M. D., ESTES, E. H., JR., HARLAN, W. R., TROUT, D. L., & KIRSCHNER, N. (1960).   Metabolic and cardiovascular changes during a state of acute central nervous system arousal. *Journal of Clinical Endocrine Metabolism, 20,* 1333–1340.

BOGDONOFF, M. D., WEISSLER, A. M., & MERRITT, F. L. (1960).   Effect of autonomic ganglionic blockade upon serum free fatty acid levels in man. *Journal of Clinical Investigation, 39,* 959–965.

BONDAREFF, W. (1980).   Compensatory loss of axosomatic synapses in the dentate gyrus of the senescent rat. *Mechanisms of Ageing and Development, 12,* 221–229.

BOTWINICK, J. (1978).   *Aging and behavior.* New York: Springer.

BOTWINICK, J. & KORNETSKY, C. (1959).   Age differences in the frequency of the GSR during a conditioning experiment. *Journal of Gerontology, 14,* 503.

BOTWINICK, J. & KORNETSKY, C. (1960).   Age differences in the acquisition and extinction of GSR. *Journal of Gerontology, 15,* 83–84.

BRAUN, H. W. & GEISELHART, R. (1959).   Age differences in the acquisition and extinction of the conditioned eyelid response. *Journal of Experimental Psychology, 57,* 386–388.

BUCHSBAUM, M. (1976).   Self-regulation of stimulus intensity: Augmenting/reducing and the average evoked response. In G. E. Schwartz & D. Shapiro (Eds.), *Consciousness and self-regulation,* vol. 1. New York: Plenum.

CALLNER, D. A., DUSTMAN, R. E., MADSEN, J. E., SCHENKENBERG, T. & BECK, E. C. (1978).   Life span changes in the averaged evoked responses of Down's syndrome and nonretarded subjects. *American Journal of Mental Deficiency, 82,* 398–405.

CARSKADON, M. A. (1982).   Sleep fragmentation, sleep loss, and sleep need in the elderly. *Gerontologist, 22,* 1987.

CARSKADON, M. A., BROWN, E. D., & DEMENT, W. C. (1981).   Respiration during sleep in the aged human. *Journal of Gerontology, 34,* 420–423.

CARSKADON, M. A. & DEMENT, W. C. (1981).   Respiration during sleep in the aged human. *Journal of Gerontology, 36,* 420–423.

CARSKADON, M. A., HARVEY, K., & DEMENT, W. C. (1981).   Sleep loss in young adolescents. *Sleep, 4,* 299–312.

CELESIA, G. G. & DALY, R. F. (1977).   Effect of aging on visual evoked responses. *Archives of Neurology, 34,* 403–407.

COLEMAN, R. M., MILES, L. E., GUILLEMINAULT, C. C., ZARCONE, V. P., VAN DEN HOED, J., & DEMENT, W. C. (1981).   Sleep-wake disorders in the elderly: A polysomnographic analysis. *Journal of the American Geriatrics Society, 29,* 289–296.

COULOMBE, P. J., DUSSAULT, J. H., & WALKER, P. (1977).   Catecholamine metabolism in thyroid disease. II. Norepinephrine secretion rate in hyperthyroidism and hypothyroidism. *Journal of Clinical Endocrinology and Metabolism, 44,* 1185.

DUSTMAN, R. E. & BECK, E. C. (1969).   The effects of maturation and aging on the wave form of visually-evoked potentials. *Electroencephalography and Clinical Neurophysiology, 26,* 2–11.

DUSTMAN, R. E. & SNYDER, E. W. (1981).   Life-span changes in visually-evoked potentials at central scalp. *Neurobiology of Aging, 2,* 303–308.

DUSTMAN, R. E., SNYDER, E. W. & SCHLEHUBER, C. J. (1981).   Life-span alterations in visually-evoked potentials and inhibitory function. *Neurobiology of Aging, 2,* 187–192.

EISDORFER, C. (1968).   Arousal and performance: Experiments in verbal learning and a tentative theory. In G. A. Talland (Ed.), *Human aging and behavior.* New York: Academic Press.

EISDORFER, C., NOWLIN, J. B. & WILKIE, F. (1970).   Improvement of learning in the aged by modification of autonomic nervous system activity. *Science, 170,* 1327–1329.

FEINBERG, I. (1974).   Changes in sleep cycle patterns with age. *Journal of Psychiatric Research, 10,* 283–306.

FEINBERG, I., KORESKO, R. & HELLER, N. (1967).   EEG sleep patterns as a function of normal and pathological aging in man. *Journal of Psychiatric Research, 5,* 107–144.

FORET, J. & WEBB, W. B. (1980).   Changes in temporal organization of sleep stages in men aged from 20 to 70 years. *Review of Electroencephalography and Neurophysiology Clinica, 10,* 171–176.

FROEHLING, S. (1974).   Effects of propranolol on behavioral and physiological measures in elderly males. Unpublished doctoral dissertation. Florida: University of Miami.

GAKKEL, L. B. & ZININA, N. V. (1953).   Changes of higher nerve function in people over 60 years of age. *Fiziologicheskii Zhurnal SSSR im. I. M. Sechenova, 39,* 533–539.

GALBRAITH, G. C., GLIDDON, J. B. & BUSK, J. (1970).   Visual evoked responses in mentally retarded and nonretarded subjects. *American Journal of Mental Deficiency, 75,* 341–348.

GLIDDON, J. B., BUSK, J., & GALBRAITH, G. C. (1975).   Visual evoked responses as a function of light intensity in Down's syndrome and nonretarded subjects. *Psychophysiology, 12,* 416–422.

GUILLEMINAULT, C. C. (1982).   Effect of various pills on sleep and daytime alertness in the elderly. *Gerontologist, 22,* 187.

GUILLEMINAULT, C. C. & DEMENT, W. C. (Eds.). (1978).   *Sleep apnea syndromes,* New York: Alan R. Liss.

HARKINS, S. W., MOSS, S. F., THOMPSON, L. W. & NOWLIN, J. B. (1976).   Relationship between central and autonomic nervous system activity: Correlates of psychomotor performance in elderly men. *Experimental Aging Research, 2,* 409–423.

HARTER, M. R. & WHITE, C. T. (1970).   Evoked cortical responses to checkerboard patterns: Effect of check size as a function of visual acuity. *Electroencephalography and Clinical Neurophysiology, 28,* 48–54.

HAYASHI, Y. & ENDO, S. (1982).   All-night sleep polygraphic recordings of healthy aged persons: REM and slow-wave sleep. *Sleep, 5,* 277–283.

HUBEL, D. H. & WIESEL, T. N. (1962).   Receptive fields, binocular interaction and functional architecture in the cat's visual cortex. *Journal of Physiology, 106,* 106–154.

HUBEL, D. H. & WIESEL, T. N. (1977).   Functional architecture of macaque monkey visual cortex. *Proceedings of Research Society in London (Biology), 198,* 1–59.

INSTITUTE OF MEDICINE (1979).   *Sleeping pills, insomnia, and medical practice.* Washington, DC: National Academy of Science.

JEFFREYS, D. (1977).   The physiological significance of pattern visual evoked potentials. In J. E. Desmedt (Ed.), *Visual evoked potentials in man: New developments.* Oxford: Clarendon Press.

JEROME, E. A. (1959).   Age and learning—experimental studies. In J. E. Birren (Ed.) *Handbook of aging and the individual.* Chicago: University of Chicago Press.

KAHN, E. & FISHER, C. (1969).   The sleep characteristics of the normal aged male. *Journal of Nervous and Mental Disease, 148,* 477–505.

KALES, A., WILSON, T., KALES, J., JACOBSON, A., PAULSON, M., KOLLAR, E., & WALTER, R. D. (1967).   Measurements of all-night sleep in normal elderly persons: Effects of aging. *Journal of the American Geriatrics Society, 15,* 405–414.

KIMBLE, G. A. & PENNYPACKER, H. S. (1963).   Eyelid conditioning in young and aged subjects. *The Journal of Genetic Psychology, 103,* 283–289.

KNORRING, L. VON, & JOHANSSON, F. (1980).   Changes in the augmenter-reducer tendency and in pain measures as a result of treatment with a serotonin-reuptake inhibitor—Zimelidine. *Neuropsychobiology, 6,* 313–318.

KNORRING, L. VON, & PERRIS, C. (1981).   Biochemistry of the augmenting-reducing response in visual evoked potentials. *Neuropsychobiology, 7,* 1–8.

LEE, R. G. & BLAIR, R.D.G. (1973).   Evolution of EEG and visual evoked response changes in Jakob-Creutzfeldt disease. *Electroencephalography and Clinical Neurophysiology, 35,* 133–142.

LINDSLEY, D. B. (1952).   Physiological phenomena and the electroencephalogram. *Electroencephalography and Clinical Neurophysiology, 4,* 443–456.

LINDSLEY, D. B. (1960).   Attention, consciousness, sleep, and wakefulness. In J. Field (Ed.), *Handbook of Physiology.* American Physiological Society, Section 1, Vol. 3.

LINDSLEY, D. B., SCHREINER, L. H., KNOWLES, W. B., & MAGOUN, H. W. (1950).   Behavioral and EEG changes following chronic brain stem lesions in the cat. *Electroencephalography and Clinical Neurophysiology, 2,* 483–498.

MARSH, G. R. & THOMPSON, L. W. (1977).   Psychophysiology of aging. In J. E. Birren & K. W. Schaie (Eds.)., *Handbook of the psychology of aging.* New York: Van Nostrand Reinhold.

MICHALEWSKI, H. J., THOMPSON, L. W., SMITH, D.B.D., PATTERSON, J. V., BOWMAN, T. E., LITZELMAN, D., & BRENT, G. (1980).   Age differences in the contingent negative variation (CNV): Reduced frontal activity in the elderly. *Journal of Gerontology, 35,* 542–549.

MILES, L. E. & DEMENT, W. C. (1980).   Sleep and Aging. *Sleep, 3,* 119–220.

MORUZZI, G. & MAGOUN, H. W. (1949).   Brain stem reticular formation and activation of the EEG. *Electroencephalography and Clinical Neurophysiology, 1,* 455–473.

PFEFFERBAUM, A., FORD, J. M., ROTH, W. T., HOPKINS, W. F. & KOPELL, B. S. (1979).   Event-related potential changes in healthy aged females. *Electroencephalography and Clinical Neurophysiology, 46,* 81–86.

POWELL, A. H., JR., EISDORFER, C., & BOGDONOFF, M. D. (1964). Physiologic response patterns observed in a learning task. *Archives of General Psychiatry, 10,* 192–195.

PRINZ, P. N. (1976a). Sleep patterns of healthy elderly subjects: Changes in EEG slow wave activity and REM sleep. Unpublished manuscript, University of Washington.

PRINZ, P. N. (1976b). EEG during sleep and waking states. In B. Eleftheriou & M. Elias (Eds.), *Annual review of experimental aging research.* Bar Harbor, ME: Experimental Aging Research.

PRINZ, P. N. (1977). Sleep patterns in the healthy aged: Relationship with intellectual function. *Journal of Gerontology, 32,* 179–186.

PRINZ, P. N. & HALTER, J. B. (1981). Sleep disturbances in the aged: Some hormonal correlates and some newer therapeutic considerations. In C. Eisdorfer & E. Fann (Eds.)., *Psychopharmacology of aging.* New York: S. P. Medical and Scientific Books.

SCHEIBEL, M. E. & SCHEIBEL, A. B. (1976). Structural changes in the aging brain. In R. D. Terry & S. Gerschon (Eds.), *Neurobiology of aging.* New York: Raven Press.

SCHENKENBERG, T. (1970). Visual, auditory, and somatosensory evoked responses of normal subjects from childhood to senescence. Unpublished doctoral dissertation, University of Utah.

SMITH, D.B.D., THOMPSON, L. W. & MICHALEWSKI, H. W. (1980). Averaged evoked potential research in adult aging—Status and prospects. In L. W. Poon (Ed.) *Aging in the 1980s: Psychological issues.* Washington: DC: American Psychological Association.

STRAUMANIS, J. J., SHAGASS, C. & SCHWARTZ, M. (1965). Visually-evoked cerebral response changes associated with chronic brain syndromes and aging. *Journal of Gerontology, 20,* 498–506.

SURWILLO, W. W. & QUILTER, R. E. (1965a). The influence of age on latency time of involuntary (galvanic skin reflex) and voluntary responses. *Journal of Gerontology, 20,* 173–176.

SURWILLO, W. W. & QUILTER, R. E. (1965b). The relation of frequency of spontaneous skin potential responses to vigilance and to age. *Psychophysiology, 1,* 272–276.

TECCE, J. J., RECHIK, D. A., MEINBRESSE, D., DESSONVILLE, C. L. & COLE, J. O. (1980). CNV rebound and aging: I. Attention functions. *Progress in Brain Research, 54,* 547–551.

THOMPSON, L. W. & MARSH, G. R. (1973). Psychophysiological studies of aging. In C. Eisdorfer & M. P. Lawton (Eds.), *The psychology of adult development and aging.* Washington, DC: American Psychological Association.

THOMPSON, L. W. & NOWLIN, J. B. (1973). Relation of increased attention to central and autonomic nervous systerm states. In L. F. Jarvik, C. Eisdorfer, & J. E. Blum (Eds.) *Intellectual functioning in adults.* New York: Springer.

TROYER, W. G., JR., EISDORFER, C., WILKIE, F., & BOGDONOFF, M. D. (1966). Free fatty acid responses in the aged individual during performance of learning tasks. *Journal of Gerontology, 21,* 415–419.

WEBB. W. B. (1981). Sleep stage responses of older and younger subjects after sleep deprivation. *Electroencephalography and Clinical Neurophysiology, 52,* 368–371.

WEBB. W. B. & DREBLOW, L. M. (1982). A modified method for scoring slow wave sleep of older subjects. *Sleep, 5,* 195–199.

WELFORD, A. T. (1965). Performance, biological mechanisms and age: A theoretical sketch. In A. T. Welford & J. E. Birren (Eds.), *Behavior, aging and the nervous system.* Springfield, IL: Charles C. Thomas.

WOODRUFF, D. S. (1977). *Can you live to be 100?* New York: Chatham Square Press.

CHAPTER 9

Aging of Sensory
and Perceptual Capacities

One of the more evident features of aging over the adult years is the change which occurs in the individual's ability to sense and perceive the world. Age changes occur in all of the sensory modalities, but the most apparent changes are manifest in vision and hearing. It is more or less an expected landmark that one dons reading glasses or bifocals in the mid-forties. While the use of a hearing aid is less universal, it is a common occurrence for those in their sixties to improve their failing hearing with this device. Thus, some of the major and general changes in the sensory systems with aging are familiar to laymen as well as to students of aging processes. In this chapter we will examine these well-known age changes and some of their underlying causes as well as explore some of the less apparent changes in the various modalities. Together with the sensory changes, other changes in more complex perceptual processes will be discussed.

When psychologists consider processes of sensation and perception they almost always make a distinction between them. Sensation is viewed as the activity of the sensory receptors—in the eyes, ears, nose, mouth, skin—which involves the recepiton and registration of the stimulus energy and the coding of it into signals which the brain can interpret. The response to a pinpoint of light or to a pure tone would be considered a sensation.

Perception is involved when we attach meaning and significance to sensations or combine them into a more complex whole. An example of an experiment with sensation would be the determination of how small an amount of odorant an individual could detect by smelling it on a neutral surface. A perceptual experiment would necessarily involve more complex stimuli. For example, testing individuals' responses to visual illusions would be considered to be a study of perception. Whenever interpretation of stimuli is involved, perceptual processes are present. In some sense, interpretation and decision making enter into even the simplest of studies of sensation as the subject must decide whether the stimulus was present or not. For this reason, the distinction between sensation and perception is somewhat artificial, but it is useful when we attempt to relate the behaviors of sensation and perception as to where they are processed in the nervous system. Sensation occurs at a peripheral receptor level while perception involves higher more central processes in the brain.

All sensory information, whether it is the wavelength of light, the frequency of a tone, or the intensity of pressure, is translated or transduced by sensory receptors into the firing of nerve cells. The world is never perceived directly. It is interpreted through the nervous system. From this perspective, it is important to be aware of the changes which occur in the nervous system during adulthood.

AGE CHANGES IN THE NERVOUS SYSTEM

Unlike the predictable sequence of development of the nervous system, aging processes are more random and do not occur at a demarcated rate or sequence. Aging in the nervous system cannot be described as occurring in systematic and predictable phases such as is the case for cell development in the nervous system. Instead, a number of structures change in the nervous system with age, and the changes vary among individuals.

At a cellular level, the most evident change which occurs in the nervous system is that nerve cells or neurons are lost. Neuronal loss is not unique to aging. More cells may be lost in fetal and neonatal development than at any other point in the life span, but the rate of neuronal development loss may accelerate in late adulthood.

Accurately pinpointing the amount of neuronal loss in the aging nervous system has been difficult for several reasons. There is no technique currently available to examine or count neurons in the living brain. Thus, counts must be undertaken upon autopsy and can be done at only one point in the life of the individual. Since there is variability in the number of cells in human brains, it is difficult to estimate how much has been lost when an accurate count of what was present in earlier years is simply not available. Estimates of amount of loss are based on cell counts in brains of other younger individuals. Another technical problem is that cell counts in human brains cannot commence immediately upon the death of the individual. In the intervening time between death and the beginning of the neuron count, changes can occur in the brain which would render the resulting data inaccurate. Also, in treating the brain so that the cells can be visualized in the microscope, damage to the tissue may occur to bias the count.

In spite of the difficulties in carrying out cell counts in the human brain, a number of these types of studies have been conducted, and they concur in their conclusions. Neurons are lost in the aging brain. The scientist best known for his research on estimating the number of cells in the aging brain is Harold Brody (1955, 1973, 1987; Brody & Vijayashankar, 1977). He performed some of the first hand counts of brain cells in adults, using accident victims as his subjects. He found differences in the amount of cells lost in different areas. The greatest loss was found in the top part of the temporal lobe, which is the superior temporal gyrus. All six layers of the cortex were affected, but the loss was greater in some layers than in others.

In the last decade new methods have been employed in which the cell counts can be automated. Research using the machine counts corroborates the earlier work. The number of neurons in the brains of animals have also been found to decline with age. In general the results from hand counts, machine counts, and counts of animal cells indicate that there is a 20 to 40 percent loss with age in the number of neurons in the brain.

While the findings of neuron loss in the brain were initially interpreted to signify loss of capacity, more recent interpretations have suggested that cell loss in some cases may improve functioning in the brain. The central nervous system is composed of a hundred billion neurons, and it undoubtedly includes some redundancy. By eliminating some of the neurons, the system may be more finely tuned rather than impaired. The metaphor which has been used is that of a sculpture. The young brain is like the uncarved piece of rock. Experience and aging sculpt the unformed brain into a finely-tuned piece. The rough edges are removed and the core is honed into a work of art.

The loss of neurons is one of the most significant age changes in the nervous system. There are a number of other changes as well, including changes in some of the components in the neuron such as the membrane and nucleus, a buildup in all parts of the neuron interior of a substance called lipofuscin, and an increase in the number and density of support cells (glial cells).

An age change which may have significant impact on the sensory capacities of the organism actually occurs outside the nervous system. This is the change which occurs in the arteries supplying blood to the brain and nervous system throughout the body. The arteries throughout the body lose elasticity and become more rigid and narrow in older adults. Arteries first begin to harden in the decade of the thirties and very gradually they become more rigid. This process is a part of normal aging. The elastin tissue in the arteries is replaced by collagen which is a stiffer, more rigid fiber. This constricts the arteries and often results in an increase in blood pressure as well as a decrease in blood flow. The process is exacerbated in the case of arteriosclerosis. When neurons receive less oxygen supply from blood, they function less efficiently and will die if the oxygen reduction is significant. Thus, the loss in sensitivity in some of the sensory modalities may be a result of insufficient blood supply to the receptors.

SENSORY CHANGES IN
ADULTHOOD AND OLD AGE

In the following pages on sensory changes, we will examine how aging affects sensory capacity at the receptor level. Many of these changes occur independently of one another in the different sensory modalities. Indeed, some of the changes in a given sensory receptor such as the eye are independent because the eye itself is complex and has many functioning components. Thus, the loss of muscle fibers in the iris and the increase in the thickness of the lens occur as independent phenomena in the aging eye. On the other hand, the net effect of each of these changes is the same. The amount of light reaching the retina is reduced.

In this section we will begin with the simplest of sensory systems, the sense of touch, and proceed through the sensory modalities as they increase in complexity to the sense of vision.

Touch

One example of a sensory modality affected by poor circulation in late life is the sense of touch. As can be seen in Figure 9.1, the touch receptors are located under the surface of the skin. The blood supply to these areas comes through small capillaries which can become occluded in old age. The number of receptors is less in later life, and the threshold for the sensation of touch—that is, the smallest amount of energy or change in energy which can be detected—is higher in old than in young individuals. In one study which suggested a parallel between the age differences in concentration of touch receptors and age differences in tactile sensitivity, Ronge (1943) counted the number and concentration of touch receptors in segments of the skin of the index finger in subjects ranging from one to 80 years of age. He found a decrease in the density of receptors (Meissner's corpuscles) in the first two decades of life due to the increase in size of the finger. An age difference was also found over the adult life span presumably due to the loss of receptors in later life. Bolton, Winkelmann and Dyck (1966) observed a decrease in the number of Meissner's corpuscles in the skin of fingers of older individuals, and Thornbury and Mistretta (1981) reported rather substantial age differences in the sensitivity of the index finger.

Counts of touch receptors can be carried out only at autopsy, while measures of touch threshold are made in living subjects. Thus, there is at present no means to assess tactile sensitivity and count Meissner's corpuscles in the same individuals. Nevertheless, because the number of touch receptors declines around the same age that there are age differences in tactile thresholds (during the decade of the fifties), it is assumed that the sensitivity changes result from the loss of Meissner's corpuscles.

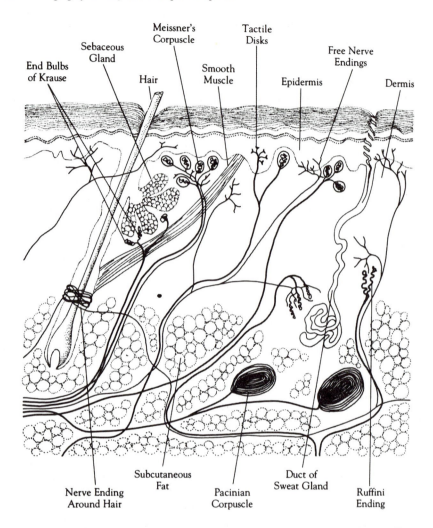

FIGURE 9.1 Cutaneous receptors. A schematic section of the nerve supply of the human skin, showing the receptors for mechanical energy (e.g., touch, pressure, temperature, and pain). Source: After Woolard, from E. Gardner (1963). *Fundemantals of Neurology*, 4th ed., Philadelphia: W. B. Saunders. Reprinted by permission.

The sense of touch is called a proximal sense along with the other cutaneous senses and the sense of taste. This means that the receptor responds to stimuli which actually have contact with it or are near. The proximal senses are the earliest senses to develop and tend to be simpler in their organization. The distal senses such as audition and vision respond to stimuli which are distant from the sensory receptor. These two senses are also the most complex in terms of their sensory receptors and brain representation. They are the last senses to develop, and since they are so complex, they are the most likely to be impaired in later life.

Pain

There has been general interest on the subject of whether pain sensitivity changes with age. Since old people are likely to suffer from at least one chronic disease and since they often adapt to it and continue to function, it has been speculated that pain sensitivity declines. Although a number of studies have been undertaken to answer this question, they have not provided compelling evidence for either side.

Early studies of pain perception used the technique of painting a black circle on the forehead of the subject with India ink, shining intense lights on the circle, and determining the amount of light energy required to elicit pain. Several of these studies found stability in pain thresholds over the adult life span (Birren, Shapiro & Miller, 1950; Hardy, Wolff & Goodell, 1943), but another (Chapman, 1944) found decreased sensitivity in older subjects. Chapman and Jones (1944) observed higher pain thresholds in relatively young adults suggesting decreasing pain sensitivity by middle age, but Schluderman and Zubek (1962) found stability in pain threshold until late in the decade of the fifties. Using a different technique, electrical stimulation of electrodes attached to the teeth to produce dental pain, Harkins and Chapman (1976, 1977) found no adult age differences in pain perception in either men or women.

The majority of studies of pain sensitivity in adulthood and old age suggest that it remains constant. However, clinical evidence implies that older people feel pain less than the young, and they appear to respond less to pain. Perhaps this means that pain tolerance increases with age while pain sensitivity remains relatively stable.

Balance

The receptors involved in the sense of balance and the ability to maintain upright posture are called the vestibular apparatus as illustrated in Figure 9.2. These receptors are located in the bony labyrinth of the inner ear. They consist of three semicircular canals, along with the saccule and the utricle. Falls and dizziness are a common complaint of older persons, and these problems may be related to changes involving the vestibular apparatus.

Orma and Koskenoja (1957) studied postural dizziness in the aged and found it to exist in 81 percent of males and 91 percent of females over the age of 65. Data from physical examination of these individuals led the investigators to conclude that the dizziness probably resulted from transient circulatory disturbances occurring during changes in body position rather than from age changes in the vestibular apparatus. Since the vestibular apparatus is located on the side of the

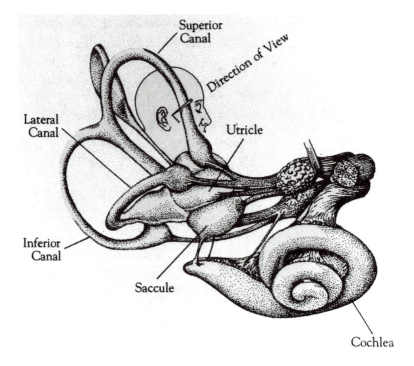

FIGURE 9.2 The vestibular apparatus. The human membranous labyrinth, showing the structural relations of the cochlear to the vestibular apparatus (the semicircular canals and the utricle and saccule). Source: Hardy, M. (1934). Observations on the innervations of the macula sacculi in man. *Anatomical Record, 59,* p. 412. Reprinted by permission.

head in a position where the cerebral arteries make the sharpest bends and thus are most likely to be adversely affected as they harden with age, it is likely that circulatory insufficiency impairs vestibular function. However, since increases in body sway along with falls and dizziness are almost universally present in older people, Szafran and Birren (1969) suggested that the vestibular apparatus itself may change adversely with age.

Smell

There is not a great deal of information about adult age changes in the sense of smell. In one of the most thorough and recent reviews of the literature on olfaction and aging, Engen (1977) asserted that the data on age changes in the sense of smell are sparse and contradictory. Nevertheless, on the basis of the few recent studies, Engen concluded that the sense of smell is not seriously affected by age. Rather, in those studies in which there are large age differences in olfactory sensitivity, the health of the older sample seems to be poor.

One of the most comprehensive studies of the sense of smell was carried out by Rovee, Cohen and Shlapack (1975). One hundred and twenty subjects ranging in age from 6 to 94 judged the intensity of seven different concentrations of an odorant. Two groups of older subjects aged 60 to 70 and 80 to 90 actually demonstrated more sensitivity than subjects in the age groups between 20 and 50. Thus, there was no evidence of any decline in olfactory sensitivity with age. Since olfactory sensitivity is particularly salient in neonates, the investigators suggested that senses developing very early in life may be the senses showing the greatest stability over the life span.

Taste

The evidence for age changes in the sense of taste is somewhat mixed, but the majority of studies suggests that there is some decline in taste sensitivity in later life. In the early studies in which small amounts of various sweet, bitter, sour, or salty substances were mixed in water and tasted by subjects, older subjects required higher concentrations of the substance to detect it (e.g., Bourliere, Cendron & Rapaport, 1958; Byrd & Gertman, 1959; Cooper, Bilash & Zubek, 1959; Richter & Campbell, 1940). Using a different method, Hughes (1969) applied a weak galvanic current to the tongue which produced a taste sensation. The amount of current necessary to elicit taste sensation in young subjects was lower than that required to elicit a response in older subjects. On the other hand, Kranz, Berndt and Wagner (1968) failed to replicate this age effect using the same method.

Most of the studies which have been carried out on taste sensitivity over the adult life span concur in indicating that there is a decline in taste sensitivity with age. However, in a review of the literature on this topic Engen (1977) cautions that this conclusion should not be accepted as a certainty without further research on taste preference as well as taste sensitivity over the life span. Indeed, since Engen made this caution, Grzegorczyk, Jones and Mistretta (1979) measured sensitivity to salt taste in subjects ranging in age from 23 to 92 and found that threshold increases over the adult life span existed but were smaller than indicated by previous studies.

Hearing

The auditory apparatus is shown in Figure 9.3. The part of the ear which seems to be most affected by processes of aging is the cochlea. However, it can be seen in Figure 9.3 that the auditory apparatus is complex, and with age, deterioration may occur in peripheral components involved in sound transmission as well as in the neural structures.

There is probably as much data on hearing acuity in adults as on any measure of human sensory capacity. Tens of thousands of adults of all ages have had their hearing tested with traditional audiometric techniques as they apply for jobs in some large corporations or as they continue in the work force. These large data sets have been combined and analyzed with the results indicating that hearing acuity begins to decline in the decade of the twenties with some hearing loss apparent

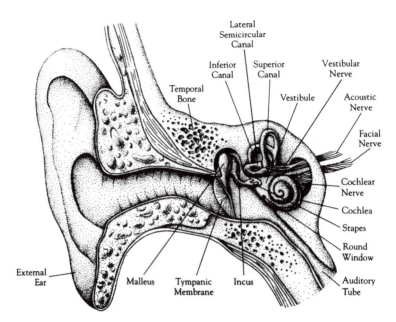

FIGURE 9.3 The auditory apparatus. A semischematic drawing of the human ear. Source: After Brodel, from E. Gardner (1963). *Fundamentals of Neurology,* 4th ed., Philadelphia: W. B. Saunders. Reprinted by permission.

beginning in the decade of the thirties (around the age of 37 for women and 32 for men). Impairment occurs mainly at the upper end of the frequency spectrum, and hearing impairment fitting this pattern is called presbycusis. Presbycusis is characterized by a progressive bilateral loss of hearing for tones of high frequency due to degenerative physiological changes in the auditory system as a function of age (Corso, 1977).

The typical pattern is for individuals to lose the most acuity for the very high frequencies, and thresholds for frequencies below 2,000 Hz show no significant deterioration. The loss in the 4,000 to 6,000 Hz frequency range is greater than in any other frequency range. Hearing loss occurs earlier in men than in women with women retaining more acuity than men. These effects are shown in Figure 9.4 which illustrates the combined data of eight studies of hearing acuity in men and women as analyzed by Spoor (1967). The relation between hearing level and age at different frequencies is demonstrated in these figures which have been modified by Lebo and Reddell (1972) to conform to the 1969 calibration data of the American National Standards Institute. It can be seen in these figures that while hearing loss over the adult years for low frequencies such as 250 Hz is at most 35 dB, the loss at higher frequencies such as 8,000 Hz is as much as 100 dB. Longitudinal data on auditory acuity collected in the Baltimore Longitudinal Study of Aging now confirm what the cross-sectional data have been illustrating for years. Parallels

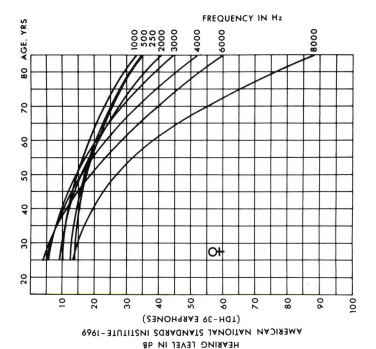

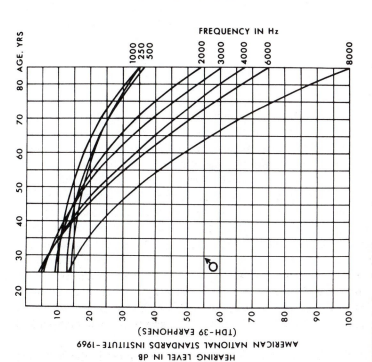

FIGURE 9.4 Spoor's (1967) composite presbycusis curves for men (♂) and for women (♀), modified to conform to ANSI-1969 standard. Source: Lebo, C. P. & Reddell, R. C. (1972). The presbycusis component in occupational hearing loss. *The Laryngoscope, 82,* pp. 1802–1803. Reprinted by permission.

between the longitudinal data and cross-sectional data as presented are almost total (Brant, Wood, & Fozard, 1986).

Some studies have demonstrated a shortening of the loudness scale in older subjects which is called recruitment. Because of recruitment, older subjects perceive an increase in the intensity of an auditory signal as being much more rapid than it actually is. Perception does not always correlate perfectly with the physical qualities of a stimulus, and in the case of recruitment, the discrepancy between the perceived and physical qualities of the stimulus is greater than normal.

Almost all older individuals show some degree of hearing loss and 13 percent of the population over the age of 65 have advanced signs of presbycusis (Corso, 1977). Hearing disability can impair an individual's capacity for social interaction as it interferes with the ability to understand conversation. Consonants are particularly difficult to understand when hearing loss is present, and women's higher frequency voice is less intelligible than men's deeper tones. Speaking in lower frequencies to one suffering from presbycusis may be as helpful as speaking more loudly.

Hearing loss has been associated with lowered intelligence test scores in the elderly (Granick, Kleban & Weiss, 1976; Schaie, Baltes & Strother, 1964). In both of these studies there was a statistically significant correlation between hearing acuity and intelligence test score. Granick et al. demonstrated in two very different samples that the relationship between hearing loss and performance IQ score was greater than the relationship between verbal intelligence and hearing loss. The implication was that hearing loss might have served as an index for some general aging factor in the individual.

Vision

Vision is the most complicated of the senses. Figure 9.5 illustrates some of the components of the eye. Not shown in Figure 9.5 is the complexity of the retina, which is like a little brain sitting on the periphery of the nervous system. Vision is the last sensory capacity to develop, and it is the sense with the most components to go wrong. A number of deleterious changes occur in the eye to make it function less efficiently in older adults. The crystalline lens of the eye thickens and yellows, scattering light as it enters the eye and requiring more light energy to permeate it. The muscles responsible for pupil accommodation lose fibers and cause the pupil to narrow. This again means that more light must be present to register on the retina. Because of these nonneural changes in the eye, it has been suggested that no increase in the magnitude of light energy of the stimulus can equate the old to the younger eye (Weale, 1965). Weale estimated that the retina of a 60-year-old receives approximately 30 percent of the amount of light reaching the retina of a 20-year-old. In contrast, Guth, Eatman and McNelis (1956) doubled the amount of light presented to the older eye and argued that perception could be equalized with this intervention.

Visual acuity with and without correction was measured in the Baltimore Longitudinal Study of Aging in several hundred men and women ranging in age

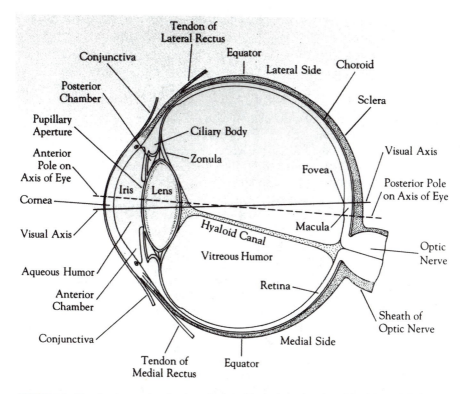

FIGURE 9.5 The visual apparatus. A schematic view of the horizontal section of the right eyeball. Source: Morris, B. J. (1966). *Human Anatomy*, 12th ed. New York: McGraw-Hill. Reprinted by permission.

from the twenties to the late eighties. Cross-sectional data from previous studies were confirmed by both the cross-sectional and longitudinal data from the Baltimore study. In 587 men representing the age decades of the twenties to the eighties, ten-year longitudinal changes in acuities revealed significant declines in corrected as well as uncorrercted acuity. Declines were greatest in men initially in their sixties and seventies (Fozard, Gittings & Schock, 1986). The researchers felt that their data were consistent with the hypothesis that less light reaches the retina of individuals as they age. As expected, uncorrected distance acuity declined precipitously between the forties and fifties, reflecting the age loss in accommodation.

Dark adaptation is the process by which the eye changes its capacity to respond as the level of illumination changes. Everyone has had the experience of walking from the brightly lit lobby of a theater into the darkness of the movie house and being temporarily blinded by the absence of light. Within a short period of time, some degree of dark adaptation occurs, and it is possible to see enough to get to a seat. For our eyes to become totally adapted to the absence of light, it takes 40 minutes. Numerous studies have illustrated how much more sensitive the eyes are to pinpoints of light after dark adapting for 40 minutes as compared to the sensitivity at the beginning of the waiting period when the eyes were adapted to bright light.

For over three decades, studies have been carried out which demonstrate that the ability of the eye to adapt to darkness declines over the adult life span. Birren, Bick and Fox (1948) examined 130 men between the ages of 18 and 83 years and found a significant decline with age in the sensitivity of the dark-adapted eye. The decline was most marked in subjects beyond the age of 60. Smaller pupil size in the older subjects did not account for the age differences in sensitivity. McFarland and Fisher (1955) observed a correlation of .89 betwen age and the final point of dark adaptation. The intensity of illumination at threshold levels almost had to be doubled for each 13 years of age between the ages of 20 and 60. The dark-adapted threshold was so closely related to age that McFarland and Fisher were able to take a given individual's threshold score and predict the subject's age with an accuracy of plus or minus three years. A striking feature of the data was the magnitude of the difference in sensitivity between the very old and the young. For example, at the second minute of dark adaptation, young subjects were almost five times more sensitive than the very old. At the fortieth minute, they were 240 times more sensitive. In this study, the rate of dark adaptation was also found to be slower in old age. However, Birren and Shock (1950) had found the rate of dark adaptation to be similar in young and old. It was only the threshold which showed age differences. The decrease in sensitivity to light was so apparent over the adult life span that McFarland suggested that the decrease in sensitivity to light might provide an index to the aging process.

The implications of these studies are considerable. In addition to the theoretical significance of the relationship between age and dark adaptation, the decline in light sensitivity with age has important significance for activities engaged in by many older individuals. For example, it is a common experience to enter a dimly lit restaurant with an older person and hear him or her complain that it is too dark to see the menu or the food. This ordeal for the older person is unpleasant, but it is in no way dangerous. However, there are activities in which the decline in light sensitivity in darkness are life threatening. The most common case is driving at night. The range of luminance in night driving is great. Thus, the rate of adaptation is exceedingly important. Older individuals are handicapped under these conditions, since their light thresholds in darkness are so much higher. They are hampered further because they are particularly sensitive to glare. Wolf (1960) examined the ability of 112 observers aged 5 to 85 to detect targets at angular distances of 4, 7, and 10 degrees around a glare intensity that varied. The intensity of target illumination needed for detection increased with age, with an abrupt increase around the age of 40. Comparing individuals between 5 and 15 to those between 75 and 85, it was found that the luminance of the target screen had to be increased 50 to 70 times for the older group to perform as well as the young. Older individuals' handicap in the face of glare, coupled with their decreased ability to adapt to darkness, severely hampers them in situations such as driving at night.

Color vision is also affected by aging of the eye. The amount and spectral distribution of light reaching the older retina decrease. The changes in spectral distribution reaching the older eye appear to affect perception of short wavelengths of light. Older individuals have greater difficulty in discriminating blues and greens.

An obvious functional change in vision over the life span is presbyopia, the impairment of the ability to focus on near objects. A normal eye at rest can focus objects at virutally an infinite distance, and it accommodates to focus near objects by shortening the focal distance of the lens. Maximal focusing accommodation is attained by around the age of 5, with a gradual decline in accommodation up to age 60, after which there is no further decline. The progressive decline in the focusing function results mainly from a loss of elasticity of the lens (McFarland, 1968). Thus, most people become farsighted as they grow older, a decline that often begins in childhood. Because most of this inability to focus near objects can be corrected with convex lenses, it presents no major problems for visual perception in middle-aged and older individuals.

The discussion of age changes in visual sensory capacity would not be complete without mention of two abnormal but common effects of aging on the eye. These are cataracts and glaucoma. While both of these afflictions are pathological and different from normal aging, they affect a large number of older adults.

The name *cataract* was given to this pathology because an advanced cataract is white and frothy like a waterfall. A cataract is any condition in the lens which makes it cloudy and less able to transmit a sharply focused image to the retina. The symptoms of a cataract involve a blurring of vision and a susceptibility to glare. The prevalence of cataracts in the United States has been estimated as 5 percent in individuals aged 52 to 62, and 46 percent in those aged 75 to 85 (Schwab & Taylor, 1985). Cataracts can be removed by trimming away the ectodermal opacity, and the procedure is performed more than 300,000 times annually in the United States (Roberts, 1987). However, cataracts are not removed until they start to produce some significant disability. After surgery, the lens is usually replaced with an artificial clear plastic lens that eliminates the need for contact lenses or thick glasses.

Glaucoma is a general term for an elevation of pressure within the eye such that damage to the nerve cells in the retina is caused. There are a number of causes of this buildup of pressure. However, glaucoma is rarely seen before the age of 40 (Anderson, 1987). When there is prolonged or severe pressure in the eye, nerve cells leaving the eye undergo progressive damage. The optic disk is damaged, and the outer areas of vision are affected first. When diagnosing glaucoma, the ophthalmologist studies the level of pressure, the appearance of the optic disc and retina, and the ability of the patient to see at the edges of the visual field. Early diagnosis is important because glaucoma is the leading cause of acquired adult blindness.

Treatment for glaucoma is through a number of modalities. The first step may by eye drops. Next may come oral medication, laser treatment, and surgery. Usually the patient does not notice any symptoms until the disease has progressed significantly. Thus, periodic eye examinations are strongly indicated for individuals over the age of 40.

PERCEPTION IN ADULTHOOD
AND OLD AGE

While the study of sensation over the life span has embraced all of the sensory modalities, the study of perception in adulthood and old age has focused primarily on the sense of vision with attention also to the auditory modality. Thus, we limit our discussion of aging and perception to these two sensory modalities.

Auditory Perception

In studies of auditory perception, attention has been directed to whether the losses observed in old age are the result of sensory changes or whether, in addition, more central changes in decision making are involved. One means to get at this issue is to conduct studies designed so that signal detection analysis can be applied. Studies of this type yield a measure of the subjects' sensitivity to the stimulus (d ') and also a measure of the criterion they have used for the judgment (β).

Craik (1966) and Rees and Botwinick (1971) used signal detection analysis in auditory tasks and found that young and old individuals did not differ in their ability to detect a pure tone in the presence of noise, but they showed a significant difference in their decision criterion. The older subjects were more cautious. They used more conservative criteria in accepting that the signal had occurred, thus waiting to be more certain that it was present before judging it as such. Using a different signal detection approach, Potash and Jones (1977) found older subjects to have poorer sensitivity as well as a more stringent decision criterion. Corso (1977) concluded that although the data are limited, the results strongly suggest that any attempt to explain decrements in adult performance solely on the basis of the physiological deterioration in sensory systems is likely to be overly restrictive.

A practical consequence of age changes in hearing ability is the increasing difficulty the aged have in understanding speech. In one study of speech perception, Feldman and Reger (1967) found that the ability to understand speech was relatively stable between the ages of 20 and 50 years. However, by the age of 80 individuals manifested a discrimination loss of 25 percent. Corso (1977) pointed out that several studies have indicated that even when the degree of pure tone hearing loss is held constant, there is a progressive decline with age in word intelligibility.

Under stressful listening conditions, the capacity of the aged to understand speech is even more greatly impaired. This phenomenon is not limited to the auditory system, as research on visual perception and aging has also indicated that whenever unusual conditions are introduced, older subjects' performance is more greatly compromised.

With regard to listening to speech in unusual circumstances, Bergman (1971) examined 282 adults in the age range of 20 to 79 years and identified very little difference in their ability to hear test sentences which were presented under ideal conditions with no distortions or interference. When he used stimuli which included overlapped words or interruptions, he observed age differences beginning in the decade of the forties. Each age group older than the group in the forties was pro- gressively worse in performance up to the oldest group in the seventies. Subjects in the seventh decade performed only half as well as the youngest subjects in con- ditions in which the speech stimuli were distorted.

Corso's (1977) interpretation of data on speech perception in adulthood and old age is that the reduced speech perception in later life may be due, in part, to a slowing of responsiveness in the central nervous system. He felt that the increase in time required to process information in the higher auditory centers is responsible for the higher error rate in the elderly. They simply miss some of the information because their nervous system cannot process it fast enough. Evidence for this inter- pretation comes from data on adults' response to accelerated speech. The word rate presented during each minute is increased to test the ability of the individual to respond quickly. With enough word acceleration, the comprehension of young subjects declines, but it is possible to offset the decline in discrimination by slightly increasing the intensity of the speech stimuli. This equalizing effect is not possible in older subjects. Calearo and Lazzaroni (1957) demonstrated that for subjects over the age of 70 years, 100 percent intelligibility can be obtained for normal word rates (140 words per minute) if the intensity is high enough; but for accelerated speech (150 words per minute), intelligibility does not exceed 45 percent regardless of intensity.

One of the aims of those who study age changes in behavior is to identify the cause of the age changes in an attempt to understand why they occur. In the domain of sensation and perception, as in other behavioral domains such as motor behavior, a question has been whether the behavioral age changes occur primarily as a function of peripheral changes in the sensory and nervous apparatus or as a function of more central changes. Corso (1977) asserted that this question was most relevant in the case of age changes in the auditory system and concluded that both central and peripheral changes led to the observed behavioral decline. In the case of the age deficit in speech intelligibility, it has been hypothesized that loss of neurons in the temporal lobe may be most responsible. Thus, a central explana- tion is offered. Slowing in central processing time perhaps caused by synaptic delays may be an additional cause of the poorer comprehension of speech. Other inter- pretations have included more peripheral factors such as lesions at the midbrain level. It may be that both peripheral and central components are involved in age changes in auditory perception, and it remains the task for future research to more explicitly relate specific behavioral losses to their locus in the auditory system.

One fact that is clearly understood at the present time is that a significant relation exists between excessive noise exposure and permanent hearing loss. This may be the primary reason why hearing loss is greater in men than in women. Men are more likely to be employed in occupations in which they are exposed to excessive noise. Corso (1977) pointed out that for several decades there has been a growing demand for the etiological evaluation of hearing losses in occupational workers of all ages so that the effects of noise exposure could be quantitatively separated from those of aging. He suggested that the problem was complex since the pathological processes for the two conditions are remarkably similar. Both involve the loss and degeneration of sensory hair cells and damage to related cochlear structures for which there is no known cure.

Visual Perception

We have considered some of the age changes in sensation and suggested that they result mainly from structural changes in the eye. However, perceptual studies indicate that physical factors cannot be held solely responsible for the decrement in visual function with age. Equating older and younger subjects for visual acuity and increasing the light intensity for aged people do not adequately compensate for visual declines in old age. Such approaches have led investigators to conclude that processes of integration and decision making, which take place in the brain, also become relatively impaired with age. Thus, declines in visual perception with age are seen as resulting from changes in the central nervous system as well.

There have been a number of methods devised to examine the manner in which stimuli are integrated in the nervous system. One of the early tests which was used rather extensively on adults of all ages is the measure called critical flicker fusion (CFF). The nervous system can perceive flicker in a stimulus only up to a certain rate. Above that rate, the light appears fused. This is the phenomenon which is used to produce motion pictures. The film is actually comprised of a large number of still pictures which appear to move when presented at the appropriate rate.

The rate at which a flashing light ceases to flicker is slower for an older person. In one study of this phenomenon, Wolf and Schraffa (1964) demonstrated that the oldest group aged 86 to 95 could perceive a rate of flashing up to 30 flashes per second when the stimulus was flashed directly at the center of their retina. Subjects in the age range of 16 to 25 could perceive up to 45 flashes per second under the same conditions. Weekers and Roussel (1946) had established that age differences in CFF thresholds were not caused entirely by the smaller pupil size in the older age groups, as dilating the pupils of subjects decreased the age differences only by half.

Another way to examine the higher-order organization and processing of visual information is to consider the susceptibility of individuals to illusions throughout the life span. In this manner, psychologists attempt to understand perceptual processes by means of the "mistakes" made by the brain in interpreting information. We all have experienced optical illusions, and apparently the impact of an illusion is different at different points in the life span.

Figure 9.6 illustrates the Muller-Lyer illusion which has been used in collecting most of the life-span data. In the presence of surrounding contours, the two physically equal lines in this figure appear to be different lengths. In general, susceptibility to this illusion decreases between the ages of 6 and 12, rises slightly from 15 to 19, reaches a plateau between 20 and 39, and increases thereafter (Comalli, 1970). Eisner (1968) obtained these results with short-term longitudinal as well as cross-sectional data. He followed up subjects and observed changes in the effect of the illusion as well as comparing effects for subjects of different ages.

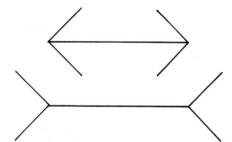

FIGURE 9.6   The Muller-Lyer illusion. These two lines are equal in length, but the bottom line looks longer because of the other lines around it.

Explanations that postulate that experiential factors lead to false interpretations of illusions cannot account for what happens with the Muller-Lyer figure because developmental functions indicate that susceptibility declines with experience and increases during old age. Pollack (1969) interpreted such functions as relating to physiological mechanisms which mature and then decline. He explains cases in which the optical illusion increases with age as being affected by intellectual mechanisms. In children, Pollack found high correlations between intelligence and the perception of those illusions to which susceptibility increases with age. There were no relationships between intelligence and the perception of illusions that decrease with age.

Comparing life-span data for four illusions, Comalli (1970) identified two general ways in which the effects of illusions changes with age. First, a declining susceptibility with age in childhood remained stable until old age, when there was an increase in susceptibility. Second, increasing susceptibility with age attained a maximal level, after which there was a plateau and then a decline in old age. Comalli suggested that these illusion patterns are consistent with the developmental notion of early-life progression followed by late-life regression. In all cases for which data on susceptibilty to illusions have been collected, the very young and the very old perceive illusions similarly even though it is in a fashion that is different from the perception of older children, adolescents, and adults.

Yet another perceptual ability that appears to change with age is the capacity to shift perceptual sets. This is the ability to reorganize a given initial perception. Figure 9.7 is an example of an ambiguous drawing that has been used to test this capacity. The figure can be perceived as either an unattractive old woman ("mother-in-law") or as an attractive young woman ("wife"). Older subjects appear to fixate on one of the two possible organizations of this figure, and they have difficulty in recognizing the alternative perception. Because this and other ambiguous figures shift less frequently for older subjects, it has been suggested that perception becomes more rigid with age.

One of the most useful hypotheses devised to explain many of the visual (and even some of the auditory) perceptual changes which occur in later life is the stimulus persistence hypothesis which was described in Chapter 8 on arousal, sleep, and aging. This hypothesis was first stated by Axelrod (1963) and one of the strongest proponents of this hypothesis has been Botwinick (1978). To review, the concept

A   B   C

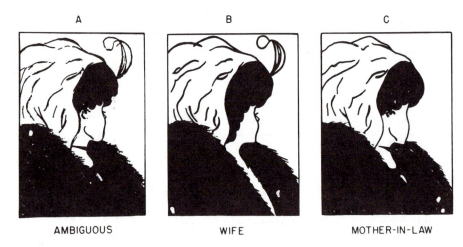

AMBIGUOUS   WIFE   MOTHER-IN-LAW

FIGURE 9.7 Ambiguous figure used to test shifts in perceptual set. In (A) the figure is ambiguous. This is the figure used most often in experiments. In (B) the "wife" aspects are highlighted. In (C) the "mother-in'law" aspects of the figures are highlighted. Source: Boring, E. G. (1930). A new ambiguous figure. *American Journal of Psychology, 42,* 444–445. Reprinted by permission.

is that in the older nervous system there is an increased persistence of the stimulus after it has once been registered. It is as if the older nervous system takes longer to process the stimulus and the aftereffects of the stimulus last longer. Another way to conceptualize it is that the rate of recovery from the effects of the stimulation may be slower. Since it is assumed that the processing of subsequent stimuli cannot take place efficiently until the effects of the first stimulus have subsided, stimulus persistence would cause interference and would impair performance in some circumstances.

Support for the stimulus persistence hypothesis has come from a number of different types of experimental paradigms. Stimulus persistence could explain why CFF occurs at a slower rate for old than for young subjects. Another type of study inovlves presenting a stimulus followed by an interval of darkenss, and then presenting a second stimulus. Using two flashes of light, Amberson, Atkeson, Pollack and Malatesta (1979) found that the interval separating the flashes had to be greater for the old subjects to perceive it than it did for the young subjects to report that they saw an interval of darkness. The dark-interval threshold had to be greater than 90 msec for 70-year-old subjects while it was 65 msec for 20-year-old subjects.

Using the letter "O" instead of light flashes, Walsh and Thompson (1978) did not support the stimulus persistence hypothesis. The dark-interval threshold was slightly greater for the young subjects. However, Kline and Schieber (1981) carried out a study quite similar in design to the Walsh and Thompson study and obtained opposite results. The mean threshold for the dark interval was greater for the older subjects.

In one of the most dramatic demonstrations of stimulus persistence in the elderly, Kline and Orme-Rogers (1978) devised a paradigm in which greater stimulus persistence actually resulted in better performance in the older subjects. The stimuli in this study were line patterns which represented parts of letters. Presented separately, the stimuli were meaningless. However, if they were to be fused, they would form a meaningful word. Hence, if a short enough interval was used to separate the first and second stimulus, the stimuli would fuse and the subject could read the word.

What Kline and Orme-Rogers (1978) demonstrated was that at longer inter-stimulus intervals, the older subjects got more words correct, as shown in Figure 9.8. It can be seen that when the two stimuli were presented simultaneously, all young and old subjects read the words correctly and got a score of 100 percent. At an interstimulus interval of 60 msec the old subjects were still performing close to 100 percent while the young adults had dropped to less than 80 percent correct. When a 120-msec interval intervened between the broken letters, less than half of them were read correctly by the young subjects. The old subjects were 70 percent correct at this interstimulus interval. It appeared that the persistence of the first stimulus in the nervous system of the aged allowed them to perform better under these unusual circumstances.

In his summation of the research relating to the stimulus persistence hypothesis, Kausler (1982) concluded, "In general, direct tests of the persistence concept have been sufficiently supportive to maintain an active interest in the concept's value for explaining the age differences over a wide range of perceptual phenomena." (p. 303). He went on to demonstrate that stimulus persistence could explain why color aftereffects as well as the spiral aftereffect involving the apparent continuation of rotation of an object after it has stopped turning last longer in

FIGURE 9.8 Percentages of young and elderly subjects recognizing words that are exposed in halves, with a varying interval separating the two exposures. Source: Adapted from Kline and Orme-Rogers, 1978 from Kausler, D. H. (1982). *Experimental psychology and human aging.* New York: Wiley. Reprinted by permission.

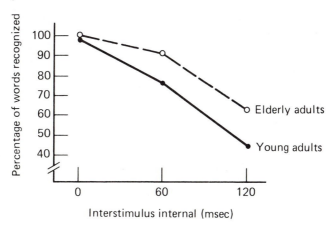

older subjects. There are also perceptual phenomena in old age such as the decrease in magnitude of some visual illusions which have not been successfully explained in terms of stimulus persistence. Nevertheless, the stimulus persistence hypothesis appears to be one of the most useful interpretations of some of the age effects on visual perception that is available at the present time.

SUMMARY

Age changes occur in all of the sensory modalities, but the most apparent changes are manifest in vision and hearing. In this chapter we differentiate between sensation, activity of the sensory receptors which registers the stimulation and codes the signals, and perception, the attachment of meaning and significance to sensations. All sensory information is transduced by sensory receptors into the firing of neurons, so the aging of the nervous system has important implications for age changes in sensory and perceptual systems.

A number of changes occur in the older nervous system, and these changes occur at different rates in different individuals. The most evident change at the cellular level is the loss of neurons. There is a 20 to 40 percent loss with age in the number of neurons. The greatest loss occurs in the superior temporal gyrus. Cell loss is not necessarily a deleterious age change; losing neurons may reduce some of the redundancy and "noise" in the brain. Another age change is a buildup inside neurons of a substance called lipofuscin. The support cells, called glial cells, increase in number and density. Outside of the nervous system, the arteries harden and become more rigid and constricted. This affects blood flow in the nervous system and may reduce the amount of oxygen available to neurons. Significant oxygen reduction to neurons causes them to die.

By the decade of the fifties, sensitivity to touch has declined significantly. There are fewer tactile receptors in the skin of older adults. The touch receptors decrease in number in later life, presumably because the small capillaries supplying the blood to the skin become occluded.

Pain sensitivity appears to remain stable over adulthood and old age. However, older adults may be able to tolerate pain better than younger adults.

Falls and dizziness are a common complaint of older people, and these problems may be related to changes involving the vestibular apparatus. Transient circulatory disturbances occurring during changes in body position may be the cause of much of the dizziness and falls. Age changes in body sway have led some investigators to suggest that the vestibular apparatus itself may become less efficient in old age.

While the data on age changes in the sense of smell are sparse and contradictory, the sense of smell does not appear to be seriously affected by age. On the other hand, taste sensitivity appears to decline with age.

Beginning in the decade of the thirties, the ability to hear high frequency tones begins to decline. Almost all older adults show some degree of hearing loss, and 13 percent of the population over the age of 65 have advanced signs of hearing loss for higher frequencies.

Many independent age changes occur in the eye. The lens thickens and yellows, scattering light. The muscles involved in accommodation deteriorate, reducing the size of the pupil. Both of these factors have the result of making more light energy necessary to stimulate the older eye. Visual acuity declines with age, especially after the age of 60. Due to a loss of elasticity and thickening of the lens, distance acuity becomes impaired between the ages of 40 and 50. Middle-aged adults develop presbyopia and require glasses for reading. The dark-adapted older eye is much less efficient than the dark-adapted younger eye. The older eye is more sensitive to glare, and it is less sensitive to the shorter wavelengths. Blues and greens are more easily confused.

Two relatively common diseases of the older eye are cataracts and glaucoma. While these eye diseases are not part of normal aging processes, they affect a large number of older adults. Cataracts are a condition of the lens making it cloudy and less able to transmit a sharply focused image to the retina. They can be removed surgically when they seriously impair visison. Glaucoma is a buildup of pressure in the eye which damages nerve cells in the retina. It can be treated in a number of ways including laser treatment and surgery.

A practical consequence of age changes in hearing ability is the increasing difficulty the aged have in understanding speech. By the age of 80, individuals manifest a 25 percent loss of speech discrimination. In stressful listening conditions, the impairment is significantly greater. The slowing of responsiveness in the nervous system may also account for some of the lowered intelligibility of speech. When older adults listen to rapid speech, their discrimination ability is reduced. The older visual system appears to respond to visual information more slowly and to fixate on one type of perception longer before shifting perceptual set. The stimulus persistence hypothesis postulates that in the older nervous system there is an increased persistence of the stimulus after it has once been registered. This hypothesis explains many of the results of studies of visual perception and aging.

REFERENCES

AMBERSON, J. I., ATKESON, B. M., POLLACK, R. H. & MALATESTA, V. J. (1979). Age differences in dark-interval threshold across the life span. *Experimental Aging Research, 5,* 423–433.

ANDERSON, B. (1987).   Eye: Clinical issues. In G. L. Maddox (Ed.), *The encyclopedia of aging.* New York: Springer.

AXELROD, S. (1963).   Cognitive tasks in several modalities. In R. H. Williams, C. Tibbits & W. Donahue (Eds.), *Processes of aging* (Vol. 1). New York: Atherton.

BERGMAN, M. (1971).   Hearing and aging. *Audiology, 10,* 164–171.,

BIRREN, J. E., BICK, M. W. & FOX, C. (1948).   Age changes in light threshold of the dark-adapted eye. *Journal of Gerontology, 3,* 267–271.

BIRREN, J. E., SHAPIRO, H. B. & MILLER, J. H. (1950).   The effect of salicylate upon pain sensitivity. *Journal of Pharmacology and Experimental Therapy, 100,* 67–71.

BIRREN, J. E. & SHOCK, N. W. (1950).   Age changes in rate and level of visual dark adaptation. *Journal of Applied Physiology, 2,* 407–411.

BOLTON, C. F., WINKELMANN, R. K. & DYCK, P. J. (1966).   A quantitative study of Meissner's corpuscles in man. *Neurology, 16,* 363–369.

BOTWINICK, J. (1978).   *Aging and behavior* (2nd ed.). New York: Springer.

BOURLIERE, F., CENDRON, H. & RAPAPORT, A. (1958).   Modification avec l'age des senils gustatifs de perception et de reconnaissance aux saveurs salee et sucree chez l'homme. *Gerontologia, 2,* 104–122.

BRANT, L. J., WOOD, J. L. & FOZARD, J. L. (1986).   Age changes in hearing thresholds. *Gerontologist, 26,* 156.

BRODY, H. (1955).   Organization of the cerebral cortex. III. A study of aging in the human cerebral cortex. *Journal of Comparative Neurology, 102,* 511–556.

BRODY, H. (1973).   Aging of the vertebrate brain. In M. Rockstein (Ed.), *Development and Aging in the Nervous System.* New York: Academic Press.

BRODY, H. (1987).   Central nervous system. In G. Maddox (Ed.), *The encyclopedia of aging.* New York: Springer.

BRODY, H. & VIJAYASHANKAR, N. (1977).   Anatomical changes in the nervous system. In C. E. Finch & L. Hayflick (Eds.), *Handbook of the biology of aging.* New York: Van Nostrand Reinhold.

BYRD, E. & GERTMAN, S. (1959).   Taste sensitivity in aging persons. *Geriatrics, 14,* 381–384.

CALEARO, C. & LAZZARONI, A. (1957).   Speech intelligibility in relation to the speed of the message. *Laryngoscope, 67,* 410–419.

CHAPMAN, W. P. (1944).   Measursements of pain sensitivity in normal control subjects and in psychoneurotic patients. *Psychosomatic Medicine, 6,* 252–255.

CHAPMAN, C. M. & JONES, C. M. (1944).   Variations in cutaneous and visceral pain sensitivity in normal subjects. *Journal of Clinical Investigation, 23,* 81–91.

COMALLI, P. E., JR. (1970).   Life span changes in visual perception. In L. R. Goulet & P. B. Baltes (Eds.), *Life-span developmental psychology: Research and theory.* New York: Academic Press.

COOPER, R. M., BILASH, M. A. & ZUBEK, J. P. (1959).   The effect of age on taste sensitivity. *Journal of Gerontology, 14,* 56–58.

CORSO, J. F. (1977).   Auditory perception and communication. In J. E. Birren & K. W. Schaie (Eds.), *Handbook of the psychology of aging.* New York: Van Nostrand Reinhold.

CRAIK, F.I.M. (1966).   The effects of aging on the direction of faint auditory signals. In *Proceedings of the 7th International Congress of Gerontology* (Vol. 6), Vienna: Viennese Medical Academy.

EISNER, D. (1968).   *Age changes in perceptual functioning in the aged.* Unpublished master's thesis, West Virginia University.

ENGEN, T. (1977).   Taste and smell. In J. E. Birren & K. W. Schaie (Eds.), *Handbook of the psychology of aging.* New York: Van Nostrand Reinhold.

FELDMAN, R. M. & REGER, S. N. (1967).   Relations among hearing, reaction time, and age. *Journal of Speech and Hearing Research, 10,* 479–495.

FOZARD, J. L., GITTINGS, N. S. & SHOCK, N. W. (1986).   Age changes in visual acuity. *Gerontologist, 26,* 158.

GARDNER, E. (1963).   *Fundamentals of neurology,* (4th Ed.), Philadelphia: W. B. Saunders.

GRANICK, S., KLEBAN, M. H. & WEISS, A. D. (1976).   Relationships between hearing loss and cognition in normally hearing aged persons. *Journal of Gerontology, 31,* 434–440.

GRZEGORCZYK, P. B., JONES, S. W. & MISTRETTA, C. M. (1979).   Age-related differences in salt taste acuity. *Journal of Gerontology, 34,* 834–840.

GUTH, S. K., EASTMAN, A. A. & McNELIS, J. F. (1956).   Lighting requirements for older workers. *Illumination Engineering, 51,* 656–660.

HARDY, J. D., WOLFF, H. G. & GOODELL, H. (1943).   The pain threshold in man. *American Journal of Psychiatry, 99,* 744–751.

HARKINS, S. W. & CHAPMAN, C. R. (1976).   Detection and decision factors in pain perception in young and elderly men. *Pain, 2,* 253–264.

HARKINS, S. W. & CHAPMAN, C. R. (1977).   The perception of induced dental pain in young and elderly women. *Journal of Gerontology, 32,* 428–435.

HUGHES, G. (1969).   Changes in taste sensitivity with advancing age. *Gerontologica Clinica, 11,* 224–230.

KAUSLER, D. H. (1982).   *Experimental psychology and human aging.* New York: Wiley.

KLINE, D. W. & ORME-ROGERS, C. (1978).   Examination of stimulus persistence as the basis for superior visual identification performance among older adults. *Journal of Gerontology, 33,* 76–81.

KLINE, D. W. & SCHIEBER, F. (1981).   What are the age differences in visual sensory memory? *Journal of Gerontology, 36,* 86–89.

KRANZ, D., BERNDT, H. & WAGNER, H. (1968).   Studies on age-dependent changes of the taste threshold. *Archiv fur Klinische und Experimenteele Ohren-Nasen, und Kehlkopfheilkunde, 192,* 258–267.

LEBO, C. P. & REDDELL, R. C. (1972).   The presbycusis component in occupational hearing loss. *Larygoscope, 82,* 1399–1409.

McFARLAND, R. A. (1968).   The sensory and perceptual processes in aging. In K. W. Schaie (Ed.)., *Theory and methods of research on aging.* Morgantown: West Virginia University Press.

McFARLAND, R. A. & FISHER, M. B. (1955).   Alterations in dark adaptation as a function of age. *Journal of Gerontology, 10,* 424–428.

MORRIS, B.J.A. (Ed.), (1966).   *Human anatomy,* (12th Ed.), New York: McGraw-Hill.

ORMA, E. J. & KOSKENOJA, M. (1957).   Postural dizziness in the aged. *Geriatrics, 12,* 49–50.

POLLACK, R. H. (1969).   Ontogenetic changes in perception. In D. E. Elkind & J. H. Flavell (Eds.), *Studies in cognitive development.* New York: Oxford University Press.

POTASH, M. & JONES, B. (1977).   Aging and decision criteria for the detection of tones in noise. *Journal of Gerontology, 32,* 436–440.

REES, J. N. & BOTWINICK, J. (1971).   Detection and decision factors in auditory behavior of the elderly. *Journal of Gerontology, 26,* 133–136.

RICHTER, C. P. & CAMPBELL, K. H. (1940).   Sucrose taste thresholds of rats and humans. *American Journal of Physiology, 128,* 291–297.

ROBERTS, J. C. (1987).   Eye: Structure and function. In G. L. Maddox (Ed.). *The encyclopedia of aging.* New York: Springer.

RONGE, H. (1943).   Altersveranderungen des Beruhrungssinnes. I. Druckpunktscjwellem und Druckpunktfrequenz. *Acta Physiologicia Scandinavica, 6,* 343–352.

ROVEE, C. K., COHEN, R. Y. & SHLAPACK, W. (1975).   Life-span stability in olfactory sensitivity. *Developmental Psychology, 11,* 311–318.

SCHAIE, K. W., BALTES, P. B. & STROTHER, C. R. (1964).   A study of auditory sensitivity in advanced age. *Journal of Gerontology, 19,* 453–457.

SCHLUDERMAN, E. & ZUBEK, J. P. (1962).   Effect of age on pain sensitivity. *Perceptual and Motor Skills, 14,* 295–301.

SCHWAB, L. & TAYLOR, H. R. (1985).   Cataract and delivery of surgical services in developing nations. In *Clinical Opthalmology,* Vol. 5, New York: Harper & Row.

SPOOR, A. (1967).   Presbycusis values in relation to noise induced hearing loss. *International Audiology, 6,* 48–57.

SZAFRAN, J. & BIRREN, J. E. (1969).   Perception. In J. E. Birren (Ed.), *Contemporary gerontology: Concepts and issues.* Los Angeles: Gerontology Center, University of Southern California.

THORNBURY, J. & MISTRETTA, C. M. (1981).   Tactile sensitivity as a function of age. *Journal of Gerontology, 36,* 34–39.

U.S. DEPARTMENT OF HEALTH, EDUCATION, AND WELFARE. (1965). *National health survey: Hearing levels of adults by age and sex, U.S. 1960–1962.* Washington, DC: U.S. Government Printing Office.

WALSH, D. A. & THOMPSON, L. W. (1978).   Age differences in visual sensory memory. *Journal of Gerontology, 33,* 383–387.

WEALE, R. A. (1965).   On the eye. In A. T. Welford and J. E. Birren (Eds.), *Behavior, aging and the nervous system.* Springfield, IL: Charles C. Thomas.

WEEKERS, R. & ROUSSEL, F. (1946).   Introduction a l'etude de la frequence de fusion en clinique. *Ophthalmologica, 117,* 305–319.

WOLF, E. (1960).   Glare and age. *Archives of Ophthalmology, 64,* 502–514.

WOLF, E. & SCHRAFFA, A. M. (1964).   Relationship between critical flicker frequency and age in flicker perimetry. *Archieves of Opthalmology, 72,* 832–843.

CHAPTER 10

Speed of Behavior and Aging

In the domain of behavioral speed, the perception that laypeople have about aging concurs with scientific observations of performance and aging. Behavior slows with age. One has only to observe an older person walking along the sidewalk or crossing the street to see that his or her responses are slower than the responses of younger adults. Indeed, the slowing of reaction time with aging can be exasperating to younger adults when they drive behind an elderly driver or when they try to shop in a supermarket crowded with elderly shoppers. In the case of older drivers, many states increase the frequency of driving examinations after the age of 70 to monitor for loss of sensory capacity as well as for slowing of speed of response. In spite of such cautions, the accident rate for older drivers is higher than for middle-aged drivers (Barret et al., 1977). Older shoppers are problematic not only because of their slowness in pushing their cart through the aisles but also because of their slowness in decision making about what to purchase. As much as a younger adult may respect the elderly, he or she can become frustrated at having to wait in a blocked aisle in a supermarket for several minutes while an older person slowly examines the products on the shelf.

Slowing of behavior is problematic for the older adult in daily living. Simple tasks like zipping a zipper or brushing teeth take longer. Table 10.1 lists some everyday tasks that have been shown to correlate with age. A high correlation with age means that the greater the age, the slower the performance on the task. These tasks such as cutting with a knife, using a fork, and dialing a telephone are highly practiced. However, even on these highly practiced tasks, reaction time slows. This

TABLE 10.1   Speed of Everyday Tasks and Correlation with Age.

Measure	Correlation with Age	Sample Size	Age Range	Source
Card sorting	0.54	49	20–80	Crossman and Szafran (1956)
Clerical perceptual speed	0.41	105	20–60	Horn et al. (1981)
	0.23	147	20–60	Horn et al. (1981)
Composite speed	0.51	161	23–60	Birren and Spieth (1962)
Copying digits	0.62	120	21–80	Botwinick and Storandt (1974)
Crossing off	0.63	120	21–80	Botwinick and Storandt (1974)
Cutting with a knife	0.32	60	18–74	Potvin et al. (1973)
Dialing telephone	0.64	60	18–74	Potvin et al. (1973)
Letter comparison substitution	0.45	102	20–70	Clark (1960)
	0.54	187	20–95	Miles (1931b)
Picking up coins	0.42	60	18–74	Potvin et al. (1973)
Squeezing toothpaste	0.55	60	18–74	Potvin et al. (1973)
Transmission rate	0.26	54	34–92	Surwillo (1964a)
Unwrapping band-aid	0.48	60	18–74	Potvin et al. (1973)
Using fork	0.33	60	18–74	Potvin et al. (1973)
Zipping garment	0.64	60	18–74	Potvin et al. (1973)

Source: Salthouse, T. A. (1985). Speed of behavior and its implications for cognition. In J. E. Birren & K. W. Schaie (Eds.), *Handbook of the psychology of aging,* (2nd Ed.), New York: Van Nostrand Reinhold, p. 404. Reprinted by permission.

result has led Birren, Woods and Williams to call the slowing of response speed with age the "most ubiquitous" of all age changes (Birren et al., 1979, p. 10).

The focus of this chapter is on the slowing of response speed with age and its causes. Reaction-time slowing is one of the most universal age changes which has been observed. It occurs in other species as well as humans, and it occurs as a function of normal aging, independent of disease processes. These observations led Birren (1965) to conclude that the speed of behavior will slow in every human if he or she lives long enough.

Psychomotor slowing does not appear to be dependent on age-related changes in health status as slowing occurs even in the healthiest of individuals (Birren et al., 1963; Szafran, 1966, 1968). Age changes in speed and timing are general inasmuch as they are not related to changes in specific sensory modalities (Koga & Morant, 1923) and because the slowing is not specific to certain tasks (Birren, Riegel, & Morrison, 1962; Chown, 1961). Data from a number of different lines of research support the notion that the slowing of psychomotor speed with age is an invariant biological transformation. Because slowing is a general phenomenon and occurs regardless of health status, it has been considered as a primary aging factor (Birren, 1965).

Reaction time is typically measured in a paradigm in which a stimulus or several stimuli are presented to a subject who is required to make a response with the shortest possible delay. Typically, the response is to press a button. The time elapsing between the onset of the stimulus and the initiation of the subject's response is operationally defined as the reaction time. Simple reaction time involves the presentation of one stimulus to the subject. Complex (also called choice or disjunctive) reaction time involves the presentation of two or more stimuli, and it can include the opportunity for two or more stimuli, and it can include the opportunity for two or more means of response (for example, with the right and left hand, or with the thumb and index finger). Reaction time to various mental tasks has been increasingly used by cognitive psychologists as a means of understanding cognitive function and aging (Salthouse, 1985).

SIMPLE REACTION TIME

Some of the first reaction time data to be collected were amassed at the International Health Exhibition in London in 1884 by Sir Francis Galton. A portion of these extensive data from more than 9,300 male and female subjects ranging in age from 5 to 80 was analyzed by Koga and Morant (1923). These data indicated that in adulthood, simple reaction time increased with age to both visual and auditory stimuli. The slowing was independent of age differences in acuity in a given sensory modality. The fastest reaction times were recorded for subjects aged 18 to 20 when mean auditory reaction time was 154 msec and mean visual reaction time was 182 msec. Subjects in the seventies had mean reaction times of 174 and 205 msec for auditory and visual reaction time, respectively. Hence, both auditory and visual reaction time increased by about 20 msec or 13 percent between the ages of 18 to 70. These figures probably underestimate the magnitude of slowing with age because Galton's sample included only the healthiest of older adults. Subjects were volunteers who came to the International Health Exhibition and actually *paid* to be tested on Galton's 17 measures. Presumably, only the most healthy and intact older adults attended the exhibition in the first place, and those willing to have themselves measured on tests presumed to assess perceptual and intellectual capacity must have been confident that they were "well preserved."

Subsequent studies confirmed Koga and Morant's (1923) results for visual and auditory reaction time. Additional confirmation of the result that psychomotor slowing occurs independently of sensory modality has been provided by studies showing age changes in simple reaction time to tactile stimuli (Hugin, Norris & Shock, 1960). Whenever speed of reaction has been compared in adult groups of different ages, older individuals have been found to be slower than younger individuals. Hicks and Birren (1970) summarized studies relating age and reaction time and found that the data demonstrated that over the adult age span from roughly 20 to 70 years, simple reaction time slowed from 11 percent to 102 percent depending on the type of stimulus, the stimulus modality, and the complexity of the task.

Exceptions to the Age-Related
Slowing Result

Three exceptions to the slowing with age phenomenon have been pointed out by Salthouse (1985). The first exception involves physical health and exercise. When younger adults in poor health are compared to healthier older adults, the age differences in reaction time disappear (Abrahams & Birren, 1973; Light, 1978; Spieth, 1964). Physically fit older adults also have faster reaction times than age-matched sedentary adults (Botwinick & Thompson, 1968; Spirduso, 1975, 1980; Spirduso & Clifford, 1978). Dustman et al. (1984) demonstrated that exercise caused reaction time to speed by exposing older adults to aerobic exercise training for four months and comparing them to a control group of unexercised older adults. Statistically significant improvement on a number of reaction time measures occurred in the older adults who exercised.

A second exception to the trend of slowing with age occurs when tasks measured vocal rather than manual reaction time. Oral versions of the digit-symbol task show smaller age differences than the written versions (Kaufman, 1968). The digit-symbol is a task which apperas on the Wechsler Adult Intelligence Scale (WAIS). It is among the tasks which show the greatest slowing as a function of age. The person is shown a table with ten different symbols, and each symbol is associated with a number from 0 to 9. In the written version, the individual is presented with rows of the various symbols and must fill in the blank underneath each symbol with the correct number. In the oral version, the person must simply say the number. The test is timed, and the score is the number of correctly filled-in or spoken numbers. In reviewing the literature on age and vocal reaction time, Salthouse (1985) cautions that the presently available evidence is not sufficient to determine if vocal response is an exception to the trend of slowing with aging. However, in many of the studies carried out thus far, age differences in vocal reaction time are minimal.

The third exception to the slowing with age phenomenon involves occasions when older adults have the opportunity to extensively practice the reaction-time tasks. Several investigations have indicated that reaction time can be improved with practice regardless of age. Mowbray and Rhoades (1959) demonstrated that with extensive practice (45,000 trials), one young subject improved at a two-choice reaction time task by 25 percent (from 392 msec to 218 msec). Improvement at a four-choice reaction-time task changed reaction time from 303 to 222 msec, or 27 percent. Such studies clearly indicate that practice is an important factor in the speed of response, and these data suggested to Murrell (1970) that the reported age differences in reaction time might represent age differences in capacity to perform an unfamiliar task. Murrell (1970) reasoned that the old may take longer to adapt to the new situation and therefore be handicapped in typical reaction-time study paradigms which involve samplings of 10 to 50 reaction-time trials. To test this notion, Murrell (1970) sampled 12,500 to 16,200 reaction-time trials with three subjects aged 17, 18, and 57 years. Initial age differences in reaction time were largely eliminated with practice, although the older subject did perform slightly more slowly on the two- and eight-choice reaction-time tasks. Younger subjects improved at the beginning of the task, while the older subject took up to 300 responses on the complex tasks before improvement showed. These data indicate that practice is an important variable in reaction-time tasks. However, the data also demonstrate that even with extensive practice, age differences in reaction time are not completely eliminated.

More recent studies of the effects of practice on reaction time in older adults have demonstrated that even with extensive practice (50 one-hour sessions), a fairly large residual age difference in reaction time remains (Salthouse & Somberg, 1982a). The basic result that age differences in overall speed persist has been replicated in studies involving practice ranging from 4 to 50 hours (Berg, Hertzog, & Hunt, 1982; Madden & Nebes, 1980; Plude & Hoyer, 1981).

Evidence that Slowing is an Age Change

All of the reaction-time studies which have been described have been cross-sectional involving different age groups on reaction time. Cohort differences could have affected the results. The evidence which establishes psychomotor slowing as an age *change* comes from several sources. First, reaction time data have been collected for over a century. Galton's data, analyzed by Koga and Morant (1923), were collected at the International Health Exhibition in London in 1884. The cohort born in 1864 that was 20 years old and at peak reaction time as measured by Galton in 1884 would be a 70-year-old group when measured around 1934. Reaction-time studies undertaken around 1934 demonstrated age differences in reaction time (Bellis, 1933; Miles, 1931), hence suggesting that age-related slowing occurred in that cohort.

Galton's data are consistent with data collected in subsequent decades on different cohorts of the same age groups. Taken as a whole, the cross-sectional data on reaction time representing age differences in adults over the period of a century suggest that reaction time slows with age.

There are also longitudinal studies of reaction time in adults. Botwinick and Birren (1965) carried out a five-year longitudinal study of reaction time on a card-sorting task. The subjects were an average of age 70 on the first testing, and they were 75 at the retest. There was a statistically significant slowing in reaction time over the five-year period. Follow-up data on the volunteers who participated in the Birren et al. (1963) study of healthy older men had slower reaction time at the 11-year retest (Granick & Patterson, 1971). Data from the Baltimore longitudinal study also indicate that reaction time slows as the participants age (Arenberg, 1982). These empirical data, coupled with the layperson's typical acknowledgment that one does indeed slow down with age, leave little doubt that the slowing of psychomotor speed is a reliable age change.

COMPLEX REACTION TIME

On complex reaction-time tasks, age-related slowing is greater than it is for simple reaction-time tasks. Increasing the number of choices makes the task more difficult for the subject, and reaction time increases. The old seem to be more hampered by the increase in task difficulty than are the young. In a classic study, Goldfarb (1941) found the difference between a 20-year-old group and a 60-year-old group on a simple reaction-time task was 11 msec, while on a two-choice task the difference was 57 msec, and on a five-choice task it was 66 msec. The age difference in reaction time increased as the number of choices increased. This result suggests that the older organism is less efficient in processing information.

The larger age difference in complex reaction time has been interpreted to mean that central nervous system processes are involved in the slowing. The reasoning is that the input time for the stimulus and the motor time for the response are similar in simple and complex reaction time. Hence, if the aged are disproportionately slowed in complex reaction-time tasks, it must be the central decision making that is slowing them down the most. The more choices they have to make, the greater the deficit as compared to the young. This means that slowing must occur in central information processing residing in the brain.

LOCUS OF THE CAUSE OF REACTION-TIME SLOWING

The older nervous system does not handle input as well as the younger nervous system. Numerous studies have been undertaken to identify the parts of the nervous system which change with age and alter the information processing capabilities of the individual.

Movement Time

One possible difference between young and old individuals which could account for age differences in reaction time is an age difference in movement time. Precisely how much movement time slows with age, compared with decision or reaction time, is difficult to determine. The reason for the difficulty lies in the fact that movements are usually measured in a context where decisions are involved. That is, movement time measurements can be easily contaminated with an undetermined contribution of time taken in the decision process governing the intent of the movement.

Tapping speed is a measure of movement time which is probably least involved with decisions. Hence, tapping speed may be a relatively pure measure of movement time. Talland (1962) reported small increases with age in tapping speed. Miles (1931) and Pierson and Montoye (1958) found that the old move more slowly, but Szafran (1951) found no age difference in movement speed when subjects were blindfolded. Older subjects are capable of moving as fast as young subjects in certain conditions. Szafran (1951) attributed the slower movement time of older subjects in normal visibility conditions to their greater tendency to visually monitor their movements.

In spite of the small increases in movement time with age, Birren (1955) argued that movement time alone could not account for increases with age in reaction time. When movement time is held constant while task difficulty is increased, the difference in reaction time between young and old increases as the task becomes more complex. This can be seen clearly in Figure 10.1. Tapping speed increases with age, but only minimally. However, handwriting speed, a more complex task than simple tapping, shows large increases with age. Movement time accounts for only a small proportion of the age-related slowing in tasks such as handwriting.

Sensory Acuity

Although a large number of independent changes occur in the receptors of all sensory modalities (which we discuss in Chapter 9 on sensation and perception), these age-related changes can account for only a small proportion of the total slowing of reaction time. When we conduct reaction-time studies, we use

FIGURE 10.1 Speeded performance for tapping and handwriting expressed as the percentage of the mean of each age group relative to the fastest performance across all age groups. *Source:* Salthouse, T. A. (1985). Speed of behavior and its implications for cognition. In J. E. Birren & K. W. Schaie (Eds.), *Handbook of the psychology of aging,* 2nd ed. New York: Van Nostrand Reinhold, p. 402. Reprinted by permission.

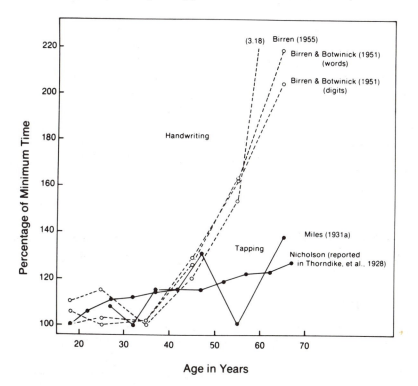

stimuli which are far above the sensory thresholds of the old as well as the young subjects. We make sure that elderly subjects can see visual stimuli clearly and hear auditory stimuli well. Since the work of Koga and Morant was published in 1923, we have known that reaction time had little relation to the acuity of sensory receptors. The correlation between visual reaction time and auditory reaction time was much higher than the correlation between sensory acuity in either of those sensory modalities and reaction time. Koga and Morant's results suggested that a process common to all sensory modalities was related to the age change in psychomotor speed.

Conduction Velocity

Since all information from sensory receptors is coded in nerve impulses and travels to the brain in neural sensory pathways, the slowing in nerve conduction velocity with age could lead to the results observed by Koga and Morant (1923). Several groups of investigators have measured conduction velocity in human peripheral nerves and have found decreases in mean conduction velocity from the ages of 30 to 80 to be 3 meters/second (Wagman & Lesse, 1952) and 10 meters/second (Norris, Shock & Wagman, 1953). Birren and Wall (1956) found no change in conduction velocity in the sciatic nerve of rats. Norris et al. (1953) pointed out that small age changes in human peripheral nerve conduction velocity could account for only 4 msec in reaction time assuming a one-meter pathway. Since simple reaction time slows by at least 20 msec over the age range of 20 to 70 years, peripheral nerve conduction velocity slowing accounts for only a fraction of the observed age change in reaction time.

Testing the possible significance of age changes in conduction velocity in another manner, Birren & Botwinick (1955) measured simple auditory reaction time of the foot, finger, and jaw in old and young subjects. The investigators reasoned that if conduction velocity was a factor in age-related slowing, the difference between the old and young in foot reaction time which is transmitted over a long peripheral nerve pathway would be relatively greater than the age difference in jaw reaction time. We discussed this study in Chapter 2 and presented the outcome in Figure 2.6. The age difference in foot, finger, and jaw reaction time was equal, with the old always slower than the young. Birren and Botwinick (1955) concluded that age changes in peripheral conduction velocity could not account for age changes in reaction time. Inference led to the conclusion that the slowness of older subjects was a function of the central nervous system rather than of peripheral structures.

Synaptic Delay

The synapse is another structure in the nervous system which might change with age, and age changes in synapses could lead to observed age change in reaction time. Wayner and Emmers (1958) measured synaptic delay in a monosynaptic reflex in rats and found a significant increase in synaptic delay from .97 msec in young rats to 1.36 msec in old rats. This represents an increase of 40 percent, suggesting that a large proportion of the slowing of behavior may be accounted for by the summation of synaptic delays in the central nervous system. Since a greater number of neurons and hence a greater number of synapses would probably be involved in a complex rather than a simple reaction-time task, age changes in synapses could also account for the greater slowing observed in complex reaction-time tasks.

Central Factors

The evidence clearly indicates that peripheral factors (movement time, sensory acuity, conduction velocity) alone cannot account for the magnitude of the age change in reaction time. Age changes in synapses and in the functioning of the brain and brain stem where sensory input and motor output are integrated seem to be the loci where the major changes leading to slowing occur. It would seem appropriate, therefore, to focus on the measurement of central factors which might be related to the age changes in psychomotor speed.

One such measure of brain activity is the EEG which is discussed in relation to aging in Chapters 5 and 8. The careful measuring techniques of Surwillo (1961, 1963, 1964a, b, 1968) have provided results suggesting that age changes in the EEG alpha frequency may be related to reaction time slowing in the aged.

The significance of Alpha slowing. Consideration of the alpha rhythm as a timing mechanism for behavior began almost with the discovery of the human EEG, and in a review of the early literature, Lindsley (1952) noted that Bishop (1933) and Jasper (1936) found relationships in animals between rhythmic cortical activity and brightness enhancement. At this time, Lindsley suggested that a cycle of approximately 10 cps as reflected in the alpha rhythm is the basic metabolic rhythm of brain cells. A large body of research literature has accumulated to support Lindsley's contention that the alpha frequency is related to excitability in the nervous system.

A proponent of the EEG excitability cycle hypothesis who has produced data called "startlingly convincing," (Sanford, 1971, p. 183) is Walter Surwillo. Surwillo's life-span data on EEG and behavior first led him to devise a model in which frequency of the EEG determined the timing of behavior (Surwillo, 1963, 1968). More recent data led Surwillo (1975) to revise this model into a two-factor model in which speed of information processing is governed by: (1) the time characteristics of the cortical gating signal; and (2) the recovery cycle of the information processing operations which are activated by the gating signals.

Because alpha waves seemed to be related to reaction time, and because older individuals had slower alpha waves and slower reaction time, Surwillo (1960, 1961) attempted to determine if reaction time and duration of alpha rhythm cycle were related. Measuring the duration of waves occurring between the onset of an auditory signal and the initiation of the subject's response, Surwillo found a statistically significant rank order correlation of 0.81 between reaction time and alpha period in a group of 13 subjects between the ages of 18 and 72 years. On the basis of these results, Surwillo hypothesized that the period of the alpha rhythm, or some multiple of the alpha cycle, serves as the master timing mechanism in behavior.

In other investigations, Surwillo attempted to replicate his first results with a larger sample and more sophisticated reaction-time tasks. Simultaneously measuring reaction time and average period of EEG between stimulus and response for 100 subjects ranging in age from 28 to 99 years, Surwillo (1963) confirmed his previous findings. In this study, a correlation of 0.72 was obtained between average reaction time and average EEG period. In another sample (Surwillo, 1964a), choice reaction time was related to alpha period with a correlation of 0.76. In both experiments there was a low but statistically significant correlation between reaction time and age which disappeared when brain wave period was partialled out. The presence of slow brain potentials appeared to be necessary for the occurrence of slow reaction time in old age, and this fact suggested to Surwillo that EEG frequency is the factor behind age-associated drops in processing capacity of the brain. He further speculated that the frequency of the EEG may reflect the operation of a "biological clock" within the CNS which is a determining factor in how rapidly and effectively information can be processed (Surwillo, 1968).

Failure to replicate Alpha significance.   Surwillo (1975) claimed that his work summarized in 1968 led to a model which could account for the prolonged reaction time in senescence. Data collected by Birren (1965) and Boddy (1971) in attempts to replicate Surwillo's work did not provide consistent support for the model, but these failures at replication were explained in terms of technical incompatibilities between the studies. In an attempt to replicate Surwillo (1963) with the data collected in a biofeedback study, Woodruff (1975) correlated reaction time and EEG data collected in a baseline condition before biofeedback began. While between subject correlations were statistically significant ($r = 0.40$, $p < .05$), they were only about half of the magnitude of Surwillo's correlations. Within-subject correlations ranged from -0.31 to 0.35 and in no way approximated Surwillo's results.

Woodruff (1975) used spectral analysis to assess EEG frequency, and Surwillo contended that the spectral analysis measure combined amplitude and frequency information and was therefore not a pure frequency measure. He argued that this was the reason for Woodruff's failure to replicate. Woodruff and Baum (1982) replicated Surwillo's (1963) technique exactly by performing manual analysis of EEG alpha activity recorded during the reaction time task and again found within-subject correlations which averaged to 0. Comparison of Woodruff and Baum's within-subject EEG alpha period and reaction-time correlation data on 80 adult subjects to Surwillo's data on 99 adult subjects is presented in Figure 10.2. The between-subject correlation for alpha period and reaction time in Woodruff and Baum's sample of 80 subjects ranging in age from 20 to 75 was 0.41 ($p < .05$).

It was Surwillo's (1971) own data on children below the age of 11 which led him to modify his model from a one- to a two-factor model. While young children's alpha rhythms are slow along with their reaction time, developmental changes in

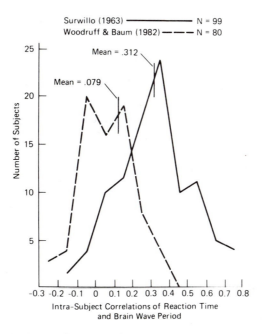

FIGURE 10.2 Comparison of intraindividual correlations between brain wave period and reaction time for the data of Surwillo (1963) and Woodruff and Baum (1982). The latter study was not able to replicate the large number of positive correlations within individuals. *Source:* Woodruff, D. S. (1985). Arousal, sleep, and aging. In J. E. Birren & K. W. Schaie (Eds.), *Handbook of the psychology of aging,* 2nd ed. New York: Van Nostrand Reinhold, p. 275. Reprinted by permission.

the EEG period could account for only a small fraction of the high correlations between age and reaction time in childhood. To explain this phenomenon, Surwillo (1975) added the notion of refractory period to his model, stipulating that gating signals could be missed if the information processing system was still refractory when the gating signal passed. This model was supported for reaction time and EEG relationships in childhood (Surwillo & Titus, 1976) but it did not account for the reaction time data as well in older adults (Woodruff & Kramer, 1979).

A major criticism of Surwillo (1963, 1968) is that he based a model predicting causal relationships on correlational data. He was aware of this problem and stated, "It is worth noting here that our hypothesis also demands that experimental alterations of brain wave frequency should be accompanied by corresponding changes in speed of response. This interesting proposition also deserves investigation." (Surwillo, 1963, p. 113). Indirect manipulation of the EEG alpha rhythm leads to changes in the timing of behavior (Creutzfeit, Arnold, Becker, et al., 1976; Harter, 1967; O'Hanlon, McGrath & McCauley, 1974). However, such relationships could be mediated by metabolic factors affecting EEG and behavior independently. More direct means for affecting alpha frequency were attempted by

Surwillo (1964b) who used photic driving and by Woodruff (1975) who used biofeedback.

Surwillo (1964b) applied flickering visual stimulation at frequencies above and below the modal alpha frequency in an attempt to drive subjects' alpha at faster and slower rates. Only 5 of the 40 subjects tested manifested adequate synchronization of alpha with flash rate, and there was some evidence of correlation between alpha period and reaction time in those subjects. These limited results did not provide conclusive support for Surwillo's model.

Biofeedback as an Intervention

Biofeedback is a technique that involves providing individuals with information about the activity of bodily processes of which they are unaware. When individuals become aware that they are producing a certain type of brain wave rhythm, that their heart is beating at a certain rate, or that their blood pressure is at a certain level, they can learn to alter or maintain these physiological rates. Connecting individuals to an electronic system which amplifies physiological signals and then activates signals which provide them with information about their internal states makes it possible for them to control those internal states. The electronic system provides the individuals with information about bodily activity (such as blood pressure, heart rate, or EEG frequency) of which they are normally unaware.

It appears that once individuals become aware of an internal state, the state can be altered. Thus, the electronic system—the biofeedback system—provides individuals with knowledge about the activity of internal organs, and when people have this awareness they become capable of consciously regulating to some extent the function of the organ. For example, in the case of the EEG alpha rhythm, a person typically is now aware of whether he or she is producing brain waves in the 8 to 13 cps (alpha) range. If he or she is placed in a situation in which the brain waves are measured and the information is "fed back" in the form of a tone or light to signal whether or not he or she is producing alpha activity, the person can learn to increase or suppress that brain wave activity.

With biofeedback it became possible to determine if the slowing of the dominant brain wave frequency in older people could be reversed. That is, it was possible to determine if old subjects could increase the time they spent producing alpha waves in the frequency bandwidths of young subjects. This biofeedback technique also made it possible to test the hypothesis by Surwillo postulating that the alpha frequency was the master timing mechanism in the nervous system. Surwillo argued that the slowing of the alpha rhythm could account for the slowing of reaction time in old age.

We designed an experiment in which young and old subjects learned to increase the abundance of EEG alpha activity at the modal frequency and at frequencies 2 cps faster and slower than the mode. Old subjects were just as capable of manipulating brain wave frequency in this manner as were young subjects, suggesting that some of the alpha slowing may be reversible. The data showing the performance of the young and old training groups at three brain wave frequencies are presented in Figure 10.3.

In this experiment it was also determined that when subjects produced fast brain wave frequencies, their reaction time was faster than when they produced slow brain wave frequencies. This is shown in Figure 10.4. Thus, biofeedback provided a means to help older individuals produce faster brain waves and possibly speed their reaction time (Woodruff, 1975; Woodruff & Birren, 1972).

Subsequent research involved examination of concurrent and long-term effects of biofeedback on brain wave frequency and behavior (Woodruff, 1981, 1982). Biofeedback training consisted of a sequence of ten one-hour training sessions after baseline performance on EEG and behavioral measures had been determined. In this research very stringent criteria for success at the biofeedback task were used, and not all subjects could control their brain activity to the specified degree. More older than younger subjects were able to demonstrate remarkable control of alpha

FIGURE 10.3 Change in abundance of modal alpha frequency is shown for 10 young and 10 old experimental subjects who received biofeedback at three different brain wave frequencies (modal frequency, 2 Hz slower than modal frequency, 2 Hz faster than modal frequency). It is apparent that the task of producing alpha frequency 2 Hz slower than mode was carried out much more quickly than the task of producing alpha frequency 2 Hz faster than mode. This difference was statistically significant at the .001 level of confidence. *Source:* Copyright © 1975, The Society for Psychophysiological Research. Reprinted with permission of the publisher from Woodruff, D. S. (1975). Relationship among EEG alpha frequency, reaction time, and age: A biofeedback study. *Psychophysiology, 12,* p. 677.

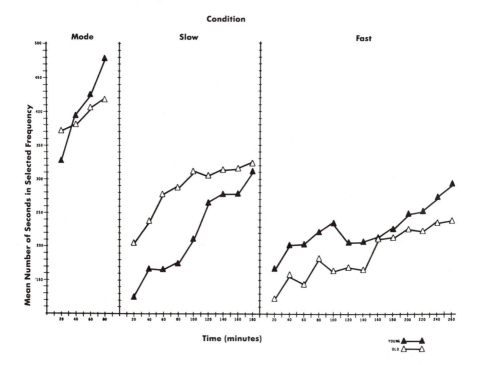

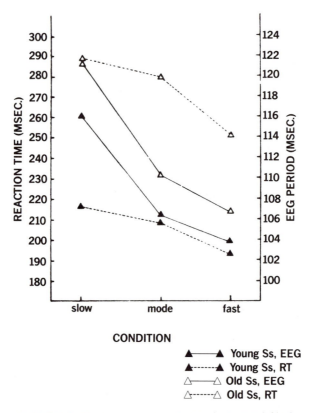

FIGURE 10.4   EEG frequency and reaction time in young and old subjects in the three brain wave conditions. Modest changes in the EEG alpha frequency with biofeedback resulted in significant changes in reaction time between the speed and the slow condition. *Source:* Copyright © 1975, The Society for Psychophysiological Research. Reprinted with permission of the publisher from Woodruff, D. S. (1975). Relationship among EEG alpha frequency, reaction time, and age: A biofeedback study. *Psychophysiology, 12,* p. 678.

activity. This result was interesting inasmuch as older subjects perform more poorly on most learning tasks.

Woodruff (1975) felt that the arousal hypothesis could account for the biofeedback results. Correlations between alpha period and reaction time were low between subjects and not apparent within subjects. However, when reaction times between biofeedback conditions were compared, the differences were statistically significant. This suggests that subjects producing fast alpha activity may have been more aroused and thus had faster reaction time.

Reducing arousal level may be associated with production of EEG frequencies bordering on the theta range. Research indicates that reaction time and performance decline when subjects' brain waves verge into theta bandwidths (Davies & Krkovic, 1965; Groll, 1966; Kornfield, 1974; Morrell, 1966; Williams, Granda,

Jones et al., 1962). Beatty, Greenberg, Deibler & O'Hanlon (1974) used biofeedback of theta over the right occipital hemisphere during a long radar watch and successfully achieved changes in the efficiency of detection. Operantly produced increases in theta activity decreased the efficiency of performance, whereas controlled decreases in theta activity removed the decrement.

Brain wave frequency itself may not serve as a biological clock, but it may be correlated with arousal level which does influence behavior. The fact that older individuals have slower modal brain wave frequencies and the fact that slow brain wave activity is associated with lowered states of arousal had been used as one of the rationales for suggesting that compared to young individuals, the aged are in a state of underarousal (Thompson & Marsh, 1973). As we ponited out in Chapter 8, the underarousal model is used to explain why older adults perform more slowly. There have been many other hypotheses to explain the slowing of behavior with age, and many of the physiological hypotheses have been presented in this chapter and in Chapters 5 and 8. We have been discussing a psychophysiological approach to the slowing of reaction time with age. Now we turn to an information processing approach to examine potential causes for age-related slowing.

POTENTIAL CAUSES
OF AGE-RELATED SLOWING

In his review of the literature on the speed of behavior, Salthouse (1985) attempted to identify possible mechanisms involved in age-related slowing. Salthouse felt that the six following alternatives appeared to encompass most of the hypotheses proposed to explain age-related slowing of behavior. It will become clear as we describe them that much remains to be done to explore carefully all of the hypotheses.

Input and/or Output Rate

This hypothesis simply predicts that as a result of sensory and motor changes in the older organism, information gets into the system more slowly and it is physically responded to on the output side more slowly. We have reviewed much of the research relevant to this hypothesis in discussing peripheral nervous system factors in reaction time. What is clear is that sensory factors, neural conduction velocity, and movement time *do not* account for the magnitude of slowing with age. If input/output rate were responsible for reaction-time slowing, age differences on all tasks, regardless of complexity, would be constant. As long as the input and output processes remain the same, a constant delay should be added to all reaction-time tasks with age. This is clearly not the case. Birren, Riegel and Morrison (1962) held input and output constant but varied what the subject had to do mentally with the stimuli. Age differences increased as the mental manipulations became more complex. It is relatively clear that the slowing observed with increased age cannot be localized simply to either input or output processes.

Inefficient Processing

Another cause for slowing in older adults could be that they deal with information in a less efficient manner than do the young. The inefficient processing hypothesis suggests that the strategies used by younger adults are more efficient than those used by older adults.

The inefficient processing hypothesis does not emphasize whether or not the age changes are conscious. The change in strategies on the part of the older person could be a conscious attempt to compensate for known or suspected deficits. On the other hand, it could be an unintentional shift in the manner in which the task is approached and performed.

Salthouse identified three specific inefficient processing hypotheses proposed to account for age-related slowing. These are (1) poor preparation, (2) inefficient use of stimulus information, and (3) differential emphasis on accuracy as opposed to speed. Salthouse's own work has demonstrated that when accuracy bias is eliminated by equating young and old adults for accuracy, age differences in speed are still present (Salthouse, 1970; Salthose & Somberg, 1982c). Because little clear support for the poor preparation or the inefficient use of stimulus information exists, Salthouse concluded that at the present time there simply is not much convincing evidence to support the inefficient processing hypothesis.

Internal Representation of Control Processes

The predictions for this hypothesis are similar to the predictions for the inefficient processing hypothesis. Age differences in speed should be eliminated with extensive practice because recent frequency of usage should lead to the optimum state of availability for all relevant operations. However, practice does not completely eliminate age differences in response speed. The only study which apparently supports the internal representation of control hypothesis was one carried out by Rabbit and Birren (1967). However, the perspective is rather novel and unique, and it has yet to be tested completely.

Capacity of Working Memory

As we note in Chapter 12 on human learning, memory, and cognition, research suggests that working memory, or primary memory as it is also called, may not be affected by aging. The size of working memory may remain the same over the adult life span. Salthouse (1982) argued that the evidence for the claim that primary memory is invariant across adulthood is still equivocal. He felt that the major prediction of the capacity of working memory hypothesis has been supported. This hypothesis is that age differences in reaction time to simple tasks should be small, while they should be increasingly larger with more complex tasks. Thus,

Salthouse concluded that the capacity of working memory hypothesis should be given further serious attention.

Concurrent Processing Demands

The overarousal and underarousal hypotheses reviewed in Chapter 8 are considered to be included in the concurrent processing demands hypothesis to explain slowing of response with age. The older adult does not have use of full capacity in the case of underarousal hypothesis, while his or her capacity is interfered with in the case of overarousal. As we saw in Chapter 8, the underarousal hypothesis receives a great deal of support, as does the concept of chronic underarousal with some phasic overarousal.

Salthouse argued that since studies designed to eliminate arousal differences with electric shock (Botwinick, Brinley & Robbin, 1958; Weiss, 1965) or monetary incentive (Salthouse, 1979; Salthouse & Somberg, 1982c) failed to eliminate age differences in reaction time, at least a simple version of the concurrent processing demands hypothesis could not be supported. On the other hand, there is little evidence that these studies equated arousal level in the young and old or that it is even possible to do so. The concurrent processing demands hypothesis has not yet been given an adequate test.

Physical Differences

A variety of hypotheses in the aging literature could be considered analogous to the physical differences hypothesis. For example, the neural noise hypothesis stipulates that there is more randomness in the older nervous system and that the signal-to-noise ratio decreases with age (Crossman & Szafran, 1957; Welford, 1958, 1981). It suggests that the older nervous system is less efficient. Neurons fire more randomly, and it is more difficult to tell what is a meaningful stimulus and what is a random firing. Thus, it takes more time to process information.

The hypothesis by Surwillo that the EEG alpha rhythm is the master timing mechanism in behavior and that the slowing of this cycle is responsible for age-related slowing is another form of the physical differences hypothesis. We have described Surwillo's ideas earlier in this chapter and concluded that it cannot account for the magnitude of response time slowing with age.

Although Surwillo's approach does not support the physical differences hypothesis, Salthouse found many other forms of evidence which he interpreted to support it. This hypothesis would predict that no single information processing stage should be uniquely responsible for age-related slowing. Slowing should be generalized and evident at all stages. Salthouse and Somberg (1982b) found that increased age affected all stages of processing and could not be localized in any one stage.

A second prediction of the hypothesis is that age differences should increase in absolute magnitude as the task increases in complexity. Birren et al. (1962) are

among the investigators who have demonstrated this to be the case. A third prediction is that there should be a general speed factor reflected in increasing intercor-
relations between measures in the aged. Many of the postulates of the physical
differences hypothesis have been supported. It is viewed as among the more
promising of hypotheses to pursue in the search for the cause of age changes in
response speed.

SUMMARY

Slowing of behavior is a normal age change affecting everyone who lives long
enough. It occurs even in the the healthiest of older adults. The slowing of response
speed with age is the most ubiquitous of all age changes. It affects everything from
simple activities in daily living to complex processes of thought.

Since reaction time was first measured over the adult age span at the International Health Exhibition in London in 1884 by Sir Francis Galton, the data have
indicated that slowing occurs with age. Galton's data demonstrated that reaction-
time slowing was independent of sensory modality. One survey of the research
on speed of response and aging reported that simple reaction time slowed anywhere
from 11 to 102 percent.

There are three exceptions to the slowing with age phenomenon. When
younger adults in poor health are compared to healthier older adults, the age differences in reaction time disappear. Physically fit older adults also have faster
reaction times than sedentary older adults. A second exception to slowing with
age occurs when young and old adults are compared on vocal reaction time.
Responding with the voice on tasks such as the digit-symbol subtest of the WAIS
is apparently not slowed with aging. However, far fewer studies have compared
vocal reaction time in aging than have compared manual reaction time. The third
exception to the slowing with age phenomenon occurs in older adults highly practiced on reaction-time tasks. After practicing for thousands of trials on the task,
the magnitude of the age difference in reaction time is reduced.

Reaction-time studies carried out over a large number of cohorts coupled
with reaction-time data in longitudinal studies indicate that the slowing is an age
change rather than simply an age difference. Reaction-time slowing with age also
occurs in other species.

Age differences in complex reaction time in which the individual must choose
between at least two alternatives of response are greater than age differences in
simple reaction time. The greater the number of choices on the reaction-time task,
the more disproportionately slowed is the older adult. This result had led gerontologists to conclude that the cause of the slowing must be central rather than
peripheral.

In attempting to isolate the locus of the cause of age-related slowing, investigators have examined age differences in phenomena at all levels of the nervous

system. Movement time, sensory acuity, and neural conduction velocity have all been ruled out as the primary source of the slowing, although they each add to reaction time in old age. Synaptic delay, particularly in the brain, and other central factors contribute more to the slowing. Research to determine if the slowing of the EEG alpha rhythm with age is the primary cause of the slowing of reaction time has indicated that alpha slowing cannot account for the magnitude of the slowing of reaction time. Underarousal may account for the relationship between slower alpha frequencies and slower reaction time in older adults.

Biofeedback can be used to train older adults to produce more fast alpha in the EEG, and this speeds simple reaction time by about 10 percent. However, changing alpha activity with biofeedback requires a great deal of time and effort, and the effect is difficult if not impossible to maintain outside the laboratory. Interestingly, older adults perform slightly better on a biofeedback task than do younger adults.

Six alternative hypotheses were presented to encompass most of the explanations for age-related slowing of behavior. Among the hypotheses not adequately accounting for the slowing are the input and/or output rate hypothesis which predicts that sensory and motor changes cause the slowing. The hypotheses of inefficient processing posits that older adults deal with information in a less efficient manner. This hypothesis also has little convincing data to support it. The internal representation of control processes hypothesis holds that the operations most efficient in reaction-time tasks are not readily available to the older adult. This hypothesis has not been put to an adequate test.

The capacity of working memory hypothesis argues that primary memory capacity changes with age. As memory load gets greater with the increasing complexity of the reaction-time task, older adults perform more slowly. Thus, the prediction of this hypothesis is supported. However, most studies of working memory and aging suggest that there are no age changes in this capacity.

The hypothesis of concurrent processing demands includes the state of the older adult as involved in affecting information processing. Thus, overarousal and underarousal would explain age-related slowing in this model. There is a great deal of evidence suggesting that older adults are in a chronic state of underarousal. In this manner the concurrent processing demands hypothesis receives support.

A variety of hypotheses in the gerontology literature could be considered analogous to the physical differences hypothesis. Among them are the neural noise hypothesis and the alpha frequency slowing hypothesis. Although neither of these hypotheses have been fully supported, many of the predictions of the physical differences hypothesis have been documented. Slowing is generalized and evident at all stages, age differences increase in absolute magnitude as the task increases in complexity, and a general speed factor emerges in old age which is not present in the data of younger adults. Thus, the physical differences hypothesis is considered to be one of the most promising of hypotheses to explain age changes in the speed of response.

REFERENCES

ABRAHAMS, J. P. & BIRREN, J. E. (1973).   Reaction time as a function of age and behavioral predispositions to coronary heart disease. *Journal of Gerontology, 28,* 471–478.

ARENBERG, D. (1982).   Changes with age in problem solving. In F.I.M. Craik & S. Trehub (Eds.), *Aging and cognitive processes.* New York: Plenum.

BARRETT, G. V., MIHAL, W. L., PANEK, P. E., STERNS, H. L. & ALEXANDER, R. A. (1977).   Information processing skills predictive of accident involvement for younger and older commercial drivers. *Industrial Gerontology, 4,* 173–182.

BEATTY, J., GREENBERG, A., DIEBLER, W. P. & O'HANLON, J. F. (1974).   Operant control of occipital theta rhythm affects performance in a radar monitoring task. *Science, 183,* 871–873.

BELLIS, C. J. (1933).   Reaction time and chronological age. *Proceedings of the Society on Experimental Biological Medicine, 30,* 801.

BERG, C., HERTZOG, C. & HUNT, E. (1982).   Age differences in the speed of mental rotation. *Developmental Psychology, 18,* 95–107.

BIRREN, J. E. (1955).   Age changes in speed of response and perception and their significance for complex behavior. In *Old age in the modern world.* London: Livingstone.

BIRREN, J. E. (1965).   Age changes in speed of behavior: Its central nature and physiological correlates. In A. T. Welford & J. E. Birren (Eds.), *Behavior, aging and the nervous system.* Springfield, IL: Charles C. Thomas.

BIRREN, J. E. & BOTWINICK, J. (1955).   Age differences in finger, jaw, and foot reaction time to auditory stimuli. *Journal of Gerontology, 10,* 429–432.

BIRREN, J. E., BUTLER, R. N., GREENHOUSE, S. W., SOKOLOFF, L. & YARROW, M. R. (1963).   *Human aging.* Washington, DC: U.S. Public Health Service.

BIRREN, J. E., RIEGEL, K. F. & MORRISON, D. F. (1962).   Age differences in response speed as a function of controlled variations of stimulus condition: Evidence of a general speed factor. *Gerontologia, 6,* 1–18.

BIRREN, J. E. & WALL, P. D. (1956).   Age changes in conduction velocity, refractory period, number of fibers, connective tissue space and blood vessels in sciatic nerve of rats. *Journal of Comparative Neurology, 104,* 1–16.

BIRREN, J. E., WOODS, A. M. & WILLIAMS, M. V. (1979).   Speed of behavior as an indicator of age changes and the integrity of the nervous system. In F. Hofmesiter & C. Mueller (Eds.), *Brain function in old age,* Berlin: Springer-Verlag.

BISHOP, G. H. (1933).   Cyclic changes in excitability of the optic pathway of the rabbit. *American Journal of Physiology, 103,* 213–224.

BODDY, J. (1971).   The relationship of reaction time to brain wave period: A reevaluation. *Electroencephalography and Clinical Neurophysiology, 30,* 229–235.

BOTWINICK, J. & BIRREN, J. E. (1965).   A follow-up study of card-sorting performance in elderly men. *Journal of Gerontology, 20,* 208–210.

BOTWINICK, J., BRINLEY, J. F. & ROBBIN, J. S. (1958).   The effect of motivation by electric shocks on reaction in relation to age. *American Journal of Psychology, 71,* 408–411.

BOTWINICK, J. & THOMPSON, L. W. (1968).   Age differences in reaction time: An artifact? *The Gerontologist, 8,* 25–28.

CHOWN, S. M. (1961).   Age and the rigidities. *Journal of Gerontology, 16,* 353–362.

CREUTZFELT, O. D., ARNOLD, P. M., BECKER, D., LANGENSTEIN, R., FIRSCH, W., WILHEIM, H. & WUTTKE, W. (1976).   EEG changes during spontaneous and controlled menstrual cycles and their correlation with psychological performance. *Electroencephalography and Clinical Neurophysiology, 40,* 113–131.

CROSSMAN, E.R.F.W. & SZAFRAN, J. (1957). Changes with age in the speed of information intake and discrimination. *Experientia Supplement, 4,* 128–145.

DAVIES, D. R. & KRKOVIC, A. (1965). Skin conductance, alpha activity, and vigilance. *American Journal of Psychology, 78,* 304–306.

DUSTMAN, R. W., RUHLING, R. O., RUSSELL, E. M., SHEARER, D. E., BONEKAT, H. W., SHIGEOKA, J. W., WOOD, J. S. & BRADFORD, D. C. (1984). Aerobic exercise training and improved neuropsychological function of older individuals. *Neurobiology of Aging, 5,* 35–42.

GOLDFARB, W. (1941). An investigation of reaction time in older adults and its relationship to certain observed mental test patterns. *Teachers College Contributions to Education* No. 831. New York: Teachers College, Columbia University, Bureau of Publications.

GRANICK, S. & PATTERSON, R. D. (1971). *Human aging II: An eleven-year followup biomedical and behavioral study.* Washington, DC: U.S. Government Printing Office.

GROLL, E. (1966). Central nervous system and peripheral activation variables during vigilance performance. *Aeitschrift Fur Experimentelle und Augenwandte Psychologie, 13,* 148–264.

HARTER, M. R. (1967). Effects of carbon dioxide on the alpha frequency and reaction time in humans. *Electroencephalography and Clinical Neurophysiology, 23,* 561–563.

HICKS, L. H. & BIRREN, J. E. (1970). Aging, brain damage, and psychomotor slowing. *Psychological Bulletin, 74,* 377–396.

HUGIN, R., NORRIS, A. H. & SHOCK, N. W. (1960). Skin reflex and voluntary reaction times in young and old males. *Journal of Gerontology, 15,* 388–391.

JASPER, H. H. (1936). Cortical excitatory state and snychronism in the control of bioelectric autonomous rhythms. In H. H. Jasper, L. D. Proctor, R. S. Knighton, W. C. Noshay & R. T. Costello (Eds.), *Reticular formation of the brain.* Boston: Little, Brown.

KAUFMAN, A. (1968). Age and performance in oral and written versions of the substitution test. In S. Chown & K. F. Riegel (Eds.), *Psychological functioning in the normal aging and senile aged.* Basel, Switzerland: S. Karger.

KOGA, Y. & MORANT, G. M. (1923). On the degree of association between reaction times in the case of different senses. *Biometrika, 15,* 346–372.

KJORNFIELD, C. M. (1974). EEG spectra during a prolonged compensatory tracking task. Unpublished doctoral dissertation. Los Angeles: University of California.

LIGHT, K. C. (1978). Effects of mild cardiovascular and cerebrovascular disorders on serial reaction time performance. *Experimental Aging Research, 4,* 3–22.

LINDSLEY, D. B. (1952). Psychological phenomena and the electroencephalogram. *Electroencephalography and Clinical Neurophysiology, 4,* 443–456.

MADDEN, D. J. & NEBES, R. D. (1980). Aging and the development of automaticity in visual search. *Developmental Psychology, 16,* 377–384.

MILES, W. R. (1931). Measures of certain human abilities throughout the life span. *Proceedings of the National Academy of Sciences, 17,* 627–633.

MORRELL, L. K. (1966). EEG frequency and reaction time: A sequential analysis. *Neuropsychologica, 4,* 41–48.

MOWBRAY, G. H. & RHOADES, M. V. (1959). On the reduction of choice reaction time with practice. *Quarterly Journal of Experimental Psychology, 2,* 16–23.

MURRELL, F. H. (1970). The effect of extensive practice on age differences in reaction time. *Journal of Gerontology, 25,* 268–274.

NORRIS, A. H., SHOCK, N. W. & WAGMAN, I. H. (1953). Age changes in the maximum conduction velocity of motor fibers in human ulnar nerves. *Journal of Applied Physiology, 5,* 589–593.

O'HANLON, J. F., McGRATH, J. J. & McCAULEY, M. E. (1974).   Body temperature and temporal acuity. *Journal of Experimental Psychology, 102,* 788-794.

PIERSON, W. R. & MONTOYE, H. J. (1958).   Movement time, reaction time and age. *Journal of Gerontology, 13,* 418-421.

PLUDE, D. J. & HOYER, W. J. (1981).   Adult age differences in visual search as a function of stimulus mapping and processing level. *Journal of Gerontology, 36,* 598-604.

RABBIT, P.M.A. & BIRREN, J. E. (1967).   Age and responses to sequences of repetitive and interruptive signals. *Journal of Gerontology, 22,* 143-150.

SALTHOUSE, T. A. (1979).   Adult age and the speed-accuracy tradeoff. *Ergonomics, 22,* 811-821.

SALTHOUSE, T. A. (1982).   *Adult cognition: An experimental psychology of human aging.* New York: Springer-Verlag.

SALTHOUSE, T. A. (1985).   Speed of behavior and its implications for cognition. In J. E. Birren & K. W. Schaie (Eds.), *Handbook of the psychology of aging,* (2nd Ed.), New York: Van Nostrand Reinhold.

SALTHOUSE, T. A. & SOMBERG, B. L. (1982a).   Skilled performance: The effects of adult age and experience on elementary processes. *Journal of Experimental Psychology: General, 111,* 176-207.

SALTHOUSE, T. A. & SOMBERG, B. L. (1982b).   Isolating the age deficit in speeded performance. *Journal of Gerontology, 37,* 59-63.

SALTHOUSE, T. A. & SOMBERG, B. L. (1982c).   Time-accuracy relationships in young and old adults. *Journal of Gerontology, 37,* 349-353.

SANFORD, A. J. (1971).   A periodic basis for perception and action. In W. P. Colquhoun (Ed.), *Biological rhythms and human performance.* London: Academic Press.

SPIETH, W. (1964).   Cardiovascular health status, age, and psychological performance. *Journal of Gerontology, 19,* 277-284.

SPIRDUSO, W. W. (1975).   Reaction and movement time as a function of age and physical activity level. *Journal of Gerontology, 30,* 435-440.

SPIRDUSO, W. W. (1980).   Physical fitness, aging and psychomotor speed: A review. *Journal of Gerontology, 35,* 850-865.

SPIRDUSO, W. W. & CLIFFORD P. (1978).   Neuromuscular speed and consistency of performance as a function of age, physical activity level and type of physical activity. *Journal of Gerontology, 33,* 26-30.

SURWILLO, W. W. (1960).   Central nervous system factors in simple reaction time. *American Psychologist, 15,* 419.

SURWILLO, W. W. (1961).   Frequency of the "alpha" rhythm, reaction time and age. *Nature, 191,* 823-824.

SURWILLO, W. W. (1963).   The relation of simple response time to brain wave frequency and the effects of age. *Electroencephalography and Clinical Neurophysiology, 15,* 105-114.

SURWILLO, W. W. (1964a).   The relation of decision time to brain wave frequency and to age. *Electroencephalography and Clinical Neurophysiology, 16,* 510-514.

SURWILLO, W. W. (1964b).   Some observations on the relation of response speed to frequency of photic stimulation under conditions of EEG synchronization. *Electroencephalography and Clinical Neurophysiology, 17,* 194-198.

SURWILLO, W. W. (1968).   Timing of behavior in senescence and the role of the central nervous system. In G. A. Talland, (Ed.), *Human aging and behavior.* New York: Academic Press.

SURWILLO, W. W. (1971).   Human reaction time and period of the electroencephalogram in relation to development. *Psychophysiology, 8,* 468-482.

SURWILLO, W. W. (1975).   Reaction time variability, periodicities in reaction time distribution, and the EEG gating-signal hypothesis. *Biological Psychology, 3,* 247-261.

SURWILLO, W. W. & TITUS, T. G. (1976). Reaction time and the psychological refractory period in children and adults. *Developmental Psychobiology, 9,* 517–527.

SZAFRAN, J. (1951). Changes with age and with exclusion of vision in performance at an aiming task. *Quarterly Journal of Experimental Psychology, 3,* 111–118.

SZAFRAN, J. (1966). Age differences in the rate of gain of information, signal detection strategy and cardiovascular status among pilots. *Gerontoligia, 12,* 6–17.

SZAFRAN, J. (1968). Psychophysiological studies of aging in pilots. In G. A. Talland (Ed.), *Human aging and behavior.* New York: Academic Press.

TALLAND, G. A. (1962). The effect of age on speed of simple manual skill. *Journal of Genetic Psychology, 100,* 69–76.

THOMPSON, L. W. & MARSH, G. R. (1973). Psychophysiological studies of aging. In C. Eisdorfer & M. P. Lawton (Eds.), *The psychology of adult development and aging.* Washington, DC: American Psychological Association.

WAGMAN, I. H. & LESSE, H. (1952). Maximum conduction velocities of motor fibers of ulnar nerves in human subjects of various ages and sizes. *Journal of Neurophysiology, 15,* 235–244.

WAYNER, M. J. & EMMERS, R. (1958). Spinal synaptic delay in young and aged rats. *American Journal of Physiology, 194,* 403–405.

WEISS, A. D. (1965). The locus of reaction time change with set, motivation and age. *Journal of Gerontology, 20,* 60–64.

WELFORD, A. T. (1958). *Aging and human skill.* London: Oxford University Press.

WELFORD, A. T. (1981). Signal noise, performance, and age. *Human Factors, 23,* 97–109.

WILLIAMS, H. L., GRANDA, A. M., JONES, R. C., LUBIN, A. & ARMINGTON, D. C. (1962). EEG frequency and finger pulse volume as predictors of reaction time during sleep loss. *Electroencephalography and Clinical Neurophysiology, 14,* 64–70.

WOODRUFF, D. S. (1975). Relationships among EEG alpha frequency, reaction time, and age: A biofeedback study. *Psychophysiology, 12,* 673–681.

WOODRUFF, D. S. (July 1981). Successful biofeedback conditioniong in young and old and its predictors. Paper presented at the 12th International Congress of Gerontology, Hamburg, Germany.

WOODRUFF, D. S. (1982). Long-term biofeedback conditioning at two EEG frequencies in young and older subjects. *Psychophysiology, 19,* 593.

WOODRUFF, D. S. & BAUM, M. R. (1982). EEG and reaction time relationships in adulthood and old age. *Gerontologist, 22,* 151.

WOODRUFF, D. S. & BIRREN, J. E. (1972). Biofeedback conditioniong of the EEG alpha rhythm in young and old subjects. *Proceedings of the 80th Annual Meeting of the American Psychological Association,* Washington, DC: American Psychological Association, 673–674.

WOODRUFF, D. S. & KRAMER, D. A. (1979). EEG alpha slowing, refractory period, and reaction time in aging. *Experimental Aging Research, 5,* 279–292.

CHAPTER 11

Psychobiology of Learning, Memory, and Aging

Progress in research on the major behavioral changes with aging has made it clear that decline in learning and memory is a common phenomenon in many species (Craik, 1977; Walker & Hertzog, 1975). At the same time, basic research on the psychobiology of learning and memory has made dramatic progress (Thompson, 1986). The aim of this chapter is to relate the advances in understanding of basic psychobiological learning and memory processes with the problem of memory loss in old age. The attempt is to explain some of the basic neural substrates of acquisition and retrieval and to isolate mechanisms responsible for their decline as organisms age. We use the example of classical conditioning of the eyelid response in rabbits, the most advanced model system for the understanding of the neurobiology of mammalian learning and memory, throughout this chapter to illustrate the rapid progress of research and knowledge about the neurobiological causes of decline in learning and memory with age.

Older adults often say that one of the most disturbing outcomes of advancing years is a decline in the efficiency of memory processes. While this decline is not seen in all aging individuals, in those people who are affected, the consequences are often severe and prevent efficient functioning in the environment. Until recently, the task of identifying those neurobiological changes underlying impaired memory in the aged has received little attention from behaviorally oriented researchers. However, the need for data about the physiological and psychological bases of memory loss will become progressively more acute in the coming years because, as stated in Chapter 3, an ever-increasing proportion of the population will exceed 65 years of age and will be potentially at risk.

It has been pointed out by Jensen et al. (1980) that the disorders of learning and memory associated with behavioral aging are generally not recognized as national health problems, in contrast to diseases such as cancer or cardiovascular disorders. However, in terms of the number of affected individuals, difficulty with learning and memory in old age should come to be recognized as a major problem in health care. Therefore, gaining an understanding of the neurobiological processes underlying age-related impairments in learning, memory, and cognitive functioning must be a primary goal of researchers in the 1980s. Effective and rational therapies for the disorders of memory associated with advanced age can be developed only with a foundation of knowledge provided by basic research.

The decline in the efficiency of learning and memory processes in the aged has been extensively documented, and a number of excellent articles and reviews describing many aspects of this deficit are available (Arenberg & Robertson-Tchabo, 1977; Botwinick & Storandt, 1974; Craik, 1977; Craik & Byrd, 1982; Poon, 1985; Talland, 1968; Thatcher, 1976). An overview of these age-related changes is presented in Chapter 12 on aging in human learning, memory, and cognition. It will become apparent that the magnitude of the decline in memory processes in the aged is not uniform and is dependent not only on which aspect of memory function is being measured but also on the type of assessment techniques employed.

From a psychological standpoint, the nature of the memory deficit in the aged is unclear. It can be interpreted as being a decrease in mental flexibility, a deficit in information processing power, a storage or retrieval deficit, or a simple decrease in effective mental capacity (Craik, 1977). It is also quite possible that it results from a variety of interactions among several of these phenomena. In addition, the neurophysiology of age changes in memory is almost entirely unknown.

Landfield and Lynch (1977) argued that basic neurophysiological information is required to determine which of the many chemical-anatomical correlates of brain aging are specifically relevant to functional impairment. We need to measure neurophysiological function while the organism is performing the learning and memory tasks in order to link specific aging changes with the behavioral deficits. This means that we must measure the brain with invasive techniques while aging organisms are learning and remembering. To undertake this kind of research, we must use aging animals instead of aging humans.

CLASSICAL CONDITIONING IN
THE AGING RABBIT AND CAT

Thompson et al. (1976) presented a rationale for the usefulness of classical conditioning of the eyeblink or nictitating membrane (NM) response of the rabbit as a model system for analysis of brain substrates of associative learning and memory.

He pointed out that the behavioral aspects of this type of classical conditioning have been well characterized by the elegant studies of Gormezano and associates (Gormezano, 1966, 1972; Gormezano, Kehoe & Marshall, 1983; Gormezano & Moore, 1969). Thompson et al. (1976) argued that this systsem had many advantages as a model for neurophysiological analysis of associative learning and memory, and in subsequent years he has documented the importance of this model (Thompson, 1982, 1986).

Figure 11.1 presents a diagrammatic explanation of the procedures involved in classical conditioning of the NM and eyelid response in humans and rabbits. The model is extremely useful in neurophysiological analysis. Furthermore, it shows behavioral changes with aging similar to changes shown in humans. Hence, this model should be useful in elucidating neurophysiological changes associated with memory loss in aging (Thompson & Woodruff-Pak, 1987; Woodruff-Pak & Thompson, 1985; Woodruff-Pak & Thompson, 1988).

The first study using aging rabbits in the classical conditioning paradigm was carried out by Powell, Buchanan and Hernandez (1981). Using tone conditioned stimulus (CS) and shock unconditioned stimulus (US), Powell et al. found that three- to five-year old rabbits required an average of 100 more trials to criterion of conditioned responses (CRs) which was significantly more trials than the average number required by young rabbits (mean age of six months).

In a subsequent experiment, Powell, Buchanan and Hernandez (1984) trained young and older rabbits in a similar paradigm which involved a discrimination. The CS + and CS − were two different frequencies of tone, with the CS + always followed by the shock US and the CS − never followed by the shock US. The animal learned a discrimination between the two tones by blinking to the CS + but not to the CS −. Rabbits 40 months old showed slower acquistion, and older males learned more poorly than older females, while young males outperformed young females.

FIGURE 11.1   Experimental set up for classical conditioning of the eyelid response in rabbit and human. (A) The rabbit's third eyelid (nictitating membrane, NM) and the human's eyelid are used. A thread is attached to the NM in the rabbit and connected to a transducer, a device that measures movement of the thread and hence the NM. An infrared device is typically used instead of a thread in humans. Air puffed from a nozzle near the eye serves as the unconditioned stimulus (US). A tone from a speaker (or delivered through earphones in humans) is the conditioned stimulus (CS).

(B) The transducer measures movement of the NM. The movement is recorded and displayed by a computer. The example shown here occurs early in training before conditioning has developed. Note that the tone does not eleict an NM response. Shortly after the airpuff US is delivered the NM begins to close; this is recorded as an upward movement displayed on the computer. After the airpuff is turned off, the NM is pulled back so that the eye is open. Closing the NM to an airpuff is an UR, also called a reflex response.

(C) To deveop a conditioned response (CR), the airpuff is paired with a tone. On the first trial, the eyelid responds only to the airpuff, a UR as in (B). After a few training trials, conditioning begins to develop. Shown here on trial 20, the eyelid begins to close while the tone is on, just before the airpuff starts. As training proceeds, eyelid closure in the initial tone-alone period begins to occur earlier (shown in trial 40). After the CR is well established (by trial 80, for example), it will occur even on test trials where the airpuff is omitted (as in trial 81). The development of the conditioned response has two important features: (1) It begins to occur earlier and earlier after the tone CS is turned on. (2) The point of maximum resonse always remains at about the time when the airpuff US would occur, even on test trials where no airpuff is present. Acquisition as shown to occur in 80 trials here in rabbits occurs in about 40 trials for young human adults. *Source:* Lindzey, G., Hall, C. S. & Thompson, R. F. (1978). *Psychology*. New York: Worth, pp. 208–209. Reprinted by permission.

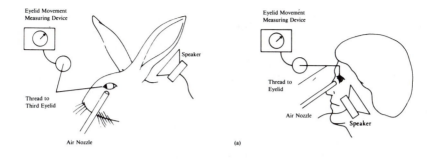

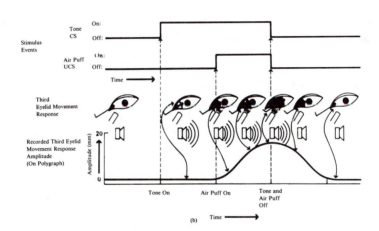

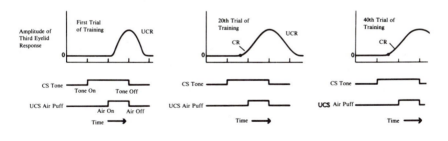

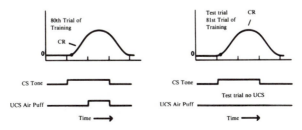

Using the delay classical conditioning paradigm with a tone CS and a shock US, Graves and Solomon (1985) found no age differences in trials to criterion for 6-month and 36- to 60-month-old rabbits. The task employed by Graves and Solomon may have been both easier and less aversive than Powell et al.'s (1981) task. In unpublished observations, Berry and Thompson found that five-year-old rabbits learned more slowly than young rabbits in the delay paradigm when an airpuff US was used. Taken together, these results indicate that seemingly small variations in the quality of the CS and US affect age differences in acquisition. These variations in parameters provide us with an opportunity to determine specific aspects in aging which result in the age differences in learning.

While Graves and Solomon (1985) found no age differences in classical conditioning in the delay paradigm, they did find large age differences in the trace paradigm. The trace classical conditioning paradigm involves turning off the CS for a period of time (e.g., 500 msec) before the US onsets. Thus, the interval between the CS and US is extended, and the CS and US never overlap. This task is more difficult for younger rabbits who take on average five times as long to meet learning criterion in the trace task as they do in the delay task (Woodruff-Pak, Lavond & Thompson, 1985). Comparison of the trace and delay task is presented in Figure 11.2. In the Graves and Solomon (1985) study, young and old animals were

FIGURE 11.2 The standard delay (above) and trace (below) classical conditioning paradigms. CS, conditioned stimulus (in our laboratory typically a 1,000 Hz tone); US, unconditioned stimulus (corneal airpuff or shock). The trace interval for all of the trace paradigm studies discussed in this chapter is 500 msec.

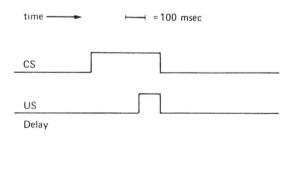

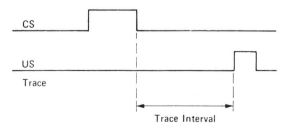

conditioned in a trace paradigm. The older group took a mean of 340 more trials to criterion than the younger group.

With a corneal airpuff US and a 500 msec trace interval, Woodruff-Pak, Lavond, Logan and Thompson (1987) found highly significant differences in conditioning between the three age groups of rabbits. These results are shown in Figure 11.3. Three-month-old rabbits attained criterion in a mean of 3.2 days (349 trials), while 30-month-old rabbits took a mean of 9.4 days (1,058 trials) to criterion, and 45-month-old rabbits took a mean of 11.75 days (1,392 trials) to criterion. These age differences in trials to criterion were statistically significant.

Variability between rabbits in trials to criterion also increased dramatically with age. While the youngest rabbits all attained criterion within a four-day period, criterion performance in the 30-month-old rabbits ranged over 16 days, and it ranged over 15 days for the 45-month-old group. These results suggest that aging of conditioning capacity occurs at different rates in different rabbits. Some of the 30- and 45-month-old rabbits performed as well as the 3-month-old rabbits, while others learned much more slowly.

Age differences in trials to criterion in the delay paradigm run in sessions immediately after overtraining in the trace paradigm were not as great as age differences in the trace paradigm. In an effort to measure retention of the conditioning task in older rabbits, five of the older rabbits (mean age = 38 months) were retested on the delay task over an interval of two to five months. The correlation between trials to criterion in the initial learning of trace conditioning and the trials

FIGURE 11.3 Mean number of days to criterion (126 paired trials per day) in the trace classical conditioning paradigm for three age groups of rabbits of an average age of: 3 months old (*N* = 6), 30 months old (*N* = 5), and 45 months old (*N* = 4).

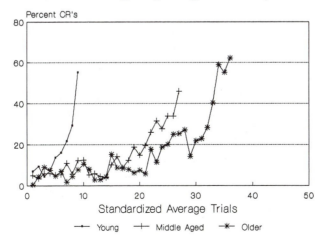

Conditioning By Age In Rabbits

to criterion (corrected for the time interval between training and retraining) on delay conditioning was .99 ($p < .01$). The correlation between acquisition of the delay paradigm and retention of the delay paradigm two to five months later (corrected for the time interval between training and retraining) was .95 ($p < .01$).

These high correlations indicate that retention of the task is strongly related to acquisition. The longer an older rabbit took to learn the trace and the delay conditioning tasks, the longer it took to relearn the delay conditioning task several months later. Young animals tested for retention in the delay paradigm several months after training need little or no retraining to attain criterion on the task (Lavond & Thompson, unpublished data).

The result that 2½-year-old rabbits take three times as many trials to attain criterion in the trace paradigm is surprising in that this is a relatively young age for a rabbit. Although the life expectancy of New Zealand white rabbits has not been empirically determined, Fox (1980) estimated on the basis of his extensive experience developing and maintaining a large aging rabbit colony that rabbit life expectancy is around eight years. If we were to interpolate from that figure to human life expectancy, we might say that one rabbit year is roughly equivalent to one human decade. Our 2½-year-old rabbits showing a deficit in conditioning in the trace paradigm are comparable in this scheme to 25-year-old humans. The oldest rabbit tested in this research was 50 months old at the beginning of the study. This rabbit took the longest to attain criterion. For a rabbit, 50 months old is middle age. Our human equivalent would be 42 years old. While we found less efficient performance in terms of total percent CRs in the delay paradigm for adults in the decade of the forties, we found no age differences in subjects in their mid-twenties (Woodruff-Pak & Thompson, 1986). On the basis of our human data, we predict that an 8-year-old rabbit would be extremely difficult to condition and would require an extensive acquisition period. Unfortunately, obtaining a disease-free rabbit of a documented age of 8 years or older is close to impossible.

Classical conditioning of the eyelid response in cats shows aging effects remarkably similar to the effects reported in rabbits and humans. Harrison and Buchwald (1983) conditioned young and old cats in a relatively difficult paradigm in which the 4 KHz tone CS+ onset 1,500 msec before the 50 msec shock US. CS− were loud and soft clicks presented randomly throughout the session. Ten young cats aged one to three years met the criterion of 80 percent CRs in a mean of 270 trials. Nine of the 15 old cats aged 10 to 23 years failed to develop CRs at criterion level with 1,000 trials. The six old cats who did develop criterion level CRs did so in a mean of 522 trials. Thus, old cats showed a marked deficit in a difficult classical conditioning paradigm. When old cats which had not demonstrated learning at the 1,500 msec CS–US interval were trained at a 400 msec CS–US interval with no CS−, they attained criteiron in a mean of 170 trials. These data along with the trace conditioning data in rabbits suggest that extending the time between the CS and US onset amplifies age differences in learning in animals.

BRAIN SITES IMPLICATED IN MEMORY AND MEMORY LOSS

Thompson (1982) stated that the first issue that must be addressed in the "search for the engram" is the identification and localization of neuronal structures and systems that appear to be involved in learning. He has approached this question using electrophysiological recording of neural unit activity as the initial method of identification. In terms of engagement of neuronal activity during learning, at least the following structures are involved: regions of the brain stem and midbrain, the cerebellum, the hippocampus and related structures, and portions of the neocortex. Other structures which do not appear to be involved include the basal ganglia and most nuclei of the amygdala.

Hippocampus

Thompson (1982) pointed out that the hippocampus is of particular interest with regard to memory. He has documented that even in the short delay classical conditioning paradigm, activity of pyramidal neurons always grows rapidly over training to form a temporal model of the behavioral conditioned response. This relationship is shown in Figure 11.4.

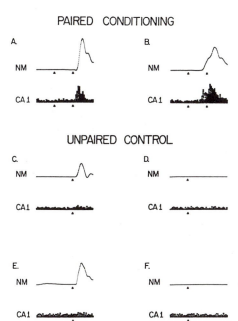

PAIRED CONDITIONING

UNPAIRED CONTROL

FIGURE 11.4 Role of hippocampus in classical conditioning in the rabbit. Examples of eight-trial-averaged behavioral NM responses and associated multiple unit histograms of hippocampal activity for a conditioning (A, B) and a control (C–F) animal at the beginning and end of training. Note the very large increase in hippocampal unit activity that develops in the conditioning animal. Upper trace: Average nictitating membrane response for one block of eight trials. Lower trace: Hippocampal unit poststimulus histogram (15 msec time bins) for one block of eight trials. (A) First block of eight paired conditioning trials, Day 1. (B) Last block of eight paired conditioning trials, Day 1, after conditioning has occurred. (C) First block of eight unpaired CS-alone trials, Day 1. (D) Last block of eight unpaired US-alone trials, Day 2. (E) First block of eight unpaired CS-alone trials, Day 1. (F) Last block of eight unpaired CS-alone trials, Day 2. *Source:* Berger, T. W. & Thompson, R. F. (1978a). Neuronal plasticity in the limbic system during classical conditioniong in the rabbit nictitating membrane response. I. The hippocampus. *Brain Research, 145,* p. 330. Reprinted by permission.

Pyramidal neurons in the dorsal hippocampus develop a very clear model of the behavioral response (Berger & Thompson, 1978b). This model of the behavioral response generated by pyramidal neurons is not present in the first few trials of training, develops rapidly, initially in the US period and then in the CS period as the learned behavioral response develops, and grows considerably in amplitude. The increased neural unit activity follows the pattern of the entire behavioral response, both the learned CS period response and the response in the US period (which probably reflects both learned and reflexive behavioral components). This learning-induced increase in pyramidal neuron activity does not develop in control animals in which the CS and US are not presented together.

Thompson and associates have characterized the learning-induced hippocampal unit response over a wide range of conditions. The learning-induced increase in hippocampal unit activity invariably precedes and accurately predicts subsequent behavioral learning performance. The hippocampal response has all the properties of a direct measure of the inferred processes of learning and memory in the brain.

In summarizing his research on learning and memory in relation to the hippocampus, Thompson stated:

> All of our results can be summed up in the following rather simple statement: In the learning paradigm we employ, the growth of the hippocampal unit response is completely predictive of subsequent behavioral learning. If the hippocampal response does not develop, the animal will not learn. If it develops rapidly, the animal will learn rapidly. If it develops slowly, the animal will learn slowly. Further, the temporal form of the hippocampal response predicts the temporal form of the behavioral response. (Thompson, 1980, p. 212).

The human hippocampus is one of the structures affected earliest and most consistently by the histopathology of aging (Malamud, 1972), and aging changes have been documented in the hippocampus of the rat (Landfield & Lynch, 1977) and the rabbit (Balzer, Sclabassi & Berger, 1986; Hernandez et al., 1979). Tissue changes in the human brain such as degeneration of neurons involve pyramidal cells of the hippocampus more than any other structure. These hippocampal changes are more observable in senile dementia of the Alzheimer's Type (SDAT), a disease known to involve dramatic memory loss (Jervis, 1970). Senile plaques are found most densely in the hippocampus as are neurofibrillary tangles which are most obvious in the pyramidal cells of the hippocampus and in the pyramidal cells in the third layer of the cerebral cortex in the prefrontal and superior temporal areas (Scheibel & Scheibel, 1975). Tomlinson (1972) stressed that when neurofibrillary tangles are present in the apparently intellectually intact aged, they are found almost exclusively in the hippocampus. It is interesting to note that Berger and Thompson (1978a, 1978b) found in rabbits that pyramidal cells are the critical elements in hippocampal neuronal plasticity during learning, and hippocampal pyramidal cells are the cells most affected in human aging.

Because the hippocampus has been associated with memory processes and has been shown to be vulnerable to aging, Drachman and Hughes (1971) examined temporal EEG abnormalities and behavior in an aged sample and compared these results to the EEG and behavior of a group with hippocampal lesions and to a group of normal young controls. Aged subjects showed a mild diffuse impairment of all cognitive functions, memory and nonmemory alike. Hippocampal lesion patients performed far worse than aged subjects on tests of memory storage but better on nonmemory cognitive tests. Thus, aged subjects failed to show isolated impairment of memory storage as is seen in patients with hippocampal complex lesions. Almost half the aged subjects showed temporal abnormalities in EEG which did not correlate with memory impairment. Temporal EEG abnormalities were significantly related to impairment on an organicity index. It was concluded that the EEG and cognitive findings in normal aged subjects reflected a diffuse degenerative process rather than a relatively localized degeneration of the hippocampal complexes. While aging subjects do not perform like individuals who have lost their hippocampal complexes, some of the memory loss in aging may result from degeneration in the hippocampus.

The more precise measurement of neurophysiological mechanisms possible in aging animals suggests hippocampal involvement in memory deficits. Landfield, McGaugh and Lynch (1977) reported that the strength of certain electrophysiological responses in the hippocampus of aging rats was deficient. These hippocampal responses were predictive of poorer learning in older rats. Landfield (1979) trained aging and young rats to actively avoid a foot shock in a Y-maze. All 8 young animals exhibited good retention of this avoidance, but only 6 of the 20 rats aged 25 months showed evidence of good avoidance. All animals were subsequently studied neurophysiologically, and the only parameter that significantly separated avoiding aged animals from nonavoiders was the electrophysiological response in the hippocampus. A highly significant correlation of 0.85 existed between avoidance retention performance and strength of the electrophysiological hippocampal response.

Recording neural modeling activity in the hippocampus in rabbits age 3 to 50 months, Woodruff-Pak et al. (1987) found that hippocampal activity in older rabbits produced a model similar to the hippocampal model in younger rabbits shown previously in Figure 11.4. Figure 11.5 shows hippocampal modeling activity for a 50-month-old rabbit. It is similar to the hippocampal activity in a young rabbit. What was different between the young and old rabbits was the number of trials it took the modeling to appear. Just as the behavioral learned response was delayed in the older rabbits, so was the hippocampal modeling delayed. Thus, the hippocampal activity in the older animals appeared normal, but its onset was delayed. It could not be determined if abnormalities in the older hippocampus caused the delay in acquisition or if aging in another brain structure such as the cerebellum was responsible for delayed acquisition.

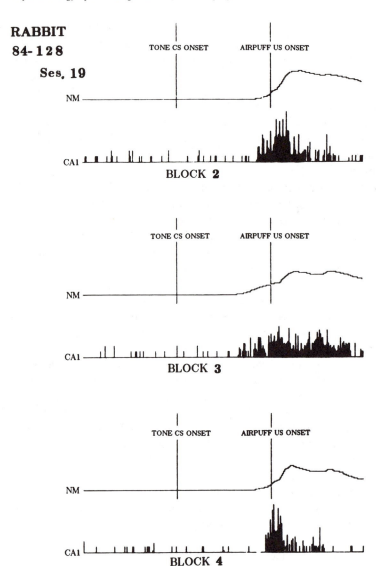

FIGURE 11.5 Hippocampal modeling in a 45-month-old New Zealand white rabbit. Each average represents nine trials presented in the delay classical conditionign paradigm. The NM response shown on the top tracing of each of the three averages is an average of nine trials. The hippocampal unit response shown below is a summation of activity in those same nine trials. The first vertical line in each of the three averages is the onset of the tone CS, while the second vertical line represents the onset of the corneal airpuff US. The total time period represented by each average is 750 msec. *Source:* Woodruff-Pak, D. S., Lavond, D. G., Logan, C. G. & Thompson, R. F. (1987). Classical conditioning in 3-, 30-, and 45-month-old rabbits: Behavioral learning and hippocampal unit activity. *Neurobiology of aging, 8,* p. 105. Reprinted by permission.

Cerebellum: Essential Site
for the Memory Trace

Animals with all brain tissue removed above the thalamus are able to learn the standard delay eyelid conditioned response (Norman, Buchwald & Villablanca, 1977). Further, animals that are acutely decorticated following training show robust retention of the CR (Mauk & Thompson, 1987). These results demonstrate that the primary memory trace circuit is below the level of the thalamus. Systematic mapping of the entire midbrain, brain stem, and cerebellum by recording neuronal unit activity in trained animals indicated a substantial engagement of the cerebellar system in the generation of the conditioned response. Studies involving recording of neuronal unit activity from the interpositus nucleus of the cerebellum over the course of training have revealed a striking pattern of learning-related growth in activity (McCormick, Clark, Lavond & Thompson, 1982; McCormick & Thompson, 1984a, 1984b).

FIGURE 11.6 Summary figure of the essential neural circuit involving the cerebellum in classical conditioning in the rabbit. *Source:* Thompson, R. F. (1986). The neurobiology of learning and menory. *Science, 233,* p. 943. Reprinted by permission of the American Association for the Advancement of Science.

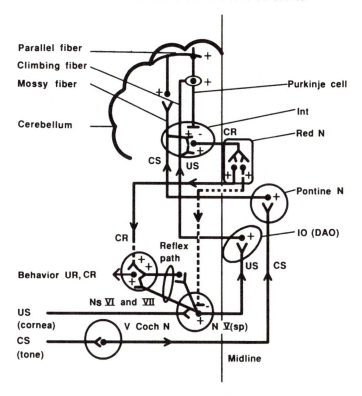

Evidence from stimulating, recording, and lesion studies argue strongly that the ipsilateral cerebellum is the site of the primary memory trace for the classically conditioned eyelid response. Furthermore, additional studies suggest that the memory trace for learning of all classically conditioned discrete, adaptive somatic motor responses occurs in the cerebellum (e.g., Donegan, Lowry, & Thompson, 1983; Woodruff-Pak, Lavond, & Thompson, 1985; Yeo, Hardiman & Glickstein, 1984). Figure 11.6 illustrates the memory trace circuit for classical conditioning in the rabbit brain.

A Cerebellar Model
for Learning and Memory

In the laboratory of Richard Thompson, a hypothetical scheme or model has been developed of the neuronal system that could serve as the essential memory trace circuit for discrete, adaptive learned somatic motor responses. This model is presented in Figure 11.7.

To illustrate the model, eyelid closure and leg flexion learning are used as the two behavioral examples. The site of the memory trace is assumed to be at the principal cells (labeled in the upper left as Purkinje cells). Principal cells are shown as Purkinje cells of the cerebellar cortex to demonstrate similarities with the models of Albus, Marr, Ito, and Eccles on cerebellar cortical function. The current data argue that the memory traces for the basic CRs are stored in the interpositus nucleus as well as in the cerebellar cortex, presumably by analogous circuitry (e.g., Woodruff-Pak, Lavond, Logan, Steinmetz, & Thompson, 1985).

In the model, the CS "learning" input to a large number of principal cells comes from parallel fibers which have been activated by mossy fibers. The US "teaching" input arrives at a specific and limited number of principal cells via climbing fibers from the inferior olive. A given US activates only specific principal cells coding the motor program for the defensive response related to the US (eyelid closure, leg flexion). The concept is essentially the following: (1) the principal cells (that is, Purkinje cells in cerebellar cortex; cells of origin of superior cerebellar peduncle axons in the interpositus nucleus) for a specific motor program such as the eyeblink are activated (along with many other principal cells) by a neutral CS such as a tone; (2) shortly thereafter, the principal cells for the eyeblink response are selectively activated by climbing fibers (responding to the airpuff US); (3) with repeated pairing of the tone CS and airpuff US, the pathway involving the tone CS and the motor program for eyeblinks will be facilitated.

The basic assumption is that the memory trace circuit is "prewired" but the CS activation is "soft-wired" before learning. The connections from any CS to any motor program already exist before training, but they are too weak to elicit any behavioral responses before training. Activation of the CS circuit shortly prior to activation of the powerful motor-program-specific climbing fiber US input (the teaching or reinforcing input) results in a long-lasting facilitation of the previously weak "soft-wired" connections. The CS channel to the specific set of principal cells for a motor program becomes facilitated. This change is learning.

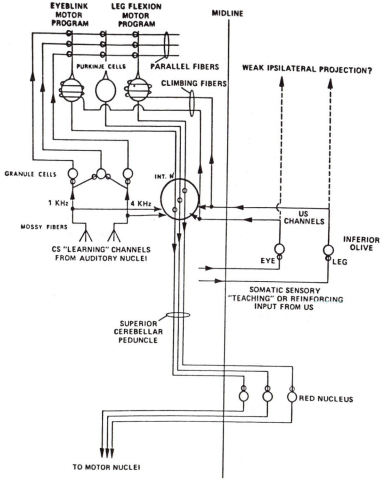

FIGURE 11.7 Scheme of hypotehtical memory trace system for learning of discrete, adaptive somatic-motor responses to deal with aversive unconditioned stimuli. Interneurons are omitted. It is assumed tha the site of the memory trace is at the principal neurons shown in the upper left under "motor programs" and/or at associated interneurons. The principal cells are labeled Purkinje cells of cerebellar cortex to show similarity with theories of cerebellar plasticity (Albus, Marr, Eccles, Ito), but our data suggest that the basic memory trace is stored in the interpositus nucleus, we assume by an analogous circuitry. A given CS (1 KHz) activates a subset of parallel fibers that in turn weakly activate all principal cells. A different tone also activates all principal cells but by a partially different group of "parallel fibers." The US pathway is assumed to be via the inferior olive and "climbing fibers." A given US is assumed to activate only a limited group of principal cells coding the motor program for the defensive response that is specific for the US (eyelid closure, leg flexion). When "parallel fiber" activation occurs at the appropriate time just prior to "climbing fiber" activation, the "connections" of the parallel fibers to the principal cells activated by the particular US are strengthened. The efferent pathway from principal cells to motor neurons is by way of the superior cerebellar peduncle and red nucleus. This scheme accounts for stimulus specificity, i.e., the fact that CRs show a stimulus generalization gradient, for response specificity of learned responses, transfer and lesion-transfer effects (such as training one eye and then the other before or after cerebellar lesion) and is consistent with all evidence to date. Although hypothetical, each aspect and assumption is amenable to experimental test. *Source:* Thompson, R. F., McCormick, D. A. & Lavond, D. G. (1986). Localization of the essential memory trace system for a basic form of associative learning in the mammalian brain. In S. Hulse (Ed.), *One hundred years of psychological research in America.* Baltimore: Johns Hopkins University Press, p. 131. Reprinted by permission.

Of course, this theoretical scheme is tentative and hypothetical, but it does account for all of the available data. Each aspect and assumption of the scheme is amenable to experimental test. Indeed, since developing the scheme, strong evidence has been amassed to support it.

The inferior olive is the source of climbing fibers to the cerebellum while other afferents reach the cerebellum as mossy fibers. Evidence suggests that the inferior olive-climbing fiber input is the essential teaching input for the learning of discrete, adaptive behavioral responses. Thus, lesions of the critical region of the inferior olive result in behavioral extinction of CRs with continued paired training (McCormick, Steinmetz, & Thompson, 1985).

It has also been recently demonstrated that stimulation of the rostromedial dorsal accessory olive can serve as the US. Stimulation of that area elicits an unconditioned response (UR) which in some cases is an eyeblink. Pairing a tone CS with the stimulation US resulted in the development of CRs within 100 to 200 trials. This is similar to the rate of acquisition using a corneal airpuff US (Mauk & Thompson, 1984).

Additional support for the model comes from studies using microstimulation of mossy fibers. Stimulation of the pontine nuclei or middle cerebellar peduncle demonstrated that mossy fiber stimulation can serve as an effective CS for classical conditioning (Steinmetz, Lavond, & Thompson, 1985a; Steinmetz, Rosen, Chapman, Lavond, & Thompson, 1986). Lesions of the middle cerebellar peduncle, the pathway for pontine afferents to the cerebellum, prevents conditioning (Solomon, Lewis, LoTurco, Steinmetz, & Thompson, 1986). Stimulation of the pontine nucleus as a CS and the dorsal accessory olive as a US mimics conditioning using a tone and airpuff (Steinmetz, Lavond & Thompson, 1985b).

Evidence that the plasticity for learning occurs in the cerebellum rather than afferent to it comes from a recent study in which stimulating electrodes were placed symmetrically into the right and left dorsolateral pontine nuclei. Rapid transfer of training occurred from the left to the right stimulating electrode indicating that the common area of cerebellar cortex stimulated by the symmetrical right and left dorsolateral pontine mossy fibers was involved as the site of plasticity (Steinmetz, Rosen, Woodruff-Pak, Lavond, & Thompson, 1986).

Finally, aging is known to affect acquisition and retention of the classically conditioned eyelid response in three species—humans, rabbits, and cats (Braun & Geiselhart, 1959; Gakkel & Zinina, 1953; Graves & Solomon, 1985; Harrison & Buchwald, 1983; Kimble & Pennypacker, 1963; Powell, Buchanan, & Hernandez, 1981; Woodruff-Pak, Lavond, Logan, & Thompson, 1987; Woodruff-Pak & Thompson, 1986). The model identifies sites in the cerebellum related to learning and memory to examine for changes during aging.

Aging in the Cerebellum

The discussion on aging in the cerebellum is based on studies in humans, monkeys, and rats. Ellis (1920) made a painstaking count of human cerebellar

Purkinje cells and found them to decrease with age in adulthood. He found greater loss in the anterior lobe than in the hemispheres. Harms (1944) reported that in the human cerebellum up to 25 percent of the Purkinje cells were lost in very old patients. This result has been verified using more recently developed techniques by Hall, Miller, and Corsellis (1975). In the Hall et al. study, 90 normal cerebella were assessed in subjects ranging from childhood to over the age of 100 years. Wide individual variations were found at all ages, but a mean reduction of 2.5 percent of the Purkinje cells per decade was found which represents a 25 percent reduction over the 100-year period of life which was studied.

Assessing Purkinje cell electrophysiology in Sprague-Dawley rats, Rogers, Silver, Shoemaker, and Bloom (1980) identified a number of cell-firing parameters which were affected by age. In particular, increasing numbers of aberrant, very slow-firing cells were encountered in older animals. Nandy (1981) reported a 44 percent decrease in the number of Purkinje cells in the left cerebellar cortex of 20-year-old rhesus monkeys as compared to 4-year-old monkeys. The number of granule cells in the same area were relatively equal in the two age groups. Purkinje neurons from old rats were significantly less sensitive to locally applied neurotransmitters than neurons from young rats (Marwaha, Hoffer, & Freedman, 1981). Marwaha et al. hypothesized that there was a senescent postsynaptic change in noradrenergic transmission in Purkinje cells. Subsequent work in that laboratory demonstrated that there is diminished interaction of norepinephrine with climbing fiber, mossy fiber, and granular-parallel fiber inputs to cerebellar Purkinje neurons in aged rats (Bickford, Hoffer, & Freedman, 1985, 1986).

Consistent with the electrophysiological and biochemical data showing age pathology of the cerebellar Purkinje cell are the anatomical changes in old rats reported by Rogers, Zornetzer, Bloom, and Mervis (1984). Many 26-month-old Purkinje cells appeared to have lost their dendrites. They appeared defoliated. There was a significant decrease in the mean Purkinje cell area between 6-month-old rats and 26-month-old rats. In every part of the cerebellum which was examined, there was a significant senescent decrease in Purkinje neuron density. The mean number of Purkinje cells/mm of Purkinje cell layer declined from 16.6 cells/mm in young rats to 12.5 cells/mm in old rats. Related to the Purkinje cell loss was a loss in synaptic density.

Additional evidence for loss of synapses in the cerebellar cortex of the rat has been provided by Glick and Bondareff (1979). Numbers of synapses were compared in the cerebellar cortex of 12-month-old and 25-month-old rats, and the total number of axon synapses on dendrites (called axodendritic synapses) was found to be 24 percent lower in the older rats. While there were no age differences in synapses on dendritic shafts, there was a 33 percent decrease in synapses involving the dendritic spines in older rats. Glick and Bondareff hypothesized that granule cells, the axons of which form the majority of synaptic contacts with dendeitic spines of Purkinje cells, may be preferentially impaired.

Undertaking a comparative neuropathological study of aging using the brains of 47 species of vertebrates, Dayan (1971) observed that changes in the cerebellum generally resembled those seen in other parts of the brain. The loss of Purkinje cells was readily apparent. Indeed, Dayan concluded that there is a generalized loss of neurons in the brain "most easily detected as fall-out of Purkinje cells from the cerebellar cortex" (Dayan, 1971, p. 37).

Aging may differentially affect the two major input systems in the hypothetical schematic for classical conditioning shown in Figure 11.7. These two input systems are (1) the climbing fiber input from the olivocerebellar system providing the US "teaching" information, and (2) the parallel fiber input from the sensory systems providing CS "learning" information. Data from the rat suggest that aging deficits may be greater in the parallel fibers. Analysis of the excitatory projection of single climbing fiber efferents from the inferior olive making multiple synaptic contacts onto dendritic shafts of single Purkinje neurons revealed no apparent change in the number of climbing fiber mediated bursts or climbing fiber spikes in rats from 3 to 28 months of age (Rogers et al., 1980). However, a number of measures of the parallel fiber system in rats aged 5 to 7 and 24 to 26 months indicated senescent changes in the parallel fiber system (Rogers, Zornetzer & Bloom, 1981). From the perspective of the model, this would mean that the CS input is less efficient in old organisms.

Aging in the Cerebellum:
Implications for Classical Conditioning

The age change in the cerebellum which has been reported most frequently is a decline in Purkinje cells. Purkinje cells are the output neurons of the cerebellar cortex. The output cells of the cerebellar nuclei are of course by definition the principal cells. Our model presented in Figure 11.7 suggests that an important focus of aging research should be on the Purkinje and principal cells. If they show changes similar to age changes in Purkinje cells in other species, this would provide evidence for age-related decline in the central component of the memory trace. If there is defoliation of the synaptic tree or the total loss of Purkinje and/or principal cells in aging, the net effect would be to eliminate the central coordination between the climbing fiber "teaching" input and the money fiber "learning" input.

The result of Purkinje and principal cell elimination in this model would be the absence of the memory trace. Reducing the number of Purkinje and principal cells might reduce the conditionability of the organism—as a result comparable to the behavioral data on classical conditioning of the eyelid responses previously presented. Indeed, Braun and Geiselhart (1959) and Kimble and Pennypacker (1963) used the terms, "relative unconditionability" and "difference between the conditionability of old and young subjects," respectively, to describe their results with aging human subjects.

With regard to testing hypotheses about input channels to the cerebellum including the mossy fiber "learning" input, our initial explorations of the aged rabbit cerebellum support the hypothesis that the CS input channels are less efficient (Woodruff-Pak, Steinmetz, & Thompson, 1986). Age differences in peripheral portions of the auditory CS pathway could account for the observed age differences in conditioniong rabbits. In this study we bypassed peripheral portions of the CS pathway and input the CS more centrally by electrical microstimulation of mossy fibers from the dorsolateral pontine nucleus.

Results indicated that older rabbits could be trained with dorsolateral pontine stimulation as the CS, but they take many more trials to criterion than 3-month-old rabbits. Older rabbits took about five times as long to condition in this manner than did younger animals. Figure 11.8 presents the acquisition data for a younger and an older rabbit which had close to identical placement of CS stimulating electrode in the pons. Acquisition took 173 trials in the younger rabbit and 921 trials in the older rabbit.

These results indicate that the age differences in eyelid classical conditioning which have been observed in rabbits cannot be entirely attributed to age differences in the peripheral CS pathway. Changes in the nervous system occurring more centrally in the cerebellum appear to be more important for age differences in learning. We are currently in the process of isolating the age changes in the cerebellum which are responsible for age changes in acquisition and retention. Once

FIGURE 11.8 Acquisition to a stimulation CS in a 3- and a 44-month-old rabbit with stimulating electrodes placed in almost identical locations in the paramedian pontine nucleus (PMN). The insert shows a coronal section approximately 11 mm caudal to bregma where the stimulating electrode was located in each rabbit's PMN. Although the stimulation CS was located in almost the identical site in the PMN, the 44-month-old rabbit attained learning criterion in 921 trials while the 3-month-old rabbit achieved criterion in 173 trials.

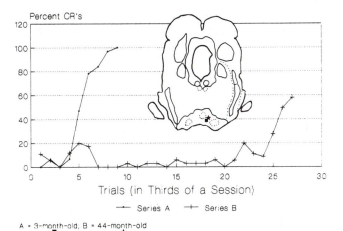

Paramedian Pontine Nucleus
% CR's in 3- & 44-Month-Old Rabbit

we identify the age changes involved, we will move in the direction of designing interventions to improve function in the cerebellum and behavior. For example, if the problem is primarily a deficit in postsynaptic response to norepinephrine, drug therapy to improve the efficiency of postsynaptic response to norepinephrine could be devised. If Purkinje and principal cell loss are the major source of the deficit, then the cause of the loss of these neurons must be determined with a consequent intervention designed to maintain the cells. Alternatively, transplants of fetal cerebellar components might be attempted.

EVENTUAL GOALS
IN PSYCHOBIOLOGICAL
RESEARCH

One major goal of research on the psychobiology of learning, memory, and aging is understanding. In Chapter 1 we explored some of the reasons for studying aging, and we likened the scientist to the mountain climber. Just as the mountain climber meets the challenge of Mt. Everest because it is there, so the scientist is challenged to study processes of aging because they occur and are one of the more complex problems of our time to understand. However, scientists are driven by more than just the need for understanding. Another goal in the study of the psychobiology of learning, memory, and aging is to understand the cause of the deficits so that we can design intervetnions to alleviate the problem of memory loss.

For some time, gerontologists have been working toward creating a memory drug. As new breakthroughs are made in comprehending the psychobiology of learning and memory, we get closer to devising therapies that will work. In the case of SDAT, a progressive disease that devastates memory capacity, patients have been fed precursors of the neurotransmitter acetylcholine. This is because the neurons manufacturing and transmitting that neurotransmitter appear to be selectively abolished by the disease. Whether there is any improvement in patients treated in this manner is not clear. The effects of the precursors appear to be minimal at best.

The effects of providing a neurotransmitter precursor have received notable success in the case of Parkinson's disease. This disease does not typically affect memory, although it does in about 30 percent of the cases. However, Parkinsonism drastically affects the motor systems causing tremor, lack of coordination, and inability to move efficiently. The precursor to dopamine, el dopa, reduces the symptoms of many Parkinson's disease patients to the point where they can function normally.

An even more dramatic development in the treatment of Parkinson's disease is brain surgery in which tissue from the adrenal medulla cortex of the patient is surgically removed and implanted in the substantia nigra of the brain. Figure 11.9 illustrates the source of tissue in the adrenal medulla and the brain site where it

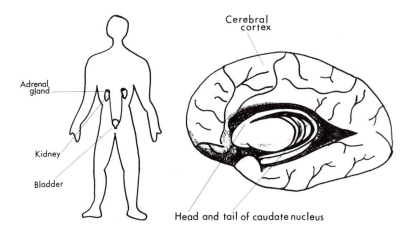

FIGURE 11.9   Schematic drawing showing source of tissue in adrenal gland which has been transplanted into the substantia nigra in the brain of Parkinson's disease victims.

is implanted. The substantia nigra is the part of the brain that produces dopamine, and it is close to totally destroyed in Parkinson's disease. Adrenal medulla tissue also produces dopamine, and it will apparently function when transplanted to the brain. The patients who have experienced this surgery have improved dramatically. However, the surgery is so new that we do not yet know the long-term prognosis for these patients.

Science is on the frontier of brain implant surgery (Blakeslee, 1987). Attempts have been made to implant fetal animal tissue to older animals' hippocampi with some success. The eventual implications of these studies are that we may have the potential to replace damaged brain tissue with functioning tissue. If aging in the hippocampus affects our memory capacity, we may be able to replace that part of the hippocampus with more viable tissue. Since memory storage probably does not reside in the hippocampus, personality and long-term memory presumably would not be affected by such surgery. Only our ability to acquire new memories would be affected, and this is the ability that appears to be most affected in old age.

SUMMARY

Research in psychology and aging along with numerous anecdotal reports of older adults have made it clear that learning and memory are behaviors showing a decline with age. Age changes in learning and memory have been documented in many subhuman species as well. Recent advances in the psychobiology of learning and memory have significant implications for the understanding of learning, memory, and aging. With some of the newer model systems of learning and memory, it is becoming possible to identify the locus of the age changes involved in the loss of these behavioral capacities at a cellular and synaptic level.

Classical conditioning of the eyelid response is the model system presented in this chapter to illustrate the depth of understanding we have of neurobiological substrates of learning and memory. Age differences have been demonstrated in classical conditioning of the eyelid response in rabbits, cats, and humans. In some conditioning paradigms, rabbits show age differences in acquisition when they are as young as 2½ years old. This is roughly equivalent to 25 years old in the human life span. Age difference in classical conditioning appear in humans by the decade of the forties.

The major brain sites which have been demonstrated to be involved in classical conditioning of the eyelid response in rabbits are the hippocampus and the cerebellum. Both of these brain sites show significant change with age in humans and in subhuman species. The hippocampus has been widely implicated in research on memory loss in humans and animals. The pyramidal cells of the dorsal hippocampus model the behavioral eyelid response in rabbits, and it is pyramidal cells that are the most extensive affected by aging. While age changes in the hippocampus are likely involved in memory loss in normal human aging (and especially in pathological aging such as SDAT), classical conditioning may not be affected by aging in the hippocampus.

The interpositus nucleus of the cerebellum is essential for classical conditioning of the eyelid response in rabbits. The neural circuitry involved in classical conditioning of the eyelid response has been almost entirely identified. Knowledge about this model system has led to the identification of age changes in the cerebellum which might account for age changes in conditioning. Among the relevant age changes being examined for their role in conditioning deficits in aging are the loss of Purkinje cells and loss of granular cell synapses on Purkinje cells. These losses may delay acquisitions and impair retention. Another age change in the cerebellum apparent in mossy fiber-granule cell-parallel fiber synapses and climbing fiber synapses as they affect Purkinje cell response is the loss of postsynaptic responsiveness to norepinephrine. Again, this change would diminish the effectiveness of stimulus input and could delay acquisition.

The model system approach to the psychobiology of learning, memory, and aging has provided us with a number of specific hypotheses to test about how aging affects the brain and consequently, affects behavior. We are in the process of isolating the age changes and relating them to loss of behavioral capacity. It is likely that when we know more specifically the causes of age changes in learning and memory, we will be able to devise effective interventions to ameliorate the deficits. Among the intervention tools presently at our disposal are drug therapy and brain implants. These techniques may be used in human aging in the future to prevent memory loss from occurring at all.

REFERENCES

ARENBERG, D. & ROBERTSON-TCHABO, E. A. (1977). Learning and aging. In J. E. Birren and K. W. Schaie (Eds.), *Handbook of the psychology of aging.* New York: Van Nostrand Reinhold.

BALZER, J. R., SCLABASSI, R. J. & BERGER, T. W. (1986). Effects of aging on system properties of the hippocampus as revealed by nonlinear systems analysis. *Society for Neuroscience Abstracts, 12,* 274.

BERGER, T. W. & THOMPSON, R. F. (1978a). Neuronal plasticity in the limbic system during classical conditioning of the rabbit nictitating membrane response. I. The hippocampus. *Brain Research, 145,* 323–346.

BERGER, T. W. & THOMPSON, R. F. (1978b). Identification of pyramidal cells as the critical elements in hippocampal neuronal plasticity during learning. *Proceedings of the National Academy of Sciences, 75,* 1572–1576.

BICKFORD, P. C., HOFFER, B. J. & FREEDMAN, R. (1985). Interaction of norepinephrine with Purkinje cell responses to cerebellar afferent inputs in aged rats. *Neurobiology of Aging, 6,* 89–94.

BICKFORD, P. C., HOFFER, B. J. & FREEDMAN, R. (1986). Diminished interaction of norepinephrine with climbing fiber inputs to cerebellar Purkinje neurons in aged Fischer 344 rats. *Brain Research, 385,* 405–410.

BLAKESLEE, S. (1987). On the frontiers of brain surgery: Transplants advance quickly but are still experimental. *New York Times,* April 7, C1, C11.

BRAUN, H. W. & GEISELHART, R. (1959). Age differences in the acquisition and extinction of the conditioned eyelid response. *Journal of Experimental Psychology, 57,* 386–388.

CRAIK, F.I.M. (1977). Age differences in human memory. In J. E. Birren & K. W. Schaie (Eds.), *Handbook of the psychology of aging.* New York: Van Nostrand Reinhold.

CRAIK, F.I.M. & BYRD, M. (1982). Aging and cognition deficits: The role of attentional resources. In F.I.M. Craik & S. Trehub (Eds.). *Aging and cognitive processes.* New York: Plenum.

DAYAN, A. D. (1971). Comparative neuropathology of ageing: Studies on the brains of 47 species of vertebrates. *Brain, 94,* 31–42.

DONEGAN, N. H., LOWRY, R. & THOMPSON, R. F. (1983). Effects of lesioning cerebellar nuclei on conditioned leg-flexion responses. *Society for Neurosciences Abstracts, 9,* 331.

DRACHMAN, D. A. & HUGHES, J. R. (1971). Memory and the hippocampal complexes: III. Aging and temporal EEG abnormalities. *Neurology, 21,* 1–14.

ELLIS, R. S. (1920). Norms for some structural changes in the human cerebellum from birth to old age. *Journal of Comparative Neurology, 32,* 1–34.

FOX, R. R. (1980). The rabbit (*Oryctolagus cuniculus*) and research on aging. *Experimental Aging Research, 6,* 235–248.

GAKKEL, L. B. & ZININA, N. V. (1953). Changes of higher nerve function in people over 60 years of age. *Fiziolog. Zhurnal., 39,* 533–539.

GLICK, R. & BONDAREFF, W. (1979). Loss of synapses in the cerebellar cortex of the senescent rat. *Journal of Gerontology, 34,* 818–822.

GORMEZANO, I. (1966). Classical conditioning. In J. B. Sidowski (Ed.)., *Experimental methods and instrumentation in psychology.* New York: McGraw-Hill.

GORMEZANO, I. (1972).   Investigations of defense and reward conditioning in the rabbit. In A. H. Black & W. F. Prokasy (Eds.), *Classical conditioning II. Current research and theory.* New York: Appleton-Century-Crofts.

GORMEZANO, I., KEHOE, E. J. & MARSHALL, B. S. (1983).   Twenty years of classical conditioning research with the rabbit. In J. Sprauge & A. N. Epstein (Eds.), *Progress in psychobiology and physiological psychology,* vol. 10. New York: Academic Press.

GORMEZANO, I. & MOORE, J. W. (1969).   Classical conditioning. In M. H. Marx (Ed.), *Learning processes.* London: Macmillan.

GRAVES, C. A. & SOLOMON, P. R. (1985).   Age related disruption of trace but not delay classical conditioning of the rabbit's nictitating membrane response. *Behavioral Neuroscience, 99,* 88–96.

HALL, T. C., MILLER, K. H. & CORSELLIS, J.A.N. (1975).   Variations in the human Purkinje cell population according to age and sex. *Neuropathology and Applied Neurobiology, 1,* 267–292.

HARMS, J. W. (1944).   Altern und somatod der Zellverbandstiere. *Z. Alternsforsch., 5,* 73–126.

HARRISON, J. & BUCHWALD, J. (1983).   Eyeblink conditioning deficits in the old cat. *Neurobiology of Aging, 4,* 45–51.

HERNANDEZ, L. L., BUCHANAN, S. L., POWELL, D. A. & SHAH, N. S. (1979).   A comparison of biogenic amine concentrations in discrete brain areas of 'old' and 'young' rabbits. *IRCS Medical Science, 7,* 356.

JENSEN, R. A., MESSING, R. B., MARTINEZ, J. L., JR., VASQUEZ, B. J. & McGAUGH, J. L. (1980).   Opiate modulation of learning and memory in the rat. In L. W. Poon (Ed.), *Aging in the 1980s: Psychological issues.* Washington, DC: American Psychological Association.

JERVIS, G. A. (1970).   In P. J. Vinken & G. W. Bruyn (Eds.), *Handbook of clinical neurology.* Amsterdam: Elsevier.

KIMBLE, G. A. & PENNYPACKER, H. S. (1963).   Eyelid conditioning in young and aged subjects. *Journal of Genetic Psychology, 103,* 283–289.

LANDFIELD, P. W. (1979).   Neurobiological changes in hippocampus of aging rats: Quantitative correlations with behavioral deficits and with endocrine mechanisms. In H. Orimo, K. Shimada, M. Iriki & D. Maeda (Eds.), *Recent advances in gerontology: Proceedings of the XI International Congress of Gerontology.* Amsterdam: Excerpta Medica.

LANDFIELD, P. W. & LYNCH, G. (1977).   Impaired monosynaptic potentiation in *in vitro* hippocampal slices from aged, memory-deficient rats. *Journal of Gerontology, 32,* 523–533.

LANDFIELD, P. W., McGAUGH, J. L. & LYNCH, G. (1977).   Impaired synaptic potentiation in the hippocampus of aged, memory-deficient rats. *Brain Research, 150,* 85–94.

MALAMUD, N. (1972).   Neuropathology of organic brain syndrome associated with aging. In C. M. Gaitz (Ed.), *Aging and the brain.* New York: Plenum.

MARWAHA, J., HOFFER, B. J. & FREEDMAN, R. (1981).   Changes in noradrenergic neurotransmission in rat cerebellum during aging. *Neurobiology of Aging, 2,* 95–98.

MAUK, M. D. & THOMPSON, R. F. (1984).   Classical conditioning using stimulation of the inferior olive as the unconditioned stimulus. *Neuroscience Abstracts, 10,* 122.

MAUK, M. D. & THOMPSON, R. F. (1987).   Retention of classically conditioned eyelid responses following acute decerebration. *Brain Research, 403,* 89–95.

McCORMICK, D. A., CLARK, G. A., LAVOND, D. G. & THOMPSON, R. F. (1982).   Initial localization of the memory trace for a basic form of learning. *Proceedings of the National Academy of Science, 79*(8), 2731–2742.

McCORMICK, D. A., LAVOND, D. G. & THOMPSON, R. F. (1982).   Concomitant classical conditioning of the rabbit nictitating membrane and eyelid responses: Correlations and implications. *Physiology and Behavior, 28,* 769–775.

McCORMICK, D. A., STEINMETZ, J. E. & THOMPSON, R. F. (1985).   Lesions of the inferior olivary complex cause extinction of the classically conditioned eyeblink responses. *Brain Research, 359,* 120–130.

McCORMICK, D. A. & THOMPSON, R. F. (1984a).   Cerebellum: Essential involvement in the classically conditioned eyelid response. *Science, 223,* 296–299.

McCORMICK, D. A. & THOMPSON, R. F. (1984b).   Neuronal responses of the rabbit cerebellum during acquisition and performance of a classically conditioned nictitating membrane/eyelid response. *Journal of Neuroscience, 4,* 2811–2822.

NANDY, K. (1981).   Morphological changes in the cerebellar cortex of aging *Macaca nemestrina. Neurobiology of Aging, 2,* 61–64.

NORMAN, R. J., BUCHWALD, J. S. & VILLABLANCA, J. R. (1977).   Classical conditioning with auditory discrimination of the eyeblink in decerebrate cats. *Science, 196,* 551–553.

POON, L. W. (1985).   Differences in human memory with aging: Nature, causes, and clinical implications. In J. E. Birren & K. W. Schaie (Eds.)., *Handbook of the psychology of aging.* New York: Van Nostrand Reinhold.

POWELL, D. A., BUCHANAN, S. L. & HERNANDEZ, L. L. (1981).   Age related changes in classical (Pavlovian) conditioning in the New Zealand albino rabbit. *Experimental Aging Research, 7,* 453–465.

POWELL, D. A., BUCHANAN, S. L. & HERNANDEZ, L. L. (1984).   Age-related changes in Pavlovian conditioning: Central nervous system correlates. *Physiology and Behavior, 32,* 609–616.

ROGERS, J., SILVER, M. A., SHOEMAKER, W. J. & BLOOM, F. E. (1980).   Senescent changes in a neurobiological model system: Cerebellar Purkinje cell electrophysiology and correlative anatomy. *Neurobiology of Aging, 1,* 3–11.

ROGERS, J., ZORNETZER, S. F. & BLOOM, F. E. (1981).   Senescent pathology of cerebellum: Purkinje neurons and their parallel fiber afferents. *Neurobiology of Aging, 2,* 15–25.

ROGERS, J., ZORNETZER, S. F., BLOOM, F. E. & MERVIS, R. E. (1984).   Senescent microstructural changes in rat cerebellum. *Brain Research, 292,* 23–32.

SCHEIBEL, M. E. & SCHEIBEL, A. B. (1975).   Structural changes in the aging brain. In H. Brody, D. Harman & J. M. Ordy (Eds.)., *Aging* Vol. 1. New York: Raven.

SOLOMON, P. R., LEWIS, J. L., LoTURCO, J. J. STEINMETZ, J. E. & THOMPSON, R. F. (1986).   The role of the middle cerebellar peduncle in acquisition and retention of the rabbit's classically conditioned nictitating membrane response. *Bulletin of the Psychonomic Society, 24,* 75–78.

STEINMETZ, J. E., LAVOND, D. G. & THOMPSON, R. F. (1985a).   Classical conditioning of the rabbit eyelid response with mossy fiber stimulation as the conditioned stimulus. *Bulletin of the Psychonomic Society, 28,* 245–248.

STEINMETZ, J. E., LAVOND. D. G. & THOMPSON, R. F. (1985b).   Classical conditioning of skeletal muscle responses with mossy fiber stimulation CS and climbing fiber stimulation US. *Society for Neuroscience Abstracts, 11,* 982.

STEINMETZ, J. E., ROSEN, D. J., CHAPMAN, P. R., LAVOND, D. G. & THOMPSON, R. F. (1986).   Classical conditioning of the rabbit eyelid response with a mossy fiber stimulation CS. I. Pontine nuclei and middle cerebellar penduncle stimulation. *Behavioral Neuroscience, 100,* 871–880.

STEINMETZ, J. E., ROSEN, D. J., WOODRUFF-PAK, D. S., LAVOND, D. G. & THOMPSON, R. F. (1986).   Rapid transfer of training occurs when direct mossy fiber stimulation is used as a conditioned stimulus for classical eyelid conditioning. *Neuroscience Research, 3,* 606–617.

TALLAND, G. (1968).   *Human aging and behavior: Recent advances in research and theory* (Vol. 1). New York: Academic Press.

THATCHER, R. W. (1976).   Electrophysiological correlates of animal and human memory. In R. D. Terry & S. Gerschon (Eds.), *Neurobiology of aging.* New York: Raven Press.

THOMPSON, R. F. (1980).   The search for the engram, II. In D. McFadden (Ed.), *Brain mechanisms in behavior.* New York: Springer-Verlag.

THOMPSON, R. F. (1982).   The engram found?—Initial localization of the memory trace for a basic form of associative learning. In *Progress in psychobiology and physiological psychology.* New York: Academic Press.

THOMPSON, R. F. (1986).   The neurobiology of learning and memory. *Science, 233,* 941–947.

THOMPSON, R. F., BERGER, T. W., BERRY, S. D., HOEHLER, F. K., KETTNER, R. E. & WEISZ, D. J. (1980).   Hippocampal substrate of classical conditioning. *Physiological Psychology, 8,* 262–279.

THOMPSON, R. F., BERGER, T. W., CEGAVSKE, C. F., PATTERSON, M. M., ROEMER, R. A., TEYLER, T. J. & YOUNG, R. A. (1976).   A search for the engram. *American Psychologist, 31,* 209–227.

THOMPSON, R. F., DONEGAN, N. H. & LAVOND, D. G. (1986).   The psychobiology of learning and memory. In R. C. Atkinson, R. J. Herrnstein, G. Lindzey & R. D. Luce (Eds.), *Steven's handbook of experimental psychology,* (2nd ed.) New York: Wiley.

THOMPSON, R. F., McCORMICK, D. A. & LAVOND, D. G. (1986).   Localization of the essential memory trace system for a basic form of associative learning in the mammalian brain. In S. Hulse (Ed.), *One hundred years of psychological research in America.* Baltimore: Johns Hopkins University Press.

THOMPSON, R. F. & WOODRUFF-PAK, D. S. (1987).   A model system approach to age and the neuronal bases of learning and memory. In M. W. Riley, J. D. Matarazzo & A. Baum (Eds.), *The aging dimension.* Hillsdale, NJ: Erlbaum.

TOMLINSON, B. (1972).   Morphological brain changes in non-demented old people. In H. M. Van Praag & A. K. Kalverboer (Eds.), *Aging of the central nervous system.* New York: De Ervon F. Bohn.

WALKER, J. & HERTZOG, C. (1975).   Aging, brain function, and behavior. In D. S. Woodruff & J. E. Birren (Eds.)., *Aging: Scientific perspectives and social issues.* New York: D. Van Nostrand.

WOODRUFF-PAK, D. S., LAVOND, D. G., LOGAN, C. G., STEINMETZ, J. E. & THOMPSON, R. F. (1985).   The continuing search for a role of the cerebellar cortex in eyelid conditioning. *Society for Neuroscience Abstracts, 11,* 333.

WOODRUFF-PAK, D. S., LAVOND. D. G. & THOMPSON, R. F. (1985).   Trace conditioning: Abolished by cerebellar nuclear lesions but not lateral cerebellar cortex aspirations. *Brain Research, 348,* 249–260.

WOODRUFF-PAK, D. S., LAVOND, D. G., LOGAN, C. G. & THOMPSON, R. F. (1987).   Classical conditioning in 3-, 30-, and 45-month-old rabbits: Behavioral learning and hippocampal unit activity. *Neurobiology of Aging, 8,* 101–108.

WOODRUFF-PAK, D. S., STEINMETZ, J. E. & THOMPSON, R. F. (1986).   Classical conditioniong of rabbits 2½ years old using mossy fiber stimulation as a CS. *Society for Neuroscience Abstracts, 12,* 1315.

WOODRUFF-PAK, D. S. & THOMPSON, R. F. (1985).   Classical conditioning of the eyelid response in rabbits as a model system for the study of brain mechanisms of learning and memory in aging. *Experimental Aging Research, 11,* 109–122.

WOODRUFF-PAK, D. S. & THOMPSON, R. F. (1986).   Delay classical conditioning of the human eyelid response with an auditory CS in 20-, 40-, and 60-year-olds. *Gerontologist, 26,* 90.

WOODRUFF-PAK, D. S. & THOMPSON, R. F. (1988).   Neural correlates of classical conditioning across the life span. In P. B. Baltes, D. M. Featherman & R. M. Lerner (Eds.), *Life span development and behavior,* (Vol. 9). Hillsdale, NJ: Erlbaum.

YEO, C. H., HARDIMAN, M. J. & GLICKSTEIN, M. (1984).   Discrete lesions of the cerebellar cortex abolish classically conditioned nictitating membrane response of the rabbit. *Behavioural Brain Research, 13,* 261–266.

CHAPTER 12

Aging in Human Learning, Memory, and Cognition

Few behavioral domains contain more uncertainties and myths about aging than do learning, memory, and cognition. For example, many people still think that senility is the inevitable outcome of aging if an individual lives long enough. Let us assert with certainty that this is not the case. In the first place, senility is a term that is often used loosely, especially when the young are describing the old. True senility is characterized by severe intellectual impairment, poor memory, and labile emotions. The senile person does not recognize relatives or long-time friends. Disorientation about time and place is common in senility, and the sleep-waking cycle is disrupted so that the individual is likely to awaken and wander around during the night.

It is difficult to estimate precisely the incidence of senility in the aging population, but since senile individuals need around-the-clock care, we will start with aged who are institutionalized. Less than 5 percent of the elderly are institutionalized at any one time, and even among these individuals who cannot live independently, all are not senile. Since a senile person requires close to 24-hour care, relatively few senile individuals reside with relatives. Hence, gerontologists typically use the estimate of around 5 percent for the number of elderly who become senile. This means that 95 percent remain mentally competent throughout old age until death.

We have begun this chapter on learning, memory, and cognition in aging with the worst case scenario involving the most negative outcome for normal cognitive functioning: senility. Senility, and its primary cause, senile dementia of the Alzheimer's Type (SDAT) will be discussed in greater detail in Chapter 16 on psychopathology and clinical intervention in the aged.

Now that we have disposed of the worst outcome for intellectual capacity, what, if any, are the effects of aging on learning and memory in the 95 percent of the elderly whose cognitive functions remain intact?

At age 74 Donald Hebb, a pioneering scientist in the study of brain and learning, wrote an article entitled "On Watching Myself Get Old" (Hebb, 1978). He first noticed signs of aging when he was 47. While reading a scientific paper, he decided that he really must make a note of an observation. As he turned the page, he discovered the very note he was planning to write in his own handwriting. He had no memory of having read the paper or having made the note. He then realized that he was stressing his memory capacity through overactivity. At the time he had been involved in extensive research, and he had been teaching, writing, chairing a department, and traveling a great deal. He was not in fact suffering from a memory deficit. His memory systems were simply overloaded. He cut back somewhat on his activities, and his memory returned to its "normal haphazard effectiveness."

In his 74th year, Hebb did notice changes. He termed them a slow, inevitable loss of cognitive capacities. However, these losses were not apparent to the outside world. The editor of the journal in which Hebb's article appeared commented that if Hebb's faculties continue to deteriorate in the same manner as he suggests, by the end of the next decade, Hebb will be only *twice* as lucid and able as the rest of us!

To put it succinctly, compared to young adults, older adults experience some difficulty with acquiring new information, and they also find the retrieval of some information from memory more difficult. In everyday life, these changes in ability are noticeable to the elderly, but they are hardly incapacitating. Furthermore, some evidence is emerging which suggests a greater capacity in older individuals for integrating information. Old people, with all their experience, are more likely to have wisdom and to see greater meaning in the whole they have assembled through their integration.

In this chapter we will begin by examining age differences in simple forms of learning and retention such as classical conditioning and paired associate learning and then move to a discussion of more complex types of learning and memory tasks and higher cognitive processing in the elderly.

AGE DIFFERENCES IN CLASSICAL CONDITIONING

One of the most simple and yet basic forms of learning is the association between a reflexive response and a neutral stimulus. This kind of learning is called classical conditioning. We discussed classical conditioning of the eyelid response in Chapter 11 on the psychobiology of learning, memory, and aging because it is with this type of learning that we are discovering the most about psychobiological substrates of behavior.

From the beginning of infants' experience, classical conditioning is a way that people and objects take on meaning. The appearance of mother means food is coming. Hence, young infants are often observed to suck reflexively at the sight of mother. Ivan Pavlov, the first scientist to describe the phenomenon and components of classical conditioning, worked with dogs and with the reflexive response of salivation to food. He called the stimulus that always elicited the reflexive response (the food), the unconditioned stimulus (US). The response (salivation) was called the unconditioned response (UR). When he presented the neutral stimulus of a bell shortly before the food, he found that the UR would become associated with the bell as well as the food. He called the bell the conditioned stimulus (CS), and the response to the bell alone was the conditioned response (CR).

If we were to analyze the classically conditioned sucking response in the infant in this manner, the food is the US, sucking is the UR, the mother is the CS, and sucking at the sight of the mother is the CR. Figure 11.1 identified the components of classical conditioning for eyelid conditioning, which is the most frequently used paradigm in contemporary classical conditioning research.

As was seen in Figure 11.1, in eyelid conditioning a tone is usually the CS (although it can also be a light, or less frequently, a tactile stimulus), and the US is an airpuff directed at the cornea. The US can also be a shock presented close to the eye so that it causes a blink. Ernest Hilgard who carried out some of the early human eyelid conditioning remembers that in the early human studies a slap in the face was the US. Naturally, shocks and face slaps as the US in humans have given way to the corneal airpuff US. The eyeblink is the UR, and it becomes the CR when it occurs to the tone alone on test trials when only the tone CS is presented (trial 81 in Figure 11.1) and when the blink occurs before the onset of the airpuff (trials 20, 40, and 80 in Figure 11.1).

This simple form of learning shows rather large age differences in humans and also in rabbits, the mammalian species in which we know a great deal about the neural circuitry involved in classical conditioning (Thompson, 1986). Indeed, we feel that classical conditioning in rabbits and humans holds great promise for unlocking some of the secrets of the neurobiology of learning, memory, and aging (Thompson & Woodruff-Pak, 1987; Woodruff-Pak & Thompson, 1985; Woodruff-Pak & Thompson, 1988).

The first study of human aging and eyelid conditioning was undertaken in the U.S.S.R. by Gakkel and Zinina (1953) and reported in this country by Jerome (1959). Only nursing home patients had been used as subjects, and there was no young control group. The older subjects were extremely slow to condition. Several eyelid conditioning studies in the United States used community residing young and elderly subjects and observed very large age differences in classical conditioning (Braun & Gieselhart, 1959; Kimble & Pennypacker, 1963).

To examine classical conditioning over the adult age range, we tested 76 subjects ranging in age from 18 to 83 years (Woodruff-Pak & Thompson, 1986). Age differences in eyelid conditioning are presented in Figure 12.1. By the decade

FIGURE 12.1 Age differences in simple delay classical conditioning of the eyelid response in human adults ranging in age from 18 to 83 years. The tone CS is on for 400 msec when the airpuff US onsets for 100 msec. Then the tone and airpuff coterminate. Shown in (A) is acquisition for the four age groups of subjects by blocks of eight paired trials over the entire session. In (B) is shown the groups' averages for the total percent CRs for the 96 paired and 12 test trials.

A. Conditioning in Adults 18-83
Acquisition in Percent CR's by Block

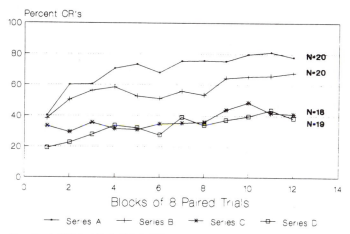

Mean Age A=20.2; B=44.9; C=52.8; D=73.1

B. Conditioning in Adults 18-83
Total Percent CR's

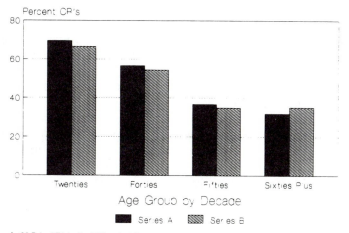

A=96 Paired Trials; B=12 Unpaired Trials

of the forties, adults are conditioning at a lower rate than adults in the twenties. Even larger age differences emerge in the decade of the fifties. Adults over the age of 60 have the lowest rate of classical conditioning. The data we have collected on eyelid conditioning and aging in rabbits indicate that the neural mechanisms involved in age differences in eyelid conditioning are in the cerebellum (Woodruff-Pak, Steinmetz, & Thompson, 1986). We presented some of these data in Chapter 11. What we learn about neurobiological age differences causing deficits in performance in older rabbits may well generalize to explain the performance deficits we have observed in older humans.

Thus, for a very simple and basic form of learning, we find rather large age differences. These differences are probably caused by aging in the nervous system. We have not discovered that the aged are unable to learn. Rather, we have observed that beginning as early as the decade of the forties, this simple reflexive learning takes more trials to occur. Individuals in the decade of the forties need more exposure to the stimuli to achieve criterion, but the 108 trials presented in our study were not sufficient for the group in the forties to achieve the same level of learning as demonstrated by the 20-year-olds. Since 55 percent of the group in the fifties and 86 percent of the group aged 60 and older in our study never achieved criterion, we do not know what number of trials would be required for most older subjects to attain criterion. Indeed, we cannot be certain that all individuals in the older age groups would achieve criterion in this simple classical conditioning task. Clearly, this ability to form associations shows large age differences.

PAIRED-ASSOCIATE AND SERIAL LEARNING

The kind of learning which a number of different studies has demonstrated to be more difficult for the elderly is the formation of new associations (Arenberg & Robertson-Tchabo, 1977). Since Gilbert (1941) first presented younger and older adults with a variety of learning and memory tasks, the result that paired-associate learning is especially difficult for the aged has been replicated (Walsh, 1983). Paired-associate learning involves presenting a series of two-word pairs for the subject to learn and then presenting the first word and asking what the associated word is. While initially, age-related deficits in paired-associate learning were interpreted as evidence that the associative machinery of learning declined with age, more recent interpretations include noncognitive factors.

When psychologists test for a behavioral ability, they rely on the performance of the subject as their assessment of the ability. However, many factors besides the subject's ultimate competence can affect how he or she performs on the task. Overton (1985) has commented extensively on the competence-performance distinction in developmental psychology. In the aging and learning literature, at least three noncognitive performance factors have been identified which affect the results of studies on learning in the aged (Woodruff & Walsh, 1975). These are:

(1) speed of presentation of stimuli and time available for responding; (2) arousal level of subjects; and (3) meaningfulness of the task and stimuli to the elderly.

One of the first investigators to identify speed as a problem in paired-associate studies of learning and aging was Canestrari (1963). He presented the stimuli to be learned at three different rates and found that age differences were greatest in the fastest paced condition (1.5 seconds), less in the medium paced condition (3.0 seconds), and minimal in the self-paced condition.

Eisdorfer (1965) demonstrated that the aged needed more time to respond as well as more time to learn in serial learning tasks. These are tasks in which a list of words is learned in sequence. When the words were presented at a slower rate so that learning could occur, and when the interval given for responding to each word was longer, older subjects performed better.

We have discussed issues of arousal in Chapter 9. Briefly, in studies of verbal learning, Powell, Eisdorfer and Bogdonoff (1964) found that older subjects were overaroused, and this interfered with their performance. A tranquilizing drug actually relaxed the elderly learners and improved their performance (Eisdorfer, Nowlin, & Wilkie, 1970). Froehling (1974) demonstrated that overarousal may be a transitory state experienced by older adults in their initial visit to a learning laboratory. Once they become accustomed to the surroundings, overarousal does not appear to interfere with their performance.

When old subjects are bored with a task, they may be underaroused, and this will affect their performance (Shmavonian & Busse, 1963). Paired-associate tasks are notoriously boring. Learning to associate the word *apple* with letters such as *TL* are typical stimuli in a paired-associate task. In Hulicka's (1967) study many older subjects simply quit when she presented them with such a task. It is no wonder that the aged do more poorly. They consider what they are doing to be nonsense! When Hulicka changed the task so that names were to be associated with occupations, the elderly agreed to participate.

Even when the paired-associate task is meaningful to older adults, they still perform more poorly. One strategy they apparently fail to use is verbal and visual mediators. Making a sentence with the two words to be paired, or creating visual images and relating the words in the image facilitate learning. Older adults are less likely to use verbal or visual mediation spontaneously (Hulicka & Grossman, 1967). When trained to use mediators, old subjects dramatically improve their performance, while young subjects perform about the same as they did before training (Canestrari, 1968). Nevertheless, even with training, the elderly still do not perform quite as well as the young.

In an analysis of the paired-associate and aging studies, Kausler (1982) examined the trial-by-trial performance data. In some studies he found that the elderly had trouble activating their learning processes, but once these processes were activated, the elderly progressed as well as the young. However, what he observed in most of the studies was a slower rate of learning for elderly subjects than for young adult subjects. Hence, while we often think that the problem of aging is with memory, what we may be observing is poorer acquisition in the first place. What older people do not learn sufficiently well, they will not remember later.

MEMORY

Often the question is asked, "Is learning or memory affected by aging?" The research evidence suggests that it is neither one nor the other alone that is affected by aging. Both processes show moderate aging effects.

Research on Forgetting

In an analysis of adult age differences in retention, Kausler (1982) points out that even when attempts are made to equate younger and older adult subjects on learning, success at this endeavor is unlikely. The number of trials to attain criterion is greater for the older subjects, so they may overlearn the simpler aspects of the task to a greater degree than the young. Since older subjects are less likely to use mediators, they may learn by rote. This is a qualitatively different way of storing information, and it is less resistant to forgetting (e.g., Adams & Montague, 1967; Bugelski, 1968). Hence, quantitatively and qualitatively what has been learned is different between young and old subjects, even in studies in which attempts have been made to equate acquisition.

Given these problems in assessing age differences in retention, Kausler (1982) observed that laboratory research indicates that aging has little effect on the retention of new material that has been learned fairly thoroughly. Similarly, forgetting in real life was found to be minimal for well-learned material. Kausler suggested that the laboratory studies offered a time-compressed simulation of forgetting in the real world. The course of forgetting over weeks for artificial laboratory material corresponded closely to the course of forgetting over years for material learned outside of the laboratory.

Research on memories for material learned years earlier indicates that whatever is retained five years after the material was learned will probably be retained for life. For example, in a study of 1,000 individuals who had learned Spanish in high school or college, Bahrick (1979) found that most of what people forgot was forgotten in the first three to five years after finishing the language course. Of the Spanish that remained, little was forgotten over the next 25 years. In another study, Bahrick, Bahrick, and Wittlinger (1975) showed pictures of classmates to people who had graduated from high school 35 years ago. People could recognize about 90 percent of the names and faces. Fifty years after graduation, they could still identify 70 to 80 percent of them.

Do older people remember past memories better than they remember more recent events? In-depth observational studies by memory and aging researcher, Irene Hulicka (1982), indicate that older adults remember events from various decades about equally well. They may talk about the past memories more because they are involved in the life review process (which is described in Chapter 17) or because they think it will interest a listener more than their comments about recent events. The following excerpt presents some of Hulicka's record of a very old man whom she interviewed extensively:

Case 5

This is my most complete report, derived from approximately 150 hours spent over a 3-year period with a man who was 90 when I first began to record the content of the conversational topics introduced by him. Categorizing the content of his conversations was facilitated because his personal history could be subdivided neatly into age and geographical categories as follows:

To age 20	Location I	Europe
Age 21–65	Location II	Farm in western Canada
Age 65–89	Location III	New farm, 500 miles from previous farm
Age 90–93	Location IV	Nursing home in strange city

About three quarters of the conversations reported were with one or more other persons involved, primarily family members or neighbors, from one of the two farm locations. It was possible to categorize fairly well 1,061 topics introduced by him, according to historical periods, general content, and relationship to guest...

The first column of Table 4 [Table 12.1] summarizes the distribution of the 614 personal memories by historical period. The percentage of personal memories was relatively constant over the development periods of childhood and youth, young adulthood, middle age, and old age. The last column indicates that the percentage of personal memories which were about or shared with his guests rather than about himself alone increased steadily by developmental period, an increase from 23% to 83%. This trend of course makes sense; by age 90 there was almost no one with whom he could share memories of events during his youth, whereas there were some people with whom he could share memories of events that occurred during his middle and late adulthood.

TABLE 12.1   Distribution of Memories of a Man Aged 90–93[a]

Developmental Period	Number of Memories	Percentage of Personal Memories by Developmental Period	Percentage of memories by Developmental Period That Were Self- Versus Other-Oriented	
			Self-Alone	Shared with or About Guest
Up to age 20	138	22	77	23
Approximately 21–40	146	24	55	45
Approximately 41–65	160	26	30	70
Approximately 66–89	123	20	19	81
Approximately 90–93	47	8	17	83

[a]By developmental period and by memories of self versus shared memories.
Source: Hulicka, I. M. (1982). Memory functioning in late adulthood. In F.I.M. Craik & S. Trehuk (Eds.) *Aging and cognitive processes.* New York: Plenum. p. 347.

Table 5 [Table 12.2] presents the content of his topical choice by category of guests....

TABLE 12.2   **Distribution by Category of Guests of Topics Introduced by Man Aged 90–93**

Category of Guest and Frequency of Association	Total of Topics Introduced	Self-Oriented Topics	Other-Oriented Topics: Shared Memories and Questions	Topics About Present Situation or Politics
Sisters: Frequent contacts until age 65, sporadic thereafter	99	14%	78%	8%
Offspring and spouses: most offspring left home by age 16 but visited at least once a year	492	25%	65%	10%
Neighbors, Location II: frequent contacts with neighbor families from age 21 to 65, sporadic thereafter	139	20%	70%	10%
Neighbors, Location III: met after age 65	71	31%	56%	13%
Grandchildren: variable	231	31%	55%	14%
Professionals: associated with nursing home	29	17%	45%	38%

Source: Hulicka, I. M. (1982). Memory functioning in late adulthood. In F.I.M. Craik & S. Trehuk (Eds.), *Aging and cognitive processes.* New York: Plenum. p. 348.

The pattern of this gentleman's choice of conversational topics suggests that his memory for all periods of his life was equally good and that he had no memory fixation on or preference for a single developmental period. Further, his selection of memories for use in conversation appeared to be strongly influenced by his desire to be a courteous host. Possibly also guests served as stimuli for the retrieval and selection of specific memories. One third of his conversational topics involved memories about his guests or memories of experiences shared with his guests, and almost as many topics were questions about their activities, with many of the questions utilizing memories about their interests and families. Further, some of his memories about himself, particularly when his guests were young people, reflected their interest in learning about the "old days."

His choice of conversational topics suggests that perhaps some old people may talk about memories of their childhood and youth, not because memories from other developmental periods are less available, but rather because such memories are judged to be of greater interest to audiences with whom the old person has no shared experiences. A 90-year-old might decide judiciously that his personal experience of 20 years ago would be of little interest to a relatively new acquaintance, while his personal experiences of 70 years ago, because of relative uniqueness, might be interesting. And many of the very elderly may converse primarily with acquaintances with whom they have few shared experiences (Hulicka, 1982, pp. 346–348).

Information Processing Analysis of Memory and Aging

Information processing approaches to memory attempt to break down various stages of memory to understand memory processes more completely. The initial perceptual aspect of the stimulus as it is first recorded is called sensory memory. The span of immediate memory which is the number of items you can hold in memory after just seeing or hearing them is called primary or short-term memory. What is remembered for longer periods of time is called secondary or long-term memory. Table 12.3 identifies features of each of these three parts of memory.

TABLE 12.3   An Outline of Information-Processing Theories of Memory

Features	Sensory Memory	Short-Term Memory	Long-Term Memory
1. Entry of information	Preattentive	Requires attention	Rehearsal
2. Maintenance	Not possible	Continued attention (rehearsal)	Repetition/organization
3. Form of information	Literal copy of input	Phonemic	Semantic
4. Capacity	Large	Small (4–7 items)	Unlimited
5. Information loss	Decay	Displacement	Loss of accessibility
6. Trace duration	¼-2 sec	Up to 30 sec	Minutes to years
7. Retrieval	Readout	Items in consciousness	Retrieval cues

Source: Craik, F.I.M. & Lockhart, R. S. (1972). Levels of processing: A framework for memory research. *Journal of Verbal Learning and Verbal Behavior, 11,* p. 672.

The age differences which have been identified from an information processing perspective are greatest in the long-term memory capacity. No clear aging effects which would be significant enough to affect registration of information in later memory states have been found in sensory memory, and age differences in short-term memory capacity are minor and simply involve encoding.

Craik (1968) presented word lists of varying lengths and also of varying commonness of the words to younger and older adult subjects and found that older subjects recalled fewer items than the young from longer lists and recalled fewer items from the lists of rarer words. He interpreted these results as evidence for the decline in long-term memory with age and argued that some part of the decline was attributable to an inability to retrieve information. This interpretation was based on the result that older adults showed poorer performance when the pool of alternatives was large.

A classic study on long-term memory and aging was carried out by Schonfield and Robertson (1966). They presented younger and older subjects with a list of 24 words. First the subjects were required to recall the words. Then they performed a recognition task in which each of the words on the list was presented embedded among three other nontarget words. The subject had to recognize the word from the list. While age differences existed on the recall task, there were no age differences in recognition. Figure 12.2 illustrates these results.

While not all subsequent studies have replicated the absence of age differences in recognition, many studies have indicated much smaller age differences in recognition than in recall tasks (e.g., Craik, 1971; Erber, 1974; Shaps & Nilsson, 1980). These results indicate that while there may be a problem with encoding, diminished proficiency in the search process is also a contributor to age differences in long-term memory proficiency.

Although a large number of studies on aging and memory have been under-

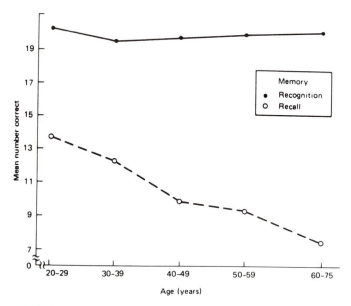

FIGURE 12.2   Mean recall and recognition scores as a function of age. While recall showed large age differences between the decades of the twenties and sixties, recognition showed no age differences. *Source:* Botwinick, J. (1973). Adapted from Schonfield & Robertson (1966). *Aging and Behavior.* Nw York: Springer Publishing Co. Reprinted by permission.

taken from the information processing perspective, some investigators in the forefront of research on memory and aging are critical of this approach. For one thing, the independence and clarity of the separate storage functions hypothesized in information processing theories has been lost (Craik & Lockhart, 1972). The model does not focus on the qualitative aspects of memory which apparently are most affected by aging. In this regard, Kausler stated:

> Moderate deficiencies of long-term memory phenomena for elderly subjects have been reported in numerous studies. Undoubtedly these deficiencies reflect those found in the real world. Our review has implicated both encoding processes and retrieval processes in this overall age-related decline in the proficiency of long-term memory. It is here that the shortcomings of the dual-store [information processing] model become apparent. Both encoding and retrieval processes are treated rather superficially by proponents of the model. Little effort is made to distinguish between quantitative and qualitative changes in processes. The possibility that age deficits in episodic memory may be due to qualitative changes that may be modified by appropriate training is largely ignored. It is with such qualitative changes that the levels of processing model has been most useful (Kausler, 1982, p. 451).

Levels of Processing Model and Aging

Moving away from an information processing approach, some psychologists have suggested that the nature of the processing of information at the time it is being perceived affects the way it is stored and retrieved. Hyde and Jenkins (1969) carried out a study with young adults which demonstrated how processing activities influenced how well items were remembered. Three groups of subjects were presented with the same 24-item word list, but each group had a different orienting task. Group I was given instructions to rate each word for how pleasant or unpleasant it was. Group II was to scan each word to see if it contained an *e*. Group III was asked to estimate the number of letters in each word. A fourth group, a control group, was asked simply to commit the list to memory. After the groups performed the orienting tasks, they were asked to recall as many of the words as they could. In those groups dealing with nonmeaningful aspects of the words, the number of letters or whether an *e* was present, recall was poor. They only remembered an average of ten words. The orientation task which involved thinking about how each word made subjects feel resulted in the greatest recall with an average of 17 words. Only the control group instructed to memorize the words came close to this level of performance.

To theorists taking the levels of processing perspective, encoding is most effective when items are processed deeply. Deep processing involves thinking about the meaning of a word. Thus, when subjects are asked to examine a word for its pleasant/unpleasant evoking qualities, they must examine the word's meaning as it is stored in their memory. To make the examination, subjects must encode the item deeply. This kind of encoding leads to a relatively permanent memory trace which is likely to be available for recall. Young adults engage in this kind of deep processing naturally when they are instructed to memorize a list of words. Thus, levels of processing theorists would predict that there should be little difference in the recall performance between young adults instructed to memorize the list and those given an orienting task which serves to make them process the words deeply. Only shallow processing is required to determine the number of letters (group III) or to scan whether an *e* is present in the word (group II). The result is a more fragile memory trace. Consequently, recall scores of groups II and III were significantly lower than for group I or the control group given intructions to recall the words.

The levels of processing perspective gave gerontologists an opportunity to examine whether elderly adults were less proficient on recall tasks because they have suffered a true decrement in the ability to engage in deep processing or if they simply do not engage in deep processing spontaneously when instructed to memorize a word list. By replicating the Hyde and Jenkins (1969) study in a group of older subjects, one could compare older subjects using deep processing (in the pleasant/unpleasant condition), to old subjects using shallow processing (counting letters, searching for *e*s), and to old subjects instructed to recall the list.

Eysenck (1974) was the first to follow Hyde and Jenkins' procedure closely with older as well as younger adult subjects. Four incidental memory groups were included in Eysenck's study. Two of the orientation tasks involved deep processing (form an image of each object and rate the image for vividness; name a modifying adjective for each item), and two involved shallow processing (count the number of letters in each word; name a rhyming word for each item). Control groups instructed to remember the words were also included. Figure 12.3 presents Eysenck's results. There were no age differences in shallow processing, but age differences in deep processing and intentional memory are apparent. This result has been replicated in several laboratories (Erber, Herman, & Botwinick, 1980; Lauer, 1976; Mason, 1979; Perlmutter, 1979; Smith, 1979; S. White, as reported in Craik, 1977). The implication is that processing proficiency appears to be less in older adults.

Craik reported on an additional test of this procedure which modifies the interpretation of these results. White, working in Craik's laboratory, replicated Eysenck (1974) under recall conditions, but after the subjects attempted to recall the words, White and Craik gave them a recognition task. In recognition conditions, older subjects performed as well as younger subjects in both the deep and shallow processing conditions. The only age differences were in the control groups instructed simply to memorize the words. Craik (1977) interpreted these results to suggest that older adults have not lost the capacity to process information deeply, but they simply do not do so spontaneously. Also, even when durable memory traces have been built with deep levels of processing, older adults are less able to retrieve memory traces.

While Craik and Simon (1980), Erber et al. (1980), and Perlmutter (1979) replicated White and Craik's results on depth of processing and recognition in the

FIGURE 12.3   Age differences in recall of items as a function of depth of processing. *Source:* Craik, F.I.M. & Lockhart, R. S. (1972). Levels of processing: A framework for memory research. *Journal of Verbal Learning and Verbal Behavior, 11,* 671–684. Copyright © Academic Press, Inc. Reprinted by permission.

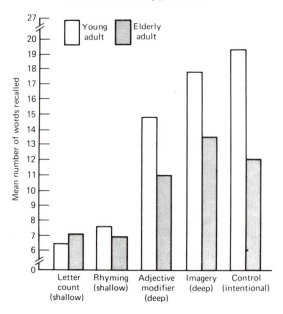

aged, Mason (1979) and Smith and Winograd (1978) did not. In the later two studies, pronounced age differences in recognition as well as recall occurred. Cued recall has been attempted in some studies as an alternative to recognition in order to separate encoding and retrieval processes. After reviewing the depth of processing work, Kausler concluded:

> Our best guess is that there is a modest age deficit in encoding proficiency, and the degree of that deficit has been overestimated in a number of studies. Why the overestimation? Our best guess, here, is that any task involving the recall of a lengthy list of items is viewed suspiciously by many elderly subjects as being trivial and of dubious ecological relevance (Kausler, 1982, p. 459).

Walsh (1983) commended the levels of processing approach because it suggests ways in which the "processing deficiencies" can be overcome through the use of more effective strategies by older learners. He also pointed out that the manipulation of processing strategies has not generally resulted in a total elimination of age differences on these tasks. Even when very serious attempts have been made to develop and implement memory improvement techniques for older adults, performance of the elderly is seldom brought to the level of the young (Poon, Walsh-Sweeney & Fozard, 1980). Nevertheless, older adults can be trained to improve their performance on memory tasks (Poon, 1985). Although processing deficiency may account for some of the age-related differences in performance on memory tasks, it does not totally account for the differences between younger and older adult groups.

Memory Tasks Requiring More or Less Effort

We have seen from the results of depth of processing studies that on tasks which require the expenditure of effort and deep, meaningful processing, older adults perform more poorly. What happens when older adults are compared to young and middle-aged subjects on memory tasks which require less effort? These simple tasks have sometimes been given the name *automatic processes.* The idea is that there may be some encoding processes which occur naturally in the organism without the expenditure of effort. These processes include the accumulation of information that might be called incidental to the learning situation.

An example of incidental learning which is stored in memory (at least for a short while after the learning has occurred) follows. Suppose you are sitting on a crowded beach for an hour looking at the passers-by. You might be listening to the radio and sipping a drink as well. After an hour had passed and someone asked you how many men and how many women had walked by, you would probably make a relatively accurate estimate. You would have "automatically" stored those numbers in your memory. It would also be likely that you would remember how many women in fire-engine red bikinis passed by, and how many people with noses whitened with sunscreen you had seen passing. The number of children running by with sandpails would also be registered in your memory.

The laboratory counterpart to this task is not as much fun as sitting on the beach. It involves sitting subjects down in a room in which there is a slide projector or computer screen and presenting them with long lists of words, some of which appear once, some twice, some five times, and so on. This measure of the "automatic" process has mistakenly been referred to as frequency of occurrence information. However, words in the frequency of occurrence paradigm are not presented one per so many other words as the name, frequency, implies. Rather, words are repeated some total number of times over the entire length of the study. The same word is not even repeated at equal intervals between the other words.

The actual meaning of the term *frequency* is the *rate* of occurrence of a phenomenon over a precise period of time. The EEG alpha frequency is ten cycles per second. A complete alpha cycle or alpha wave crosses the baseline precisely ten times per second. Hence, a more accurate term than frequency of occurrence information for this form of "automatic" processing would be encoding of *number of repetitions.*

Kausler (1982) reported several number of repetitions studies, some of which were carried out in his own laboratory, demonstrating that older adults remember the number of repetitions of words as accurately as do middle-aged and younger adults. These same subjects in Kausler's studies showed large age differences in the number of paired associates they learned. While some investigators interpreted these results to support the notion that "automatic" processes show no age differences and "effortful" processes such as those involved in memory for paired associates do show age differences, Kausler (1982) argued that it is too early to accept this interpretation. When subjects are asked to remember the actual number of repetitions of words, older subjects underestimate the number of presentations of the most often repeated words to a significantly greater degree than do younger subjects (e.g., Freund & Witte, 1978). Using categories of items as a means to question subjects about the number of repetitions of certain types of words also puts older adults at a disadvantage. For example, Kausler, Lichty, and Hakami (1984) asked whether there had been more men's names, more names of states, or more names of religions after presenting younger and older subjects with lists of words. Younger subjects were significantly more accurate on this presumably "automatic" task.

Kaulser and Puckett (1981) demonstrated that when subjects were instructed to note the sex of the individual on a tape recorder saying the sentences to be remembered, this seriously impaired memory for the sentences in the older but not the younger adults. Regardless of instructions, "automatic" processes are not predicted to impinge on "effortful" processes. However, in the older adults, encoding of the nonsemantic information occurred at the expense of encoding of the semantic information. Here, again, the postulation of "automatic" and "effortful" processes does not accurately predict memory performance in aging.

Perlmutter and Mitchell (1982) pointed out that the notion that automatic processing does not change with age is probably incorrect. These authors argued that the concept that there is one single processing capacity and that there is a *processing surplus* in younger adults is a better interpretation of the data. These and other results led Welford (1987) to conclude that there is a single system for episodic memory rather than two systems represented as "automatic" and "effortful." Furthermore, this single system appears to show a decline in efficiency with age.

Metamemory in Older Adults

Knowing about remembering—that is, knowing one's own capacities for memory—is what we mean by metamemory. Studies by Lachman, Lachman, and Thronesbery (1979) and Perlmutter (1978) suggested that metamemory is stable across the adult age span. Older people appear to know what facts they know or do not know as well as young adults do.

Another aspect of metamemory, knowledge of skills needed to store information, may not be equal between younger and older adults. Two experiments by Murphy, Sanders, Bariesheski, and Schmitt (1981) provided insights about age differences in this type of metamemory and also indicated ways in which the elderly might improve their memory skills. A series of pictures of common objects was given to younger and older adult subjects to study. The task was to recall the names of the objects in serial order. Some of the series were of memory-span length (5 to 7 items), some were of subspan length (2 items less than memory span), and some were of supraspan length (2 items more than memory span). Subjects were given as much time with the pictures as they wanted to enable them to study and rehearse the items. Older subjects spent considerably less time (20 to 30 seconds less) studying both the span- and supraspan-length series, and their performance was much poorer than the performance of the young. For example, in the supraspan condition, the elderly got 73 percent of the items correct, while the young got 96 percent correct. The older subjects simply did not appreciate the difficulty of the task, and they did not practice enough with the longer lists to succeed. Most research comparing young and old on strategies indicates that the old are more cautious. In the Murphy et al. study, the aged were more careless in their study of items to remember.

Following up on these results, Murphy et al. (1981) performed a second experiment in which they forced elderly subjects to spend at least as much time studying the items to be recalled as the young had spent in the first experiment. The older subjects had to increase the time they spent with span-length series to 32 seconds, and they were made to study supraspan-length series for 59 seconds. Forced to study in this manner, the older adults recalled as many series without error as did the young subjects in the first experiment.

The Murphy et al. (1981) study has important implications for researchers interested in memory and aging as well as for the aged in real life. In the Canestrari (1963) study of paired-associate learning, self-pacing helped older adults, but they still performed more poorly than the young. Older people may have underestimated the time needed to study and learn the lists. Perhaps older individuals overestimated their own competence and failed to give themselves sufficient time to rehearse the items.

In the real world the elderly may terminate their rehearsal of material they need to learn too soon. With a little more time and effort put into study and practice of the material to be remembered, the aged might find that their memory is not failing at all. Maybe it is patience with practicing that declines with age, rather than memory capacity! If the elderly were to recognize that there is only a moderate change in the capacity to learn and remember, they might be willing to make a bit more effort to deeply process and rehearse what they learn. The reward could be memory performance in old age at the level the individual had maintained throughout his or her young adult life.

COGNITIVE PROCESSES

Gisela Labouvie-Vief (1977) criticized the typical practice in the study of aging of adapting tasks designed to assess learning, memory, and cognition in adolescents and young adults and applying them to studies of aging. It may be more appropriate in exploring adult cognition to seek age-appropriate constructs rather than merely altering the content of the tasks. For the most part, gerontologists appear to have been more concerned with the acquisition of new information and new skills while overlooking the potential for acquired knowledge in facilitating problem solving in aging. In this regard, Labouvie-Vief (1976) discussed ways of optimizing cognitive competence in later life.

One approach to explore a developmental progression in adult cognition has resulted in attempts to formulate a model of adult cognitive development from within a Piagetian framework (Arlin, 1975; Koplowitz, 1984; Kramer, 1983; Labouvie-Vief, 1980; Pascual-Leone, 1983; Pascual-Leone & Goodman, 1979; Riegel, 1973; Sinnott, 1984). All of these formulations maintain their unique features, but there does appear to be considerable agreement on the overall qualities of mature thought. In general, postformal operational reasoning is believed to involve: (1) an understanding of the relativistic, nonabsolute nature of reality and knowledge; (2) acceptance of contradiction as part of reality; and (3) an integrative approach to thinking.

In a study of decision making in successful middle-aged executives, Birren (1969) observed that the thinking of these individuals appeared more integrative. They "chunked" large amounts of information rather than dealing with smaller "bits" as the younger executives did. The older executives had developed fewer solutions with age, but the solutions were proven ones. Unsuccessful strategies had been eliminated leaving fewer, more successful solutions. Thus, chunking information or adopting a more integrative style was not seen as regressing to a less complex, dedifferentiated mode of thinking which is characteristic of children's thought. Rather, integration is seen as a progressive manner of reasoning gained from experience.

Results from a variety of areas support the hypothesis that older adults chunk information into fewer units, and some studies demonstrate that the aged employ a more integrative style of processing this information. From the area of categorization, it has been demonstrated repeatedly that older adults construct fewer categories in organizing information with tasks using familiar objects (Cicirelli, 1976; Kogan, 1974) and simulations of real-life situations (Sabatini & Labouvie-Vief, 1979).

Kramer and Woodruff (1984) found empirical evidence for a more integrative classification strategy in highly educated older adult women. Since it was the highest achieving older women in the sample who showed the greatest integration in their classification schemes, the data suggest that this mode of thinking is not indicative of regression to a childlike phase. In a subsequent study, Kramer and Woodruff (1986) examined formal operational, relativistic, and dialectical thought processes in young, middle-aged, and older adults and found that relativistic and dialectical thought may increase in later life. In support of continuing development in adult thinking, dialectical, but not relativistic thought was postformal operational.

Cognitive phenomena such as wisdom, ego, integrity, and life review have been associated with old age. All of these phenomena involved a greater synthesis of ideas reflecting an integration to a more mature stage of cognition. Schaie (1977–1978) devised a model of the development of adult cognition which had at its final stage a period he called "reintegrative." He contended that in old age, cognition is oriented toward integrating one's life experiences in order to make sense of one's life and to find continuity. Such a stage parallels Erikson's (1968) stage of integrity versus despair, the final of his eight stages of personality development over the life span.

Consideration has also been given to the concept of wisdom, a quality often associated throughout history with thinking in old age (Clayton & Birren, 1980). Clayton (1982) compared and contrasted wisdom and intelligence and concluded that intelligence focuses on questions of how to accomplish tasks, while wisdom involves considerations of whether a particular course of action should be pursued. Wisdom also involves an integration of affect and cognition. Roodin, Rybash, and Hoyer (1984) suggested that it is precisely the integration between cognition and affect which characterizes adult development.

SUMMARY

We began this chapter by attempting to explode the myth that senility is the inevitable outcome of the aging of cognitive processes. At the very most, 5 percent of us will become senile in very old age. The vast majority of us will retain our cognitive capacities. Our ability to learn and remember new information may not be what it used to be by the time we reach our seventh and eighth decades, but the age changes will not be enough to affect our lives in any dramatic way. Furthermore, by the time we are 70 to 80 years of age, we will have amassed so much information and experience that our ability to make judgments about our lives might be greatly enhanced from what it was when we were 20.

One of the simplest forms of learning, classical conditioning, shows a decline with age that appears sometime in the decade of the forties. This age change is apparent in other species such as rabbits and cats. In rabbits, that age change in classical conditioning has been associated with age changes in the cerebellum.

The kind of learning which a number of different studies has demonstrated to be more difficult for the elderly is the formation of new associations. Sometimes performance factors interfere with the actual learning capacity of older adults. The rate of presentation of stimuli to be learned impairs learning in older adults if the presentation is too rapid. Arousal level can interfere with learning, especially when the older adult feels stressed and uncomfortable in the learning setting. The boredom and meaninglessness inherent in many learning tasks is another perform- ance factor that results in lower scores for older adults. They are not willing to put up with the "nonsense" that many younger subjects will tolerate.

Older adults appear to learn new information at a slower rate than younger adults. Thus, when they are tested for memory, older adults may perform more poorly simply because they have not learned the material well enough in the first place.

In learning experiments it is very difficult to equate younger and older adults for acquisition. This means that interpretation of laboratory studies of memory and aging is difficult. Studies of forgetting have demonstrated that once material is learned well, it will be retained for long periods of time. For example, middle- aged adults readily recognized 90 percent of the names and faces of classmates in their high school yearbooks 35 years after graduation, and older adults recognized 70 to 80 percent of their classmates 50 years after graduation. Older adults do not appear to remember early life experiences much better than they remember more recent experiences. Rather, they remember events from various decades about equally well.

Information processing approaches to memory attempt to break down various stages of memory to understand the processes more completely. Age dif- ferences identified from an information processing perspective are greatest in the long-term memory capacity. Older adults have a more difficult time in retrieving information from memory. They do relatively well at recognition memory tasks such as multiple-choice tests where the answer is there and requires correct iden- tification. When the item must be recalled from memory, such as in a fill-in ques- tion, older adults perform more poorly. However, it is true for all of us that recall is more difficult than recognition.

The levels of processing model examines the nature of the processing of information as it is encoded into memory. When information is encoded mean- ingfully (or more deeply), it is more likely to be remembered. While deep process- ing helps older adults to remember material better, they apparently do not carry out as much deep processing as do younger adults. The levels of processing model provides ways in which some of the processing deficiencies of older adults can be overcome.

Another approach in adult cognition has been to suggest that some aspects of encoding are "automatic" while others are "effortful." The prediction for aging has been that automatic processes show no age change, while effortful processes are less efficient in older adults. In some cases no age differences in "automatic" processing have been observed. However, other methods of assessing "automatic" processes have shown age differences. Thus, this distinction has shown itself to be not particularly useful. Episodic memory is best viewed as a single process, and it appears to be a process in which age differences occur.

Knowledge about one's own memory abilities, metamemory, appears to be stable over the adult years. However, an awareness of the skills required to successfully remember things appears to show age differences. Evidence indicates that older adults overestimate their own competence and fail to give themselves sufficient practice to learn and remember items.

Most of the studies of adult learning, memory, and cognition simply take behavioral tasks designed from observations of young adults and apply them to older adults. Seldom do psychologists look to older adults first before they design the learning and memory tasks. However, there is a trend in the study of psychology and aging to examine more carefully the actual abilities of older adults.

One of the newer approaches to cognition in psychology and aging is to investigate how cognitive abilities develop. In many cases the cognitive developmental theory of Jean Piaget has been used as a basis from which to explore further cognitive development in adulthood. Other approaches have involved the observation of cognitive behavior in middle and old age to extract what aspects may develop. These approaches have led to suggestions that the ability to integrate information to synthesize a broader perspective may develop in later life. Ego integrity, life review, and wisdom are other dimensions of cognition which have been associated with later life.

REFERENCES

ADAMS, J. A. & MONTAGUE, W. E. (1967).   Retroactive inhibition and natural language mediation. *Journal of Verbal Learning and Verbal Behavior, 6,* 528–535.

ARENBERG, D. & ROBERTSON-TCHABO, E. A. (1977).   Learning and aging. In J. E. Birren & K. W. Schaie (Eds.), *Handbook of the psychology of aging.* New York: Van Nostrand Reinhold.

ARLIN, P. K. (1975).   Cognitive development in adulthood: A fifth stage? *Developmental Psychology, 11,* 602–606.

BAHRICK, H. P. (1979).   Maintenance of knowledge: Questions about memory we forgot to ask. *Journal of Experimental Psychology: General, 108,* 296–308.

BAHRICK, H. P., BAHRICK, P. O. & WITTLINGER, R. P. (1975).   Fifty years of memory for names and faces: A cross-sectional approach. *Journal of Experimental Psychology: General, 104,* 54–75.

BIRREN, J. E. (1969).   Age and decision strategies. In A. T. Welford & J. E. Birren (Eds.), *Decision making and age.* Basel, Switzerland: S. Karger.

BRAUN, H. W. & GEISELHART, R. (1959).   Age differences in the acquisition and extinction of the conditioned eyelid response. *Journal of Experimental Psychology, 57,* 386–388.

BUGELSKI, B. R. (1968).   Images as mediators in one-trial paired-associate learning: II. Self-timing in successive lists. *Journal of Experimental Psychology, 77,* 328–334.

CANESTRARI, R. E., JR. (1963).   Paced and self-paced learning in young and elderly adults. *Journal of Gerontology, 18,* 165–168.

CANESTRARI, R. E., JR. (1968).   Age changes in acquisition. In G. A. Talland (Ed.), *Human aging and behavior.* New York: Academic Press.

CICIRELLI, V. G. (1976).   Categorization behavior in aging subjects. *Journal of Gerontology, 31,* 676–680.

CLAYTON, V. (1982).   Wisdom and intelligence: The nature and function of knowledge in the later years. *International Journal of Aging and Human Development, 15,* 315–321.

CLAYTON, V. & BIRREN, J. E. (1980).   The develpoment of wisdom across the life span: A reexamination of an ancient logic. In P. B. Baltes & O. G. Brim (Eds.), *Life-span development and behavior,* (Vol. 3), New York: Academic Press.

CRAIK, F.I.M. (1968).   Two components in free recall. *Journal of Verbal Learning and Verbal Behavior, 7,* 996–1004.

CRAIK, F.I.M. (1971).   Age differences in recognition memory. *Quarterly Journal of Experimental Psychology, 23,* 316–323.

CRAIK, F.I.M. (1977).   Age differences in human memory. In J. E. Birren & K. W. Schaie (Eds.), *Handbook of the psychology of aging.* New York: Van Nostrand Reinhold.

CRAIK, F.I.M. & LOCKHART, R. S. (1972).   Levels of processing: A framework for memory research. *Journal of Verbal Learning and Verbal Behavior, 11,* 671–684.

CRAIK, F.I.M. & SIMON, E. (1980).   Age differences in memory: The roles of attention and depth of processing. In L. W. Poon, J. L. Fozard, L. S. Cermak, D. Arenberg, & L. W. Thompson (Eds.), *New directions in memory and aging.* Hillsdale: NJ: Erlbaum.

EISDORFER, C. (1965).   Verbal learning and response time in the aged. *Journal of Genetic Psychology, 107,* 15–22.

EISDORFER, C., NOWLIN, J. & WILKIE, F. (1970).   Improvement of learning in the aged by modification of the autonomic nervous system activity. *Science, 170,* 1327–1329.

ERBER, J. T. (1974).   Age differences in recognition memory. *Journal of Gerontology, 29,* 177–181.

ERBERT, J. T., HERMAN, T. G. & BOTWINICK, J. (1980).   Age differences in memory as a function of depth of processing. *Experimental Aging Research, 6,* 341–348.

ERIKSON. E. H. (1968).   *Identity and crisis.* New York: W. W. Norton.

EYSENCK, M. W. (1974).   Age differences in incidental learning. *Developmental Psychology, 10,* 936–941.

FREUND, J. S. & WITTE, K. L. (1976).   Paired-associate transfer: Age of subjects, anticipation interval, association value, and paradigm. *American Journal of Psychology, 89,* 695–705.

FROEHLING, S. (1974).   Effects of propranolol on behavioral and physiological measures of elderly males. Unpublished doctoral dissertation. Florida: University Miami.

GAKKEL, L. B. & ZININA, N. V. (1953).   Changes of higher nerve function in people over 60 years of age. *Fiziolog. Zhurnal., 39,* 533–539.

GILBERT, J. G. (1941).   Memory in senescence. *Journal of Abnormal and Social Psychology, 36,* 73–86.

HEBB, D. O. (1978).   On watching myself get old. *Psychology Today, 12,* 15–23.

HULICKA, I. M. (1967).   Age changes and age differences in memory functioning. *The Gerontologist, 7,* 46–54.

HULICKA, I. M. (1982).   Memory functioniong in late adulthood. In F.I.M. Craik & S. Trehub (Eds.), *Aging and cognitive processes.* New York: Plenum.

HULICKA, I. M. & GROSSMAN, J. L. (1967). Age-group comparisons for the use of mediators in paired-associate learning. *Journal of Gerontology, 22,* 46-51.

HYDE, T. S. & JENKINS, J. J. (1969). Differential effects of incidental tasks on the organization of recall of a list of highly associated words. *Journal of Experimental Psychology, 82,* 472-481.

JEROME, E. A. (1959). Age and learning—Experimental studies. In J. E. Birren (Ed.), *Handbook of aging and the individual.* Chicago: University of Chicago Press.

KAUSLER, D. H. (1982). *Experimental psychology and human aging.* New York: Wiley.

KAUSLER, D. H., LICHTY, W. & HAKAMI, M. (1984). Frequency judgments for distractor items in a short-term memory task: Instructional variation and adult age differences. *Journal of Verbal Learning and Verbal Behavior, 23,* 660-668.

KAUSLER, D. H. & PUCKETT, J. M. (1981). Adult age differences in memory for sex of voice. *Journal of Gerontology, 36,* 44-50.

KIMBLE, G. A. & PENNYPACKER, H. W. (1963). Eyelid conditioning in young and aged subjects. *Journal of Genetic Psychology, 103,* 283-289.

KOGAN, N. (1974). Categorization and conceptualizing styles in younger and older adults. *Human Development, 17,* 218-230.

KOPLOWITZ, H. (1984). A projection beyond Piaget's formal-operations stage. In M. L. Commons, F. A. Richards & C. Armon (Eds.), *Beyond formal operations: Late adolescent and adult cognitive development.* New York: Praeger.

KRAMER, D. A. (1983). Post-formal operations? A need for further conceptualization. *Human Development, 26,* 91-105.

KRAMER, D. A. & WOODRUFF, D. S. (1984). Categorization and metaphoric processing in young and older adults. *Research on Aging, 6,* 271-286.

KRAMER, D. A. & WOODRUFF, D. S. (1986). Relativistic and dialectical thought in three adult age groups. *Human Development, 29,* 280-290.

LABOUVIE-VIEF, G. (1976). Toward optimizing cognitive competence in later life. *Educational Gerontology, 1,* 75-92.

LABOUVIE-VIEF, G. (1977). Adult cognitive development: In search of alternative interpretations. *Merill-Palmer Quarterly, 23,* 227-263.

LABOUVIE-VIEF, G. (1980). Beyond formal operations: Uses and limits of pure logic in life-span development. *Human Development, 23,* 141-161.

LACHMAN, J. L., LACHMAN, R. & THRONESBERY, C. (1979). Metamemory through the adult life span. *Developmental Psychology, 15,* 543-551.

LAUER, P. A. (1976). The effects of different types of word processing on memory performance in young and elderly adults. *Dissertation Abstracts International, 36,* 5833-B. (University Microfilms No. 76-11, 591).

MASON, S. E. (1979). Effects of orienting tasks on the recall and recognition performance of subjects differing in age. *Developmental Psychology, 15,* 467-469.

MURPHY, M. D., SANDERS, R. E., GABRIESHESKI, A. S. & SCHMITT, F. A. (1981). Metamemory in the aged. *Journal of Gerontology, 36,* 185-193.

OVERTON, W. F. (1985). Scientific methodologies and the competence-moderator-performance issue. In E. Neimark, R. D. Lisi & J. Newman (Eds.)., *Moderators of competence.* Hillsdale, NJ: Erlbaum.

PASCUAL-LEONE, J. (1983). Growing into human maturity: Toward a metasubjective theory of adult stages. In P. B. Baltes & O. Brim (Eds.), *Life-span developmental psychology,* (Vol. 5), New York: Academic Press.

PASCUAL-LEONE, J. & GOODMAN, D. (1979). Intelligence and experience: A neo-piagetian approach. *Instructional Science, 8,* 301-367.

PERLMUTTER, M. (1978). What is memory the aging of? *Developmental Psychology, 14,* 330-345.

PERLMUTTER, M. (1979). Age differences in adults' free recall, cued recall, and recognition. *Journal of Gerontology, 34,* 533-539.

PERLMUTTER, M. & MITCHELL, D. B. (1982).   The appearance and disappearance of age differences in adult memory. In F.I.M. Craik and S. Trehub (Eds.), *Aging and cognitive processes*. New York: Plenum.

POON. L. W. (1985).   Differences in human memory with aging: Nature, causes, and clinical implications. In J. E. Birren & K. W. Schaie (Eds.), *Handbook of the psychology of aging*. New York: Van Nostrand Reinhold.

POON, L. W., WALSH-SWEENEY, L. & FOZARD, J. L. (1980).   Memory skill training for the elderly: Salient issues on the use of imagery mnemonics. In L. W. Poon, J. L. Fozard, L. S. Cermak, D. Arenberg & L. W. Thompson (Eds.), *New directions in memory and aging*. Hillsdale: NJ: Erlbaum.

POWELL, A. H., JR., EISDORFER, C. & BOGDONOFF, M. D. (1964).   Physiological response patterns observed in a learning task. *Archives of General Psychiatry, 10,* 192-195.

RIEGEL, K. F. (1973).   Dialectic operations: The final period of cognitive development. *Human Development, 16,* 371-381.

ROODIN, P. A., RYBASH, J. & HOYER, W. J. (1984).   Affect in adult cognition: A constructivist view of moral thought and action. In C. Z. Malatesta & C. E. Izard (Eds.), *Emotion in adult development*. Beverly Hills, CA: Sage Publishers.

SABATINI, P. P. & LABOUVIE-VIEF, G. (1979).   *Age and professional specialization in formal reasoning*. Paper presented at the 86th Annual Meeting of the Gerontological Society, Washingtron, DC: November.

SCHAIE, K. W. (1977-1978).   Toward a stage theory of adult cognitive development. *International Journal of Aging and Human Development, 8,* 129-136.

SCHONFIELD, D. & ROBERTSON, B. A. (1966).   Memory storage and aging. *Canadian Journal of Psychology, 20,* 228-236.

SHAPS, L. P. & NILSSON, L. (1980).   Encoding and retrieval operations in relation to age. *Developmental Psychology, 16,* 636-643.

SHMAVONIAN, B. M. & BUSSE, E. W. (1963).   Psychophysiological techniques in the study of the aged. In R. H. Williams, C. Tibbitts & W. Donahue (Eds.), *Processes of aging*. New York: Atherton Press.

SINNOTT, J. D. (1984).   Postformal reasoning: The relativistic stage. In M. M. Commons, R. A. Richards & C. Armon (Eds.), *Beyond formal operations: Late adolescent and adult cognitive development*. New York: Praeger.

SMITH, A. D. (1979).   The interaction between age and list length in free recall. *Journal of Gerontology, 34,* 381-387.

SMITH, A. D. & WINOGRAD, E. (1978).   Adult age differences in remembering faces. *Developmental Psychology, 14,* 443-444.

THOMPSON, R. F. (1986).   The neurobiology of learning and memory. *Science, 233,* 941-947.

THOMPSON, R. F. & WOODRUFF-PAK, D. S. (1987).   A model system approach to age and the neuronal bases of learning and memory. In M. W. Riley, J. D. Matarazzo & A. Baum (Eds.), *The aging dimension*. Hillsdale, NJ: Erlbaum.

WALSH, D. A. (1983).   Age differences in learning and memory. In D. S. Woodruff & J. E. Birren (Eds.), *Aging: Scientific perspectives and social issues,* (2nd Ed.), Monterey, CA: Brooks/Cole.

WELFORD, A. T. (1987).   Automaticity. In G. L. Maddox (Ed.), *The encyclopedia of aging*. New York: Springer.

WOODRUFF, D. S. & WALSH, D. A. (1975).   Research issues in adult learning. *Gerontologist, 15,* 424-430.

WOODRUFF-PAK, D. S., STEINMETZ, J. E. & THOMPSON, R. F. (1986).   Classical conditioning in rabbits 2½ years old using mossy fiber stimulation as a CS. *Society of Neuroscience Abstracts, 12,* 1315.

WOODRUFF-PAK, D. S. & THOMPSON, R. F. (1985).   Classical conditioning of the eyelid response in rabbits as a model system for the study of brain mechanisms of learning and memory of aging. *Experimental Aging Research, 11,* 109–122.

WOODRUFF-PAK, D. S. & THOMPSON, R. F. (1986).   Delay classical conditioning of the human eyelid response with an auditory CS in 20-, 40-, and 60-year-olds. *The Gerontologist, 26,* 90.

WOODRUFF-PAK, D. S. & THOMPSON, R. F. (1988).   Cerebellar correlates of classical conditioning across the life span. In P. B. Baltes, D. M. Featherman & R. M. Lerner (Eds.), *Life-span development and behavior,* (Vol. 9), Hillsdale, NJ: Erlbaum.

CHAPTER 13

Intelligence and Aging

There is no behavior which has been studied more intensively in life-span developmental psychology than intelligence. Many of the earliest studies in the psychology of aging involved intellectural behavior, and this is still a central issue in the study of geropsychology. A great deal of controversy has been generated over the debate about whether intelligence declines with age. To this day, investigators do not agree about this issue. They interpret the data from different perspectives and reach conflicting conclusions. Thus, in intellectual behavior, we have a topic receiving intensive study which has led to multiple perspectives with no complete resolution.

One of the major issues in the study of intellectual behavior is the definition of intelligence. The concept of intelligence encompasses the totality of the human mind and imagination, but performance on one or another of the numerous intelligence tests has become the critical metric for intellectual capacity. Intelligence has alternatively been viewed as the ability to carry on abstract thinking by Louis Terman, who first brought intelligence testing to the United States. It has also been viewed as the aggregate or global capacity of the individual to act purposefully, to think rationally and to deal effectively with the environment by David Wechsler who adapted his scale to measure adult intelligence. Jean Piaget saw intelligence as any behavior indicating adaptive thinking or action, while nativists such as Arthur Jensen view intelligence more as an innate general cognitive ability. J. P. Guilford has devised a structure of intellect model which posits 120 independent abilities as measures of human intelligence. Contrasted to this is Raymond Cattell's model involving two major components in all human intellect. Underlying Guilford's and Cattell's models are different factor analytic techniques which combine the data in different manners and thus lead to different conclusions.

Inferences about intellectual capacity must be drawn from observable performance on a task, and intelligence tests consist of samples of behavior on a variety of tasks designed to tap whatever the investigators' definitions of intelligence may include. The particular tasks making up each intelligence test may vary as widely as do the psychologists' definitions. What constitute intelligent behavior in one test battery may not be included in another. In addition to the basic differences in the test material, the statistical manipulations and combinations of the responses may be different. This leads to divergent perspectives on the nature of human intelligence and contributes to the controversy about whether there is stability or change in intelligence over the adult years.

One of the most difficult problems facing contemporary geropsychologists is how to measure intellectual capacity in adulthood. This leads to the general issue of the external validity of intelligence tests in adulthood. Intelligence tests were initially designed to measure ability in children and to predict how well children would perform in school. The tests have been relatively successful in this task, and they are valid in predicting school performance. What do intelligence scores predict in adulthood? The problem is that there is no good criterion measure against which all adults can be assessed. In adulthood, no longer is there one activity in which all individuals of the same age are required to participate. Thus, it becomes more difficult to test the validity of the measure.

One of the great problems with adult intelligence tests is that they are instruments which have been designed for children and adapted for adults. The very basis of the intelligence test is to assess abilities exhibited by children which help them to succeed in school. Those abilities may be no longer relevant in adulthood. There may be whole new categories of abilities more salient in adulthood and old age which are simply not tapped by our current battery of tests. Thus, as we discuss the available data on intelligence in adulthood, it must be kept in mind that we are discussing adults' performance on test batteries adapted from childhood tests designed to measure abilities predictive of school performance. We are assessing adults on the basis of a young person's scale. If we find that the older person falls short, he or she is falling short only in the sense that they do not have the same amount of ability as the young person. The test tells us little or nothing about what new abilities the adult may have developed with experience.

It is the thesis of this chapter that perspectives about intelligence in adulthood and old age have gone through four major phases in the twentieth century. The phases are roughly chronological, but at the same time, research continues to be undertaken in all categories with the possible exception of the first phase. The term *phase* and a Roman numeral has been used to identify each of the four broad perspectives on intelligence in adulthood and old age which have been influential in this century. The sequential numbering of each of the perspectives is intended to imply that subsequent phases emerged from previous ones. The term *phase* is used to suggest that the perspective, while pervasive at the time, is transitory rather than permanent. Thus, it is argued here that in the twentieth century developmental psychologists have progressed through four major ways of thinking about intelligence in later life.

THE SOCIO-CULTURAL
PROCESS MODEL

The causes for changing perspectives on intelligence in later life are viewed as emanating from social, cultural, and historical forces combined with an expanding data base on psychometric intelligence and evolving methodololgy. Changing attitudes about older adults coupled with an evolving and sometimes contradictory data base on adult intelligence forced investigators to take new perspectives. Thus, the theoretical orientation used to explain the progression through the four phases is called the socio-cultural process model. The combination of prevailing socio-cultural and historical viewpoints and discontinuities or discrepancies in the empirical data on psychometric measures of intelligence in adulthood and old age resulted in the emergence of four distinct phases in the study of aging and intelligence. Only one of these perspectives, the first, has been superceded by the current research. Investigations into the nature of adult intelligence in the latter part of the twentieth century continue to involve one or more of the perspectives identified as Phases II–IV.

The four phases of conceptualization on intelligence in later life along with the social forces and empirical results responsible for changing the perspectives are schematically represented in Figure 13.1. Phase I with its unidimensional view of age-related decline emerged in the 1920s based on cross-sectional studies of psychometric intelligence. This was a period when faith in psychometric measures of intelligence was almost absolute, and the rapid industrialization of American society favored youth and the acquisition of new skills. Characteristic of this period is a quotation from the August 28, 1913 *Independent,* "In the search for increased efficiency, begotten in modern time by the practically universal worship of the dollar...gray hair has come to be recognized as an unforgivable witness of industrial imbecility," cited by Achenbaum and Kusnerz (1978, p. 33).

The long duration of the perspective of Phase I was clearly superceded only in the 1950s when longitudinal data on intelligence became available and suggested at a minimum that adult intelligence was stable until the age of 50, which was the oldest age for which longitudinal data were available. Social attitudes toward aging were changing in the 1950s. Life expectancy had increased dramatically, and the percentage of people over 65 in the population had more than doubled since the turn of the century. The aged were becoming more visible and more vocal. Legislation to provide social supports for the later years, beginning with the Social Security Act in 1935 and culminating in the Older Americans Act in 1965, reflected a positive change in attitudes about older adults.

Socio-Cultural Process Model

Phase I
Age-Related Decline

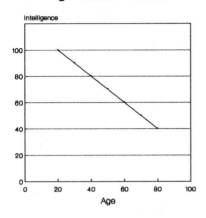

Simple, unidirectional model

Phase II
Stability Vs. Decline

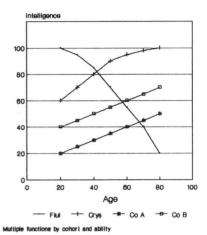

— Flui —+— Crys —*— Co A —□— Co B

Multiple functions by cohort and ability

Phase III
Manipulation of Adult IQ

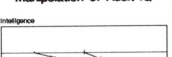

— Normal IQ —+— Post intervention

Intervention to ameliorate performance

Phase IV
Growth of Adult Intellect

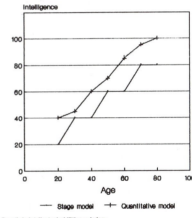

— Stage model —+— Quantitative model

Growth in intellectual abilities; wisdom

FIGURE 13.1 Schematic representation of the socio-cultural process model presenting the four phases of research on aging and intelligence. The Phase I perspective reflected in the research literature between 1920 and the mid- to late-1950s was a unidimensional model of age-related decline. Negative stereotypes of the aged in a period of rapid industrialization coupled with cross-sectional data on intelligence measures designed to predict academic success yielded the Phase I view. As life expectancy increased and the aged became more visible in society, perceptions began to change. Phase II beginning in the 1960s emerged because of the changing social climate, but more importantly, as a result of longitudinal studies demonstrating stability in intelligence. Multiple age-functional relationships were recognized arising from cohort differences and from differential effects of development and aging on different abilities such as fluid and crystallized measures of intelligence. In the post-Great Society period of the 1970s interventions to ameliorate intelligence in the aged are representative of the Phase III perspective. Phase IV with its search for developmental changes in adult intelligence recognizes the potential for even a stage-like progression in adulthood. The Phase IV perspective involves a rejection of traditional psychometric measures of academic success in favor of assessment of competence in the everyday world.

Phase II embraced a more sophisticated view of adult intelligence with intellect varying by cohort and by specific type of ability. Age functions could be incremental or decremental, and linear or quadratic. From the contradiction between longitudinal and cross-sectional data emerged a new synthesis in Phase II of a more complex perspective of intelligence in later life.

The acknowledgment in Phase II that environmental forces could affect intelligence scores of a given cohort led investigators to consider that manipulation of environmental contingencies might affect intelligence scores within a cohort as well. If experience in the environment could result in differences in IQ scores as a function of when one was born, then within an individual at some point in the life span environmental manipulations might affect performance on intelligence tests. The social context for this Phase III perspective was a result of the Great Society program in which intervention into many forms of social problems were being attempted. In some ways Project Head Start as an intervention in early development served as a model for the Phase III approach involving attempts to modify older adults' performance on intelligence tests.

While gerontologists found in Phase III that performance on intelligence tests could be manipulated, it became more apparent that training was simply familiarizing older people with abilities which were novel or unused by them. At a time when the context in which intelligence was defined and measured was seen as an increasingly important issue, the relevance of the psychometric tasks to the lives of the aged was questioned, and the search for new age-appropriate tasks was begun.

The Phase IV perspective emerged in the mid-1970s at a time when the growing size and social and economic power of aging adults was being recognized in all segments of society. The Phase IV perspecvtive challenged the validity of existing psychometric measures of intelligence for assessment of older adults and introduced the notion of growth in intellectual ability over the adult years.

What follows is an elaboration and documentation of each of the four phases of the model. The emphasis is on the empirical data collected in each phase and on how those data were interpreted. It should be emphasized that the socio-cultural process model does not imply that ideas representative of the four phases emerged exclusively at the beginning of each of the subsequent phases. The foundation of the concept of differential age functions for fluid and crystallized measures of intelligence which characterizes Phase II can be traced to data collected at the height of Phase I in the late 1920s. Achenbaum and Kusnerz (1978) pointed out that respect for the wisdom and experience of the aged which identifies Phase IV was representative of attitudes toward aging in the period between 1790–1864 in the United States.

The socio-cultural process model represents an attempt to explain why each of the four identified twentieth-century phases represents the predominating bias of research on psychometric intelligence in that period. The largest number of empirical studies undertaken during a selected period in the twentieth century between 1920 and the present can be categorized into one of the four phases. Since research, however, is still undertaken in the late 1980s from three of the four phases, each subsequent phase is less singularly dominant than the previous phase. Phase IV which explores the development of intelligence in adulthood is less predominant in contemporary research than was the intervention approach of Phase III in the 1970s and early 1980s, and Phase III never predominated as much as the stability versus decline debate of Phase II in the 1960s and early 1970s. This in turn was never as singular as the decline model of Phase I which dominated our conceptualization of adult intelligence for at least 30 years.

The socio-cultural process model stresses the social, cultural, and historical phenomena fostering a particular view of intelligence in later adulthood along with the insights provided by the empirical data as the two primary factors contributing to the changing perspectives from Phase I to Phase IV. Social and historical impacts on behavior and aging have been elaborated by social scientists such as Havighurst, Neugarten, and Riegel (e.g., Havighurst, 1973; Neugarten & Havighurst, 1976; Riegel, 1973a, 1977). Hence, in the following sections the emphasis will be on the empirical data on psychometric intelligence over the adult life span and how those data contributed to new perspectives on adult intelligence.

PHASE I:
AGE-RELATED DECLINE

The prototype for contemporary intelligence tests was designed early in the twentieth century in France by Alfred Binet who worked with the psychiatrist, Theodor Simon, to identify those school children in the Paris school system who simply did not have the cognitive capacity to benefit from normal training along with those who were of normal or above-normal ability. Binet and Simon succeeded in devising such an instrument which was comprised of a set of 30 problems emphasizing judgment, comprehension, and reasoning (Binet & Simon, 1905). In the United States, Louis Terman reworked the test considerably and called it the Stanford-Binet Intelligence Test. Such tests were quite successful with children, and they were adapted to test adults by 1911 (Anastasi, 1976).

The first group tests for intelligence were devised for the United States Army in the second decade of the twentieth century. At that time the United States became involved in World War I, and large numbers of young men had to be inducted into the service. Intelligence tests were used to screen out candidates who simply did not have the mental capacity to perform in the military. The test was called the Army Alpha Examination, and it was administered to thousands of recruits.

One of the major results of this first intelligence testing of large numbers of adults was that it was observed that older adults performed more poorly than younger adults. This was the first indication that investigators had that over the age of twenty, there appeared to be a "decline" in intelligence. This was not a comparison of young to very old individuals. It was a comparison ranging from the age of 18 to a maximum age of 60 years. Nevertheless, the older men in the sample performed more poorly, and even past the age of 25 there appeared to be "decline."

The first of these data were published in 1921 by the National Academy of Sciences (Yerkes, 1921). An analysis of the data on over 1.7 million men tested during World War I was included, although the analysis by age was carried out only on officers. Jones (1959) recalculated Yerkes' data and Figure 13.2 shows the results. Men between the ages of 18 and 20 scored higher than all other individuals on the examination. Men in the late twenties were already scoring .2 of a standard deviation lower than the youngest men, and the difference between the 51–60-year-old group and the 18–20-year-old group was a whole standard deviation or 15 points on total intelligence score. This sample was not the general group of soldiers but the actual leaders of the corps—the officers who would be expected to be among the brightest of the group.

Yerkes stated about these data that, "The most reasonable surmise is that older officers are selected more on the basis of their specific experience or training, professional or military, and less on native intelligence than are young officers who have as yet little valuable experience" (1921, p. 813). However, Yerkes recognized that the data were problematical because of the selective bias in cross-sectional samples. He stated, "...it is unsafe for us to assert that the apparent relation is not spurious" (1921, p. 813).

In spite of slight reservations by investigators such as Yerkes, the initial perspective of intelligence in adulthood and old age was one of decline. This perspec-

FIGURE 13.2   Age deficits in successive age groups of World War I Army officers in terms of the mean and standard deviation for ages 18 to 20. Data from Yerkes (1921) as reanalyzed by Jones (1959). *Source:* Jones, H. E. (1959). Intelligence and problem-solving. In J. E. Birren (Ed.), *Handbook of Aging and the Individual.* Chicago: The University of Chicago Press. Reprinted by permission.

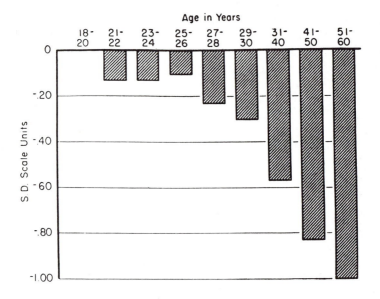

tive had a lasting impact on the psychology of aging, and it would prevail for more than 30 years before significant challenge to it was presented.

The Yerkes report showing older officers to score lower on the Army Alpha Examination was the first study of intelligence in a large sample of indiviuduals in the normal population. The only two other reports on intelligence and age at that point has been carried out with samples of old people in hospitals and nursing homes compared to healthy younger individuals (Beeson, 1920; Foster & Taylor, 1920). In both of these studies the older adults scored considerably more poorly on a number of abilities. The only ability which had shown stability in later adulthood was vocabulary.

Willoughby (1927) reported the first study on intellectual ability carried out on the entire middle-age range of community residing adults. He sampled 141 children aged 13 who were in the school system and residing near Stanford University, and then he tested their parents ($N = 190$) and their siblings ($N = 280$). One of the contributions of Willoughby was to note that different abilities showed different functions with age. For example, a test of analogies was performed best by individuals assessed between the ages of 16 and 20, and individuals older than 20 performed more poorly on the task. On the other hand, a test of arithmetic reasoning was performed well by subjects older than 16 years, but it was performed about equally well by subjects in their thirties, forties, and fifties.

Willoughby anticipated the theory of fluid and crystallized intelligence by Cattell and Horn which has played a prominent role in the study of adult intellectual capacity by stating that the functions characterized by sharp peaks (such as analogies) are essentially maturational in nature, acquired as a matter of normal growth and relatively free from influences of school training. Tests such as arithmetic and vocabulary, on the other hand, reflect accumulated experience and may be relatively easier for adults.

Other research on adult intelligence published in the 1930s and 1940s replicated the results of the earliest studies. All were cross-sectional in design, comparing the scores of individuals of different ages tested at one point in time (e.g., Jones & Conrad, 1933; Miles & Miles, 1932).

In 1944 David Wechsler standardized his Wechsler-Bellevue Intelligence scales on a sample of 1,751 individuals chosen to be representative of the occupational distribution of the United States census. He found that the verbal scores in this cross-sectional sample were much more stable across the age range of 20 to 60 than were the performance scores. This result was replicated in the standardization of the Wechsler Adult Intelligence Scale (WAIS) in 1955. On the basis of these results, Wechsler concluded that intelligence declined with age, and he devised standardized scores for his test such that an older adult received an average score of intelligence of 100 for a lower raw score than a young adult.

The perspective of Phase I is one of intellectual decline with adulthood. This was the perspective generated with the initial studies of intelligence in 1920 and apparently confirmed in studies conducted throughout the 1930s, 1940s, and even into the 1950s. So pervasive was this model that the standardized scores of the

WAIS were designed to conform to a "decline" in intelligence with age. At this point in history, it was widely held that intellectual ability peaked between the ages of 15 and 20, and that decline in ability was inevitable after that point.

The only data that had been available at this period were cross-sectional studies comparing individuals of different age and experience at one point in time. Little consideration was given to the appropriateness of the tests, to the different experiences of the individuals including different educational levels, or to the degree of similarity between the individual's daily experiences and activities and the testing material. All of the many factors which might bias cross-sectional testing were not clearly apparent to investigators during this period. A number of studies converged to confirm that older people scored lower on intelligence tests, and psychologists and laymen simply accepted the conclusion that intelligence declined with age. It was not until longitudinal data became available and revealed a different pattern of age and intellectual function that a new level of awareness began to pervade the interpretation of research on age and intelligence.

PHASE II:
STABILITY VERSUS DECLINE

From the period in which intelligence tests were first used to assess intellectual capacity in adults in the 1920s until the 1950s, it was accepted on the basis of cross-sectional evidence that intelligence declines beyond the age of 20. The first longitudinal data to be published were collected by Owens (1953). The study was a 31-year follow-up of 127 young men who had been tested on the Army Alpha Examination in 1919. All of the men had been freshmen entering Iowa State College, and their average age had been 19. Upon retest, they were middle-aged, and on the basis of 30 years of cross-sectional data, they would be predicted to show declines in their performance. Instead, the total scores of these individuals showed a gain of over half of a standard deviation. None of the eight subtests showed loss while four of the subtests (practical judgment, vocabulary, disarranged sentences, information) showed statistically significant improvement. Four other subtests showed no change (following directions, arithmetical problems, number series completion, analogies). These results were remarkable considering that the magnitude of gain in these individuals was about equal to the predicted loss in other cross-sectional samples.

Several explanations for Owens' (1953) results were offered by scholars of the period who were still imbued with the notion that intelligence declined with age (Jones, 1959). It was argued that Owens' sample was selected from a group of college students with initially higher ability level. The implication was that intellectual ability at the highest levels shows greater maintenance than ability at average or lower levels. The college freshmen in the sample also received four years of additional education, and it was argued that if they had been tested four years after the initial test as college seniors, their intellectual level would have been even higher than it was in the 1950 retest. Thus, education was thought to have affected the results.

Sampling was another factor contributing to the outcome, according to initial interpretations. In 1919, 363 freshmen had been tested at Iowa State College, and 162 of the original sample could not be located or were deceased. An additional 63 of the 201 who were located refused to participate. Owens argued that there were zero level correlations between initial scores and gain scores within the retested group and concluded that the sampling bias was unimportant. Jones (1959), on the other hand, asserted that the alumni who had been successful in life were more likely the ones to have been found or to have come forward, and he felt that the bias of the selective sampling produced a more favorable picture of intellectual change with time than would have been found in the sample as a whole. It was also pointed out by Jones that a large part of the gain in total score was contributed by gains in information and vocabulary subtests. These are abilities which had shown stability in cross-sectional studies and which would be expected to show continued adult acquisition particularly among college graduates.

Two additional longitudinal studies which appeared in the decade of the 1950s replicated Owens' (1953) findings and made it more difficult to maintain the perspective that intelligence inevitably declined with age. In a 16-year follow-up in the Oakland Growth Study when the subjects were 33 years old, the test-retest correlation between the last adolescent testing and the first adult testing was .84 for the men and .90 for the women. The group gain over the 16-year period was about one year in mental age months (Jones, 1959). As in the Owens study, the subtests which showed the most gain were vocabulary and information. The results were different from Owens' findings in that they showed no correlation between gains in intelligence scores and years of education beyond high school.

Bayley and Oden (1955) reported gains in intelligence test scores in the Terman gifted sample. The Concept Mastery Test which measures subjects' knowledge of concepts in different fields through an analogies test and a synonym-antonym test was administered to this sample in 1939–1940 and 12 years later in 1951–1952. Regardless of whether they were tested in the decade of their twenties, thirties, or forties, all age groups showed increments. The gains were of a magnitude of about half a standard deviation. On the one hand, this is a group of highly intelligent people, but on the other hand, they demonstrated gains in tests demanding analogical reasoning—an ability which had been thought to fail in adulthood.

It is interesting to note that even when these results appeared, the perspective of adult decline in intelligence was so pervasive that Jones stated, "Although other studies of tests requiring analogical reasoning have shown a decrement in this age range, a group as exceptional as this might be expected to have a delayed decline" (1959, p. 709). The Bayley and Oden data showed nothing but increment to the age of 50, and there were no data beyond that age. There is not one shred of evidence for decline in this study. However, Jones was so convinced of the inevitable decline in adult intellectual capacity, that he surmised that decline in this sample was simply delayed.

The perspective developed in Phase II is one of conflict. It arose from the impact between 30 years of replication of cross-sectional results indicating age decline, and the emerging longitudinal results documenting intellectual stability or gain. What was once a simple and relatively straightforward age and behavior relationship became an age function for which there was no consistent picture. Phase II shifted the interpretation of adult intellectual behavior to a new level of complexity. It was acknowledged that the earlier model simply did not fit all of the data, and never since in the history of the study of adult intelligence has one model been successful in gaining unqualified support. The controversy engendered in Phase II has never been totally resolved. From the 1950s to the present, investigators have debated the perspectives of stability versus decline. What differentiates Phase II from Phase I is that no simple, unidirectional model prevails.

The period after the appearance of longitudinal data on intelligence was one of puzzlement, with investigators pursuing a number of avenues for interpretation of the discrepant age functions. Articulation of the various biasing factors in cross-sectional and longitudinal designs had begun as early as 1940 when Raymond Kuhlen first acknowledged the potential bias in comparing individuals of different age and experience and interpreting the results only in terms of maturational aging effects. Kuhlen (1940) pointed out that sex, occupation, education, and cultural differences accounted for more of the variance in cross-sectional studies than did age. During that period, Raymond Cattell (1943) identified fluid and crystallized intelligence measures and suggested that aging might affect these two components of intelligence differently.

Jones presented some of the major practical problems and difficulties of interpretation involved in longitudinal research designs in a 1958 article. Many of the problems with longitudinal and cross-sectional designs were elaborated by James Birren (1959) when he pointed out that true developmental age functions could only be viewed with longitudinal data and that cross-sectional designs were flawed by experiential differences between different age groups. It was during the 1960s that the clear inadequacies of cross-sectional and longitudinal designs were fully elaborated along with proposals for strategies to remedy the weaknesses (Baltes, 1968; Schaie, 1965).

Emergence of Sequential Strategies

The first of two landmark proposals which were to cause controversy and debate over the next several decades was published by K. Warner Schaie. While this paper was directed to the study of life-span development of all behaviors, it had been written while Schaie was puzzling over the empirical results of a seven-year longitudinal follow up of a large cross-sectional study on intelligence and rigidity (Schaie, 1979, 1982). The model has also had its greatest impact on the study of intelligence in adulthood.

Schaie (1965) identified certain inadequacies inherent in all longitudinal and cross-sectional approaches. He defined three variables which are confounded in all developmental research. The first variable, age, is the one developmentalists purport to measure. This involves stability or change in behavior with increasing age. The second variable, called cohort, refers to the total population of organisms born at the same point or interval in time. These individuals share a common gene pool and similar historical experience. The third variable is time of measurement. This is the impact of the environment occurring over given temporal points.

Schaie felt that cross-sectional studies could not reveal clear aging effects because they confounded age with cohort effects. Not only do individuals vary by age in cross-sectional studies, they vary by cohort. According to Schaie, cohort effects should encompass both genetic and environmental variation. Longitudinal studies, on the other hand, confounded age and time of measurement. Environmental effects as well as maturational change are incorporated into the data. Longitudinal data were also biased in reflecting the aging of only one cohort; they lacked external validity.

To remedy the weaknesses of the conventional designs, Schaie proposed the use of sequential strategies in which the effects of age, cohort, and time of measurement could be separated. These strategies involve elaborate combinations of cross-sectional and longitudinal sampling or repeated random sampling of cross sections of cohorts.

A student of Schaie's, Paul Baltes (1968), elaborated Schaie's criticisms of conventional cross-sectional and longitudinal designs. Baltes described five major methodological shortcomings of the designs: selective sampling, selective survival, selective dropout, testing effects, and generation effects. These biases could account for the major discrepancies between cross-sectional and longitudinal data on intelligence tests.

After proposing sequential strategies to remedy the weaknesses of conventional longitudinal and cross-sectional designs, Schaie and his collaborators conducted a series of sequential studies of intelligence in adulthood to demonstrate the usefulness of the strategies. In 1956 Schaie established and tested a random sample stratified by age and sex of 500 individuals over the age range of 20 to 70. There were 25 men and 25 women tested in each five-year interval over the age range, and these individuals were selected from a roster of 18,000 individuals participating in a prepaid medical plan. Cross-sectional data on the Primary Mental Abilities (PMA) intelligence test and on the Test of Behavioral Rigidity (TBR) were presented by Schaie in 1958 and demonstrated the typical pattern of age differences observed previously in numerous cross-sectional studies of intelligence.

In 1963 Schaie followed up his research by finding and retesting 302 of the original 500 participants and by generating and testing a different random sample from the original pool of 18,000 which had been identified in 1956. Thus, he was following ten cohorts longitudinally and also testing another cross-sectional sample of cohorts who had no prior experience with the PMA. In this manner, Schaie achieved several goals. He controlled for the effect of retesting on a longitudinal sample by adding a group of comparable subjects who had never been tested on the PMA, he collected longitudinal as well as cross-sectional data, and he tested the hypotheses he had devised to interpret why cross-sectional and longitudinal data on intelligence were inconsistent.

The results of this first follow-up research published in 1968 (Schaie & Strother, 1968a, 1968b) provided clear evidence for the magnitude of the effect of the cohort variable on intelligence data. On most of the subtests of the PMA, there appeared to be large cohort differences which remained stable over the longitudinal testing. Over the seven-year period that was covered by the study, age changes on most intellectual variables were negligible, but cohort differences tended to be large. Many of the subtests followed the pattern of increasing performance levels with younger cohorts. More recently born groups were achieving higher performance levels in young adulthood. These performance levels were being maintained over time. Examples of these results can be seen clearly in the subttests of reasoning and space shown in Figure 13.3.

From this early demonstration of sequential design methodology in the domain of aging and intelligence, Schaie and Strother concluded:

> The most important conclusion to be drawn from this study is the finding that a major portion of the variance attributed to age differences in past cross-sectional studies must properly be assigned to differences in ability between successive generations. Age changes over time within the individual appear to be much smaller than differences between cohorts, and textbook age gradients may represent no more than the effects of increased environmental opportunity and/or genetic improvement in the species. The findings on longitudinal age changes suggest further that levels of functioning attained at maturity maybe retained until late in life except where decrement in response strength and latency interferes (1968a, p. 679).

Cohort differences in intelligences were greater than age changes, and stability over the adult period rather than decline was indicated.

One of the major emphases of the Phase II perspective is the realization of a much more complex picture of adult intellectual performance. The initial perspective of Phase I was that of a univariate measure of intelligence changing with age in one direction—the direction of decline. Phase II evolved from the discrepancy between cross-sectional and longitudinal data. The picture which emerged was more than a simple picture of cross-sectional decline and longitudinal stability. Age functions were identified which varied by cohort in terms of level. Baltes and his colleagues have continued to elaborate the logical status of cohort as a design variable and to point out implications of cohort effects for research and theory in developmental psychology (Baltes, Cornelius, & Nesselroade, 1979; Dixon, Kramer, & Baltes, 1985).

In addition to the identification of the cohort effect in Phase II, it became clearer that subcomponents of intelligence varied differently over time. Some abilities showed stability or increment, while others showed decline. Almost any direction and shape of age function was present when the data were analyzed for individual abilities and individual cohorts. Thus, the notion of generalized age curves of intelligence appeared to be less useful than a perspective which recognized

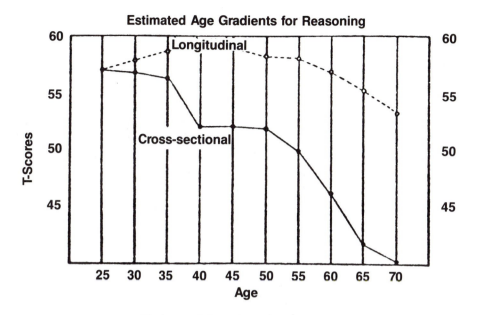

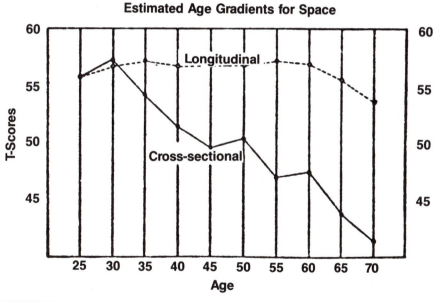

FIGURE 13.3   Age gradients obtained on the basis of the current performance of individuals at different ages who are members of different cohorts with the estimated longitudinal age gradient for a single cohort. The longitudinal estimation was carried out by beginning with the level of the cohort aged 25 and estimating change from that initial level of performance based on the change observed over the seven-year period in the various older cohorts. The estimated age gradients are for the space and reasoning subtests of the Primary Model Abilities intelligence test. Cross-sectional comparisons indicated that the youngest cohorts performed the best on those tasks with earlier-born individuals performing successively more poorly. *Source:* Schaie, K. W. & Strother, C. R. (1968a). A cross-sequential study of age changes in cognitive behavior. *Psychological Bulletin, 70,* 671–680. Copyright © 1968. The American Psychological Association. Reprinted by permission.

the complexity and individuality of age changes and age differences in intelligence over the life span.

Theory of Fluid
and Crystallized Intelligence

A theoretical model created during the period when the Phase II perspective was most influential is the theory of Cattell and his student, John Horn, of fluid and crystallized intelligence (Cattell, 1971; Horn,1968). These investigators argued that there were two basic and general types of intelligence and that all measures of intellectual performance could be factor analyzed into one of the two categories. Fluid intelligence (Gf) represents the fluidity of the mind. It involves the biologically determined capacity to take in information quickly and deal with it efficiently. Tests of intelligence involving skills which are unlearned, skills of dealing with new information in a novel manner are considered tests of fluid ability. Examples of tests of fluid intelligence would be measures of memory, manipulation of objects in space, inductive reasoning, and attention. Brain damage and physiological incapacity are thought to interfere most with fluid ability. The developmental gradient of fluid intelligence was hypothesized to increment up until the age of 20 to 25 when it reaches its asympote and then gradually decline along with the decline in biological capacity in middle and later adulthood.

The other component of intelligence in this theory is called crystallized intelligence (Gc). This ability is analogous to the "crystals" of knowledge which accumulate with experience. Crystallized ability is learned information. Tests which measure the accumulation of knowledge are considered tests of crystallized ability and include measures of vocabulary, mathematical ability, stored information, and the like.

Horn and Cattell (1967) provided empirical support for their theory in the form of cross-sectional data collected on a highly heterogeneous sample of adults. The age functions generated from this sample approximated the age functions generated by the theory. More recently, Horn (1982) presented an overview of a series of studies on fluid and crystallized intelligence in which paid volunteers from the inmate population of a penitentiary served as subjects. Horn argued that losses in capacities for maintaining spontaneous alertness, focused intensive concentration, and awareness of possible organization for otherwise unorganized information were largely responsible for age differences in fluid intelligence measures.

Research demonstrating the plasticity of older adults' performance on fluid as well as crystallized intelligence measures (Phase III perspective) as well as skepticism about the relevance of psychometric test batteries for older subjects (Phase IV perspective) have provided challenges to the usefulness of the theory of fluid and crystallized intelligence. On the other hand, the theory has been widely adopted by gerontologists and serves as a useful framework to organize data on abilities which remain stable as opposed to abilities which are impacted by age.

Phase II Perspectives
in Contemporary Research

Many controversies arose during the emergence of Phase II, and many of them have yet to be completely resolved. Thus, while the Phase I perspective has been almost completely supplanted with an awareness of the greater complexity of intellectual age functions, the Phase II perspective is still reflected in contemporary published research. Although some researchers have moved to Phases III and IV, others have pursued the issues raised by Phase II and continue to design and carry out research describing age changes and age differences in intelligence.

One of the controversies which continues to be debated is whether or not it is useful to describe generalized age functions of intelligence. Schaie, Baltes, and their colleagues emphasized the impact of the environment and historical time on the aging of different cohorts and the diversity and multiple shapes and direction of age functions. They question the probability of finding any universal age functions in adult intelligence.

Others have continued to search for one or two universal age functions to generalize over a number of cohorts. Horn and Cattell's theoretical approach represents one form of continuing endeavor to find major age functions. Another proponent of general age functions is Botwinick who has maintained that the divergence between cross-sectional and longitudinal measures of intelligence is not as great as suggested by the originators of sequential strategies. Botwinick has presented a picture of generalized age funtions on the basis of integration of the data. Botwinick (1967, 1977) stated that there is a classic pattern of age change in intelligence which is reflected in cross-sectional and longitudinal designs. There may be quantitative differences between the magnitude of the effects as estimated by the different designs, but the qualitative differences between the studies do not exist according to Botwinick. This classic pattern is one of relative stability of verbal functions on intelligence measures such as the WAIS with decline in nonverbal, psychomotor tasks called performance tests on the WAIS.

Data for sequential designs have demonstrated relative stability in performance as well as verbal abilities, at least until subjects are aged in their late sixties. Cohort differences were found to be of much greater magnitude than age changes (Schaie, 1979, 1983; Schaie & Hertzog, 1983; Schaie & Labouvie-Vief, 1974; Schaie & Parham, 1977; Schaie & Strother, 1968a). In this case, Botwinick and Arenberg (1976) pointed out that in sequential studies, the time period typically represented by the cross-sectional analysis is much greater than the time period represented by the longitudinal analysis. Subjects might differ in age by as much as 50 years in the cross-sectional analyses while the longitudinal gradients are at most 21 years.

An empirical comparison of the magnitude of age changes and cohort differences was presented by Botwinick and Siegler (1980). The investigators analyzed WAIS data collected in the Duke Longitudinal Study using a sequential strategy. The age period covered was the period between the sixties and the eighties, and four cohorts were selected which ranged in age intervals of three to four years.

The subjects were tested four times, and only subjects who were tested all four times over a 12-year period were included in the sample. According to the analyses made by Botwinick and Siegler, there was little difference between the cross-sectional and longitudinal gradients. Longitudinal decline achieved statistical significance while cross-sectional differences did not. These data were used to argue for the importance of equality of time intervals covered by the cross-sectional and longitudinal analyses.

While the point Botwinick and Siegler (1980) addressed is important, a limitation of their study is the sampling technique and the age of the sample. This was a post-hoc analysis of data on elderly adults carried out after all the data had been collected as part of the larger Duke study. By holding to the requirement that all subjects had to be tested at all four times, Botwinick and Siegler (1980) introduced a bias which would be expected to minimize cross-sectional differences. To be included, subjects of an average age of 73 had to have survived for the next 12 years along with the younger subjects who began the study at an average age of 62. The older subjects were a select group to begin with, and there were fewer of them to be found ($N = 11$ as compared to $N = 20$ for the 62-year-olds).

Intelligence is correlated with survival, with higher scoring individuals more likely to live longer (Riegel, Riegel & Meyer, 1967). Indeed, in the very Duke longitudinal sample used by Botwinick and Siegler, McCarty, Siegler, and Logue (1982) found a clear difference between older subjects who remained in the sample and those who dropped out.

> Participants who remained in the study longer and were present at all waves tended to score higher than those who dropped out earlier in the study . . . Older participants present for Waves 2–11 often not only scored higher than older participants who dropped out earlier, they also frequently scored higher than the younger participants present throughout the study'' (McCarty et al., 1982, pp. 173–174).

By stipulating that the oldest group must have still been alive at a mean age of 85, sample selection was being carried out in such a way that the earlier-born cohorts were a more select group and hence a more highly intelligent group. By selecting each earlier-born cohort to be more intelligent, the difference which might emerge in a cross-sectional comparison was erased.

One of the points Schaie and his colleagues made was that the differences between one or two adjacent cohorts 7 to 14 years apart in date of birth were greater in magnitude than were changes over a 7- to 14-year period in a given cohort. Schaie and Parham (1977) carried out cohort-sequential analysis with data from over 700 subjects retested after a 7-year interval on the Primary Mental Abilities Test and the Test of Behavioral Rigidity. With the exception of the highly speed-related Word Fluency Test, cohort variance was more important than age variance until the late sixties, while age changes were more heavily implicated in the seventies. The 14-year cohort-sequential analysis of these data continued to confirm larger cohort differences than age changes until the late sixties (Schaie & Hertzog, 1983).

The Phase II perspective is still evident in research in the 1980s in the interpretation of the literature on adult intelligence. The perspective of conflict and complexity in the data on adult intellectual performance and the interest in the continued generation of data on descriptive age functions continues to be maintained. Emerging from Phase II is the concept that adult age functions in intelligence are not singular or unidirectional. What continues to be debated is the degree of convergence of the data from studies using various designs, the number of age functional relationships which actually exists, and the usefulness in continuing the attempt to describe existing relationships between age and IQ in adulthood.

PHASE III:
MANIPULATION OF ADULT
INTELLIGENCE

While Phases I and II involve descriptive methodology, Phase III is involved with experimentation. In its formative decades, the psychology of aging involved the descriptive identification of the nature of behavioral aging. Researchers focused on the normative aspects of aging and primarily identified behavioral decline. Kastenbaum captured the essence of Phases I and II by stating that researchers in gerontology up to the 1960s were largely satisfied with, "counting and classifying the wrinkles of aged behavior" (1968, p. 280). This was an important first step in the understanding of processes of aging, but it had limitations.

The step taken in Phase III was to move to causal-analytic work involving manipulative-experimental research. The question of why and how much plasticity in aging generated a new intellectual climate of optimism. The possibility of redesigning the aging process was suggested, and practitioners were given an emerging set of tools for intervention.

The beginnings of the Phase III perspective roughly paralleled the interventionist movement in the study of intelligence in child development. In addition to the impetus from developmentalists studying younger age periods was the empirical demonstration that cohort differences in intelligence scores were often greater than age changes. The cohort variable could be explained in part by forces operating in the environment. Thus, it was reasoned that if environmental forces such as education led to differences in adults' intelligence test scores, manipulation of these factors should alter the scores. In this sense, Phase III was a direct outcome of one of the models evolving in Phase II.

Many of the arguments for moving in a new direction away from the descriptive designs characteristic of Phase II to the experimental designs of Phase III were presented in an article by Baltes and Goulet in 1971. One argument for the experimental perspective was that a goal of science is to explain, and explanation relies upon experimental demonstration. Enough descriptive data had been accumulated to suggest that different experiences of different cohorts might account for some of the age differences in intelligence scores. Providing that experience in an experimental format would provide a test of the environmental hypothesis.

Another rationale for the interventionist approach was humanitarian. If older cohorts had certain experiential deficiencies which led to their poorer performance on intelligence tests, then it was desirable to ameliorate these deficiencies. A third argument for experimental studies was expedience. Longitudinal and sequential research designs required tremendous time and resources to collect data. If age differences could be simulated and manipulated in experimental studies, then a great deal of time and effort could be saved. Knowledge would also advance more quickly with this approach as experimental studies could be completed sooner than most longitudinal or sequential studies.

The intervention approach was initiated primarily in the 1970s, and we currently have over a decade and a half of research results which have been generated from this perspective. By the end of the decade of the 1970s, Sterns and Sanders (1980) identified 15 published intervention studies on manipulation of intellectual performance in the aged. Since their review, many additional studies on the plasticity of adult intelligence have been reported.

One of the simplest and yet most effective strategies used to improve performance on intelligence tests by older adults is practice. Indeed, much of the training involved in intervention studies may work simply because it provides familiarization and practice to old people on tasks which had initially been novel to them.

A direct test of the effect of practice was undertaken by Hofland, Willis, and Baltes (1981) when they administered tests of figural relations and induction over eight retest trials. Induction and figural relations were chosen because they are indices of fluid intelligence which has been suggested as evidencing a high level of sensitivity to intellectual decline with aging (Horn, 1978). Figure 13.4 shows the outcome of this study. Over eight retest sessions, continuous increments in performance were observed. Even after eight sessions, no evidence for an asym-

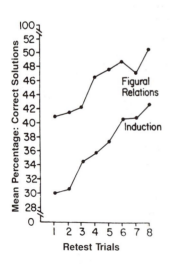

FIGURE 13.4 Mean percentage of correct solutions across retest trials for older adults aged 60 to 80 years for measures of figural relations and induction. *Source:* Hofland, B. F., Willis, S. .L. & Baltes, P. B. (1981). Fluid intelligence performance in the elderly: Intraindividual variability and conditions of assessment. *Journal of Educational Psychology, 73,* 573–586. Copyright © 1981 American Psychological Association. Reprinted by permission.

pote is apparent. The 30 older adults in this sample continued to improve with practice. Such results indicate that the aged can perform at higher levels than indicated by normative or average test scores.

Denney (1979) evaluated the existing literature on intervention in cognitive abilities and concluded that the cognitive performance of older people is modifiable when training is targeted on specific cognitive skills. She extended this perspective by developing a theory of unexercised and optimally exercised cognitive abilities (Denney, 1982). The theory postulates that there are two types of developmental functions in adulthood: (1) untrained, unpracticed ability; and (2) optimally trained or exercised ability. The mental activities an individual practices or exercises in adulthood continue to develop, while the activities which go unpracticed tend to deteriorate. Research by Cornelius (1984) supported this theory in that younger and older adults reported measures of exercised abilities to be equally familiar, difficult, effortful and speeded. However, older adults viewed measures of unexercised abilities to be less familiar, more difficult, more effortful, and more highly speeded than did younger adults. Denney's theory predicts that intervention works by providing practice and/or training on abilities of older adults which have gone unused.

There have also been reviews of the available evidence on intervention in psychometric intelligence abilities (Baltes & Willis, 1979, 1982; Labouvie-Vief, 1976; Sterns & Sanders, 1980). All of these reviewers have concluded that the evidence to date supports the conclusion that older individuals can and do benefit from training aimed at enhancing psychometric intelligence.

A comprehensive and systematic attempt to enhance psychometric intelligence in the elderly was undertaken by Baltes and Willis (1982) at Pennsylvania State University. This program was aimed at examining the limits of intraindividual plasticity in intellectual performance in older individuals. The name of the program is Adult Development and Enrichment Project (ADEPT). It used healthy community residents in rural Pennsylvania aged 60 to 85 and measured dependent variables covering the major dimensions of psychometric intelligence as formulated in the theory of fluid and crystallized intelligence (Horn, 1978).

Synthesis of Phase II and Phase III Perspectives

An interesting marriage between Phases II and III occurred when the Seattle sample which had been used in Schaie's sequential research since 1956 became the target for intervention research in a collaboration between Schaie and Willis (1986; Willis & Schaie, 1986). A training study was undertaken in which five hours of individual training was given to 229 older persons ranging in age from 64 to 94. The training was either on spatial orientation or inductive reasoning. All of the subjects had been assessed at least 14 years before the study, and about half of the sample had shown decline. Of those who declined, more than half gained significantly from the training, and about 40 percent returned to their predecline level of performance. About a third of the group which showed no decline improved their performance above previous levels. This degree of plasticity suggests that disuse rather than irreversible physiological decline accounts for the change with age in performance.

Emerging from his work on sequential strategies and intervention is Baltes' conception of adult intelligence which includes four major concepts: plasticity, multidimensionality, multidirectionality, and interindividual variability (Baltes, Dittmann-Kohli & Dixon, 1984; Dittmann-Kohli & Baltes, 1984). This model takes into account the Phase III perspective that training and practice can improve older adults' performance on intelligence measures. It also incorporates the notion originating in Phase I and elaborated in Phase II that intellectual ability is comprised of a number of dimensions which demonstrate varying age functions. The cohort concept elaborated in Phase II is a major cause of the interindividual variability component.

Phase III denies the inevitable deterioration of intellect with aging, or at a minimum, the empirical work undertaken from this perspective demonstrates that the decrement can be compensated with other skills. The aim is to maximize intellectual performance in the elderly. This perspective emphasizes the existence of plasticity in behavior in the aged and points out that decremental age functions can be altered with training and practice. From this point of view, the number of possible age functions of intelligence is unknown and unknowable until all possible attempts at manipulation have been made. Intervention research has contributed to a better understanding of theories of adult intelligence, and it has also provided practitioners with new tools with which they can help the elderly.

PHASE IV:
DEVELOPMENT OF ADULT
INTELLIGENCE

One of the major limitations of Phases I through III is that all perspectives base information about intellect in older adulthood on tests initially designed for children. All three perspectives accept psychometric measures of intelligence as valid measures for the aged. Old people are assessed with the yardstick designed to measure the young, and if they deviate from the young pattern, they are labeled deficient. A number of researchers have questioned the usefulness of this approach (Baltes et al., 1984; Kramer, 1986; Labouvie-Vief, 1980; Labouvie-Vief & Chandler, 1978; Schaie, 1978; Woodruff, 1983).

Thus, one of the characteristics of Phase IV is that it reexamines the psychometric approach in an attempt to determine what the most appropriate tests of intellect are in late life. The ecological validity of traditional intelligence tests is questioned in the case of the aged. In this regard, Sternberg's (1985) triarchic theory of intellectual development is relevant. One of the three components of the triarchic theory is the context in which intelligence is expressed. Different contexts foster the expression of different abilities. Hence, what intelligence tests measure may not relate to the context of older adults' lives.

Berg and Sternberg (1985) examined applications of the triarchic theory to adulthood and aging and emphasized the role of intelligence in successful adaptation to the environment. Since the contextual aspect of the three-part theory highlights differences in the environment for different age groups, the resulting implication is that different measures of intellectual competence should be used for older adults.

The two new subtheories which Sternberg (1985) has added to his unidimensional componential theory of intelligence (Sternberg, 1977) to make it a triarchic theory are representative of the manner in which investigators use the Phase IV perspective to augment their views of intelligence in adulthood and old age. Componential theory represents an information processing approach to psychometric intelligence in which human abilities contributing to performance on psychometric measures are analyzed. Componential theory has become one of the three subtheories in triarchic theory, and it is the two subtheories which Sternberg added in the 1980s which have the greatest implications for intelligence and aging. The contextual subtheory has already been mentioned as reflecting one aspect of the Phase IV perspective: Intelligent or adaptive behavior is different in differnt contexts and cannot necessarily be measured accurately at different points in the life span with the same test battery.

The experiential subtheory of triarchic theory is clearly relevant in adult development. This subtheory stipulates that measures of intelligence assess novel and automated behavior. With experience, behaviors change from being novel to becoming automated, and as a behavior becomes automated, expertise emerges. When individuals differ in the amount of experience they have on a task, then the measure is assessing different components in these individuals.

The experiential subtheory for intelligence and aging has two implications. (1) If measures of psychomotor intelligence are novel to middle-aged and older people inasmuch as they have not used skills designed originally to predict academic performance for the past 30 to 50 years, then the measures are assessing novel behaviors in older and automated behaviors in younger cohorts. (2) Experience improves abilities, and behaviors adults perform repeatedly over the adult life span become automated. Clearly, expertise with continued improvement on an ability can emerge over the adult period.

This capacity for continued improvement in intellectual ability is an underlying assumption of the Phase IV perspective. Characteristic of Phase IV is the notion that intelligence is dynamic over the adult years and that certain abilities change and even improve with age. Gisela Labouvie-Vief captured the essence of this assumption when she stated, "Thus, adulthood is no longer to be seen as the cessation of growth and development (and, consequently, as the beginning of aging) but as a life stage programmed for plasticity and further growth" (Labouvie-Vief, 1985, p. 501).

To assume that a competent middle-aged executive has not successfully mastered cognitive strategies is naive from the Phase IV perspective. Given that we have no intelligence tests designed for the aged and that intelligence develops during the adult years, one of the tasks of researchers working in this mode is to begin as in the manner of Piaget to observe carefully the behavior of older problem solvers to discover what is unique about their approach. A complimentary approach would be to use Sternberg's (1977, 1985) componential analysis to identify the information processing strategies used by adults in middle age and later life. This approach is exemplified in the work of Salthouse who has analyzed behavioral components in task performance of younger and older typists to explain their expert performance (Salthouse, 1984). The important point is to develop theory and methods which are based on observations of aging adults.

A related aspect of Phase IV is the search for qualitative changes in adult intelligence and cognition using the available data and measuring instruments as well as novel methodology. Working in this paradigm are investigators who are applying statistical techniques such as factor analysis to the psychometric intelligence data to determine if the factor structure and hence the quality of adult intelligence would change over time. We will briefly examine these approaches to the Phase IV perspective and then determine if any consensus is being reached from the divergent pathways taken to examine development and change in adult intellect.

The Search for Ecologically Valid Adult Intelligence Tests

The initial attempts to devise age-appropriate tests of intelligence did not represent a break with the psychometric intelligence or cognitive psychology approaches for the most part, but involved instead the attempt to make standard tests more relevant to old people. To devise more age-appropriate cognitive tasks, Sinnott (1975) used stimuli and problems encountered in everyday life and compared classification of these stimuli with traditional, formal stimuli. Comparing groups of middle-age and older individuals, Sinnott used three classification tasks, including simple classification, class inclusion, and multiple classification. Familiar materials facilitated simple classification in both younger and older adults, but it facilitated the performance of older adults considerably more than younger adults. There was 100 percent improvement in older adults and 53 percent improvement in younger adults. There was also an interaction between education and type of material. College graudates scored significantly higher on the formal, traditional tasks than did noncollege graduates.

In the interpretation of her results, Sinnott stated, "If formal operations are developed by the dialectical activity of assimilation/accommodation, older persons would most likely do better on familiar tasks to a greater extent, since their experience is even further removed from the academic environment of the children for whom the tasks were designed" (Sinnott, 1975, p. 439).

Older adults are typically very removed from the academic environment which would most likely sustain formal, abstract modes of thinking. Their average educational attainment is much less than the educational achievement of even the middle-aged cohort, and many more years have elapsed since they attended school as compared to the young and middle aged with whom they are evaluated. It is not surprising that the aged perform better on tests tapping practical experience. Furthermore, in Sinnott's study, older noncollege graduates scored even proportionately higher on the familiar set of materials than any other group. They scored 113 percent higher on the familiar materials than on the formal materials, and this was more than twice that of any other group.

Traditional cognitive tests may alienate older individuals because the tests seem trivial and fail to tap cognitive operations that occur in daily thinking and problem solving. Hulicka (1967) reported an 80 percent attrition rate of older adults on an attempted memory task. Because older adults may find the tasks presented to them by psychologists displeasing, we must consider the context within which the individuals live in order to study their cognitive processes.

Change in Adult Cognition

It may be more appropriate in exploring adult cognition to seek age-appropriate constructs rather than merely altering the content of the tasks (Labouvie-Vief, 1977). It is known that tests can be constructed to favor performance in the aged (Demming & Pressey, 1957; Gardner & Monge, 1977). Such tests generally tap experiential, practical skills. Cornelius and Caspi (1987) demonstrated that over the age range of 20 to 78, everyday problem solving and crystallized intelligence were greater in older cohorts while measures of fluid intelligence indicated deficits after middle age. The most salient difference between everyday and academic types of intelligence occurred in the greater emphasis placed on practical abilities and social competence in everyday intelligence (Cornelius & Caspi, 1987).

It was documented in the Phase I perspective that older adults maintained vocabulary and information scores. It was indicated from the Phase II perspective that these abilities may increase with age, and it continues to be demonstrated that tests which tap memory for general information favor performance by middle-aged and older adults (Camp, Lachman & Lachman, 1977). For the most part, however, gerontologists appear to have been more concerned with the acquistion of new information and new skills while overlooking the potential for acquired knowledge in facilitating problem solving in aging. The emphasis appears to be gradually changing, as psychologists study possible forms of progressive cognitive development in adulthood. Kramer (1986) suggested that this Phase IV perspective reflects a shift from analytic to synthetic world views of aging and intelligence.

The approach to explore a developmental progression in adult intelligence has resulted in attempts to formulate a model of adult cognitive development from within a Piagetian framework (Arlin, 1975; Koplowitz, 1984; Kramer, 1983; Labouvie-Vief, 1980; Pascual-Leone, 1983; Pascual-Leone & Goodman, 1979; Riegel, 1973b; Sinnott, 1984). This approch was discussed in Chapter 12.

Empirical evidence for a more integrative classification strategy in highly educated older adult women was presented by Kramer and Woodruff (1984). The highest achieving older women in the sample showed the greatest integration in their classification schemes. This is an important result because the data suggest that broader classification schemes are not indicative of regression to a childlike phase. The results of this study showing a higher level of performance in older women are presented in Figure 13.5.

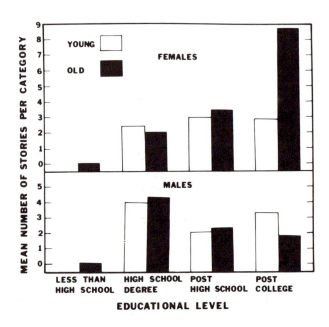

FIGURE 13.5   Age differences in breadth of categorization in men and women of varying educational levels. Young subjects had an average age of 28 years. Old subjects had an average age of 72 years. Highly educated older women had significantly greater breadth in their categorization. *Source:* Kramer, D. A. & Woodruff, D. S. (1984). Categorization and metaphoric processing in young and older adults. *Research on Aging, 6,* p. 284. Reprinted by permission of Sage Publications, Inc.

Factor-Analytic Evidence for Integration in Old Age

Evidence from factor-analytic approaches to psychometric intelligence test data in young and old samples provides some support for the notion of greater integration in old age. Several studies have revealed higher interrelatedness among cognitive skills in the elderly (Baltes, Cornelius, Spiro, Nesselroad & Willis, 1980;

Reinert, 1970; Schultz, Hoyer & Kaye, 1977). Earlier interpretations focused on the concept of "dedifferentiation," but Baltes et al. (1980) suggested that the results may also be viewed as higher integration, or "neointegration."

A study which provided partial support for the concept of neointegration was carried out by Cunningham (1980) in which the generality of ability factor structure in adulthood and old age was investigated using simultaneous maximum likelihood procedures. Data for 198 young, 156 younger old (age range of 53–68), and 156 older (age range of 69–91) on nine tests marking three ability factors (verbal comprehension, sensitivity to problems, and semantic redefinition) were factor analyzed. There were no age differences in the number of factors and no psychologically important differences in salient factor loadings. However, increasingly larger factor covariances were obtained in the two older groups. The increased factor covariances could be construed as suggestive of greater integration in the aged, although Cunningham noted that alternative hypotheses could also be used to interpret the data. Examining longitudinal data on intelligence for increased factor correlations in the older groups, Cunningham and Birren (1980) and Hertzog and Schaie (1986) found higher average correlations when subjects were older.

SUMMARY

The main contention of this chapter has been that in the twentieth century, sociocultural forces coupled with an expanding data base and improving research methodology have led to changing perspectives of intelligence and aging. Research on age changes in adult intelligence can be divided into four basic perspectives which reflect an evolving consciousness of the methodological issues and theoretical complexity involved in the understanding of adult intellect. When intelligence tests initially designed to predict academic performance were adapted and applied to World War I recruits, a picture emerged of steep decline in intelligence after the age of 20.

The initial view of adult intelligence was the Phase I: age-related decline perspective. The Phase II: stability versus decline model emerged in the mid-1950s when longitudinal data contradicted cross-sectional results. Longitudinal results suggested maintenance or increment in intellectual ability over the adult years, and the controversy generated by the discrepancy between cross-sectional and longitudinal results is still a contemporary issue. After sequential strategies had been presented and descriptive research data had suggested environmental explanations for age differences in performance on intelligence tests, experimental-analytic approaches were undertaken to explain and modify adult age functions on intellectual measures.

The Phase III: manipulation of adult intelligence model and the interventionist movement was introduced to gerontology. A number of studies designed to modify adult cognitive and intelligence test behavior have been carried out and have demonstrated that performance on these tests can be manipulated and optimized. The Phase IV: development of adult intelligence perspective evolved in part from research indicating that improvement on intelligence tests was possible, but it also emerged as a reaction against the prevalence of the psychometric testing model in Phases I through III. In Phase IV the question of the ecological validity of tests designed to predict academic performance and applied to a population of relative educational deprivation is raised. The search for new and more appropriate measures is initiated, and a reanalysis of the existing psychometric data is pursued with the outcome providing evidence that adult intelligence may be more integrated. In Phase IV the search for intellectual abilities which develop over the adult life span has been initiated, and in this perspective older adults are finally being assessed for their wisdom and experience.

Research on aging and intelligence in the future is likely to be more pluralistic than in the past. The singular and dominating perspective of Phase I is no longer possible at a point where a large data base and increasingly sophisticated research methodologies and designs are available. The fact that Phases II through IV are still represented in the current literature argues that no one perspective can be as dominant as Phase I or even Phase II was in the past.

A survey of the most recent publications on aging and intelligence in the newest and most prestigious psychological journal on aging, *Psychology and Aging,* which initiated volume 1 in 1986 revealed three articles on psychometric intelligence and aging: Baltes, Dittmann-Kohli & Kliegl, 1986 (Phase III); Hertzog & Schaie, 1986 (Phase II); Willis & Schaie, 1986 (Phase III). The publication of these articles in an important new journal on the psychology of aging attests to the continued importance of psychometric intelligence to psychologists studying aging. Three of the 44 (6.8 percent) full articles published in volume 1 of this major journal which covers all aspects of psychology and aging were dedicated to aging and psychometric intelligence. The variety of phases into which the articles can be categorized points out the current state of the field as heterogeneous in its approach to the study of intelligence. While the sample is too small to discern a trend, it is clear that research activity in Phases II and III is still vital. Since the endeavor at Phase IV is new and techniques and theory are less well-established, no Phase IV article appeared in volume 1 of this new journal. However, the socio-cultural process model would predict that as aging adults become increasingly prominent and powerful in society, and as methodologies to assess intelligence in adulthood evolve, in *Psychology and Aging* and in other leading research journals, the Phase IV perspective of development of intelligence will become more completely represented.

REFERENCES

ACHENBAUM, W. A. & KUSNERZ, P. A. (1978). *Images of old age in America: 1790 to the present.* Ann Arbor, MI: Institute of Gerontology, University of Michigan.

ANASTASI, A. (1976). *Psychological testing.* (4th ed.) New York: Macmillan.

ARLIN, P. K. (1975). Cognitive development in adulthood: A fifth stage? *Developmental Psychology, 11,* 612–616.

BALTES, P. B. (1968). Longitudinal and cross-sectional sequences in the study of age and generation effects. *Human Development, 11,* 145–171.

BALTES, P. B., CORNELIUS, S. W. & NESSELROADE, J. R. (1979). Cohort effects in developmental psychology. In J. R. Nesselroade & P. B. Baltes (Eds.), *Longitudinal methodology in the study of behavior and development.* New York: Academic Press, p. 61–87.

BALTES, P. B., CORNELIUS, S. W., SPIRO, A., NESSELROADE, J. R. & WILLIS, S. L. (1980). Integration versus differentiation in fluid/crystallized intelligence in old age. *Developmental Psychology, 16,* 625–635.

BALTES, P. B. & DITTMANN-KOHLI, F. & DIXON, R. A. (1984). New perspectives on the development of intelligence in adulthood: Toward a dual-process conception and a model of selective optimization with compensation. In P. B. Baltes & O. G. Brim, Jr. (Eds.), *Life-span development and behavior* (Vol. 6), New York: Academic Press, p. 33–76.

BALTES, P. B., DITTMANN-KOHLI, F. & KLIEGL, R. (1986). Reserve capacity of the elderly in aging-sensitive tests of fluid intelligence: Replication and extension. *Psychology and Aging, 1,* 172–177.

BALTES, P. B. & GOULET, L. R. (1971). Exploratiaon of developmental variables by manipulation and simulation of age differences in behavior. *Human Development, 14,* 149–170.

BALTES, P. B. & SCHAIE, K. W. (1976). On the plasticity of intelligence in adulthood and old age. Where Horn and Donaldson fail. *American Psychologist, 31,* 720–725.

BALTES, P. B. & WILLIS, S. L. (1977). Toward psychological theories of aging and development. In J. E. Birren & K. W. Schaie (Eds.), *Handbook of the psychology of aging.* New York: Van Nostrand Reinhold, p. 128–154.

BALTES, P. B. & WILLIS, S. L. (1979). The critical importance of appropriate methodology in the study of aging: The sample case of psychometric intelligence. In F. Hoffmeister & C. Muller (Eds.), *Brain function in old age.* New York: Springer, p. 164–187.

BALTES, P. B. & WILLIS, S. L. (1982). Plasticity and enhancement of intellectual functioning in old age: Penn State's adult development and enrichment project (ADEPT). In F.I.M. Craik & S. Trehub (Eds.), *Aging and cognitive processes.* New York: Plenum Press, p. 353–389.

BAYLEY, N. & ODEN, M. H. (1955). The maintenance of intellectual ability in gifted adults. *Journal of Gerontology, 10,* 1–107

BEESON, M. F. (1920). Intelligence at senescence. *Journal of Applied Psychology, 4,* 219–234.

BERG, C. A. & STERNBERG, R. J. (1985). A triarchic theory of intellectual development during adulthood. *Developmental Review, 5,* 334–370.

BINET, A. & SIMON, T. (1905). Methodes nouvelles pour le diagnostic du niveau intellectual des arnormaux. *Annee Psychologique, 11,* 191–244.

BIRREN, J.E . (1959). Principles of research on aging. In J. E. Birren (Ed.), *Handbook of aging and the individual,* Chicago: University of Chicago Press, p. 3–42.

BIRREN, J. E. (1969).   Age and decision strategies. In A. T. Welford & J. E. Birren (Eds.), *Decision making and age*. Basel: Karger.

BOTWINICK, J. (1967).   *Cognitive processes in maturity and old age*. New York: Springer.

BOTWINICK, J. (1977).   Intellectual abilities. In J. E. Birren & K. W. Schaie (Eds.), *Handbook of the psychology of aging*. New York: Van Nostrand Reinhold, p. 580–605.

BOTWINICK, J. & ARENBERG, D. (1976).   Disparate time spans in sequential studies of aging. *Experimental Aging Research, 2,* 55–66.

BOTWINICK, J. & SIEGLER, I. C. (1980).   Intellectual ability among the elderly: Simultaneous cross-sectional and longitudinal comparisons. *Developmental Psychology, 16,* 49–53.

CAMP, C., LACHMAN, R. & LACHMAN, J. (1977).   *Age and the retrievability of world knowledge*. Paper presented at the 30th annual meeting of the Gerontological Society, Dallas, November.

CATTELL, R. B. (1943).   The measurement of adult intelligence. *Psychological Bulletin, 40,* 153–193.

CATTELL, R. B. (1971).   *Abilities: Their structure, growth, and action*. Boston: Houghton Mifflin.

CICIRELLI, V. G. (1976).   Categorization behavior in aging. *Journal of Gerontology, 31,* 676–680.

CLAYTON, V. (1982).   Wisdom and intelligence: The nature and function of knowledge in the later yearss. *International Journal of Aging and Human Development, 15,* 315–321.

CLAYTON, V. & BIRREN, J. E. (1980).   The development of wisdom across the life span: A reexamination of an ancient logic. In P. B. Baltes & O. G. Brim (Eds.), *Life-span development and behavior* (Vol. 3), New York: Academic Press, p. 103–135.

CORNELIUS, S. W. (1984).   Classic pattern of intellectual aging: Test familiarity, difficulty, and performance. *Journal of Gerontology, 39,* 201–206.

CORNELIUS, S. W. & CASPI, A. (1987).   Everyday problem solving in adulthood and old age. *Psychology and Aging, 2,* 144–153.

CUNNINGHAM, W. R. (1980).   Age comparative factor analysis of ability variables in adulthood and old age. *Intelligence, 4,* 133–149.

CUNNINGHAM, W. R. & BIRREN, J. E. (1980).   Age changes in the factor structure of intellectual abilities in adulthood and old age. *Educational and Psychological Measurement, 40,* 271–290.

DEMMING, J. A. & PRESSEY, S. L. (1957).   Testing 'indigenous' to the adult older years. *Journal of Counseling Psychology, 4,* 144–148.

DENNEY, N. W. (1979).   Problem solving in later adulthood: Intervention research. In P. B. Baltes & O. G. Brim, Jr. (Eds.), *Life-span development and behavior* (Vol. 2). New York: Academic Press.

DENNEY, N. W. (1982).   Aging and cognitive changes. In B. B. Wolman (Ed.), *Handbook of developmental psychology*. Englewood Cliffs, NJ: Prentice Hall, p. 37–66.

DITTMANN-KOHLI, F. & BALTES, P. B. (1984).   Towards an action-theoretical and pragmatic conception of intelligence during adulthood and old age. In C. N. Alexander & E. Langer, (Eds.), *Beyond formal operations: Alternative endpoints to human development*. Oxford: Oxford University Press.

DIXON, R. A., KRAMER, D. A. & BALTES, P. B. (1985).   Intelligence: A life-span developmental perspective. In B. B. Wolman (Ed.), *Handbook of intelligence: Theories, measurements, and applications*. New York: Wiley, p. 301–350.

ERIKSON, E. H. (1968). *Identity and crisis.* New York: W. W. Norton.

FOSTER, J. C. & TAYLOR, G. (1920). The applicability of mental tests to persons over fifty years of age. *Journal of Applied Psychology, 4,* 39-58.

GARDNER, E. F. & MONGE, R. H. (1977). Adult age difference in cognitive abilities and educational background. *Experimental Aging Research, 3,* 337-383.

HAVIGHURST, R. J. (1973). History of developmental psychology: Socialization and personality development through the life span. In P. B. Baltes & K. W. Schaie (Eds.), *Life-span developmental psychology: Personality and socialization.* New York: Academic Press, p. 3-52.

HERTZOG, C. & SCHAIE, K. W. (1986). Stability and change in adult intelligence: 1. Analysis of longitudinal covariance structures. *Psychology and Aging, 1,* 159-171.

HOFLAND, B. F., WILLIS, S. L. & BALTES, P. B. (1981). Fluid intelligence performance in the elderly: Intraindividual variability and conditions of assessment. *Journal of Educational Psychology, 73,* 573-586.

HORN, J. L. (1968). Organization of abilities and the development of intelligence. *Psychological Review, 75,* 242-259.

HORN, J. L. (1978). Human ability systems. In P. B. Baltes (Ed.), *Life-span development and behavior* (Vol. 1). New York: Academic Press, p. 212-255.

HORN, J. L. (1982). The theory of fluid and crystallized intelligence in relation to concepts of cognitive psychology and aging in adulthood. In F.I.M. Craik & S. Trehub (Eds.) *Aging and cognitive processes.* New York: Plenum Press, p. 237-278.

HORN, J. L. & CATTELL, R. (1967). Age differences in fluid and crystrallized intelligence. *Acta Psychologica, 26,* 107-129.

HULICKA, I. M. (1967). Age differences in retention as a function of interference. *Journal of Gerontology, 22,* 180-184.

JONES, H. E. (1959). Intelligence and problem-solving. In J. E. Birren (Ed.), *Handbook of aging and the individual.* Chicago: University of Chicago Press, p. 700-783.

JONES, H. E. & CONRAD, H. S. (1933). The growth and decline of intelligence: A study of homogeneous group between the ages of ten and sixty. *Genetic Psychology Monographs, 13,* 223-298.

KASTENBAUM, R. (1968). Perspectives on the development and modification of behavior in the aged: A developmental-field perspective. *The Gerontologist, 8,* 208-283.

KOGAN, N. (1974). Categorizing and conceptualizing styles in younger and older adults. *Human Development, 17,* 218-230.

KOPLOWITZ, H. (1984). A projection beyond Piaget's formal-operations stage. In M. L. Commons, F. A. Richards & C. Armon (Eds.), *Beyond formal operations: Late adolescent and adult cognitive development.* New York: Praeger, p. 272-295.

KRAMER, D. A. (1983). Post-formal operations? A need for further conceptualization. *Human Development, 26,* 91-105.

KRAMER, D. A. (1986). Practical intelligence and adult development: A world views perspective. *International Society for the Study of Behavioral Development Newsletter, 1,* 1-3.

KRAMER, D. A. & WOODRUFF, D. S. (1984). Categorization and metaphoric processing in young and older adults. *Research on Aging, 6,* 271-286.

KRAMER, D. A. & WOODRUFF, D. S. (1986). Relativistic and dialectical thought in three adult age groups. *Human Development, 29,* 280-290.

KUHLEN, R. G. (1940). Social change: A neglected factor in psychological studies of the life span. *School and Society, 52,* 14-16.

LABOUVIE-VIEF, G. (1976). Toward optimizing cognitive competence in later life. *Educational Gerontology, 1,* 75-92.

LABOUVIE-VIEF, G. (1977). Adult cognitive development: In search of alternative interpretations. *Merill-Palmer Quarterly, 23,* 227–263.

LABOUVIE-VIEF, G. (1980). Beyond formal operations: Uses and limits of pure logic in life-span development. *Human Development, 23,* 141–161.

LABOUVIE-VIEF, G. (1985). Intelligence and cognition. In J. E. Birren & K. W. Schaie (Eds.), *Handbook of the psychology of aging.* New York: Van Nostrand Reinhold, p. 500–530.

LABOUVIE-VIEF, G. & CHANDLER, M. J. (1978). Cognitive development and life-span developmental theory. Idealistic versus contextual perspectives. In P. B. Baltes (Ed.), *Life-span development and behavior* (Vol. 1), New York: Academic Press.

McCARTY, S. M., SIEGLER, I. C. & LOGUE, P. E. (1982). Cross-sectional and long-itudinal patterns of three Wechsler Memory Scale subtests. *Journal of Gerontology, 37,* 169–175.

MILES, C. C. & MILES, W. R. (1932). The correlation of intelligence scores and chrono-logical age from early to late maturity. *American Journal of Psychology, 44,* 44–78.

NEUGARTEN, B. L. & HAVIGHURST, R. J. (Eds.), (1976). *Social policy, social ethics, and the aging society.* Washington, DC: U.S. Government Printing Office.

OWENS, W. A., JR. (1953). Age and mental abilities: A longitudinal study. *Genetic Psychology Monographs, 48,* 3–54.

PASCUAL-LEONE, J. (1983). Growing into human maturity: Toward a metasubjective theory of adult stages. In P. B. Baltes & O. Brim (Eds.), *Life-span development and behavior* (Vol. 5), New York: Academic Press, p. 117–156.

PASCUAL-LEONE, J. & GOODMAN, D. (1979). Intelligence and experience: A neo-piagetion approach. *Instructional Science, 8,* 301–367.

REINERT, G. (1970). Comparative factor analytic studies of intelligence throughout the human life span. In L. R. Goulet & P. B. Baltes (Eds.), *Life-span developmental: Research & theory.* New York: Academic Press, p. 468–484.

RIEGEL, K. F. (1973a). Developmental psychology and society: Some historical and ethical considerations. In J. R. Nesselroade & H. W. Reese (Eds.), *Life-span developmental psychology: Methodological issues.* New York: Academic Press, p. 1–23.

RIEGEL, K. F. (1973b). Dialectic operations: The final priod of cognitive development. *Human Development, 16,* 371–381.

RIEGEL, K. F. (1977). History of psychological gerontology. In J. E. Birren & K. W. Schaie (Eds.), *Handbook of the psychology of aging.* New York: Reinhold, p. 70–102.

RIEGEL, K. F., RIEGEL, R. M. & MEYER, G. (1967). A study of drop-out rates in longitudinal research on aging and the prediction of death. *Journal of Personality and Social Psychology, 5,* 324–348.

ROODIN, P. A., RYBASH, J. & HOYER, W. J. (1984). Affect in adult cognition: A constructivist view of moral thought and action. In C. Z. Malatesta & C. E. Izard (Eds.), *Emotion in adult development.* Beverly Hills, CA: Sage Publishers, p. 297–316.

SABATINI, P. P. & LABOUVIE-VIEF, G. (November, 1979). *Age and professional specialization in formal reasoning.* Paper presented at the 86th annual meeting of the Gerontological Society, Washington, DC.

SALTHOUSE, T. A. (1984). Effects of age and skill in typing. *Journal of Experimental Psychology: General, 113,* 345–371.

SCHAIE, K. W. (1965).   A general model for the study of developmental problems. *Psychological Bulletin, 64,* 92–107.

SCHAIE, K. W. (1977–1978).   Toward a stage theory of adult cognitive development. *International Journal of Aging and Human Development, 8,* 129–136.

SCHAIE, K. W. (1978).   External validity in the assessment of intellectual development in adulthood. *Journal of Gerontology, 33,* 695–701.

SCHAIE, K. W. (1979).   Theh Primary Mental Abilities in adulthood: An exploration of psychometric intelligence. In P. B. Baltes & O. G. Grim, Jr. (Eds.), *Life-span development and behavior* (Vol. 2). New York: Academic Press.

SCHAIE, K. W. (1982).   The Seattle Longitudinal Study: A twenty-one year exploration of psychometric intelligence in adulthood. In K. W. Schaie (Ed.), *Longitudinal studies of adult psychological development.* New York: Guilford Press.

SCHAIE, K. W. (1983).   Age changes in adult intelligence. In D. S. Woodruff & J. E. Birren (Eds.), *Aging: Scientific perspectives and social issues* (2nd Ed.), Monterey, CA: Brooks/Cole.

SCHAIE, K. W. (1986).   Beyond calendar definitions of age, time, and cohort: The general developmental model revisited. *Developmental Review, 6,* 252–277.

SCHAIE, K. W. & BALTES, P. B. (1975).   On sequential strategies in developmental research: Description or explanation. *Human Development, 18,* 384–390.

SCHAIE, K. W. & HERTZOG, C. (1982).   Longitudinal methods. In B. B. Wolman (Ed.), *Handbook of developmental psychology.* Englewood Cliffs, NJ: Prentice Hall, p. 91–114.

SCHAIE, K. W. & HERTZOG, C. (1983).   Fourteen-year cohort-sequential studies of adult intellectual development. *Development Psychology, 19,* 531–543.

SCHAIE, K. W. & LABOUVIE-VIEF, G. (1974).   Generational versus ontogenetic components of change in adult cognitive behavior: A fourteen-year cross-sequential study. *Developmental Psychology, 10,* 305–320.

SCHAIE, K. W. & PARHAM, I. A. (1977).   Cohort-sequential analyses of adult intellectual development. *Developmental Psychology, 13,* 649–653.

SCHAIE, K. W. & STROTHER, C. R. (1968a).   A cross-sequential study of age changes in cognitive behavior. *Psychological Bulletin, 70,* 671–680.

SCHAIE, K. W. & STROTHER, C. R. (1968b).   The effects of time and cohort differences on the interpretation of age changes in cognitive behavior. *Multivariate Behavioral Research, 3,* 259–294.

SCHAIE, K. W. & WILLIS, S. L. (1986).   Can decline in adult intellectual functioning be reversed? *Developmental Psychology, 22,* 223–232.

SCHULTZ, N. R., HOYER, W. J. & KAYE, D. B. (1977).   *Spontaneous flexibility and rigidity in adulthood and old age: A multitrait-multimethod analysis.* Paper presented at the 30th annual meeting of the Gerontological Society, San Francisco, November.

SINNOTT, J. D. (1975).   Everyday thinking and Piagetian operativity in adults. *Human Development, 18,* 430–443.

SINNOTT, J. D. (1984).   Postformal reasoning: The relativistic stage. In M. L. Commons, R. A. Richards, and C. Armon (Eds.) *Beyond formal operations: Late adolescent and adult cognitive development.* New York: Praeger, p. 298–325.

STERNBERG, R. J. (1977).   *Intelligence information processing, and analogical reasoning: The componential analysis of human abilities.* Hillsdale, NJ: Erlbaum.

STERNBERG, R. J. (1985).   *Beyond IQ: A triarchic theory of human intelligence.* Cambridge, England: Cambridge University Press.

STERNS, H. L. & SANDERS, R. E. (1980).   Training and education of the elderly. In R. R. Turner & H. W. Reese (Eds.) *Life-span developmental psychology: Intervention*. New York: Academic Press, p. 307–330.

WILLIS, S. L. & SCHAIE, K. W. (1986).   Training the elderly on the ability factors of spatial orientation and inductive reasoning. *Psychology and Aging, 1,* 239–247.

WILLOUGHBY, R. R. (1927).   Fmaily similarities in mental-test abilities (with a note on the growth and decline of these abilities). *Genetic Psychology Monographs, 2,* 235–277.

WOODRUFF, D. S. (1983).   A review of aging and cognitive processes. *Research on Aging, 5,* 139–153.

YERKES, R. M. (1921).   Psychological examining in the United States Army. (National Academy of Science). Washington, DC: U.S. Government Printing Office.

CHAPTER 14

Personality and Aging

One of the most fascinating aspects of psychology is the study of personality. Few dimensions of behavioral science draw more attention and interest than phenomena related to personality. We think of personality as somehow at the core of what gives an individual a unique identity. When we consider personality in adulthood and old age, we are interested in knowing if there are characteristic changes in personality with aging. Are there certain personality characteristics which lead to more successful aging? What qualities foster adjustment in old age? As one of the most notable scholars on personality over the life span, Bernice Neugarten has asserted that two of the major questions about personality and aging are: Does aging affect personality? Does personality affect the way a person ages? In this chapter we will attempt to answer these and other questions about consistency and change in personality over the adult age span.

The first step necessary to a discussion of personality in the adult years is to define what we mean by personality. This is more difficult than it might appear because scholars do not agree on the definition of the concept of personality. Indeed, some psychologists have suggested that personality as an enduring characterization of an individual may not even exist. Investigators of Skinnerian persuasion reject the concept of personality, choosing to focus instead on behaviors which can be observed and manipulated. Others such as Mischel (1973) have criticized the study of personality traits. The argument is that humans are so adaptable and fluid in their ability to react differently in different situations that there may be no stable set of qualities by which any one person can be identified.

In spite of the many critics of the concept of personality, the traditional conception of personality has been defined as the pattern of traits characterizing an individual person. The meaning of trait is any psychological characteristic of a person, such as reacting consistently despite changing stimulus conditions. Other examples of personality traits include values, abilities, motives, defenses, and aspects of temperament, identity, and personal style. The full pattern or organization of traits becomes apparent only over the enitre life span, although the term *personality* is typically used to refer to the observable pattern of traits at any one point in time.

One of the first means that was used to assess whether the traits characterizing individuals went through any kind of systematic change with age was to carry out cross-sectional studies over the adult age span using standard psychometric personality tests. While these early studies were useful only in identifying age differences in personality characteristics in groups of people with widely divergent backgrounds, they did serve as a first step in isolating traits which might change. Of course, the only manner in which true age *changes* in personality can be identified is through longitudinal research. Some of the early longitudinal studies used clinical interviews to assess personality, and it is often difficult to quantify the interview data and generalize from it. Nevertheless, some insights have been gained from this information. In addition, longitudinal and follow-up studies of psychometric personality inventories have been carried out. These studies combined with studies using both interview and psychometric assessment of adults as they age provide us with information about personality in adulthood.

PERSONALITY TRAITS
IN ADULTHOOD AND OLD AGE

One way that psychologists have measured personality in adulthood is to devise psychometric test batteries designed to assess individual traits. The tests are comprised of a large number of questions, and each question is associated with a specific trait. An individual's score on a trait would be computed on the basis of how he or she responded to the 15 to 30 questions representing that trait. For example, the question, "I enjoy interacting with other people," might be included as one of 30 questions measuring the trait of introversion-extroversion. Instead of answering simply yes or no, the respondent could circle any number between 1 and 9 with 1 representing full agreement and 9 representing full disagreement. On the basis of the individual's responses, the personality test assesses his or her configuration of personality traits.

A number of psychometric personality inventories have been developed. One of the best known is the Minnesota Multiphasic Personality Inventory (MMPI) which was designed to identify abnormalities in personality. It was standardized by being administered to patient populations diagnosed by other means as having the various abnormal traits it was designed to identify. The responses of the clinical populations were compared to the responses of clinically normal individuals, and items distinguishing the abnormal group were used to test for that trait. Other inventories such as the Eysenck Personality Inventory, the Cattell Sixeen Personality Factor Questionnaire, the Guilford-Zimmerman Temperament Survey and the Comrey Personality Inventory have been designed to measure normal personality characteristics in the general population. Personality traits and the questions used to measure them have been selected on the basis of factor-analytic techniques.

A number of cross-sectional studies have been carried out using psychometric personality inventories. Some age differences have been identified, but surprisingly few personality traits consistently differentiated adults of various ages. The most reliable age differences which were observed were on the traits of extroversion-introversion and rigidity. Some studies also identified age differences in cautiousness, depression, and hypocondriasis.

Extroversion-Introversion

More than any other trait measure of personality, extroversion-introversion has been shown to differentiate younger and older adult age groups. Questionnaire measures of extroversion-introversion reveal a small but consistent trend. A number of independent investigators using a variety of subject populations have found a small age difference in favor of greater introversion in the older subjects. Brozek (1955) compared the MMPI social introversion scores of 157 male college students to comparable scores for 233 business and professional men in their forties and found that the older men scored significantly higher in the direction of greater introversion.

Also using the MMPI social introversion scale, Calden and Hokanson (1959) assessed 160 male tuberculosis patients over the age range of 20 to 70. In the decades of the twenties and thirties the scores were similar, but beginning with the decade of the forties, social introversion scores were increasingly in the direction of greater introversion in the older men. Hardyck (1964) reported that the age differences in social introversion scores on the MMPI also existed in women. There were 189 female college students and middle-aged women tested in Hardyck's study, and the age differences in introversion were found to be of about the same magnitude as in men over the same age range.

The MMPI social introversion scale is not the only scale which has been used to demonstrate age differences in introversion. The sociability scale of the Heron Inventory was used by Craik (1964) and by Heron and Chown (1967) to identify age differences in introversion. The age range of the 240 British male volunteers in the Craik study was 20 to 80, and in each decade there was a higher introversion score with some leveling off occurring after the forties. There were 540 British male and female volunteers matched for social class and intelligence in the Heron and Chown study. Both men and women showed age differences in introversion, and as in the Craik study, there was a plateau in introversion scores after the forties.

Other personality inventories which have been used to demonstrate greater introversion in middle and old age are the Guilford-Zimmerman Temperament Scale (Bendig, 1960) and the Maudsley Personality Inventory (Gutman, 1966). Bendig analyzed the scores from 400 men tested for employment or promotion in business who were in their twenties to fifties. While the introversion score was slightly higher in each age group, the greatest difference was between men in their mid-twenties and mid-thirties. The Gutman study involved 1,419 Canadian male and female volunteers over the age span of the twenties to the nineties. In this sample, higher introversion scores did not appear until the decade of the fifties.

Age changes to increased introversion is only one of a number of possible explanations for the observed trend. Cohort differences could account for the apparent age differences in extroversion-introversion, and one attractive hypothesis is that social interaction has been valued more by succeeding generations. Some evidence for this position was provided in a short-term longitudinal study covering a seven-year period in the lives of adults over the age range of 21 to 84 (Schaie & Parham, 1976). While there were cohort differences in introversion, there were no age changes in that direction. The investigators suggested that people born in different generations were taught different things about the proper amount of reserve to show in social situations. Additional longitudinal data covering a longer time period is required before it is clear that the age differences in introversion are only cohort differences rather than age changes.

A study by Swenson (1961) limited to 160 subjects around the age of 70 demonstrated the need for validation of personality inventories in older populations. Using the MMPI, Swenson found that between one fourth and one third of the normal subjects scored in the abnormal range on a number of the subtests. He also found that geriatric patients scored significantly higher in the direction of greater introversion than did the community-residing sample. He concluded that the observed trend to introversion could result from inadequate measurement tools for older subjects.

The data indicating that sick elderly individuals score more in the direction of introversion than healthy elderly support yet another hypothesis to explain age differences in introversion. Slater and Scarr (1964) found that introversion scores increased with age in a longitudinal study. To examine their results more thoroughly, the compared profiles of eight subjects who died during the study to eight matched living subjects. The deceased subjects tended to demonstrate less introversion. Slater and Scarr suggested that the observed trend to introversion with age could be a result of selection. Introverts might live longer than extroverts.

Another speculative hypothesis regarding the observed trend of higher introversion scores in older cohorts defined introversion-extroversion in terms of Eysenck's theory which postulates two levels of personality: excitation-inhibition balance in the nervous system and introverted-extroverted behavior patterns. According to this hypothesis, aging represents a shift to extroversion on the physiological level (resulting from a decline in nervous system inhibition) and a shift to introversion (in terms of decreasing social interaction) on the behavior pattern level. Chown (1968) noted that tests showing increasing introversion with age rely on items related to social events. Thus, the personality inventories may measure the social behavior alone; this hypothesis would accurately predict the trend.

In addition to all the interpretations suggesting that the observed age differences in introversion-extroversion are simply generational differences or are only part of the total picture of the aging personality is the real possibility that introversion increases with age. Individuals may become more introspective as they get older. Personality researchers such as Neugarten describe what they call an increasing interiority with age which they have found repeatedly in their observations. It appears that old people may turn inward as they reach the end of their lives, and this increasing interiority registers on trait inventories of introversion.

Rigidity

One of the common stereotypes we have about older people is that they are more "set in their ways." They often appear to have strict patterns in their life styles and to adhere rigorously to their own point of view. This stereotype was reinforced with empirical data when early cross-sectional studies indicated that older people scored higher on tests of rigidity. One such test, a task requiring cognitive flexibility, is the Luchin's Water Jar Test. In this task the subject is told about different-sized water jars and asked to pour water in and out of them to arrive at some desired volume. One strategy solves the early problems while the first strategy or a short-cut strategy solves the middle series of tasks. Finally, the last tasks can only be solved by the second strategy. Subjects must switch strategies to succeed.

Heglin (1956) tested three groups of 100 subjects each in the teens, thirties, and sixties on this and other measures of rigidity and found that the old subjects had the highest degree of rigidity. Other cross-sectional studies replicated these results. In one of the largest of these early studies, Schaie (1958) tested 500 adults ranging in age from 20 to 70 years in age groups spaced five years apart. For the study he devised his own Test of Behavioral Rigidity in which he identified three major types of rigidity: motor-cognitive, personality-perceptual, and psychomotor speed. Of these three types of rigidity Schaie stated:

> The motor-cognitive rigidity factor seems to indicate the individual's ability to shift without difficulty from one activity to another; it is a measure of effective adjustment to shifts in *familiar* patterns and to continuously changing situational demands. The personality-perceptual rigidity factor seems to indicate the individual's ability to adjust readily to *new* surroundings and change in cognitive and environmental patterns; it seems to be a measure of ability to perceive and adjust to *unfamiliar* and *new* patterns and situations. The psychomotor speed factor finally indicates an individual's rate of emission of familiar cognitive responses. A high score on this factor would seem to imply superior functioning efficiency in coping with familiar situations requiring rapid response and quick thinking (Schaie, 1958, p. 4).

Schaie also administered an intelligence test (Thurstone's SRA Primary Mental Ability Test) to the subjects. Over the adult age span Schaie observed statistically significant age differences in the direction of decline on the mental abilities and significant age differences in the direction of an increase in all measures of behavioral rigidity. The correlations between the mental abilities scores and the rigidity scores were high. This same result was obtained from an English sample of 200 men and women over the age range of 20 to 82, tested on 16 measures of rigidity and the Raven Progressive Matrices test of intelligence (Chown, 1961). Indeed, from her own studies of age, intelligence, and rigidity, Chown (1961, 1972) concluded that age differences on intelligence tests could account for most of the variance in age differences in rigidity. When Chown statistically controlled for the variance contributed by age differences in intelligence, the age differences in rigidity disappeared. Scores on tests of rigidity were more closely related to intelligence than to chronological age.

There was some evidence that age differences in rigidity related to age differences in intelligence were also involved with age differences in psychomotor speed. Several studies demonstrated that while measures of the speed of behavior formed a discrete and relatively independent factor in groups of young subjects, it was a more general factor related to variables including nonverbal intelligence in older subjects (Birren, Butler, Greenhouse, Sokolov & Yarrow, 1963; Chown, 1961). Birren (1964) suggested that behind the age differences in rigidity and intelligence there might be a basic process of aging—slowing in the central nervous system. On this topic, he stated:

> Here is one of the most basic issues in the psychology of aging—that psychomotor speed in its changes with age is correlated with measures of nonverbal intelligence, and that these in turn are related to personality variables. One senses not only that the variable of speed is expressing a change in a basic property of the nervous system of the older organism, but also that the changes involve the personality and the individual's social functioning (Birren, 1964, p. 233.).

The cross-sectional studies completed by the early 1960s were convincing in their documentation of age differences in rigidity so that geropsychologists were willing to accept rigidity as one of the personality traits which changed with age. Subsequent data gathered with short-term longitudinal research designs make it less clear that adults become more rigid with age.

Schaie followed up his original sample tested on rigidity and intelligence and retested them at seven-year intervals (Schaie & Labouvie-Vief, 1974). To avoid the effect of repeated testing, he also generated a new sample at each of the seven-year intervals and tested them on the same measures (Schaie, Labouvie & Buech, 1973). In this manner, Schaie had two replications of measures of groups of adults over the age range of 20 to 70 (and older in the follow-up studies) covering a 14-year period. These studies indicated little increase in rigidity with age. The increases which occurred were small and were not consistent over many age groups. In the case of motor-cognitive rigidity, only the oldest group in the follow-up study and the youngest and a middle-aged group in the independent-measures study showed an increase. Personality-perceptual rigidity showed an increase in all of the follow-up groups above the age of 53, but the changes in the independent-measures group were inconsistent. The oldest groups in the follow-up study were the only groups to show increased psychomotor speed rigidity.

To summarize the current perspective on rigidity and aging, it would appear that contemporary older adults score higher than younger adults on tests of rigidity. However, it is not clear that the existing age differences result from processes of aging. Higher rigidity scores of older cohorts may result from cultural and experiential factors. A clear articulation of the current position on aging and rigidity was made by Botwinick as he stated:

> While the elderly of today may be seen as more rigid than their younger counter-parts, the elderly of tomorrow are likely to be less rigid than present-day elderly people, and perhaps not more rigid than their junior contemporaries. The reasons for this conjecture are the results of longitudinal investigations, on one hand, and of increasingly greater opportunities for continued intellectual growth on the other (Botwinick, 1978, p. 111).

Cautiousness

None of the personality inventories used to assess age differences and age changes in personality include a trait called cautiousness. The trait appearing on the Cattell sixteen Personality Factor Questionnaire (16 PF) is called *surgency-desurgency*. People with the personality trait of surgency are thought to be care-free, happy-go-lucky, and even rash. They are full of zest for life and are enthusiastic about everything. In contrast, desurgent individuals are sober and serious. Most importantly for this discussion, they are cautious. Almost all of the studies using the 16 PF to test personality in adulthood have yielded results indicating that older people score higher on desurgency (Cattell, 1950; Fozard, 1972; Sealy & Cattell, 1965).

If data on surgency-desurgency were the only evidence to suggest age differences in cautiousness, it would probably not be considered enough to highlight cautiousness as one of the personality traits showing age differences. However, a large body of evidence on increased cautiousness in old age has accumulated from laboratory studies. Old people appear to adopt more cautious strategies when they make perceptual judgments, when they give their answers in studies of learning and memory, as well as when they respond to personality questionnaires. Thus, the evidence for age differences in cautiousness comes from the experimental psychology laboratory as well as from studies of personality and aging.

The perspective presented by the data on cautiousness is that older people are uncomfortable in situations they find novel and uncertain. This may occur because there has been a loss of self-confidence and because there is an expectation or fear of failure. While evidence for greater cautiousness in older adults has accumulated over the past six decades and thus spans a number of cohorts of elderly, all of the data linking cautiousness to old age are cross-sectional. There are no data showing individuals becoming more cautious as they age. Thus, while greater cautiousness may characterize contemporary cohorts of aged, it is inappropriate to conclude that they have changed this way with age.

Botwinick (1978) compares the performance of older and younger workers to the story of the tortoise and the hare. In performing a task the old work at a slow, steady pace, and they sacrifice speed for accuracy. Indeed, in carrying out a task older adults appear to place so much importance on accuracy and the avoidance of mistakes that when they err, it is in the direction of *errors of omission.* Errors of omission occur when the respondent fails to give an answer. *Errors of commission* occur when the respondent gives an answer which is incorrect. Rather than make a mistake, the older adult appears more willing to leave a blank or to fail to respond. What he or she most wants to avoid is giving an answer which is wrong.

The observation that old subjects make more errors of omission has been made repeatedly, and it was first made in one of the earliest studies of age and behavior. Reporting on older adults' performance on intelligence tests, Thorndike, Bregman, Tilton and Woodyard (1928) found that there was a substantial increase in the number of omission errors in the performance of older adults. At this time Thorndike and associates interpreted these results to signify an increase in caution or a decrease in impulsiveness in the intellectual operations of the old. In studies of learning in which the subject must produce the correct answer, older subjects have again showed their preference for withholding a response instead of producing an incorrect one (e.g., Eisdorfer, Axelrod & Wilkie, 1963; Korchin & Basowitz, 1957).

Another type of laboratory task in which the old have been shown to adopt a more cautious strategy involves measures of perceptual ability. When the signal detection design is used so that a measure of the subject's decision criterion as well as a measure of his or her sensitivity can be derived, it has been repeatedly observed that the older subjects' decision criteria are more cautious (Craik, 1969; Potash & Jones, 1977; Fees & Botwinick, 1971).

There are other types of tasks such as those involving social situations and opinion poll responses which have been used to demonstrate greater cautiousness in older cohorts. Thus, cautiousness has been a trait identified in many of the behavior strategies of older adults. Cautiousness can be ascribed to the actions of older people as well as to the manner in which they describe their behavior. Because the adoption of a cautious strategy can be viewed as a natural outcome of the slowing of response speed and the decline of sensory and motor capacities, it is tempting to view age differences in cautiousness as reflecting a true age change. This would mean that we would all become more cautious in old age. Because this unwarranted conclusion is so appealing, it must be reiterated that all of the data demonstrating greater cautiousness in old age are cross-sectional. It remains to be demonstrated whether cautiousness is a genuine aging phenomenon or if it is simply another manifestation of the consequences of rapid social change and differing levels of experience and education for people born at different points in history.

Depression

One of the subscales of the MMPI measures the degree to which an individual feels depressed, and some comparisons of young and old respondents have indicated that older subjects score higher on this measure of depression (Botwinick & Thompson, 1967; Britton & Savage, 1966; Swenson, 1961). Depression is one of the main psychiatric complaints of the elderly. However, the individuals tested on the MMPI represented a normal rather than a clinical population. Nevertheless, even normal elderly score higher on depression.

There has been some debate as to whether there is a continuum of depression and as to where "normal" depression ends and abnormal response begins. Depression in the elderly appears to occur as a response to loss. At this time of life individuals lose loved ones, and they can also lose some of their physical health and vigor and even some of their personal wealth. Many also feel the loss of status and identity resulting from retirement. Minor depression is a normal response to some of these losses. Depression becomes abnormal and debilitating when the individual cannot see beyond the loss to any hopeful future. It is at this point that some type of intervention must be taken to help the person to function once again. Clinical depression and the interventions used to combat it is discussed more fully in Chapter 16 on psychopathology and clinical intervention. In terms of our discussion of age and personality, it appears that depression is one of the traits which is manifested at a higher level in older as compared to younger adults. The studies were cross-sectional and thus do not implicate depression as an age change.

Hypochondriasis

In addition to scoring higher on the MMPI scales of social introversion and depression in cross-sectional studies, normal older individuals score higher on the scale of hypochondriasis (Calden & Hokanson, 1959; Swenson, 1961). This scale measures individuals' abnormal preoccupation with their bodies and with illness. The *Dictionary of Behavioral Science* (Wolman, 1973) defined hypochondriasis as "an exaggerated and morbid concern with one's health often focused on a single organ and accompanied by the belief that one is plagued by serious bodily illnesses." Populations of elderly psychiatric patients are more likely to exhibit hypochondriasis, but this trait is also present in normal aged.

It is possible that since contemporary elderly have been socialized to deplore any kind of mental illness that they reformulate their complaints into what they perceive as the more acceptable physical complaints. Thus, their hypochondriasis is really a form of mental distress. Busse and Pfeiffer (1977) have suggested that hypochondriasis may be an escape from feelings of personal failure. It may be easier to tolerate the sick role than the role of failure. Hypochondriasis may be the preferred outlet for mental distress in contemporary elderly who feel that it is more socially acceptable to suffer from physical as opposed to mental disease. However, future cohorts of elderly may not opt for this form of symptom expression. The cross-sectional studies of age differences in personality traits which have shown greater hypochondriasis in the elderly may not be replicated in the future, and longitudinal studies using personality inventories may not find increases in hypochondriasis with age.

While we can only guess about future cohorts of elderly, our best guesses are based on the evidence we have at present. Because of the differences in socialization which have occurred during the twentieth century, people's attitudes about physical and mental illness have changed. Contemporary young adults appear to be more willing to admit to neurotic and socially unacceptable traits (Woodruff & Birren, 1972). Thus, they might be more willing to attribute distress to mental rather than physical causes. This hypothesis requires testing in the future, but from the present vantage point it would appear that age differences on the MMPI social introversion and depression scales may well reflect age changes on these dimensions. The age difference on the hypochondriasis scale is more likely to be simply a cohort difference which will not be expressed in future generations of the elderly.

Support for the interpretation that higher hypochondriasis scores in older adults result from cohort differences has been provided by Costa and associates (Costa & McCrae, 1985; Costa, Zonderman, McCrae et al., 1987). In a ten-year follow-up of almost 5,000 adults aged 24 to 74 in a national sample, Costa and associates found no changes over time in how older adults described their concerns about health. However, there were cross-sectional differences in health concern, with older adults having higher scores. The frequency of health problems increases with age, but these changes are to be expected. They do not lead to increased worry or concern about health in most people. The stability of psychological well-being and health concern scores which Costa et al. (1987) found in the ten-year longitudinal data provide striking support for the contention that aging individuals are not hypochondriacs.

CONSISTENCY AND CHANGE
IN ADULT PERSONALITY

After the many years of research which have been invested in the study of personality and aging, one of the major conclusions which can be drawn is that there is both consistency and change in personality over the adult years (Neugarten, 1977). On the one hand, there is pressure for continuity as an individual ages surrounded by family and friends who expect certain personality patterns from him or her. The self becomes an institution, and deviations from the normal self are not easily accepted. Change occurs in personality as a function of the individual's increasing repertoire of experience. It may also be paced by changes in health and the normal physical aging processes. We have already seen that changes in the central nervous system which result in the slowing of psychomotor speed may also be involved in behavioral patterns of rigidity. Introversion which is greater in older adults may also be influenced by physical changes including a decline in energy and vigor which make the individual less inclined to be socially oriented and more inclined to focus on the self.

Most of the previous discussion of personality traits in adulthood and old age has been based on cross-sectional data. In order to consider consistency and change in individuals, we must turn to longitudinal data. It is only by studying the same individuals over the span of their adult lives that we can really determine if they demonstrate consistency, change, or both.

The two main types of data collection procedures used in longitudinal studies of personality have been assessment with trait inventories of personality and less structured assessment in the form of interviews. Both of these types of studies are not without weaknesses. In the case of the personality inventories, important advances in the design and construction of these tests have been made since they were first used in the 1930s, but to make the longitudinal follow-up data consistent, the early tests initially administered must be used. Hence, we are sometimes limited by a 50- to 60-year-old inventory as to the kind of generalizations we can make. Longitudinal interview studies are often limited by lack of consistency in the questions which were asked and by changes in the interviewers. The rapport one interviewer may have with a subject may be different from the relationship between a second or third intereviewer. Thus, the data gathered under these differnt conditions may be unreliable. In spite of these problems, longitudinal personality data have provided valuable insights.

The Perspective from Personality Inventories

It has been pointed out by McCrae and Costa (1982) that personality inventories and scales can be interpreted as assessments of self-conceptions. These measures assess how an individual rates himself or herself on aspects of the personality provided by the investigator through the personality inventory.

General personality.   The remarkable result which has been repeatedly replicated in longitudinal studies using personality inventories is great consistency of personality during the adult years. Some of the earliest longitudinal data on a personality inventory were provided by Kelly (1955) in following up a group of almost 500 former college students who had been admitted to the sample only if they were an engaged couple. They were retested after 20 yeras of marriage. The Bernreuter Personality Inventory was used in addition to Strong's Interest Inventory, the Allport-Vernon Scale of Values, and Remmer's Generalized Attitude Scales. Values and interests showed the greatest stability over time while attitudes changed the most. The degree of stability of scales on the Bernreuter Personality Inventory was intermediate between the consistent values and interests and the less stable attitudes. Another interesting feature of this study was that the personalities of the married couples were compared to see if they had changed in the same manner or become more alike. Moderate or low positive correlations were observed between the engaged couples at the first testing, but 20 years later there was no increase in the congruencies between the partners.

A 25-year follow-up study over the early to middle-aged years of life was conducted by Woodruff and Birren (1972) using the California Test of Personality. College students tested in 1944 were found and retested in 1969. While many of the original subjects could not be located, the 1944 tests scores of the available subjects were not significantly different from the scores of lost subjects. This provided some evidence that the follow-up sample was representative.

The results of the Woodruff and Birren follow-up study were striking in demonstrating consistency of personality. Mean personality test scores for the men changed only five points (2.7 percent) and for the women the mean change was one point. In addition to the similarity of average scores for the group over the 25-year period, there was consistency in individuals' rankings within the group. The test-retest correlations give evidence of this. For the men this correlation was .58 and for the women it was .65. Individuals followed up in their mid-forties responded to a personality questionnaire very much in the same manner as they had answered it in their early twenties.

The personality consistency of this group was all the more remarkable when it was compared to a group of contemporary college students. The average personality test scores of college students tested in 1969 at the same university where the follow-up subjects had attended was 20 points different from the mean score of the follow-up group. This study indicated that cohort differences in personality test scores were large while age changes in personality were small. Studies such as this provide all the more reason to be suspicious of cross-sectional studies of personality as accurate reflections of the aging of personality.

Longitudinal personality measurement over the later adult years has also indicated stability. Schaie and Parham (1976) used the Cattell 16 PF to assess subjects ranging in age from 21 to 84. They were tested once in 1963 and followed up seven years later in 1970. Over this period, only one trait—excitability—appeared to increase systematically with age. As in the Woodruff and Birren study, larger and more cohort differences were found than age changes. One of the biggest cohort differences in this study was in introversion. Cohorts born earlier in the century tended to be more reserved and less outgoing. This led Schaie and Parham to question the assumption held by so many personality and aging specialists that introversion increases with age.

Another short-term longitudinal study using the 16 PF was carried out by Siegler, George and Okun (1979) on 331 men and women aged 54 to 70. The study represented a follow up over an eight-year period. Almost no age changes were observed in this sample and test-retest correlations were extremely high.

The Guilford-Zimmerman Temperament Survey was used in a longitudinal study of 915 men whose ages spanned the adult life cycle (Costa, McCrae & Arenberg, 1980; Douglas & Arenberg, 1978). Over a 12-year period only two traits showed change. As they grew older, the men reported being less masculine and their attitudes appeared less "macho" than in younger years. Activity level increased for men in the their twenties and then it showed decline in men over 50. Older men indicated a preference for a slower, more deliberate pace. Retest correlations of these men's scores were high. The retest correlation was .73 for the average scale and this correlation was raised to between .80 and 1.00 when it was corrected for the unreliability of the personality test.

In an overview of studies which used personality inventories to investigate adult personality, Bengtson, Reedy and Gordon (1985) concluded that correlational studies indicated considerable stability across wide age ranges in adulthood. In the longitudinal studies, introversion-extroversion and neuroticism in particular appeared quite stable over most of the adult life span. This is in contrast to the cross-sectional studies on introversion-extroversion previously reviewed. Indeed, another of Bengtson et al.'s conclusions was that cohort membership had a more significant impact than did maturation on personality. Gender, social/cultural trends, and life-stage experiences also had very significant impact on self-conceptions. Table 14.1 presents an overview of 13 longitudinal or cross-sequential studies which used personality scales over periods of adulthood as they were summarized by Bengtson et al. (1985).

Memory and the personality test.   The longitudinal studies of personality using personality trait inventories have provided evidence for impressive consistency in personality whether they have covered the early or the late portions of the adult life span. Mean scores on retest have been extremely similar and retest correlations have been high. These data have not been accepted without criticism. Skeptics have argued that the participants in these longitudinal studies may be motivated to give the appearance of consistency and may remember how they answered the personality inventory at the initial testing and replicate their answers.

This hypothesis about the role of memory in personality studies was tested by Woodruff (1983) who had follow-up data spanning a 25-year period. In addition to asking subjects to describe their own personality in the present on the California Test of Personality, Woodruff asked them to describe themselves as they had been when they were students in 1944. Under these conditions the subjects' mean scores were 11 to 18 points different from the scores they actually achieved in 1944, and the test-retest correlations for the 1944 actual and the 1969 attempt to replicate were .17 for the men and .45 for the women. These correlations were far lower than the correlations of .58 and .65 for men and women respectively which they achieved by simply describing themselves on both occasions. Thus, it appears that subjects cannot accurately remember how they answered a personality inventory on a previous occasion. They replicate their previous answers better if they respond describing themselves in the present than if they try and remember how they had responded in the past. These results suggest that the consistency which has been observed on longitudinal studies of personality in adulthood is real rather than an artifact of the test-retest design.

TABLE 14.1 Summary of Studies Using Personality Scales: Age Changes or Age Differences in the Cognitive Components of Self-Concepts

AUTHORS	SAMPLE	METHOD	VARIABLES	MEASURES	RESULTS
Bray and Howard (1983)	422 M Age in 20s, 1956–1960 266 M 20 year follow-up 204 M,F Age in 20s, 1977 (AT&T Longitudinal Studies of Managers)	Longitudinal × 20 years X-sectional Mean level	15 personality needs	Edwards Personal Preference Schedule	Age change on eight needs; need autonomy increased the most No cohort differences in need autonomy; cohort differences in need dominance
Costa and McCrae (1977–78)	104 M Age, 25–35 711 M Age, 35–54 118 M Age, 55–82 (Normative Aging Study)	Longitudinal × 10 years X-sectional Correlation	Anxiety/neuroticism Extraversion Openness to experience	16 PF	Correlational stability across age groups and over time for all three dimensions ($r = 0.58$ to 0.84 over 10 years)
McCrae, Costa, and Arenberg (1980)	114 M Age, 17–85; three age groups; three measurement points	X-Sequential × 12 years Correlation	10 personality variables	Guilford-Zimmerman Temperament Survey	Correlational stability across age groups and over time ($r = 0.59$ to 0.87 over 12 years)
Douglas and Arenberg (1978)	915 M Age, 17–98; tested 1958–74 336 M Retested seven years later (Baltimore Longitudinal Study)	X-Sequential × seven years Mean scores	10 personality variables	Guilford-Zimmerman Temperament Survey	Mean level stability with aging for emotional health and sociability Maturational decline in general activity and masculine interests Later born cohorts lower on restraint; higher on ascendance Period declines for thoughtfulness, personal relations, friendliness Significant attrition effects

Study	Sample	Design/Analysis	Variables	Instrument	Results
Kelly (1955)	227 couples Age, 25 and 45	Longitudinal × 20 years Mean scores Correlation	Many personality variables	Bernreuter Personality Inventory 36-Trait Personality Rating Scale	Mean level stability for most personality variables; decrease in energy Correlational stability for personality variables
Leon, Gillum, Gillum, and Gouze (1979)	71 M Age, 49–77; four measurement points	Longitudinal × 30 years Mean scores Correlation	MMPI Validity and Clinical Scales	MMPI	Mean level increases in depression, hypochondriasis, hysteria, and introversion Correlational stability, with extroversion most stable
McCrae, Costa, and Arenberg (1980)	769 M Age, 17–97 346 M Age, 25–91 171 M Age, 33–86 (Baltimore Longitudinal Study)	X-sequential × nine years; three measurement periods Factor analysis	Emotional health Extraversion Thinking introversion	Guilford-Zimmerman Temperament Survey	Structural stability of three factors in three age groups and across time
Schaie and Parham (1974)	2151 M,F Age, 21–84; independent X-sectional and repeated meas. data, tested in 1956, 1963, 1970	X-sequential Mean scores	Social responsibility	Social Responsibility Scale	Social responsibility showed a differential course over time as a function of cohort and sex
Schaie and Parham (1976)	2500 + F,M Age, 21–84; tested in 1963, 1970	X-sequential × seven years Mean scores	13 personality variables 6 attitudinal variables	75-Item Questionnaire	Maturation effects on two of 19 variables Cohort effects on 10 out of 19 variables Period effects on seven out of 19 variables

TABLE 14.1 (con't)

AUTHORS	SAMPLE	METHOD	VARIABLES	MEASURES	RESULTS
Whitbourne and Waterman (1979)	76 M, 71 F College age in 1966; Age 30 in 1976 224 F,M College age in 1976	Longitudinal × 10 years X-sectional Mean scores	Overall: Trust-mistrust Autonomy-shame Initiative-guilt Industry-inferiority Identity-diffusion Intimacy-isolation	Inventory of Psycho-social Development	Found maturational trend toward increased psychosocial development Period effects found to have differential impact on male-female development
Woodruff and Birren (1972)	85 M,F Age, 20 and 45; tested in 1944 and 1969 34 M,F Age, 19 43 M,F Age, 16; tested in 1969	Longitudinal × 25 years X-sectional Mean scores	Personal adjustment	California Test of Personality	No age-change in personal adjustment Cohort differences Subjective perception of positive change in the self

Psychological well-being.   Psychological well-being is another measure on inventories which has been shown to be stable over time (Costa et al., 1987). Psychologists have paid extraordinary attention to the topics of morale, life satisfaction, and psychological well-being (George, 1981; Larson, 1978; Liang, 1985; Nydegger, 1977). These measures are thought to assess quality of life, and as such, they are presumed to be useful in documenting the needs of elderly adults and identifying targets for interventions. Psychological well-being is an important indicator of the subjective experience of aging.

While literature reviews about psychological well-being have indicated that well-being does not decline with age (Larson, 1978), the stereotypical view of old age is a time of depression and dejection. It is believed that poor health reduces feelings of well-being and that health worries increase markedly. Lowered income due to retirement and death of loved ones are other life events more frequent in old age that have been assumed to lessen feelings of psychological well-being.

To explain the stability in overall levels of psychological well-being, some researchers have proposed the emotional blunting hypothesis (Malatesta, 1981; Schultz, 1985). This hypothesis stipulates that global well-being has both positive and negative components, and well-being is sometimes measured by subtracting the negative affect scale from the positive affect scale (Bradburn, 1969). It could be that older adults maintain a stable level of well-being because the frequency and intensity of both positive and negative emotions declines with age. The idea is that emotions become blunted in later life.

Costa et al. (1987) tested the emotional blunting hypothesis, and they also assessed age, cohort, and time of measurement effects in a large national sample of adults. A national probability sample of community-residing individuals aged 10 to 74 was surveyed at 100 locations in the 48 coterminous states of the United States between April 1971 and October 1975 (National Center for Health Statistics, 1973, 1978), and 14,407 of these individuals aged 24 and older were selected to be retested approximately ten years later between January 1981 and August 1984 (Cornoni-Huntley, Barbano, Broda et al., 1983). In-person interviews were conducted with 10,149 of these participatns. A subgroup of the first sample completed extensive psychological testing, and this procedure was also carried out on the follow up. Thus, there were 4,986 individuals ranging in age from 32 to 87 for whom there were data on psychological well-being.

Over the ten-year span of this large representative sample, there were no changes in psychological well-being. None of the age groups (younger than 35, 35–44, 45–54, older than 64) showed any longitudinal change on how they answered questions about: positive affect (e.g., "How happy, satisfied, or pleased have you been with your personal life during the past month?"); negative affect (e.g., "Have you been anxious, worried, or upset during the past month?"); health concern (e.g., "Have you been bothered by any illness, bodily disorder, pains, or fears about your health, during the past month?"); and on total well-being (negative subtracted for positive well-being score).

In the cross-sectional analysis, Costa et al. (1987) found age differences in the form of lower positive and negative affect which had the net result of making the total well-being score stable across birth cohorts. The fact that cross-sectional differences in positive and negative affect were not replicated by the longitudinal change analyses suggested to Costa and associates that cohort differences may have been responsible for the emotional blunting hypothesis. Individuals raised in earlier generations may be less willing to express their feelings, both positive and negative, than are later-born individuals.

Costa et al. summarized their results in the following manner:

> Viewed positively, the present data provide compelling evidence for the stability of levels of well-being in adulthood. To the extent that levels of well-being reflect the operation of underlying personality dispositions such as neuroticism and extroversion, the data also support the view that personality shows neither growth nor decline in adulthood (McCrae & Costa, 1984). If, as is widely believed, well-being measures also reflect the influence of recent life experiences, the findings of the present study suggest either that life on the whole neither improves nor worsens with age, or that individuals adapt quickly to whatever circumstances they find themselves in (Murrell et al., in press; Palmore et al., 1979) (Costa et al., 1987, p. 54).

The Perspective from Interviews

Longitudinal studies using the clinical interview method also suggest consistency in personality, but they present a more complex picture than the one presented by personality inventories. The staff of the Institute of Human Development at the University of California at Berkeley have evaluated personality over a 50-year period. Participants in the Oakland Growth Study and the Guidance Study who have had their personality assessed by clinical psychologists since early adolescence continue to be followed up as they reach their sixtieth birthdays and beyond. Haan, Millsap and Hartka (1986) reported on these long-term observations of personality made by professional observers rather than being the self-reports of the participants.

The California Q-sort technique was used by Haan et al. to study six major dimensions of personality called: self-confident/victimized, assertive/submissive, cognitively committed, outgoing/aloof, dependable, warm/hostile. Fifty years of observation on these six dimensions are summarized in Figure 14.1. The following is Haan et al.'s summary of their results:

> Considered in relation to unusual conceptualization of personality development, this complex array of findings presents a paradox. On the one hand, orderly progression seemed to occur: (a) when sex and sample were controlled, all of the dimensions but assertive had highly significant effects of time in analyses of repeated measures; (b) all of the dimensions except assertive had highly significant, unidirectional, accelerating trends.... But on the other hand, the usual supposition that personality develops in a linear and orderly fashion is plainly incorrect (1986, pp. 226–227).

Haan et al. observed relative stability of personality in childhood with substantial change occurring in adulthood up to late maturity. The adult changes were especially apparent in women.

When data archived in the Institute of Human Development are analyzed from the perspective of individual differences, there are certain personality characteristics which remain stable over long periods in the life span. One trait which appeared to show great consistency was an active, energetic style. Individuals who manifested this characteristic early in childhood tended to demonstrate it throughout adolescence and adulthood and on into later maturity.

That an active, energetic personality is maintained from adolescence through adulthood was also demonstrated in a sample of Harvard undergraduates who were followed through middle age (Von Eckartsberg, Burdick & Ono, 1959). A group of 103 undergraduates were evaluated on activity-passivity personality dimensions. Ratings were made on 25 dimensions involving vitality and energy level. Those 24 subjects scoring the highest on the ratings were called the "vital" group, and the 14 lowest scorers comprised the "bland" group. A follow-up of these men was carried out 20 years after the initial study when the subjects were in their forties. The degree to which these individuals were dynamic in their lives appeared to affect their whole careers. The differences between the groups in income, occupation, and social status were significant. Individuals in the vital group were far more likely to be at the top of their profession of chosen career while individuals in the bland group were less successful and had initially chosen less prestigious occupations. The active or passive personality pattern had remained consistent in these men and had dramatically affected their aspirations and achievement.

The consistency of that aspect of the personality which is energetic, extroverted and active has been observed in the Berkeley Growth studies which followed individuals from infancy and childhood, and it has also been observed in Von Eckartsberg's study over the early to middle adult years. Since this characteristic appears to be established early in the life span and remains stable over long periods, it has been suggested that vitality may be biologically or constitutionally determined. The vigor and energy level of an individual which determines the dynamic qualities of his or her personality may depend on physical health, metabolic rate, and the biological efficiency of the body. If extroverted, energetic personality characteristics are even partly related to peak physical efficiency, then it is not surprising that in later life when physical capacity is waning that we observe more introversion and less social interaction in many individuals.

Another clear documentation of the greater interiority in old age was provided by a series of studies carried out by a group of investigators from the University of Chicago (Neugarten and Associates, 1964). These studies are often called the Kansas City studies after the city in which they were conducted. The investigators used a multidimensional approach working with projective tests, questionnaires, and structured and unstructured interview data. A large and representative sample of individuals aged 40 to 80 was assessed over a ten-year period. The projective test data were summarized by Neugarten and Gutmann (1958). It was observed that there was a change from outer-world to inner-world orientation which was described as increased interiority. This result which was based primarily on projective test data was interpreted to support the personality trait inventory results indicating greater introversion in old age. Older people had a tendency to direct their perspective away from the external world and more into themselves.

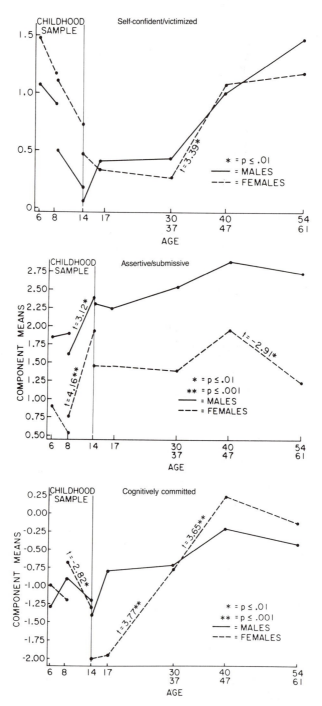

FIGURE 14.1 California Q-sort scores over a 50-year period on six major dimensions of personality. *Source:* Haan, N., Millsap, R. & Hartka, E. (1986). As time goes by: Change and stability in personality over fifty years. *Psychology and Aging, 1,* pp. 228–230, Copyright © 1986 American Psychological Association. Adapted by permission of the publisher and author.

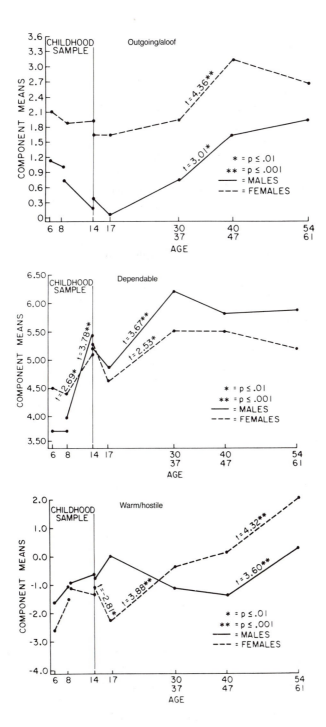

Another observation in this series of studies using projective tests was that a change from active to passive mastery in relating to the environment occurred. The elderly were more content to let things happen to them. The third conclusion was in the domain of sex differences. Older men became more receptive of their affiliative, emotional feelings while older women accepted more of their aggressive and egocentric impulses. In this manner older men and women were more accepting of personality characteristics of the opposite sex. They become more androgynous.

It is interesting to note how closely the empirical results of the Kansas City studies parallel the theoretical perspective on aging of the personality of Carl Jung. Unlike his mentor, Sigmund Freud, Jung was willing to consider the potential for personality change in adulthood and old age. Jung considered extroversion-introversion to be one of the major personality dimensions and on this basis of his analysis he concluded that in young adulthood there would be a balance favoring extroversion while in middle to old age introversion should predominate. He also considered the masculine-feminine dimensions and argued that in youth the individual tends to suppress all of the opposite-sex tendencies and emphasize the purely masculine or feminine characteristics. With age, the suppressed part of the personality emerges, and the individual becomes more tolerant of all aspects of his or her personality. Thus, Jung's analyses based on his interaction with patients and his brilliant insights have been supported by a number of independent empirical observations.

MODELS OF ADULT PERSONALITY

Until quite recently we had only two major psychosocial theories of personality which covered the adult years. These were Erik Erikson's psychosocial crisis theory in which he divided the life span into eight stages and identified major issues to be resolved at each point, and Robert Havighurst's developmental task theory in which he divided the life span into six periods and identified the tasks necessary to accomplish at each stage. Erikson's theory and to a lesser extent Havighurst's were primarily armchair theories. The theories were inductively derived on the basis of the theorists' insights about human development. The theories have generated research, and there has been support for some of the formulations. Indeed, the search for identity in adolescence as conceptualized by Erikson is accepted as an almost universal rite of passage. Thus, the theories have received wide application.

The models of adult personality which have been developed more recently have been derived directly from empirical evidence. The investigators conducted studies of adult personality and based their models on the results of their investigations. Three investigators who have used this approach are Roger Gould (1978), Daniel Levinson (1978) and George Vaillant (1977).

Gould was the only one of the three investigators who has developed models of pesonality over the adult years to base his conclusions on cross-sectional data.

He administered a questionnaire to a large group of middle-class individuals over the age range of 16 to 60, and he also got responses from a group of psychiatric outpatients (Gould, 1972). Results indicated that the central concerns of adolescence involved ambivalence about growing up and leaving home. In his model the central goal of young adulthood is establishment in a primary relationship, in an occupation, and in an appropriate social milieu.

Mid-life is viewed as a troubled time in which turmoil and uncertainty about the future abound. The individual is in a period of reassessment and often suffers personal discomfort at this point, according to Gould. Introspection increases, and the person becomes aware that he or she has a limited number of years left to live. The unstable period in mid-life gives way to more fulfillment in later life. Individuals entering their sixties are characterized as feeling new freedom and flowering after the turmoil of middle age.

The results and interpretation of the Levinson, Darrow, Klein, Levinson & McKee (1974) longitudinal study of 40 men in four occupational groups have probably received the most popular attention because his data and analysis provided the basis for the best seller *Passages*. Levinson interviewed blue-collar and white-collar workers, business executives, and academicians, and from their biographies he extracted generalizations about personality development in adulthood. In adolescence, the major task is to separate oneself from the family, both physically and psychologically. The twenties is a time for attempting to enter the adult world. Possibilities are explored, an initial life structure is developed, and an occupation and mate are chosen.

Deeper commitments to work, family, and valued interests are made in the thirties. This is a period for settling down. There is a desire for stability and security and to be free and unfettered of excessive outside commitments. The middle or late thirties often involve a desire to become one's own person. Relationships with mentors are terminated, and attempts to function independently of authority figures are made. The early forties is the time of mid-life transition. The disparity between achievements and aspirations leads to this unease. Major issues in this period include a sense of bodily decline, an increasing sense of personal mortality and aging, and a greater openness to formerly devalued parts of the self. This includes an openness to traits characteristic of the opposite sex. The middle to late forties involve restabilization. A new life structure emerges following the reassessment and reevaluation of the previous period.

A book has been written by Vaillant (1977) to report some of the extensive data from a 40-year longitudinal study of 268 men who have been followed since they were undergraduate students at Harvard between 1939 to 1944 (Vaillant & McArthur, 1972). Because of the composition of the sample, the study reveals the nature of personality development in adult men in the most favorable of circumstances. The results are based on clinical interview data. Not surprisingly, from young adulthood to middle age there is an increasing tendency to use mature as opposed to immature defense mechanisms. Thus, there is indeed a developmental progress of the personality in adulthood.

Middle age in this study was also observed to be a time of reassessment, a time for reordering the past, and a time of self-appraisal and depression. However, Vaillant observed positive affect in middle age as well. There was a renewed sense of personal vitality and an increasing ability to handle stress and change. The crises of middle age were not viewed as terribly painful or negative by these men. They accepted the turmoil as a normal part of this period of life, and many of the men judged as the best adjusted described the years between 35 and 49 as the best phase of their lives. The sense of the men's competence and mastery continued to grow as they were followed into their fifties along with their feelings of autonomy and authority. In these competent and privileged men, it becomes quite apparent that growth and development of the personality continues throughout adulthood.

The three models which have been described represent a consolidation of an extensive number of observations over time of adult personality. The two longitudinal studies were conducted only with men serving as subjects, and the generalizations are undoubtedly more appropriate for men than for women. Characteristic in all three studies was the period of stress and discomfort in mid-life, usually during the decade of the forties. Also characteristic was the resolution in the early fifties with increasing stability and even "flowering," according to Gould.

The point has been made by Schaie and Geiwitz (1982) that there is some scientific controversy over the extent and degree to which the mid-life crisis is experienced. Levinson (1978) argued that this crisis was experienced by 80 percent of his subjects, thus making it a very common event. Similarly, Gould (1978) and Vaillant (1977) report that the majority of individuals experienced distress during the forties. All of these studies used in-depth interview techniques to examine the experiences and feelings of the subjects.

Contrasted to these results are the findings of studies surveying job satisfaction, personal happiness, and life satisfaction (Bray & Howard, 1983; Cameron, 1975; Clausen, 1976; Palmore & Luikart, 1974). These studies found no evidence for crisis in middle age. For the most part the controversy appears to exist between investigations conducted with in-depth interviews and those using questionnaires on happiness and life satisfaction. Schaie and Geiwitz have suggested that the in-depth interviews may simply give respondents more of an opportunity to "bellyache." Furthermore, as Vaillant (1977) pointed out, the crisis may not be viewed as terribly stressful. Many of the men experienced stimulation from their difficulties. They viewed it as a challenge and an opportunity. Indeed, in Vaillant's study, a number of men reported this so-called crisis period as the happiest time of their lives.

What is especially apparent in Vaillant's descriptions covering the longest period of times in the men's lives is the dynamic quality of personality in adulthood. This quality emerges from all of the studies. Individuals continue to mature and change throughout adulthood. They face new concerns and are consumed with new issues with each succeeding decade of their adult years, and their capacity to deal with these matters appears to develop and mature.

Throughout most of the first parts of this chapter, we examined the cross-sectional data indicating that some personality traits showed age differences.

Evidence was also presented to suggest that it was more likely that these were cohort differences than age changes, although introversion may increase with age. Longitudinal data repeatedly emphasized stability in personality over long periods of the adult age span. The final section on models of adult personality adds an additional perspective. While people tend to show consistency in personality traits, their motivations and aspirations do change. Personality continues to mature. Coping strategies and decision making capacities change and grow during adulthood, making this period of life dynamic for the individual.

SUMMARY

Personality is the pattern of traits characterizing an individual person. In adulthood there appears to be both stability and change in personality. Cross-sectional studies of personality traits suggests that there are age differences in extroversion-introversion, with older adults becoming more introverted. Social introversion is greater in older adults, but this may be a cohort difference rather than an age change in personality. Longitudinal studies suggest consistency in individuals in the way they score on trait measures of extroversion-introversion. Age differences in rigidity clearly appear to be a cohort effect. Since all data indicating that older adults are more cautious than younger adults are cross-sectional, this result may also reflect cohort differences rather than age changes. Cohort differences on scales of depression and hypochondriasis have also been reported. The effect of cohort is very large on personality trait measures.

Longitudinal data on personality typically indicate stability over the adult age span. Personality inventory measures which assess self-conceptions and professional observations of personality over long periods of time suggest stability more than change. However, people subjectively report that they have changed, when given the opportunity to retrospectively report their personality adjustment. Psychological well-being also appears stable in adulthood and into old age.

Gould, Levinson, and Vaillant have developed models of adult personality which describe primarily how men adjust in young and middle adulthood. Characteristic of all models was a period of stress and discomfort in mid-life, usually during the decade of the forties. Resolution occurred in the early fifties with increasing stability at that time. Personality continues to mature. Growth and change in coping strategies and decision-making capacities occur during later adulthood, again emphasizing that there are dynamic factors in adult personality as well as stable ones.

REFERENCES

BENDIG, A. W. (1960).   Age differences in the interscale factor structure of the Guilford-Zimmerman Temperament Survey. *Journal of Consulting Psychology, 24,* 134–138.

BENGTSON, V. L., REEDY, M. N. & GORDON, C. (1985). Aging and self-conceptions: Personality processes and social contexts. In J. E. Birren & K. W. Schaie (Eds.). *Handbook of the psychology of aging* (2nd Ed.), New York: Van Nostrand Reinhold.

BIRREN, J. E. (1964). *The psychology of aging.* Englewood Cliffs, NJ: Prentice Hall.

BIRREN, J. E., BUTLER, R. N., GREENHOUSE, S. W., SOKOLOFF, L. & YARROW, M. R. (1963). *Human aging.* Washington, DC: U.S. Government Printing Office.

BOTWINICK, J. (1978). *Aging and behavior* (2nd Ed.), New York: Springer.

BOTWINICK, J. & THOMPSON, L. W. (1967). Depressive affect, speed of response, and age. *Journal of Consulting Psychology, 31,* 106.

BRADBURN, N. M. (1969). *The structure of psychological well-being.* Chicago: Aldine.

BRAY, D. W. & HOWARD, A. (1983). The AT&T longitudinal studies of managers. In K. W. Schaie (Ed.), *Longitudinal studies of adult psychological development.* New York: Guilford Press.

BRITTON, P. G. & SAVAGE, R. D. (1966). The MMPI and the aged: Some normative data from a community sample. *British Journal of Psychiatry, 112,* 941–943.

BROZEK, J. (1955). Personality changes with age: An item analysis of the MMPI. *Journal of Gerontology, 10,* 194–206.

BUSSE, E. W. & PFEIFFER, E. (1977). Functional psychiatric disorders. In E. W. Busse & E. Pfeiffer (Eds.), *Behavior adaptation in late life.* Boston: Little, Brown.

CALDEN, G. & HOKANSON, J. E. (1959). The influence of age on MMPI responses. *Journal of Clinical Psychology, 15,* 194–195.

CAMERON, P. (1975). Mood as an indicant of happiness: Age, sex, social class, and situational differences. *Journal of Gerontology, 30,* 216–224.

CATTELL, R. B. (1950). *Personality: A systematic, theoretical, and factual study.* New York: McGraw-Hill.

CHOWN, S. M. (1961). Age and the rigidities. *Journal of Gerontology, 16,* 353–362.

CHOWN, S. M. (1968). Personality and aging. In K. W. Schaie (Ed.), *Theory and method of research on aging.* Morgantown, WV: West Virginia University.

CHOWN, S. M. (1972). The effect of flexibility-rigidity and age on adaptability in job performance. *Industrial Gerontology, 13,* 105–121.

CLAUSEN, J. A. (1976). Glimpses into the social world of middle age. *International Journal of Aging and Human Development, 1,* 99–106.

CORNONI-HUNTLEY, J., BARBANO, H. E., BRODA, J. A., COHEN, B., FELDMAN, J. J., KLEINMAN, J. C. & MADANS, J. (1983). National Health and Nutrition Examination I—Epidemiologic Followup Survey. *Public Health Reports, 98,* 245–251.

COSTA, P. T., JR. & McCRAE, R. R. (1977–1978). Age differences in personality structure revisited: Studies in validity, stability and change. *International Journal of Aging and Human Development, 8,* 261–275.

COSTA, P. T., JR. & McCRAE, R. R. (1978). Objective personality assessment. In M. Storandt, I. C. Siegler, & M. F. Elias (Eds.), *The clinical psychology of aging.* New York: Plenum.

COSTA, P. T., JR. & McCRAE, R. R. (1985). Hypochondriasis, neuroticism, and aging: When are somatic complaints unfunded? *American Psychologist, 40,* 19–28.

COSTA, P. T., JR., McCRAE, R. R. & ARENBERG, D. (1980). Enduring dispositions in adult males. *Journal of Personality and Social Psychology, 38,* 793–800.

COSTA, P. T., JR., ZONDERMAN, A. B., McCRAE, R. R., CORNONI-HUNTLEY, J., LOCKE, B. Z. & BARBANO, H. E. (1987). Longitudinal analyses of psychological well-being in a national sample: Stability of mean levels. *Journal of Gerontology, 42,* 50–55.

CRAIK, F.I.M. (1964). An observed age difference in responses to a personality inventory. *British Journal of Psychology, 55,* 453–462.

CRAIK, F.I.M. (1969). Applications of signal detection theory to studies of ageing. In A. T. Welford (Ed.), *Interdisciplinary topics in gerontology, 4.* New York: S. Karger.

DOUGLAS, K. & ARENBERG, D. (1978). Age changes, cohort differences, and cultural change on the Guilford-Zimmerman Temperament Survey. *Journal of Gerontology, 33,* 737–747.

EISDORFER, C., AXELROD, S. & WILKIE, F. L. (1963). Stimulus exposure time as a factor in serial learning in an aged sample. *Journal of Abnormal and Social Psychology, 67,* 594–600.

FOZARD, J. L. (1972). Predicting age in the adult years from psychological assessments of abilities and personality. *Aging and Human Development, 3,* 175–182.

GEORGE, L. K. (1981). Subjective well-being: Conceptual and methodological issues. In C. Eisdorfer (Ed.), *Annual review of gerontology and geriatrics* (Vol. 2), New York: Springer:

GOULD, R. C. (1972). The phases of adult life: A study in developmental psychology. *American Journal of Psychiatry, 129,* 521–531.

GOULD, R. C. (1978). *Transformations.* New York: Simon & Schuster.

GUTMAN, G. M. (1966). A note on the MPI: Age and sex differences in extroversion and neuroticism in a Canadian sample. *British Journal of Social and Clinical Psychology, 5,* 128–129.

HAAN, N., MILLSAP, R. & HARTKA, E. (1986). As time goes by: Change and stability in personality over fifty years. *Psychology and Aging, 1,* 220–232.

HARDYCK, C. D. (1964). Sex differences in personality changes with age. *Journal of Gerontology, 19,* 78–82.

HEGLIN, H. J. (1956). Problem solving set in different age groups. *Journal of Gerontology, 11,* 310–317.

HERON, A. & CHOWN, S. N. (1967). *Age and function.* London: Churchill.

KELLY, E. L. (1955). Consistency of the adult personality. *American Psychologist, 10,* 659–681.

KORCHIN, S. J. & BASOWITZ, H. (1957). Age differences in verbal learning. *Journal of Abrnomal and Social Psychology, 54,* 64–69.

LARSON, R. (1978). Thirty years of research on the subjective well-being of older Americans. *Journal of Gerontology, 33,* 109–125.

LEVINSON, D. J. (1978). *The seasons of a man's life.* New York: Knopf.

LEVINSON, D. J., DARROW, C. N., KLEIN, E. G., LEVINSON, M. H. & McKEE, B. (1974). The psychosocial development of men in early adulthood and the mid-life transition. In D. F. Ricks, A. Thomas, & M. Roff (Eds.), *Life history research in psychopathology* (Vol. 3). Minneapolis: University of Minnesota Press.

LIANG, J. (1985). A structural integration of the Affect Balance Scale and the Life Satisfaction Index. *Journal of Gerontology, 40,* 552–561.

MALATESTA, C. Z. (1981). Affective development over the lifespan: Involution of growth? *Merrill-Palmer Quarterly, 27,* 143–173.

McCRAE, R. R. & COSTA, P. R., JR. (1982). Self-concept and the stability of personality: Cross-sectional comparisons of self-reports and ratings. *Journal of Personality and Social Psychology, 43,* 1282–1292.

McCRAE, R. R. & COSTA, P. R., JR. (1984). *Emerging lives, enduring dispositions: Personality in adulthood.* Boston: Little, Brown.

McCRAE, R. R. & COSTA, P. R., JR. & ARENBERG, D. (1980). Constancy of adult personality structure in males: Longitudinal, cross-sectional, and times-of-measurement analysis. *Journal of Gerontology, 35,* 877–883.

MISCHEL, W. (1973). Towards a cognitive social learning reconceptualization of personality. *Psychological Review, 80,* 252-283.

MURRELL, S. A., HIMMELFARB, S., & PHIFER, J. F. (in press). Effects of bereavement/loss and pre-event status on subsequent physical health in older adults. *Aging and Human Development.*

NATIONAL CENTER FOR HEALTH STATISTICS. (1973). *Plan and operation of the Health and Nutrition Examination Survey: United States, 1971-1973.* (DHEW Publication No. PHS 79-1310), Washington, DC: U.S. Government Printing Office.

NATIONAL CENTER FOR HEALTH STATISTICS. (1978). *Plan and operation of the HANES I Augmentation Survey of Adults 25-27 Years: United States, 1974-1975.* (USDHEW Publication No. PHS 78-1314), Washington, DC: U.S. Government Printing Office.

NEUGARTEN, B. L. (1977). Personality and aging. In J. E. Birren & K. W. Schaie (Eds.), *Handbook of the psychology of aging.* New York: Van Nostrand Reinhold.

NEUGARTEN, B. L. & ASSOCIATES. (1964). *Personality in middle and late life.* New York: Atherton.

NEUGARTEN, B. L. & GUTMANN, D. L. (1958). Age-sex roles and personality in middle age: A thematic apperception study. *Psychological Monographs: General and Applied, 17,* whole no. 470.

NYDEGGER, C. N. (Ed.) (1977). *Measuring morale: A guide to effective assessment.* Washington, DC: Gerontological Society.

PALMORE, E. B., CLEVELAND, W. P., JR., NOWLIN, J. B., RAMM, D. & SIEGLER, I. C. (1979). Stress and adaptation in later life. *Journal of Gerontology, 34,* 841-851.

PALMORE, E. & LUIKART, C. (1974). Health and social factors related to life satisfaction. In E. Palmore (Ed.), *Normal aging II.* Durham, NC: Duke University Press.

POTASH, M. & JONES, B. (1977). Aging and decision criteria for the detection of tones and noise. *Journal of Gerontology, 32,* 436-440.

REES, J. & BOTWINICK, J. (1971). Detection and decision factors in auditory behavior of the elderly. *Journal of Gerontology, 26,* 133-136.

SCHAIE, K. W. (1958). Rigidity-flexibility and intelligence: A cross-sectional study of the adult life span from 20 to 70 years. *Psychological Monographs, 72,* no. 9.

SCHAIE, K. W. & GEIWITZ, J. (1982). *Adult development and aging.* Boston: Little, Brown.

SCHAIE, K. W. & LABOUVIE-VIEF, G. (1974). Generational versus ontogenetic components of change in adult cognitive behavior: A fourteen-year cross-sequential study. *Developmental Psychology, 10,* 305-320.

SCHAIE, K. W., LABOUVIE, G. V. & BUECH. B. U. (1973). Generational and cohort-specific differences in adult cognitive functioning. *Developmental Psychology, 9,* 151-166.

SCHAIE, K. W. & PARHAM, I. A. (1976). Stability of adult personality traits: Fact or fable? *Journal of Personality and Social Psychology, 34,* 146-158.

SCHULZ, R. (1985). Emotion and affect. In J. E. Birren & K. W. Schaie (Eds.), *Handbook of the psychology of aging.* (2nd ed.), New York: Van Nostrand Reinhold.

SEALY, A. P. & CATTELL, R. B. (1965). Standard trends in personality development in men and women of 16 to 70 years, determined by 16 PF measurements. Paper read at the British Psychological Society Conference, London, April.

SIEGLER, I. C., GEORGE, L. K. & OKUN, M. A. (1979). Cross-sequential analysis of adult personality. *Developmental Psychology, 15,* 350-351.

SLATER, P. E. & SCARR, H. A. (1964). Personality in old age. *Genetic Psychology Monographs, 70,* 229-269.

SWENSON, W. M. (1961). Attitudes toward death in an aged population. *Journal of Gerontology, 16,* 49-52.

THORNDIKE, E. L., BREGMEN, E. O., TILTON, J. W. & WOODYARD, E. (1928). *Adult learning.* New York: Macmillan.

VAILLANT, G. E. (1977). *Adaptation to life.* Boston: Little, Brown.

VAILLANT, G. E. & McARTHUR, C. C. (1972). Natural history of male psychological health: The adult life cycle from eighteen to fifty. *Seminars in Psychiatry, 4,* 415–427.

VON ECKARTSBERG, R., BURDICK, H. A. & ONO, H. (1959). Two experiments in social power. *Psychology Reports, 5,* 781–789.

WOLMAN, B. B. (Ed.), (1973). *Dictionary of behavioral science.* New York: Van Nostrand Reinhold.

WOODRUFF, D. S. (1983). The role of memory in personality continuity: A 25-year follow-up. *Experimental Aging Research, 9,* 31–34.

WOODRUFF, D. S. & BIRREN, J. E. (1972). Age changes and cohort differences in personality. *Developmental Psychology, 6,* 252–259.

CHAPTER 15

Work and Retirement

Work and retirement are extremely significant aspects in the lives of adults as they age. The work of an individual shapes his or her daily schedule of activities and contributes greatly to life satisfaction. Employment sets the stage for growing old by contributing to a sense of identity for most men and for an increasing number of women. It also affects the health and income of an individual, and these are two major determinants of adjustment and satisfaction in later life. Retirement is a major event in the life of an adult. It involves a total shift in the activity pattern of the individual, and it may represent a significant change in economic status. Symbolically, it signifies the transition into old age. The event of retirement, whether viewed as a crisis or a normal part of aging, demonstrates to the individual and to society that a major role shift has transpired.

Retirement and aging are often viewed as synonymous in contemporary society. However, this was not the case in the past, and it is not likely to be the case in the future. Retirement was created in Western Europe in the nineteenth century at a time when almost none of the working population survived to the age of 65 let alone 70, which was the age at which retirement was first set. In the United States in the twentieth century, retirement has become a major institution as a result of the increasing life expectancy of the population and the shift from an agrarian to an industrialized economy. The rising standard of living in the twentieth century along with the relatively greater number of younger workers permitted the growth of retirement to an almost universal rite of passage.

At present, retirement might be considered an institution under attack. The problems with the system of mandatory retirement at the age of 65 come from a number of sources. First, life expectancy has risen dramatically. The great majority of individuals will live to the age of 65, and life expectancy at 65 is 14.5 years for men and 18.6 years for women. This means that half the population of 65-year-olds will live longer by 14 to 18 years and will need to sustain and entertain themselves in those years of retirement.

Another problem for the retirement system is the result of continuing inflation which has rendered what appeared to be an affluent retirement income to an inadequate means of support. Furthermore, Social Security and pension systems are buckling under the pressure of the greater numbers and longevity of the retired. Finally, the declining birth rates in the decades of the sixties through the eighties have supplied a far smaller number of young workers to support the retirement system as it was initially structured. Thus, to be old and to be retired may be a status which will be abolished by the twenty-first century. Those born in the post-World War II baby boom generation and later may find that they have to work to the age of 75 or more. Employment may become a necessity in later life as well as in the middle years.

In order to understand the influences of work and retirement on adulthood and aging, we will first examine some of the attributes of employment and changing patterns of employment for men and women. Then we will look at the institution of retirement, first from a historical perspective and then as it impacts contemporary retirees and how it may be reshaped in the future. A final section will examine leisure time and activities and how they relate to employment and retirement in the adult years.

WORK

Work has a central role in the life of most adults. Indeed, Troll (1982) stated that adulthood itself (at least for men) is defined by working at a job. Some of the multiple factors determined by type of employment include the location and expense of the home, the style, quality, and amount of clothing, the hours of awakening and going to sleep, the kind and quality of food, the people with whom individuals meet and interact, friends, recreational activities, and membership in organizations. Personal identity, feelings of self-worth, and health are affected by employment. Not only has life expectancy been found to be related to occupation, life expectancy of the spouse is also correlated with the worker's occupation (Woodruff, 1977). Throughout most of adulthood, life is organized around work.

McConnell (1983) has asserted that employment is one means of enhancing the economic well-being of older persons. Also, it is a means for rescuing the fiscally unsound Social Security and private pension systems. If the average retirement age is not increased, the retiree-to-worker ratio which is called the dependency ratio will decline over the next 30 years from three workers for each retiree to only two workers per retiree. Social Security is a system constructed so that workers' contributions at the present time are immediately transferred to present-day retirees. The problem created by the change in the dependency ratio is that fewer workers will have to pay higher taxes to support those who are retired. The other alternative is to reduce benefits for the retirees. Neither of these solutions is satisfactory, and employment of older workers appears to be a more appealing solution.

Toward the goal of retaining individuals in the work force longer, Congress amended the Age Discrimination in Employment Act (ADEA) in 1978 to raise the mandatory retirement age from 65 to 70 in the private sector. For most federal employees, the mandatory retirement age was abolished. Legislators such as Congressman Claude Pepper have worked to abolish all upper age limitations for employment in the private sector as well. The 1978 amendments to the ADEA also expanded protection for workers in the age range of 40 to 70. In some states and in some companies, the mandatory retirement age for the private sector has also been eliminated. Nevertheless, the average retirement age has continued to decline as an increasing number of middle-aged and older workers choose to retire early.

The main reason that individuals are choosing to retire earlier rather than taking advantage of their right to work to the age of 70 or beyond is that there are financial incentives to do so. For example, under the directives of the 1978 Age Discrimination in Employment Act, employers are permitted to freeze all contributions and accrual of pension benefits at the age of 65. Social Security allows only a 3 percent increase in benefits for each additional year worked beyond the age of 65.

McConnell (1983) argued that to be actuarially fair, the benefit increase should be as high as 7 to 9 percent per year. Another means by which Social Security discourages continued employment beyond the age of 65 is called the "retirement test." Wages earned above a fixed limit cause the individual to receive less than his or her full Social Security benefit. Private pensions provide similar disincentives for working beyond the age of 65 (Bankers Trust Company, 1980).

After reviewing the policies affecting employment of older workers, McConnell concluded:

> Thus, older workers are confronted with mixed messages. The ADEA protects their right to continue working until age 70 in most jobs (and indefinitely in federal jobs), but Social Security and private pensions provide strong incentives to leave the labor force early. Moreover, those who retire and find they cannot make ends meet financially are confronted with age discrimination, inadequately funded jobs programs and, via the Social Security retirement test, economic disincentives to work after retirement. A consistent set of policies guiding work and retirement decisions is needed. If an early retirement age is desirable then retirement income systems should provide an adequate and inflation-proof income for all retirees. If, on the other hand, later retirement is desirable, incentives should be developed to delay retire-

ment, and all obstacles to continued work should be eliminated (McConnell, 1983, p. 344).

Trends in Employment
of Older Workers

As pointed out by McConnell (1983) and others, there are a large number of disincentives to work in old age. Thus, it is not surprising that the number of older persons choosing to remain in the work force is declining. Indeed, labor force participation among those 65 and over has declined dramatically since 1950, and there has also been a decline in the percentage of individuals working in the 60 to 64 age bracket (Sheppard, 1977). Total labor force participation rate for those 65 and over has declined by 50 percent since 1950.

By far the greatest proportion of the change in labor force participation is accounted for by men leaving the labor force. The rate for women over 65 in the labor force between 1950 and 1980 remained almost stable. In the 55 to 64 age group the rate of participation for men over the last three decades has declined by 16 percent. However, during that same period, the employment rate for women aged 55 to 64 has increased by 50 percent. Thus, the net change in employment rate for this age group is negligible. Employment for women in the 45 to 54 age group has shown a comparable increase.

Labor force participation by women is touted as a new phenomenon by Sheppard (1976). He stated that the growth of paid employment among women over the past quarter century is of great import in industrial gerontology. From 1947 to 1973, women's rate of participation in the work force of the United States increased at a rate of over 40 percent. During this time male participation rates declined at a rate of over 8 percent. Such major changes in activity of large segments of the population undoubtedly will have significant impact on patterns of aging for both men and women. Reasons for the great increase in women's participation in the work force include the changing social values regarding acceptable roles for women, declining home responsibilities resulting from decreased family size and automization of household chores, increasing numbers of families living in urban areas which offer more employment opportunities, the increasing cost of living along with the rise in expectations for a higher standard of living requiring two wage-earners per family, rise in divorce rates, and increasing availability of jobs to women.

Some occupations appear to lend themselves to employment over longer periods of the work life while other occupations are associated with earlier retirement. Table 15.1 identifies rate of employment in various occupations by individuals between the ages of 58 to 63. It can be seen that people working in professional capacities are far more likely to remain in their jobs than are people working as laborers. Older workers are less likely to be involved with physically demanding jobs. It is easier to remain employed as a self-employed professional such as a physician or to continue running one's own farm. In both cases the individual can choose

TABLE 15-1   1969 Labor Force Participation of Men 58-63,
by Occupation

Occupation of Longest Job	Percent in Labor Force
Professional	9
Farmer	88
Manager	87
Clerical	83
Sales	89
Craftsmen	84
Operative	79
Service	79
Farm Laborer	76
Nonfarm Laborer	73

Source: Schwab, 1974.

when to retire with no external guidelines regarding the age at which retirement should take place.

In addition to being concentrated in certain occupations, older workers are also more likely to be working part time. Deuterman and Brown (1978) reported that 39 percent of men and 54 percent of women over 65 had part-time jobs. While part-time work may be more satisfactory for older workers, the wages for this type of employment tend to be considerably less than the wages for full-time work.

Multiple Careers

At a point in history when the work-life expectancy of an individual may be 50 or more years, it is becoming increasingly common to change occupations and embark on a second or third career. In the case of a man, this can involve learning several occupations or professions sequentially, and in the case of a woman it might mean moving from working as a housewife to becoming employed outside the home. Often the choice to begin a second career is forced due to technological change and worker obsolescence. In one survey, just over a third of the employees expressed an interest in second careers (Sheppard & Belitsky, 1966). The investigators found that those most interested in a career change were different from their colleagues who wanted to maintain the status quo in that they showed more interest in the social-psychological characteristics of jobs, and they also tended to have higher achievement motivation. Those seeking a change also had lower perceived mobility chances and lower job satisfaction.

With regard to the issue of multiple careers, Troll stated:

> Multiple careers may be related to personal development and creativity if they include opportunities for acquiring new perspectives. It may be that there is an optimal duration for any one pursuit. After 15 years, for instance, a person may have "drawn out" all the "juice" from one activity but may start a whole new cycle of creativity by shifting to a different arena. Some of the dramatic productivity of women in recent years who have returned to careers after a period spent in child rearing sug-

gests that regular switching of arenas of achievement may encourage cognitive and creative development in many people (Troll, 1982, p. 187).

RETIREMENT

Retirement has become so common in Western society in the last several decades that many accept it as a univesal phenomenon which has been occurring throughout history. When we examine the history of retirement, we find that this is not the case. Retirement is a relatively new rite of passage which is neither universal nor long established. It is only really since the mid-twentieth century that we have had large cohorts of retired individuals in the population. Until quite recently, people simply did not live long enough to retire.

While it is commonly understood that by retirement it is meant that an individual is no longer gainfully employed, it may be useful to be more specific about how we are using the term *retirement* in this discussion. The definition used by McConnell (1983) will be adopted. Retirement is defined as the point at which a person (1) withdraws fully or partially from the labor force *and* (2) begins collecting a pension, Social Security benefits or other retirement income. Both conditions must be met in order to qualify as retirement. Excluded in this definition are individuals who retire from one job with a pension but accept another full-time job, individuals who reduce their work hours but do not begin drawing retirement income, and individuals who never worked in the first place.

History

The actual creation of retirement as an officially designated event has been attributed to the German Chancellor Otto von Bismarck. In 1891 Chancellor von Bismarck enacted the Old Age and Survivors Pension Act. This established the age of 70 as the retirement age (Meier & Dittmar, 1979). However, very few German workers survived to the age of 70 to receive their pension. It was a law that presented the government in a favorable light to workers while it did almost nothing for them.

The push for legislation for economic security in old age in the United States began after World War I when a government-sponsored national pension system was sought. However, it was not until the Great Depression in the 1930s that the country really seriously considered the plight of its older citizens. In 1935 the Social Security Act became law, and this was the first step in the United States toward providing support for the elderly. At the same time this act provided some economic security to individuals aged 63 and older, it also set into motion a trend toward labor force exit at or before the age of 65 (McConnell, 1983).

It is quite apparent that retirement is a twentieth-century phenomenon and that large numbers of individuals were not involved in retirement until the mid-twentieth century. The history of retirement has closely paralleled the history of industrialization in the United States and in other Western European nations. In an agrarian economy, retirement is not an issue as it is possible and desirable for an individual to labor until he or she goes to the grave. Prior to industrialization, workers were tied to their jobs because of the need for their labor and also because they simply could not afford to retire.

McConnell (1983) identified four forces which acted simultaneously during the period of American industrialization to create an atmosphere conducive to the emergence of retirement as an institution. The first major economic force was the decline in the demand for labor. This trend began in the 1870s and reached its peak with 30 percent unemployment in the Great Depression. A second important trend in industrialization was the rapid technological transformations in industry which led to major changes in the kinds of skills which were required of workers. This meant that many of the skills of older workers were obsolete. It appeared cheaper to train young, new workers than to retrain old, former employees. A third trend which facilitated the firing of older workers was the growth of large-scale bureaucracies with impersonal rules and regulations governing all aspects of employment policies including the retirement decision. The fourth force that existed almost as a sanction for terminating older workers was the growth of private pensions and Social Security. These funds provided an economic base to supoprt retirement.

As a consequence of the forces which have been described along with the increasing life expectancy of the population, the rate of individuals retiring increased dramatically during the 1950s. In 1900 more than 60 percent of men over the age of 65 were in the labor force. By 1950 only 39 percent of retirement-aged men were working, and by the 1980s only 20 percent in the over-65 age bracket were employed.

In absolute numbers of older workers, the figures have not changed as dramatically as indicated by the statistics just presented. At the turn of the century only 4 percent of the population was over the age of 65. By 1980, over 11 percent of a much greater population was over the age of 65. Thus, the actual number of men over the age of 65 who are working in the 1980s is about twice the number of men in the same age group working in 1900. Nevertheless, a major trend toward retirement has taken place in this century with the majority of men over 65 remaining on the job in 1900, while the vast majority of contemporary men retire.

Changes have continued to take place in the policies governing retirement. In 1956 legislation enabling women to retire at the age of 62 with reduced Social Security benefits was enacted. This early retirement "opportunity" was extended to men in 1961. These new provisions along with the expansion of benefits such as disability and private pensions have led to a decrease in the labor force participation among those younger than 65. Between 1950 and 1979 the labor force participation rates for men aged 55 to 64 declined by 16 percent. During this same period the labor force participation for men aged 45 to 54 declined by 5 percent. Thus, in the latter half of the twentieth century we are seeing retirement among the middle-aged as well as among those 65 and over.

The employment and retirement cycle for women is quite different from the pattern reported for men. While men in the age range of 45 to 64 are leaving the work force at an increasing rate, women in that age range are actually increasing their rate of employment. Many women reenter the work force when they are in this age range. Since 1950 women between the ages of 45 to 64 have increased their participation in the work force by 50 percent. In spite of the fact that women are returning to work later in their lives, they still tend to retire at the age of 65. Thus, in 1979 only 8.3 percent of all women continued working beyond the age of 65.

The Decision to Retire

Making the decision to retire is one of the major steps in later life. Employees seek to make this decision in a fashion which will provide them with the most social and economic benefits, and employers attempt to understand the determinants of this decision so that they can maintain control over the composition of their labor forces. In this manner they provide either incentives or disincentives for retirement.

There are many reasons for making the decision to retire. Some workers are bored or dissatisfied with their jobs while others are in such poor health that they simply cannot continue to work. Others are forced off the job by mandatory retirement, and still others are lured to retire by lucrative pension benefits. The pace of the retirement decision also varies. Some plan for many years for their retirement while others retire unexpectedly due to a sudden change in health, family relationships or company policies.

One reason that the retirement decision is so varied is that the age at which people retire has a wide range. Four age categories for retirement have been described by McConnell (1983). These include the very early retirement (younger than age 61), early retirement (62–64), normal retirement (65), and late retirement (66 or older). McConnell has described how each retirement category has associated with it a unique set of causes.

Very early retirement. Retirement before the age of 61 represents one of the most interesting and complex phenomena in the study of retirement. There appear to be several very different groups who retire at this time of their lives, according to one longitudinal study conducted by the University of Michigan (Morgan, 1980). In that study very early retirees were either in good health with high incomes or in poor health with low incomes. Those in the fortunate group retired because they were sufficiently affluent to do so. Those in the other group were forced to retire due to poor health. Kingson (1979) found that the majority of very early retirees were in the second category, and a large number of them died within a few years of retirement.

There is a third category of retirees falling into the very early retirement group which has little in common with the retirees described previously. These are employees in hazardous occupations. In the case of fire fighters, police officers, airline pilots, and bus drivers, very early retirement is typically mandatory. In the cases of these occupations, age is considered to be part of the occupational qualification. The quick reflexes and strength essential to these occupations have been observed to change enough with age so that the older worker can no longer qualify. Thus, individuals in these occupations retire after 20 to 30 years of service, and often before they are 50 years of age.

Early retirement.   It has been documented by the Social Security Administration (1980) that most workers retire between the ages of 62 and 64. More than two thirds of all workers covered by Social Security accepted reduced benefits for early retirement in 1979. The most typical age for retirement in that year was 62.

In one large study of employees in the auto industry, the major determinants in the decision to retire early appeared to be finances, health, retirement attitudes, and job-related attitudes (Barfield & Morgan, 1975). The single most important factor in early retirement decisions was finances. There was a high correlation between expected retirement income and plans for retirement. The higher the expected retirement income, the higher the probability that there were plans for early retirement. The converse of this result was found by Morgan (1980). Inadequate or unstable income acted as a deterrent to early retirement.

In the case of early retirement, health is often an important factor in the decision. Jacobsen (1972) reported in a study of 145 British male factory workers that 80 percent of those who reported themselves to be in poor health wanted to retire, while 70 percent of those reporting good health wanted to continue working beyond retirement age. Nearly two thirds of older men who were not working reported some type of chronic health problem (Bowen & Finegan, 1969). In a longitudinal study sponsored by the Department of Labor it was found that workers who reported health limitations in a 1966 survey were more likely to be out of the labor force in a 1973 survey (Sheppard, 1977). The relationship between health and retirement is significant regardless of the age at retirement, and this issue will be explored more fully in a later section of this chapter.

While attitudes are important in the decision to retire, they appear to run a distant third place in significance when compared to finances and health. Job dissatisfaction can play a role in the decision to retire early, but only if adequate retirement income is assured. In a study of nonacademic employees at a university medical center it was found that it was only when the job was of prime importance as the central organizing factor of the individual's life that it affected retirement attitude (Fillenbaum, 1971). Thus, early retirement occurs when retirement income is anticipated to be adequate, health is perceived to be poor, or attitudes toward retirement are very positive. Job dissatisfaction affects the decision to retire early only if the job is of central importance to the individual.

Normal retirement.   The concept of retirement is almost synonymous with the age of 65. Indeed, when undergraduates are asked to name the point in life at which old age begins, they almost invariably say the age of 65. This is because we have literally legislated old age and retirement to begin at that time. It is interesting then that with the availability of early retirement benefits from Social

Security and private pensions, fewer workers are remaining in the work force until the age of 65. The "normal" age for retirement is becoming abnormal.

Although there is a trend on the one hand for increasing numbers of individuals to retire early and on the other hand for Congress to push the mandatory retirement age to 70, the age of 65 still retains social significance. Social Security pays full retirement benefits at the age of 65 and not before. Legislation governing private pension plans also uses the age of 65 as the point in the work life of the individual that pension plan benefits reach maturity. Furthermore, employers are permitted to discontinue contributions to an employee's pension at the age of 65 even though the mandatory retirement age has been set at 70. As has been mentioned previously, this discrepancy in the law is one of the factors resulting in retirement by the age of 65, as to go on working beyond that point with no further pension contributions on the part of the employer is to take a decrease in salary.

Late retirement. Individuals who prefer to continue working beyond the age of 65 tend to come from the professional occupational levels and they also are frequently self-employed. These are usually individuals who are committed and invested in their work and who prefer being on the job to a life of leisure. A study of older members of the Writers Guild of America revealed that many television, motion picture and radio writers over the age of 60 viewed retirement as dull when compared to the lives they were currently leading. Fully a third of these self-employed professionals wanted to continue working as long as they possibly could (McConnell & Fiske, 1980).

In a summary of the factors affecting the retirement decision, McConnell stated:

> Thus, the decision to retire is influenced by many factors. Economics plays a central role, both for its direct impact on perceptions about the feasibility of retirement and indirectly as a contributor to worker health and job satisfaction. Health is the second most important influence on retirement decisions. Poor health, when it is combined with an adequate retirement income, results in early or very early retirement. In contrast, poor health and an inadequate income tends to delay retirement, out of necessity. Attitudes about retirement and work enter into the decision process, but often only indirectly. For example, those who work at physically demanding or stressful jobs tend to retire early because they are less satisfied with their jobs, whereas those who are self-employed retire late, largely due to higher levels of job satisfaction. Mandatory retirement provisions affect only a minority of workers, but retirement income policies are often discriminatory and discourage most workers from continuing beyond age 65 (McConnell, 1983, p. 339).

Retirement and Mortality

There have been a number of studies comparing the mortality of older workers who stayed on the job to the mortality of those who retired. All of these studies, regardless of the occupation involved, demonstrated that life expectancy was shorter for the retired individuals. More of the retirees died, and right after retirement the death rate was particularly high. Thus, it became common in medical folklore to believe that an individual who was forced to retire would die much earlier than if he or she were allowed to continue working. Retirement was seen as a stress which had deleterious physiological consequences which often proved fatal before the individual could adapt to the new life style. The individual lost income, companionship, activity and stimulation, prestige, and identity, and these losses proved overwhelming.

While this retirement impact theory still has some adherents, it is generally believed that the studies demonstrating a relationship between retirement and death are seriously flawed because the health of the retirees was never considered. The reason many people retire early is because they are in poor health and can no longer go on working. Thus, when the life expectancy of the people who have retired due to poor health is compared to the life expectancy of people who have been able to continue working, it is not surprising that the workers live longer. Retirement has been the *result* rather than the cause of poor heath, and poor health results in an earlier death for the retirees. From the studies which have been carried out specifically on retirement and longevity, there is no conclusive evidence that retirement causes death. It appears more likely that people who are nearer to death choose to retire because their poor health precludes them from working longer.

But what about those individuals who are faced with mandatory retirement? Is it possible that they would live longer if allowed to continue in what they considered to be a productive work role? This is a question to which we do not have the answer, although some prominent longevity experts believe that retirement may cause early death. It is highly likely, however, that retirement has different effects on different kinds of people.

Adjustment to retirement is associated with a number of variables including income after retirement, health, and leisure activity. Other factors undoubtedly influencing how much of an impact retirement has on health and longevity are dependent on the extent a person derived his or her identity and enjoyment from the job and the number of interesting alternative hobbies and activities an individual has to occupy his or her time and interest after retirement. There may be some people who could be considered at high risk for health problems after retirement because their occupation was the center of their lives and their life outside of the job was not very interesting to them. It has been shown that white-collar workers find retirement more stressful immediately after they leave their job than blue-collar workers, but appear to adjust well several years later (Rowe, 1972). Blue-collar workers are happy to retire, but they become bored with retirement after several years (Streib & Schneider, 1971). Thus, individual patterns may dispose some people to suffer after retirement, but it is not clear that the difficulty in adjustment is stressful enough to cause death.

In recent years people seem to anticipate retirement and to plan for it. They are better prepared financially, their health is generally better, and they have developed leisure time hobbies and interests to carry them into retirement. More firms have established preretirement counseling and have prepared their employees and their families for the transition from work to leisure.

There is no question that people today anticipate retirement more than they have in the past because retirement has become more widespread. However, it is not clear that people enjoy retiring any more in the 1980s than they did in earlier decades. Indeed, many fought mandatory retirement as individuals in the courts and as lobbying groups in Congress. They were successful inasmuch as the mandatory retirement age has been increased, but financial incentives are such that more people are retiring at younger rather than older ages.

While it is not clear that retirement leads to an earlier death, it is certain that having a meaningful, fulfilling life in the later years is associated with longer life. Thus, if we can develop a system both as individuals and as a society that provides for a meaningful and productive existence at all points of the life span, it will aid in the goal of maximizing the adulthood and aging years.

Adjustment to Retirement

One of the classic studies undertaken to examine adjustment to retirement just when retirement was becoming a life stage experienced by large numbers of Americans in the 1950s was carried out in California by Reichard, Livson and Petersen (1962). These invetigators interviewed a group of men as they were about to retire and then followed them longitudinally over several years as they adjusted to their new mode of living.

From the large body of data these investigators amassed, they were able to identify five major personality types among the men. Reichard and associates felt that these personality typologies had characterized the men throughout most of their adult lives and the personality types were predictive of adjustment to retirement. The researchers concluded that three of the personality types resulted in adjustment to retirement while two did not. The personality types included the *mature* individuals who were still active in pastimes which were meaningful to them and were satisfied with their life as retirees. They had been happy when they were employed as well. They were individuals who took life as it came, made adjustments, and made the best of events which happened to them. Some admitted to have had adversity in their lives, but they had dealt with it and emerged to move on with their lives.

The *rocking chair* types took a different path to adjustment in retirement. Their attitude was that they had worked hard throughout their lives and now they wanted to relax. They preferred to stay at home and take it easy and disassociate themselves from all of the activities which had kept them so busy in the past. Their life satisfaction was high, but they wanted passive rather than active roles for the rest of their lives.

The third group which evidenced a high degree of life satisfaction in retirement was called the *armored* personality. This was a group of men who had developed strong defenses against what they considered to be the deleterious processes of aging. They were quite fearful of poor health and they remained physically active to defend against processes of aging. Thus, in retirement they were denying their age and trying to act younger to maintain their vigor.

The two personality types which Reichard et al. identified as poorly adjusted to retirement were called the *angry* and the *self-haters*. The angry individuals felt that their lives had not been successful and they regretted having to retire. They were depressed in retirement and dwelt on the failures they had experienced. They were angry because they blamed external forces for all that had gone wrong in their lives. They did not see their lack of success as their own personal weakness but as something which had been done to them from the outside. On the other hand, the self-haters blamed themselves for their unsatisfactory lives. They experienced the same depression in retirement as those labeled angry, but they felt that the responsibility for the failure resided in themselves.

The Reichard et al. (1962) study was important in and of itself in demonstrating that long-term personality patterns laid down in early life play a major role in adjustment to retirement. It gained further significance when Neugarten and associates identified similar personality patterns in relation to adjustment to retirement in a large sample in Kansas City. Several major studies of adjustment to retirement now concurred that lifelong personality patterns more or less set the stage for adjustment to retirement.

The data on personality and adjustment to retirement should not be interpreted to suggest that personality alone determines adjustment to retirement or that an individual cannot prepare for retirement and thus affect his or her adjustment to it. Indeed, Davidson and Kunze (1965) demonstrated that retires who have experienced formal retirement preparation tend to feel more positive about retirement. Two other factors that play a major role in adjustment to retirement are income and health. Individuals with high incomes are most likely to retire early, and they generally enjoy retirement. Those with low incomes tend to postpone retirement as long as they can and are less happy when they do retire. Income seems to be related to decline in satisfaction after retirement as well. When poor health is the cause for retirement, life satisfaction is usually low.

To summarize the information about adjustment in retirement, there appears to be a number of factors involved in life satisfaction during retirement. An important predictor of adjustment is the individual's personality, and the patterns of coping he or she has adopted throughout life will be similar to the manner in which retirement is faced. Most people are satisfied in retirement, especially if they have at least a moderate income and are in good health. Those who are the least satisfied with retirement are either in poor health or have a low income, or both.

SUMMARY

Work and retirement are extremely significant factors in adulthood and aging. Work shapes the pattern of individuals' lives, and retirement requires major adjustment. Retirement in the future may be quite different from retirement in its present state. Nevertheless, retirement as it exists for contemporary cohorts of older adults is the focus of discussion in this chapter.

For the major part of adulthood, life is organized around work. However, as individuals age, they face a growing number of disincentives to work. Financially, people are encouraged to retire early, and many do. Professionals are the most likely to remain in the work force after they reach retirement age. With life expectancy and health improvements, increasing numbers of adults have multiple careers.

Retirement is a twentieth-century phenomenon resulting from increases in life expectancy and from legislation enacted to provide support for individuals in old age. The history of retirement closely parallels the history of industrialization in the United States and other Western nations. Four forces created an atmosphere conducive to the emergence of retirement as an institution: (1) the decline in the demand for labor; (2) technological transformations in industry changing the skills required of workers; (3) the growth of large, impersonal bureaucracies; (4) the growth of private pensions and Social Security.

A major step taken in later life is making the decision to retire. Four age categories for retirement represent individuals making the retirement decision for quite different reasons. Very early retirement before the age of 61 occurs in individuals who are affluent and can afford to retire, and in individuals in poor health. A third group of very early retirees are individuals working in hazardous occupations such as fire fighter and police officer. Early retirement occurs between the ages of 62 and 64, and the majority of workers retire in this age bracket. Financial status and health are the major determinants of the decision to retire at this point in life. Normal retirement age has been 65, and this is the age when Social Security pays full retirement benefits. Late retirement or retirement after the age of 65 is most often taken by professionals and self-employed individuals. These are individuals who prefer their work to a life of leisure. They are also in a position of control over their employment and thus avoid an employer dictating the terms of their retirement.

There is a correlation between age of retirement and age of death. However, the data should not be interpreted to mean that retirement causes death. Rather, individuals in poor health are more likely to retire at a younger age and to die at a younger age. Poor health leads to early retirement and also to an earlier demise.

Since retirement is a major life change, it is often a difficult adjustment for both the retiree and for his or her family. Individuals adapt to retirement in ways similar to the manner they have previously adjusted to other hurdles. Those who experienced formal retirement preparation tend to feel more positive about retirement.

REFERENCES

BANKERS TRUST COMPANY. (1980). *Corporate pension plan study: A guide for the 1980s.* New York: Bankers Trust Company.

BARFIELD, R. E. & MORGAN, J. N. (1975). *Early retirement: The decision and the experience and a second look.* Ann Arbor, MI: University of Michigan.

BOWEN, W. G. & FINEGAN, T. A. (1969). *The economics of labor force participation.* Princeton, NJ: Princeton University Press.

DAVIDSON, W. & KUNZE, K. (1965).   Psychological, social, and economic meanings of work in modern societies: Their effects on the worker facing retirement. *Gerontologist, 5,* 129–133.

DEUTERMAN, W. & BROWN, S. (1978).   Voluntary part-time workers: A growing part of the labor force. *Monthly Labor Review, 101,* 3–10.

FILLENBAUM, G. (1971).   On the relation between attitude to work and attitude to retirement. *Journal of Gerontology, 26,* 244–248.

JACOBSEN, D. (1972).   Willingness to retire in relation to job strain and type of work. *Journal of Industrial Gerontology, 2,* 65–74.

KINGSON, E. (1979).   Men who leave work before age 62: A study of advantaged and disadvantaged very early labor force withdrawal. Unpublished doctoral dissertation, Brandeis Unviersity.

McCONNELL, S. R. (1983).   Retirement and employment. In D. S. Woodruff & J. E. Birren (Eds.), *Aging: Scientific perspectives and social issues,* 2nd ed. Monterey, CA: Brooks/Cole.

McCONNELL, S. R. & FISKE, S. J. (1980).   The survey of older writers. Unpublished report, Andrus Gerontology Center, University of Southern California, Los Angeles, California.

MEIER, E. & DITTMAR, C. (1979).   *Varieties of retirement ages.* Staff working paper of the President's Commission on Pension Policy, Washington, D. C.

MORGAN, J. (1980).   Economic realities of aging. Paper presented at the Convocation on Work and Retirement, University of Southern California, Los Angeles, California.

REICHARD, S., LIVSON, F. & PETERSEN, P. G. (1962).   *Aging and personality.* New York: Wiley.

ROWE, A. (1972).   The retirement of academic scientists. *Journal of Gerontology, 27,* 113–118.

SCHWAB, K. (August 1974).   Early labor force withdrawal of men: Participants and nonparticipants aged 58–63. *Social Security Bulletin.*

SHEPPARD, H. L. (1976).   Work and retirement. In R. H. Binstock & E. Shanas (Eds.), *Handbook of aging and the social sciences.* New York: Van Nostrand Reinhold.

SHEPPARD, H. L. (1977).   Factors associated with early withdrawal from the labor force. In S. Wolfbein (Ed.), *Men in the preretirement years.* Philadelphia: School of Business Administration, Temple University.

SHEPPARD, H. L. & BELITSKY, A. H. (1966).   *The job hunt.* Baltimore: The Johns Hopkins University Press.

SOCIAL SECURITY ADMINISTRATION. (1980).   OASDI cash benefits—Table Q-6. *Social Security Bulletin,* USDHEW, *43,* 75.

STREIB, G. & SCHNEIDER, G. (1971).   *Retirement in American Society,* Ithaca, NY: Cornell University Press.

TROLL, L. E. (1982).   *Continuations: Adult development and aging.* Monterey, CA: Brooks/Cole.

WOODRUFF, D. S. (1977).   *Can you live to be 100?* New York: Chatham Square Press.

CHAPTER 16

Psychopathology and Clinical Intervention in the Aged

Throughout this book we have discussed normal aging phenomena. Some of the biological, behavioral, and social facets of aging which affect the vast majority of adults as they age have been presented. In this chapter we turn to a smaller segment of the aging population. This is the group that experiences maladjustment and/or brain pathology in late life. Those individuals who have been adjusted throughout the major part of their adult lives and who experience the onset of psychopathology in late life are the subject of this chapter. They may break down when they have difficulties with the social and psychological phenomena accompanying aging. They may suffer from organic neurological syndromes which interfere with normal mental processes, or they may have a combination of environmental stressors and organic deficits which result in an inability to cope.

There are relatively few psychopathologies which have their onset in later life. If an individual has adjusted throughout adulthood to the various psychosocial crises and nonnormative life events causing unusual stress, it is likely that he or she will adjust to old age. Clearly, the incidence in psychopathology is no greater in aged individuals. However, the type of psychopathology which begins in late life may be different.

The most common form of psychopathology with first onset in late life is depression. This does not necessarily mean that the incidence of depression increases with age, although there is a debate about this issue in the literature on the psychopathology of aging. It means that of those individuals who have mental health problems late in life, a majority are depressed. There are other late-life psychopathologies such as paranoia and hypochondriasis, but they are less prevalent than depression.

The incidence of organic pathology as a cause of psychological distress increases in old age. Strokes and brain tumors result in behavioral impairment which may or may not be reversible. Late-life onset diseases such as Parkinson's disease can result in dementia. However, severe memory impairment to the degree that the individual must be institutionalized is relatively rare in old age, and occurs only in about 5 percent of individuals who live to the age of 65 or older. The most common cause of senility in old age is Alzheimer's disease.

Rather than present an exhaustive overview of the psychopathology of late life, this chapter will focus on two examples of late-life psychopathology: the major psychological incapacity in late life, depression; and the major organic disease with onset in late life, senile dementia of the Alzheimer's type (SDAT). It should be clear from the beginning of the discussion that depression can have organic as well as social and psychological causes, and Alzheimer's disease has devastating social and psychological consequences.

The prognosis for depression is significantly better than the prognosis for SDAT. Old people who are depressed often get over their sadness, but victims of SDAT lose their memory, lose control of their normal bodily functions, and eventually die. At the same time, interventions are being designed and tested for both depression and SDAT. In the case of depression, the interventions are often successful. Psychotherapists in previous decades with negative stereotypes of the rigidity of the adult personality might not have predicted such positive results. SDAT is a terminal disease, so no intervention has been identified to reverse the torturous progress of the loss in capacity. Interventions to maintain memory and lucidity as the disease progreses and to relieve depression as the inevitable losses proceed have had some success. Interventions to help family members and caretakers cope with the awful toll of SDAT have also been developed and used effectively.

DEPRESSION

To present a specific definition of depression for which there would be general agreement among psychologists, psychiatrists, psychiatric nurses, and other mental health specialists is simply not feasible in the late 1980s. Beck (1967) dramatized this contemporary dilemma by pointing out that the condition that we label today as depression is not new to humankind. It has been described by ancient writers for centuries under the classification of "melancholia." The first clinical description of melancholia was made by Hippocrates in the fourth century B.C. Aretaeus, a second century A.D. physician, described the malancholic patient as "sad, dismayed, sleepless. . . They become thin by their agitation and loss of refreshing sleep. . . At a more advanced stage, they complain of a thousand futilities and desire death'' (Beck, 1967, p. 4). Although we have acknowledged the existence of depression in human behavior since at least the fourth century B.C., we still cannot agree as to exactly what defines this affective disorder. Unfortunately, defining depression in old age is even more problematic than defining it in younger adulthood.

While there is not general agreement about a definition of depression, most mental health professionals could agree to the following attributes of the disorder as presented by Beck (1967, p. 6):

1. A specific alteration in mood: sadness, loneliness, apathy.
2. A negative self-concept associated with self-reproaches and self-blame.
3. Regressive and self-punitive wishes: desires to escape, hide, or die.
4. Vegetative changes: anorexia, insomnia, loss of libido.
5. Change in activity level: retardation or agitation.

Incidence of Depression in Late Life

The lifetime risk for developing a major depression is between 6 and 18 percent (Boyd & Weissman, 1981). The reason that this figure is presented as a range of 12 percentage points rather than a more precise estimate is that the actual incidence of depression is extremely difficult to pinpoint. Variability is introduced in population estimates due to the definition of depression which is adopted, the assessment instruments used, and the sample populations selected. While popular belief has it that depression has a higher prevalence among the elderly, epidemiological surveys of the incidence of depression in the adult population indicate that the aged are not any more prone to depression than younger adults (Blazer, 1982b; Boyd & Weissman, 1982; Craig & Van Natta, 1979; Hirschfield & Cross, 1982).

Age differences in depression were assessed by self-report on the Center for Epidemiological Studies Depression scale, which has recently become a prominent measure of depression. A total of 1,330 male and female respondents aged 20 to 100 years completed the scale. The group in the age range of 55 to 69 actually had significantly *lower* depression scores than the youngest and oldest groups. Adults over the age of 70 scored no higher on the depression scale than subjects aged 20 to 54 years (Gatz, Hurwicz & Weicker, 1986). The researchers concluded that overall, older adults were not more depressed. However, on items asking whether the person had a hopeful outlook, old adults were more likely to respond that they lacked such positive feelings.

Although the incidence of depression is no greater in older adults, and although older adults do not score higher on self-report scales of depression, the most common psychiatric disorder among the elderly is depression (Blazer, 1982b; Butler, 1975; Storandt, Siegler & Elias, 1978; Zung, 1967, 1973).

In a cross-national study carried out in the United States and Great Britain, only 5 percent of the patients over the age of 65 were diagnosed as depressed by psychiatrists participating in the study (Gurland, 1976). Boyd and Weissman (1981) estimated the prevalence at one point in time for nonbipolar depression diagnosed with current techniques to be about 3.7 to 4.3 percent in the adult population. A comparison of the cross-national study data on the incidence of depression in the elderly with the Boyd and Weissman estimates for the total adult population suggests about the same rate of depression for older adults as for the adult population in general. However, Gurland (1976) pointed out that apart from the psychiatrists' diagnoses in the cross-national study, many more older patients gave themselves high depression ratings on a symptom checklist. Gurland concluded that psychiatrists may diagnose older adults as clinically depressed less frequently because the older adults may be subject to a higher incidence of transient depressive episodes which are frequently precipitated by external events. For example, the aged are more likely to experience grief reactions resulting from the death of a spouse, relative, or friend. Grief reactions mimic the symptoms of depression, but they are not enduring.

Another problem with diagnosing depression in the elderly is that the diagnostic criteria are unclear. These criteria vary across the mental health professions, and they were developed with younger populations.

Diagnosis of Depression in Old Age

The most common symptoms of clinical depression in the aged include helplessness, despair, feelings of worthlessness, apathy, pessimism, suicidal thoughts, and less frequently, guilt over real or imagined past failures (Salzman & Shader, 1979). Problematic in the diagnosis of depression in the elderly are physical complaints. Whereas scales assessing depression include somatic complaints as symptoms of depression, many of the typical somatic symptoms of depression in younger adults (such as disturbances of sleep and appetite) may be the result of normal processes of aging, other diseases common in the elderly, or a number of medications commonly prescribed for older adults. This leads some mental health professionals to argue that self-rating scales for depression such as the Zung Self-Rating Depression Scale (Zung, 1965) identifies more elderly as depressed than are actually clinically depressed (Gallagher, Thompson & Levy, 1980). Similar problems arise with the Beck Depression Inventory (Zemore & Eames, 1979) and the MMPI Depression scale (Harmatz & Shader, 1975).

Ratings provided by a professional external observer may provide more accurate diagnosis of depression in the elderly. An observer rating scale which has been used in a number of studies involving older patients is the Hamilton Psychiatric Rating Scale (Hamilton, 1967). Gallagher, Thompson and Levy (1980) endorse the structrured interview technique provided by the Schedule for Affective Disorders and Schizophrenia (SADS) as promising in the reliable assessment of depression in the elderly. Whatever assessment technique is used, it is important to supplement the measure with screening measures for organic dysfunction and health function so that the older individual's depressive symptoms can be evaluated from a realistic perspective of physiological health status and perceived physical health.

Causes of Depression in the Elderly

At both a biochemical level and an environmental level, the elderly may be predisposed toward depression. Losses initiated in the external environment such as loss of income and loss of employment through retirement along with psychological losses such as the loss of loved ones due to death or loss of physical health are tangible factors causing older individuals to feel depressed. Losses in physical capacity and energy level also undoubtedly play a role. Additionally, some evidence suggests that on a biochemical level, production of certain neurotransmitters in the aging brain may be altered. This may also predispose old people to feel depressed. Thus, the aged may be in a state of double jeopardy. Whether biological changes are caused by these environmental stresses, whether the biological and physiological changes are completely independent, or whether they exacerbate one another has not clearly been determined.

Perhaps we will find that biologically older organisms are more predisposed toward depression without any environmental stresses. This is clearly the view of Blazer who stated, "Any attempt to understand and explain the phenomenon of depression that excludes biologic factors is severely limited" (Blazer, 1982a, p. 55). The loss of physical vigor and health is extremely depressing to many older people, and this loss is thought to account in part for the steep increase in the suicide rate in elderly white men. The decline in physical health which accompanies aging may be the most severe stressor the elderly experience (Lieberman, 1982).

A summary of what may be some of the major psychological and social causes of depression in the aged are : (1) physical illness and sensory loss, (2) bereavement and loss of significant others, (3) economic deprivation and poor living conditions, (4) retirement and loss of social roles. While only the fourth cause is specific to old age, the first three causes of depression are also more likely to affect the elderly.

With hypotheses about the cause of depression in old age including explanations ranging from biological to social-environmental, it is clear that gerontologists have no precise understanding of the causes of depression in the aged. Furthermore, it appears that there are some myths about depression in aging. In an exhaustive search of the literature on aging and depression, Hybels (1986) identified several false premises held about depression in the elderly.

First, it is assumed that geriatric depression is of a different nature from that found in younger people. Hybels (1986) pointed out that reviewers of the objective data, including the American Psychiatric Association Task Force on Nomenclature and Statistics which designed the DSM-III diagnostic system, have reached the conclusion that no clinical justification exists for retaining a separate category of depression based on old age. There are some differences in presentation of symptoms because old people are more willing to present physical symptoms than they are to discuss sadness and psychological problems. However, the substance of the depression is similar to depression in younger individuals.

Second, it is often assumed that the prevalence of geriatric depression is greater than for younger groups. Hybels (1986) argued that while the number of symptoms of depression may be greater in older populations, it is incorrect to interpret that the prevalence of depression is greater. Symptoms of actual physical illness and of grief reactions must be excluded before a diagnosis of clinical depression in the elderly is accurate. When physical illness and grief reaction symptoms are excluded, the prevalence of clinical depression in the aged is roughly the same or even less than in the younger adult age groups.

Given the numerous potential causes for depression in the elderly, it is indeed remarkable that only 5 percent of the aged suffer a clinical depression late in life. Hybels (1986) made the point that we should be asking why 95 percent of the individuals over the age of 65 *do not* get clinically depressed rather than dwelling so much on the causes for depression in old age!

Nevertheless, clinicians are faced with older individuals who have adjusted successfully throughout their lives and then suffered their first serious mental health problem in old age. We now turn to what constitutes successful treatment of depression in later life.

Psychotherapeutic Treatments for Late-Life Depression

It has already been pointed out that depression is the most common psychiatric complaint among the elderly, and it is essential to treat depressive symptoms in older adults because a common outcome of depression in the elderly is suicide. The actual number of suicides in the over-65 age group, including those not reported, may exceed 10,000 annually, according to Miller (1979).

Two aspects about depression making it particularly troublesome to treat were pointed out by Gatz, Smyer and Lawton (1980). The first is that loss is a central aspect of old age, and there are clear reasons why older people should be feeling depressed. As we have mentioned previously, when the actual number of depressive *symptoms* is counted, older people have more. However, when the prevalence of depressive *disorders* as diagnosed by psychiatrists is examined, the rate is highest between the ages of 25 and 65.

The other problematic aspect of depression in the elderly is that family and friends find it difficult to be around the depressed individual. Elderly people typically have fewer living relatives and friends, and when they alienate these few potential helpers with the dependent and demanding behaviors characteristic of depressed individuals, they become isolated. Gatz, Smyer and Lawton (1980) suggested that the families and caretakers need assistance, and interventions to maximize the helpers' effectiveness are required as well as interventions for the depressed elderly.

In the late 1980s it is fortunate that several relatively long-term follow-up studies have been conducted to examine the effectiveness of various treatments for elderly depressives. Evidence to date indicates that several forms of individual psychotherapy and some forms of group therapy are effective in helping the elderly overcome their depression. It is only very recently that such a positive picture for the efficacy of treatment of depression in the aged has been presented.

Gallagher, Thompson and Breckenridge (1986) reported one-year follow-up results on three modalities of individual psychotherapy: behavioral, cognitive, or psychodynamic. The invetsigators had selected 120 older people over the age of 60 who had evidenced a major depressive disorder as assessed by Research Diagnostic Criteria (Spitzer, Endicott & Robins, 1978). Participants had been depressed an average of two years before participating in the study. The program lasted for four months with weekly sessions in one of the three types of psychotherapy.

Common characteristics in the three types of individual psychotherapy used in the study were:

1. A strong therapeutic alliance between the therapist and elderly client. This alliance was equivalent in all of the three therapy modalities.
2. A clear focus on mutually defined goals. The therapist and client had a contract.
3. All the therapies were brief, lasting four months, and the client and therapist were aware of the need to use the time effectively. There was structure to the sessions.
4. There were individual difference variables which predicted success in the various therapies.

While patients were randomly assigned to treatment in the study, data from it can be used to assign individuals to the most effective therapy for them in future treatment programs.

Of the 91 participants who completed the study, 52 percent had complete remission of their depression, 18 percent had reduced the level of depression to minor, and 30 percent were still as depressed as in the beginning of the study. This posttreatment assessment of depression was based on the SADS assessment. There was no difference in the outcome as a function of the type of individual psychotherapy. All three treatments were equally effective.

A year after the treatment, 82 of the patients were assessed again, and at this point 57 percent were still not depressed, while 13 percent had experienced minor depression of brief episodes. Major depression existed in 27 percent of the subjects, and 3 percent had other diagnoses at the time of the one-year follow-up. Thus, a clear majority of older depressed patients were successfully treated in four months and maintained their improved mental health status for one year.

Beutler and his associates (1986) described a study of older depressed patients in which they compared the effects of cognitive group therapy and the drug, Alprazolam, in the treatment of depression. Alprazolam is commonly prescribed for depression in older adults. Fifty-six older adults carefully screened for depression were randomly assigned to one of four groups: drug, placebo, cognitive group therapy and drug, cognitive group therapy and placebo. Therapy lasted ten weeks with a three week follow-up assessment. As sleep disorders are a common problem in depression, sleep efficiency was also stressed in these patients for four nights.

Assessment with the Beck Depression Inventory indicated that there was some improvement in the cognitive therapy group. Sleep efficiency improved about 5 percent in this group, while sleep efficiency in the groups not receiving cognitive group therapy decreased by 12 percent. While cognitive group therapy was somewhat effective in this group of older depressed patients, Alprazolam was not effective. Beutler et al. (1986) found no evidence that prescription of this drug is indicated in the case of elderly depressed patients.

Beutler suggested that the individual psychotherapy intervention used by Gallagher and associates was probably more effective than the cognitive group therapy he used. That treatment results in these studies was not an outcome due to spontaneous remission is indicated in several different ways. In the Gallagher study patients on the waiting list who were tested for depression but not accepted for several months for treatment did not show improved scores on depression until after treatment. Beutler's study had nontreatment control groups, and these individuals showed no improvement. Age of onset of depression also did not predict improvement in either study. Thus, regardless of how old an individual is when depression occurs, he or she can still be treated and show improvement.

Depression is frequently seen in older adults in the early stages of Alzheimer's disease. Indeed, who would not be depressed to find one's mental capacities gradually failing? Teri, Uomoto and Stoffel (1986) have undertaken the treatment of depression in Alzheimer's disease, both for the caregivers and the patients. In this behavioral approach, the patient as well as the caregiver are involved. Teri and her associates pointed out that all too often patients are left sitting outside in the hall while the family discusses the patient with the doctors and mental health personnel. Even if the patient has deteriorated cognitively, he or she still has an emotional reaction to being literally left out in the hall. It is Teri's recommendation that the patient always be included in these conferences, regardless of his or her capacity to understand what is being discussed.

One of the therapies used by this group is to get the patient involved in activities similar to things that used to give the patient pleasure. For example, if the patient used to enjoy corssword puzzles, find easier crossword puzzles, including large crossword puzzles for children, that the patient can still master. When the patient can no longer undertake those puzzles, find simple word rhymes and games. If the patient used to enjoy sewing, introduce sewing cards. While it is important never to infantalize older adults, in the case of Alzheimer's disease mental capacities do regress severely, and simple children's activities relating to the patient's past interests do not insult the individual at this point.

In a typical seven-week treatment program, Teri's group would first interview the patient and caregivers and identify pleasant activities the caregivers can introduce for the patient. In the first two weeks of the program these pleasant activities involving things the patient used to enjoy are introduced, and caregivers are encouraged to use these activities and identify other pleasant activities for the patient throughout the time they are providing care. In the third week of the program relaxation training for the caregiver is introduced, and in the fourth week problem solving with the caregiver is undertaken by the mental health professionals. Relaxation training and problem solving continue with the caregivers until the end of the treatment program. Finally, in the seventh week a review of the entire period is carried out. The effect on patients' mood of working at a pleasant activity such as the kind identified by Teri's group can be dramatic. Although Alzheimer's patients regress in their cognitive capacity, their emotions can be positively affected with sensitive interventions.

While depression is probably the most common emotional problem of the elderly, senile dementia of the Alzheimer's type (SDAT) is undboutedly the most feared. When a young person misplaces the keys, little concern is experienced. It is quite a natural thing to forget where you put the keys. However, when an old person misplaces something, he or she wonders if this is the beginning of senility. There is a tremendous fear among the elderly that they are going to "lose their mind." A common symptom of depression in the aged is memory loss. The most devastating progressive degeneraiton of cognitive and eventually physical capacity occurs in SDAT.

SENILE DEMENTIA
OF THE ALZHEIMER'S TYPE

Alzheimer's disease or senile dementia of the Alzheimer's type (SDAT) is not the inevitable outcome of normal aging. It is not a disease to which we will all succumb if we live long enough. Rather, it is a rare disease affecting about 4 percent of the older population at any given time. Mortimer (1983) has estimated that after the age of 65 about 1 percent of the aged per year will suffer the onset of Alzheimer's disease. This means that the cumulative risk to individuals surviving to 85 years of age is 15 percent to 20 percent (Mortimer, Schuman & French, 1981; Sluss, Gruenberg & Kramer, 1981).

While the prevalence of Alzheimer's disease makes it appear to be a relatively rare disease, even this small percentage is significant because there is an increasing number of older people in the population. Also, it is difficult to count accurately the number of Alzheimer's victims because of the difficulty of diagnosis. Thus, various estimates of the number of victims of Alzheimer's disease exist. Government statistics published by the National Institute on Aging estimate that two million people currently suffer from Alzheimer's disease. It has been projected that the number of Americans over the age of 65 in the year 2020 will reach 43 million, nearly twice the older population of the late 1980s. If the prevalence of Alzheimer's disease remains similar to what it is at the present time, then we could have four to five million victims of this devastating disease. However, to diagnose, understand, and prevent the occurrence of SDAT in future cohorts of the elderly, since 1976 the federal government has increased support of research on dementia by more than 800 percent.

The Significance of Alzheimer's
Disease for Psychology

Alzheimer's disease is significant to psychology because its main presenting symptom is behavioral. Profound cognitive impairment is the hallmark of SDAT. Alzheimer's disease accounts for a major portion of senility in older people. Robert Katzman (1984), an authority on the disease, estimated that of 1,000 autopsies of individuals who had been demented, 53 percent would be diagnosed as having Alzheimer's disease, 23 percent would have had cerebral vascular pathology, 14 percent would have had mixed cerebral vascular pathology and Alzheimer's disease, and 10 percent would have had various other pathologies. Thus, the majority of dementia cases are caused by SDAT.

The disease does not always strike down its victims in old age. Alois Alzheimer diagnosed the first case in 1907 in a patient just over 50 years of age. Until recently, a sharp distinction had been made between patients with onset of the disease when they were younger than 65. This was called presenile dementia of the Alzheimer's type, while onset after age 65 was called SDAT. However, the three major neuropathological symptoms of presenile and SDAT are similar and involve:

1. Neuronal cell loss—in some sites up to 90 percent loss.
2. Senile plaques—small masses of degenerating tissue.
3. Neurofibrillary tangles—paired helical twisted filaments comprised of proteins which exist inside neural cells.

Evidence presented in 1985 at the International Congress of Gerontology by investigators such as Sir Martin Roth indicated that brain degeneration in patients with onset when they are younger is more profound, especially in the frontal lobes. There is also a stronger case for the genetic basis of the early onset type.

It is important to emphasize some of the limitations of our knowledge about SDAT. A major problem is that even at a histopathological level during postmortem examination of the brain, diagnosis of SDAT is based on elimination of other neuropathologies. Furthermore, we use quantitative analysis of neuronal cell loss, senile plaques, and neurofibrillary tangles to identify the disease. Matsuyama (1983) demonstrated that all of the pathological brain changes characteristic of Alzheimer's disease occur in normal aging in individuals who show no signs of senility. What is different in Alzheimer's disease is the incidence of senile plaques and neurofibrillary tangles. There is a higher number of plaques and tangles per field of brain tissue. Hence, we have no unique identifying neuroanatomical feature of SDAT at the present time.

One of the things which must be done is to develop a differential diagnosis positive to Alzheimer's disease. We must find pathology unique to SDAT and qualitatively different from normal aging. At present we diagnose the disease only by exclusion of other dementing diseases such as cerebral arteriosclerosis and tumors and by quantitatively greater neuropathology than seen in normal aging.

Behavioral signs of SDAT.   Alzheimer's disease begins with mild impairment in memory and semantic knowledge capacities. The patient is conscious of his or her difficulties, and an attempt is made to compensate. Notes will be written as reminders. Indeed, the homes of some Alzheimer's patients in the early stages of the disease are littered with little pieces of paper with indecipherable notes. One of the tragedies of the disease is that its onset is so gradual that patients become aware that they are beginning to lose their mind. Indeed, the unprovoked spontaneous sobbing frequently observed after SDAT has progressed is interpreted as a conscious or unconscious mourning by the victim for the loss of intellect (Reisberg, 1983).

Reisberg (1983) presented a seven-stage categorization of the behavioral progression of SDAT which he developed with Ferris and Crook. While others such as Jarvik (1985) have pointed out that not all cases present the seven stages and that a three-stage categorization is usually adequate for treatment, we will discuss the seven stages to elaborate on the progression of the disease.

Stage 1 is normal functioning with no cognitive decline. Very mild cognitive decline characterizes Stage 2, and this stage is difficult to distinguish from normal aging or from overload in a younger adult. The patient is forgetful of where familiar things have been placed and of the names of well-known people or places.

Stage 3 marks the onset of confusion, and clear-cut deficits begin to appear. Co-workers notice a decline in performance; the patient forgets what he or she has just read; the patient may lose or misplace an object of value. Also, at this point the patient may start to deny the cognitive losses. In Stage 4 denial becomes more apparent. When asked, "Who is the President of the United States?" a patient might answer, "I don't follow politics very closely." Patients at this stage manifest decreased knowledge of current and recent events, they begin to forget their own personal history, they can no longer carry out such tasks as serial subtractions, and they experience difficulty with traveling, handling their personal finances, and their daily affairs. At this point they begin to withdraw from challenging situations.

Stage 5 is called the early dementia stage, and the patient can no longer survive without assistance. Things as familiar as their long-time address or telephone number cannot be recalled, nor can the names of their grandchildren. They become disoriented to time and place. However, they still know their own name, and the name of their spouse and children. They can eat, but they may have difficulty dressing themselves.

By Stage 6 severe cognitive decline is apparent to the point that they may forget the name of the spouse or child upon whom they are totally dependent. They cannot remember recent events, and they can only partly remember past experiences. They are unaware of time or place and may have difficulty counting to 10. They may become incontinent, and to the consternation of caretakers, they may fail to discriminate between day and night.

Finally, at Stage 7 involving very severe cognitive decline, all verbal abilities are lost. There may be no speech, only grunting. Assistance with feeding and toileting is required; even the ability to walk is lost. The brain no longer controls the body, and the patient eventually dies in this extremely deteriorated state.

Death usually ensues about five to seven years after the first symptoms, but survival time can be as long as 14 or more years after diagnosis. At the present time there is no cure or even much effective treatment for the alleviation of symptoms. Thus while long-time experts in this area assert that in the last six to seven years we have made remarkable advances, knowledge about Alzheimer's disease is still in a preliminary stage.

Causes of SDAT

While the causes of Alzheimer's disease are unknown, there are some hypotheses about its origin. All of the research we describe here is rapidly changing our perspective about SDAT. At the same time, one acknowledged leader in research on the biology of aging, Caleb Finch, sadly acknowledged, "At this point in time, we don't even know what we don't know about Alzheimer's disease" (Finch, 1985).

Slow virus studies.   One approach to understanding the causes of SDAT continues with studies on central nervous system diseases believed to be caused by slow-acting transmissible viruses. Scrapie is a central nervous system disease affecting sheep, and it has provided a model for the study of dementing disorders in humans, including SDAT. It is difficult to identify an animal model for SDAT because dementia involves the loss of cognitive capacities animals never have in the first place. Nonetheless, scientists are actively pursuing an animal or other model. Scrapie is similar to kuru and Creutzfeldt-Jakob disease, two rare diseases in humans which cause progressive, irreversible dementia. This fact, plus the well-established evidence that scrapie is the result of a slow-acting infectious agent, encouraged a new avenue of research of the possible causes of central nervous diseases in humans.

Prusiner (1982) at the University of California at San Francisco has suggested that Alzheimer's disease may involve something like a slow virus. He has proposed that a small proteinaceous infectious particle which he calls a "prion" may be a component of the amyloid plaques in Alzheimer's disease. However, scientists pursuing this line of research have consistently failed in their efforts to identify and isolate any component of the infectious agent. At the present time, Prusiner's research tentatively suggests that the amyloid plaques seen in victims of Creutzfeldt-Jakob disease and kuru, two transmissible degenerative brain diseases, may be composed of prions. Amyloid plaques are also present in the brains of the victims of SDAT.

Prions have many properties which distinguish them from typical viruses. Although viruses contain nucleic acids which carry all of the information necessary for the virus to multiply and spread infection, prions may or may not contain a nucleic acid. Since nucleic acids are necessary for proteins to replicate, molecular biologists are challenged by the puzzle of how prions transmit their effect.

The work of Prusiner and associates remains to be confirmed. If this avenue of research on SDAT continues to prove promising, it might significantly alter our understanding of the nature of this particular form of virus and how it works. The research might also provide insights about how to treat and cure degenerative diseases in the central nervous system including disorders such as SDAT.

Trace metal studies. Perl and associates (1982) at the University of Vermont have developed an environmental hypothesis based on parallels between the high aluminum content in the affected neurons of Alzheimer's patients and the dementia and aluminum content in the brains of Chamorra natives of Guam dying of amyotrophic lateral sclerosis (ALS). The research suggests that aluminum may contribute to the development of SDAT and ALS.

In SDAT patients the neurons affected by the disease have accumulations of aluminum within them along with neurofibrillary tangles. In a collaborative study, Perl and a group of other scientists reported high accumulations of aluminum, iron, and calcium in the brains of Chamorra natives of Guam who had died of ALS or of parkinsonism-dementia (Perl et al., 1982). This population is adversely affected by these two chronic disorders, both of which were previously suspected to be transmitted by a slow-acting virus.

Researchers in the field of aging have carefully observed the studies in Guam because of the similarities between the parkinsonism-dementia syndrome and SDAT. In both disorders, there is an excessive accumulation of neurofibrillary tangles in the brains of victims that is associated with severe dementia and death.

The latest results of Perl's research confirm his earlier work linking concentrations of aluminum in the brain to the development of neurofibrillary tangles. Samples of garden soil and drinking water in Guam as well as in parts of Japan and New Guinea similarly plagued by high incidences of ALS and dementia indicate low levels of calcium and magnesium and unusually high levels of aluminum. All of these elements have similar chemical structures. Scientists have never been able to prove that aluminum alone predisposes a person to or causes SDAT. It may be that high intake of aluminum over a long period of time, coupled with chronic low intake of vital minerals such as calcium and magnesium, ultimately results in a breakdown of the normal mechanisms which metabolize minerals. This, in turn could result in what investigators find are toxic levels of these elements in the brain cells and in the walls of major blood vessels in the brain.

Scientists have yet to determine how or why low intake of calcium and magnesium can lead to high levels of these elements in the brain, but there appears to be a link since the same phenomenon occurs in three different high incidence areas. One hypothesis is that the body is overcompensating for the lack of vital minerals by storing these in combination with other available trace elements in the bones. Ultimately this may lead to deposits in the central nervous system.

Future studies in this area will determine whether accumulations of metals in the brain are a primary cause of SDAT or if other factors or circumstances might combine with environmental factors to trigger the onset of chronic, but ultimately fatal, diseases of the nervous system. At the present time, we simply do not know whether the accumulation of trace metals results as a consequence of the breakdown of the central nervous system in SDAT or whether exposure to excessive levels of these metals initiates the disease process.

Genetic studies. For several decades there have been hints that SDAT in either its early onset form or senile form might be hereditary. In what amounts to a handful of studies on genetic influence, researchers have found an increased incidence of some form of dementia among parents and siblings of SDAT victims. Some studies show a slight increase; others show a considerable one over the occurrence of dementia in the general population. Researchers have suggested that early-onset SDAT poses a greater risk to relatives than late onset. Practically no data are available on risk to children. The studies appear to show a clustering of dementia cases in some families of SDAT victims but no consistent pattern of genetic transmission.

Genetic research may eventually indicate whether there is one disease or more than one in the presenile and senile forms of SDAT. Studies may also provide a way to diagnose dementia accurately using a "marker" for the disease. Jarvik at the University of California at Los Angeles School of Medicine has found something unusual in the behavior of white blood cells taken from patients with SDAT (Matsuyama & Jarvik, 1982). The cells appear "disoriented" when they are exposed to temperatures which generally elicit a specific response from cells in healthy individuals. Additional research will attempt to determine if the change is consistent and to identify what causes it.

Brain neurotransmitter studies. Since the first reports in the mid-1970s, research scientists have been studying evidence of a significant and progressive decrease in the activity of the enzyme choline acetyltransferase (ChAT) in the brain tissue of SDAT patients. ChAT is a crucial ingredient in the chemical process which produces acetylcholine, a neurotransmitter involved in learning and memory. One of the most interesting results indicates a link between a change in levels of acetylcholine in the brain and changes in cognition such as memory loss and disorientation and in the neuroanatomy in brains of patients with SDAT. The number of plaques (degenerated nerve cell pieces which form around a fibrous core in the cerebral cortex) was higher when ChAT and acetylcholine concentrations were decreased. In order to explore further the relationship between ChAT and SDAT, scientists are using techniques such as monoclonal antibodies to help map areas of the brain where ChAT is present.

Recent work at the Johns Hopkins University has been at the forefront of the neurotransmitter research on SDAT. In studying the brains of SDAT victims, Price and Coyle found a marked loss of nerve cells in a part of the base of the brain called the nucleus basalis (Coyle et al., 1983). Some patients with classical SDAT have been shown to lose as much as 90 percent of these cells. There is likely to be a link between the loss of cells in the nucleus basalis and the decrease in cholinergic activity.

The nucleus basalis produces acetylcholine and utilizes the neurotransmitter and its enzymes in communicating with the cerebral cortex via connecting pathways. In SDAT cholinergic cells are lost at a much higher rate than most other types of cells. Between 75 and 95 percent of cholinergic cells are lost in SDAT patients. Since the loss of acetylcholine is so detrimental to these patients, and the nucleus basalis appears to be a major source of the substance, researchers aim to learn why nerve cells of the nucleus basalis seem to be selectively destroyed in SDAT. Another reason for interest in the nucleus basalis is because it may be one of the earliest centers hit by the disease. The neurotransmitter approach is apparently looking at an early consequence of SDAT, rather than the cause of the disease. However, the neurotransmitter research does indicate a cause for the cognitive deterioration.

A Biochemical Marker
for Alzheimer's Disease?

The first fully accurate diagnostic indicators of SDAT in living humans may have recently been discovered. At the present time, enough clinical trials have not been run. However, it appears likely that we may be able to identify the disease with a biochemical test of spinal fluid. With possible positive diagnosis in the living patient rather than the present positive diagnosis only at autopsy, appropriate treatment for SDAT patients may become easier to implement.

Scientists Davies and Wolozin from New York City's Albert Einstein College of Medicine have found an abnormal protein in the brains of SDAT victims (Wolozin & Davies, 1986). They named the protein A-68 and find that it is unique to SDAT. Patients with dementing diseases other than SDAT do not have this protein. Whether this protein has a role in causing SDAT is unknown. However, if the result that A-68 is unique to SDAT patients continues to hold, then Davies feels that within a year a routine laboratory test for SDAT could be available.

The technique used to isolate A-68 was monoclonal antibodies. Davies and his graduate student, Wolozin, worked with brain tissue from SDAT patients, examining the tissue for abnormal proteins that might be inflicting damage. Monoclonal antibodies bind to specific proteins, thus identifying which ones are present. Davies and Wolozin eventually isolated and identified A-68. In a subsequent series of autopsies as well as in two rare brain biopsies of living SDAT patients, it was found that A-68 was present it all cases. Further tests indicated that A-68 also appeared in the spinal fluid. Additionally, and perhaps most significantly, A-68 has not been found in patients or autopsies of other known diseases affecting the central nervous system.

There would be numerous benefits for a simple diagnostic test for SDAT. One benefit would be that physicians could eliminate a large number of patients currently misdiagnosed with SDAT. Many victims of stroke, malnutrition, depression, brain tumor, and other diseases are misdiagnosed as SDAT patients and not given proper treatment. With the correct diagnoses, these people have a much better prognosis.

A second benefit is that early detection of SDAT could increase the chances for treatment and cure. Davies has found that the appearance of A-68 appears to be one of the very early pathological effects of SDAT. The earlier the disease is found, the better the chances of stabilizing patients to help them maintain normal cognitive function. Although the disease is progressive and terminal at the present time, if a cure were to be found, early detection would save many lives.

Perhaps the most significant potential benefit from the discovery of A-68 is the potential for finding a cure to SDAT. Among the hypothesis we have explored about the cause for SDAT (slow virus, trace metals, and genetic), Davies favors the genetic hypothesis. He believes that the disease is at least activated, if not actually caused, by a defective human gene. Davies feels that the defective gene is not normally turned on in the brain, but when it is turned on, it produces A-68. The search for the defective gene centers on the twenty-first chromosome. This is the chromosome which, when present in triplicate instead of the normal duplicate, produces Down's syndrome.

Down's syndrome results in severe mental retardation in the children who have it, and when they reach the end of their lives in the forties and early fifties, they all have neurological signs seemingly identical to SDAT. Thus, Davies' hypothesis about the cause of SDAT involves a gene likely to reside on the twenty-first chromosome which only causes the disease when "by mistake" it is turned on. If Davies is correct, identifying the gene and preventing the mistake that turns it on will save millions of future elderly from the devastating experience of SDAT.

The Role of Psychologists
in Differential Diagnosis of SDAT

We need to develop behavioral indexes which more precisely differentiate normal aging from SDAT. As emphasized previously, early and accurate diagnosis of SDAT can have a major impact on the progression of the disease. One of the problems in treating the disease is that it is often diagnosed in its late stages so that the few interventions we do have are no longer effective. For example, the cholinergic facilitator, physostigmine, shows some promise in ameliorating memory loss in SDAT, but it is most effective in the early stages of the disease (Davies, 1985). Drugs which improve memory must be administered before the cells which can use them are lost.

Khachaturian (1985) has pointed out that the only practical way to screen for SDAT in the aged population as a whole would be to use short, easily administered measures. We simply cannot bring all old people to the hospital or laboratory even for simple biochemical tests if A-68 proves to be a successful marker for SDAT. We also need to discover a reliable neuropsychological "marker" which would single out a patient in the early stages of Alzheimer's disease from an individual showing normal cognitive aging. To develop such a measure we need to undertake longitudinal studies on large samples of middle-aged and aged individuals so that we can identify behavioral profiles of those who eventually develop SDAT. The discovery of such a profile would revolutionize the care and treatment of

Alzheimer's disease by allowing us to begin care early. Early diagnosis might also speed up the identification of the causes.

It is really up to psychologists to develop an Alzheimer's profile, as psychology is the domain of cognitive and behavioral measurement. Devising such tests would demand that we improve our description of normal cognitive age changes as a baseline against which to compare SDAT. We know something about how abilities change with age, but our measurement lacks precision. It is as if we are at the light microscopic stage of neuropsychological testing of cognitive age changes in the late 1980s. To identify cognitive and behavioral markers early in the progression of Alzheimer's disease, psychologists must progress to the electron microscopic stage of neuropsychological testing in cognition and aging.

SUMMARY

The focus of this chapter is on psychopathological aging which affects a minority of the elderly. However, it is a needy minority and one that requires a great deal of care.

While the incidence of depression is no greater in old age, depression is the most frequent diagnosis of psychopathology in late life. The most common symptoms are helplessness, despair, feelings of worthlessness, apathy, pessimism, suicidal thoughts, and less frequently, guilt. Loss is a common cause of depression in old age; loss of spouse, loss of friends, loss of income, and loss of employment through retirement are all more frequent occurrences in the lives of older adults. Age changes in neurotransmitters may also preclude older adults to depression. Given the numerous potential causes for depression in late life, it is surprising that more older adults do not exhibit clinical symptoms of depression.

Interventions to alleviate depression in old age have been successful. Individual psychotherapy using behavioral, cognitive, or psychodynamic approaches have all been successful in treating depression in elderly clients. In one study of older adults who had been depressed an average of two years, after a four-month therapy, 52 percent of the patients had no signs of depression. A year later, 57 percent of the patients were still not depressed. In another study, cognitive group therapy helped to alleviate depression in some elderly patients. Individual therapy has even been shown to be effective in patients depressed as a consequence of being in the initial stages of senile dementia of the Alzheimer's type (SDAT).

SDAT is the most feared disease of old age. It is a devastating progressive degeneration of cognitive and physical capacity ending in death. There is no cure for SDAT at the present time. Although SDAT affects only about 4 percent of the older population, that older population is growing so large that SDAT affects two million people. Unless a cure is found, the number of SDAT victims will more than double as the numbers of older adults increase.

Profound cognitive impairment is the hallmark of SDAT. The majority of older people who are senile have SDAT. The disease was first diagnosed in 1907 by Alois Alzheimer, and there are three major neuropathological symptoms: (1) neuronal cell loss, up to 90 percent in certain regions of the brain; (2) senile plaques—which are small masses of degenerating tissue; and (3) neurofibrillary tangles, paired helical twisted filaments comprised of proteins which exist inside neural cells. Diagnosis of SDAT can only be confirmed presently after death at autopsy. However, rapid advances in research on SDAT may make a test for the disease using a patient's spinal fluid available soon.

Behavioral signs of SDAT begin with mild impairment of memory and semantic knowledge. Gradually the individual begins to show signs of confusion, and performance at work and at home declines. The patient tries to compensate by withdrawing from challenging situations. At some point the patients become a threat to themselves and require full-time care. If they go out, they get lost. If they try to cook, they burn themselves and may set the house on fire. They loose track of time and place and even forget the name of a spouse and children. Eventually, even physical functions fail, and the patient is confined to bed, unable to talk, walk, or eat without assistance. Death usually ensues about five to seven years after the first symptoms, but some SDAT patients survive twice that long.

The causes of SDAT are not known, but there are several hypotheses about its origin. One approach is to attribure SDAT to a slow-acting transmissible virus. Another hypothesis is that trace metals in the brain such as aluminum are involved in the disease. Genetic research suggests that the early-onset SDAT may be inherited, and a gene on the twenty-first chromosome has been implicated. Brain neurotransmitter studies have identified a significant and progressive decrease in the activity of the enzyme choline acetyltransferase. Finally, a biochemical marker for SDAT has been identified.

REFERENCES

BECK, A. T. (1967). *Depression: Causes and treatment.* Philadelphia: University of Pennsylvania Press.

BEUTLER, L., SCOGIN, F., MEREDITH, K., SCHRETLIN, D., HAMBLIN, D., POTTER, R. & CORBISHLEY, A. (1986). Efficacy of cognitive group therapy for depressed older adults. *Gerontologist, 26,* 214.

BLAZER, D. G. (1982a). *Depression in late life.* St. Louis: Mosby.

BLAZER, D. G. (1982b). The epidemiology of late life depression. *Journal of the American Geriatrics Society, 30,* 581–592.

BOYD, J. H. & WEISSMAN, M. M. (1981). Epidemiology of affective disorders: A reexamination and future directions. *Archives of General Psychiatry, 38,* 1039–1046.

BOYD, J. H. & WEISSMAN, M. M. (1982). Epidemiology. In E. S. Paykel (Ed.), *Handbook of the affective disorders.* New York: Guilford, p. 109–125.

BUTLER, R. N. (1975). *Why survive? Being old in America.* New York: Harper and Row.

COYLE, J. T., PRICE, D. L. & DeLONG, M. R. (1983). Alzheimer's disease: A disorder of cortical cholinergic innervation. *Science, 217,* 1053–1055.

CRAIG, T. J. & VAN NATA, P. A. (1979). Influence of demographic characteristics on two measures of depressive symptoms: The relation of prevalence and persistence of symptoms with sex, age, education, and marital status. *Archives of General Psychiatry, 36,* 149–154.

DAVIS, K. L. (1985). Alterations of cholinergic and peptide mechanisms in Alzheimer's disease. Invited paper presented at the XIII International Congress of Gerontology, New York.

DAVIS, K. L. & MOHS, R. C. (1982). Enhancement of memory processes in Alzheimer's disease with multiple-dose intravenous physostigmine. *American Journal of Psychiatry, 139,* 1421–1424.

FINCH, C. E. (1985). Research on the biochemistry of Alzheimer's disease. Invited symposium presented at the 93rd Annual Meeting of the American Psychological Association, Los Angeles.

GALLAGHER, D., THOMPSON, L. W. & BRECKENRIDGE, J. S. (1986). Efficacy of three modalities of individual psychotherapy: One year follow-up results. *Gerontologist, 26,* 214.

GALLAGHER, D., THOMPSON, L. W. & LEVY, S. M. (1980). Clinical psychological assessment in older adults. In L. W. Poon (Ed.), *Aging in the 1980s: Psychological issues.* Washington, DC: American Psychological Association, p. 19–40.

GATZ, M., HURWICZ, M. & WEICKER, W. (1986). Are old people more depressed? Cross-sectional data on CES-D factors. Paper presented at the annual meeting of the American Psychological Association, Washington, DC: August.

GATZ, M., SMYER, M. A. & LAWTON, M. P. (1980). The mental health system and the older adult. In L. Poon (Ed.), *Aging in the 1980s: Psychological Issues.* Washington, DC: American Psychological Association, p. 5–18.

GURLAND, B. J. (1976). The comparative frequency of depression in various adult age groups. *Journal of Gerontology, 31,* 283–292.

HAMILTON, M. (1967). Development of a rating scale for primary depressive illness. *British Journal of Social and Clinical Psychiatry, 6,* 278–296.

HARMATZ, J. & SHADER, R. (1975). Psychopharmacologic investigations in healthy elderly volunteers: MMPI Depression Scale. *Journal of American Geriatrics Society, 23,* 350–354.

HIRSCHFIELD, R.M.A. & CROSS, C. K. (1982). Epidemiology of affective disorders: Psychosocial risk factors. *Archives of General Psychiatry, 39,* 35–46.

HYBELS, D. C. (1986). Depression in the elderly: An application of the reformulated learned helplessness model. Unpublished doctoral dissertation, Temple University.

JARVIK, L. F. (1985). Genetics and Alzheimer-type dementia. Invited symposium presented at the 93rd Annual Meeting of the American Psychological Association, Los Angeles.

KATZMAN, R. (1984). Clinical and pathologic aspects of Alzheimer's disease. Invited paper presented at the 14th Annual Meeting of the Society for Neuroscience, Anaheim, CA.

KHACHATURIAN, Z. S. (1985). Progress of research on Alzheimer's disease: Research opportunities for behavioral scientists. *American Psychologist, 40,* 1251–1255.

LIEBERMAN, M. A. (1982). The effects of social support on responses to stress. In L. Goldberger & S. Breznitz (Eds.), *Handbook of stress: Theoretical and clinical aspects.* New York: Free Press.

MATSUYAMA, H. (1983). Incidence of neurofibrillary change, senile plaques, and granulovacuolar degeneration in aged individuals. In B. Reisberg (Ed.) *Alzheimer's disease.* New York: Free Press.

MATSUYAMA, S. S. & JARVIK, L. F. (1982). Genetics: What the practitioner should know. *Generations, 56,* 19–21.

MILLER, M. (1979).   *Suicide after sixty: The final alternative.* New York: Springer.

MORTIMER, J. A. (1983).   Alzheimer's disease and senile dementia: Prevalence and incidence. In B. Reisberg (Ed.), *Alzheimer's disease.* New York: Free Press.

MORTIMER, J. A., SCHUMAN, L. M. & FRENCH, L. R. (1981).   Epidemiology of dementing illness. In J. A. Mortimer & L. M. Schuman (Eds.) *The epidemiology of dementia.* New York: Oxford University Press.

PERL, D. P., GAJDUSEK, D. C., GARRUTO, R. M. et al. (1982).   Intraneuronal aluminum accumulation in amyotrophic lateral sclerosis and parkinsonism-dementia of Guam. *Science, 217,* 1053–1055.

PRUSINER, S. B. (1982).   Novel proteinaceious infectious particles cause scrapie. *Science, 216,* 136–144.

REISBERG, B. (1983).   Clinical presentation, diagnosis, and symptomatology of age-associated cognitive decline and Alzheimer's disease. In B. Reisberg (Ed.), *Alzheimer's disease.* New York: Free Press.

SALZMAN, C. & SHADER, R. I. (1979).   Clinical evaluation of depression in the elderly. In A. Raskin & L. F. Jarvik (Eds.), *Psychiatric symptoms and cognitive loss in the elderly.* Washington, DC: Hemisphere.

SLUSS, T. K., GRUENBERG, E. M. & KRAMER, M. (1981).   The use of longitudinal studies in the investigation of risk factors for senile dementia-Alzheimer's type. In J. A. Mortimer & L. M. Schuman (Eds.), *The epidemiology of dementia.* New York: Oxford University Press.

SPITZER, R. L., ENDICOTT, J. & ROBINS, E. (1978).   *Research diagnostic criteria (RDC) for a selected group of functional disorders.* New York: New York State Psychiatric Institute.

STORANDT, M., SIEGLER, I. C. & ELIAS, M. F. (Eds.) (1978).   *Clinical psychology of aging.* New York: Plenum.

TERI, L., UOMOTO, J. & STOFFEL, C. (1986).   Treatment of depression in Alzheimer's disease: Helping caregivers to help themselves and their patients. *Gerontologist, 26,* 214.

WOLOZIN, B. L. & DAVIES, P. (1986).   Characterization of the Alz-50 antigen. *Society for Neuroscience Abstracts, 12,* 944.

ZEMORE, R. & EAMES, N. (1979).   Psychic and somatic symptoms of depression among young adults, institutionalized aged and noninstitutionalized aged. *Journal of Gerontology, 34,* 716–722.

ZUNG, W.W.K. (1965).   A self-rating depression scale. *Archives of General Psychiatry, 12,* 63–70.

ZUNG, W.W.K. (1967).   Depression in the normal aged. *Psychosomatics, 8,* 287–291.

ZUNG, W.W.K. (1973).   From art to science: The diagnosis and treatment of depression. *Archives of General Psychiatry, 29,* 328–337.

CHAPTER 17

Autobiography and Life Review

The late adulthood years, according to Erik Erikson, are a time when the major psychosocial crisis revolves around the achievement of ego integration versus despair. It is a time when personal adjustment involves the ability to sort through the memories of one's life and pull them together into a meaningful whole. In this sense, autobiography as the ability to describe one's own life, is a therapeutic exercise for older adults.

Biography and autobiography have become more popular in recent years (Birren & Hedlund, 1985). These means of describing lives have received attention in popularly written books as well as in scholarly works. The increase in literature on the subject of biography and autobiography has been noted in such journals as *The Chronicle of Higher Education* (Paul, 1982). More and more often courses are being taught on how to create your own autobiography, and in some cases groups at senior centers and nursing homes work together to tell individual members' autobiographies (Butler & Lewis, 1982).

Years ago Butler (1963) emphasized the need for psychological adjustment in late life through the reminiscing process he called "life review." Butler felt that an awareness of the closeness of death led elderly individuals to reminisce about the events of their life. Life review in Butler's conceptualization was less systematic than an autobiography, as the individual might focus on a certain period of life or on certain limited aspects of life in his or her memories. While a preoccupation with one's past could result in depression, bitterness, and even anger, Butler felt that in many cases the insights gained from the life review process could lead to serenity and even wisdom in old age.

In his developmental task theory, Havighurst identifies adjustment to the death of a spouse and to one's own death as two of the developmental tasks of late life. Life review, including systematically undertaking one's own auto-biography, is a means of adjusting to impending death. We have seen in Chapter 16 on psychopathology and clinical intervention that much of what presents itself as late-life depression is really a grief reaction to the loss of loved ones. It is something that an individual experiences intensely for a period of time, but then the pain subsides. In the case of a spouse of many decades, it is a loss which can never be compensated. However, the intensity of the despair is reduced by time. Death is faced by individuals at all points in the life span, but it is associated with old age because that period of life is the natural time to die. Old age is usually the time of life that we are faced most frequently with death—of friends, loved ones, our spouse, and eventually ourselves.

In this chapter, we will discuss autobiography in older adults as a means to integrate life as part of the life review process. We will consider how proximity to death changes one's attitudes and activities and results in reminiscence as part of the individual's effort to achieve ego integration. In the next chapter, we will consider death and the psychological aspects of the dying process.

AUTOBIOGRAPHY

Everyone has a certain fascination with the events that have happened in one's life. At many periods of life we think about our past, and we may reinterpret the same events in a number of different ways as we look back from different vantage points of maturity. In old age when there are fewer time constraints due to retirement and reduction in responsibilities, reminiscing becomes more frequent. Indeed, we often think of old people as overly concerned with the past or even living in the past. Furthermore, we come to resent that they always want to talk with us about their experiences, as indicated in the following anecdote recounted by James Birren as he heard it from a student in one of his courses on autobiography:

> When I was a child, my grandfather used to tell me stories. One of his favorite stories was about the great distance he used to have to walk to school. It seems that all sorts of misadventures befell him on his long trek to school, and each time he told the story, the distance got longer and the tale became more embellished.
>
> One day he started, "Did I ever tell you the story about the time I was walking to school...?"
>
> I quickly interrupted and said, "Yes, Grandpa, you *did*."
>
> He looked at me very intently for a moment, and then replied, "Well, I'm gonna tell it again, 'cause I *like* it!"

Everyone has a story to tell, and usually these stories are fascinating to hear. For the most part, the dictum that fact is stranger than fiction is true, and these strange facts are often amusing. People of every age and from every type of background have stories about who they are, what has happened to them, and how they got to be where they are today. They exchange bits of their stories in the process of getting to know one another; they regale their friends at parties with particularly interesting stories; they console each other in times of sadness and loss with mutual tales of tragedy and failure. Nothing seems to be as interesting or as natural to people as telling their life stories.

Part of the fascination we have for telling and hearing stories is that we learn from our own and others' experiences. Listening to stories is fun and a relatively painless way to gather new and important information. This aspect of anecdotal, personal information is one of the rationales for presenting autobiographical material to illustrate various empirical phenomena about psychology and aging throughout this book.

Imparting knowledge about psychological aging is the purpose of this text, and it is important for the student to be acquainted with elderly people in order to better understand them. Unfortunately, in our age-segregated society, we have few opportunities to encounter the elderly. Through their stories, we hope to impart a better understanding of old people.

Another reason for presenting life history material is to demonstrate one of the most reliable observations about aging: the vast range of individual differences. The aged are probably the least homogeneous group in society. As we age we become more and more differentiated, more and more unique. Neugarten, an acknowledged authority on personality and aging, has characterized aging individuals as becoming more like themselves (Neugarten, 1968). Each and every individual has his own personal story which is unlike the story of any other. This diversity is apparent in the material which follows.

A third reason for presenting real-life interviews is that increasing focus on the issues of life span development, growth, and aging in institutions of higher education and in society at large is bringing with it a demand to address these issues (Birren & Hedlund, 1985). The rapidly emerging field of gerontology and the increased awareness of the real and potential social problems resulting from enhanced longevity have created the need for further specialized training in fields such as educational counseling, clinical and counseling psychology, social work, and pastoral counseling, among others. Thus, interest in the topic of autobiography has recently flourished, and the number of courses on the subject proliferate across the country, even into other countries.

Courses in autobiography and life history are being offered in such diverse disciplines as anthropology, English, history, psychology, religion, and sociology. They are offered in community colleges, at state and private universities, religious academic institutions, and colleges of continuing education, as well as in nonacademic settings such as church adult education programs, nursing homes, senior centers, women's clubs, and therapy groups (Birren & Hedlund, 1985).

Autobiography as a topic is gaining increasing attention from laypeople and scholars alike. Techniques have been developed to stimulate the writing of autobiographies, and individuals are meeting in groups to write about and share their life experiences. In addition to the amusement of telling and hearing life stories, autobiography appears to have a number of useful purposes.

The autobiographical impulse does not appear to be limited to any particular age group or educational background. The urge to "take stock" of one's life can come at any time, and usually occurs several times during a person's life. Young people often feel the need to assess where they have been before they decide where they are going as they prepare to launch into new worlds of college, career, marriage, or family. Middle-aged people spend a lot of time assessing themselves, their careers, their relationships and families, and their value systems as they go through various forms of mid-life transitions and "crises." Children leaving home, career changes, strained marital relationships, disillusionment with current goals and lifestyles all prompt the middle-aged person into looking back at where he or she has been before setting new directions for the future years. Older persons also find the process of life review to be fruitful, as they finish careers and relinquish previous roles. Indeed, a portion of this chapter will be devoted to the life review process as it is seen as a significant part of the last phases of one's life (Butler, 1961; Butler & Lewis, 1982).

The task of the elderly is to review decades of experience, integrating often discontinuous life events and finding meaning in existence. Erik Erikson (1959) has identified the characteristic feature of late life as accomplishing the goal of ego integrity as oposed to ending life in despair. Old people need to find that in all of those years and in all of that experience, there is something which can be extracted as an essence which gives meaning to the life they have lived. Indeed, exercises in life history have been initiated in hospitals for terminal care with great success. Patients have "work" to anticipate each day, they feel that they are leaving behind something of value for those whom they love, and it gives the nursing staff an interesting project to offer their dying patients along with some relief for themselves from the hopelessness of terminal care.

The following material is autobiographical in that it was written by the person who had the experience, Amy Phillimore Fowler. She wrote the following autobiographical material when she was 89 years old, and she was most pleased recently at the age of 93 to hear that her writing was being published in this book. She is a widow of over 20 years, living in an exclusive retirement community in California.

Mrs. Wilson S. Fowler's parents provided her with a comfortable middle-class upbringing, and with her very successful husband, she experienced an upper middle-class adult life. She has visited every state in the United States and has traveled around the world, even in her seventies. Although childless, she has numerous friends spread all over the country. Each year her birthday is an "event" as calls come to her from throughout the day and evening from friends she has made and kept over a period of close to a century.

Mrs. Fowler is an exceptional woman. One feature that makes her exceptional is her mind. Her memory is remarkable even a she progresses through her ninth decade, and it has been remarkable all of her life. She is a brilliant and knowledgeable woman. Her values are also ahead of her generation. She developed a deep love of blacks as a girl in Atlanta. Each year, one of her birthday telephone calls has been from Alonzo, a black man who worked for her husband's firm and who occasionally helped her when she entertained in her home on both the east and the west coasts. When he finally retired, Alonzo moved to New York, but he faithfully called Mrs. Fowler each year until he died in 1985 at the age of 94. Now his daughter makes the birthday call.

Among Mrs. Fowler's closest friends is a Japanese family. During World War II when the Japanese were sent to internment camps, the Fowlers invited a Japanese teenage girl into their home to work. This girl and her sister who worked in a home close by became the Fowlers' dear friends. When the girls married and had families, one of them named her daughter Amy in honor of Amy Fowler. Mrs. Fowler recently donated a large sum to purchase equipment for Amys husband's research laboratory at a university. Thus, Mrs. Fowler has reached across culture, race, and generations of friendship and found "family" in many places.

The author asked Mrs. Fowler whom she calls "Aunt Amy" to tell her autobiography into a tape recorder, but instead Mrs. Fowler sent a ten-page single-spaced, typed document stating, "I would never be able to pull my thoughts out of the recesses of my mind without my fingers on my typewriter. Inasmuch as I can see neither the keys or the typewriter roll clearly, I know that there are typing and perhaps spelling mistakes, as well as poor composition. . . for it is impossible with my limited central vision to make any corrections." She has macular degeneration, a loss of the foveal or fine vision, which makes it impossible for her to read.

In her letter accompanying the autobiographical statement, Aunt Amy wrote, "Not being sure just what you would find useful, I thought it would be well to start at the beginning and let the continuity unfold straight from my memory as I thought back through the years. Surely I have given just a skeleton without detail or incident. Even though my limitation of energy and vision have forced me to rest along the way, the task has not been a burden but rather a needed challenge to review the long years that have been given to me and to stimulate my thinking processes."

The following are excerpts from the material Mrs. Amy Fowler wrote as her autobiography to be included in this book.

AUTOBIOGRAPHICAL STATEMENT
OF MRS. AMY PHILLIMORE FOWLER

A meaningful page from the life of one approaching four score and nine is a challenge to balanced retrospection! I was born in Atlanta, Georgia, the largest metropolis of the deep South which only 25 years earlier had been almost totally destroyed by Sherman's marching army. My father was Canadian, my mother Pennsylvanian. Racial prejudice was the way of life in the South. That prejudice

FIGURE 17.1 Photograph of Amy Phillimore Fowler as she looked in her early 50s. (Courtesy of Mrs. W. S. Fowler).

totally covered those of Negro blood—and most particularly those who had a drop of white blood! We had a Negro cook and "wash-woman." They were always kind and loving to my brother and me and we loved them. But from our school mates and friends we learned the "dos and don'ts" in our association with Negroes.

At the turn of the century Father was transferred to Philadelphia. We were there almost two years. I dearly loved living in Philadelphia. The beautiful parks, both small and large, the museums, the Schuykill and Delaware Rivers. The pleasant, friendly neighborhood and the splendid school. I was not happy about it when Father was again transfererd, and we went to New York to live.

I was just past ten when we settled into a typical New York apartment on the West Side of Manhattan Island. We were within a short walking distance of Central Park, Riverside Drive, which ran along the majestic Hudson, and our very excellent schools. For the first time, I attended a girls' school and my brother was assigned to a boys' school. My brother who was just 11 months younger, was utterly heartbroken by this separation but was soon consoled when by the special help of one of his fine teachers he soon surged ahead of me! What a privilege we had in attending the New York schools of the early days of this twentieth century. I owe so much to the wonderful teachers of those years. With classes of 46 or more pupils we had teachers who exacted discipline and at the same time were inspiring. Often I was chosen by the students to be president for the term. And from time to time I was sent by the principal to substitute for the day when a teacher was absent. My teachers and even the principal of my school encouraged me to become a teacher. I did not have the heart to tell them that I did not want to be an "old maid." All the teachers I had known were old maids. [Mrs. Fowler said that at that time it was against the rules for a teacher to be married.]

New York in the teens of the twentieth century was an exciting place in which to live! Father joined a boat club and we had a boat on the Hudson. During the summer on in to late October we spent much time living on board and sailing all the waters around New York. We dug clams and picked wild plums on Sandy Hook. We anchored for weeks on the Shrewsbury River, and sitting on the back deck, we netted a pail full of crabs in a short time.

The nearby Carnegie Library was almost my daily haunt. Our school had special days to visit the Museum of Natural History where I learned so much about the peoples of the world and their cultures.

During fall and winter a favorite trip was to take the "L" to the Battery at the south end of Manhattan Island where we could see the magnificent New York harbor, the Statue of Liberty, the aquarium which was housed in Manhattan's first opera house, where the world famous Lily Lantry had sung. My brother, Bud, and I were especially interested in watching the boat from Ellis Island unload the immigrants who were pouring into our land from all of the European countries. In that day there were no quotas, but there was a strict law that immigrants had to speak and read enough English to apply for citizenship!

Knowledge of words and their use came through the constancy of my reading habits. Almost every day during school would find me walking to the nearby Carnegie Library, returning several books and taking home two or three. Reading was a "must." No matter what else occupied my days, a book was always with me. The fiction of my day, from *The Rover Boys, The Alger Series, The Lamp Lighter, Rebecca of Sunnybrook Farm,* and on to *Jane Eyre,* just to mention a few which set patterns of understanding the "dos and don'ts" which made one a desirable person. I loved beautiful, self-sacrificing love stories that ended "happily ever after" even as the fabulous fairy tales told it. I loved Scott and Dickens for they depicted real people. I detested *The Iliad* and *The Odyssey* because it did not belong to humanity. And of course I was delighted with biography, in both the first and third persons. I loved history with the accounting of what led to wars and the consequences. The Revolutionary and Civil Wars of our country were fascinating to me. As a child I even knew about the Spanish-American War. As a captain in the Governor's Horse Guards of the state of Georgia, my father was likely to be called.

Having a strong desire to launch into the mainstream of the city, which was the business world, I persuaded my parents to send me to a secretarial school. We found that the course at the Harlem Y.W.C.A. in upper Manhattan had an excellent reputation, and my parents decided that I would be "safe" under the influences there. [Harlem at the time was an excellent area.] I was indeed fortunate in this choice for many new experiences came into my life there. Upon graduation I was immediately placed in the educational department of the West Side Y.M.C.A. at 57th and Seventh Avenue. This was the largest Y.M.C.A. in the world! I was assigned to answering letters regarding the wide range of courses that were offered there. In those days both the Y.W.C.A. and the Y.M.C.A. offered a strong Christian influence. Enquiries from all over the world came into our department. Each day was a challenge and an opportunity to increase in knowledge. I was delighted with the opportunity to earn and at the same time learn.

Meanwhile, I attended the David Mannes School of Music, took private lessons in voice and sang successively in large New York churches of four different denominations. Along the way I was blessed with many friends, while still retaining contact—even to this day—with three closest school friends. . . .

A particularly handsome dividend during my five years with the "Y" was a full month's vacation every July. Mother and I took the train to Haines Falls, a beautiful resort area in the heart of the Catskill Mountains where we stayed at a highly recommended summer resort boarding house which was well known as a gathering place for delightful young people. We took the train because there was practically no automobile travel at that time. Father came later in the month for his vacation. It was there on July 18, 1914, while on my first vacation, that I met the wonderful man whom I would marry five years later.

The war in Europe had been raging, fought mostly in the trenches. This was World War I, which started in August 1914. The United States did not enter the war until after the sinking of the Lucitania in April 1917. Most of the young men I knew signed up for officers' training at Lake Champlain, New York. My "boss" had already left to join the Army when his friend who was Oliver Morosco's secretary appeared at my office and introduced himself in person. Morosco was a leading theatrical producer on New York's prestigious Broadway, and his secretary was fascinating and very handsome. In the course of time I almost made the mistake of being married to him. Meanwhile, before the secretary left for the Army, he recommended me to Morosco and Morosco accepted me, his first woman secretary.

Financially, the job was a big step up, and my daily contact with the successful actors and those seeking ways to climb the ladder to fame on Broadway were exhilarating. I was interacting with the biggest names in theater. It was a challenge to learn by observation and conversation the potentials of those whom I was meeting.

While working at the Y.M.C.A. I was always addressed as Miss Phillimore. In the Morosco offices where we had a switchboard operator, general manager, booking agent, and press agent, I was always called Amy, with the inclusion of Mr. Morosco. However, the Morosco stage hands, electricians, and elevator man all addressed me as Miss Phillimore. Of course I was known by my first name among the people of the theater. The offices of all the big-time theatrical people were familiar to me. I knew their phone numbers and whom to contact by heart—Belasco, Shubert, Henry Miller, etc. Broadway and Times Square were the "Great White Way"—very prestigious!

In 1918 Morosco decided to give a one-night benefit show to raise money for the Stage Women's War Relief Fund. He asked me if I had any ideas to offer for it. He accepted my suggestion, staging the Morosco offices as the focal setting and bringing the stars from his companies in New York and from his many road shows. He gave me the part of the receptionist and telephone operator, and I was the first speaker on the stage as the curtain rang up. I was the only totally non-professional in the entire production! That could not happen today with the existing labor laws.

Wilson S. Fowler and I were married in November 1919, and at Morosco's enticing offer of time arrangements, I remained with him for three more years. . . .

The 41 years of our marriage were filled with the joy of a love and devotion that never failed. Wilson was already on the first rungs of officialdom in the great communications corporation [Western Union] in which he spent his entire business career. He carried a heavy load of responsibility with equanimity. In those days the telegraph was the heartbeat between the media and the world, as well as every point of commercial, governmental, labor, and social activity in our country. During Wilson's 55 years of service there were two world wars, the Great Depression. . . . Through most of the years Wilson's responsibility was national which required traveling to every division headquarters in the country. I traveled with him from time to time. On two different trips we traveled in the company's private railroad car. . . . It was my great privilege to travel in every state in the union, and to see almost every town and hamlet. This gave me the privilege of meeting hundreds of our Western Union people and to have enjoyed their loving friendship through all these years, even since Wilson's death. He was greatly loved by all who knew him, as well as highly respected by those who worked with him. I count this loving loyalty a rare inheritance from him.

In the course of time Wilson headed four different divisions for the company, each division comprising nine or more states. The headquarters cities were Omaha, Denver, San Francisco, and New York. He became a vice president in New York while World War II was on, and we lived in beautiful Montclair, New Jersey where we spent nine very happy years. Mother had died the year before we moved to Montclair. I nursed her through her final illness with cancer. When she went I felt that my hands were completely empty. But God had prepared me for this separation and his abiding presence in my heart had taken away the fear I suffered in my childhood, and replaced it with the joy of knowing that "because He lives" my beloved mother now lives with Him. . . .

All my young life had been filled with strain, anxiety, and what is so much spoken of today, insecurity. From my earliest memory my mother suffered the debilitation of constant pain which no doubt was consequent to the ignorance of the doctor who delivered me, and only 11 months later, my brother. From a strong, healthy young woman of 21, she became a frail invalid. At 27 a surgeon performed a complete hysterectomy, and it was thought she would not live. However, she lived through years spent with severe headaches during which she spent days in a darkened bedroom, and complete quiet was required of us children. . . . I was five when mother had her operation, and for years I lived in fear that she would die. About a year later she contracted diptheria. My brother, Bud, and I were given the antitoxin so that we need not be quarantined from Mother's room. About a year after that Bud came down with typhoid fever. He was very low for many weeks. During his convalescence he had to learn to walk and talk again. I was held back a year from starting school in order that I could be in the same calss and watch over him. . . .

Father had become well known in Atlanta as he was the Southern representative of Otis Elevator. This required that he travel the southern states and also that he have membership in various clubs with required attendance at many social functions. The men of Atlanta were addicted to heavy social drinking. My father became addicted to the regular use of alcohol but never to the point of drunkenness. At all times he was able to "hold his liquor." But it was a strong influence, and to be critical and stern, it resulted in consequent unhappiness for our family. It was also a heavy financial drain, added to the constant medical bills. . . .

[In 1919 when he experienced a Christian conversion along with his wife, Mr. Phillimore overcame his alcoholism immediately. It was following the conversion of her parents that Aunt Amy experienced a Christian conversion that totally changed her motivation and values in her life. Indeed, she states that the two "greatest gifts" in her life have been her husband and her Christian faith.]

When we moved into our spacious beautiful new home, high on the upper side of upper Mountain Avenue in Montclair, with its magnificent view of the New York skyline, Father came to be with us. He happily and contentedly entered into our way of life, driving to business in New York every day.

Looking ahead to retirement, Wilson chose to come to San Francisco with a few years ahead in which to put down our roots and prepare to "live out our days" where the climate was so delightful. We came and settled on the Peninsula and love it! Father retired from his very active life in the elevator business in New York. He, too, loved being out here, and at once became active in many projects. So many dear friends came out to see us, we did not find time to be homesick. I might add that Father retired from his extremely active career at the age of 77 to come and be with us in California. He had made a tremendous contribution in the field of elevator engineering inasmuch as his company served the five boroughs of Manhattan where perhaps the greatest usage of elevators in the entire world is to be found. The New York papers carried articles of his retirement naming him dean of elevator engineering.

Our home in Hillsborough, a beautiful suburb of San Francisco, was finally located after almost three months of searching on both sides of the bay. There we spent our last 12 happy years as a family of three. . . . We had been living in California about eight years when Father's health began to fail, and suddenly he went home to be with the Lord. He had been such an active, wonderful member of our family for 17 years. How very much we missed him!

Two years later Wilson retired after 55 years of service with one company, Western Union. His associates of the Pacific division arranged a truly heartwarming occasion at the St. Francis Hotel in San Francisco. From all over the

United States, Wilson's colleagues of the years together with their wives came to honor this occasion. Several of his staff members spent a year of Saturdays researching newspaper archives and libraries for pictures and articles of human and historic value which had been published during each of the 55 years Wilson had served in the company.... The program was well received as it revealed the march of history through more than half of the twentieth century, and, delightfully, the presentation was a total surprise to Wilson!

Six months later Wilson had a severe heart attack from which he made a limited recovery. Following a regular routine of rest, diet, and walking, he was encouraged by his doctor to try a short round of golf. On the seventh hole he fell and was gone immediately. With the exception of my brother, Bud, who lived in Arizona battling a losing cause with cancer, I felt completely alone in this world. But God, in that very hour of Wilson's going, raised my eyes to heaven and filled my heart with acceptance. Standing alone beside that still body that had been so precious for more than 41 years, I thanked my Lord for the wonderful husband who loved me so completely to the end of his days....

Three and a half years earlier, Wilson and I had contracted to enter the Sequoias upon its completion. Within six months I moved to beautiful Portola Valley and took up life at the Sequoias.... Almost 22 years have passed over my head [since Wilson's death] as my heart has reached out to love and serve "because *He* first loved me."

An "around the wolrd" trip in 1966 was such a privileged encounter with the inhabitants of our world! In addition I made further trips four times with groups under the escort of *Eternity* magazine. Getting acquainted with the peoples of the world gave me such a warm feeling of belonging to each other. I recognized what a rich contribution has been made to the development of my own country by all the ethnic groups of the world who had bravely come to our shores during the earliest days. I had learned so much about this through my travels with Wilson to every state in the union, together with the fact that I had lived in seven of them.

Early in life I discovered that a strong body is a prime requirement for success in traveling. During my traveling days I observed old ladies who were enduring rather than enjoying their trip, and this led me to terminate my desire to go hither and yon unless it was of dire necessity. By the mid-1970s my two physical handicaps grounded me for distant traveling. I have macular degeneration of the retina. This destroys central vision but side vision permits one to get about. In addition, by some unknown cause, the cartilage has been torn away gradually from both shoulder sockets, and the use of my arms is very painful at all times. These conditions have no known cure, and they have worsened gradually over the past ten years. Now, every physical effort has been confined to short periods with a bit of rest along the way.

When I realized that the time had come to stop driving, I made arrangements for a driver for my church and [PEO] chapter attendance and then gave my car to someone who could make good use of it. Long ago I found that a life of peace and contentment depended upon acceptance of "whatsoever place in which I find myself." Also, there is always a thrill in the satisfaction of finding another way to compensate.... However, being unable to read is perhaps my most trying deprivation. It meets me at every turn.... Now, I keep my mind alive with the excellent Bible studies that come through the air by radio every morning and evening.... In addition I receive tapes sent by friends, and last Christmas I was given the priceless gift of the entire King James version of the Bible on tapes with the matchless diction of Alexander Courby. "My cup runneth over." In addition to this I can hear—and partially see—interesting documentaries on television, and once or twice during the night I hear a complete rundown of the news or prominent people in government or world affairs being interviewed....

This saga of reflections is at last drawing to a close. But perhaps I need to touch lightly on the warmth and joy that fills my being as I remember all the beautiful people who have embroidered all my days with the warmth of their love and constancy. The young, the very young, the middle-aged, and those who are walking up the last long hill with me have shared so much of themselves through the years. You have made me aware of my debt to all humankind, with gratitude to my heavenly father for His gifts.

LIFE REVIEW

Writing an autobiography such as the one excerpted in this chapter is a relatively systematic means of undertaking a life review. The psychiatrist and first director of the National Institute on Aging, Robert Butler (1963, 1968), pointed out the significance of the life review process for adjustment in late life.

While the tendency of older individuals to turn inward and become reflective about their past has often been viewed as the beginning of senility and indicative of a decline in the ability to remember recent events, Butler indicated that reminiscence in the aged may be part of a normal life process. The cause for the life review, according to Butler, is the realization of approaching dissolution and death.

The life review process is characterized by the progressive return to awareness of past experience. Especially common in this process is the resurgence of memories about unresolved conflicts that can be examined again and reintegrated into one's perspective of one's life.

In the autobiography of Amy Fowler, recall her vivid description of the death of her husband on the golf course from a second heart attack not too long after he had suffered the first major heart attack. Upon reading this, the author felt anger at the physician who approved of Wilson Fowler's premature return to the golf course and suspected that Aunt Amy might have had a similar feeling. Remember that she had suggested that the suffering of her mother was, "no doubt consequent to the ignorance of the doctor." However, upon discussing this, Aunt Amy emphatically stated that she felt no anger toward Wilson's physician. Rather, she felt relief that her husband did not linger and suffer, and she believed, "He was now with the Lord." Rather than becoming bitter, she resolved the conflict with positive emotion and expressed gratitude for the 41 years she had lived with her husband. This reflects the successful reintegration of conflict in reminiscence.

Butler and Lewis (1982) indicated that when reintegration is successful, it can give new significance and meaning to the life of the older person. It prepares the individual for death by mitigating fear and anxiety. Research on the process of life review has suggested that the life review is not necessarily a preoccupation of the aged until death. It is a relatively temporary process. It is undertaken through reminiscence and inner searching, and then the older adult returns to an external, future orientation (Havighurst & Glasser, 1972; Gorney, 1968).

From the time that he first presented the concept of the life review, Butler (1963) has maintained that the process occurs universally in all persons sometime during the final years. Indeed, in the opening sentence of the original 1963 article, Butler wrote, "The universal occurrence of an inner experience or mental process of reviewing one's life in older people is postulated" (Butler, 1963, p. 65). Not all older people are completely aware that they are involved in reminiscence, and some may defend themselves from realizing its presence. Life review is spontaneous, and the memories are not particularly selected by the individual, rather, they emerge into consciousness. While life review is seen in other age groups, particularly during adolescence and middle age, the intensity and emphasis on putting life in order are most striking in old age, undoubtedly motivated by the conscious or unconscious awareness of impending death.

Butler has observed that in late life people have a particularly vivid imagination and memory for the past. They can recall with sudden and remarkable clarity early life events. Think of the detail contained in Amy Fowler's autobiography. She describes with great intensity sights, sounds, locations, and feelings she had in New York City 80 years ago. According to Butler, who is a psychiatrist, and quite contrary to the beliefs of the original psychoanalyst, Sigmund Freud, in old age during the life review process there is a renewed ability to free associate and to bring up material from the unconscious. "Individuals realize that their own personal myth of invulnerability and immortality can no longer be maintained," (Butler & Lewis, 1982, p. 59).

When Butler first wrote about his insights on life review in 1963, he believed that reminiscence contributed to the occurrence of certain late-life disorders, particularly depression. He also suspected that reminiscence was involved in the evolution of such characteristics as candor, serenity, and wisdom among certain of the aged. Certainly, Amy Fowler's autobiography reflects expression of the latter qualities. The following excerpts from an interview of a 92-year-old woman exemplify a life review characteristic of poorer adjustment.

Interview with a Famous Artist

The woman to whom we will give the fictitious name of May Helsen had been a famous painter and was in the 1930s one of the few women listed in *Who's Who in American Art*. Her real name has not been used.

May Helsen resides in a private room in a nursing home. While she is ambulatory, she is quite deaf, and her hearing problem precludes much interaction with peers. Her eyesight is also failing, although otherwise her health is excellent for a nursing home resident. May had been in the facility for one year, and prior to that she spent almost another year shuffled through the health care system—first to a hospital, then to another nursing home where she appeared weak, confused, and not improved. She has no living relatives, and she never had children. She lived alone, widowed, on her farm near New Hope, Pennsylvania, an artist colony.

May is an oil painter who grew up in Philadelphia, the daughter of a painter. She achieved recognition for her art, even though in her lifetime it was difficult for female artists to succeed.

In the 1930s she married and moved to New Hope where she remained for the next 50 years of so. After her husband died, she remained on their farm, but living alone in her late eighties began to be difficult. She had been consuming large quantities of liquor, and at the age of 90 she was found unconscious in her yard. It was this event that precipitated her entry into the Pennsylvania health care system. During this period all of her property was sold, without her consent, to pay for her medical expenses. He first nursing home placement was unsuccessful. She was confused and depressed. When she was moved to a second nursing home, she appeared to recover, and she started to paint again. On her 92nd birthday, she had an opening exhibit at a gallery.

During an inverview with May Helsen, she was asked why she had not painted during the previous week. Her reply was, "I'm waiting for the ocean to speak to me. It's just about ready to—and then I'll paint." After commenting about her failing eyesight, she reminisced, "I'm going blind and lame just like an old horse my grandfather used to have. He was very old but they kept him anyway. I remember when that horse, Czar, used to be with my grandfather in Philadelphia. My sister and I lived with him in the city. Those were very wonderful days of my life. I used to go to the Pennsylvania College of Art on the train, and in the evening grandfather's boy would pick me up at the station in the carriage. He knew that horse so well, all he had to do was shake the reins and up that Czar would go—flashing up the hill. It's wonderful to know an animal that well."

When asked to describe the artist colony at New Hope in the 1930s and 1940s, Mrs. Helsen said, "Oh, we learned a lot from each other. In that artist colony we all painted each other and hung paintings in one anothers' homes. Mostly we had lots of fun. I knew them all. I could tell you trash about all of them. But sometimes artists disappointed me as people. I knew one man in New Hope who was a painter. He always said he hated all artists. His wife used to make his brushes out of his hair. . . .

"It churns me up inside to think about the past, about my farm. Everything sold right down to my nail clippers. No, I'll never get over that—all my paintings, my photographs, collections of pink china, my cats, my exotic bulb gardens, my mother's wedding dress from the 1800s. It was in the attic. All sold at auction.

"No, I'm old. It would be good to go somewhere in Italy to die where no one knows me."

Consequences of Life Review

It is common for the life review process to uncover feelings of regret that are increasingly painful. Severe forms reminiscence can yield anxiety, guilt, despair, and depression. In extreme cases when an individual is unable to resolve the previously experienced problems or to accept them, terror and panic, or even suicide can result. The most tragic life review is that in which a person decides that life was a total waste. Yet we discussed in Chapter 14 on personality and aging that just such outcomes do occur. Reichard, Livson and Petersen (1962) identified personality patterns they named the "angry" and the "self-hater," which were men who expressed after their retirement feelings of the futility of their lives. The angry men blamed others for their troubles, while the self-haters blamed themselves. In his assessments of reminiscence characteristics, Coleman (1974) also observed depression as well as acceptance or satisfaction as outcomes of the life review.

Butler and Lewis (1982) have pointed out some of the positive results of life review as being a righting of old wrongs, making up with enemies, coming to an acceptance of mortal life, developing a sense of serenity, feeling pride in accomplishment, and gaining a feeling of having done one's best. Reviewing one's life gives individuals the opportunity to decide what to do with the remaining months or years. They come to a recognition that emotional and material legacies must be worked out. While they are in no hurry to die, they are prepared for death.

Younger people may have the most difficult time with the life review process when older relatives and friends want and need to discuss their legacies and put their affairs in order. Even listening thoughtfully to the reminiscences of older people may be difficult. However, life review is a necessary and healthy process which is to be encouraged in older adults. Indeed, attempts are being made to develop life review therapy to aid older adults in undertaking this process (Lewis & Butler, 1974; Merriam, 1980).

Life review can also be conducted as part of a group activity. Groups of all kinds such as nursing home residents, senior center participants, social groups, church groups, and therapy groups can engage in the life review to help older individuals reevaluate their lives (Dietsche, 1979). Several guidebooks to aid groups and individuals in the life review are available (Daniel, 1980; Hendricks, 1979), and Butler and Lewis (1982) urge friends, relatives, and mental health professionals to be supportive and attentive when older adults reminisce because life review is a necessary and essential aspect of the final stage of life.

SUMMARY

Adjustment in later life includes the ability to sort through the memories of earlier years and to assemble them into a meaningful whole. Three well-known experts on adulthood and old age have addressed various aspects of the process of look-ing back on one's life and evaluating it. Erikson called this the process of achiev-ing ego integrity. The reminiscence which occurs spontaneously in old age is what Butler has called the process of life review. Birren has identified autobiography as a useful source of information about the development of individuals.

Autobiography can be written at any point in an individual's life, but when it is written in late life, it can become a therapeutic exercise. It helps the older adult to carry out a life review and achieve ego integrity. In this manner the older adult prepares to face death. Autobiography helps us to learn in an interesting and enjoyable way from our own and others' experience. Presenting autobiographical material in this textbook helps the student to become acquainted with older adults, it demonstrates the vast range of individual differences in old age, and it presents autobiography as a tool for studying aging.

Presented in this chapter is an autobiographical account of Mrs. Amy Phillimore Fowler who clearly has achieve ego integrity at this point in her long and full life. Also presented is an interview with a well-known artist whose life review process gives her pain. It is common for the life review process to uncover feelings of regret that are increasingly discomforting. In severe forms, reminiscence can yield anxiety, guilt, despair, and depression.

Some of the positive outcomes of life review can include the righting of old wrongs, making up with enemies, and developing a sense of serenity. Reviewing life gives individuals the opportunity to think about what to do with the time they have remaining. One of the things individuals need to do at this pont is to discuss their legacy with their spouse, children, and friends. While younger adults may find it difficult to let their beloved relative or friend talk about his or her coming death, it is an important aspect of the life review process. Friends and relatives are urged to be supportive and attentive when older adults reminisce. Life review is a necessary and essential aspect of the final stage of life.

REFERENCES

BIRREN, J. E. & HEDLUND, B. (1985).   Adult development through autobiography. In N. Eisenberg (Ed.), *Current perspectives in developmental psychology*. New York: Wiley.

BUTLER, R. N. (1961).   Re-awakening interest. *Nursing Homes, 10,* 8–19.

BUTLER, R. N. (1963).   The life review: An interpretation of reminiscence in the aged. *Psychiatry, 26,* 65–76.

BUTLER, R. N. (1968).   Toward a psychiatry of the life cycle: Implications of socio-psychologic studies of the aging process of the psychotherapeutic situation. In A. Simon & L. J. Epstein (Eds.), *Aging in modern society*. Washington, DC: American Psychiatric Association.

BUTLER, R. N. & LEWIS, M. I. (1982).   *Aging and mental health: Positive psychosocial and biomedical approaches* (3rd Ed.), St. Louis: Mosby.

COLEMAN, P. G. (1974).   Measuring reminiscence characteristics from conversation as adaptive features of old age. *International Journal of Aging and Human Development, 5,* 281–294.

DANIEL, L. (1980). *How to write your own life story: A step by step guide for the non-professional writer*. Chicago: Chicago Review Press.

DIETSCHE, L. M. (1979). Facilitating the life review through group reminiscence. *Journal of Gerontological Nursing, 5*, 43-46.

ERIKSON, E. H. (1959). The problem of ego identity. *Identity and the life cycle: Psychological Issues, 1*, 101-164.

GORNEY, J. E. (1968). Experiencing and age: Patterns of reminiscence among the elderly. Unpublished doctoral dissertation, University of Chicago.

HAVIGHURST, R. J. & GLASSER, R. (1972). An exploratory study of reminiscence. *Journal of Gerontology, 27*, 245-253.

HENDRICKS, L. (1979). *Personal life history. Writing for older adults. A handbook for teaching personal life history classes*. Tallahassee, FL: Leon County School Board.

LEWIS, M. I. & BUTLER, R. N. (1974). Life review therapy: Putting memories to work in individual and group psychotherapy. *Geriatrics, 29*, 165-169, 172-173.

MERRIAM, S. (1980). The concept and function of the reminiscence: A review of the research. *The Gerontologist, 20*, 604-609.

NEUGARTEN, B. L. (1968). The awareness of middle age. In B. L. Neugarten (Ed.), *Middle age and aging*. Chicago: University of Chicago Press.

PAUL, A. (1982). Biography is one sign of what may be new life in the art of recounting lives. *Chronicle of Higher Education, 24*, 19-25.

REICHARD, S., LIVSON, F. & PETERSEN, P. G. (1962). *Aging and personality*. New York: Wiley.

CHAPTER 18

Living, Dying, and Death

In this chapter we consider what for many decades in the United States has been a taboo subject. While we are finally maturing in the late 1980s in our professional and personal approaches to dying and death, until recently researchers and writers on this topic have described death as the "new pornography" (Sheskin, 1979). A pioneer in the study of death is Herman Feifel, who wrote in 1959 in the preface to *The Meaning of Death:*

> Even after looking hard at the literature, it is surprising how slim is the systematized knowledge about death. Far too little heed has been given to assessing thoroughly the implications of the meaning of death. There is no book on the American scene which offers a multifaceted approach to its problems. The purpose of this volume is a first attempt to narrow that gap by coming to grips with the problem of death as seen by philosophers, religionists, and scientists from varying bases (Feifel, 1959, p. v).

A decade and a half after the appearance of Feifel's book, attitudes toward the topic of death and dying in America were still defensive and grim. Ernest Becker wrote in *The Denial of Death:*

> . . . the idea of death, the fear of it, haunts the human animal like nothing else; it is a mainspring of human activity—activity designed largely to avoid the fatality of death, to overcome it by denying in some way that it is the final destiny for men (Becker, 1973, p. ix).

It is no wonder that in this climate of fear and repression about death that efforts to avoid or escape it were made. In 1964 Robert Ettinger, a physicist, published *The Prospect for Immortality*. In this book Ettinger proposed the practice of cryonics which involves freezing the body for an indefinite period until a cure for the cause of the frozen patient's death can be found. While the scientific community was not impressed, the book appealed to Americans so fearful of death of loved ones and of their own dying, and the book was quite successful. Cryonics societies were created in several regions of the country, and some individuals were "suspended," that is, frozen and kept in liquid nitrogen at a temperature of − 320 degrees Fahrenheit.

A dramatically opposite approach to dying is suicide, an option which is taken strikingly more often in later life, especially by older white males. Edwin Schneidman, a noted authority on death, dying, and suicide, has maintained that the role of the individual in contribuitng to his or her death should be noted on every death certificate. That is, whether the patient contributed not at all to the death, a little, moderately, or completely. Schneidman feels that many kinds of suicide go unreported, and that the incidence of suicide is much greater than acknowledged (Schneidman, 1976).

Euthanasia, or mercy killing, can be a form of suicide, executed by the dying person or at the request of the dying individual by a relative or friend. With the availability of medical technology to keep parts of the body in a state considered legally alive, even the definition of euthanasia is becoming difficult. Is turning off the respirator euthanasia? In some cases relatives of the dying patient and the physicians and hospital administrators have been forced into court to make such decisions.

The right-to-die movement, formally initiated in 1938, works for the recognition of the individual's right to die with dignity and has been active in establishing legislation such as living-will laws now enacted in 16 states. The living will, made when the patient is alert and functioning, directs the attending physician to withhold or withdraw treatment that merely prolongs dying in the case of an incurable or irreversible mental or physical condition with no reasonable expectation of recovery.

The state of the medical care system is technologically advanced to prolong life, but often this system works to defeat the wishes of the dying patient. For example, when asked what they would do if they had a terminal illness and death was imminent, 60 percent of a sample of older adults answered that they would prefer to go home to die as opposed to remaining in the hospital where more life prolonging measures would be taken (Mathieu & Peterson, 1970).

A third option that was not available in 1970 when Mathieu and Peterson's study was carried out reflects the increasing awareness of the needs of the terminally ill patient. This is the hospice. The hospice provides a supportive, comfortable setting for dying patients and their families. Doctors, nurses, staff, and family members are trained to help the patient with positive supports. Pain-killing medication is given freely, but no heroic measures are taken to prolong life. The advent of the hospice in the United States represents a clear example of progress in the way Americans deal with living, dying, and death.

ATTITUDES TOWARD DEATH

Attitudes toward death is a topic which has been studied since the very beginning of the modern era of research on the psychology of aging. The work was initiated by G. Stanley Hall at the end of the nineteenth century. Hall developed a questionnaire on conceptions of death and reported on the attitudes of 299 respondents in an article entitled, "A study of fears" (Hall, 1897). He devoted a long last chapter in *Senescence: The Last Half of Life* (Hall, 1922) to "the psychology of death." A conclusion of Hall's which received support in studies of attitudes toward death for decades was that fear of death was more a preoccupation of the young. "But the fear of death and the forms of mitigating this fear are chiefly because man still dies young. If we had experienced and explored senescence fully we should find that the lust of life is supplanted later by an equally strong counterwill to die" (Hall, 1922, p. 514). Of course, when Hall undertook his survey, life expectancy at birth in the United States was less than 50 years. A much greater percentage of the population died young, and death was a more likely presence in youth than it is today.

A number of studies have replicated Hall's original result that fear of death is greatest in adolescence and that young adults fear death while older adults worry more about the circumstances of their death (Kalish, 1976; Kastenbaum & Aisenberg, 1972). Other studies have not found significant age differences in anxiety about death past adolescence (Oleshansky, Gamsky & Ramsmeyer, in press; Templer, Ruff & Franks, 1971). Indeed, clinical studies of death anxiety suggest that those individuals who assert with the greatest certainty that they are not afraid of death may be the ones who give evidence of having the greatest unconscious fears of death (Feifel & Branscomb, 1973; Feifel & Jones, 1968; Magni, 1972). Unconscious fears were assessed by examining people's sensitivity to death stimuli on projective tests.

DEALING WITH DYING
AND DEATH

The individual who is credited with having the greatest impact on contemporary attitudes toward dying and death is psychiatrist Elizabeth Kubler-Ross. While her theory about the dying process has not received empirical support, her sensitivity to the dying patient and her prolific writing about her experience with the dying, especially her 1969 best seller, *On Death and Dying,* have made her almost a cult figure and have impacted our attitudes about death and dying.

It was during the mid-1960s that Kubler-Ross began her work with the dying; a period when the topic of death was still a taboo. At first, she simply wanted to interview a dying patient for a medical school seminar. However, when she searched a 600-bed hospital for dying patients, asking staff on each floor to locate one, none could be found. Although the hospital was reporting deaths on a daily basis, no one wanted to identify a terminally ill patient. Sudnow (1967) was one of the first to describe this phenomenon that was experienced by Kubler-Ross. There was a systematic organization of events through which institutions attempted to conceal the near dead and the dead. It was only when Kubler-Ross went back and asked about specific patients that doctors admitted that the patient was terminally ill. The topic of death and dying was clearly avoided in medical schools at that time.

European attitudes about death and dying are different from American attitudes, and Kubler-Ross's natural openness toward the dying might have been a reflection of her experience as a child in Switzerland. There death was confronted with honesty and dignity. Maria Domenici, aged 92 at the time of her interview, came to the United States from Sicily in 1919. Interviewed in Italian which she preferred to speak, she expressed the attitude more typical of the European attitude to dying. She said that she rarely thinks about dying. She feels that it is just as much a part of life as birth, but Americans do not understand that. She feels that people spend too much money and time grieving. Life must go on no matter what age you are. Her favorite proverb which her father taught her is, "E'meglio vivere un giorno du leone che cent' anni du perona." It is better to live one day as a lion, than 100 years as a lamb.

Based on the thousands of hours she spent with over 200 patients facing death, Kubler-Ross developed a stage theory about the process of dying. She suggested that these stages were characteristic of all dying individuals, once they know that they are terminally ill (Kubler-Ross, 1969). The first reaction of the dying patient when learning of the prognosis is *denial.* Kubler-Ross (1969) reported that almost all of the patients she interviewed initially responded, "No, not me, it cannot be true." This denial stage may result in isolation by the patient, but he or she cannot sustain denial for very long, and eventually they accept that the diagnosis was not a mistake.

Upon acceptance of the diagnosis, the second stage of *anger* sets in. The preoccupation becomes, "Why me?" After the anger comes the third stage of *bargaining.* The patient holds out some hope and rationalizes, "If God has decided to take us from this earth and he did not respond to my angry pleas, he may be more favorable if I ask nicely" (Kubler-Ross, 1969, p. 82). *Depression* occurs as the patient weakens and his or her body shows clear signs of the impending death.

The fifth stage, which Kubler-Ross admits is not attained by all terminally ill patients, is *acceptance.* If a patient has had enough time before death ensues, and if help has been given by caretakers in working through the previous stages, the individual will attain a state of freedom from depression and anger. This is not a happy state; it is almost void of feeling, including pain. One patient called it "the final rest before the long journey" (Kubler-Ross, 1969, p. 113).

While lauding Kubler-Ross for stimulating attention to the dying process and sensitizing caretakers to attend to rather than withdraw from the terminally ill, Kastenbaum (1985) criticized the stage theory itself. The theory has not been confirmed empirically (Hinton, 1975; Metzger, 1979; Schultz & Anderman, 1974)

Weisman and Kastenbaum (1968) emphasized the great individual differences in the way people die. Kastenbaum objected to any theory which might imply the standardization of death. Consider the death of "Gramp," affectionately portrayed in photographs and writing by his two grandsons (Jury & Jury, 1976).

> On February 11, 1974, Frank Tugend, age 81, removed his false teeth and announced that he was no longer going to eat or drink. Three weeks later, to the day, he died.
>
> Frank Tugend was our grandfather. He was born in Scranton, Pennsylvania in 1892. Although he went into the mines as a slatepicker when he was 11 years old, he had a happy childhood.
>
> He married Anna Margaret Schmidt, a young lady he met in Sunday-school class, and they took a house within walking distance of the mines.
>
> In 1924, with three children added to the family, Gramp made a bold move for a Scranton coal miner. He purchased a tract of land in the country and moved his young brood into a hastily constructed garage. Each night after work, Gramp would hammer, nail, saw, and plaster until he had built a splendid house in the woods.
>
> The overpowering experience of our growing-up years was the joyous two weeks we spent each summer with Gramp and Nan. We didn't just love them; we worshiped them. Our vacations were full of crazy, wild fun. It was not unusual for my grandmother to throw a sack of water from an upstairs window on an unsuspecting victim.
>
> After his retirement, Gramp was cursed with an infirmity that's lumped under titles like senility or hardening of the arteries or generalized arteriosclerosis.
>
> The camera has always been part of our family life. We photographed Gramp through his years of strength, and we saw no reason to stop when he became ill (Jury & Jury, 1976).

Mr. Tugend's approach to death, willing himself to die, would be difficult to mold into a stage theory. It is relatively unique, as was his family's ability to support him, even in his atypical approach to the end of life. Of this, his grandsons commented:

> When Gramp stopped eating, we checked with his doctor. He said there was no way to force nourishment on Gramp short of hospitalization and intravenous feeding. That possibility had always been something the family wanted to avoid. To see this wiry, independent, sometimes exasperating but thoroughly decent man strapped to a hospital bed with tubes protruding from his arms was completely alien to the person of Gramp and the life he'd led. We would not take Gramp's destiny from him; to die was a decision his inner force had obviously decided upon. While newspapers debate the right to die, death researchers find that many old people control the time and the manner of their going. If he became racked with pain, we would insist on medical treatment to relieve the suffering. Beyond that, it was Gramp's show. We continued to cajole him about eating, but he was adamant. He told Nink, his daughter, "I'm just going to lay here until it happens" (Jury & Jury, 1976).

Many of the conceptual and methodological deficiencies of Kubler-Ross's stage theory approach have been pointed out (Kastenbaum, 1981; Kastenbaum & Costa, 1977; Schneidman, 1980). The tendency to limit attenton to the hypothetical states is a feature which Kastenbaum (1985) viewed as most problematic.

Kastenbaum felt that the control gained through naming and predicting phases of response was an illusion. Health care personnel used the theory to reduce anxiety. Fortunately, according to Kastenbaum (1985), theory and research into the dying process appear to be becoming liberated from the inadequacies of stage theory.

ROLE OF THE LIVING IN HELPING
DURING THE DYING PROCESS

It is mentioned in Chapter 17 on autobiography and life review that one of the last things younger people want to do is listen to the reminiscing of older people. A typical negative stereotype of the old is that they are garrulous and living in the past. Younger people attempt to escape listening. This typical avoidance in the young, coupled with a societal aversion to discussing death, frequently precludes the possibility of an older adult's putting his or her affairs in order and talking about their death. Many research sources address the value of allowing dying persons to talk about the process of dying and what will happen after their death (Schwartz & Peterson, 1979). The Harvard psychiatrist, Avery Weissman (1972), emphasized the need for sensitive responding by the caretaker. Making oneself accessible for intimate sharing and remaining open and responsive during the discussions are necessary to allow the dying individual to express his or her feelings and needs.

Mathieu (1972) conducted research on the kind of supports most important to people when they think about death. The results of that study are presented in Table 18.1. One of the interesting results was that the outcome was similar for three quite divergent groups of older people. The Laguna Hills group were upper middle class retirees residing in an exclusive retirement community in southern California. The Pasadena sample was comprised of suburban southern California community-dwelling elderly. The mountain state sample involved an older group of community-residing individuals from rural Montana. Memories of a full life were most comforting to two of the three samples, and in the third sample, memories and religion were equal as providing the most comfort.

TABLE 18.1 Religion As A Comfort When Thinking of Death

Which of the Following Comforts You Most As You Think of Death?	Pasadena (N = 189)		Laguna Hills (N = 183)		Mountain State (N = 115)	
	N	%	N	%	N	%
My religion	62	32.8	58	31.7	43	37.4
Love from those around me	49	25.9	51	27.9	29	25.2
Memories of a full life	78	41.3	74	40.4	43	37.4

Source: Mathieu (1972).

The Hospice

Until quite recently the medical care system did not provide older adults (or terminally ill individuals of any age) with the option to die naturally in a facility staffed with health care personnel. The options were either to abandon hospital care entirely to go home or to remain in a nursing home or hospital where heroic measures including intravenous feeding and other medical technologies would be used. The expense for such measures is prohibitive, and for the cost as well as for distaste of these measures, patients objected. In 1970, Mathieu and Peterson wrote, "The medical care system that functions in our society has not been, nor is it presently a socialization agency or agent for dying and death. In fact the strong taboo on death has enabled the medical care system to function almost as an anti-socialization process in society" (Mathieu & Peterson, 1970, p. 4).

Interviewing 183 men and women aged 50 years and older living in Leisure World, Laguna Hills, California, Mathieu and Peterson (1970) found that the majority wanted to die at home, they wanted all treatments withdrawn except those to reduce pain, and they wanted to know that they had a terminal illness. Some of the results of the survey are presented in Table 18.2. At that time the traditional medical practices involving dying and death were almost in exact opposition to people's desires.

Herman Feifel described the situation in the following manner in 1963:

> We have been compelled, in unhealthy measure, to internalize our thoughts and feelings, fears and even hopes concerning death. . . . Some think and say that it is cruel and traumatic to talk to dying patients about death. Actually, incoming data indicate that patients want very much to talk about their thoughts and feelings about death, but feel that we, the living, close off the avenues for their accomplishing this. A good number of them prefer honest and plain talk from physicians about the seriousness of their illness. They have a sense of being understood and helped rather than becoming frightened or panicking when they can talk about their feelings concerning death (Feifel, 1963, pp. 66–67).

In London, Dr. Cicely Saunders as medical director of St. Christopher's Hospice developed an innovative response to dying patients which has served as a model for hospice care in the United States. The aim is to create institutional care which meets the needs of the terminally ill patient and his or her family. Doctors, nurses, and staff receive special training which they then use to train dying patients and their families. In this manner the last weeks of life are humanized, and physical pain is minimized. Pain killers are given freely, but no life-prolonging technologies are used. Staff members and families are trained in their attitudes toward death and they are instructed to be open to discussing death so that the dying person is surrounded by positive supports throughout the terminal illness. Families can continue to receive counseling after the death as well. Thus, both the dying patient and his relatives are treated in the hospice, and the attempt is to provide the patient with a decent appropriate death in a dignified manner.

TABLE 18.2   Orientation Dimension

a.: If a person has an incurable disease and death is imminent, should a doctor

Response:	Value	Frequency	Percentage
Use every medical treatment and device available to keep the person alive	1	7	3.8
Continue to use reasonable life-maintaining treatment, but avoid "heroic" methods	2	55	30.1
Withdraw all treatments except those designed to maintain comfort and reduce pain	3	121	66.1

$N = 183$ Mean = 2.6

b: If you suffered an incurable illness, would you like the doctor to

Response:	Value	Frequency	Percentage
Keep information to himself	1	7	3.8
Inform the nurses and staff	2	7	3.8
Inform your family	3	23	12.6
Tell you	4	146	79.7

$N = 83$ Mean = 3.7

c.: If you had a choice, would you rather die

Response:	Value	Frequency	Percentage
In a hospital	1	68	37.1
In a neighborhood nursing home	2	3	1.6
At home	3	112	61.2

$N = 183$ Mean = 2.3

Source: From Mathieu & Peterson (1970).

The hospice approach emphasizes the individuality of each patient and the needs and rights of families and caregivers as well. Thus, if the patient prefers to die at home, hospice personnel arrange to provide supports similar to those provided in the hospice setting itself. Some hospices are housed in buildings set off by themselves, while others are located in a wing of a regular hospital. Kastenbaum (1985) is optimistic about the hospice movement for treatment of the dying aged. While he admits that support for the terminally ill older patient is not yet within the total health care system, the hospice influence is reaching into more conventional medical practice. Kastenbaum feels that the hospice influence may result in improved care for the terminally ill aged in all settings.

There is now an ongoing National Hospice Study through which we can expect to gain further knowledge about care for the terminally ill elderly (Mor, 1982; Morris, 1982). Already from St. Christopher's Hospice have come useful studies of pain relief (Twycross, 1974) and family dimensions of care (Parkes, 1975). Thus, in the 1980s in the United States we have seen a genuine change in attitudes and provision of care to the terminally ill which accurately reflects the desires for care of the dying articulated by elderly in earlier decades.

WILLING DEATH: SUICIDE, EUTHANASIA, AND THE RIGHT TO DIE

On the one hand, individuals go to great lengths to remain alive and to avoid death. On the other hand, some people seek death and welcome it. In this discussion of willing death, we will turn to what G. Stanley Hall (1922) referred to as the opposite force to the lust for life, the "counterwill to die."

Suicide

The incidence of suicide increases with age and reaches the highest rate in the group aged 75 to 84 years (National Center for Health Statistics, 1986). Adolescent suicide receives more media coverage, perhaps leading us to believe that the suicide rate is highest in that period of life. The suicide rate in the group aged 17 to 24 years is 12.5 per 100,000, while the rate for the 75 to 84 age group is 22 per 100,000. Older adults are almost twice as likely to take their own life as adolescents. Also, since death is a more likely event for old people, the suicide rate in late life may be underestimated. Older adults are likely to have one or two chronic diseases which are life threatening, but adolescents typically enjoy excellent health. Thus, it is easier to cover up a suicide in late life to make it appear to be naturally caused than it is in a healthy adolescent.

Suicide is a relatively common occurrence in contemporary society. Of the 15 leading causes of death, suicide ranks eighth. Men are far more likely than women to succeed at suicide. The age-adjusted death rate for suicide was 3.6 times higher for men than for women in the most recently available health statistics (National Center for Health Statistics, 1986). In the United States the most likely individual to commit suicide is an older white male. By the 35 to 44 age period, the suicide rate for white men exceeds the rate for all other groups, and it surges dramatically until it is over three times the rate for other racial groups and women in the 75 to 83 age group.

Failing health may be the primary reason that older men take their own lives. Losses they have experienced in old age may be another cause. Social and economic loses felt as a result of retirement, and the loss of identity from the work role may be felt especially strongly by older white males who previously had experienced a position of power and prestige in their community.

When older men decide to commit suicide, they usually succeed. In their case, suicide is not a cry for help, and they do not choose a means such as an overdose of sleeping pills from which there is a chance for rescue. The following case of Joseph Parlucci is an example.

Joseph Parlucci was a 68-year-old retired police officer who lived with his wife in their house in Long Beach, California, a suburb of Los Angeles. Joe had been on the Long Beach police force for 40 years and was well known in the community. He did some volunteer work with troubled adolescents several days a week and kept busy with projects around the house and with fishing trips to the nearby coast. Joe and his wife attended weekly mass at the nearby Catholic church and were recognized affectionately by almost everyone in the parish. Joe loved seeing any or all of his nine grandchildren, and he enjoyed the frequent visits of his four sons and their families, all of whom lived less than an hour away. It was very apparent that Joe had adjusted well to retirement.

Shortly after his 68th birthday, Joe had began to experience headaches which were relatively mild at first but got more and more severe. Since his health had always been good, the headaches alarmed him. However, he suffered with them for several months without telling his wife. One day when he awoke, he had difficulty talking. What words he could manage to get out were slurred. This symptom he couldn't hide from his wife, and it also frightened him even more than the headaches. He agreed to go to his longtime physician who examined Joe and immediately referred him to a neurologist. The neurologist gave Joe a number of tests, including a CAT scan, an X-ray picture of Joe's brain. The CAT scan indicated a tumor about the size of a baseball in the left parietal lobe of Joe's brain. From Joe's previous health records the neurologist had been able to obtain an earlier CAT scan taken just before Joe retired. In pursuing a suspect, Joe had gotten hit in the head and knocked out. The previous CAT scan showed no sign of a tumor, and the neurologist suspected that the tumor he could see now was malignant and spreading rapidly. He gave Joe the name of a neurosurgeon and recommended that Joe see him immediately.

Joe's headaches got worse, his speech was often impaired, and he sometimes experienced numbness in his right arm and fingers. He visited the neurosurgeon and agreed to surgery which was scheduled a month later. A week before the surgery, Joe cancelled it without telling his wife. In the early evening he sent her to the market across town for some Italian candy which was his favorite. When she returned she found Joe slumped in his chair with a bullet hole in his skull. She discovered that he was still alive, and she called the paramedics. She quickly hid the gun that Joe had dropped on the floor and told the paramedics and later the police that they had been burglarized and that she had seen a man fleeing from her house as she returned home. Later the next day she drove to the pier and dropped the gun in the ocean.

Joe died on the operating table. He was buried in the parish cemetery, and his funeral was attended by well over 500 mourners. His death was recorded as a homicide. The case remained open as the killer was never found.

In this example we have a man who has adjusted well to retirement, but he committed suicide as a result of his drastic change in health status. The stigma of suicide was avoided by the family due to their religious beliefs. However, Joe's former connections with the local police force probably helped to suppress further investigation. His suicide is typical of a suicide in an older white male in that it was violent and almost certain to succeed.

Euthanasia

Euthanasia means the "good death," and it is usually not as dramatic as Joe's suicide, although technically suicide is one form of active euthanasia. Passive euthanasia means allowing the person to die by not taking artificial measures to keep him or her alive. The care occurring at a hospice might be termed passive euthanasia.

Active euthanasia, which is the deliberate shortening of a life, has several forms. One type would be when the patient voluntarily hastens death. Gramp, as previously described, is a clear example of this form of active euthanasia. He stopped eating and drinking to terminate his life. Another type of active euthanasia is to decide yourself that if certain circumstances are met, then life should be terminated. The living will exemplifies this type of active euthanasia. A person may decide in advance that if they become comatose with no hope for recovery, they want to die. Sixteen states now recognize this living will. Sometimes friends make pacts with one another without signing a document like a living will, and one friend may have to gently ease the other out of life.

The third kind of active euthanasia is what we know as mercy killing. Without the permission of the dying individual, but when the dying person may be in a great deal of pain with no hope of recovery, he or she is helped to die. Evidence has emerged that a mercy killing occurred in 1936 in the case of King George V of England, grandfather to Queen Elizabeth II. Lord Dawson of Penn, physician of the king, hastened the monarch's end by injecting him with fatal doses of cocaine and morphine. Euthanasia is illegal in Britain, but Lord Dawson apparently had several overriding motives. He wanted the king to die painlessly with dignity, and he wanted to make sure the king died in time to make the morning's newspapers and *The Times* in partiuclar. The evening journals were deemed less worthy of heralding King George V's death.

The Right to Die

The issue of death can stir heated emotions at any point in the life span. Certainly abortion is a controversial issue for which there is no simple answer. Euthanasia and the right to die are similarly complicated and difficult to resolve. On the one hand, moral and religious arguments prohibit killing under any circumstances. This is why a majority of states compel hospitals and physicians to use artificial measures to keep patients alive. In line with what is practiced in a majority of states, Appelbaum and Klein (1986) deplore the popularization of euthanasia in media, legal, and medical circles and advocate an undivided commitment by physicians to healing the sick and preserving life.

Opposed to this perspective is the Society for the Right to Die, and this society has apparently gained the support of the powerful American Medical Association. In March 1986, after two years of study, the Council on Ethical and Judicial Affairs of the American Medical Association issued the opinion that it is ethically permissible for doctors to withold all life-prolonging treatment, including artificial nutrition and hydration, from patients in irreversible coma and from dying patients.

The battle emerging over the right to die has expanded to include the question, "When, if ever, should nasal tubes or other life-sustaining artificial feeding be withheld or withdrawn from the terminally ill, the permanently unconscious and other incurable men and women unable to relate to life in any meaningful way?" Rather than being a private concern between the physician and the family, the debate has become public (Otten, 1986). The right-to-life movement views the removal of tubes as starving patients to death. "These decisions withdrawing artificial nutrition are a direct movement towards widespread euthanasia," says John Wilke, head of the National Right to Life Commimttee, "and we will strenuously oppose that. Our legislation will say, in effect, that under no circumstances will you starve this person to death. We are the spear carriers in this battle" (Otten, 1986).

At the present time, what has come to be called the food-and-water debate is the most controversial issue in the right-to-die area. Medical and legal practices as well as the courts have moved to accept the right-to-die perspective when technological interventions are involved. "Pulling the plug" on a terminally ill patient is no longer very controversial. However, the practice of withdrawing nutrition and hydration still cause a furor. As John Rowe, a geriatrician at the Harvard Medical School, stated, "I do see a heightened awareness of the issue, but withdrawal of food and water is a barrier that a good many people aren't ready to cross" (Otten, 1986).

CRYONICS

A very different approach to dying is taken by individuals involved in the cryonics movement. While an individual must be legally dead before he or she can be frozen, subscribers to the cryonics approach redefine death to fit their practice. They view the individuals they suspend as in an intermediary stage. Cryonicists define death as the point at which resuscitation technology is insufficient to revive the frozen patient (Sheskin, 1979). They feel that in the future medical science will be able to repair almost any damage to the body. Thus, freezing the damaged human body at this point in time preserves it for a future time when it can be thawed and repaired.

At least 12 cryonics societies exist at the present time, and many of them are involved in the suspension of human bodies. Cryonic suspension begins as soon as death is pronounced by lowering the temperature of the individual. He or she is packed in ice, and special attention is given to the head region. Cryonic practitioners believe that the immediate lowering of body temperature prevents deterioration and thus halts the damage brought about by death. *Patient* is the term cryonicists use to refer to the body at this point. They put the patient in a strong, thin, watertight sack. Ringers lactate solution is perfused through the circulatory system to prevent cell damage. Then a solution of cooled glycerol in Ringers lactate solution is used. Heavy foil is wrapped around the body, and a separate facial piece is used to permit easy removal for viewing.

At this point the patient is placed in a capsule. The capsule is eight feet tall, 31 inches in diameter, and has a removable top. The patient is suspended vertically in it and is surrounded by liquid nitrogen maintained at a temperature of -320 degrees Fahrenheit. The liquid nitrogen is replaced on a monthly basis. The suspension and maintenance are expensive. The Eastern Cryonics Society estimates that $50,000 should be adequate for the suspension procedure and maintenance.

Robert Ettinger, the founder of the cryonics movement, got the idea for freezing human bodies after reading an article about the use of glycerol to freeze frog sperm. While some scientific research has been undertaken with freezing and reviving various species of animals, no success has ever been achieved in freezing and then reviving any healthy mammal, let alone a diseased one which has already died.

BEYOND-DEATH EXPERIENCES

Over the past decade as the taboo against discussing death has been gradually lifted, some attention has been focused on individuals reporting sensations they had during a near-death experience. Impetus to the publicity about near-death experiences was given by Elizabeth Kubler-Ross who claimed on the basis of interviews with people who had been resuscitated that "beyond a shadow of a doubt" there is life after death (Briggs, 1976). Most scientists assert that the available evidence from near-death experiences proves little or nothing about the afterlife and equate the sensations to vivid dreams or hallucinations. However, for most of those individuals who have had the experience of nearly dying, the visions they had significantly changed the way they led the rest of their lives.

For about a year and a half, from early 1980 to September 1981, the Gallup organization polled American adults about their attitudes and beliefs about immortality (Gallup, 1982). Of the sample, 15 percent reported near-death experiences. On the basis of this national survey, Gallup estimated that eight million Americans have had near-death episodes. The 15 percent in the sample who reported a verge-of-death encounter were given in-depth questionnaires calling for open-ended, detailed descriptions of their experience. Ten basic positive feelings were expressed by some proportion of the individuals having a near-death experience. These were:

An out of body senstaion: 9 percent of adults with a near-death experience.

Visual perception of something going on around them, either in the earthly realm or some other dimension or level of consciousness: 8 percent.

Audible sounds of human voices, either on earth or in some other dimension: about 6 percent of adults with a near-death experience.

An overwhelming sense of peace and painlessness: approximately 11 percent.

The sight of a single light or several bright lights: about 5 percent.

The impression of reviewing or reexamining the individual's past life in a brief, highly compressed period of time: a solid 11 percent of those polled.

A special sensation of feeling, such as being in another world: about 11 percent.

A feeling that another being or beings, other than the living humans who had been left behind, were present during the near-death adventure: approximately 8 percent.

A sense of the presence of some sort of tunnel: about 3 percent.

Premonitions about some event or events that would happen in the future: about 2 percent. (Gallup, 1982, p. 32.)

There are many accounts of near-death experiences presented by Gallup (1982). The following account was described as distinctive because it was so detailed. However, many of the points such as the immediate movement into an out-of-body consciousness and the great mobility and acute perceptive abilities coincide with what other people told the Gallup interviewers. The women in this excerpt is a middle-aged Oklahoma housewife who was in the process of giving birth to her third child when she almost died.

I was in hard labor from two A.M. until two P.M. I was yelling for a 'C section' just before Daniel was born, but my doctor said, 'Shut up!'

I wanted to die of shame for yelling. I wanted to die more than anything! At that moment, I just popped out of my body and was about two or three feet above myself and everyone in the room. My doctor said, 'My God! My God!!'

Someone moved to my side and pounded on my chest. (I wondered why he was hitting my chest.) Daniel was coming out and was handed to a nurse and wrapped in a blanket. I looked up and saw many beings waiting on me but not talking. We all *knew* each other's thoughts. (This was very beautiful.)

I turned around wondering about my husband and started to go out the door, but only floated through the door and down the hall to where he was standing in a doorway with my eight-year-old daughter. They were fine—I went back to the birth room.

The 'beings' were waiting on me to decide to stay with them or reenter my body. It was *my* decision! I wanted to stay on the other side, but felt I should stay and raise my baby until he was 11 years old.

Immediately, I popped back into my body. My boy is now 13 years old, and I keep finding another project to start or finish before I leave again (Gallup, 1982, pp. 34–35).

Two small scale surveys of national leaders in the fields of science and medicine were also conducted by Gallup in conjunction with the special focus on near-death experiences. The scientists and physicians interviewed in Gallup's study, along with other scientists who have commented on near-death experiences, do not see the experiences as "proving" the existence of an afterlife. Rather, they account for the phenomenon as the result of exceptionally heightened awareness, perhaps resulting from the release of endorphins activated in the brain in this time of extreme stress. Pain reduction and the runner's high are other consequences of the secretion of endorphins. The effects of endorphins are comparable to morphine and may result in hallucinatory behavior.

Regardless of the origin of the sensations, near-death experiences appear to change the lives of those who have had them. One of the founders of the International Association of Near-Death Studies, psychiatry professor Kenneth Ring, stated that near-death experiences are a catalyst for spiritual development (*New York Times,* October 28, 1986). People who have these experiences often believe that they have escaped death to fulfill a special mission in life. The Oklahoma woman whose verge-of-death experience was presented came back to raise her baby.

Another example of a near-death experience changing a life was experienced by Virgina Sendor. In 1969 Mrs. Sendor had a near-death experience when suffering from uremia. She said, "I knew I came back for a reason, but I had no idea what that reason was." In the late 1970s she began to work with terminally ill patients and their families. She realized it was her mission to open a hospice in Long Island in the early 1980s. She founded Long Island Foundation for Hospice Care and Research, Inc. This organization provides a range of counseling and support services to patients and their families. Mrs. Sendor used her verge-of-death experience to help others, and this response is fairly typical of those who have come close to death. They fear death less, and they frequently try to use their experience to provide insight and support to others in the dying process.

WIDOWHOOD, GRIEF, AND MOURNING

The stress of losing a spouse or a close relative can be so great that it can result in the death of the surviving relative. Parkes pointed out that grief resembles a physical injury more closely than any other type of illness. "The loss may be spoken of as a 'blow'" (1972, p. 5). In an exhaustive review of the literature on the loss of a significant other as a predictor of death, Rowland (1977) concluded that death often results from the loss of a spouse. Indeed, Young and colleagues (1963) observed an increase in mortality rate among almost 4,500 widowers over the age of 54 of close to 40 percent during the first six months of bereavement.

Rowland (1977) observed that the most convincing evidence came from studies in which recently bereaved were followed for a period of years after the death of their spouse. The mortality rate in these people was much greater than it was in people matched for age and health status who had not lost their spouse. The death rate for the bereaved was greatest in the first 6 to 12 months following bereavement. After this period the mortality rate returned gradually to the level of married people.

The loss of a spouse appears to be more stressful for men, who died at a greater rate than women during bereavement. There is also some evidence that loss of a parent or sibling results in an increase in mortality among close family members. The loss of close emotional ties appears to be the most stressful event we can experience as humans. If we have not developed other relationships and activities which can sustain us over this difficult period, we may not be able to adapt to the change.

In an effort to understand what the bereaved found most supportive after the death of their spouse, Rigdon (1986) interviewed 570 bereaved aged 55 years or older and followed bereavement for a two-year period. The average length of marriage for the sample before the death of the spouse had been 40.9 years. No sex differences emerged in the responses. There were three issues addressed in Rigdon's study: (1) the kind of help appreciated most; (2) what others can do to be more helpful; and (3) identification of who helped the most.

The help the widows and widowers appreciated most was people keeping in touch. Phone calls and brief visits to see how they were doing were very comforting to the bereaved. Rigdon stated that telephone calls and visits were "lifelines" for these respondents. After a year of widowhood they appreciated expressions of concern. Two years after the death of the spouse, these adults expressed a need for "strong arm" help, that is, help with chores such as grocery shopping and laundry. They also appreciated social invitations.

When first asked how others can be more helpful, the respondents typically said that people had done so much, they could not do more. However, when she pressed them, Rigdon found that 93 percent of the widows and widowers wanted help in the form of contact and communication to continue well after the death of their spouse. They were afraid that they would be forgotten.

Along with a desire for more frequent communication, the bereaved wanted to talk about their spouse. They noted that friends felt awkward mentioning the deceased in front of them, and they regretted not being able to talk more about him or her. Finally, the bereaved resented individuals who told them that they understood or that it would get easier. They felt that they alone knew how it felt to lose a spouse of more than four decades. Many asserted that the pain of loss would always be there.

The person who helped the most was identified as the daughter. No other specific person was named as being the second most helpful; many people helped. The third most frequent answer was that the son helped the most. Apparently older parents receive more support from daughters than from sons.

Troll (1982) commented that there are sex differences in mourning. Women express a feeling of being abandoned, while men feel dismembered. Troll viewed these differences as an extension of the fact that women in the United States have been socialized to affiliation and to a focus on others, but men are socialized to autonomy and external mastery.

Once widowed, women are more likely to remain in that status. Women greatly outnumbered men in the decades of the fifties and older due to sex differences in longevity. In addition, women tend to marry older men. Hence, widowers usually remarry within a couple of years, while widows are less likely to do so.

SUMMARY

Dying and death are difficult topics to discuss. In this chapter we have examined a number aspects of dying and death. First we explored attitudes toward death, and then we considered the literature on dealing with the dying patient. The hospice as a new place to die was described. Next the topic of willing death was addressed including aspects of suicide, euthanasia, and the right-to-die movement. Cryonics, the practice of freezing the dead body with the hope of curing the disease that caused death and returning the individual to life, was the next topic. We also considered beyond-death experiences. Finally, we considered those left behind in a discussion of widowhood, grief, and mourning.

Attitudes toward death is a topic which has been studied since the very beginning of the modern era of research on the psychology of aging. Since 1897 it has been documented that fear of death is more a preoccupation of the young. Older adults worry more about the circumstances of their death than about death itself.

Elizabeth Kubler-Ross is the person credited with having the greatest impact on contemporary attitudes toward dying and death. She has brought a more humanistic approach to the care for the dying. Kubler-Ross developed a stage theory about how the dying individual deals with death. She hypothesized that the dying go through the phases of denial, anger, bargaining, depression, and acceptance. While the stage theory has sensitized investigators to examine the attitudes of the dying patient, the theory has not been supported empirically.

The living usually find it difficult to help and support a patient in the process of dying. However, the dying individual needs to talk about his or her impending death. Dying people also prefer to die in familiar surroundings away from a hospital environment. This desire is being met now by the hospice, a setting devoted to making the final days of the patient comfortable with staff trained to provide support for the dying patient and the family. The hospice represents a genuine change in attitudes and provision of care to the terminally ill.

The incidence of suicide increases with age and reaches the highest rate in the group aged 75 to 84 years. The suicide rate is highest among older white men, and they often take their life because of failing health. Social and economic losses in old age are another common cause of suicide. Suicide is one form of active euthanasia. Passive euthanasia means allowing the person to die by not keeping the individual alive artifically. Active euthanasia is the deliberate shortening of a life. Right-to-life and right-to-die groups are battling over the legal rights of individuals to choose when, how, and under what circumstances they can be allowed to die.

Cryonics involves freezing a body after an individual has been pronounced dead. Cryonicists do not consider the person dead at that point becuase they define death as the point at which resuscitation technology is insufficient to revive the frozen patient. However, at the present time the technology to revive mammals which have been frozen alive (let alone dead) has not advanced to a point where it is successful.

In a national poll 15 percent of the individuals reported that they had near-death experiences. These experiences seem to involve a heightened awareness in the individuals who have them, and the experience frequently changes the life of the individual who has it. Ofter near-death experiences are a catalyst for spiritual development.

The loss of a spouse or close relative is tremendously stressful. Indeed, it can result in the death of the individual left behind. Health and psychological well-being are significantly impaired for a year after the death of a loved one. Although some say they never get over the loss, the intensity of the grief decreases with time.

One of the things that is most helpful to widows and widowers is the effort others make to keep in touch. Phone calls and visits have been called "lifelines" to those in mourning, and they are deeply appreciated. Those in mourning also appreciate the opportunity to talk about the deceased. Daughters are the most likely to be identified as the ones who helped in the mourning. When a woman becomes a widow it is likely that she will keep this status the rest of her life. Widowers usually remarry within two years of the death of their wife. This disparity in experience between widows and widowers occurs because of the large sex differences in life expectancy.

REFERENCES

APPELBAUM, P. S. & KLEIN, J. (1986).   Therefore choose death? *Commentary, 81,* 23–29.

BECKER, E. (1973).   *The denial of death.* New York: Free Press.

BRIGGS, K. A. (1976).   New studies of the dying process provide impetus for scientific inquiries on the question of life after death. *New York Times,* April 20, C15.

ETTINGER, R. (1964).   *The prospect for immortality.* New York: Doubleday.

FEIFEL, H. (1959).   *The meaning of death.* New York: McGraw-Hill.

FEIFEL, H. (1963).   The taboo on death. *The American Behavioral Scientist, 6,* 66–67.

FEIFEL, H. & BRANSCOMB, A. B. (1973).   Who's afraid of death? *Journal of Abnormal Psychology, 81,* 282–288.

FEIFEL, H. & JONES, R. (1968).   Perception of death as related to nearncss to death. *Proceedings of the 76th Annual Convention of the American Psychological Association, 3,* 545–546.

GALLUP, G., JR. (1982).   *Adventures in immortality.* New York: McGraw-Hill.

HALL, G. S. (1897).   A study of fears. *American Journal of Psychology, 8,* 147–249.

HALL, G. S. (1922).   *Senescence, the last half of life.* New York: Appleton.
HINTON, J. M. (1975).   Facing death. *Journal of Psychosomatic Research, 10,* 22–28.
JURY, M. & JURY, D. (1976).   *Gramp.* New York: Viking Press.
KALISH, R. A. (1976).   Death and dying in a social context. In R. H. Binstock & E. Shanas (Eds.), *Handbook of aging and the social sciences.* New York: Van Nostrand Reinhold.
KASTENBAUM, R. J. (1981).   *Death, society and human experience,* (2nd Ed.) St. Louis: Mosby.
KASTENBAUM, R. J. (1985).   Dying and death: A lifespan approach. In J. E. Birren & K. W. Schaie (Eds.), *Handbook of the psychology of aging.* New York: Van Nostrand Reinhold.
KASTENBAUM, R. J. & AISENBERG, R. (1972).   *The psychology of death.* New York: Springer.
KASTENBAUM, R. J. & COSTA, P. T., JR. (1977).   Psychological perspectives on death. In M. R. Rosenzweig & L. W. Porters (Eds.), *Annual review of psychology,* (Vol. 28), Stanford, CA: Stanford University Press.
KUBLER-ROSS, E. (1969).   *On death and dying.* New York: Macmillan.
MAGNI, K. G. (1972).   The fear of death. In A. Godin (Ed.), *Death and presence.* Brussels: Luman Vitae Press.
MATHIEU, J. T. (1972).   Dying and death role-expectation: A comparative analysis. Unpublished doctoral dissertation, University of Southern California.
MATHIEU, J. T. & PETERSON, J. A. (1970).   Death and dying: Some social psychological dimensions. Paper presented at the 23rd Annual Scientific Meeting of the Gerontological Society, Toronto, October.
METZGER, A. M. (1979).   A Q-methodological study of the Kubler-Ross stage theory. *Omega, 10,* 291–302.
MOR, V. (1982).   The National Hospice Study: Progress Reports. Providence, RI: School of Medicine, Brown University.
MORRIS, J. (1982).   Technical reports, National Hospice Study. Hebrew Home for Rehabilitation of the Aged: Social Gerontology Research Unit, Boston, MA.
NATIONAL CENTER FOR HEALTH STATISTICS. (1986).   Advance report of the final mortality statistics, 1984. *Monthly Vital Statistics Report,* Vol 35, No. 6, Supp. (2). DHHS Pub. No. (PHS) 86–1120. Hyattsville, MD: Public Health Service, September 26.
New York Times. (October 28, 1986).   Near-death experiences illuminate dying itself, C8.
OLESHANSKY, M. E., GAMSKY, N. R. & RAMSEYHER, G. C. (in press).   Activity level, purpose in life and repression as predictions of death anxiety in the aged. *Omega.*
OTTEN, A. L. (1986).   Life or death: Issue of force-feeding to keep patients alive enters political arena. *Wall Street Journal,* June 9.
PARKES, C. M. (1972).   *Bereavement.* New York: International Universities Press.
PARKES, C. M. (1975).   Evaluation of family care in terminal illness. Alexander Ming Fisher Lecture, Columbia University.
RIGDON, I.S . (1986).   Help and hope for the elderly bereaved. *Gerontologist, 26,* 128.
ROWLAND, K. F. (1977).   Environmental events predicting death for the elderly. *Psychological Bulletin, 84,* 349–372.
SCHNEIDMAN, E. S. (1976).   *Death: Current perspectives.* Palo Alto, CA: Mayfield.
SCHNEIDMAN, E. S. (1980).   *Voices of death.* New York: Harper & Row.
SCHULTZ, R. & ANDERMAN, D. (1974).   Clinical research on the stages of dying. *Omega, 5,* 137–144.
SCHWARTZ, A. N. & PETERSON, J. A. (1970).   *Introduction to gerontology.* New York: Holt, Rinehart, & Winston.

SHESKIN, A. (1979).   *Cryonics: A sociology of death and bereavement.* New York: Irvington Publishers.

SUDNOW, D. (1967).   *Passing on.* Englewood Cliffs, NJ: Prentice Hall.

TEMPLER, D., RUFF, C. & FRANKS, C. (1971).   Death anxiety: Age, sex, and parental resemblance in diverse populations. *Developmental Psychology, 4,* 108–114.

TROLL, L. E. (1982).   *Continuations.* Monterey, CA: Brooks/Cole.

TWYCROSS, R. G. (1974).   Clinical experience with diamorphine in advanced malignant disease. *International Journal of Clinical Pharmacology Therapy & Toxicology, 9,* 184–198.

WEISMAN, A. D. & KASTENBAUM, R. (1968).   The psychological autopsy: A study of the terminal phase of life. *Community Mental Health Journal Monography No. 4.* New York: Behavioral Publications.

WIESSMAN, A. (1972).   *On dying and denying.* New York: Behavioral Publications.

YOUNG, M. B., BENJAMIN, B. & WALLIS, C. (1963).   The mortality of widowers. *Lancet, 2,* 454–456.

CHAPTER 19

Aging and the Future

In discussing aging and the future, we are writing about you. While some students who read this textbook may be 60 years old or older already, the vast majority of college students are still in their twenties or younger. Thus, when we discuss aging in the twenty-first century, we are considering what aging may be like for you.

A central point about aging in the future for you as an individual is that you are not going to be aging alone. Estimates of the size of the aging population in the twenty-first century continue to be revised upward (Zopf, 1986). Projections based on data from the United States Bureau of the Census anticipate that by 2030 the population over the age of 65 will number about 65 milion and comprise 21.2 percent of the general population (U.S. Department of Health and Human Services, 1986).

Demographers have made these projections on the basis of health and longevity in the present decade. If medical breakthroughs dramatically affect mortality rates for diseases such as heart disease, cancer, and stroke, people aged 65 and older may number 74 million and comprise 23 percent of the population by 2025 (Gordon, 1979). Thus, in the next century, old people in the population will be even more numerous than they are at present. The large numbers of older adults in society will undoubtedly affect its social, economic, and political structure.

As we face this major increase in the size of the population of the aged in the next 30 years, we might consider it to be a major social problem. Zopf (1986) has pointed out that it is inaccurate to view aging as a social problem. Aging is a time beset by particular problems, and these problems arise more as a function of the existing social system than as a consequence of the aging process itself.

Employment and Retirement
in the Future

Significant concerns of older adults in the present center around income maintenance and health. It is likely that these concerns will also be felt by the elderly in the future. Having a decent level of living is what we all want, and the need extends to the very end of our lives. The problem is that the average income is reduced by a third when an individual retires. For those who rely completely on Social Security for income, they subsist at the poverty or near-poverty level. Certainly, it is bleak to anticipate a future in which one spends the end of life in poverty. Indeed, even the Social Security system is at risk with the declining size of contemporary birth cohorts in the looming retirement of the large post-World War II baby boom cohorts.

It seems quite apparent that the organization work and retirement in the twenty-first century will change. On the one hand, mandatory retirement has been abolished in many sectors, and the retirement age has been increased to 70 years. On the other hand, Americans are retiring at younger and younger ages. While long-range planners discuss the need to extend the working career in order to defer payment of benefits and gain a longer period of contributions, the trend is toward earlier and earlier retirement. Corporations are providing early retirement incentives to eliminate highly paid older employees and replace them with younger ones. Thus, retirement in the late fifties is not uncommon, and most individuals retire before the age of 64. This pattern of work and retirement may not be tenable in the American economy in the twenty-first century. Indeed, early retirement may not even be a satisfactory strategy in the late 1980s.

Many employees who accept early retirement regret it soon after they have remained at home for a month or two. One woman who accepted an attractive early-retirement offer later stated, "But I've never been so sad. I feel like I've lost my home" (Alsop, 1985). Alsop quoted another executive who received a large retirement bonus on top of his benefits who said, "I had seen only the dollar signs. I was too young, and my health was too good for me to retire. My wife wasn't ready for a rocking chair, either." Fortunately, his company found that they needed him again and hired him back on a temporary part-time basis.

Companies often sacrifice valuable employees when they undertake early retirement. Rep. Edward R. Roybal of California, Chairman of the House Select Committee on Aging stated, "History will prove the early-retirement incentives so prevalent in the 1980s to be a disastrous waste of human resources. The programs indiscriminately jettison the most experienced, loyal and talented members of the work force." It has been reported by management consultants that absenteeism rates often rise after a wave of early retirement because the departed older workers were more committed to their jobs and were more dependable (Alsop, 1985). It is becoming recognized that

> the mushrooming army of unemployed and unproductive retirees is placing an intolerable strain on younger workers, on Social Security, on the American pension system, and on the economy as a whole. Changing demography, occuaptional shifts, labor-force composition, pension systems, and the whole gamut of employment issues play an interactive role in affecting the health or sickness of the national economy (Forman, 1984, p. 47).

The United States at present is caught between two equally important concerns. The public is becoming increasingly conscious of the aging of the population, and current retirement practices are appearing more and more illogical and unjust. At the same time, there is concern that if present policies are changed, younger workers will have fewer prospects. One generic change in policy is not the solution to this dilemma (Forman, 1984). What appears necessary are a number of innovative programs which could serve as alternatives to current retirement policies.

Forman (1984) has pointed out that a wide variety of alternatives to total retirement are already available. Flexible approaches to retirement include combinations of delayed or postponed retirement, in-company part-time work, or temporary assignments. There are also opportunities for phased-in or "tapered" withdrawal from full employment and there are a variety of novel shared-job arrangements. Some companies offer continued accrual of pension benefits while other companies have pension benefits which are pro-rated or postponed until full retirement occurs. In-service retraining programs for redeployment of older workers is another possibility. In Denmark voluntary demotion has been tried as an alternative to involuntary retirement, and some firms in the United States have also tried this strategy.

When you think about aging and the future and consider yourself, what kind of options will you want for employment and retirment in your early sixties? You will probably be in excellent health, and your life expectancy at that point could be 90 years. What do you want to do with the rest of your life? This question that many contemporary adults have asked themselves in their mid-thirties to early forties, they may be asking again in their early sixties when they still have 30 years to live. As life expectancy and health are extended, a great number of older people are going to have a lot of time ahead of them to weigh the advantages and disadvantages of having nothing really meaningful to do.

Employment may increasingly become a favored option for adults beyond the age of 65 not only for the additional income it provides, but also for the satisfaction it provides through companionship with other workers and through meaningful, fulfilling occupation of the older adult's time. On the other hand, many of us as older adults in the twenty-first century will have no option at all. We will have to continue working into our seventies to support ourselves in the face of modified pension and Social Security systems that will not have been able to bear the weight of the staggering number of older adults in American society.

Health and Longevity in the Future

Major increases in human life expectancy have been achieved in the twentieth century. Not only do we live longer, our health is more optimal throughout our years. These facts have led Fries and Crapo (1981) to predict that life expectancy in the future will become a rectangular curve as presented in Figure 19.1. The rectangular curve is the survival curve. It depicts the age of death. A rectangular curve means that the whole birth cohort survives to a given age, and then they all die within a period of a few years.

Typical survival curves for wild animals and humans in hostile environments approximate a simple exponential decay. Death is a daily reality, and some members of the population die everyday until no one is left. For civilized human populations, the shape of the survival curve begins to bend upward to the right. This indicates that most deaths occur at increasingly advanced ages. The curve has become more and more rectangular as we have eliminated the causes of death in the early years. As we improve health in old age, the curve will become even more rectangular.

Fries and Crapo (1981) predicted that given present trends in mortality in the United States, we are on the verge of becoming a "rectangular society" in which nearly all people survive to old age and then die rather abruptly over a narrow age range centering about age 85. Other researchers argue that current trends do not fit the rectangular curve prediction. Rather the whole curve is being shifted upward. Eighty-five years may not be an accurate endpoint for human life expectancy. Thus, for your own personal aging as a 20-year-old college student, you might expect to live to the age of 85 or 90 years, and you will probably be in relatively good health throughout most of those years.

The future health and longevity of Americans depends on three major categories of biomedical research (Zopf, 1986). These are: (1) efforts to prevent, diagnose, and treat more effectively the three major causes of death which are heart disease, cancer, and stroke; (2) research designed to describe and manipulate social conditions that affect aging and death; and (3) research directed to the processes of aging including the understanding of the genetic limits on life span.

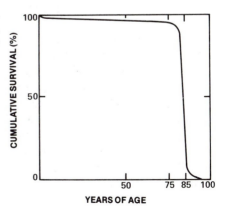

FIGURE 19.1   The rectangular survival curve. *Source:* Fries, J. F. & Crapo, L. M. (1981). *Vitality and aging.* San Francisco: W. H. Freeman, p. x. Reprinted by permission.

The rectangular curve described by Fries and Crapo (1981) will be more readily achieved as advances in research on cardiovascular disease and cancer provide insights about how to treat and eliminate these diseases. It is very reasonable to assume that we will continue to reduce mortality due to cardiovascular disease because the death rate from heart disease has fallen steadily since 1960. Research on the genetic antecedents of cancer is very promising, and it is likely that cancer too will be brought under control. Even if these major diseases are more or less eliminated, our biological potential for life averages around 85 years. By eliminating major diseases, we will maximize human life expectancy so that children born in the twenty-first century will have a life expectancy of 85 years. However, to exceed a life expectancy of 85 years, we will have to tamper with the genes and affect the human life span.

The prospect of affecting human life span is depicted in Figure 19.2 in which life expectancy (when half of the population has died and half still survives) appears to be around 95 years. Interventions into the processes of aging might include efforts to alter the ways that cells, organs, and physiological systems age. It might also involve the regeneration of tissue. These advances are more futuristic than advances to cure and prevent known disease processes. However, with the current rate of advances in molecular genetics, it is no longer in the realm of science fiction to state that extension of the human life span is possible.

The life span extending phenomena we understand currently involve interventions early in the life span to prolong it in late life. In mammals, the only life span extending intervention we know involves dietary restriction (Cutler, 1981; Schneider & Reed, 1985; Weindruch, 1984). Underfeeding young mice and rats by reducing food intake by 25 to 60 percent below what they normally would consume causes them to live almost twice as long as their normally fed littermates and results in lower incidence and later onset of senescence-associated diseases (Barrows & Kokkonen, 1984; Masoro, 1984). Dietary restriction also benefits learning and motor performance in aged mice (Ingram et al., 1987). While this intervention has implications for the human life span, the critical experiments to test this intervention will never be undertaken directly. Nevertheless, it is likely that whatever means we attempt to extend the life span in humans will have to be undertaken early in life.

Social changes which would maximize health and life expectancy include the reduction of stress, the elimination of poverty, the elimination of environmental pollutants and hazards, and the reduction of homicide and accident rates. American society is gaining some control over poverty, and Americans may be learning to cope with stress. However, we continue to pollute our environment with toxic chemicals, and we are apparently incapable of eliminating automobile accidents or lowering the crime rate. Interestingly, as the median age gets older in the United States and the proportion of young adults in the population gets smaller, the crime rate will decline. The crime rate is much lower for older adults. Nevertheless, social factors affecting health and longevity are problematic. It appears that social factors

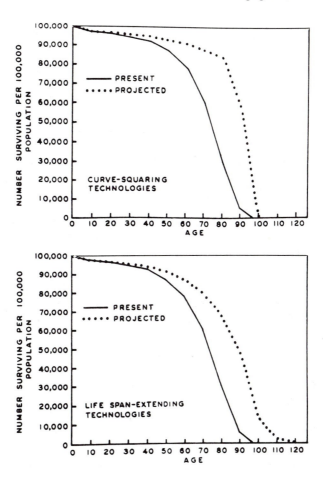

FIGURE 19.2 Effects of curve-squaring and life span-extending technologies. *Source:* Zopf, P. E., Jr. (1986). *America's older population.* Houston: Cap and Gown Press, Inc. p. 277. Reprinted by permission.

may prevent us from achieving the rectangular survival curve at any time in the predictable future.

Behavior and Aging in the Future

In considering behavior of older adults in the future, we are again thinking about you, a young adult college student, and trying to predict how aging will be for you as an individual. Remember that diversity is the hallmark of old age. There is more individual difference at the endpoint of life than during any other period. However, in spite of the diversity, we are venturing some guesses about individual behavior in old age based on what research in psychology and aging has told us about behavioral aging processes.

Response speed.   The most pervasive and apparent behavior change with aging is behavioral slowing. It is unlikely that we will be able to change that significantly in the future. However, we already know how to prevent significant slowing, and we also recognize that older adults compensate well with other strategies for the loss in speed that they suffer.

The best way to maintain response speed is to remain active. A growing number of studies has shown that physical exercise facilitates response speed. Older adults who have remained physically active throughout their lives (Dustman & Ruhling, 1986) as well as older adults who begin an exercise program in late life (Dustman et al., 1984) have more rapid reaction time than sedentary adults. Many more members of contemporary young and middle-aged cohorts have been socialized to exercise than had contemporary older adults. Thus, for aging and the future, the prospect of maintenance of response speed, or at least a smaller magnitude of slowing, is a reality.

A recent training study is also showing how new strategies can effectively speed behavior in older adults. Clark, Lanphear and Riddick (1984) exposed a group of older adults to several video games and allowed them to play the games at least two hours per week for seven weeks. The older adults who played video games were faster on several difficulty levels of a choice reaction time task than were older adults not exposed to the video games. Here again, activity in the form of playing a video game increased the speed of performance. In this case, the activity was fun. Peak scores of the older adults on Pac Man increased from an average of 687 the first week to an average of 1,997 the seventh week.

The aged in the future, even more than the aged of the present, will likely be able to compensate for the tendency in aging organisms for response speed to be slower. They will be in better health, and they will more likely be physically active. Both of these factors minimize slowing. Continued experience with an activity also buffers against slowing. Hence, the computer game playing youth of today who will be the aged of the future may maintain the speed of their performance by contiunuing to play the games and/or to operate the computer. The author's 9-year-old son has a high score of 73,198 on Pac Man. As an older adult of the future with 60 years to practice, he has the potential to score over a million on that game!

Sensation and perception.   Impairments in hearing and vision are relatively common in the elderly. In 1982, 30 percent of those 65 and older reported hearing impairments, and 10 percent had visual impairments (National Center for Health Statistics, 1985). In the most recently available survey, depending on age, from 30 percent to 58 percent of men and from 18 percent to 44 percent of women reported presence of deafness or other hearing problems (National Center for Health Statistics, 1986). In this sample visual impairment was reported by

9.5 percent to 26.8 percent of respondents, depending on age. Until the age of 85, the majority of noninstitutionalized persons are free of major sensory problems. Thus, the majority of older adults do not have problems with vision and hearing, but a significant minority do report impairment.

Projections about the incidence of sensory loss in future cohorts of aged is difficult to determine. As more is learned about the etiology of impairments of vision and audition, some sensory loss might be prevented or slowed. However, if anything, future cohorts of elderly may suffer similar or greater levels of hearing impairment as a result of loss due to high intensity sounds. While workers in noisy industrial environments are protecting their hearing by wearing headphones, large numbers of teenagers and young adults continue to expose their ears to highly amplified music. Thus, there is no evidence that the aged in the future will experience any less hearing loss than contemporary older adults.

Research breakthroughs in vision which could prevent glaucoma and macular degeneration have the potential to save the eyesight of many future elderly adults. Of course, cataract surgery now prevents blindness in large numbers of the elderly. Continuing improvements in prosthetic devices for vision and hearing including contact lenses, eyeglasses, and hearing aids also promise to make sensory loss less of a problem for future cohorts of older adults.

Learning and memory. Age changes in the speed of behavior may be the most pervasive age change, but age changes in learning and memory are the most troubling.

> The feeling that one's ability to remember and to retrieve information is not as good as it used to be is a universal complaint among middle-aged and elderly persons. The effort to substantiate these complaints and to clarify issues surrounding age-related differences in memory abilities has become the single most concentrated activity in psychological aging research (Poon, 1985, p. 427).

Research on learning, memory, and aging has already provided insights about what older adults must do to learn and remember better. Some of these strategies are discussed in Chapter 12. However, it is in Chapter 11 on the psychobiology of learning, memory, and aging that we really consider the major potential for impacting learning and memory in the future. By unlocking the secrets of the neurobiology of learning and memory we will understand how learning occurs and how memories are formed. With this knowledge we can design facilitators for these functions. Memory drugs are in the experimental stage at present. The aged of the future may carefully monitor their diet and take pills that will maintain and even enhance their ability to learn and remember.

In the case of memory loss due to disease such as senile dementia of the Alzheimer's type (SDAT), aging in the future may also be different. It is possible that the incidence of senility will become less as treatments and cures for cardiovascular disease are developed and strokes are prevented. With a clinical test for SDAT on the horizon, the identification, treatment, and even a cure seems closer to our grasp than it did even several years ago. If we do not find treatments and cures for SDAT, and if the demographic projections for as many as 65 to 75 million older adults in 2030 are realized, then we may be faced with as many as 5 million older adults with SDAT for whom we must provide care. The cost in human suffering and in health care dollars for this burden from SDAT would be enormous.

Intellectual capacity.   Cognitive aging has been presented in Chapter 12 on human learning, memory, and cognition and Chapter 13 on intelligence as something which includes growth as well as decline. What one loses in terms of performance on speeded tasks is often more than compensated by taking the bigger picture and integrating the information into a larger whole. As we age, we may lose efficiency on the activities we no longer do, but we maintain or improve our competence on the tasks we continue to perform in our occupations and in our everyday lives. What was called the Phase IV perspective in research on intelligence in Chapter 13 emphasizes continued development of cognitive faculties in later life.

Rybash, Hoyer, and Roodin (1986) have pointed out the inadequacies of information processing or even postformal operational models of cogniution to account for all aspects of cognition in aging. These authors effectively document why new and expanded views of mature cognition are needed that take account of age-related changes in processing, thinking, and knowing. Psychology and aging in the future must address cognitive abilities in older adults in a more mature fashion. With the increasing visibility of older adults in society and with our increasing need for their skills to be used rather than retired, it seems likely that future attitudes about cognitive capacity in old age will become more positive.

Personality.   Neugarten has said that as we age we become more like ourselves. If you want to imagine how aging will affect your personality, consider that as an old person in the future, you will be an exaggeration of what you are now. If you are an aggressive, angry young adult, you may become more aggressive and angry in your old age. Many of the personality types identified in research on personality and aging were consistent over the retirement period and into old age. Costa and his research associates have emphasized the vast evidence for stability of personality over the adult life period. The social system including our relatives and friends reinforce our personality and help us to maintain characteristic response patterns. Thus, you might be quite accurate in predicting your personality in old age if you simply take a look at yourself at present.

Indeed, if you take a look at your personality and like what you see, your chances for living a long, fulfilling life and adjusting well to your own old age are good. Researchers have demonstrated for years that adjustment in the present along with anticipatory socialization to future roles are excellent predictors of future adjustment. Thinking about your own aging in the future actually helps you to adjust to it better. Thus, with the knowledge about psychology and aging you have gained from this book, coupled with your own thoughts about aging in the future, you are in a better position to understand older adults, and you are better prepared for your own aging.

REFERENCES

ALSOP, R. (1985).   As early retirement grows in popularity, some have misgivings. *The Wall Street Journal,* April 24.

BARROWS, C. H., JR. & KOKKONEN, G. C. (1984).   Nutrition and aging: Human and animal laboratory studies. In J. M. Ordy, D. Harman, & R. Alfin-Slater (Eds.), *Nutrition in gerontology.* New York: Raven Press.

CLARK, J. E., LANPHEAR, A. K. & RIDDICK, C. C. (1987).The effects of videogame playing on the response selection processing of elderly adults. *Journal of Gerontology, 42,* 82–85.

CUTLER, R. G. (1981).   Life-span extension. In J. L. McGaugh & S. B. Kiesler (Eds.), *Aging: Biology and behavior.* New York: Academic Press.

DUSTMAN, R. E. & RUHLING, R. O. (1986).   Brain function of old and young athletes and nonathletes. Presented at the *39th Annual Scientific Meeting of the Gerontological Society of America,* Chicago.

DUSTMAN, R. E., RUHLING, R. O., RUSSELL, E. M., SHEARER, D. E., BONEKAT, W., SHIGEOKA, J. W., WOOD, J. S. & BRADFORD, D. C. (1984).   Aerobic exercise training and improved neuropsychological function of older individuals. *Neurobiology of Aging, 5,* 35–42.

FORMAN, B. I. (1984).   Reconsidering retirement: Understanding emerging trends. *The Futurist,* June, 43–47.

FRIES, J. F. & CRAPO, L. M. (1981).   *Vitality and aging.* San Francisco: W. H. Freeman.

GORDON, T. J. (1979).   Prospects for aging in America, In M. W. Riley (Ed.), *Aging from birth to death.* Boulder, CO: Westview Press.

INGRAM, D. K., WEINDRUCH, R., SPANGLER, E. L., FREEMAN, J. R. & WALFORD, R. L. (1987).   Dietary restriction benefits learning and motor performance of aged mice. *Journal of Gerontology, 42,* 78–81.

MASORO, E. J. (1984).   Food restriction and the aging process. *Journal of the American Geriatrics Society, 32,* 296–300.

NATIONAL CENTER FOR HEALTH STATISTICS. (1985).   Current estimates from National Health Interview Survey, United States, 1982. *Vital and Health Statistics,* Series 10, No. 150. DHHS Pub. No. (PHS) 85–1578. Public Health Service. Washington, DC: U.S. Government Printing Office, September.

NATIONAL CENTER FOR HEALTH STATISTICS. (1986).   R. J. Havlik. Aging in the eighties, Impaired senses for sound and light in persons age 65 years and over, Preliminary data from the Supplement on Aging to the National Health Interview Survey, United States, January–June 1984. *Advance Data from Vital and Health Statistics,* No. 125. DHHS Pub. No. (PHS) 86–1250. Public Health Service, Hyattsville, MD.

POON, L. W. (1985).   Differences in human memory with aging: Nature, causes, and clinical implications. In J. E. Birren & K. W. Schaie (Eds.), *Handbook of the psychology of aging.* New York: Van Nostrand Reinhold.

RYBASH, J. M., HOYER, W. J. & ROODIN, P. A. (1986).   *Adult cognition and aging.* New York: Pergamon.

SCHNEIDER, E. L. & REID, J. D., JR. (1985).   Life extension. *New England Journal of Medicine, 312,* 1159–1160.

SUBCOMMITTEE ON HUMAN SERVICES OF THE HOUSE SELECT COMMITTEE ON AGING. (1980).   *Future directions for aging policy: A human services model.* Pub. no. 96–226. Washington, DC: U.S. Government Printing Office.

U.S. DEPARTMENT OF HEALTH AND HUMAN SERVICES. (1986).   *A Profile of Older Americans.* Washington, DC: Program Resources Department, American Association of Retired Persons (AARP) and the Administration on Aging (AoA).

WEINDRUCH, R. (1984).   Dietary restriction and the aging process. In D. Armstrong, R. S. Sohal, R. G. Cutler & T. F. Slater (Eds.), *Free radicals in molecular biology, aging, and disease.* New York: Raven Press.

ZOPF, P. E., JR. (1986).   *America's older population.* Houston: Cap and Gown Press.

Index